Index Of Wills In The York Registry: 1554 To 1568...

York (England), Ely Wilkinson Crossley, Yorkshire Archaeological and Topographical Association, Yorkshire Archaeological Society

THE

Yorkshire Archæological Society.

FOUNDED, 1863.   INCORPORATED, 1893.

RECORD SERIES.
VOL. XIV.

FOR THE YEAR 1893.

York, Eng.

INDEX OF

WILLS IN THE YORK REGISTRY

A.D. 1554 TO 1568.

v. 3

PRINTED FOR THE SOCIETY.

1893.

RV

WORKSOP :
ROBERT WHITE, PRINTER.

PREFACE.

THIS Volume, compiled by Mr. A. Gibbons, is a continuation of the Calendar of the Wills proved in the Exchequer and Prerogative Courts of York, and covering the years 1554 to 1568, is an Index to Registers 14, 15, 16, and 17. The Administration Acts for the same period have, as previously, been dealt with separately and form an Appendix to the Volume, which contains, in all, references to 11,213 Wills and 1,242 Administrations. In consequence of Register 15 being divided into three parts it has been found necessary to add a third column of reference. With this exception the Calendar is continued on the same plan as in the previous Volumes.

F. COLLINS.

WILLS IN THE YORK REGISTRY.

A.D. 1554 TO 1568.

The date of the Probate precedes the Name and that of the Will follows the Name, the reference to the Register and folio following the latter. The Act Books have been freely used in making corrections and supplying deficiencies.

		Vol.	Pt.	Fol.
Oct. 28, 1555.	Abbot, Richard, Newarke, Notts., Oct. 4, 1555.	14		16
Jan. 4, 1562.	Abbott, John, Gawlle (bur. Howke), July 15, 1562.	17		140
Jan. 3, 1558.	———, John, Wintersett, par. Wragbie, Jan. 28, 1557.	15	3	35
Jun. 9, 1563.	———, Richard, Gowlle (bur. Howkk), Dec. 22, 1562.	17		257
Sep. 6, 1558.	———, Robert, Fetherstone, Jun. 1, 1558.	15	3	100
Oct. 3, 1554.	———, Sir Thomas, curate of Burnesall, Mar. 6, 1553.	14		38
May 4, 1558.	———, William, Bradmore, par. Bonney (Notts.), Nov. 18, 1559.	15	2	213
Oct. 20, 1558.	Abdie, Thomas, Abdie, par. Wath, gent., Aug. 28, 1558.	15	2	352
Jun. 2, 1564.	Abott, Margaret, Gowle (bur. Howke), May 10, 1563.	17		347
Jan. 20, 1557.	Abson, Thomas, Swynton, par. Wathe, Nov. 24, 1557.	15	2	64
Feb. 25, 1558.	Acam, William, Hutton Wansley als. Marstone, husbn., Oct. 24, 1558.	15	3	280
May 19, 1559.	Acarland, John, Armyn, par. Snaith, Mar. 24, 1559.	15	3	425
Mar. 9, 1557.	Acclam, John, Gemlinge (bur. Foston), July 31, 1557.	15	2	127
Jun. 22, 1568.	———, Thomas, Gt. Kelke (bur. Foston), Oct. 19, 1567.	17		822
Nov. 28, 1567.	———, William, Gt. Kelke (bur. Foston), Aug. 17, 1567.	17		737
Mar. 24, 1567.	Acclom, Robert, senr., Bewhollme (bur. Nunkelinge), yeoman, Jan. 26, 1567.	17		766
Mar. 16, 1559.	Acclome, Anthony, Cawode, gentleman, Aug. 16, 1558.	16		9
Feb. 15, 1558.	Ace, Thomas, Preston in Holderness, Dec. 13, 1558.	15	3	271
Apl. 19, 1559.	Acerlay, Robert, Rempstone (Notts.), Dec. 19, 1558.	15	3	373
Jan. 12, 1558.	Acey, Isabell, Kirke Elley, Sep. 8, 1558.	15	3	193
Jan. 10, 1558.	———, William, Elley, Nov. 10, 1558.	15	2	355
May 5, 1558.	Achard, John, North Collingham (Notts.), husbn., Sep. 11, 1557.	15	2	254
May 10, 1559.	Aclam, George, Rudstone, husbandman, Jan. 6, 1558.	15	3	390
Sep. 30, 1556.	———, Sir William, preist (bur. Hornesey), Jun. 3, 1556.	15	1	141
July 12, 1566.	Acome, Margaret, Houton Wanseley als. Marston, wid., Feb. 14, 1565.	17		564
Aug. 12, 1566.	Acye, Peter, Preston in Holderness, husbandman, Dec. 30, 1565.	17		568
Oct. 2, 1566.	Adam, Annas (bur. Paull), widow, Nov. 21, 1566.	17		714
Apl. 28, 1563.	———, George, Brathewyet, par. Kirke Bramvithe, Feb. 16, 1562.	17		234
Sep. 30, 1562.	———, Henry, Owston, Jun. 21, 1562.	17		114
May 24, 1563.	———, John, senr., Hecke (bur. Snathe), Mar. 11, 1562.	17		248
Mar. 23, 1557.	———, John, Pawle, Feb. 25, 1556.	15	2	172
Dec. 18, 1560.	———, Robert, Byrom (bur. Brotherton), Apl. 18, 1559.	16		136
Oct. 2, 1560.	———, Robert, Uppall in Holderness (bur. Pall), July 6, 1560.	16		115
July 5, 1557.	———, William, Athwyke by the Strete, Jun. 1, 1557.	15	1	302
(1555).	———, William, Burghwallis, labourer, Aug. 25, 1554.	14		87
Oct. 22, 1556.	Adame, Robert, Darringtone, Aug. 10, 1556.	15	1	99
Dec. 17, 1557.	———, William, Owston, yeoman, Sep. 18, 1557.	15	2	38
Oct. 9, 1560.	Adamson, Clement (bur. S. Jo. Evang.) (? Beverley), Feb. 24, 1559.	16		122
Apl. 28, 1563.	———, John, Beverley, merchaunt, Mar. 31, 1563.	17		236
Mar. 4, 1562.	———, John, Kaingham, Oct. 29, 1562.	17		150
Oct. 29, 1558.	———, Thomas, Honmanbie, May 15, 1558.	15	2	368
Apl. 17, 1567.	———, William, Beverley, bocher, Sep. 15, 1566.	17		640
May 5, 1568.	———, William, Beverley, clothier, Nov. 20, 1567.	17		778
Oct. 2, 1560.	———, William, Wrelton, par. Mydleton, husbn., Mar. 28, 1560.	16		111

I

A.D. 1554 TO 1568.

A.D. 1554 TO 1568.

		Vol.	Pt.	Fol.
Sep. 1, 1563.	Allane, William, Sykehowse, par. Fyshelake, Jun. 21, 1563.	17		207
July 15, 1567.	Allanson, Richard, West Marton, Jun. 13, 1567.	17		679
Jan. 16, 1558.	——, Thomas, Gowthrope (bur. Selbye), coriar, Sep. 3, 1558.	15	3	209
Jun. 1, 1554.	——, Thomas, Muston, Apl. 10, 1554.	14		8
July 30, 1567.	——, Thomas, Sherif Hoton, husbandman, Jun. 16, 1567.	17		683
May 26, 1567.	——, William, Burnaston, par. Scawbie, July, 7, 1566.	17		654
Oct. 23, 1566.	Allansonne, John, Ripon, cordyner, Aug. 13, 1566.	17		586
Oct. 18, 1558.	Allatson, George, Harwoddayle, par, Hackenes, Mar. 5, 1557.	15	3	93
Jun. 20, 1566.	——, Richard, senr., Semer, July, 25, 1564.	17		557
May 26, 1567.	——, Robert, Muston, par. Hunmanbie, Jan. 8, 1566.	17		653
Sep. 29, 1557.	——, William, priest (bur. Ripon), Aug. 14, 1557.	15	1	330
Sep. 21, 1557.	Allen, Agnes, Barnebye on Don, widow, Jun. 13, 1557.	15	1	356
Feb. 4, 1556.	——, Jenet, wid. of Ric. A., alderman of Doncaster, Nov. 12, 1556.	15	1	169
May 13, 1568.	——, John, Boughton, par. Walesbe (Notts.), husbn., July 5, 1567.	17		801
Apl. 23, 1556.	——, Nicollas, Barnbie on Don, Oct. 21, 1555.	15	1	37
Apl. 18, 1560.	——, Thomas, Exthorpe, par. Doncaster, Apl. 1, 1560.	16		30
Oct. 14, 1561.	—— als. Wright, John, Fyshelake, July 12, 1561.	17		36
July 26, 1558.	Allene, John, Hamlinge (bur. Wagame, Holderness) Mar. 16, 1558.	15	3	11
Oct. 20, 1558.	Allerton, Richard, Swyne in Holderness, Aug. 15, 1558.	15	2	349
Nov. 8, 1557.	——, Robert, Anston, Sep. 9, 1557.	15	2	110
May 5, 1568.	——, William, senr., Allerton, par. Bradforthe, Dec. 1, 1567.	17		792
May 9, 1563.	Allotson, Edmund, Filinge, May 16, 1563.	17		255
Oct. 29, 1555.	——, Robert, Filing, freman, Oct. 1, 1555.	14		179
Feb. 22, 1558.	——, Thomas, Filing, Dec. 10, 1558.	15	3	277
May 9, 1565.	Allott, Agnes, Wombell, par. Darfeld, Jan. 9, 1564.	17		427
Oct. 2, 1567.	——, Elizabeth, Emley, widow, Feb. 1, 1566.	17		717
Mar. 10, 1566.	——, Jennet, Lewlyn, par. Worsburgh, widow, May 17, 1559.	17		518
Mar. 27, 1560.	Alman, Clemente, Settrington, Aug. 29, 1559.	16		20
Apl. 20, 1559.	——, John, Standfurthebrigges, husbandman, Jan. 10, 1558.	15	3	378
May 10, 1559.	Almoche, John, Sandhuton, Mar. 4, 1558.	15	3	388
Sep. 16, 1558.	Almoke, Richard, Sand Hooton (bur. Thriske), May 18, 1558.	15	3	105
Feb. 15, 1558.	Almon, John, Rosse in Holderness, husbandman, Jan. 10, 1558.	15	3	267
Dec. 8, 1556.	Almonde, Thomas, Marflete, husbandman, Oct. 17, 1556.	15	1	73
Nov. 26, 1557.	Alott, Isabell, Wygfall, par. Wyrspure, widow, Aug. 14, 1557.	15	2	91
Feb. 25, 1556.	——, John, Lewlyn in Worspur (Worsburgh), Aug. 12, 1556.	15	1	165
Jan. 11, 1562.	Alrede, Thomas, Hull, gentleman, May 12, 1562.	17		142
May 17, 1565.	Alvie, Robert, Lowdam (Notts.), Jan. 13, 1564.	17		441
May 19, 1559.	Ambler, Thomas, Balne (bur. Snaith), Jan. 29, 1559.	15	3	425
Dec. 17, 1557.	Amcottes, John, the Marrys, par. Tyckell, Aug. 1, 1557.	15	2	37
May 2, 1560.	Amery, William, Edlyngton, Apl. 10, 1559.	16		48
May 5, 1564.	Amler, James, Snaythe, Jun. 4, 1563.	17		342
Nov. 4, 1557.	Ampleforth, Katherine, Lytyll Rybston (bur. Spofforth), Oct. 12, 1557.	15	2	106
Jun. 20, 1556.	——, Richard, Littell Ribston, par. Spofforthe, May 28, 1556.	15	1	50
Dec. 16, 1556.	Anbye, John, Sherwodhall, par. Kellington, yeoman, Nov. 3, 1556.	15	1	174
Aug. 16, 1560.	Anderson, Henry, Skelton in Cleveland, Apl. 25, 1560.	16		102
Oct. 28, 1563.	——, John, Billisdaill, June 15, 1563.	17		299
Jan. 11, 1563.	——, John, North cave, husbandman, July, 18, 1563.	17		309
Feb. 15, 1558.	——, John, Sprotley, Oct. 13, 1558.	15	3	268
Oct. 5, 1558.	——, Robert (bur. Kirkbe Mysperton), Sep. 6, 1558.	15	3	70
Sep. 29, 1563.	——, Thomas, Scostrope (bur. Kirkebye Mallidall), Dec. 28, 1562.	17		279
Aug. 13, 1567.	——, William, Sprotley, husbandman, Mar. 14, 1567.	17		688
Jun. 2, 1556.	Andray (or Audray), Richard, Birdsaull, May 14, 1556.	15	1	40
Oct. 29, 1558.	Andreson, Richard, Gramsmoore (bur. Burton Agnes), July 22, 1558.	15	3	239
Apl. 8, 1562.	——, William, Angram, par. Marston, Mar. 12, 1561.	17		161
Sep. 15, 1558.	Andrew, John, Langton, husbandman, Apl. 3, 1558.	15	3	104
Mar. 5, 1554.	Andrewe, Alison, Raystropp, par. Wharham Percie, 1553.	14		302
Feb. 5, 1562.	——, George, Towthrope (bur. Wharrom Percye), husbandman, July 3, 1562.	17		146
Oct. 3, 1554.	Andro, Henry (bur. Lynton), Mar. 12, 1554.	14		37
Oct. 5, 1558.	——, Hugh (bur. Gargrave), Apl. 6, 1558.	15	3	37
Jan. 11, 1558.	Androw, William, Secrofte (bur. Whitkirke), Oct. 11, 1558.	15	3	171

A.D. 1554 TO 1568.

		Vol.	Pt.	Fol.
Dec. 5, 1567.	Androwe, Peter, Hull, May 21, 1567.	17		749
May 2, 1560.	Angle, William, Hull, maryner, Sep. 23, 1558.	16		44
Aug. 27, 1557.	Angrom, Thomas, Fernelay (bur. Otley), yeoman, Jun. 4, 1557.	15	2	116
Oct. 5, 1558.	Annigson, Thomas, Newham, par. Whitby, Aug. 5, 1558.	15	3	68
Jan. 19, 1558.	Anningson, Isabell, Yowcotte, par. Whitbie, Nov. 23, 1558.	15	3	20
Oct. 5, 1558.	Annyngson, Henry, Yowcote, par. Whitby, Aug. 14, 1558.	15	3	42
Oct. 5, 1558.	Anthony *als.* Wiske, Robert, Terringham, par. Holme in Spalding-more, Mar. 10, 1557.	15	3	71
Jan. 12, 1557.	Anweke, Thomas, Skipbye, Nov. 13, 1557.	15	2	79
Dec. 5, 1558.	Apleby, John, Wrelton, par. Midleton, husbandman, Aug. 21, 1558.	15	3	149
Apl. 28, 1558.	Appelbye, Robert, senr., Keldaill, Mar. 31, 1557.	15	2	232
Jan. 24, 1558.	Appilton, Robert, Kirkby in Cleveland, husbandman, Sep. 6, 1558.	15	3	216
Jan. 13, 1558.	Applay, Henry, Claworth (Notts.), Oct. 25, 1558.	15	3	187
Mar. 5, 1559.	Applebe, John, bailife of Haknes, Feb. 6, 1558.	16		4
Sep. 28, 1560.	Applebye, Robert, Bingham (Notts.), gentleman, Aug. 7, 1558.	16		107
Mar. 12, 1561.	Applegarthe, Robert, Moremoncketon, Oct. 20, 1561.	17		6
Mar. 7, 1563.	Appleton, Richard, Lound of the Wold, husbandman, Dec. 28, 1563.	17		323
Nov. 29, 1557.	———, Richard, Skrethenbeck, Jun. 3, 1557.	15	2	95
Apl. 20, 1555.	———, Robert, Goodmanham, husbandman, Oct. 27, 1554.	14		121
Sep. 30, 1557.	———, Thomas, Goodmanham, singleman, July 29, 1557.	15	1	326
Apl. 3, 1555.	Appleyerde, Katherine, Thorpe on hill (bur. Roythwell), Oct. 1, 1554.	14		190
Dec. 22, 1557.	———, Nycholas, Rookes, par. Halyfax, Jun. 16, 1556.	15	2	48
Mar. 28, 1560.	———, Richard, senr., Eastkeswycke, par. Harwode, Apl. 5, 1559.	16		22
Dec. 30, 1556.	Appylby, John, Londsbourgh, Oct. 12, 1556.	15	1	86
May 3, 1565.	Apthorpe, William, Rednes (bur. Whitgyft), Oct. 20, 1564.	17		420
Nov. 15, 1565.	Arandale, Symond, Bainton, Feb. 14, 1565.	17		487
Apl. 15, 1562.	Archer, Alexander, Eyssingwold, Feb. 21, 1561.	17		160
Mar. 24, 1562.	———, Alice, Clifton, near York, widow, Dec. 16, 1562.	17		220
Mar. 15, 1560.	[1] ———, Thomas, Wellcottes, par. Blythe (Notts.), husbn., Jan. 6, 1560.	16		170
Mar. 26, 1560.	———, Wilfride, priest, curate of St. Olave's, York, July 9, 1559.	16		19
Oct. 7, 1563.	Ardell, Hewgh, Rodington (Notts.), husbandman, Apl. 14, 1563.	17		293
May 16, 1564.	Ardington, Jane, Woulston (bur. Tadcaster), widow, Mar. 20, 1563.	17		343
Nov. 28, 1558.	———, Jennet, Pontefracte, widow, Sep. 28, 1558.	15	3	136
May 5, 1568.	———, John, Cowike, par. Snaythe, Mar. 13, 1567.	17		793
May 3, 1565.	———, John, Cowike (bur. Snaythe), husbn., July 16, 1564.	17		420
Jun. 12, 1562.	Ardingtonn, John, Wolstonn, par. Tadcaster, Jan. 12, 1558.	17		201
May 5, 1568.	Ardyngton, Roger, Gargrave, Feb. 6, 1567.	17		786
Nov. 17, 1562.	Areson, William, Hawnebie, July 10, 1562.	17		128
May 2, 1555.	Areton, Richard, Malham, husbandman, Dec. 13, 1554.	14		28
Jan. 11, 1557.	Arkesay, John, Brandesburton, labouring man, —— 16, 1557.	15	2	75
May 9, 1563.	Arklus, John, Burton Pidsey, Apl. 7, 1563.	17		255
May 19, 1559.	Arksay, Robert, Selbie, smyth, Jan. 28, 1558.	15	3	424
Feb. 17, 1557.	Armen, Elizabeth, Rotherham, widow, Sep. 20, 1557.	15	2	143
Oct. 3, 1560.	Armestede, John, Gyglesweke, Jun. 15, 1560.	16		118
Oct. 2, 1567.	Armetsted, John, Kirkedighton, husbandman, May 26, 1567.	17		719
Apl. 16, 1562.	Armistede, Bartilmew, Hawxweke, par. Arnclyffe, Dec. 21, 1561.	17		169
Aug. 3, 1555.	Armistrange, John, Clowghton (bur. Scawby), Apl. 28, 1555.	14		22
Apl. 22, 1556.	Armitage, John, Hothersfeld, yeoman, July 1, 1555.	15	1	20
Jun. 11, 1555.	———, Thomas, Dyrker [par. Sandal Magna], Apl. 23, 1555.	14		256
May 6, 1557.	Armsteed, Richard, Painstroppe, par. Kirkbie Undeffedaill, herdman, April 10, 1557.	15	1	270
Sep. 11, 1567.	Armytage, John, Stainford (bur. Haitfeld), Mar. 19, 1566.	17		707
Oct. 8, 1562.	———, Thomas, Nottingham, Apl. 10, 1562.	17		122
Oct. 5, 1554.	Armystrange, William, Huton Rudbye, Dec. 10, 1553.	14		44
July 8, 1561.	Armyteige, John, the Ermytaige, par. Almonburie, yeoman, Jun. 4, 1561.	17		80
Apl. 12, 1559.	———, John, Honley, par. Almonburye, smyth, Nov. 10, 1558.	15	3	337
Oct. 10, 1560.	———, John, Wombewell, par. Darfelde, Apl. 22, 1559.	16		125

1 See also Hercher.

A.D. 1554 TO 1568.

		Vol.	Pt.	Fol.
Jan. 18, 1557.	Armytson, Roger, Awdbye (bur. Bossall), Dec. 1, 1557.	15	2	65
Jun. 12, 1562.	Armytte, Walter, Everingham, Apl. 2, 1562.	17		88
July 26, 1557.	Arnald, Thomas, Waikefeld, cupper, July 10, 1557.	15	1	317
Dec. 1, 1558.	Arnold, Thomas, Hull, mariner, Oct. 25, 1558.	15	3	145
Aug. 24, 1554.	Arnolde, Thomas, Rosington, Dec. 9, 1553.	14		270
Apl. 24, 1567.	Arnoll, John, Faryndon (Notts.), Mar. 6, 1566.	17		641
Dec. 2, 1561.	Arnshay, Thurston, Scheypmanthorpe, par. Tankersley, Jan. 12, 1559.	17		31
Aug. 12, 1567.	Arnysse, Thomas, Hunmanbie, Apl. 1, 1567.	17		694
May 28, 1560.	Arrundall, Henry (Pontefract Deanery), Apl. 14, 1560.	16		68
Aug. 14, 1566.	Arrundell, Thomas, East lutton (bur. Weverthorppe), husbandman, Apl. 30, 1566.	17		565
Oct. 3, 1554.	Arsum, William, Marske, 1554.	14		43
Mar. 23, 1560.	Arteis, Augustyne, Lockington, labourer, Mar. 7, 1560.	16		177
May 8, 1567.	Arthar, John (bur. Burnholme), Jun. 30, 1566.	17		650
Apl. 6, 1558.	Arthington, Elizabeth, Aithweke by streate, widow, Aug. 10, 1557.	15	2	185
Oct. 6, 1558.	————, Robert, Athwike by strete, Dec. 16, 1557.	15	3	25
Mar. 4, 1560.	————, Robert, Cowike (bur. Snaythe), Jan. 3, 1560.	16		154
May 5, 1568.	————, Thomas, Hewyk at the bridge (bur. Ripon), Dec. 3, 1567.	17		784
Sep. 30, 1557.	Arthure, Francys, Estoft (bur. Adlyngflete), July 11, 1557.	15	1	345
Jan. 11, 1557.	Asbrige, William, North Frothingham, Aug. 27, 1557.	15	2	76
Apl. 30, 1557.	Aschebe, John (bur. Bubwith), Mar. 24, 1556.	15	1	209
Jan. 11, 1557.	Ascrike, Isabell, Ulrum (bur. Skepsey), Nov. 28, 1557.	15	2	74
Apl. 13, 1559.	Ase, Henry, Swanland (bur. North Ferebe), husbn., Mar. 16, 1558.	15	3	349
July 10, 1563.	—, John, senr., Preston in Holderness, husbandman, Jun. 5, 1563.	17		262
Jun. 15, 1566.	Asey, Bryan, Wooferton, par. Elveley, Jan. 29, 1565.	17		552
Apl. 26, 1558.	Ashburne, William, Shereburne, Mar. 16, 1557.	15	2	235
Oct. 8, 1556.	Ashe, George, Nottingham, butcher, Aug. 4, 1556.	15	1	153
Oct. 2, 1555.	—, John, Doncaster, Aug. 14, 1553.	14		167
Mar. 18, 1557.	Ashebye, Myles, Spaldington (bur Bubwythe), fletcher, Mar. 5, 1557.	15	2	176
Mar. 8, 1557.	Asheley, Jennett, Barley, par. Brayton, May 25, 1553.	15	2	169
May 4, 1558.	Asher, Richard, Ruddington (bur. Flafurthe, Notts.), Nov. 8, 1557.	15	2	210
Mar. 14, 1560.	Asheton, Thomas, Darton Grange (Notts.), gent., Jan. 28, 1560.	16		162
Oct. 24, 1554.	Ashton, John, Whithill, par. Rotherham, Jun. 26, 1553.	14		309
May 24, 1555.	—, Robert, Aithwike by the Strete, 28 Oct., 1554.	14		310
Apl. 14, 1568.	Aske, John, Bubwithe, 1563.	17		770
Jun. 14, 1562.	—, John, Dighton (bur. Eskrike), Feb. 20, ——.	17		90
Mar. 19, 1562.	—, Richard, Awghton, gentleman, Feb. 25, 1562.	17		216
May 9, 1565.	Askerne, Robert, Campsall, Jan. 12, 1564.	17		428
Mar. 23, 1560.	Askewe, William, Halsam, Feb. 11, 1560.	16		177
Oct. 31, 1556.	Askewith, William (bur. Ripon), Jan. 16, 1556.	15	1	106
Aug. 4, 1563.	Askewithe, William, Osgodbie (bur. Thurkilbie), Sep. 2, 1559.	17		269
Oct. 13, 1557.	Askewythe, John, Kilburne, Jun. 8, 1557.	15	1	361
July 10, 1561.	Askwith, Symon, Wistowe, Nov. 28, 1560.	17		63
May 4, 1564.	Askwithe, William, Byshoppmonnkton (bur. Ripon), Oct. 22, 1563.	17		342
Oct. 21, 1554.	1 Aslaby, Thomas, Whitwell, par. Crambum, gent., Dec. 4, 1553.	14		49
July 27, 1558.	Aslabye, Francis, Sowthdalton, Aug. 23, 1557.	15	2	308
Aug. 28, 1561.	————, Thomas, West Markham (Notts.), May 4, 1560.	17		57
Apl. 10, 1557.	Asmoughe, Lawrence, Sourby, par. Hallifax, Sep. 30, 1556.	15	1	206
May 13, 1557.	Aspenall, John, senr., Snenton (Notts.), Jan. 8, 1556.	15	1	226
Mar. 13, 1558.	Aston, Robert, Brodsworth, Dec. 25, 1558.	15	3	159
Oct. 10, 1566.	—, William (bur. Clifton, Notts.), 1562.	17		595
Dec. 1, 1558.	Asye, Robert, Anlaby (bur. Hesle), husbandman, Oct. 5, 1558.	15	3	146
Apl. 20, 1559.	Athorwhit, Richard, Myssyn (Notts.), Dec. 16, 1558.	15	3	307
Oct. 31, 1566.	Atkin, Hawes, Cookeswold, Feb. 22, 1565.	17		585
Apl. 15, 1562.	Atkingson, Robert (bur. Braffayton), husbandman, Aug. 11, 1561.	17		160
Jun. 22, 1568.	Atkinson, Alice, East Markham (Notts.), widow, Jun. 22, 1567.	17		829
Feb. 19, 1567.	————, Arthur, Wymerslay, singleman, May 17, 1567.	17		760
July 4, 1565.	————, Francis, Lound (Harthill), Apl. 20, 1565.	17		448
Oct. 3, 1564.	————, Henry (bur. Kirkeby overblaus), Apl. 2, 6 Eliz.	17		365
Mar. 21, 1560.	————, Henry, Morker (bur. Ripon), Aug. 15, 1558.	16		174

1 See also under letter H.

A.D. 1554 TO 1568.

	Vol.	Pt.	Fol.
Jan. 14, 1558. Atkinson, Henry, (bur. Ripon), Sep. 25, 1558.	15	3	190
Oct. 5, 1558. ——, Hugh, Pontefracte, Apl. 19, 1558.	15	3	63
Apl. 27, 1564. ——, Hughe, Woodcottes, par. Fledbroughe (Notts.), husbn., Oct. 10, 1563.	17		337
Jun. 12, 1567. ——, Isabell, Beforth, widow, Feb. 13, 1566.	17		662
Oct. 13, 1565. ——, Isabell, Egton, Feb. 18, 1564.	17		475
Sep. 29, 1563. ——, James, Erneclyffe, Apl. 16, 1563.	17		279
May 2, 1555. ——, James (bur. St. Oswald churchyard, Craven), Feb. 3, 1554.	14		27
Feb. 15, 1558. ——, John, Beford, husbandman, Nov. 18, 1558.	15	3	269
Jun. 11, 1568. ——, John, Hamylton (bur. Braton), husbn., Aug. 30, 1567.	17		805
Jan. 12, 1558. ——, John, Harnoll (bur. Riston), husbandman, Sep. 15, 1558.	15	3	203
Dec. 5, 1554. ——, John, Heke, par. Snaithe, Nov. 3, 1554.	14		93
Apl. 13, 1562. ——, John, Morker (bur. Ripon), Oct. 30, 1561.	17		169
Sep. 11, 1567. ——, John, Stainford (bur. Haitfeld) Dec. 13, 1566.	17		707
Jan. 28, 1558. ——, John, Stanfurthbrigges, labourer, Jan. 12, 1558.	15	3	220
Nov. 30, 1555. ——, Margaret, Lytle Armyn, par. Drax, widow, Aug. 16, 1555.	14		182
Apl. 16, 1562. ——, Oliver, Flasbye, par. Gargrave, July 18, 1561.	17		190
July 10, 1567. ——, Rannold, Baxbe (bur. Cookeswold), Apl. 7, 1567.	17		681
Oct. 1, 1557. ——, Raufe, Seamer in Clevelande, Jun. 28, 1557.	15	1	362
Nov. 15, 1566. ——, Reginald, Atwike on Strete, Jun. 8, 1566.	17		599
Apl. 28, 1563. ——, Richard, Hothome, Feb. 19, 1562.	17		236
Sep. 29, 1557. ——, Richard (bur. Paythleybrigges), Aug. 12, 1557.	15	1	330
Nov. 17, 1558. ——, Richard, Wistow, Sep. 6, 1558.	15	3	115
Apl. 18, 1567. ——, Robert, Bentley, mylner, Feb. 12, 1566.	17		637
Aug. 13, 1567. ——, Robert, Goexall, May 28, 1567.	17		689
Dec. 8, 1556. ——, Robert, Holom, Nov. 4, 1556.	15	1	72
Oct. 2, 1567. ——, Robert, (bur. Slaidburne), Jun. 24, 1567.	17		711
May 30, 1560. ——, Thomas, Bursaye, par. Holme in Spaldingmore, Apl. 14, 1560.	16		71
Oct. 5, 1564. ——, Thomas, Gawkthorp, par. Kirkheaton, Oct. 21, 1558.	17		373
Dec. 16, 1557. ——, Thomas, Outthorne, mylner, Nov. 23, 1557.	15	2	46
Apl. 17, 1567. ——, Thomas, Pathorne (bur. Gysburne), Feb. 5, 1566.	17		619
Oct. 4, 1564. ——, William, Erneclif, July 20, 1564.	17		370
Jan. 11, 1562. ——, William, Holme in Spaldingmore, Dec. 12, 1562.	17		141
Dec. 14, 1557. ——, William, Northe Ferybie, Nov. 10, 1557.	15	2	49
May 13, 1568. ——, William, Sutton on Lounde (Notts.), husbn., Apl. 16, 1566.	17		802
May 5, 1558. Atkinsone, Thomas, Estmarkham (Notts.), Dec. 28, 1557.	15	2	333
Mar. 13, 1556. Atkyn, Richard, Hamylton, par. Braton, Nov. 20, 1556.	15	1	184
Apl. 20, 1559. Atkynson, Alis, Kelvyngton, widow, Dec. 3, 1558.	15	3	371
May 19, 1559. ——, Christopher, Ledes, Aug. 27, 1558.	15	3	426
May 5, 1558. ——, Christopher, Westretford (Notts.), Dec. 6, 1557.	15	2	242
Nov. 5, 1554. ——, Henry, Morkar (bur. Rypon), July 9, 1554.	14		291
May 7, 1559. ——, Henry, Waltenhead (bur. Kirkbye Overbloys), husbn., Aug. 24, 1558.	15	3	384
Jun. 11, 1557. ——, Hugh, Castilforth, Mar. 19, 1556.	15	1	288
Oct. 1, 1562. ——, John, Arinclif, Apl. 10, 1562.	17		110
Mar. 31, 1558. ——, John, Bawne, par. Snaythe, Mar. 9, 1557.	15	2	177
Apl. 13, 1558. ——, John, Sutton on Derwent, Feb. 7, 1557.	15	2	188
Apl. 20, 1559. ——, John, Sutton (Retford, Notts.), Dec. 2, 1558.	15	3	365
Apl. 28, 1559. ——, John, Thorganby, Sep. 10, 1558.	15	3	362
Jun. 21, 1554. ——, Lyonell, Whitley, Jun. 16, 1554.	14		12
Sep. 30, 1558. ——, Margaret, Morcar (bur. Ripon), widow, Aug. 9, 1558.	15	3	56
Apl. 27, 1558. ——, Richard, Swynden, par. Gysborne, husbn., Dec. 22, 1557.	15	2	201
Oct. 1, 1561. ——, Robert, Preston in Holderness, husbn., Mar. 13, 1556.	17		47
Mar. 7, 1559. ——, Thomas, Braffartone, yeoman, Jan. 10, 1559.	16		6
Jun. 20, 1562. ——, Thomas, Carlton Myniate (bur. Thirske), Mar. 30, 1562.	17		89
Aug. 21, 1561. ——, Thomas, Ferybe, husbandman, Mar. 20, 1561.	17		56
Dec. 3, 1561. ——, Thomas, Gysburne, Oct. 8, 1561.	17		27
Apl. 7, 1557. *als.* Cooke, Elizabeth, Addle, Mar. 2, 1556.	15	1	204
May 10, 1559. Atkynsone, Elizabeth, Boltone nye Bowland, widow, Apl. 6, 1559.	15	3	385
Apl. 30, 1556. ——, John, Ragenhill (Notts.), husbandman, Dec. 30, 1555.	15	1	29
Jun. 2, 1558. ——, Thomas, junr., Everingham, Mar. 13, 1557.	15	2	313

		Vol.	Pt.	Fol.
May 6, 1557.	Atmar, Elizabeth, Shipbie, Jun. 9, 1556.	15	1	238
Aug. 6, 1567.	Atmarre, Elizabeth, Skidbie, widow, Apl. 22, 1567.	17		699
Dec. 1, 1558.	Atmer, Thomas, Shipby (Skidby), husbandman, Aug. 11, 1558.	15	3	148
May 6, 1557.	Attkinson, John, Kirskell, par. Adle, husbandman, Mar. 20, 1556.	15	1	214
Jan. 14, 1558.	———, John (bur. Ripon), Sep. 22, 1558.	15	3	191
May 28, 1557.	———, John, Sandhowton, bucher, Apl. 30, 1558.	15	1	256
Jun. 12, 1557.	———, Richard, Goldall (bur. Snaith), May 15, 1557.	15	1	275
May 13, 1557.	———, Thomas, Kilvington (Notts.), Dec. 17, 1556.	15	1	217
Aug. 21, 1561.	Atyll, Alice, Ticton (bur. Beverley), widow, Apl. 7, 1561.	17		56
Mar. 23, 1557.	Auderdaill, Margaret, Pattrington, widow, Jan. 19, 1557.	15	2	175
Feb. ult., 1558.	Audhouse, James, Seamer, Dec. 8, 1558.	15	3	281
July 8, 1561.	Audislay, William, Osset, yeoman, Apl. 11, 1561.	17		80
Sep. 21, 1557.	Audous, Edward, Doncaster, singleman, marchante, July 5, 1557.	15	1	352
May 6, 1557.	Austaine, Philipe, Semer, Nov. 20, 1556.	15	1	247
July 16, 1562.	Austeweke, Thomas, Morley (bur. Batley), clothear, May 30, 1562.	17		97
Jan. 12, 1558.	Auston, Andrew, Beverlay, cordiner, Nov. 7, 1558.	15	2	354
Oct. 1, 1558.	Austrope, Christopher, Thornar, July 26, 1558.	15	3	89
Sep. 17, 1562.	Austweke, William, Morley (bur. Batley), clothier, Sep. 1, 1562.	17		107
Oct. 8, 1562.	Averell, William, Nottingham, Apl. 6, 1562.	17		122
Oct. 7, 1561.	Averyll, Margery, Nottingham, Dec. 6, 1559.	17		42
Apl. 27, 1558.	Aveson, Robert, Sharleston, par. Warmefelde, Feb. 2, 1557.	15	2	193
Feb. 28, 1566.	Avott, John, clerk, curate of Lyverton, Jan. 3, 1565.	17		616
Feb. 23, 1559.	Awbraye, Adam, (Darton ?) May 20, 1558.	16		1
Oct. 24, 1554.	———, Richard, Heighame, par. Darton, Apl. 22, 1554.	14		309
Feb. 6, 1558.	Awbrowghe, John, Bridlington keye, fysherman, Sep. 30, 1558.	15	3	259
May 5, 1564.	Awcoke, Bryan, Carlton (bur. Snaythe), 1563.	17		342
Feb. 9, 1557.	Awderdaill, Robert, Owtthorne, Dec. 16, 1557.	15	2	119
Feb. penult., 1556.	Awderson (or Anderson), John, Northe houses, par. Cottingham, Nov. 1, 1556.	15	1	180
Jan. 24, 1558.	Awderson, Myles, Lowsdaile, par. Kildaile, Oct. 27, 1558.	15	3	22
Nov. 10, 1563.	———, William, Norhousis, par. Cottingham, May 2, 1563.	17		300
May 9, 1565.	Awdus, William, Scardburghe, Feb. 20, 1564.	17		425
Jun. 6, 1560.	Awemonde, Lawrance, Hooton Craunsewycke, labr., Nov. 19, 1559.	16		72
Dec. 1, 1557.	Awgar, Richard, Heworth in York, Sep. 20, 1557.	15	2	95
Nov. 9, 1557.	Awger, Margaret, widow (bur. Hunttyngton), July 26, 1557.	15	2	89
Mar. 2, 1558.	Awkbarrowe, Johan, York, widow, Aug. 10, 1558.	15	3	282
Apl. 20, 1559.	Awkelay, Elizabeth, Wallesbe (Notts.), widow, Mar. 3, 1558.	15	3	368
No date.	———, John, Wallesby, Nov. 4, 1555.	14		19
Nov. 6, 1567.	Awkes, Edmunde, Newsom, par. Wressill, Sep. 30, 1567.	17		733
Apl. 15, 1558.	———, John, Bryghton (bur. Bubwythe), bachelor, Aug. 2, 1554.	15	2	179
Nov. 8, 1557.	Awkland, John, York, walker or sherman, Oct. 5, 1557.	15	2	89
Apl. 23, 1563.	Awmber, John, Haworthe, Sep. 10, 1561.	17		223
Mar. 9, 1557.	Awmon, Edward, Carnabye, yeoman, Sep. 4, 1557.	15	2	128
Sep. 30, 1557.	Awmonde, John, Cottingham, husbandman, Jun. 8, 1557.	15	1	327
Feb. penult., 1556.	Awnwyke, Edward, Cottingham, Oct. 21, 1556.	15	1	180
Aug. 4, 1558.	Awsten, James, Beverley, baker, Dec. 29, 1557.	15	3	1
Mar. 29, 1555.	———, Sir James, Harpham, Dec. 2, 1554.	14		188
July 26, 1557.	Aydon, William, Helmyshlay, May 20, 1557.	15	1	319
Nov. 12, 1556.	Aykerod, Robert, junr., Sourbie, par. Halyfax, Aug. 2, 1556.	15	1	111
Feb. ult., 1559.	Ayme, Thomas, Wheldryke, Jan. 10, 1559.	16		4
May 5, 1558.	Aynysworth, Rawffe, Kirklington (Notts.), Apl. 24, 1558.	15	2	256
Mar. 26, 1560.	Ayrson, Thomas, Great Edstone, husbandman, Aug. 31, 1559.	16		19
Oct. 4, 1564.	Ayrton, Christopher, Pathorne (bur. Gisburne), Jun. 18, 6 Eliz.	17		372
Nov. 26, 1566.	———, John, Pathorne (bur. Gisburne), July 22, 1566.	17		600
Oct. 5, 1558.	———, William, Pathorne, par. Gisburne, husbn., Jun. 26, 1558.	15	3	60
Mar. 27, 1560.	Ayseley, William, Whorleton, glover, Nov. 20, 1559.	16		21
May 2, 1560.	Babthorpe, Rawffe, Avarhame (Notts.), gentleman, Sep. 26, 1559.	16		38
Nov. 22, 1555.	Bacheler, John, York, cordwyner, Nov. 13, 1555.	14		182
Dec. 3, 1558.	Bachouse, Jennett, Over Catton, widow, Oct. 20, 1558.	15	3	149
May 13, 1557.	Bachowse, John, junr., West Retford (Notts.). Nov. 2, 1556.	15	2	134
Sep. 30, 1560.	Backhouse, Agnes, Ripon, spenster. *No date.*	16		109
Oct. 13, 1558.	Backhowse, John, West Retforth (Notts.), Aug. 13, 1558.	15	2	357

A.D. 1554 TO 1568.

		Vol.	Pt.	Fol.
Oct. 5, 1558.	Baddie, Robert, junr., Holme in Spalding More, Apl. 25, 1558.	15	3	71
Mar.15, 1558.	Badkyn, Thomas, Awghton, Sep. 7, 1558.	15	3	167
Mar,19, 1562.	Bady, William, Holme Spaldingmore, Jan. 27, 1562.	17		216
Oct. 11, 1565.	Bagelay, Richard, Cropwel Butlar (Notts.), husbn., July 18, 1565.	17		470
Oct. 7, 1557.	Bagnald, Thomas, Gresley (Notts.), May 8, 1557.	15	2	25
May 13, 1557.	Bagulaie, William, Bleasbie (Notts.), Apl. 13, 1557.	15	1	235
Oct. 7, 1557.	Baguley, Thomas, Gybsemer (bur. Blesebe, Notts.), May 25, 1557.	15	2	21
May 9, 1565.	Baildon, Danyell, Baildon, par. Otley, Feb. 13, 1564.	17		422
July 19, 1557.	———, John (bur. Howke), Apl. 7, 1557.	15	1	314
Nov.16, 1558.	Baile, George, Langtun, husbandman, Aug. 12, 1558.	15	3	124
Jan. 12, 1558,	Baillaie, Margaret, widow of Philippe B., Everthorpe, par. North Cave, Nov. 11, 1558.	15	3	194
Oct. 20, 1558.	Bailland, Robert, Hartton, par. Bossaile, yeoman, May 22, 1558.	15	3	234
Aug. 4, 1558.	Baillay, Phillipe, Everthroppe, par. Northe Cave, May 3, 1558.	15	3	6
Jun. 12, 1557.	Bailton, Thomas (bur. Whytgyft), May 1, 1557.	15	1	274
Feb. 6, 1558.	Bainton, Margaret, Fostone, Oct. 27, 1558.	15	3	259
May 13, 1557.	Baise, Miles, Lowdham (Notts.), Nov. 21, 1556.	15	1	222
Oct. 12, 1558.	Baite, John, Kingston, par. Ratliffe on Soore (Notts.), husbandman, Mar. 30, 1558.	15	3	33
Oct. 13, 1558.	Baithlaie, Robert, Westhorpe, par. Sowthwell (Notts.), June 11, 1558.	15	2	361
May 13, 1557.	Baithley, Alice (bur. Southwell, Notts.), Jan. 8, 1556.	15	1	234
Apl. 30, 1556.	Baithleye, Thomas, Southwell (Notts.), Feb. 13, 1555.	15	1	33
Aug.27, 1567.	Baittes, Nycholes (bur. Helmsley), July 13, 1567.	17		696
Sep. 19, 1566.	Bakar, Thomas, Swynflete, Nov. 5, 1566.	17		571
Apl. 20, 1559.	Bakehouse, Elizabeth, West Rettord (Notts.), wid., Sep. 20, 1558.	15	3	429
Apl. 28, 1559.	———, John, Wheldrake, Aug. 10, 1558.	15	3	361
Jun. 29, 1554.	———, Richard, Mekleby (bur. Lith), Aug. 21, 1553.	14		141
July 12, [1555].	Baker, Alexander, Whitgifte, Aug. 20, 1552.	14		261
Jan. 25, 1557.	———, Edward (bur. Adlingflete), May 13, 1557.	15	2	160
Oct. 6, 1557.	———, John, Bothumsall (Notts.), Aug. 17, 1556.	15	2	8
Sep. 18, 1564.	———, John, Hull, porter, Apl. 7, 1564.	17		361
Jan. 16, 1558.	———, John, Usflytt (bur. Whitgift), Oct. 29, 1558.	15	3	209
Feb. 28, 1566.	———, Laurance (bur. Gisburne), July 21, 1566.	17		617
May 13, 1557.	———, Seyth, Tuxford (Notts.), husbandman, Mar. 7, 1556.	15	2	134
May 11, 1557.	———, Thomas, Usflett (bur. Whytgift), Apl. 12, 1557.	15	1	252
May 5, 1558.	———, William, Kirktone (Notts.), Apl. 6, 1558.	15	2	332
Oct. 1, 1566.	———, William, Seamer, labourer, May 12, 1566.	17		583
Apl. 19, 1564.	Bakester, Symond (bur. Carlton, Craven), Mar. 8, 1564.	17		330
Mar.10, 1555.	Bakon, Robert, Halloughton (Notts.), husbandman, Oct. 26, 1554.	14		230
Dec.14, 1557.	Balay, Rauffe, North Cave, Mar. 11, 1556.	15	1	358
Dec.14, 1557.	———, Robert, North Cave, Sep. 16, 1557.	15	1	359
Mar. 6, 1567.	Balaye, Anthony, Gowle, Dec. 4, 1567.	17		762
Oct. 29, 1554.	Balding, John, Dubbham on Trent (Notts.), Nov. 16, 1547.	14		288
May 5, 1558.	Baldinge, William, senr., Dunham on Trente (Notts.), Aug. 24, 1551.	15	2	211
Oct. 6, 1557.	Baldocke Laurence, Bradmore, par. Bonney (Notts.), Sep. 13, 1557.	15	2	26
Oct. 6, 1557.	———, Laurence,junr.,Bradmore (bur.Bonney,Notts.),Jun.16,1557.	15	2	26
Aug.27, 1567.	Baley, Jane, Hoton, par. Lestingam, May 21, 1567.	17		696
Apl. 28, 1563.	———, Robert, the chapell parish, Hull, Feb. 26, 1562.	17		237
Jan. 15, 1565.	Balland, John, Tikehill, Nov. 26, 1565.	17		494
Jan. 8, 1562.	———, Richard, Great Smeton, Aug. 21, 1562.	17		141
Oct. 22, 1558.	———, Thomas, East Herlseye, yeoman, Aug. 27, 1558.	15	3	235
Sep. 30, 1557.	Ballande, Margaret, Hull, widow, Dec. 20, 1556.	15	1	326
July 15, 1561.	Ballye, Robert, Hotton Robert, mylner, May 24, 1561.	17		82
Oct. 7, 1556.	Bamfforthe, Roger, Belhowse Grange, par. Cockney (Notts.), husbn., Oct. 4, 1556.	15	1	192
Jun. 23. 1567.	Bampton, Christopher, Letheley, Mar. 25, 1567.	17		665
Apl. 24, 1559.	Banester, John, Hensall (bur. Snathe), Apl. 10, 1559.	15	3	310
Oct. 8, 1562.	———, John, Myssen (Notts.), Apl 15, 1561.	17		121
Oct. 3, 1560.	Banestre, Robert, Over Shellsaye (bur. Sladburne), gent.,Dec.24,1559.	16		118
Jan. 23, 1558.	———, William, Easington (bur. Sladburne), gent., Aug. 1, 1558.	15	3	214
May 2, 1560.	Bangke, William, Aubroughe, husbandman, Apl. 21, 1559.	16		51
Dec.17, 1557.	Banister, John, Sandhuton, Nov. 22, 1557.	15	2	88

A.D. 1554 TO 1568.

		Vol.	Pt.	Fol.
Mar.23, 1557.	Banke, Christopher, Whysted in Holderness, husbn., Dec. 27, 1557.	15	2	174
Feb. 10, 1561.	———, George, Sledmer, Feb. 14, 1559.	17		9
Apl. 7, 1554.	———, John a, Wiested, wever (bur. Winestead). *No date.*	14		158
Apl. 22, 1556.	———, Leonarde, Lithe, Feb. 10, 1555.	15	1	27
Jan. 19, 1558.	———, Margaret (bur. Eskrige), Dec. 1, 1558.	15	3	21
Aug.13, 1567.	———, Mertyn, Wynestead, beare brewer, July 1, 1566.	17		690
Apl. 28, 1563.	———, Richard, Northe Cave, yeoman, Dec. 11, 1562.	17		236
May 2, 1560.	———, Robert, Scardburgh, burgess, Mar. 9, 1558.	16		34
May 9, 1565.	———, Thomas, Banke Newton, par. Gargrave, esq., Sep. 27, 1564.	17		432
May 2, 1560.	———, Thomas, Scarburgh, marrener, May 25, 1559.	16		36
Sep. 1, 1566.	———, William, Sledmar, husbandman, Apl. 25, 1566.	17		571
Jun. 12, 1567.	Bankes, Alison, Buholme, par. Nunkelinge, Feb. 10, 1567.	17		662
Sep. 13, 1565.	———, Awstayne, Longe Preston, May 6, 1565.	17		463
Mar. 4, 1560.	———, Elizabeth, Beverlay, Aug. 3, 1559.	16		165
Mar.17, 1556.	———, John, Aldbourghe, husbandman, Jan. 30, 1556.	15	1	187
Apl. 7, 1554.	———, Martin, Thorpe par. Welwicke, Dec. 26, 1554.	14		219
Sep. 26, 1558.	———, Thomas (bur. Baddesworth), clerke, Aug. 14, 1558.	15	3	51
Sep. 21, 1557.	———, William, Rotherham, July 4, 1557.	15	1	349
May 5, 1568.	Bankus, Richard, Beverley, Dec. 26, 1567.	17		777
Jun. 6, 1558.	Banyster, John, York, May 18, 1558.	15	2	287
Nov.21, 1556.	———, Lyonell, Hensall, par. Snaithe, Apl. 20, 1556.	15	1	115
Sep. 30, 1556.	———, William, Eassington, par. Slaydburne, gent., Aug. 20, 1556.	15	1	144
Oct. 2, 1567.	Barbar, Alice, Dewisburie, widow, July 7, 1567.	17		716
Jun. 5, 1566.	Barber, James, Dewysberye, clothier, Jan. 13, 8 Eliz.	17		551
Dec. 3, 1560.	———, Roger, Kirkeheton, Oct. 13, 1560.	16		131
Apl. 29, 1559.	———, Thomas, Eskrige, Apl. 23, 1559.	15	3	361
May 10, 1567.	Barboɪ, John, Awkley co. York (bur. Fynnyngley, Notts.), husbn., Sep. 5, 1566.	17		651
May 27, 1562.	Barcar, John, Egton, Dec. 9, 1558.	17		100
Apl. 20, 1559.	———, Margaret, Ruddington (Notts.), Nov. 1, 1558.	15	3	371
Dec. 16, 1557.	Barcharde, Henry, Preston (Holderness), Nov. 13, 1557.	15	2	44
Oct. 3, 1555.	———, William, Prestone (Holderness), May 10, 1555.	14		175
May 6, 1557.	———, William (bur. Skyfflinge), Jan. 23, 1556.	15	1	241
July 9, 1563.	Barcherd, William, Rosse, husbandman, May 2, 1563.	17		265
May 17, 1557.	Barde, Ellen, Nafferton, widow, Mar. 31, 1557.	15	1	244
May 26, 1567.	Baret, Robert, Righton, Oct. 29, 1566.	17		654
Mar.23, 1557.	Barffoote, George, Hornesey, husbandman, Sep. 17, 1557.	15	2	174
Feb. 6, 1558.	Barge, Petere, Hummanbie, Sep. 1, 1558.	15	3	261
Apl. 17, 1563.	Barghe, Robert, Snytall, par. Normanton, Dec. 6, 156[2].	17		221
Feb. 15, 1558.	Barige, Thomas, Beifforth, husbandman, 1558.	15	3	269
Oct. 12, 1558.	Barkar, Thomas, Ruddington (bur. Flafurthe, Notts.), Dec. 5, 1557.	15	3	28
May 14, 1567.	Barker, Elizabeth (bur. Gysburne), Dec. 6, 1566.	17		647
July 6, 1555.	———, Elizabeth, servaunt at Sowthclif, par. North Cave, Oct. 4, 1554.	14		258
May 29, 1557.	———, Isabell, Wistow, Oct. 3, 1556.	15	1	264
Mar. 8, 1558.	———, John, Cherye Burton (bur. Cottingham), priest, Feb. 10, 1558.	15	3	285
Jan. 31, 1563.	———, John, Crambum, husbandman, Jan. 26, 1563.	17		310
Mar.20, 1559.	———, John, Clyffurthe, par. Bramham, May 12, 1558.	16		15
May 2, 1560.	———, John, Hallyfaxe, Feb. 18, 1559.	16		42
Dec. 18, 1560.	———, John, Lynton, par. Spoffurthe, Jan. 1, 1559.	16		136
Sep. 26, 1558.	———, John, Oldsteid, par. Kilborne, July 24, 1558.	15	3	87
Jun. 4, 1561.	———, John, Standley (bur. Wakfeld), May 26, 1560.	17		68
Oct. 1, 1556.	———, John, Tadcaster, Aug. 6, 1555.	15	1	135
Dec. 6, 1557.	———, John, Thormonbye, Sep. 24, 1557.	15	2	87
Oct. 11, 1565.	———, Lyones, Eastretford (Notts.), yeoman, May 27, 1565.	17		473
Mar. 2, 1558.	———, Margaret, Sandhoton, widow, Feb. —, 1558.	15	3	282
July 19, 1560.	———, Richard, Brandesdaill (bur. Kyrkedayll), husbn., May 21, 1560.	16		94
Apl. 3, 1559.	———, Richard, Bulome, par. Helmeslay, May 14, 1554.	15	3	318
Apl. 20, 1559.	———, Richard, Harworth (Notts.), labourer, Dec. 10, 1558.	15	3	370
Mar.30, 1555.	———, Richard, Tadcaster, Mar. 14, 1554.	14		190
Mar. 2, 1558.	———, Robert, Sandhoton, husbandman, Aug. —, 1557.	15	3	282
Oct. 7, 1557.	———, Sir Robert, Laxton (Notts.), clerk, May 1, 1557.	15	2	16

2

		Vol.	Pt.	Fol.
Aug.31, 1565.	Barker, Roger, Wombleton, par. Kirkedaill, husbn., Jan. 13, 1560.	17		460
Oct. 8, 1562.	———, Thomas, Bevercottes (Notts.), husbn., Mar. 8, 1561.	17		121'
Apl. 18, 1560.	———, Thomas, Brawell, Jan. 17, 1559.	16		30
Jun. 5, 1564.	———, Thomas, Carlton (bur. Helmesley), husbn., Feb. 26, 1560.	17		349
Mar.19, 1559,	———, Thomas, Dewysburye, yeoman, Jun. 12, 1557.	16		13
July 31, 1562.	———, Thomas, Nawton, par. Kyrkedaill, husbn., Aug. 9, 1558.	17		99
Dec. 3, 1560.	———, Thomas, Sutton (Holderness), Mar. 25, 1560.	16		134
Nov.11, 1558.	———, Thomas, Thormonbye, Sep. 8, 1558.	15	3	73
Apl. 7, 1557.	———, William, Chapell Haddilsay (bur. Byrkyn), Mar. 10, 1556.	15	1	204
Jun. 9, 1556.	———, William, Newton Kyme, May 19, 1556.	15	1	43
Apl. 15, 1562.	———, William, Owstone (bur. Cowkkixwolde), Feb. 13, 1558.	17		159
May 11, 1563.	———, William, senr., Owstonne (bur. Cookwold), Apl. 24, 1563.	17		240
July 22, 1558.	———, William, Tadcaster, May 29, 1558.	15	2	386
Oct. 27, 1556.	———, William, Scarcrof, par. Thornar, Sep. 12, 1556.	15	1	71
Oct. 10, 1556.	Barkeston, Anne, wid. of Edw. B., senr., Barkeston, par. Shereborne, Aug. 28, 1556.	15	1	70
Nov.17, 1558.	———, Nicholas, Barkeston, gent., Oct. 14, 1558.	15	3	115
Apl. 27, 1558.	———, Thomas, Dewesburye, gent., Nov. 4, 1557.	15	2	193
Oct. 12, 1556.	Barkestone, Edward, Shereburne in Elmett, Aug. 10, 1556.	15	1	96
Jan. 13, 1558.	Barlay, Omfray, Barnbye, par. Blythe (Notts.), husbn., Oct. 18, 1558.	15	3	185
Oct. 23, 1555.	Barlaye, James, Wistowe, Sep. 14, 1555.	14		200
Apl. 27, 1563.	Barley, Andro, Huthwhaite, par. Whorlton, yeoman, July 20, 1562.	17		226
Oct. 4, 1565.	Barmbe, John, Essingwold, May 5, 1565.	17		481
Apl. 16, 1567.	———, Laurance, Preston in Holderness, husbn., Dec. 29, 1566.	17		634
July 18, 1560.	———, Robert, Humanbye, Jan. 5, 1559.	16		94
May 10, 1559.	———, Thomas, Nafferton, husbandman, Dec. 12, 1558.	15	3	389
Mar.13, 1565.	Barmbie, Symon, Sherburne, Nov. 26, 1565.	17		503
Aug.14, 1556.	Barmby, George, Snaynton, par. Brompton, Jun. 22, 1556.	15	1	61
July 18, 1560.	Barmebie, Emmote, Hummanbie, widow, Feb. 28, 1559.	16		94
Dec.17, 1557.	Barmeburghe, George, Kymberworthe (bur. Rotherham), Nov.6,1557.	15	2	38
Aug. 3, 1563.	Barnarde, Elizabeth (bur. Locton), ———, 1563.	17		212
Mar.30, 1559.	Barne, Henry, Hornsay. *No date.*	15	3	298
Oct. 1, 1562.	———, Richard, Holyme, Jan. 27, 1561.	17		113
Jan. 20, 1557.	Barnebie, Thomas, Barnbie, par. Calthorne, Aug. 23, 1557.	15	2	66
Apl. 20, 1559.	Barneby, Richard, North Wheatly (Notts.), Aug. 6, 1558.	15	3	366
Mar. 4, 1562.	Barnes, Robert, Dripowle, Dec. 18, 1562.	17		149
Jan. 8, 1563.	———, Robert, Haitefeld, Oct. 28, 1563.	17		308
Jan. 12, 1558.	Barneyfather, William, Croppwell Buttler, par. Tithebie (Notts.), Oct. 28, 1558.	15	3	181
May 2, 1566.	Barnsley, Roger, Sheaffeld, Jan. 16, 1565.	17		521
Feb. 20, 1560.	Baroclought, William, Whytley (bur. Kellington), Jun. 17, 1560.	16		147
Oct. 31, 1556.	Barone, Kyrshen, York, widow, Oct. 26, 1556.	15	1	106
Apl. 20, 1559.	Barowe, Henry, Austerfeld (Notts.), Mar. 28, 1558.	15	3	309
Oct. 1, 1556.	——— (Barwe in Register), Hughe, Byrdsall, Sep. 6, 1556.	15	1	68
Oct. 10, 1566.	Barr, Isabell, Estwett (Notts.), widow, Apl. 26, 1566.	17		594
May 4, 1558.	Barra, John, Kirkebye in Ashefelde (Notts.), July 10, 1557.	15	2	213
Jan. 23, 1561.	Barrane, Steven, Tunstall, husbn., Apl. 30, 1559.	17		20
May 13, 1568.	Barret, William, Eperston (Notts.), husbandman, Feb. 10, 1567.	17		796
Oct. 6, 1557.	Barrett, Elizabeth, Hawxworthe (Notts.), July 26, 1557.	15	2	31
Oct. 6, 1557.	———, Thomas, Hawxworthe (Notts.), May 7, 1557.	15	2	32
May 5, 1568.	Barrette, George, Lothersdaill (bur. Carleton), July 3, 1567.	17		786
July 19, 1557.	Barrie, Nicholas (bur. Estretforde, Notts.), May 15, 1557.	15	1	287
July 15, 1567.	Barrooes, Thomas, Ripon, Dec. 9, 1565.	17		680
Jun. 5, 1556.	Barrowclughe, William, Hallifaxe, Apl. 4, 1556.	15	1	42
May 6, 1557.	Barrowe, Hewe, Skipton in Craven, Oct. 6, 1556.	15	1	253
Oct. 8, 1567.	———, Robert, Plumtrie (Notts.), Apl. 23, 1567.	17		726
Aug. 6, 1567.	———, Thomas, Hempholme, par. Leven, Apl. 15, 1566.	17		702
Oct. 11, 1565.	Barryt, William, Flintam (Notts.), husbandman, Apl. 17, 1563.	17		470
May 7, 1554.	Barstowe, Robert, Hallifax, Mar. 28, 1554.	14		2
Apl. 22, 1562.	Bartelay, John, Nottingham, gent., Sep. 1, 1561.	17		177
Nov.26, 1556.	Bartelott, Robert, Barkestone, par. Shereburn, Oct. 14, 1556.	15	1	118
Mar.20, 1556.	Barthorpe, Sir William, curate of Buttercrambe, par. Bossall, Aug. 24, 1556.	15	1	189

A.D. 1554 TO 1568.

Date	Name	Vol.	Pt.	Fol.
Nov. 5, 1561.	Barthrope, Annes, Whenbye, widow, May 4, 1561.	17		35
Dec. 1, 1558.	———, Robert, Beverlay, taylor, Sep. 27, 1558.	15	3	81
Dec. 12, 1560.	Barton, Connande, Newton on Darwent, par. Wylberfosse, gent., Jun. 5, 1559.	16		135
Aug. 3, 1555.	———, John, Kirklethome, gent., Jun. 26, 1555.	14		203
Apl. 18, 1567.	———, John, Thirske, July 19, 1566.	17		631
Apl. 23, 1554.	———, John, Whenbie, esquier, Feb. 15, 1552.	14		62
Sep. 15, 1561.	———, Margaret (bur. Scorburgh), widow, Apl. 7, 1561.	17		54
Jan. 17, 1567.	———, Mawd, Thriske, widow, Nov. 4, 1567.	17		754
Aug. 21, 1561.	———, Rauf, Scorebroughe, tayler, May 23, 1560.	17		57
Sep. 23, 1558.	———, Robert, clerk (Deanery of Ridall), Jun. 1, 1558.	15	3	87
Sep. 10, 1563.	———, Robert, Wyggynthorpe (bur. Terington), gent., Jun. 2, 1563.	17		204
Dec. 7, 1566.	———, Thomas, Appleton (bur. Bolton), Dec. 21, 1565.	17		600
Jun. 4, 1568.	———, Thomas, Thorppebassett, Mar. 7, 1568.	17		813
Sep. 6, 1565.	———, Thomas, Whenbie. esquier, July 9, 1565.	17		461
Mar. 4, 1560.	———, William, Southe Fenton, par. Kirke Fenton, May 20, 1560.	16		153
May 6, 1563.	———, William, Sutton Bonnyngton (Notts.), Aug. 8, 1562.	17		246
May 13, 1557.	Bartram, Elizabeth, Scrowbe (Notts.), widow, Feb. 12, 1556.	15	2	132
Oct. 13, 1558.	———, John, Sutton on Lound (Notts.), Apl. 19, 1558.	15	2	358 & 379
Oct. 8, 1567.	———, Jone, Sutton, par. Granbe (Notts.), widow, Sep. 10, 1566.	17		727
Oct. 8, 1561.	———, Robert, Knesall (Notts.), July 14, 1561.	17		39
Feb. 12, 1554.	Bartropp, Myles. *No place mentioned.* Dec. 13, 1554.	14		298
Oct. 1, 1556.	Barwe (Barowe, Act Book), Hughe, Byrdsall, Sep. 6, 1556.	15	1	68
Nov. 24, 1556.	Barweke, Bartilmewe, York, tanner, Oct. 23, 1556.	15	1	117
Jan. 5, 1557.	Barwhe (Bawrghe, Act Book), Robert, Scampston, par. Ryllington, Oct. 20, 1557.	15	2	72
Oct. 7, 1563.	Barwicke, Bryan, Bulcot (Notts.), Jan. 21, 1558.	17		291
Nov. 23, 1563.	———, John (bur. Cukewold), Sep. 8, 1563.	17		305
Dec. 5, 1558.	———, Sir Richard, chaplain of St. Saviour's, York, Oct. 5, 1558.	15	3	126
May 14, 1560.	———, Robert, Eskrycke, Dec. 8, 1559.	16		62
Sep. 18, 1563.	Barwyke, Richard, Bushopthorpe, husbandman, Apl. 8, 1563.	17		202
Sep. 20, 1557.	Baryman, Jennet, Wykeham, widow, Feb. 12, 1557.	15	1	334
Apl. 28, 1558.	Bas (or Basse), Anthonie, Cheryburton, husbandman, Feb. 17, 1557.	15	2	219
Apl. 26, 1559.	Basfurthe, Rauf, Thornaby (bur. Thormondby), Aug. 22, 1558.	15	3	311
Jan. 13, 1558.	Basse, William, Gamston (Notts.), husbandman, Oct. 6, 1558.	15	3	181
Apl. 27, 1556.	———, William, Northe Dalton, husbandman, Feb. 11, 1555.	15	1	14
Mar. 20, 1553.	Bassler, William, senr., York, butcher, Sep. 5, 1553.	14		213
Dec. 17, 1557.	Bate, Christopher, Treton, Apt. 13, 1557.	15	2	40
May 13, 1557.	———, John, clerk (bur. Wolanton, Notts.), 1556.	15	1	224
Dec. 4, 1554.	Bathe, Lionell, Ripon, priest, Jan. 14, 1553.	14		149
May 9, 1560.	Bathlay, Edmond, Suthewell (Notts.), Apl. 26, 1560.	16		58
Nov. 5, 1558.	Batman, John, Mekielfeild, par. Shearburne, husbn., Jan. 16, 1554.	15	3	231
May 2, 1560.	Batte, Christopher, Rawden, par. Gysslay, May 10, 1558.	16		56
Jan. 20, 1561.	———, Roger, Wakefeld, Mar. 10, 1560.	17		20
Apl. 5, 1558.	Battell, John, Lombe (bur. Sherburne), Nov. 10, 1557.	15	2	180
Jun. 18, 1557.	———, Robert, Willetofte (bur. Bubwith), yeoman, May 15, 1557.	15	1	292
July 3, 1561.	Batterisbe, Thomas, Southe house, par. Horton, Jan. 13, 1560.	17		77
May 9, 1565.	Battersbe, Thomas, Brakenbodome (Craven), Jan. 27, 1562.	17		434
May 5, 1568.	Battersbye, Alexander, Wigilsworthe, par. Longe Preston, Dec. 16, 1567.	17		787
Oct. 1, 1561.	Battie, Agnes, Albroughe in Holderness, Aug. 27, 1561.	17		47
Jan. 13, 1558.	———, Elles, Brotton, par. Clifton (Notts.), Oct. 1, 1558.	15	3	182
Dec. 13, 1557.	———, John, Darrington, husbandman, Sep. 3, 1557.	15	2	54
Oct. 1, 1562.	———, Robert (bur. Conyston), Jun. 26, 1562.	17		111
Aug. 4, 1558.	Battye, John, Swandelande (bur. North Fereby), husbn., May 26, 1558.	15	3	7
Apl. 18, 1560.	———, Thomas, Fyshelaike, labourer, Sep. 22, 1559.	16		30
No prob.	———, William, Aldbrughe in Holderness, husbn., Jan. 1, 1553.	14		295
Oct. 10, 1560.	Batyson, Robert, Kyrtlington (Notts.), husbandman, Apl. 1, 1560.	16		124
Oct. 7, 1561.	Bauldocke, Isabell, Cossall Marshe (Notts.), widow, Mar. 27, 1561.	17		43
May 4, 1556.	Bawde, Rawff (Helmesley), Oct. 9, 38 [Hen. VIII.].	15	1	28
Apl. 28, 1563.	Bawdwane, Edward, Cunnunley (bur. Kildweke), Jan. 15, 1562.	17		230
Jun. 4, 1561.	Bawdwen, James, Heptonstall, Aug. 16, 1560.	17		68
Dec. 22, 1556.	———. John, priest, curate of Derfelde, Aug. 8, 1556.	15	1	85

A.D. 1554 TO 1568.

		Vol.	Pt.	Fol.
Oct. 5, 1558.	Bawdwen, William, Colling (bur. Kildwicke), Apl. 8, 1558.	15	3	61
Oct. 5, 1558.	Bawdwyn, Edmonde, Flasby (bur. Gargrave), Jan. 7, 1557.	15	3	40
Sep. 28, 1557.	Bawdwyne, Christopher, Kyghley. Feb. 28, 1556.	15	1	338
May 5, 1568.	Bawmbrughe, George, Barton, par. Crambum, Mar. 12, 1566.	17		781
Apl. 20, 1556.	Baxbie, William, Baxbie, gent., Mar. 15, 1556.	15	1	22
Apl. 11, 1559.	Baxster, Anne, Hirst Curtnay, par. Birkyne, widow, Feb. 27, 1558.	15	3	333
Feb. 26, 1560.	———, Cicilie, widow of Richard B., senr., Marston, Jan. 18, 1560.	16		151
Jan. 12, 1558.	———, Sir John, Dunnington, par. Befford, priest, Aug. 14, 1558.	15	3	204
Apl. 23, 1556.	———, Richard, Aston, Apl. 8, 1550.	15	1	23
Apl. 11, 1559.	———, Richard, Hirst Curtney (bur. Birkyn), husbn., Apl. 12, 1556.	15	3	332
Mar. 15, 1558.	———, Richard, Marstonne, husbandman, Jan. 31, 1558.	15	3	242
Jan. 22, 1567.	Baxter, Elliner, Bowwicke, Oct. 16, 9 Eliz.	17		754
Oct. 4, 1565.	———, John, Bossall, labourer, Aug. 11, 1565.	17		482
May 17, 1554.	———, John, Cottingham, Aug. 20, 1553.	14		5
Mar. 1, 1564.	———, John, Cottingham, labourer, Jan. 4, 1564.	17		408
Feb. 10, 1557.	———, Robert, Cottingham, Jan. 13, 1557.	15	2	147
Aug. 20, 1558.	Baycheler, William, York, boucher, Jun. 4, 1558.	15	2	295
Apl. 27, 1564.	Bayckwell, William, Rodington (bur. Flafford, Notts.), husbn., Oct. 6, 1563.	17		341
Sep. 30, 1557.	Bayker, Thomas, Adlingflete, Aug. 17, 1557.	15	1	345
July 1, 1562.	Bayle, John, Bubwith, Jun. 20, 1562.	17		93
Apl. 22, 1562.	———, Richard, Ratlef on Trente (Notts.), husbn., Dec. 8, 1561.	17		192
Apl. 19, 1559.	Bayley, Thomas, Nottingham, Jan. 4, 1558.	15	3	357
Jan. 15, 1565.	Baylie, John, Barnislay, Jun. 3, 1558.	17		494
Apl. 26, 1559.	Baylles, William, Staxton, par. Whitby, Jan. 3, 1558.	15	3	364
Oct. 2, 1567.	Baylyer, Robert, Howke, Apl. 12, 1567.	17		710
May 20, 1564.	Baynbrige, Margaret, Moremonnckton, Feb. 16, 156[3-]4.	17		343
Apl. 28, 1563.	Bayne, John, Souerbie, ———, 1562.	17		239
Dec. 11, 1566.	Baynes, Adam, Nafferton, May 21, 1566.	17		601
May 13, 1557.	———, Richard, Sowthwell (Notts.), husbandman, Dec. 12, 1556.	15	1	235
Jan. 13, 1558.	———, Margaret, Sowthwell (Notts.), widow, Oct. 7, 1558.	15	3	205
Jun. 23, 1561.	———, Margaret, Thourne, widow, May 30, 1561.	17		84
Nov. 28, 1558.	Baynton, Jennett, Tunstall in Holderness, widow, Apl. 21, 1558.	15	3	76
May 15, 1564.	———, John, Norton, husbandman, May 9, 1564.	17		343
Dec. 22, 1557.	———, John, Watton, Aug. 31, 1557.	15	2	43
May 14, 1558.	———, Robert (bur. Nafferton), labourer, Dec. 30, 1557.	15	3	7
Feb. 20, 1558.	———, Thomas a, Tybthorp, par. Kirkebown, labr., Oct. 13, 1558.	15	3	275
Jan. 12, 1557.	———, Thomas, Watton, Nov. 25, 1557.	15	2	78
Dec. 9, 1556.	———, William, Tunstall, Oct. 6, 1556.	15	1	197
Dec. 22, 1557.	Bayrstow, Edward, Halyfax, Aug. 1, 1554.	15	2	48
Oct. 1, 1556.	Bayrstowe, Edward, Ovenden, par. Hallifax, Aug. 6, 1556.	15	1	142
May 4, 1557.	Bayte, Richard, Aghttone, par. Astone, Feb. 13, 1556.	15	1	276
Sep. 26, 1558.	———, Robert, Darnall, par. Sheffeld, arrowhedsmythe, July 24, 1558.	15	3	51
Sep. 30, 1563.	———, William, Gaytforthe (bur. Brayton), Apl. 6, 1563.	17		272
Oct. 7, 1557.	Bayteman, Gabriell, Bulcote (Notts.), Sep. 9, 1557.	15	2	22
July 6, 1560.	Baytes, John, Ibromedaile, par. Whytbye, Apl. 22, 1560.	16		88
Apl. 27, 1563.	———, William. Westlaithes (par. Whorlton), July 28, 1558.	17		224
Oct. 3, 1564.	Baytson, Elizabeth, Follyfate (bur. Spofforthe), Apl. 6, 1564.	17		365
Sep. 30, 1557.	———, Steven, Thurnum, par. Burton Agnes, husbn., ———, 1557.	15	1	342
May 30, 1556.	———, Thomas, Follyfaite, par. Spofforthe, Apl. 28, 1556.	15	1	39
Dec. 1, 1558.	Beale, Robert, Beverlay, cordiner, July 28, 1558.	15	3	147
Oct. 9, 1560.	Beall, Richard, Beverlay, tanner, July 12, 1560.	16		122
Mar. 19, 1559.	———, William, Egbrought (bur. Kyllyngton), Apl. 18, 1559.	16		13
Dec. 4, 1557.	Bealmeslay, Robert, Rednes (bur. Whytgyfte), May 16, 1557.	15	2	50
May 18, 1564.	Beamond, Edward, Horton, par. Bradford, Dec. 13, 1563.	17		344
Nov. 3, 1554.	Beamont, George, Almonbury, May 20, 1552.	14		290
Feb. 20, 1560.	———, John, the Hay in Lynthwayte, par. Allmonbrye, Jan. 29, 1560.	16		147
Oct. 1, 1556.	———, Thomas, Dewisberie, Aug. 13, 1556.	15	1	143
Apl. 27, 1558.	Beamonte, Agnes, wid. of Lawrance B., Meltame, par. Almunbury, Oct. 1, 1556.	15	2	194
Apl. 27, 1558.	———, William, Netherton, par. Almonburye, Oct. 4, 1557.	15	2	191

		Vol.	Pt.	Fol.
Apl. 20, 1564.	Beamount, Herrye, Southe Crosland (bur. Almonburie), Jan.10,1562.	17		327
Apl. 12, 1559.	———, Thomas, Almonbury, Oct. 8, 1558.	15	3	338
Feb. 25, 1558.	———, William, Brighouse, par. Eland, July 11, 1556.	15	3	279
May 5, 1568.	Beamounte, Umfrey. Overflockton, par. Thornell, yeom., Feb.16,1567.	17		785
May 11, 1555.	Beamund, Henrie, Danehowse in Honley, par. Almunburie, Mar. 30, 1 Mary.	14		35
Apl. 22, 1556.	Beane, William, Acworthe, gent., Jan. 4, 1555.	15	1	22
May 17, 1554.	Bearne, Robert, Burneholme, May 16, 1553.	14		5
Apl. 20, 1556.	Beaston, Richard, Escrike, Apl. 3, 1556.	15	1	15
July 27, 1567.	Bechem, John, senr., Filing, Feb. 18, 1566.	17		670
Apl. 6, 1566.	Becke, Thomas, Yearsley (bur. Cookeswold), Dec. 28, 1565.	17		509
Oct. 7, 1556.	Beckes, Thomas, Clareburghe (Notts.), Nov. 25, 1553.	15	1	149
Feb. 25, 1556.	Beckett, Myles, Meltone, par. Waithe, Jan. 12, 1556.	15	1	167
Sep. 30, 1563.	———, Rauf, Selbie, wyer drawer, Apl. 15, 1563.	17		272
Sep. 30, 1562.	Beckwith, Richard, Yarum, Aug. 11, 1562.	17		109
Feb. 6, 1558.	Beckwithe, John, South Kirkbie, Dec. 24, 1558.	15	3	255
May 5, 1568.	———, John, Wattone, preiste, Oct. 21, 1567.	17		776
May 2, 1566.	———, Robert, Yarom, Mar. 13, 1565.	17		539
July 26, 1557.	Beckwythe, Ambrose, Mydleton in Pekeringe lythe, gent.,Jun.6,1557.	15	1	320
May 2, 1560.	Becroft, William (bur. Longe Preston), Mar. 18, 1559.	16		43
Oct. 5, 1554.	Bed, Thomas, Ynglibe onder Grenehow in Cleveland, Oct. 30, 1551.	14		47
Aug. 28, 1563.	Beddforthe, William, Thornehill, yeoman, July 7, 1562.	17		211
Dec. 10, 1562.	Bedforthe, Robert, Esyngwold, Oct. 28, 1562.	17		132
Oct. 4, 1558.	Bee, Agnes, widow of John B., York, pewderrer, Sep. 28, 1558.	15	3	90
May 5, 1558.	—, Isabell, Mylneton (bur. West Markham, Notts.),wid.,Feb.16,1557.	15	2	252
Aug. 26, 1558.	—, John, York, pevderer, Aug. 2, 1558.	15	2	294
Mar. 6, 1556.	—, Laurence, Mylneton, par. West Markham (Notts.), husbn., Nov. 4, 1556.	15	1	183
Apl. 20, 1559.	—, Margaret, Bothumsall (Notts.), Mar. 12, 1558.	15	3	367
Oct. 11, 1565.	—, Richard, Mylneton, par. Markham (Notts.), husbn., Nov.5,1564.	17		473
Nov. 28, 1567.	—, Roger, Rudstone, gresseman, July 4, 1567.	17		737
Jan. 26, 1563.	Beesley, Raynold, York, advocate of the court of York, Nov. 20, 1562.	17		311
Sep. 19, 1556.	Beforthe, Thomas, Heworthe (bur. Allhallows, Peseholme), Sep. 10, 1556.	15	1	66
Oct. 9, 1561.	Begham, John, Egmunton (Notts.), July 18, 1561.	17		42
July 24, 1567.	Beilbie, John, Seaton, May 21, 1567.	17		666
Sep. 2, 1557.	———, Peter, Caiton, Aug. 15, 1557.	15	1	330
Aug. 6, 1567.	Beilbye, Robert, Bubwithe, taylliour, Mar. 29, 1567.	17		698
Apl. 17, 1567.	Beislay, James, Croke, par. Mytton, husbandman, Feb. 15, 1566.	17		622
Dec. 21, 1566.	Beiston, Robert, Beiston, par. Ledes, esquier, Mar. 31, 1566.	17		605
Sep. 26, 1558.	Beitt, Thomas, Gresbroke, par. Rotherham, Aug. 26, 1558.	15	3	50
Jun. 26, 1554.	Bekerdike, William, Newburghe (bur. Cookewald), 28 May, 1549.	14		148
Sep. 27, 1557.	Bekwythe, Sir Leonard, York, kt., Apl. 15, 1557.	15	1	336
Apl. 27, 1557.	Bekynsay, Thomas, Sandhoton, husbandman, Nov. 18, 1556.	15	1	208
Oct. 13, 1558.	Belamie, John, Eastmarkham, Dec. 28, 1557.	15	2	378
Jun. 14, 1560.	Belamye, Robert, junr., East Markham (Notts.), husbn., May 5, 1560.	16		85
Mar. 4, 1562.	Belbe, George, Nuton Rachforthe (bur. Hunmanbie,) Jun. 5, 1562.	17		153
Aug. 12, 1567.	Belbie, Thomas, Woldnewton (bur. Hunmanbie), Apl. 3, 1567.	17		693
May 18, 1559.	Beldome, William, Sturtton (Notts.), badger, Jan. 5, 1558.	15	3	405
Apl. 20, 1559.	Beldon, Robert, Est Retford (Notts.), Sep. 2, 1558.	15	3	369
Mar. 6, 1556.	Bell, Agnes, Eldmyer, par. Topclif, widow, Jan. 15, 1556.	15	1	202
Feb. 6, 1556.	——, Alison, Fawdington (bur. Cundall), Dec. 6, 1556.	15	1	171
Oct. 5, 1558.	——, Cicile, Kirklevington, widow, Jan. 16, 1557.	15	3	69
Oct. 17, 1558.	——, Davy, York (bur. Wheldrike), Sep. 14, 1558.	15	3	92
Mar. 8, 1566.	——, Henry, Holme in Spaldingmore, Dec. 27, 1566.	17		512
Mar. 30, 1559.	——, Henry, Waghen, Mar. 7, 1557.	15	3	298
May 12, 1559.	——, John, Bentlay (bur. Rowlay), husbandman, Mar. 15, 1558.	15	3	395
Sep. 9, 1558.	——, John, Bubwith, young man, July 31, 1558.	15	3	101
Oct. 3, 1560.	——, John, Hubie (bur. Sutton in Galtres), Aug. 19, 1560.	16		117
Oct. 13, 1565.	——, John, Kildall, July 29, 1565.	17		475
July 15, 1567.	——, John (bur. Rypon), Apl. 22, 1567.	17		676
Feb. 7, 1566.	——, John, Settryngton, husbandman, Jan. 24, 1566.	17		613

A.D. 1554 TO 1568.

		Vol.	Pt.	Fol.
May 4, 1558.	Bell, John, Wodborrowe (Notts.), Aug. 2, 1557.	15	2	214
Sep. 24, 1557.	——, Sir John, prest, Hawburne (bur. Bridlington), Jun. 30, 1557.	15	1	370
Mar. 10, 1554.	——, Johne, Fulsutton, Jan. 4, 1553.	14		131
Oct. 20, 1558.	——, Leonard, Dalton (bur. Topliffe), July 5, 1558.	15	2	347
Jan. 18, 1560.	——, Margaret, Hewby (bur. Sutton), Nov. 1, 1560.	16		140
Mar. 16, 1553.	——, Margaret, Woodhouse, par. Draxe, widow, Jun. 23, 1553.	14		212
Apl. 28, 1563.	——, Richard, Beverley, draper, Dec. 3, 1562.	17		237
Nov. 16, 1558.	——, Richard, Langton, labourer, Aug. 10, 1558.	15	3	125
July 8, 1558.	——, Richard, Spaldington (bur. Bubwith), Jun. 26, 1558.	15	2	325
Sep. 16, 1564.	——, Richard, Woldkirke, webster, July 18, 1564.	17		361
Mar. 29, 1555.	——, Robert, Frastrop, husbn., (bur. Carnanbye), Dec. 28, 1554.	14		188
Jun. 19, 1567.	——, Rowland, Westowe, labourer, Sep. 8, 1566.	17		656
Feb. 4, 1557.	——, Thomas, Bursay, par. Holme, Nov. 13, 1557.	15	2	163
Jun. 22, 1568.	——, Thomas, Foston, May 3, 1568.	17		824
Jan. 22, 1557.	——, Thomas, Huton Rudbye, husbandman, Sep. 28, 1557.	15	2	156
Apl. 4, 1560.	——, Thomas, Kyrtham, Mar. 24, 1559.	16		24
Mar. 4, 1562.	——, Thomas (bur. Paull), Sep, 7, 1562.	17		150
Oct. 7, 1563.	——, Thomas, Roston (Notts.), Mar. 21, 1562.	17		291
July 2, 1558.	——, Thomas, Topclif, Apl. 12, 1558.	15	2	342
Oct. 28, 1566.	——, Thomas, Westow, husbandman, Jun. 5, 1566.	17		586
Apl. 8, 1559.	——, William, Eldmire, par. Topliffe, Nov. 10, 1558.	15	3	321
July 19, 1557.	Bellamye, Anthony, Laneham (Notts.), July 1, 1557.	15	1	312
May 18, 1559.	————, James, Est Markam (Notts.), yeoman, Aug. 16, 1557.	15	3	407
Sep. 30, 1557.	Belland (or Bellerd). John, Lowthorpe, husbandman, July 22, 1557.	15	1	342
Sep. 28, 1557.	Bellerbye, Richard, Beverlay, tanner, Mar. 18, 1556.	15	1	357
Sep. 30, 1557.	Bellerd (or Belland), John, Lowthorpe, husbandman, July 22, 1557.	15	1	342
May 24, 1558.	Bellinggam, William, Harum, par. Helmesley, Sep. 27, 1557.	15	2	284
July 21, 1557.	Bellowe, William, Spaldingtone (bur. Bubwith), gresseman, July 4, 1557.	15	1	316
Nov. 12, 1556.	Beltonne, John, Newlande, par. Cottingham, Sep. 24, 1556.	15	1	109
Dec. 4, 1556.	Belwood, John, Felicekirke, Dec. 2, 1553.	15	1	119
May 10, 1554.	Bemunde, Robert, Thorp on Hill, par. Rothwell, Apl. 7, 1554.	14		136
Apl. 3, 1554.	Bemunte, Laurence, Meltame, par. Almonburie, Sep. 20, 1553.	14		222
Mar. 23, 1560.	Bende, Richard, Southe Kylvington, Jun. 9, 1559.	16		175
Oct. 4, 1564.	Benelandes, Alan, Morton, par. Bingley, Apl. 8, 1564.	17		369
Sep. 30, 1557.	Benes, Richard, Northe cave, Aug. 24, 1557.	15	1	326
Jan. 31, 1564.	Beneson, James, Kilton (bur. Brotton), Oct. 14, 1564.	17		404
Apl. 4, 1560.	Benette, William, Est Retforde (Notts.), Jan, 31, 1559.	16		24
May 5, 1568.	Benit, Thomas, Lund, labourer, Nov. 4, 1567.	17		776
Feb. 17, 1557.	Benkes, William, Royston, Jan. 18, 1557.	15	2	143
Apl. 19, 1564.	Bennes, William, Carleton (Craven), Jan. 17, 156[3-]4.	17		328
Jun. 2, 1561.	Bennet, Anthony, Nuthall (Notts.), May 4, 1560.	17		66
Apl. 22, 1563.	————, Jennet, Hillom, par. Monnckfriston, ——, 1562.	17		223
Aug. 2, 1557.	————, Thomas, Swyne, July 3, 1557.	15	1	322
July 26, 1558.	————, William, Preston in Holderness, Nov. 28, 1557.	15	3	12
Apl. 20, 1564.	————, William, Raistropp, par. Wharolme Percye, husbn., Mar. 18, 1563.	17		326
Oct. 8, 1556.	Bennett, Cuthbert (bur. Gedlinge, Notts.), Aug. 10, 1556.	15	1	152
Mar. 14, 1560.	————, John, Shelforthe (Notts.), labourer, Aug. 22, 1556.	16		163
May 5, 1558.	Benson, Christopher, Stoke next Newarke (Notts.), husbn., Mar. 29, 1558.	15	2	255
Mar. 5, 1557.	————, Christopher, Thorner, Feb. 18, 1557.	15	2	170
Mar. 23, 1559.	————, Elizabeth, Thornar, Feb. 28, 1559.	16		18
Feb. 6, 1558.	————, William, Thorne, Nov. 8, 1558.	15	3	255
May 2, 1566.	————, William, Wawplay, par. Lofthus, Nov. 28, 1565.	17		539
Oct. 1, 1556.	Bensone, Ranold, Doncaster, Mar. 10, 1555.	15	1	127
Dec. 5, 1565.	Bensonn, Alice, Thourne, May 1, 1563.	17		493
Mar. 26, 1565.	Bentame, Thomas, Northe Owrome, par. Halifax, clothier, Feb. 19, 1564.	17		416
May 13, 1557.	Bentlay, John, Gyrtton (Notts.), Apl. 6, 1557.	15	1	216
July 8, 1560.	Bentley, Edward, Clayton, par. Bradforthe, Apl. 1, 1560.	16		90
Feb. 24, 1558.	————, Elizabeth, Northowrome, par. Halifax, widow, Jan. 24, 1558.	15	3	278

		Vol.	Pt.	Fol.
Feb. 24, 1558.	Bentley, John, Northowrome, par. Halifax, Nov. 18, 1558.	15	3	278
May 8, 1567.	———, Robert, Elloughton, labourer, Dec. 20, 1566.	17		650
Sep. 9, 1561.	———, Robert, Heptenbrige, par. Heptonstall, July 14, 1561.	17		49
July 15, 1561.	Benynglay, John, Helleres (High Ellers), par. Cantlaye, May 12, 1561.	17		81
Apl. 18, 1560.	———, William, Heerles, par. Cantlay, Sep. 6, 1559.	16		32
Oct. 7, 1557.	Benytt, Richard, Lawdam (Notts), Apl. 7, 1557.	15	2	23
Apl. 28, 1558.	Berber, Christopher, Thormonbye neire the Teise (bur. Staynton), Mar. 6. 1557.	15	2	231
Dec. 1, 1563.	Berdsell, Margere, Waleswood (bur. Hartell), Oct. 28. 1563.	17		305
July 1, 1558.	Berdshay, Nicholas, Langley Carre (bur. Kirkburton), Apl. 30, 1558.	15	2	328
1553.	Bere, Beatrix, Almonbury, Jun. 4, 1554.	14		100
Apl. 28, 1563.	Berege, John, Skipsey in Holderness, Mar. 15, 1562.	17		239
Dec. 9, 1556.	———, Thomas, Skipsey in Holderness, Oct. 20, 1556.	15	1	72
Dec. 5, 1567.	———, Thomas, Skipsey in Holderness, 1567.	17		742
Oct. 6, 1558.	———, William, Wike, par. Bardsay, Aug. 18, 1558.	15	3	90
Mar. 19, 1562.	Beren (Berne), Richard, Warter, Sep. 7, 1562.	17		216
Sep. 29, 1557.	Berge, William, Salley nere Funtaunce (bur. Ripon), 1557.	15	1	330
Jan. 11, 1562.	Berie, John, Anlabie, par. Kirke Elley, July 14, 1562.	17		141
Oct. 2, 1560.	———, John, Thorner, Nov. 3. 1559.	16		113
Jun. 2, 1557.	———, Thomas, Lyttle Smeaton, par. Womerslaie, Mar. 15, 1556.	15	1	265
May 18, 1559.	Berighe, Thomas, Brandisburton, husbandman, Dec. 27, 1558.	15	3	412
Jan. 12, 1558.	Berne, William, Burnholme, Nov. 20, 1558.	15	3	201
Jan. 11, 1557.	Berrege, John, Brandesburton, husbandman, Oct. 15, 1557.	15	2	75
May 6, 1557.	Berregge, Agnes, Brandisburton, widow, Jan. 13, 1556.	15	1	238
Apl. 7, 1554.	Berrier, George, Sutton in Holdernes, Feb. 21, 1554.	14		218
May 5, 1568.	Berrye, Herrye, Bingley, Nov. 5, 1567.	17		787
Apl. 17, 1563.	Berstowe, John, Bronesherste in Ovenden, par. Halifax, yeoman, Jan. 3, 1562.	17		221
Jan. 10, 1558.	Berton, John, Eskrig, July 24, 1558.	15	3	169
Mar. 10, 1558.	Bertton, Jhone a, Newton par. Wilberfosse, husbn., Jan. 3, 1558.	15	3	158
Dec. 13, 1557.	Berye, Jennett, Allverthorpe (bur. Wakefelde), Oct. 17, 1557.	15	2	53
Nov. 12, 1567.	Beryman, Thomas, Wikam, ———, 1566.	17		734
Jan. 20, 1557.	Besacle, Edmonde, Fyshelaike, Sep. 11, 1557.	15	2	65
Dec. 2, 1562.	———, Isabell, Fyshelaike, May 12, 1562.	17		129
July 4, 1556.	———, Thomas, Fishelake, yeoman, May 4, 1556.	15	1	52
Oct. 12, 1564.	Bessacle, William, Eastbridgeforthe (Notts.), husbn., Apl. 25, 1564.	17		390
May 4, 1558.	Bessewycke, George, Normanton on Sore (Notts.), husbn., Sep. 4, 1557.	15	2	264
Mar. 21, 1564.	Best, George, senr. Cudworthe, par. Roystonne, husbn., Aug. 5, 1564.	17		410
Aug. 5, 1557.	———, James, Ovenden, par. Halifax, Jun. 15, 1557.	15	2	131
Dec. 1, 1558.	———, Jenett, Cottingham, Oct. 3, 1558.	15	3	81
Jun. 25, 1560.	———, William (bur. Kyrkebe Mysperton), Apl. 24, 1560.	16		87
Oct. 29, 1555.	Besthroppe, James, Wynthorpe (Notts.), May 1, 1554.	14		283
Jun. 22, 1568.	Bestone, Bryan, Eshalde (bur. Otteley), Apl. 13, 1568.	17		817
Oct. 12, 1558.	Bestonne, Robert, Gamston (Notts.), husbandman, July 8, 1553.	15	3	33
Feb. 18, 1556.	Bestwyke, Richard, Sylfoo, par. Hackenes, July 3, 1553.	15	1	161
Nov. 27, 1560.	Beswyke, William (Ridall Deanery), Nov. 30, 1560.	16		130
Apl. 1, 1559.	Bet, Robert, Claworthe (Notts.), husbandman, Feb. 4, 1558.	15	3	433
Apl. 20, 1559.	—, Thomas, Claworth (Notts.), husbandman, Sep. 3, 1558.	15	3	367
Feb. 1, 1554.	Betnam, Benet, Selbye, husbandman, Aug. 21, 1554.	14		297
Oct. 10, 1566.	Bett, Richard, Worksoppe (Notts.), Apl. 26, 1566.	17		587
Oct. 9, 1567.	———, Robert, Northe Whetley (Notts.), husbn., May 1, 1566.	17		721
Oct. 9, 1567.	Bette, William, Northe Wheatley (Notts.), July 14, 1567.	17		721
July 6, 1558.	Bettynsonne, Thomas, Helaugh, husbandman, Apl. 17, 1558.	15	2	325
Feb. 20, 1560.	Beuer, Robert (bur. Kyrkebyrton), Oct. 26, 1560.	16		148
Oct. 4, 1558.	Beuerlay, Edward, Whitkirke, Aug. 8, 1558.	15	3	58
Feb. 24, 1563.	Beuerley, Richard, Brustwicke (bur. Skeclinge), Nov. 7, 1563.	17		319
Sep. 29, 1557.	Bever, John, Kyrkebirton, July 20, 1557.	15	1	328
Oct. 7, 1563.	Bevercottes, Barbara, Bevercottes (Notts.), widow, Aug. 13, 1559.	17		295
May 2, 1560.	Beverlaye, Richard, Austrope, par. Whitkyrke, Sep. 10, 1559.	16		57
Aug. 8, 1562.	Beverley, William, Halifax, clothier, May 28, 1562.	17		103
Aug. 31, 1555.	Bewatter, Robert, Haymyltie (bur. Braytton), husbn., Feb. 8, 1555.	14		241
Jun. 12, 1567.	Bewbanke, Thomas, Drypoule, husbandman, Jan. 16, 1566.	17		665

A.D. 1554 TO 1568.

		Vol.	Pt.	Fol.
Apl. 11, 1559.	Bewe, William, Hamiltonne, par Braitonne, Feb. 1, 1558.	15	3	331
Jun. 12, 1557.	——, William, Stillingflete, Apl. 7, 1557.	15	1	290
No prob.	Bewes, Robert, Tikhill, Aug. 24, 1554.	14		296
Mar. 7, 1566.	Bewholme, George, Seaton, par. Seglstorne, Nov. 7, 1566.	17		515
Feb.penult.,1556.	Bewley, John, Cottingham, Dec. 10, 1556.	15	1	179
Nov.10, 1557.	Bewyke, Jerard, Beverley, waterman, Sep. 28, 1557.	15	2	99
Apl. 16, 1562.	Beye (Boys, Act Book), Richard, Edseton (Ridall), yeoman. *No date.*	17		159
Sep. 1, 1563.	Beyghton, Robert, Halome, par. Shefeld, May 20, 1563.	17		208
May 26, 1567.	Beylbye, Thomas, Waldnewton (bur. Hondmanbie), Oct. 1, 1566.	17		654
Oct. 6, 1557.	Beymonde, Henry, Shafforthe (bur. Everton, Notts.), Jul. 21, 1557.	15	2	8
Oct. 3, 1555.	Beyrd, William, Seton (bur. Silstron), Apl. 30, 1555.	14		176
Apl. 13, 1559.	Beyrley, Robert, Holme in Spaldingmore, Dec. 20, 1558.	15	3	347
Dec.18, 1562.	Beyston, Thomas, York, mylner, Nov. 20, 1562.	17		135
Dec. 2, 1561.	Beytt, William, Gresbrough, par. Rotherham, May 27, 1561.	17		31
Feb. 4, 1556.	Bibbe, John, Tychill, husbandman, Oct. 2, 1556.	15	1	168
Jun. 22, 1568.	Bickers, William, Griestrope, par. Filay, July 22, 1567.	17		820
Nov.28, 1567.	—— *als.* Vicars, Thomas, Griestrope, par. Fylay, husbn., Jun.12, 1567.	17		740
Apl. 19, 1559.	Bickerstaffe, Henry, Annsley (Notts.), yeoman, Jan. 13, 1558.	15	3	355
Mar.20, 1558.	Bickertonne, Robert, Tadcaster, Aug. 2, 1558.	15	3	289
May 4, 1558.	Bigg, Bartillmew, Nuttall (Notts.), May 3, 1557.	15	2	271
July 24, 1567.	Bigod, Katherin, Molgrave, widow, Oct. 15, 1566.	17		670
Mar. 8, 1558.	Bigott, Isabell, Beverley, wid. of Hen. B., Barton on Humbre, co., Linc., Dec. 30, 1558.	15	3	284
Nov.17, 1558.	Bilbroughe, John, Snathe, Sep. 30, 1558.	15	3	74
Jan. 21, 1567.	Bilithe, Robert, Wynsettes, par. Skefflinge, gent., Aug. 20, 1567.	17		753
Oct. 14, 1557.	Billingham, Robert, Harum, par. Helmsley, Feb. 26, 1557.	15	1	363
Jan. 22, 1567.	——————, Phillip, Paulflet (bur. Paull), Aug. 31, 1567.	17		753
Mar.14, 1560.	Biltcliffe, Thomas, Highe Hulland, Sep. 13, 1560	16		161
July 1, 1561.	Bilton, Raufe, Torworthe, par. Blythe (Notts.), husbn., Mar. 19, 1560.	17		60
May 6, 1557.	——, Richard, Aram, par. Lekingfeilde, husbn., Feb. 25, 1557 (*sic*).	15	1	251
Jan. 22, 1567.	——, Thomas, Pattrington. *No date.*	17		754
Mar. 3, 1555.	Biltone, William, Kayngham, Nov. 7, 1555.	15	1	10
Oct. 6, 1557.	Bingham, John (bur. Colston Bassett, Notts.), Aug. 8, 1557.	15	2	29
Aug. 7, 1565.	——————, John, senr., North Wheatley (Notts.), Jun. 22, 1564.	17		460
Oct. 11, 1565.	——————, William, Coston Basset (Notts.), batcheler, Feb. 15, 1565.	17		471
Feb. 20, 1560.	Bingley, John, Westhardweke, par. Wragbye, Apl. 8, 1559.	16		148
Apl. 24, 1566.	Binkes, Leonard, York, bayker, Mar. 26, 1566.	17		511
May 15, 1560.	Birch, John, Adlingflete, yeoman, Mar. 16, 1560	16		64
July 20, 1561.	Bird, Peter, Cottingham, husbandman, Mar. 16, 1560.	17		62
Jan. 12, 1558.	——, William, Roall (bur. Kellington), Nov. 16, 1558.	15	3	172
May 6, 1557.	Birde, William, Rimswell (bur. Ousthorne), Jan. 10, 1556.	15	1	239
Dec.22, 1556.	Birdsall, Edmunde, Swynton, par Waithe, Sep. 28, 1556.	15	1	76
Feb.ult.,1557.	Birkbecke, Richard, Pontfret, carpenter, Jan. 22, 1557.	15	2	147
Apl. 11, 1554.	Birke, Christopher, West Marton in Craven, husbandman, 1553.	14		160
Oct. 3, 1565.	Birkebe, Richard, Hynging Heaton, par. Dewisberie, yeom., May 6, 1565.	17		476
Mar.19, 1559.	Birkebie (or Birlbeke), Elizabeth, Pontefracte, widow, Dec. 25, 1559.	16		12
Mar.20, 1558.	Birkeby, John, Carleton, par. Roiston, husbandman, Mar. 20, 1557.	15	3	245
May 4, 1555.	Birkes, Richard, West Malton, par. Wath on Derne, husb., Feb.12,1554.	14		79
Apl. 10, 1559.	——, Thomas, Lynwheat, par. Wathe, Feb. 23, 1559.	15	3	329
May 13, 1568.	Birkit, Isabell, Knesall (Notts.), widow, Mar. 18, 1567.	17		798
July 26, 1558.	Birkwodde, Robert, Burton Pidsey, Jun. 10, 1558.	15	2	380
Oct. 13, 1558.	Birkwood, Thomas, Gaytfurth, par. Worsoope (Notts.), May 11, 1558.	15	2	356
Sep. 29, 1557.	Birlay, Robert, Wragbye, Jun. 26, 1557.	15	1	328
Mar.19, 1559.	Birlbeke (or Birkebie), Elizabeth, Pontefracte, wid., Dec. 25, 1559.	16		12
Jun. 3, 1558.	Birley, Henry, Bradfeilde, July 17, 1551.	15	2	339
Apl. 17, 1567.	Birtwysill, Robert, Calton (bur. Kirkbie Malhomdaill), husbandman, Nov. 22, 1566.	17		619
Apl. 10, 1559.	Bisbie, Robert, Felkirke, Aug. 8, 1558.	15	3	325
May 19, 1554.	Bishoppe, Thomas, Normanton on Soore (Notts.), husbn. Nov.18,1553.	14		111
Apl. 3, 1554.	Bitterworthe. Robert, Meltam, par. Almunburghe, July 4, 1553.	14		221
May 5, 1557.	Biwatter, William, Friston by water, husbandman, Apl. 6, 1557.	15	1	213

		Vol.	Pt.	Fol.
Apl. 19, 1564.	Blackburne, Alice, Heton (bur. Relston), Jan. 3, 1563.	17		330
Sep. 16, 1557.	————, Edward, Myrfelde, Jun. 10, 1557.	15	1	334
Jun. 21, 1565.	————, John, Bentley (bur. Rowley), husbn., Feb. 6, 1564.	17		447
Sep. 11, 1567.	————, John, Wentbridge, par. Kirke Smeton, Jun. 16, 1567.	17		707
Feb. 7, 1567.	————, Thomas, Seaton, Oct. 2, 1567.	17		757
Nov. 1, 1565.	Blackebourne, Henry, Mydelsbrugh, yeoman, Oct. 4, 1564.	17		489
May 23, 1564.	Blackeburne, William, Marton in Cleveland, gent., Jan. 30, 1563.	17		346
Jun. 17, 1554.	Blackhouse, John, bur. Foxholl. *No date.*	14		12
Sep. 29, 1563.	————, Margaret, Foxeholls, widow, Mar. 26, 1563.	17		275
Sep. 30, 1562.	Bladeworth, Heughe, Bromwith, yeoman, July 26, 1562.	17		114
Jan. 15, 1561.	Bladworthe, George, Bramwith, Feb. 8, 1559.	17		25
Sep. 30, 1557.	————, Hughe, Barnby on Done, Aug. 22, 1557.	15	1	369
Jan. 8, 1563.	————, Steven (bur. Bramwith), husbn., Nov. 8, 1563.	17		308
Mar. 18, 1559.	————, William, Branwith, Nov. 24, 1559.	16		10
May 13, 1568.	Blage, Henry, Sutton, par. Granebie (Notts.), husbn., Apl. 22, 1568.	17		800
Apl. 19, 1559.	Blagge, Thomas, Barnestone, par. Langer (Notts.), husbn., Oct. 20, 1558.	15	3	359
Jun. 27, 1562.	Blaidworthe, Robert, Wodhouse, par. Bramwithe, Apl. 24, 1559.	17		90
May 13, 1557.	Blaike, Robert, Papulwicke (Notts.), Feb. 8, 1556.	15	1	237
Dec. 16, 1556.	Blakburne, Giles, Ripon, glover, Oct. 15, 1556.	15	1	195
May 18, 1559.	————, Robert, Morlay, par. Batlay, Oct. 16, 1558.	15	3	413
Oct. 4, 1563.	Blake, Frauncis, Scorby (? clerk), Jun. 20, 1563.	17		290
May 6, 1563.	————, George, Barmiston, par. Langar (Notts.), Nov. 22, 1562.	17		245
Sep. 6, 1566.	————, Thomas, Cattonparke, Aug. 31, 1566.	17		571
Sep. 26, 1558.	Blakeman, William, Raumershe, husbandman, Aug. 1, 1558.	15	3	52
Mar. 23, 1557.	Blakett, Robert, Ottringham, Jan. 16, 1557.	15	2	173
Feb. 24, 1563.	Blakithe, Christopher, Preston in Holderness, husbn., Aug. 13, 1563.	17		320
July 23, 1560.	Blakker, John, Chappellthorp, par. Sandall Magna, Jun. 28, 1560.	16		95
Oct. 30, 1567.	Blakston, Elizabeth, Burnbie, Sep. 8, 1567.	17		730
Apl. 26, 1558.	Blanchard, Robert, Harlthrope (bur. Bowbwyth), Feb. 18, 1557.	15	2	221
Feb. 6, 1558.	Blanche, Sir Robert (bur. Shereburne), clerk, Dec. 14, 1558.	15	3	266
Feb. 20, 1558.	Blancherd, Alexander, Everingham, Nov. 25, 1558.	15	3	276
May 6, 1557.	Blande, Robert, Apletrewicke, par. Burnsall, Jun. 20, 1556.	15	1	254
Apl. 27, 1558.	————, William, Langardon (bur. Burnesall), Feb. 11, 1557.	15	2	200
May 5, 1558.	Blanke, John, Sutton on Trent (Notts.), Aug. 19, 1557.	15	2	262
Mar. 19, 1562.	Blanshart, Rauf, Augheton, Jan. 20, 1561.	17		217
Oct. 2, 1566.	Blansherd, James, Holme on Wolde, husbandman, Apl. 18, 1566.	17		572
Jun. 28, 1566.	————, Robert, Brighton (bur. Bubwith), May 23, 1566.	17		553
Apl. 10, 1567.	Blasham, John, Bubwithe, husbandman, Feb. 17, 1566.	17		618
July 18, 1554.	————, Katherine, Bubwith, widow, June 11, 1554.	14		143
July 9, 1554.	Blathwate, John, Estkeswike, par. Harwoode, husbn., July 12, 1554.	14		142
Dec. 14, 1557.	Blathwayt, Elizabeth, Estkesweyke, par. Harwood, Sep. 1, 1557.	15	2	94
May 13, 1557.	Blaunke, Thomas, Sutton on Trente (Notts.), July 25, 1556.	15	1	218
Apl. 26, 1558.	Blaybye, John, Thorne, Nov. 31 *(sic)*, 1557.	15	2	225
Jun. 12, 1562.	Blayston, Thomas, Lockyngton, Mar. 29, 1562.	17		88
Oct. 19, 1556.	Blaystone, Christopher, Ettone, Aug. 26, 1556.	15	1	105
Aug. 13, 1555.	Blencherd, John, Ellerton, July 16, 1555.	14		206
Mar. 21, 1560.	Blenkensopp, John, Sherifhooton, yeoman, Feb. 28, 1560.	16		175
Sep. 26, 1558.	Blenkeorne, James, Settrington, Aug. 3, 1558.	15	3	88
Jan. 18, 1560.	Blenkerne, Alice, Ferlington (bur. Sheryfhuton), wid., Sep. 22, 1560.	16		140
Apl. 26, 1558.	Blenkynsopp, William, Doncaster, glover, Aug. 11, 1557.	15	2	227
Oct. 5, 1558.	Blewet, Thomas, Metheley, Sep. 12, 1557.	15	3	63
Jan. 11, 1558.	Blewmer, Robert, Shearborne, labourer, Nov. 2, 1556.	15	3	171
Dec. 18, 1567.	Blithe, Peter, Cawood, Jan. 10, 1566.	17		746
Oct. 5, 1564.	Blome, Robert, Mydlewood, par. Darfeld, May 23, 1564.	17		377
May 31, 1557.	Blumbley, William, Whetlaie, par. Doncaster, Jan. 11, 1556.	15	1	260
Mar. 10, 1555.	Blunt, Thomas, Staneforthe on Soore (Notts.) Nov. 20, 1554.	16		231
Jun. 15, 1566.	Blyethe, John, Ellerton, Oct. 26, 1565.	17		553
May 6, 1557.	Blyth, Thomas, Kaingham in Holderness, Mar. 15, 1556.	15	1	238
Sep. 30, 1562.	Blythe, Thomas, Hemphollme, par. Leaven, Dec. 15, 1559.	17		118
Nov. 10, 1563.	Bocher, John, Beverley, July 19, 1563.	17		300
Sep. 7, 1558.	Bockill, John, Stillingflete, Nov. 28, 1557.	15	3	101
Apl. 14, 1558.	Boes (Boyes, Act Book), John, Yereslay, par. Cookeswold, Dec. 18, 1557.	15	2	226

3

A.D. 1554 TO 1568.

	Vol.	Pt.	Fol.
Apl. 24, 1555. Bointon, Roland a, Shereburne (Buckros), husbn., Feb. ult., 1554.	14		192
Oct. 5, 1558. Bois, Richard, Esington, Jan. 29, 1558.	15	3	69
Apl. 16, 1562. Boisman, William, Muscotes, par. Kirkedaylle, husbn., Feb. 17, 1561.	17		159
July 19, 1557. Boith, William, Laneham (Notts.), May 20, 1557.	15	1	313
Oct. 2, 1560. Boithe, Lawrance, Netherthownge, par. Almonburye, July 28, 1560.	16		113
Sep. 20, 1561. ———, Richard, Leedes, clothier, Aug. 10, 1559.	17		61
Apl. 27, 1558. ———, William, Horburye, par. Waikefelde, Nov. 13, 1557.	15	2	194
May 20, 1557. Boithes, William, North[o]rom, par. Halifax, Feb. 15, 1556.	15	1	212
Mar. 26, 1557. Bokyll, Thomas, Spawdyngeton (bur. Bubwith), husbn., Feb.16,1556.	15	1	203
Jun. 25, 1568. Bolbie, John (bur. Helmesley), Mar. 22, 1567.	17		815
July 11, 1558. Bold, Thomas, Sykehowsse, par. Fyshelake, Mar. 10, 1557.	15	2	316
Feb. 5, 1555. Bolde, Annable, York, widow, Apl. 26, 1553.	15	1	5
Jan. 14, 1558. Bolling, Marye, Skipwith, Nov. 25, 1557.	15	3	190
Jun. 4, 1561. ———, Trystram (bur. Bradford). *No date.*	17		69
Mar. 3, 1563. Bollynge, Robert, Wybsey, par. Bradforth, Jan. 3, 1563.	17		322
Sep. 2, 1563. Bolton, James, Hornsey. *No date.*	17		205
Feb. 1, 1555. ———, John, junr., Brotherton, Apl. 13, 1554.	15	1	5
Apl. 17, 1567. ———, Richard, Emsaye, par. Skipton in Craven, Dec. 11, 1566.	17		622
Dec. 22, 1556. ———, Robert, Kirke Smeton, May 14, 1556.	15	1	79
May 5, 1559. ———, William, Bolton Percye, Feb. ult., 1558.	15	3	381
Nov. 10, 1563. ———, William, Swyne, May 23, 1563.	17		302
May 2, 1560. Bomforthe, James, Ovenden, par. Hallyfaxe, Dec. 22, 1558.	16		42
Mar. 15, 1558. Bond, Thomas, Spaldington par. Aughton, husbandman, Oct. 16,1558.	15	3	167
Apl. 5, 1558. Bonde, Katheren, widow of Randall B., Brighton, Mar. 10, 1557.	15	2	179
Jan. 29, 1555. ———, Randall, Brighton (bur. Bubwith), husbandman, Oct. 18, 1555	15	1	1
Mar. 9, 1557. Bone, Harman, Bridlington, July 12, 1557.	15	2	129
Oct. 29, 1558. Bonike, William, Nafferton, carpenter, Aug. 16, 1558.	15	2	369
July 10, 1557. Bonnbie, Christopher, Elkesley (Notts), Apl. 13, 1557.	15	1	287
Jun. 23, 1558. Bonnd, John, Spaldington, May 23, 1558.	15	2	337
Dec. 12, 1564. Bonner, John, Burton Agnes, yongman, Sep. 2, 1564.	17		400
Aug. 12, 1556. ———, John (bur. Ottley), Sep. 25, 1556.	15	1	113
Jun. 16, 1561. Bonton, Roger, Knapton par. Wyntringham, Oct. 31. 1558.	17		71
Mar. 27, 1555. Bonyson, John, Hull, cowper, Oct. 13, 1555.	15	1	-13
May 18, 1559. Bonyvant, Edmund, Worksop (Notts.), Mar. 5, 1558.	15	3	422
Oct. 8, 1562. Boothbie, Adam, South Leverton (Notts.), husbandman, May 6, 1561.	17		122
May 10, 1565. Boothe, Thomas, Beverley, draper, Aug. 3, 1561.	17		424
Oct. 8, 1562. ———, Thomas, Lanham (Notts.), May 13, 1562.	17		120
Feb. 24, 1563. Borall, Jenett, Bransburton, Oct. 28, 1563.	17		318
May 9, 1565. Bordall, Thomas, Thirgond (?) (bur. Heptonstall), Feb. 4, 7 Eliz.	17		422
Sep. 13, 1565. Borell, Richard, Potter Newton (bur. Leedes), tayler, Aug. 30, 1565.	17		465
Oct. 5, 1558. Boroo, Lawrence, Waikefeilde, Sep. 2, 1558.	15	3	62
May 13, 1557. Borowe, William, Gotham (Notts.), husbn., Nov. 12, 1556.	15	1	221
Oct. 1, 1556. Borows, Richard, Tynneslawe, par. Rotherham, May 6, 1556.	15	1	123
Dec. 1, 1558. Borrell, Roger, Cottingham, Sep. 14, 1558.	15	3	84
Jun. 12, 1567. Borrill, William, Pattrington, Feb. 25, 1567.	17		664
Mar. 15, 1562. Boshowe, Robert, Eskirke, Feb. 19, 1562.	17		154
Apl. 27, 1558. Bosmunde, Henry, Muscottes, par. Kirkedaill, Sep. 1, 1557.	15	2	239
Oct. 3, 1562. Bosomworth, Jenet, Sutton under Whistenclyf (bur. St. Felix), wid., May 4, 1562.	17		115
Feb. 18, 1567. Bossell, Jeyne, Calton (bur. Gillinge), Oct. 3, 1567.	17		758
Apl. 3, 1559. ———, Richard, Cawton (bur. Gilling), Aug. 6, 1558.	15	3	319
Sep. 28, 1557. Bosswell, John, Sherebnrn, Aug. 14, 1557.	15	1	371
May 17, 1565. Bostocke, Elizabeth, Chilwell, par. Addenber (Notts.), wid., Dec. 7, 1561.	17		440
Jan. 11, 1558. Boswell, Alice, Shearburne, Sep. 6, 1558.	15	3	169
Feb. 17, 1557. ———, Jasper, Staynton, gentleman, Jan. 6, 1557.	15	2	140
Feb. 6, 1558, ———, Miles, Wistoe (bur. South Kirkebie), gent., Jan. 21, 1558.	15	3	254
Feb. 4, 1556. ———, Richard, Tykhill, Oct. 6, 1556.	15	1	169
July 4, 1556. ———, Robert, Criston (Clifton), par. Cunsburghe, husbn., Apl. 20, 1556.	15	1	52
Oct. 2, 1566. ———, Thomas, Rotherham, Apl. 28, 1566.	17		576
May 6, 1563. Bosworth, Edmund, Cotgrave (Notts.), Oct. 9, 1562.	17		247
Jun. 21, 1568. Bosworthe, Richard, Willobie (Notts.), Oct. 10, 1567.	17		830
May 5, 1558. Boteler, John, Weston (Notts.), July 17, 1557.	15	2	259

		Vol.	Pt.	Fol.
Apl. 28, 1558.	Botell, Richard, Lekenfelde, husbandman, Feb. 15, 1557.	15	2	218
May 9, 1566.	Bothe, John, Hucknall Torkerd (Notts.), housewright, Jan. 8, 1565.	17		546
Apl. 22, 1562.	——, Richard, Brygeforthe on Hyll (Notts.), yeom., Mar. 22, 1558.	17		179
Oct. 13, 1558.	——, Robert, Elston (Notts.), husbn., Apl., 25, 1557.	15	2	365
Aug.26, 1561.	——, .William, Neytherthowng, par. Almonburie, Dec. 16, 1560.	17		55
Mar.21, 1559.	Bother, John, Lellay, par. Preston, husbn., Dec. 15, 1559.	16		18
July 26, 1557.	Bothom, Thomas, Waikefeld, Jun. 5, 1557.	15	1	317
Apl. 27, 1558.	Bothome, Jane, Waikefelde, widow, Sep. 20, 1557.	15	2	191
Apl. 10, 1555.	Bothomleye, John, Hallifaxe, ——, 1554.	14		120
Oct. 6, 1558.	Bottrell, Robert, Menethorpe (bur. Westoe), husbn., Aug. 22, 1558.	15	3	26
Apl. 12, 1557.	——, Thomas, Cowlton (bur. Hounyngham), Mar. 7, 1556.	15	1	207
May 9, 1566.	Boulcott, Edward, Haitfeild Graunge, par. Cuckney (Notts.), Oct. 31, 1565.	17		542
May 5, 1558.	Bounbie, John, Elkesley (Notts), July 3, 1557.	15	2	250
Apl. 18, 1555.	Bounde, Agnes, Otleye, widow, Mar. 5, 1554.	14		120
Apl. 19, 1559.	Boune, Edward, Nuthall (Notts.), gentleman, Oct. 26, 1558.	15	3	431
Nov.15, 1566.	Bouthe, Elizabeth, Askarne, par. Campsall, widow, Aug. 3, 1566.	17		599
Apl. 20, 1559.	——, John, Wodhouse, par. Claworthe (Notts.), Dec. 6, 1558.	15	3	308
Dec. 11, 1567.	——, Richard, York, pynner, Dec. 4, 1567.	17		748
Apl. 16, 1562.	Bovell, John (bur. Kettlewell), Feb. 8, 1561.	17		169
Apl. 28, 1558.	——, Richard, Beverley, milner, Jan, 2, 1557.	15	2	222
Feb. 3, 1561.	——, Margaret, Wheldricke, widow, Apl. 18, 1561.	17		11
May 5, 1558.	Bowear, Robert, Woodhouse, par. Blythe (Notts.), husbn., Mar.9,1557.	15	2	241
Apl. 12, 1559.	Bowell, William, Wheldryke, July, 25, 1558.	15	3	335
Jan. 17, 1560.	Bowelt, John, Sutton, par. Brotherton, Dec. 9, 1560.	16		142
Nov.29, 1558.	Bower, Agnes, Fenweke, par. Campsall, Sep. 22, 1558.	15	3	110
May 18, 1559.	——, Ambrose, Barnyslay, wyer drawer, Nov. 28, 1557.	15	3	417
Mar.15, 1558.	——, Ellyne, Spaldington, widow, Jan. 29, 1558.	15	3	167
Apl. 24, 1556.	——, Henry, Sheffelde, hardwareman, Mar. 11, 1555.	15	1	34
Jan. 20, 1557.	——, Jennett, Bramwith, Sep. 20, 1557..	15	2	67
Sep. 18, 1565.	——, John, Doncaster, Jun. 4, 1565.	17		468
Jan. 30, 1555.	——, Robert, Sheffield, cutler, Oct. 18, 1555.	15	1	2
May 13, 1557.	Bowering, Margaret, Wallesbie (Notts.), widow, Apl. 3, 1557.	15	1	234
Aug.22, 1566.	Bowes, Elizabeth, York, widow, Feb. 8, 1564.	17		570
Jun. 26, 1565.	——, Robert, York, miller, Jan. 25, 1564.	17		444
May 10, 1559.	Boweser,William,Burton Flemynge(bur.Hawmanbye),Nov.17,1558.	15	3	390
July 15, 1567.	Bowker, John, Mytton (bur. Waddington), May 24, 1567.	17		675
Oct. 2, 1560.	Bowland, Richard, Hartofte, par. Mydleton, Mar. 31, 1559.	16		111
Jan. 28, 1556. 1	——, William, Hartofte (bur. St. Hilda, Egton), Sep. 29, 1556.	15	1	92
May 9, 1565.	Bowle, John, Louersall, Mar. 9, 1564.	17		427
Oct. 12, 1558.	Bowler, William, Nottingham, July 28, 1558.	15	3	29
Dec. 9, 1556.	Bowmer, John, Preston, Nov. 1, 1556.	15	1	198
Oct. 23, 1566.	——, Margaret, widow of Bryan B., Hull, Jan. 6, 1564.	17		585
Sep. 29, 1563.	——, Richard, Great Kelcke, par. Foston, Nov. 24, 1562.	17		275
May 18, 1559.	Bowne, Steven, Bownehill, par. Sandall Magna, Mar. 13, 1558.	15	3	414
Nov.29, 1557.	Bownton, William, Eastheslarton, Oct. 8, 1557.	15	2	95
Oct. 5, 1558.	Bowr, Margaret, Welburie, widow, Jan. 10, 1557.	15	3	68
May 13, 1557.	Bowreing, John, Wallesbie (Notts.), husbn., Dec. 11, 1556.	15	1	234
May 5, 1558.	Bowringe, Richard, Perlethorpe (Notts.), husbn., Nov. 14, 1557.	15	2	245
May 18, 1559.	——, Thomas, Westretford (Notts.), Aug. 24, 1558.	15	3	423
May 28, 1560.	Bowrton, George, Baxbie, par. Cookeswold, Sep. 20, 1558.	16		69
May 17, 1565.	Bowt, George, Barton in the Bayns (Notts.), Feb. 14, 1564.	17		437
July 19, 1557.	Bowth, Richard. Estretford (Notts.), Jun. 13, 1557.	15	1	308
May 5, 1558.	Bowthe, Thomas, Newark on Trent (Notts.), yeom., Mar. 14, 1556.	15	2	260
May13, 1557.	Boxton, Henry, Estretford (Notts.), Sep. 7, 1556.	15	2	132
Jan. 11, 1558.	Boy, Edward, Wortley, par. Leedes, Sep. 29, 1558.	15	3	171
Apl. 10, 1557.	——, John, Northowrom, par. Hallifax, July 3, 1556.	15	1	205
Oct. 6, 1558.	Boye (Registered Loy), Conisburghe, husbandman, Aug. 24, 1557.	15	3	223
Apl. 20, 1556.	——, Christopher, Hetton, par. Seasey, husbandman, Oct. 22, 1555.	15	1	16
May 5, 1557.	——, John, Harum, par. Helmeslaie, Jan. 26, 1556.	15	1	251

1 Visited wt. the hand of God at Egton.

A.D. 1554 TO 1568.

		Vol.	Pt.	Fol.
Apl. 26, 1559.	Boye, Richard, Ovenden, par. Halifax, Feb. 16, 1558.	15	3	363
Apl. 28, 1558.	Boyes, James, Witby, Sep. 28, 1557.	15	2	230
May 9, 1563.	——, John, Sneton, Apl. 13, 1563.	17		256
Apl. 14, 1558.	—— (Registered Boes), John, Yearesley, par. Cookeswold, Dec. 18, 1557.	15	2	226
Jun. 22, 1562.	——, Richard, Cowborne, par. Esington, yongman, Apl. 20, 1562.	17		90
Sep. 20, 1557.	——, Thomas, Great Edstone, Oct. 24, 1556.	15	1	334
July 19, 1566.	——, William (bur. Kirkbemysperton), Jan. 5, 1563.	17		562
Jan. 9, 1560.	Boynton, Jennat, Estheslerton, Feb. 21, 1558.	16		145
Apl. 16, 1562.	Boys, Homffray, Sandon, par. Brompton, Jan. 14, 1561.	17		158
Apl. 16, 1562.	—— (Registered Beye), Richard, Edseton (Ridall), yeom. *No date.*	17		159
May 5, 1558.	Boythe, Robert, Sowthe Wheatley (Notts.), Feb. 17, 1556.	15	2	207
May 5, 1568.	————, William, Cowike, par. Snaythe, Dec. 23, 1567.	17		793
Oct. 5, 1564.	Boythes, Edward, Northowrome, par. Halifax, clothier, Feb. 22, 1563.	17		374
Sep. 30, 1556.	Brabenare, Edward, Bridlington, husbandman, July 2, 1556.	15	1	134
Oct. 25, 1558.	Brabyner, William, Nonnington, husbandman, Oct. 6, 1558.	15	3	237
Jan. 12, 1558.	Bradbelt, Richard, North Cave, Nov. 27, 1558.	15	3	200
May 13, 1557.	Bradberie, Christopher, Poplewicke (Notts.), yeoman, Oct. 16, 1556.	15	1	225
Apl. 24, 1567.	Bradbery Nicholas, Eastwaythe (Notts.), labourer, Oct. 5, 1566.	17		644
Feb. 6, 1558.	Bradforde, Brian, Standley (bur. Waikefeild), gent., Nov. 20, 1558.	15	3	257
Apl. 26, 1558.	Bradforth, William, Fyshlaike, yeoman, Nov. 19, 1557.	15	2	197
Apl. 26, 1558.	Bradforthe, Cycylye, wid. of Jo. B., Alomholme (bur. Arkesey), Aug. 15, 1556.	15	2	198
Mar. 11, 1562.	———— ——, Hew, yong man, servant to Will. B., Fyshlaike, Jan. 31, 1557.	17		155
Oct. 2, 1566.	————, Robert, junior, Bentley (bur. Arksey), Sep. 1, 1566.	17		577
Dec. 16, 1556.	————, Robert, Morlay, par. Batley, Aug. 18, 1556.	15	1	193
July 8, 1561.	————, Robert, Osset (bur. Dewisbury), husbn., May 30, 1561.	17		79
Jun. 10. 1563.	Bradfourthe, Hellene, Hillom, par. Monkefriston, Sep. 10, 1562.	17		257
July 11, 1558.	Bradfurth, Jenett, wid. of John B., Bentley (bur. Arkesey), May 16, 1558.	15	2	305
Jun. 3, 1558.	————, John, Bentley, par. Arkesay, Apl. 23, 1558.	15	2	313
Aug. 8, 1561.	Bradfurthe, Anthony, Hillom, par. Monkefriston, husbn., July 20, 1561.	17		64
Apl. 6, 1558.	————, Peter, Bentley, par. Arkesay, Feb. 12, 1557.	15	2	185
May 6, 1557.	Bradlaie, James, Cononlaie, par. Kildwicke, Feb. 27, 1555.	15	1	255
Oct. 4, 1564.	Bradlay, George, the aighe (bur. Thorneton), Jun. 30, 1564.	17		371
July 8, 1560.	————, Isabell, Wombewell, par. Derffelde, wid., Jun. 23, 1553.	16		81
Sep. 1, 1563.	————, John, Smythlay, par. Derfeld, husbandman, Apl. 20, 1563.	17		208
Sep. 27, 1558.	————, Thomas, Cottingwith (bur. Aughton), Aug. 30, 1558.	15	3	88
Dec. 4, 1553.	Bradlaye, John, Leithlay, Mar. 1, 1553 *(sic)*.	14		92
Mar. 14, 1560.	Bradley, Elizabeth, Maylbeke (Notts.), widow, Oct. 30, 1540.	16		157
Oct. 3, 1564.	————, Elizabeth, wid. of Richard B., Watterfryston, Jun. 12, 1564.	17		367
Jan. 13, 1558.	————, Oliver, Mapulbecke (Notts.), Sep. 15, 1558.	15	3	17
Jun. 20, 1568.	-———, Roger, Bayley, par. Mytton, Apl. 21, ——.	17		808
Apl. 24, 1567.	————, Thomas, Crumwell (Notts.), Dec. 8, 1566.	17		641
Oct. 13, 1558.	Bradlye, Olyver, Maplebecke (Notts.), husbandman, Sep. 9, 1558.	15	2	363
Apl. 21, 1562.	Bradsha, Elizabeth, Marnham (Notts.), Feb. 16, 1561.	17		175
Oct. 10, 1566.	Bradshawe, Roger, Stanton on Wouldes (Notts.), July 28, 1566.	17		596
Mar. 14, 1560.	Bradshay, Robert, Clifton (Notts.), husbandman, Jan. 31, 1560.	16		156
Apl. 20, 1554.	Bradshaye, Robert, Worksope (Notts.), Jan. 25, 1553.	14		59
Jan. 12, 1558.	Braidie, John, Whenbie, labourer, July 21, 1558.	15	3	177
May 21, 1554.	Braidley, Thomas, Ellerton, May 10, 1554.	14		113
Feb. 6, 1558.	Braisbrige, Robert, Gaithfurthe, par. Braiton, Aug. 8, 1557.	15	3	265
Oct. 2, 1567.	Braisbrigge, William, Brayton, May 23, 1567.	17		710
Oct. 1, 1556.	Bramelaye, George (Ottley), Feb. 23, 1549.	15	1	135
Dec. 1, 1557.	Bramham, Margere, Ledstone (bur. Kepax), Nov. 17, 1557.	15	2	84
Aug. 16, 1566.	————, Robert, Gaytfurthe, par. Braton, Jan. 9, 1565.	17		569
Mar. 23, 1563.	Bramley, Richard, Kirkbyeouerblowes, husbandman, Dec. 14, 1563.	17		324
Dec. 1, 1557.	Bramman, Brian, Ledston (bur. Kepax), Nov. 12, 1557.	15	2	86
May 5, 1568.	Brand, John, Beverley, barbor, July 4, 1567.	17		776
Sep. 21, 1557.	——, John, Eglesfeld, Jan. 23, 1556.	15	1	356
Jan. 20, 1557.	Brande, Johan, Hestley, par. Eglesfelde, widow, Apl. 21, 1557.	15	2	67
July 1, 1558.	Brandisbie, Gregorie, Nafferton, husbandman, Apl. 6, 1558.	15	2	323

A.D. 1554 TO 1568.

		Vol.	Pt.	Fol.
Oct. 12, 1558.	Branlay, Thomas, Cossall (bur. Trowell, Notts.), husbn., ——, 1558.	15	2	367
Sep. 7, 1556.	Bransby, Maulde, Naffreton, July 28, 1556.	15	1	64
Apl. 20, 1559.	——, Robert, Sutton on Trent (Notts.), Mar. 20, 1558.	15	3	371
Mar. 15, 1556.	Bransbye, Ralfe, Yeddingham, Jan. 26, 1556.	15	1	185
Mar. 24, 1567.	Brasbrige, Alice, Gaitefurthe (bur. Braton), widow, Jun. 24, 1567.	17		766
Feb. 6, 1558.	——, Thomas, Burne, par. Braiton, Mar. 12, 1558.	15	3	264
Oct. 1, 1562.	Brashawe, John, Kirkbie Malhomedall, May 3, 1562.	17		112
July 12, 1558.	——, Robert, Ledstone (bur. Kepax), Mar. 20, 1557.	15	2	308
Mar. 15, 1558.	Brasse, Robert, Stokysley, servand to Chris. Rowntrie (bur. Barweccke), July 14, 1558.	15	3	165
Mar. 30, 1559.	Brassebrige, John, Humbleton, Mar. 3, 1558.	15	3	298
Jun. 2, 1558.	——, William, Burne, par. Brayton, Mar. 30, 1558.	15	2	215
Nov. 1, 1557.	Brathwatt, John, Denton, Oct. 11, 1557.	15	2	101
May 2, 1560.	Bratwhat, Alyson, Denton (bur. Otlaye), widow, July 6, 1559.	16		54
Feb. 4, 1556.	Brawell, Richard (bur. Cantley), Dec. 2, 1556.	15	1	170
Jun. 28, 1561.	Braydlay, John (bur. Thornton), Jan. 31, 1561.	17		75
July 27, 1560.	Braye, Robert (bur. Wheldrike), 1556.	16		96
Oct. 7, 1563.	Braylsforde, Rauffe, Nottingham, May 13, 1563.	17		293
Mar. 6, 1559.	Breare, Adam, Helwycke, par. Bynglaye, Aug. 22, 1559.	16		5
May 19, 1559.	Brearlay, William, Armyne (bur. Snaithe), Nov. 4, 1558.	15	3	429
Dec. 20, 1558.	——, William, Raynber, par. Wathe, Oct. 21, 1558.	15	3	154
Apl. 10, 1559.	Brearley als. Locksmyth, John, Barmbrough, Jan. 22, 1558.	15	3	327
Nov. 26, 1557.	Brears, Richard, Skelbroke, July 5, 1557	15	2	92
July 2, 1561.	Brearwood, Elizabeth, Lowthorpe, widow, Mar. 3, 1560.	17		78
Oct. 12, 1564.	Breatt, George, Broughton Sulney (Notts.), husbn., July 14, 1564.	17		392
Jan. 13, 1558.	Bredon, John, Annslay (Notts.), husbandman, Nov. 12, 1558.	15	3	183
Feb. 24, 1563.	Breerwood, Robert, Hornsey, yeoman, Oct. 4, 1562.	17		319
Dec. 10, 1566.	Bregame, Jennet (bur. Holme in Spawdingmore), wid., Apl. 1, 1566.	17		605
Apl. 24, 1567.	Breitt, William, Broughton Sulney als. Over Broughton (Notts.), husbandman, May 16, 1566.	17		644
Apl. 11, 1554.	Brennand, Christopher (bur. Slatburn), Feb. 4, 1553.	14		160
Feb. 19, 1557.	Brerhey, Thomas, Menstone (bur. Otteley), yeoman, Nov. 20, 1557.	15	2	143
Feb. 5, 1557.	Brerley, Mawde, Armyn (bur. Snaythe), widow, Nov. 11, 1557.	15	2	164
May 5, 1558.	Brethwytt, Jennett, Westretforth (Notts.), wid. of John B., Mar. 10, 1557.	15	2	246
Jan. 7, 1562.	Bretton, Richard, West Bretton, par. Sandall Magna, yeom., Sep. 13, 1556.	17		139
Oct. 1, 1561.	Breuer, Christopher, Skipton in Craven, July 6, 1561.	17		48
May 6, 1563.	Brewer, Thomas, Northgayte nigh Newarke (Notts.), husbandman, Mar. 30, 1562.	17		241
July 1, 1561.	Brewit, William, Walkringham (Notts.), husbandman, May 6, 1561.	17		61
May 2, 1560.	Brewster, Margaret, Waugham, widow, Apl. 9, 1560.	16		51
Feb. 6, 1558.	Brian, Robert, Carnabie, Oct. 8, 1558.	15	3	261
Apl. 22, 1556.	Bridge, Richard, junr., Warley, par. Hallifaxe, Aug. 6, 1555.	15	1	19
May 10, 1559.	Bridkirke, Thomas, Yrton, par. Seamer, Dec. 10, 1558.	15	3	389
May 17, 1557.	——, William, Seymer, Jan. 29, 1556.	15	1	245
May 2, 1566.	Brig, Henry, Staynton (bur. Gargrave), yeoman, May 1, 1565.	17		527
Apl. 12, 1559.	Brige, George, Altoftes (bur. Normantone), husbn., Aug. 29, 1558.	15	3	337
Jan. 18, 1558.	——, John, Hallifax, Sep. 20, 1558.	15	3	211
Apl. 12, 1559.	——, Juliane, Altoftes, par. Normanton, Mar. 20, 1558.	15	3	339
Feb. 20, 1560.	——, Robert, Altoft, par. Normanton, Jan. 26, 1560.	16		149
Mar. 20, 1560.	Brigg, Elizabeth, wid. of Chris. B., Stanton Cotte (bur. Gargrave), Oct. 26, 1556.	16		172
Oct. 2, 1566.	——, John, Stainton (bur. Gargrave), husbandman, May 1, 1566.	17		575
Apl. 27, 1558.	——, Robert, senr., Catwyke, Sep. 20, 1557.	15	2	206
Oct. 2, 1567.	——, Thomas, Broughton (Craven), July 7, 1567.	17		711
Apl. 14, 1559.	Briggame, John, Housum, par. Skraynggame, husbn., Sep. 3, 1558.	15	3	351
Oct. 1, 1562.	Brigge, Thomas, Conunley, par. Kildweke, July 20, 1560.	17		111
Dec. 22, 1556.	Brigges, Agnes, Norton, par. Campsall, widow, Sep. 12, 1556.	15	1	85
Oct. 12, 1558.	——, Henry, Selston (Notts.), May 2, 1558.	15	3	28
May 13, 1557.	——, John, Bonneie (Notts.), Sep. 20, 1556.	15	1	230
Sep. 1, 1563.	——, Thomas, Mosse, par. Campsall, Apl. 12, 1563.	17		208
Sep. 16, 1555.	——, William, the eldest, Sikehous, par. Fishelake, Aug. 12, 1553.	14		65
Jan. 8, 1563.	——, William, Sykehouse, par. Fyshelake, Apl. 24, 1563.	17		309

		Vol.	Pt.	Fol.
July 26, 1557.	Brigham, George, Sherifhoton, Mar 14, 1552.	15	1	320
Feb. 15, 1558.	————, Raulfe, Witon, par. Swyne, gentleman, May 24, 1558.	15	3	268
Apl. 13, 1559.	————, Thomas, Holme in Spaldingmore, Oct. 25, 1558.	15	3	347
July 10, 1556.	Brighowse, Richard, senr., Hipperham, par. Hallifaxe, Sep. 12, 1555.	15	1	44
Oct. 4, 1558.	Brisse, Robert, Leedes, Aug. 14, 1558.	15	3	58
Jun. 20, 1568.	Brobe (Brooke, Act Book), John, Woodheade in Wombewell, par. Darfeld, Jun. 22, 1567.	17		816
Oct. 2, 1566.	Brockesbanke, Edward, Warley, par. Halifaxe, clothier, Apl. 7, 1566.	17		580
Feb. 18, 1562.	Brocton, Anthony, Wymerslay, husbandman, Dec. 21, 1562.	17		146
May 5, 1568.	Brockden, Christopher. LittleNewton)bur. LongePreston, Jan. 17, 1567.	17		783
Jan. 14, 1564.	Brodbent, Thomas, Scholles (bur. Rotherham), Jan. 9, 1563.	17		403
Mar. 30, 1560.	Brodberye, Ellys, Moregren, par. Greslaye (Notts.), Nov. 26, 1559.	16		23
May 2, 1566.	Brodeheade, John, Overthonge, par. Almonburie, May 30, 1565.	17		534
Aug. 28, 1563.	Brodehede, John, Brige, par. Burton, Oct. 13, 1562.	17		208
July 6, 1558.	Brodes, Emot, York, widow, Jan. 31, 1557.	15	2	325
Jan. 7, 1562.	Brodhead, John, Bradsha, par. Almonbure, Aug. 27, 1562.	17		140
Jan. 15, 1565.	————, Richard, Rotherham, Dec. 2, 1565.	17		495
May 27, 1557.	————, Thomas, Ecclesfelde, servant, Aug. 30, 1556.	15	1	215
May 6, 1568.	————, William, Notton, par. Roiston, husbn., Mar. 6, 1566.	17		771
Mar. 13, 1558.	Brodhed, Jennett, Monkbretton, par. Roiston, widow, Oct. 24, 1558.	15	3	161
Sep. 9, 1561.	Brodley, Edward, Shelff, par. Hallifax, Jan. 20, 1558.	17		50
Mar. 9, 1557.	————, Richard, Hiperome, par. Hallyfax, Oct. 12, 1557.	15	2	168
Dec. 28, 1562.	————, Robert, Hipperholme, par. Halifax, Dec. 22, 1560.	17		136
Mar. 26, 1561.	Brodrycke, Richard, Hull, inholder, Mar. 1, 1560.	16		178
Jan. 12, 1557.	Brodynge, Ellene, wid. of Wm. B., Beverlay, tanner, Dec. 23, 1557.	15	2	80
Jun. 7, 1557.	Brogdon, Christopher, Womerslay, husbandman, Oct. 13, 1556.	15	1	288
Sep. 16, 1555.	Broghton, Robert, Rotherham, Apl. 17, 1555.	14		66
Oct. 31, 1554.	Broike, Robert, Brayton, clerk, Oct. 20, 1554.	14		284
Apl. 12, 1559.	Broikysbanke, John, Thornton, par. Bradford, Feb. 14, 1558.	15	3	336
Apl. 12, 1559.	Brokbanke, Necolas, Eland, Jan. 10, 1558.	15	3	339
Apl. 19, 1564.	Brokden, Henry, Elingthrope (bur. Gisburne), Nov. 11, 1563.	17		328
Apl. 12, 1559.	————, John, Bradford, Mar. 2, 1558.	15	3	336
May 6, 1559.	Broke, Agnes, Woodhouse, par. Hudderfelde, Aug. 6, 1558.	15	3	382
Aug. 16, 1566.	——, Christopher, Snaith, Mar. 8, 1565.	17		570
May 2, 1566.	——, Edmund, Grenehouse, par. Huddersfeild, July 2, 1565.	17		533
Nov. 3, 1558.	——, George, Scooles, par. Burstall, July 3, 1558.	15	3	133
Jan. 7, 1562.	——, James, Bradford, Oct. 6, 1562.	17		140
Mar. 26, 1565.	——, John, Adwallton, par. Bristall, Aug. 19, 1564.	17		416
Mar. 22, 1558.	——, John, Ackworth, Jan. 12, 1558.	15	3	296
Oct. 5, 1558.	——, Richard, Adwalton, par. Burstall, Aug. 12, 1558.	15	3	41
Feb. 6, 1558.	——, Richard, Adwalton, par. Bristall, Aug. 12, 1558.	15	3	256
[? Aug. 2, 1561.]	——, Roger, Huddersfeld, yeoman, Jan. 29, 1560.	17		65
Apl. 18, 1559.	——, Thomas, Bylling (bur. Sherefhoton), husbn. Sep. 2, 1558.	15	3	353
Jan. 13, 1558.	——, William, Coddington (Notts.), husbandman, Feb. 3, 1557	15	3	17
May 18, 1559.	Brokebanke, Agnes, Eland, widow, Mar. 3, 1558.	15	3	413
Oct. 14, 1561.	Brokesbanke, Anne, Gyls, par. Doncaster (bur. Arkesey), Apl. 15, 1561.	17		38
May 18, 1559.	————, James, Arksey, yeoman, Jan. 26, 1558.	15	3	402
Sep. 30, 1557.	————, Thomas, Sourbye, par. Halyfax, Aug. 22, 1557.	15	1	324
Oct. 5, 1558.	Brokesope, Nicholas, Bolton (Craven), —— 30, 1558.	15	3	61
Aug. 4, 1558.	• Brokylbunke, John, Sounlande, par. N. Feribe, husbn., Apl., 18, 1558.	15	3	8
Mar. 20, 1560.	Brome, Elizabeth, widow of Henry B., Wrenthorpe, par. Waikefelde, Oct. 12, 1559.	16		155
July 28, 1556.	————, Henry, Wrenthorp (bur. Wakefeld), gent., Mar. 27, 2 and 3, Philip and Mary.	15	1	59
Apl. 16, 1562.	Bromehed, Charles, Bradfeld, Aug. 10, 1561.	17		173
Apl. 16, 1562.	————, John Dongworthe, par. Bradfeld, Feb. 15, 1560.	17		174
Oct. 14, 1561.	————, Richard, Bradfeld, Jan. 31, 1560.	17		37
Oct. 1, 1556.	Bromhead, William, Warmesworthe, par. Doncaster, Jan 20, 1554.	15	1	127
Apl. 7, 1562.	Bromhed, Thomas, Faringdon (Notts.), husbandman, Feb. 11, 1561.	17		186
May 5, 1558.	Bromskale, Steven, Eykeryng (Notts.), husbandman, Oct. 22, 1557.	15	2	255
Oct. 8, 1562.	Bronley, John, Gamilston (Notts.), 1562.	17		121
Feb. 1, 1558.	Bronye, John, York, wright, Dec. 10, 1558.	15	3	23

		Vol.	Pt.	Fol.
May 31, 1557.	Broodhead, William, Roistonne, Mar 14, 1555.	15	1	260
Jun. 20, 1568.	Brooke (Registered, Brobe), John, Woodheade in Wombwell, par. Darfeld, Jun. 22, 1567.	17		816
Jun. 27, 1554.	———, Thomas, Newhouse, par. Huddersfeld, Jan. 8, 1553.	14		115
Apl. 6, 1554.	Brotherton, Richard, Wallehowse (bur. Gisburn), yeom., Jan. 23, 1553.	14		154
Apl. 26, 1558.	Broughton, John, Arkesey, Mar. 4, 1555.	15	2	197
No date.	Brouke, William, Wentworthe, husbandman, Apl. 19, 1554.	14		83
Mar. 22, 1564.	Broune, Rauf, Ruston, par. Wikham, Jan. 3, 1563.	17		412
Oct. 1, 1562.	———, William, Malhame More (bur. Kirkbie Malh.), Aug. 18, 1562.	17		110
Apl. 19, 1564.	Browghton, Johan (bur. Mytton), widow, Oct. 19, 1554.	17		329
Mar. 20, 1558.	Browinge, William, Carleton, par. Snayth, gresman, Nov. 12, 1558.	15	3	289
Jun. 13, 1560.	Browit, William, Walkeringham (Notts.), husbn, Feb. 20, 2 Eliz.	16		84
Mar. 3, 1555.	Browmflet, James, Stonefere, par. Sutton in Holdernes, Sep. 23, 1555.	15	1	11
Apl. 19, 1564.	Brown, John, Pathorn (bur. Gysburne), husbandman, Aug. 26, 1563.	17		330
Mar. 15, 1562.	———, John, Sneton (bur. Whytbie), Feb. 2, 1561.	17		162
Oct. 6, 1557.	Browne, Cristine, Rampton (Notts.), widow, Apl. 14, 1557.	15	2	6
Aug. 12, 1566.	———, Christopher, Downyngton in Holderness, Apl. 30, 1556.	17 ·		568
May 2, 1560.	———, Edmonde, Walton, July 10, 1559.	16		55
Jun. 6, 1560.	———, Henry, Everthorpe (bur. Northe Cave), July 1, 1559.	16		76
Dec. 11, 1566.	———, Henry, Thwenge, husbandman, Nov. 5, 1565.	17		601
May 4, 1568.	———, Hewe, Raskell, Apl. 1, 1568.	17		769
Oct. 6, 1558.	———, Isabell, Hovingham, widow, Sep. 23, 1558.	15	3	91
Oct. 2, 1555.	———, James (bur. Gargrave), Feb. 20, 1554.	14		169
Dec. 1, 1557.	———, James, Gyesley, Aug. 15, 1557.	15	2	84
Apl. 27, 1558.	———, Jane (bur. Gargrave), widow, Apl. 13, 1557.	15	2	202
May 2, 1560.	———, Jarret, Hylston, Apl. 17, 1559.	16		51
Jun. 14, 1561.	———, Jenet, Sneton (bur. Whitbye), Jan. 13, 1560.	17		71
Jan. 21, 1558.	———, John, Acastre Malbis, Nov. 28, 1558.	15	3	213
July 11, 1558.	———, John, Barnesley, July 29, 1557.	15	2	306
Mar. 4, 1562.	———, John (bur. Brandseburtone), Jan. 3, 1562.	17		150
Jun. 4, 1568.	———, John, Collom, Aug. 28, 1567.	17		812
May 2, 1566.	———, John, Kirkbemoreshed, Feb. 4, 1565.	17		519
May 1, 1555.	———, John, Mydlehowse (bur. Kirkbie Malhamdall), Feb. 26, 1554.	14		126
Apl. 3, 1559.	———, John, senr., Nonington, par. Stayngrayve, Sep. 21, 1558.	15	3	318
Dec. 5, 1567.	———, John, Preston in Holderness, husbandman, May 28, 1567.	17		742
Apl. 11, 1554.	———, John, Rathmell (bur. Gigleswicke), Sep. 27, 1553.	14		159
Apl. 4, 1560.	———, John, Rosyngton, Jun. 17, 1559.	16		25
Apl. 6, 1554.	———, John, Skipton in Craven, Jan. 18, 1553.	14		154
Nov. 18, 1558.	———, John, Snathe, Sep. 9, 1558.	15	3	73
Dec. 3, 1560.	———, John, Sutton in Holderness, Nov. 24, 1559.	16		133
Apl. 23, 1567.	———, Leonarde, Cawood, Dec. 5, 1556.	17		638
Oct. 27, 1564.	———, Margaret, Sneton (bur. Whitbie), widow, Feb. 22, 1563.	17		394
Oct. 6, 1557.	———, Myghell, Shelfelde (Notts.), May 6, 1557.	15	2	27
Jun. 2, 1564.	———, Nicholas, Hensall (bur. Snaythe), Aug. 1, 1563.	17		347
Apl. 14, 1557.	———, Peter, Cawood, Feb. 27, 1556.	15	1	208
May 18, 1559.	———, Phillip, Hilstone in Holderness, Jan. 26, 1558.	15	3	412
No date.	———, Richard, Amonderby in Ridall, husbandman, Nov. 5, 1554.	14		101
May 9, 1565.	———, Richard, the Stores (bur Bolton), Apl. 3, 1565.	17		431
Oct. 4, 1558.	———, Richard, Barley, par. Braton, Jun. 1, 1558.	15	3	59
Oct. 6, 1558.	———, Richard, Hovingham, husbandman, Sep. 10, 1558.	15	3	90
May 13, 1568.	———, Richard, Willowbie, par. Walesbe (Notts.), husbn., Nov. 11, 1567.	17		802
Mar. 8, 1558.	———, Robert, Beverley, Aug. 5, 1558.	15	3	288
July 12, 1564.	———, Robert, Pattrington, husbandman, Feb. 10, 1563.	17		357
Mar. 20, 1558.	———, Thomas, Adle, Oct. 21, 1553.	15	3	290
July 10, 1567.	———, Thomas, Ecclesfeld, Mar. 21, 1567.	17		685
May 5, 1568.	———, Thomas, Gargrave, Jan. 16, 1567.	17		787
May 17, 1557.	———, Thomas, Garton on the Wold, Apl. 12, 1557.	15	1	245
Aug. 2, 1560.	———, Thomas, Horneseye. No date.	16		100
Sep. 20, 1557.	———, Thomas, Newmalton, chapman, Apl. 20, 1557.	15	1	334
Sep. 29, 1557.	———, Thomas (bur. Ripon), Sep. 8, 1557.	15	1	329
Dec. 18, 1560.	———, Thomas, Selbie, Mar. 28, 1560.	16		136

A.D. 1554 TO 1568.

		Vol.	Pt.	Fol.
Dec. 1, 1557.	Browne, Thomas, curate of Walton (Aynstie), Jan. 2, 1555.	15	2	85
Feb. 15, 1558.	———, William, Alburgh (bur. Swyne), daryeman, Nov. 21, 1558.	15	3	267
Oct. 20, 1554.	———, William,.Crakill, par. Topcliffe, Sep. 18, 1554.	14		49
Mar. 1, 1556.	———, William, Newe Malton, Oct. 9, 1556.	15	1	176
Feb. 15, 1558.	———, William, Northe Skirley (bur. Swyne), labr., Dec. 26, 1558.	15	3	270
Feb. 15, 1558.	———, William, Riston in Holderness, Oct. 2, 1558.	15	3	270
Aug. 28, 1561.	———, William, Rosington, husbandman, May 25, 1561.	17		58
May 5, 1558.	———, William, Rosingtone, Aug. 11, 1556.	15	2	332
Apl. 26, 1558.	———, William, Towton, par. Saxton, Oct. 27, 1557.	15	2	233
Oct. 4, 1565.	———, William, Walkenton, husbandman, Feb. 20, 1559.	17		484
Dec. 20, 1558.	———, William, Worsburghe, clerke, Jun. 2, 1557.	15	3	151
Jun. 30, 1558.	———, William, York, tanner, May 19, 1558.	15	2	342
Jun. 21, 1565.	Brownell, George, Hardenbee, par. Bradfeld, Feb. 14, 1564.	17		446
Oct. 1, 1556.	———, Robert, Dalton, par. Rotherham, May 25, 1556.	15	1	127
Mar. 22, 1558.	Brownye, Richard, Standley (bur. Waykefeild, husbn., Feb. 3, 1558.	15	3	296
July 1, 1562.	Broykesbanke, William, Arkesay, clerk, Mar. 23, 1561.	17		92
Dec. 22, 1557.	Brucke, Charles, Southowrome, par. Halyfax, Oct. 23, 1557.	15	2	71
Oct. 21, 1561.	Brugh, Agnes, Rither, Dec. 24, 1558.	17		44
May 13, 1557.	Brumbie, Thomas, Bonnay (Notts.), Nov. 12, 1556.	15	1	228
Apl. 20, 1554.	Brushe, Thomas, Averham (Notts.), Dec. 13, 1 Mary.	14		232
Sep. 1, 1563.	Bruster, John, Kyrkby, May 8, 1563.	17		206
Mar. 29, 1555.	Bruyster, Robert, Lowthorpe, husbandman, Feb. 19, 1554.	14		189
Jun. 12, 1563.	Bryan, Alison, Cawood, widow, Feb. 18, 1562.	17		258
Oct. 12, 1564.	———, Bartholmew, Scroby (Notts.), May 6, 1564.	17		389
Mar. 9, 1557.	———, Rauffe, Carnabye, Jan 10, 1557.	15	2	127
May 18, 1559.	———, William (bur. Est Retford, Notts.), Mar. 3, 1557	15	3	421
Jan. 13, 1558.	———, William, Myssyn (Notts.), Nov. 10, 1558.	15	3	207
Jun. 2, 1558.	Bryde, Richard, Skeclynge, Apl. 23, 1558.	15	2	337
July 10, 1564.	Brydkirke, William, Brompton, Feb. 1, 1563.	17		355
Sep. 14, 1563.	Brygam, Richard, Brygam, par. Kyrkebe in Grenedalyth, Mar. 1, 5 Eliz.	17		203
Sep. 21, 1557.	Brygg, Richard, Rawmarshe, Feb. 3, 1556.	15	1	354
Apl. 26, 1558.	Brygges, Richard, Sykehouse, par. Fyshlaike, Jan. 10, 1557.	15	2	195
Nov. 29, 1557.	Bryggom, John, West Luttone (bur. Weverthroppe, Dec. 29, 1557.	15	2	95
Sep. 26, 1565.	Brygnall, Richard, Bickerton, Apl. 20, 1565.	17		469
Apl. 22, 1562.	Brymlay, Thomas, Sutton (Bingham, Notts.), husbn., Jan. 23, 156[1-]2.	17		179
Jun. 6, 1560.	Brysco, Robert, Northburton als. Chereburton, Sep. 18, 1559.	16		74
Aug. 5, 1557.	Bryttayne, John, Anslye, Dec. 28, 1556.	15	2	117
Oct. 2, 1567.	Bubwithe, Richard, Bubwithe House, gentleman, May 12, 1567.	17		717
Jun. 8, 1564.	Bucke, George, Coulthrop, May 5, 1564.	17		348
Oct. 2, 1566.	———, George, Darnebroncke, Jun. 10, 1566.	17		573
Sep. 30, 1558.	———, John, Wallerqueite (bur. Ripon), husbn., Nov. 18, 1557.	15	3	57
May 28, 1560.	———, Robert, Thorganbye, Mar. 21, 1558.	16		70
Jan. 18, 1560.	Buckebarrowe, John, Hewbie (bur. Sutton), July 15, 1560.	16		140
Nov. 26, 1558.	Buckell, Elizabeth, Stillingflete, Aug. 12, 1558.	15	3	75
Jan. 31, 1558.	———, John, Eskrig, Apl. 24, 1558.	15	3	221
May 10, 1554.	Bucklay, Richard, Heptonstall, Jan. 7, 1553.	14		131
Feb. 17, 1561.	Buckley, John, Allerton in Sherwood (Notts.), husbn., Dec. 14, 1558.	17		14
Mar. 13, 1565.	Bucktrowte, Elizabeth (bur. Otley), widow, May 2, 1565.	17		503
Apl. 28, 1558.	Bucton, Rauffe, Gisburne, Sep. 25, 1557.	15	2	231
Sep. 30, 1557.	Bud, Nynyan, Carleton, par. Snaythe, May 5, 1557.	15	1	343
May 19, 1559.	———, Richard, Carletone, par. Snathe, Mar. 28, 1558.	15	3	428
Nov. 28, 1567.	Buka, Richard, Sewirbie (bur. Bridlington), husbn., July 6, 1567.	17		736
Apl. 20, 1559.	Bulbye, Edmonde, Westhorpe (bur. Southwell, Notts.), tanner, Dec. 26, 1558.	15	3	370
May 2, 1560.	Bule, John (bur. Selbye), Apl. 1, 1560.	16		53
May 30, 1566.	Bulie, Johan, Ledstonne, par. Ledesham, widow, Mar. 11, 1565.	17		544
July 30, 1567.	Bullacy, John, Topclif, Apl. 20, 1567.	17		686
Nov. 10, 1563.	Buller, Henry, Burton Pidsay, July 23, 1563.	17		302
Mar. 8, 1558.	———, John, Eske, par. St. John, Beverley, Dec. 16, 1558.	15	3	286
Jan. 11, 1557.	———, John, Preston (Holderness), Dec. 8, 1557.	15	2	73
Jan. 11, 1557.	———, Robert, Sutton in Holderness, husbandman, Nov. 25, 1557.	15	2	76

		Vol.	Pt.	Fol.
Dec. 10, 1561.	Buller, William, Skeflyng, Apl. 7, 1561.	17		28
May 6, 1557.	Bullesse, John, Killwington, Feb, 20, 1556.	15	1	241
Jun. 8, 1557.	Bullie, Jenett, Emmottland, par. North Frothingham, widow, Apl.13, 1557.	15	1	268
No date.	Bullocke, Nicholas, Eastnes (bur. Hovingham), gentleman, Dec. 9, 1558	15	3	379
Jun. 22, 1561.	——, Nicholas (bur. Eskerige), Jan. 9, ——.	17		84
Oct. 24, 1558.	——, Richard, Sowth Holme (bur. Hovingham), Apl. 20, 1557.	15	3	131
Mar. 6, 1556.	Bulloke, William, Allerton in Sherwood (Notts.), husbn., Sep. 13, 1556.	15	1	179
Jan. 11, 1557.	Bullye, Elizabeth, Emotland, par. North Frodingham, Nov. 9, 1557.	15	2	76
Jan. 28, 1563.	Bulmer, Bryan, Hull, maister mariner, July 23, 1563.	17		311
May 10, 1559.	——, Elizabeth, South Ottrington, widow, Apl. 20, 1559.	15	3	387
Aug. 7, 1565.	Bunbe, William, Lanham (Notts.), Mar. 8, 1564.	17		457
Oct. 7, 1557.	Buntinge, Richard, St. Peter's, Nottingham, Jun. 8, 1557.	15	2	22
Mar. 6, 1556.	Buntyng, John, Allerton in Sherwod (Notts.), husbn., Nov. 19, 1556.	15	1	181
Nov. 29, 1554.	Burddus, John, Wenthorpe (? Bugthorpe, bur. St. Andr.), Jun. 2, 1554.	14		91
Jun. 11, 1562.	Burde, Alice, Nafferton, widow, Jan. 6, 1559.	17		99
Nov. 6, 1557.	——, Edwarde, Lanam (Notts.), Sep. 24, 1557.	15	2	106
May 6, 1557.	——, Katherin, Owthorne, Feb. 13, 1557.	15	1	241
Apl. 4, 1555.	——, Symond, Hull, taylior, Feb. 21, 1554.	14		191
Apl. 17, 1563.	Burdeas, Thomas, Whitley (bur. Kellington), Jan. 12, 1562.	17		222
July 11, 1558.	Burdett, Charles, Norcrofte, par. Cawthawrne, Aug. 21, 1557.	15	2	305
Dec. 16, 1557.	Burdon, Katherine, vyrgyne (bur. Wylberfosse), Mar. 25, 1557.	15	2	88
Apl. 20, 1559.	—— *als.* Taylor, John (bur. Wallesby, Notts.), Mar. 19, 1558.	15	3	366
Aug. 21, 1561.	Burdsall, Elizabeth, Downswall, par. Cottingham, Apl. 1, 1561.	17		56
Dec. 21, 1562.	Burdus, Thomas, Boynton, husbandman, Aug. 23. 1562.	17		137
Jun. 9, 1563.	Burellt, John, senr. (bur. Brandisburton), Mar. 5, 1563.	17		254
Jun. 21, 1568.	Burgaine, Richard, Beverley, July 30, 1567.	17		815
Apl. 13, 1559.	Burgayn, Robert, Garton, Mar. 1, 1558.	15	3	346
July 5, 1557.	Burges, John, Doncastre, Nov. 17, 1556.	15	1	300
Jun. 30, 1558.	Burges, Margaret, Newe Malton, widow, May 16, 1558.	15	2	341
Aug. 4, 1554.	——, Robert, Newmalton, Apl. 12, 1554.	14		267
Dec. 12, 1554.	——, Thamas, Tyckell, Aug. 6, 1554.	14		96
Apl. 10, 1557.	Burgh, Alice, Wodkyrke, Dec. 23, 1556.	15	1	206
Feb. 26, 1557.	——, Lionell, Wyghell, yeoman, Aug. 27, 1557.	15	2	145
Mar. 20, 1558.	——, William (bur. Snaithe), Aug. 15, 1558.	15	3	252
No date.	Burghe, Elizabeth, Ruston, Jan. 22, 1553.	14		87
Apl. 16, 1567.	——, John, Woodkirke, bagger, Jan. 8, 1566.	17		624
Nov. 7, 1565.	——, Thomas, Skerthenbecke, husbandman, May 12, 1565.	17		491
Apl. 5, 1565.	——, William, Skrethenbecke, husbandman, Mar. 8, 1564.	17		419
Oct. 22, 1556.	——, William, Woodkyrke, May 26, 1556.	15	1	101
Jan. 12, 1557.	Burgon, John, Hull, maryner, Nov. 4, 1557.	15	2	79
Feb. 13, 1558.	——, Mabill, widow of John B., Hull, Feb. 3, 1558.	15	3	266
Sep. 2, 1563.	Burke, John, Garton, husbandman, May 18, 1563.	17		205
Jan. 12, 1557.	Burlay, Robert, Northe Dalton, husbandman, Oct. 28, 1557.	15	2	79
Jan. 22, 1563.	Burman, Margaret, Rillington, widow, July 21, 1563.	17		310
Mar. 22, 1556.	Burn, John, Cheriburton, husbandman, Dec. 20, 1556.	15	1	190
Aug. 2, 1560.	Burnam, James, Waxam, par. Outhorne, husbn., May 29, 1560.	16		100
Apl. 20, 1559.	Burne, George, North Wheatly (Notts.), Dec. 20, 1558.	15	3	368
Nov. 5, 1564.	——, Henry, Beiswicke, par. Kelwicke, Feb. 8, 1563.	17		395
Jan. 12, 1558.	——, Richard, Eskrigge, Aug. 4, 1558.	15	3	172
May 17, 1554.	——, William, Tibthorpe, par. Kirkburne, Nov. 24, 1553.	14		4
Oct. 5, 1554.	Burneley, John, Selby, drapper, Jun. 5, 1554.	14		47
July 16, 1562.	——, Richard, Halifax, clothier, May 3, 1562.	17		96
Oct. 20, 1558.	Burnell, Alice, Catton (bur. Topliffe), widow, Sep. 2, 1558.	15	2	347
May 2, 1566.	——, William, Beiston (bur. Leedes), labourer, Mar. 29, 1566.	17		520
Oct. 2, 1567.	Burnet, Henry (bur. Bylton), Apl. 11, 1567.	17		720
July 5, 1557.	——, John, Markynton (bur. Ripon), husbandman, Dec. 10, 1556.	15	1	304
May 2, 1566.	——, Thomas, Raskell, Feb. 12, 1565.	17		520
May 2, 1566.	——, William, Raskell, Jan. 26, 1565.	17		520
Sep. 30, 1557.	Burnsall, Richard, Rednes (bur. Whytgyft), Mar. 9, ——.	15	1	344
May 13, 1557.	Burnslay, John, Bawtre, Mar. 30, 1557.	15	2	133
Oct. 2, 1560.	Burnum, John, Preston in Holderness, husbandman, Mar. 16, 1559.	16		117

A.D. 1554 TO 1568.

		Vol.	Pt.	Fol.
Nov. 28, 1558.	Byrnum, Thomas, Preston in Holderness, Sep. 2, 1558.	15	3	79
May 7, 1568.	Burr, Francis, Roclif, par. Snaythe, Mar. 17, 1567.	17		781
Jun. 10, 1557.	Burraie, Dorothe, Cottingham, widow, Dec. 16, 1556.	15	1	270
Jan. 12, 1558.	Burrell, John, Hubie (bur. Sutton), Aug. 24, 1558.	15	3	176
Feb. 24, 1563.	———, William, Northe Frothingham, May 5, 1563.	17		318
Jun. 20, 1568.	Burros, Richard, Darnall, par. Sheffeld, Apl. 7, 1567.	17		815
Apl. 6, 1558.	———, William, Sheffelde, yeoman, Jan. 12, 1557.	15	2	180
Jan. 11, 1562.	Bursay, Thomas, Cottingham, labourer, Dec. 18, 1562.	17		142
Nov. 7, 1564.	———, William, Sutton (Holderness), July 13, 1564.	17		399
Jan. 20, 1561.	Bursee. William, Wakefeld, Nov. 25, 1559.	17		22
May 2, 1566.	Burstal, John, Rihill, par. Skeclinge als. Brustwicke, Nov. 15, 1565.	17		526
Jun. 12, 1567.	Burstall, John, West Halsam, Dec. 24, 1566.	17		662
Jun. 12, 1567.	———, William, West Halsam, Sep. 20, 1566.	17		665
Apl. 20, 1559.	Burton, Agnes, Shafforth, par. Everton (Notts.) Dec. 9, 1558.	15	3	370
Jan. 14, 1562.	———, Anthony, Hillom (bur. Monkefriston), Oct. 30, 1562.	17		142
Oct. 7, 1557.	———, Averey, Stapleforthe (Notts.), May 9, 1557.	15	2	25
Aug. 21, 1561.	———, Barthelmew, Kirke Elley, Mar. 24, 1560.	17		56
Oct. 3, 1565.	———, Ellis, Methellay, Jan. 3, 1564.	17		475
Feb. 1, 1563.	———, George, Hodroide (bur. Felkirke), gentleman, Aug. 21, 1563.	17		314
Apl. 28, 1563.	———, George, Trepland (bur. Relston), Nov. 5, 1562.	17		229
Jan. 11, 1558.	———, Henry, Bardsay, yeoman, Aug. 28, 1558.	15	3	169
Dec. 11, 1566.	———, Hughe, Besingbie, husbandman, Nov. 9, 1557.	17		603
Oct. 1, 1566.	———, Jarrat, Thercklebe, par. Kirkabe in Grendalleth, July 28, 1566.	17		572
Mar. 11, 1562.	———, Jennet, Wattonn Carre, widow, Nov. 28, 1562.	17		156
May 24, 1558.	———, John, Cawod, Jun. 18, 1557.	15	2	284
Feb. 28, 1566.	———, John, Great Busby, par. Stokesley, Feb. 11, 1564.	17		617
May 2, 1566.	———, John, Hymsworth, badger, July 26, 1565.	17		521
May 5, 1568.	———, John, Selside in Hortonn, Apl. 4, 1567.	17		787
Apl. 7, 1554.	———, John, Threpeland, par. Rilston, Nov. 2, 1 Mary.	14		155
May 2, 1560.	———, John, junr., Wallesgrave, par. Scarbrughe, Sep. 15, 1558.	16		40
Jan. 11, 1558.	———, Margery, Monkfriston, widow, Aug. 9, 1558.	15	3	171
May 28, 1568.	———, Michaell, Brayton, Apl. 1, 1568.	17		795
Oct. 17, 1567.	———, Myles, Lealam, par. Danbie, yeoman, Apl. 21, 1567.	17		731
Feb. 25, 1558.	———, Rawphe, Mylforth, par. Shereburne, ———, 1558.	15	3	280
Mar. 6, 1556.	———, Richard, Mathersay (Notts.), Sep. 3, 1556.	15	1	182
May 13, 1557.	———, Richard, St. Peter's, Nottingham, Apl. 9, 1557.	15	1	224
May 13, 1557.	———, Richard, Sutton on Trente (Notts.), Mar. 7, 1555.	15	1	219
Sep. 26, 1558.	———, Robert, Bentlay, par. Arkesay, July 20, 1558.	15	3	55
Oct. 6, 1557.	———, Robert, Blythe (Notts.), Aug. 11, 1557.	15	2	14
May 10, 1559.	———, Robert, senr., Bridlingtone, Mar. 13, 1559.	15	3	391
Apl. 24, 1560.	———, Robert, Everingham, Mar. 24, 1559.	16		33
Sep. 30, 1557.	———, Robert, Marflete, husbandman, July 15, 1557.	15	1	341
Jan. 11, 1557.	———, Robert, Ryston in Holderness, Nov. 24, 1557.	15	2	73
May 13, 1568.	———, Thomas, Bonnay (Notts.), Apl. 27, 1568.	17		800
Oct. 6, 1557.	———, Thomas, Bonney (Notts.), Jun. 9, 1557.	15	2	33
Jun. 11, 1556.	———, Thomas, Carleton in Cleveland, May 1, 1556.	15	1	57
May 12, 1555.	———, Thomas, Pontefract, clerk, late fellow of Trinity College, (bur. Metheleye), Apl. 29, 1555.	14		35
Jun. 4, 1568.	———, Thomas, Sherburne, husbandman, Feb. 2, 1566.	17		814
Apl. 18, 1567.	———, Thomas, Topclif, Oct. 19, 1566.	17		631
Feb. 17, 1561.	———, William, Bole (Notts.), Jan. 3, 1560.	17		15
July 24, 1564.	———, William, Hoton Cransewicke, labourer, Dec. 4, 1563.	17		359
Oct. 9, 1560.	———, William, Hull, porter, Aug. 3, 1559.	16		123
July 1, 1555.	———, William, Keldome, par. Kirkebye Moresyde, walker, May 16, 1555.	14		257
Aug. 21, 1561.	———, William, Weille (bur. Beverley), Jan. 10, 1559.	17		56
[Nov.] 9, 1557.	Burtonne, William, Metheley, Aug. 24, 1557.	15	2	103
Apl. 27, 1564.	Busbe, John, Cossall (Notts.), husbandman, Sep. 10, 1563.	17		338
Jun. 8, 1557.	Busbie, Robert, Siglesthorne, Jan. 9, 1556.	15	1	268
May 14, 1568.	Bushell, Wenefride (bur. Cunsebrughe), widow, Mar. 19, 1567.	17		804
May 5, 1558.	Busse, Walter, Fyskerton, par. Rowlestone (Notts.), Nov. 12, 1557.	15	2	255
Jun. 14, 1554.	Bustarde, Leonard, Drax Manor (late Priory), Apl. 22, 1554.	14		4

A.D. 1554 TO 1568.

		Vol.	Pt.	Fol.
Nov.17, 1558.	Butcher, Ales, Braton, Sep. 8, 1558.	15	3	113
Mar.20, 1558.	Buterfeld, John (bur. Selbie), Jan. 3, 1558.	15	3	251
Aug.20, 1558.	Butlar, Robert, Thorganby, Aug. 11, 1558.	15	2	295
Jan. 26, 1556.	Butler, Alexander, Morton, par. Byngley, Jan. 15, 1556.	15	1	90
Jun. 5, 1554.	———, Alison, Willerbie, par. Elley, Jan. 26, 1553.	14		9
Dec. 14, 1557.	———, James, Willarbye, par. Kerke Elley, Oct. 17, 1557.	15	1	359
Mar. 8, 1558.	———, Margett, Chereburton, Jan. 1, 1558.	15	3	157
Aug.28, 1561.	———, Margaret, Eyton (Notts.), widow, Feb. 26, 1560.	17		57
Jun. 2, 1558.	———, Sir Richard, Lesset, par. Befurth, priest, Mar. 23, 1557.	15	2	288
Nov.12, 1567.	———, Robert, Wheldrake, husbandman, Jun. 22, 1567.	17		733
Nov.14, 1554.	———, Thomas, Eskrig, labourer, Sept. 25, 1554.	14		294
Apl. 28, 1558.	———, Thomas, Hull, maryner, Jan. 19, 1557.	15	2	221
Mar.15, 1560.	———, William, Elksley (Notts.), Feb. 6, 1560.	16		168
Feb.19, 1556.	———, William, Wheldryke, ———, 1556.	15	1	176
May 12, 1566.	Butterfeild, Alexander, West Morton, par. Byngley, ———, 1558.	17		549
Nov.22, 1558.	———, John, Kighley, yeoman, Oct. 21, 1558.	15	3	128
July 18, 1558.	Butterfeyld, Edward, Norland, par. Hallyfax, Mar. 3, 1557.	15	2	316
Apl. 14, 1562.	Butterne, Thomas, Rosse, May 18, 1561.	17		184
Dec. 3, 1561.	Butterwicke, Jennet, Gysburne, July 7, 1561.	17		27
July 11, 1558.	Butterworth, Randall, Barnesley, Jan. 14, 1557.	15	2	315
Apl. 20, 1564.	Butterworthe, Gregorie (bur. Thirske), Feb. 1, 1563.	17		334
Dec.16, 1563.	———, Rauff (bur. Thirske), Mar. 2, 1562.	17		306
Feb.20, 1558.	Butterwyke, Richard, Yarum, Nov. 4, 1558.	15	3	276
Jan. 24, 1558.	———, William, Gisburne, Sep. 14, 1558.	15	3	214
Jan. 12, 1558.	Buttler, William, Cheriburton, yeoman of the chamber to the King and Queen, Oct. 12, 1558.	15	3	198
May 4, 1558.	Button, William, Bradmore, par. Bonney (Notts.), Sep. 24, 1557.	15	2	266
Feb.26, 1560.	Buttre, John (bur. Hawnbie), Jan. 28, 1560.	16		151
Jun. 4, 1568.	Buttres, Leonard, Leppington, Mar. 7, 1567.	17		813
Oct. 6, 1557.	Buxham, Thomas, Codlingstocke (Notts.), Apl. 19, 1557.	15	2	33
Dec. 2, 1561.	Byamount, Richard, Blaker in Wyrspur, Apl. 14, 1561.	17		31
Mar. 4, 1562.	Byckers, Richard, Grisestrupe (bur. Fylaye), 1562.	17		154
May 29, 1563.	Byeres, John, Sheryfhoton, husbandman, Mar 29, 1562.	17		251
Feb. 11, 1557.	Byggyn, William (bur. Rippon), Oct. 9, 1557.	15	2	166
Jun. 20, 1558.	Bygod, Robert, Adlingflete, May 10, 1557.	15	2	335
Mar.23, 1557.	Bylby, Edward, Hempholme, par. Leven, Jun. 10, 1557.	15	2	153
July 11, 1558.	Bylkclif, John, Thurelstone, par. Penystone, Aug. 24, 1558.	15	2	301
Aug. 2, 1560.	Byllamye, Robert (bur. Skeiflinge), Apl. 20, 1560.	16		99
Apl. 14, 1562.	Byllanye, Steven, Rosse, husbandman, Feb. 8, 1561.	17		183-2
Apl. 22, 1562.	Byllton, Richard, Torworthe, par. Blythe (Notts.), labr., Feb.ult., 1561.	17		194
Feb.26, 1562.	Bylton, Jennet, Stillingfleet, Feb. 19, 1562.	17		147
Oct. 6, 1557.	———, Margerye, Thorwell, par. Blythe (Notts.), Sep. 25, 155[4?].	15	2	12
Jan.30, 1557.	———, Robert, Acaster Selbye, par. Styllyngflete, Sep. 9, 1557.	15	2	161
May 15, 1559.	Byltone, Roger, Prestone in Holderness, husbandman, Jan. 3, 1558.	15	3	408
Apl. 27, 1564.	Bylyalde, John, East Markham (Notts.), yeoman, May 1, 1562.	17		336
July 11, 1558.	Bynd, Nicholas, Fyshelacke, yeoman, Nov. 19, 1557.	15	2	321
Mar.10, 1555.	Byngham, John, Burton (Notts.), May 7, 1554.	14		224
July 15, 1555.	Byngley, John, Naytherton, par. Thornell, yeoman, Apl. 24, 1555.	14		261
May 5, 1558.	———, Richard, Blythe (Notts.), Sep. 8, 1557.	15	2	245
July 8, 1561.	———, William, Netherton, par. Thornell, labourer, Apl. 2, 1561.	17		79
Oct. 6, 1557.	———, William, Torworthe (bur. Blythe, Notts.), yeom., Sep.3, 1557.	15	2	10
May 6, 1568.	Bynkes, Christopher, Felkirke (bur. Roiston), Aug. 14, 1567.	17		770
Sep. 24, 1567.	———, John, Royston, yeoman, May 1, 1567.	17		709
Aug.14, 1554.	———, William, Kyngstone on Hull, maryner, Apl. 27, 1554.	14		146
Mar.14, 1560.	Bynne, Richard, Todwicke, Sep. 19, 1560.	16		159
Oct. 5, 1564.	———, William, Harthill, husbandman, Apl. 22, 1564.	17		377
Sep. 30, 1556.	Bynnyngtone, Robert, Garton on the Walde, husbn., Aug. 22, 1556.	15	1	133
May 9, 1563.	Byrd, Alison, Wysteid, Jun. 24, 1562.	17		255
Oct. 1, 1562.	———, Henry, Esington (Holderness), May 17, 1562.	17		112
Oct. 1, 1565.	———, John, Roall (bur. Kellington), Sep. 10, 1565.	17		487
Mar.17, 1556.	———, Robert, Dymylton (bur. Esington), Nov. 3, 1556.	15	1	188
Apl. 16, 1567.	Byrde, Christopher, Essyngton. Sep. 1, 1566.	17		634

	Vol.	Pt.	Fol.
Jun. 10, 1560. Byrde, Leonarde, Owtnewton (bur. Esington), Apl. 13, 1559.	16		82
Jan. 11, 1563. ——, Margaret, Cottingham, widow, Sep. 6, 1563.	17		309
July 15, 1562. ——, Robert, Wynesteade, Apl. 14, 1562.	17		95
Aug. 2, 1557. ——, Steven, Withestede in Holderness, husbandman, Apl. 2, 1557.	15	1	322
Oct. 2, 1566. ——, Thomas, Beverley, tanner, Apl. 18, 1566.	17		572
Dec. 1, 1557. Byrdsall, Isabell, Tadkaster, widow, Aug. 24, 1557.	15	2	86
Apl. 26, 1558. ——, John, Monkefryston, Mar. 1, 1557.	15	2	236
Feb. 15, 1558. Byrke, Richard, Ottringham, Oct. 15, 1558.	15	3	268
May 6, 1557. ——, Thomas, Syglisthron, Feb. 23, 1557.	15	1	240
Apl. 2, 1562. Byrkebye, Alyce, Dewesbury, widow, Feb. 3, 1561.	17		181
Jun. 12, 1567. Byrket, Henry, Merflet in Holderness, yeoman, Jan. 6, 1566.	17		661
Oct. 8, 1561. Byrkett, Alice, Knesall (Notts.), widow, July 8, 1561.	17		39
May 13, 1557. Byrkhead, John, Knesall (Notts.), husbandman, Apl. 9, 1557.	15	1	217
Oct. 2, 1566. Byrkinshay, Thomas, Thorneton, par. Bradford, Jun. 5, 1566.	17		580
Oct. 2, 1556. Byrkynshawe, John, Golldale, par. Snaythe, Aug. 18, 1556.	15	1	132
Sep. 18, 1565. Byrley, John, Lawasshe in Bradfeld, Feb. 23, 1564.	17		467
Oct. 2, 1566. ——, John, Sheffeld, May 18, 1566.	17		577
Feb. 17, 1557. ——, William, Eglesfeld, Aug. 21, 1557.	15	2	137
May 31, 1567. Byron, Sir John, Newsted (bur. Collwicke, Notts.), knight, Aug. 17, 1558.	17		656
May 6, 1563. Bysshepe, William, Langar (Notts.), husbandman, Sep. 20, 1562.	17		246
Apl. 17, 1567. Bysshopp, Robert, Elslaike (bur. Broughton), Dec. 4, 1566.	17		621
Jan. 17, 1560. Bywater, Agnes, Swillington, Mar. 24, 1560.	16		142
Nov. 12, 1556. ——, John, Litle Prestone, par. Kyppax, Sep. 27, 1556.	15	1	112
Aug. 15, 1562. Bywatter, Thomas, Saxton, July 25, 1562.	17		105
Oct. 30, 1554. Bywayter, George, Swillington, Aug. 24, 1554.	14		280
Aug. 20, 1567. Bywell, Agnes, York, widow, Aug. 9, 1567.	17		697
May 13, 1557. Cadde, Robert, Adbolton, par. Holme Perpoynte (Notts.), husbn., Sep. 23, 1556.	15	1	231
Nov. 28, 1558. Cadebye, William, Hornesaye. *No date.*	15	3	78
Oct. 13, 1558. Caid, Robert, Rotherham, Mar. 12, 1557.	15	2	356
Mar. 21, 1560. Caide, John, Southcliffe (bur. North Cave), Dec. 23, 1560.	16		173
Jan. 19, 1558. Caige, Edmund, Eskrige, Apl. 23, 1558.	15	3	21
Oct. 13, 1558. Calai, Lawrence, Westhorpe, par. Sowthwell (Notts.), Sep. 24, 1558.	15	2	360
July 27, 1557. [1] Calam, Hewgh, Newmalton, cordyner, July 4, 1557.	15	1	321
Apl. 26, 1558. Calbek, Robert, Huslett, par. Ledes, yeoman, Feb. 16, 1557.	15	2	236
May 9, 1565. Calbeke, Robert, Huntslett, par. Ledes, husbandman, Nov. 16, 1564.	17		421
Apl. 27, 1558. Cale, Christopher (bur. Waddington), Sep. 12, 1557.	15	2	200
Dec. 14, 1566. Calf, William, Sherburne, Jun. 22, 1566.	17		604
Mar. 15, 1556. Calffe, Annes, Sherburne (Bucrose), widow, Feb. 8, 1555.	15	1	185
Jan. 31, 1560. [1] Calome, Nicholas, York, Jan. 16, 1558.	16		146
Apl. 17, 1567. Calvard, Leonard, Owlcottes, par. Arnclif, Feb. ult., 1565.	17		620
July 10, 1561. ——, Richard, Wistow, Aug. 24, 1559.	17		65
Mar. 20, 1559. Calvarde, William, Raskell, husbandman, Mar. 2, 1558.	16		14
Oct. 1, 1557. Calvart, Adam, Huton Rudbye, mylner, Apl. 24, 1557.	15	1	362
May 10, 1565. Calverd, John, Morsom, par. Skelton, Oct. 10, 1562.	17		427
Apl. 6, 1557. Calverley, Dame Anne, Mylnegrene, par. Ledes, Dec. 31, 1556.	15	1	191
Dec. 22, 1556. ——, Christopher, Fishelake, labourer, May 28, 1556.	15	1	80
Sep. 27, 1554. ——, Christopher, Hewbie (bur. Sutton), Aug. 14, 1554.	14		273
Oct. 24, 1554. ——, Robert, Tikehill, Aug. 1, 1553.	14		309
May 9, 1565. Calvert, John, Oulcotes, par. Arneclif, Dec. 7, 1564.	17		434
Oct. 5, 1558. ——, William, Potto, par. Whorleton. *No date.*	15	3	44
May 9, 1566. ——, William, Widmerpoole (Notts.), Jan. 17, 1566.	17		550
Oct. 4, 1564. Calverte, Robert, Oulcottes, par. Arneclif, Apl. 10, 1564.	17		369
May 5, 1558. Cam, William, Rosington, husbandman, Nov. 21, 1557.	15	2	332
Apl. 22, 1562. Came, Thomas, Walkryngham (Notts.), Feb. 23, 1562.	17		193
Apl. 29, 1568. Cammage, George, Cawood, Feb. 23, 1567.	17		769
Aug. 18, 1562. Campleon, William, Semer, Apl. 3, 1562.	17		106
Apl. 28, 1559. Camplechone, Richard, Wilberfosse, husbandman, Oct. 12, 1558.	15	3	361
Dec. 5, 1567. Campon, William, Kayngham, husbandman, Sep. 16, 1567.	17		743
Oct. 6, 1557. Campsall, Edmonde, Blythe (Notts.), husbandman, Aug. 18, 1557.	15	2	13

1 See also under letter K.

		Vol.	Pt.	Fol.
May 7, 1554.	Campynet, Thomas, Ovenden, par, Hallifax, Mar. 21, 1552.	14		2
Jun. 1, 1556.	Campyon, Robert, Danbie, Apl. 22, 1556.	15	1	40
Dec. 4, 1561.	Camys, Nicholas, Skelton, par. Overton, husbandman, Oct. 25, 1561.	17		30
Aug.18, 1562.	Candler, Robert, Urton, par. Seamer, July 19, 1562.	17		105
Sep. 29, 1563.	Canlare, John, Aytton, par. Semer, Nov. 28, 1562.	17		274
Apl. 14, 1559.	Cannum, Edward, Newton, par. Wyntryngham, Sep. 18, 1558.	15	3	350
Apl. 13, 1559.	Cannan, William, Garton, Jan. 15, 1557.	15	3	344
Oct. 27, 1557.	Canson or Causon als. Edrington, Henry, Heworthe, York, Sep.4,1557.	15	1	365
Jun. 2, 1558.	Cantie, Michael, Hornesey, fisherman, Oct. 30, 1558.	15	2	337
Apl. 22, 1556.	Cantley, John, Hensaull (bur. Snathe), Jan. 11, 1555.	15	1	18
Oct. 8, 1556.	Canyet, Nicholas, Newarke (Notts.), cowper, Jun. 27, 1556.	15	1	153
Apl. 20, 1559.	Capistoke, William, Carleton in Lindreke (Notts.),husb.,Mar.27,1558.	15	3	309
Mar. 6, 1556.	Capper, Robert, Wyston, par. Claworthe (Notts.), Aug. 3, 1556.	15	1	181
Jun. 17, 1556.	Cappes, Thomas, Cawood, labourer, Jan. 19, 1555.	15	1	48
May 13, 1557.	Caprons, Thomas, preist (bur. Eperston, Notts.), Dec. 1, 1556.	15	1	226
Jan. 22, 1561.	1 Car, Robert (bur. Sutton), Aug. 10, 1561.	17		24
July 2, 1561.	—, William, Gristrope, par. Fyley, Mar. 20, 1561.	17		78
Aug.18, 1565.	Carbott, Henry, Towlston, par. Newton Kyme, husbn., Jun. 21, 1565.	17		455
Mar.20, 1565.	Care, Robert, Aston, Apl. 19, 1564.	17		506
Apl. 13, 1559.	——, William, Weton (bur. Wellweke), Feb. 10, 1558.	15	3	345
Jun. 5, 1563.	Carelill, Leonard, Icopp (bur. Adle), husbandman, May 19, 1563.	17		253
Mar. 3, 1562.	Carie, Hew, Howke, July 1, 1562.	17		148
Oct. 7, 1557.	1 Carington, John, Stoike, par. Gedlynge (Notts.), Aug. 8, 1557.	15	2	26
May 4, 1558.	Caringtonne, William, Trowell (Notts.), husbandman ——, 1557.	15	2	275
Oct. 5, 1558.	Carlell, James, Whitby, Jun. 28, 1558.	15	3	42
May 18, 1559.	——, John, Great Houghton, par. Derfield, Aug. 30, 1558.	15	3	417
Sep. 6, 1558.	——, John, Wilberfosse, husbandman, Aug. 4, 1558.	15	3	100
Jun. 10, 1557.	——, Roger, Whenby, yeoman, Apl. 24, 1557.	15	1	288
Jun. 1, 1556.	——, Thomas, Humbleton, ——, 1556.	15	1	40
May 5, 1558.	——, William, Bothomsall (Notts.), Nov. 16, 1557.	15	2	246
Apl. 22, 1556.	——, William, Dunsley, par. Whitbie, Feb. 23, 1549.	15	1	27
Oct. 1, 1557.	Carleton, Beatrix, Stoxley in Cleveland, widow, May 19, 1556.	15	1	362
Jan. 13, 1558.	——, Hugh, Nottingham, priest, Oct. 29, 1558.	15	3	14
Dec. 1, 1561.	Carlill, John, Scostrope, Sep. 20, 1560.	17		33
Jan. 3, 1558.	——, William, Wilberfosse, yeoman, Oct. 28, 1558.	15	3	199
Oct. 6, 1558.	Carlinglay, Robert, Bolton on Derne, Sep. 7, 1558.	15	3	223
Mar.22, 1554.	Carllell, Henry, Newham, par. Whitbye, Jan. 8, 1551.	14		187
Sep. 5, 1565.	Carlton, Thomas, Old Malton, Jun. 2, 1565.	17		460
Nov. 5, 1564.	Carnabye, Edward, Leckenfeild, husbandman, Apl. 27, 1564.	17		395
Mar.19, 1559.	Carpmell, Bryan, Stayndlaye (bur. Waikefelde), husbn., Feb.12,1558.	16		13
Sep. 30, 1557.	1 Carr, Henry, Bylton in Holdernesse, Aug. 17, 1557.	15	1	341
Apl. 27, 1558.	——, Thomas, Longe Gill, par. Longe Preston, Sep. 22, 1557	15	2	204
July 3, 1565.	——, Thomas, York, baker, Jun. 18, 1565.	17		450
Dec.22, 1557.	——, William, Santon, Oct. 8, 1557.	15	2	43
Feb. 1, 1563.	Carre, Catherine, Atterclif, par. Sheffeld, Sep. 28, 1563.	17		313
May 5, 1568.	——, Christopher, the Heighe in Thornton in Craven, gentleman, Dec. 30, 1567.	17		782
Jan. 16, 1558.	——, George, Skamston, par. Rillington, Oct. 12, 1558.	15	3	20
Apl. 22, 1558.	——, Henry (bur. Skarburgh), Nov. 9, 1557.	15	2	234
May 2, 1560.	——, James (bur. Santon), Nov. 30, 1559.	16		43
July 20, 1557.	——, Robert, Carnabie, labourer, Apl. 20, 1557.	15	1	314
Jan. 12, 1558.	Carrocke, Christopher (bur. Swine), Oct. 23, 1558.	15	3	178
Apl. 7, 1562.	——, Robert, Appleton (bur. Bolton Percye), Mar. 6, 1561.	17		161
Jun. 21, 1568.	——, William, Nottingham, Nov. 10, 1567.	17		830
Apl. 28, 1554.	Carroke, Robert, Colton (bur. Bolton), Jan. 29, 1553.	14		55
Sep. 26, 1558.	Cartar, William, Scakellthorpe (bur. Settrington), Aug. 3, 1558.	15	3	88
Mar.20, 1558.	Carter, Edmond, Thorp, par. Baddisworth, husbandman, Jan.20,1558.	15	3	243
Nov.20, 1563.	——, Edward, Gysburne in Cleveland, yeoman, Jun. 18, 1561.	17		304
Oct. 22, 1560.	——, Henry, Easton, par. Burlington, husbandman, May 9, 1560.	16		127
Mar. 4, 1562.	——, Isabell, Righton, widow, Jan. 7, 1562.	17		152

1 See also under letter K.

A.D. 1554 TO 1568.

	Vol.	Pt.	Fol.
Jun. 14, 1567. Carter, John, Belfeld, par. Stellingfleite, Apl. 26, 1566.	17		656
July 26, 1558. ——, John, Rysse in Holderness, husbandman, Apl. 5, 1558.	15	3	10
Sep. 28, 1557. ——, Martyn (bur. Beverlay), Apl. 20, 1557.	15	1	357
Jun. 22, 1568. ——, Mathewe, Auborn, par. Bridlington, husbn., Mar. 2, 1567.	17		824
Dec. 22, 1556. ——, Richard, Thorpe, par. Badsworthe, Nov. 20, 1556.	15	1	86
Mar. 20, 1558. ——, Roger, Kelfeild, par. Stilllingflete, Oct. 21, 1558.	15	3	248
Oct. 31, 1564. ——, Thomas, Drynghouses (bur. York), husbandman, May 2, 1563.	17		393
Jan. 20, 1557. ——, Thomas, Hewton Robert, husbandman, Oct. 28, 1557.	15	2	67
May 2, 1566. ——, Thomas, Nubigginhill, par. Sandall Magna, Jan. 31, 1565.	17		533
Dec. 4, 1557. ——, Thomas, Selbye, tanner, Nov. 13, 1557.	15	2	52
Jun. 3, 1568. ——, William, Kelfeld, husbandman. *No date.*	17		831
Oct. 5, 1558. ——, William, Stappleton, par. Darrington, husbn., Aug. 10, 1558.	15	3	63
Sep. 30, 1557. ——, William, Thyrkelbye, par. Kyrkebye in Gryndall lythe, Feb. 16, 1557.	15	1	324
Dec. 15, 1557. Cartewright, George, Warsopp (Notts.), Sep. 12, ——.	15	2	59
Feb. 26, 1562. Cartmell, Thomas, York, barbor and chandler, Jan. 7, 1562.	17		147
Dec. 15, 1557. Cartwright, Agnes (bur. Warsopp, Notts.), Nov. 14, 1557.	15	2	59
May 18, 1559. ————, Henry, Babworth (Notts.), July 26, 1558.	15	3	422
May 2, 1555. ————, Richard, Newland, par. Cottingham, Apl. 23, 1554.	14		32
Dec. 17, 1557. ————, Richard, Pigburne, par. Brodsworthe, Nov. 2, 1557.	15	2	39
May 2, 1566. ————, Robert, Edlington, Feb. 26, 1565.	17		522
Aug. 6, 1567. ————, Thomas, Newland, par. Cottingham, husbn., July 8, 1566.	17		699
Jan. 22, 1561. ————, William, Newland, par. Cottingham, yeom., Sep. 1, 1561.	17		24
Mar. 14, 1560. ———— *als.* Vicars, William (bur. Athewyke), Sep. 9, 1560.	16		161
Oct. 9, 1567. 1 Carver, Robert, Thorney (Notts.), husbandman, May 14, 1567.	17		722
No date. ————, Thomas, junr., Blesby, Notts., Oct. 12, 1555.	14		18
Jun. 2, 1562. Casse, Thomas, Brompton, Dec. 1, 1562 (*sic*).	17		86
July 10, 1564. ——, Thomas, Sowden, par. Brompton, Apl. 13, 1561.	17		355
Oct. 2, 1560. —— (or Crosse), William, Hoton bushell, husbandman, Dec. 10, 1558.	16		110
Jun. 2, 1557. Casson, German, Fullam, par. Womerslaie, Apl. 10, 1557.	15	1	267
Mar. 4, 1560. ——, John, Hunslett Woodhouse, par. Ledes, tanner, Nov. 8, 1560.	16		152
Mar. 20, 1558. ——, Margaret, Holbeke (bur. Leedes), widow, Oct. 8, 1558.	15	3	289
Aug. 28, 1561. ——, Robert, Hulslet Wodhouse, par. Leedes, Apl. 10, 1561.	17		53
Dec. 15, 1557. ——, William, Carleton in Lynryke (Notts.), labr., Aug. 10, 1557.	15	2	56
July 26, 1563. ——, William (bur. Waikefeild), Jan. 12, 1562.	17		267
Oct. 7, 1556. Castelyne, John, Worsope (Notts.), Aug. 1, 1556.	15	1	144
May 5, 1558. Casteven, William, Sokam, par. Warsope (Notts.), Sep. 8, 1557.	15	2	332
July 1, 1561. Castylforthe, Peter, Ranskyll, par. Blythe (Notts.), yeom., Feb. 28, 1560	17		61
Nov. 9, 1557. Castyll, Gylbart, Hogley, par. Allmonburye, Sep. 22, 1557.	15	2	89
Oct. 12, 1564. Catfosse, John, Gedling (Notts.), yeoman, Dec. 13, 1564.	17		392
Sep. 18, 1565. Catlin, Thomas, Silkeston, Jan. 14, 1563.	17		466
May 2, 1566. 1 Catterall, James, Heyton, par. Burnesall, Nov. 27, 1565.	17		531
Jan. 13, 1558. Catterson, Richard, Balderton (Notts.), wedower, Sep. 12, 1558.	15	3	17
Apl. 3, 1555. Catton, Richard, Kyrkbie Underdale, Mar. 6, 1554.	14		191
Nov. 3, 1557. ————, Thomas, Everyngham, Sep. 1, 1557.	15	2	105
Oct. 8, 1567. Caulcroft, Raufe, Barnston (bur. Granbe, Notts.), Apl. 10, 1567.	17		726
Apl. 26, 1560. Causon or Canson *als.* Edrington, Henry, Heworthe, Sep. 4, 1557.	16		33
May 2, 1560. Cavart, Nicholas, Tunstall (bur. Aton), Nov. 6, 1559.	16		42
Dec. 21, 1562. Cave, Christopher, Otley. *No date.*	17		136
Oct. 3, 1566. ——, Elizabeth, Thornton, par. Foston, handmaid, July 3, 1566	17		579
Jun. 22, 1568. ——, John, Carlton (bur. Gyseley), Jan. 12, 1566.	17		819
Jun. 22, 1568. ——, John, Righton, Mar. 27, 1568.	17		823
Jun. 3, 1558. ——, John, Staneburne, Mar. 18, 1557.	15	2	288
Oct. 2, 1567. ——, John, Thornton, par. Foston, husbandman, Jun. 13, 1567.	17		711
Dec. 16, 1556. ——, Thomas, Burlay, par. Otley, Mar. 16, 1555.	15	1	195
Oct. 21, 1557. Caverte, Christopher, Tunstall, (bur. Ayton), Oct. 4, 1557.	15	2	35
July 17, 1565. Cavvard, George (bur. Swyne), Dec. 21, 1564.	17		453
Jan. 22, 1557. Cawarde, Robert, Thorneton in Pickeryngelythe, Nov. 24, 1557.	15	2	159
Sep. 9, 1561. Cawdey, Richard, Baildon, priest, Jun. 24, 1561.	17		52
Jun. 4, 1561. Cawdrey, John, Bramhoppe, par. Otley, husbandman, Apl. 25, 1561.	17		67

1 See also under letter K.

A.D. 1554 TO 1568.

		Vol.	Pt.	Fol.
Mar. 6, 1556.	Cawerd, John, Sturton (Notts.), husbandman, Nov. 30, 1556.	15	1	179
Oct. 11, 1554.	Cawode, George, Newton Kyme, Sep. 1, 1554.	14		50
May 4, 1558.	Cawood, William, Lamley (Notts.), husbandman, Aug. 11, 1557.	15	2	278
Jun. 2, 1561.	Cawpe, John, Kyrkebye in Asshefeld (Notts.), smythe, Jan. 18. 1560.	17		66
Dec. 11, 1557.	Cawston, Rowland, Newsom, par. Kyrkeby on Wyske, Oct. 12, 1557.	15	2	83
Jun. 16, 1564.	Cawthorne, Henry, Beubanke. par. Sylkeston, Mar. 20, 1562.	17		350
Sep. 30, 1557.	Cawton, John, Catton (bur. Topclyffe), Oct. 10, 1541.	15	1	346
May 6, 1563.	1 Cawuer, Isabell, Sturton (Notts.), widow, May 3, 1558.	17		244
Mar. 20, 1559.	Cawvarde, Alyson (bur. Raskell), Oct. 3, 1559.	16		15
Oct. 8, 1562.	1 Cawver, Robert, Sturton (Notts.), husbandman, May 9, 1562.	17		120
Sep. 7, 1567.	Cawvert, Margerie, Wistowe, widow, Mar. 26, 1567.	17		703
Feb. 12, 1566.	Cayde, Elizabeth, Wresle, widow, Jan. 24, 1566.	17		612
May 25, 1554.	Certayn (? Kirton), Alan, Redker, par. Marske, Aug. 30, 1553.	14		134
Sep. 30, 1556.	Chabylman, Robert, Burton Flemyne, July 17, 1556.	15	1	134
Mar. 26, 1562.	Chace, Esabell, York, widow, Jan. 8, 1561.	17		157
Oct. 7, 1558.	Chadweke, James, Soyland, par. Eland, Apl. 25, 1558.	15	3	226
May 5, 1558.	———, Katheryn, West Retforde (Notts.), widow, Nov. 25, 1556.	15	2	252
Oct. 3, 1556.	Chadwike, John, Campsall, Sep. 6, 1556.	15	1	69
Oct. 13, 1558.	———, Richard, West Markham (Notts.), Sep. 8, 1558.	15	3	31
Mar. 6, 1556.	———, Robert, West Retford (Notts.), Nov. 3, 1556.	15	1	176
Nov. 6, 1557.	Chadwyck, William, Scruby (Notts.), Apl. 9, 1557.	15	2	109
Mar. 28, 1560.	Chaice, Margaret, Overton, widow, May 14, 1559.	16		22
Oct. 1, 1556.	Chalener, John, Lityll Hapton, par. Kirkbymysperton, July 19, 1556.	15	1	67
Mar. 30, 1555.	Challand, Richard, Orston, Notts., husbandman, Nov. 23, 1553.	14		15
Jun. 23, 1568.	Challaner, William, Sandesend, par. Lythe, Mar. 14, 1567.	17		828
Oct. 12, 1564.	Chalon, John, Flaboro, par. Staunton (Notts.), husbn., July 7, 1564.	17		379
Oct. 10, 1555.	Chalonour, Robert, Stanleye (par. Wakefield), July 7, 1555.	14		311
Aug. 6, 1562.	Chamber, Agnes, Wintringham, Dec. 1, 1561.	17		104
Sep. 30, 1557.	———, Jennet, Newton, par. Wyntringham, Aug. 10, 1557.	15	1	324
May 31, 1557.	———, John, Adwicke of Derne, mylner, Oct. 10, 1556.	15	1	260
May 31, 1560.	———, John, York, parish clerk, Apl. 26, 1559.	16		71
Apl. 20, 1564.	———, Richard, Astlay, par. Swillington, husbn., Dec. 3, 1563.	17		332
Oct. 6, 1557.	Chamberlayn, Thomas, Flyntam (Notts.), husbandman, Jun. 10, 1557.	15	2	26
Oct. 8, 1556.	Chamberlayne, Richard (bur. Slafurthe, Notts.), Jun. 20, 1556.	15	1	151
Oct. 12, 1564.	Chamberlen, William, Wollaton (Notts.), Jun. 5, 1564.	17		392
Sep. 28, 1560.	Chamberleyne, John, Ruddington (Notts.), husbn,, Mar. 26, 1560.	16		107
May 13, 1557.	Chambers, George, Darleton (Notts.), Jan, 12, 1554.	15	1	235
Mar. 15, 1560.	———, James, Clomber, par. Wurshopp (Notts.), Nov. 14, 1559.	16		168
Apl. 19, 1559.	———, John, Staplefurth (Notts.), husbandman, Aug. 8, 1558.	15	3	353
July 14, 1558.	———, John, Wresle, Mar. 26, 1558.	15	2	322
Oct. 7, 1561.	———, Margaret, Staplefurthe (Notts,), widow, Mar. 6, 1561.	17		42
Nov. 28, 1558.	———, Richard, Gristwatt (bur. Topcliffe), July 26, 1558.	15	3	126
May 2, 1560.	———, Robert, Newarke (Notts.), smythe, July 21, 1559.	16		40
Mar. 22, 1560.	Chambre, William, Newton, par. Wyntringham, May 1, 1559.	16		176
Nov. 10, 1557.	Chamer, Robert, Ferybrigge, par. Waterfryiston, husbn., Sep. 15, 1557.	15	2	97
Apl. 28, 1563.	———, Umfrey, Bridlington, Aug. 10, 1562.	17		231
Feb. 4, 1557.	Chamles, Alyson, Holme in Spldingmore, Nov. 20, 1557.	15	2	163
Mar. 15, 1558.	———, Robert, Holme in Spaldingmore, Feb. 4, 1558.	15	3	168
Mar. 4, 1555.	Chamney, Olyver, Barnebie, yeoman (bur. St. Michael,[C]althorne), Nov. 4, 1554.	14		191
Jun. 12, 1567.	Champlay, Thomas, Bubwithe, husbandman, Mar. 11, 1566.	17		657
Feb. 17, 1557.	Champnay, Robert, Bubwyth, husbandman, Oct. 28, 1557.	15	2	148
Oct. 6, 1557.	Champyon, Henry, Codgrave (Notts.), Apl. 19, 1557.	15	2	28
Apl. 16, 1562.	Chansey, E[m]ote (bur. Brompton), Mar. 23, 1571 (sic).	17		157
Apl. 16, 1562.	Chansie, William, Brompton, Jan. 23, 1561.	17		158
Nov. 29, 1558.	Chantre, Avis, Barneby (Doncaster), July 1, 1558.	15	3	142
Oct. 7, 1556.	Chantrie, Thomas, Schaftworthe, par. Evertone (Notts.), Sep. 27, 1555.	15	1	148
May 18, 1559.	Chapill, George, Darton, Sep. 16, 1558.	15	3	400
Dec. 19, 1555.	Chaplayn, William, Thernum, par. Burton Agnes, husbn. *No date.*	14		247
May 10, 1559.	Chaplayne, Thomas, Burton Agnes, husbandman, Jan, 3, 1558.	15	3	391

1 See also under letter K.

		Vol.	Pt.	Fol.
Sep. 29, 1563.	Chapman, Agnes, Flambrughe, widow, Mar. 13, 1562.	17		275
Dec. 5, 1567.	———, Alison, Holme in Spaldingmore, May 9, 1567.	17		750
Oct. 20, 1558.	———, Anne, Cornbroughe (bur. Sheriffe Howtone), widow, Sep. 20, 1558.	15	3	232
Feb. 17, 1557.	———, Bryan, Felkyrke, yeoman, Dec. 30, 1557.	15	2	141
Mar. 15, 1562.	———, Cecilie, Esingeton, Jan. 5, 1561.	17		163
Jun. 6, 1556.	———, Christopher, South Dalton, May 19, 1556.	15	1	41
Oct. 6, 1558.	———, George (bur. Berithorpe), Aug. 5, 1558.	15	3	224
Mar. 5, 1555.	———, George, Cawton in Ridall, yeoman, Jan. 4, 1554.	14		107
Apl. 26, 1558.	———, George, Harswell, Jan. 28, 1557.	15	2	222
Sep. 1, 1565.	———, Henry, Danbye, May 18, 1565	17		462
Jan. 22, 1557.	———, Janet, Hawnbye, widow, Jan. 3, 1557.	15	2	158
Apl. 3, 1559.	———, Jenet, Harpham, Sep. 18, 1558.	15	3	360
Jan. 17, 1557.	———, John, Carnabye, husbandman, Sep. 7, 1557.	15	2	61
Oct. 28, 1563.	———, John, Everingham, Sep. 10, 1563.	17		299
Oct. 27, 1564.	———, John, Filinge, Dec. 28, 1563.	17		393
Apl. 13, 1559.	———, John, Goodmanham, Mar. 4, 1558.	15	3	350
Apl. 3, 1567.	———, John, Hull, husbandman, Feb. 13, 1566.	17		618
Jan. 12, 1558.	———, John (bur. Middleton), Dec. 4, 1558.	15	3	193
Oct. 9, 1560.	———, John, South Cleffe, par. North Cave, Apl. 4, 1560.	16		123
Jun. 7, 1560.	———, Lawrance, Nafferton, clerk, Feb. 12, 1558.	16		79
Feb. 4, 1561.	———, Percivall, Esyngton, Oct. 9, 1561.	17		12
Mar. 17, 1556.	———, Richard, Beverlay, fisher, Jan. 25, 1556.	15	1	188
July 27, 1567.	———, Richard, Hinderwell, May 20, 1567.	17		671
Nov. 2, 1565.	———, Richard, Naburne, par. Acaster, May 28, 1565.	17		487
Mar. 2, 1555.	———, Richard, Ryge House, par. Esington, July 31, 1554.	15	1	9
Jan. 24, 1558.	———, Robert, Gisborne, Apl. 28, 1558.	15	3	23
Jun. 25, 1561.	———, Robert, Kirkbye Underdaile, husbandman, Sep. 25, 1560.	17		74
May 17, 1565.	———, Robert, Lenton (Notts.), Apl. 7, 1565.	17		441
May 31, 1559.	———, Roger (bur. Egton), Feb. 9, 1557.	15	3	434
Oct. 21, 1557.	———, Roger, Marske, husbandman, Jun. 16, 1551.	15	2	35
Apl. 5, 1554.	———, Thomas, Carnabie, May 1, 1553.	14		216
July 12, 1557.	———, Thomas, Estherlsay, husbandman, 1557.	15	1	306
Jan. 24, 1558.	———, Thomas, Fylyng, Sep. 25, 1558.	15	3	22
Apl. 22, 1563.	———, Thomas, Holme in Spaldingmore, Dec. 13, 1562.	17		222
Feb. 25, 1558.	———, Thomas, Myddleton, Feb. 1, 1558.	15	3	278
Feb. 15, 1558.	———, Thomas, Rowton (bur. Swyne), wever, Sep. 20, 1558.	15	3	270
Jan. 8, 1556.	———, William, Faydmore (bur. Kirkeby Moreshead), Jan. 21, 1556.	15	1	87
Apl. 18, 1567.	———, William, Fernley, par. Ledes, husbandman, Jan. 18, 1565.	17		632
Jan. 17, 1557.	———, William, Flambroughe, fyshemonger, Oct. 30, 1557.	15	2	62
Sep. 30, 1557.	———, William, Harpham, Aug. 29, 1557.	15	1	342
Oct. 7, 1557.	———, William, Nottingham, Mar. 29, 1557.	15	2	23
Aug. 23, 1563.	———, William, Thornton in Pykeringe, husbn., Dec. 27, 1562.	17		211
Apl. 3, 1559.	———, William, Womelton (bur. Kirkdayle), husbn., Oct. 30, 1558.	15	3	317
Feb. 28, 1566.	———, William, Ynglebie under Grenowe, Nov. 7, 1566.	17		616
Feb. 10, 1557.	Chappeman, Richard (bur. Kyrkeburne), Oct. 20, 1557.	15	2	147
Jan. 28, 1555.	Charlesworth, Agnes, Derton, widow, Dec. 22, 1555.	15	1	1
Nov. 15, 1557.	———, Richard, Cottyes, par. Kyrkburton, yeom., July 1, 1557.	15	2	89
Mar. 22, 1558.	———, Thomas, Holyngreve, par. Kirkeburton, Jan. 13, 1558.	15	3	294
Oct. 1, 1556.	Char[l]esworthe, John, Royston, Dec. 7, 1555.	15	1	130
July 1, 1558.	Charlesworthe, Raufe, Austonleye, par. Almonburye, Mar. 21, 155[7-]8.	15	2	331
Apl. 28, 1563.	Charlisworth, Thomas, Darton, Oct. 4, 1562.	17		231
July 8, 1561.	Charlsworthe, John, Austonley, par. Almonburie, May 6, 1561.	17		79
Jan. 13, 1558.	Charrier, Elizabeth (bur. South Leverton, Notts.), Sep. 7, 1558.	15	3	18
Jan. 24, 1565.	Chasse, Thomas, Hull, marchaunt, July 24, 1564.	17		497
July 1, 1556.	Chasterton als. Yedall, Thomas, Kyrkestall, par. Ledes, Aug. 7, 1555.	15	1	51
Nov. 29, 1558.	Chatburne, James, Baddisworthe, Nov. 19, 1558.	15	3	109
Apl. 13, 1559.	Chauncell, William, Hulbridg, par. St. John, Beverley, Mar. 6, 1558.	15	3	350
Oct. 13, 1558.	Chauntre, John, Woodhowse, par. Cowkney (Notts.), Aug. 2, 1558.	15	2	356
May 31, 1557.	———, Thomas, Barmbie on Dunne, husbandman, Mar. 25, 1556.	15	1	262
July 11, 1558.	Chauntrie, William, Barnebye on Done, husbn., Mar. 6, 1557.	15	2	301
May 16, 1554.	Chawmer, John, Newland, par. Cottingham, Nov. 16, 1553.	14		3

		Vol.	Pt.	Fol.
Apl. 19, 1559.	Chaworthe, Sir John, Wyverton (bur. Langor, Notts.), knt., Aug. 30, 1558.	15	3	300
Apl. 28, 1563.	Cheister, Charles, Haitfeld Woodhous, Jan. 30, 1563.	17		235
Dec. 18, 1560.	Chelloye, John (bur. Sherburne), Aug. 11, 1560.	16		136
May 19, 1559.	Cheriholme, Thomas, Drax, Apl. 24, 1559.	15	3	426
Nov. 3, 1558.	Chermley (Registered, Hermelay), William, York, innholder, Oct. 27, 1558.	15	3	232
Apl. 20, 1559.	Cheryholme, William, Newland, par. Drax, Dec. 2, 1557.	15	3	305
Feb. 5, 1557.	————, William, Roclyffe (bur. Snaythe), Nov. 21, 1557.	15	2	164
May 2, 1560.	Cheryolme, Cicilie, wife of William, C., Newland, par. Draxe, Apl. 16, 1559.	16		52
July 27, 1564.	Cheseman, John, Wrellton (bur. Myddleton), husbn., Jun. 24, 1564.	17		359
May 21, 1560.	————, Thomas, Symmyngton, Aug. 16, 1559.	16		66
Jun. 2, 1562.	Chesman, Ales, Thornton in Pickeringlith, Mar. 24, 1561.	17		86
Apl. 16, 1562.	————, Robert, Thornton in Pykrynclith, husbn., Aug. 21, 1561.	17		157
May 4, 1558.	Chester, George, Clyfton by Nottingham (Notts.), Sep. 24, 1557.	15	2	270
Jan. 22, 1557.	————, William, New Malton, coverlet weaver, Dec. 15, 1557.	15	2	159
Oct. 6, 1558.	Chettill, William, Laugton, Mar. 27, 1558.	15	3	27
1554.	Chewe, Richard, Bridlington, husbandman, Feb. 8, 1554	14		100
Mar. 13, 1558.	Child, Alis, Billinglay, par. Darfeld, widow, Nov. 21, 1558.	15	3	161
May 2, 1566.	————, James, Leverseige, par. Bristall, Dec. 6, 1564.	17		535
Nov. 28, 1567.	————, John, Hunmanebie, July 19, 1567.	17		737
Mar. 9, 1567.	————, Thomas, Skellowe, par. Ousten, Dec. 3, 1567.	17		764
Aug. 28, 1563.	Childe, Richard, Hertyshead, par. Deusburye, Sep. 4, 1559.	17		209
Apl. 24, 1567.	————, Richard, Rolston (Notts.), husbandman, Jan. 30, 1566.	17		641
Nov. 29, 1558.	————, Thomas, Billinglay (bur. Darfeld), husbn., Oct. 21, 1558.	15	3	139
Apl. 14, 1563.	Chimley, John, Sherburne, husbandman, Dec. 27, 1562.	17		203
May 13, 1557.	Chosyng, John, Weston (Notts.), Jan. 3, 1556.	15	1	217
July 11, 1561.	Choyston, William, Welbourne (bur. Kyrkedaill), husbn., Oct. 12, 1553.	17		81
Mar. 1, 1564.	Chreswell, Joseph (bur. Trinity, Hull), Jun. 10, 1564.	17		407
Sep. 10, 1555.	Chrispyn, Elles, Fledburgh, Aug. 13, 1555.	14		305
July 20, 1561.	Christalson, Henry, Beverley, May 2, 1561.	17		63
Jan. 22, 1567.	Christie, Isabell, Patrington, widow, Jun. 26, 1565.	17		754
Apl. 28, 1563.	————, Nicholas, Ostwicke, par. Rosse, husbn., Mar. 16, 1562.	17		238
Mar. 4, 1562.	————, William, Kaingham, Jan. 22, 1561.	17		151
Mar. 23, 1557.	Chyarder (or Charder), Thomas, Attynweke, husbn., Nov. 14, 1557.	15	2	172
Nov. 12, 1556.	Claghton, John, Bramley, par. Leedes, May 26, 1556.	15	1	112
May 31, 1557.	Claie, Rawffe, Sheaffeld, Apl. 2, 1557.	15	1	262
Sep. 6, 1558.	Claiton, Sir John, priest, curate of Standfurthbrige, Aug. 26, 1558.	15	3	100
Nov. 28, 1558.	————, William, Whitlay, par. Kellington. *No date.*	15	3	138
Sep. 19, 1558.	————, William, York, Aug. 6, 1558.	15	3	108
Apl. 12, 1559.	Clapam, Richard, Thorlbye (bur. Skipse), July 23, 1558.	15	3	341
Sep. 30, 1556.	Clapham, Christopher, Long Preston, Aug. 17, 1556.	15	1	173
Apl. 19, 1564.	————, Thomas, Exley (bur. Kyghley), gentleman, Nov. 18, 1563.	17		328
Sep. 16, 1557.	————, Thomas, Wakefelde, Nov. 2, 1556.	15	1	334
Oct. 13, 1558.	Clark, Robert, Skegbe (bur. Marnham, Notts.), Jan. 31, 1557.	15	2	363
Feb. 24, 1563.	Clarke, Agnes, Thurnhome (bur. Burton Agnes), widow, May 29, 1563.	17		320
Apl. 27, 1558.	————, Alyson, Whytby, widow, July 10, 1557.	15	2	238
Sep. 1, 1565.	————, Christopher (bur. Gisburne), May 27, 1565.	17		462
July 10, 1567.	————, Christopher, Rawmarshe, July 21, 1566.	17		684
July 9, 1562.	————, George, Felchurche, Jun. 3, 1562.	17		95
Jun. 25, 1561.	————, George, Kirkbe Underdaile, husbandman, Mar. 5, 1561.	17		74
Oct. 2, 1567.	————, Harrye, Hollifeld (bur. Longe Preston), July 7, 1567.	17		712
Jan. 12, 1558.	————, Henry, Lockington, husbandman, Dec. 15, 1558.	15	3	193
Aug. 13, 1567.	————, Henry (bur. Owthorne), Apl. 23, 1567.	17		691
Nov. 3, 1558.	————, Isabell, Beffurth, servande, Oct. 20, 1558.	15	2	232 & 3 236
Apl. 15, 1562.	————, James, Huby (bur. Sutton), Feb. 2, 1561.	17		160
May 6, 1557.	————, Jenett, wid. of John C., Hellefelde (bur. Longe Preston), Nov. 6, 1556.	15	1	253
Oct. 6, 1564.	————, John, Barrake Grainge (bur. Kirkebie Overblaus), Jun. 8, 1564.	17		367
Aug. 12, 1567.	————, John, Burton Agnes, Dec. 24, 1566.	17		693
Jun. 7, 1564.	————, John, Fayrburne, par. Ledesham, husbn., May 11, 1564.	17		349
Jan. 11, 1563.	————, John, Hull, scryvener, July 21, 1563.	17		310

A.D. 1554 TO 1568.

		Vol.	Pt.	Fol.
May 2, 1560.	Clarke, John, Hunmanbe, husbandman, ——, 1559.	16		35
July 12, 1564.	——, John, Rose in Holderness, husbandman, Mar. 6, 1563.	17		357
Apl. 20, 1559.	——, John, Shafforth, par. Everton (Notts.), Feb. 5, 1557.	15	3	369
Mar. 9, 1559.	——, John, Shupton in Gawltres (bur. Overton), Nov. 25, 1559.	16		7
Dec. 16, 1557.	——, John, South Frodingham, par. Outthorne, Sep. 30, 1557.	15	2	47
Apl. 22, 1562.	——, John, Teversall (Notts.), Oct. 25, 1561.	17		176
Mar. 20, 1558.	——, John, Ulley, par. Treetonne, Mar. 1, 1558.	15	3	246
Mar. 11, 1558.	——, John, West Cottingwith (bur. Thorganby), Jan. 15, 1558.	15	3	159
May 5, 1557.	——, Sir John, Thornton in Pykerynglythe, Apl. 5, 1557.	15	1	251
Jun. 9, 1563.	——, Lyonell, Golldall, par. Snaythe, Apl. 10, 1562.	17		257
July 11, 1564.	——, Nicholas, Harton. par. Bossall, Jun. 10, 1564.	17		355
July 15, 1562.	——, Paterike, Preston in Holderness, husbandman, Mar. 30, 1562.	17		94
May 2, 1566.	——, Peter, Rowith in Holderness, husbandman, Mar. 23, 1566.	17		527
Oct. 20, 1558.	——, Richard, senior (bur. Braffarton), husbn., Aug. 25, 1558.	15	2	347
Mar. 7, 1566.	——, Richard, Roos, juvenis, Dec. 26, 1566.	17		515
Sep. 29, 1563.	——, Richard, Sowth Kirkby, July 16, 1563.	17		285
Oct. 2, 1566.	——, Richard, Swynden (bur. Gysburne), yeoman, Apl. 24, 1566.	17		574
Mar. 23, 1557.	——, Robert, Coldum (bur. Awdebrought), Aug. 16, 1557.	15	2	153
Jun. 6, 1554.	——, Robert, Flixton, Feb. 7, 1554.	14		71
July 23, 1558.	——, Robert, Goldaill (bur. Snaithe), Mar. 14, 1557.	15	2	386
Sep. 30, 1557.	——, Robert, Haudenby (bur. Adlyngflete), Aug. 2, 1557.	15	1	343
May 18, 1559.	——, Robert, Howbecke Woodhouse, par. Cuckney (Notts.), Jan. 3, 1558.	15	3	421
Dec. 16, 1557.	——, Robert, Preston (Holderness), Oct. 26, 1557.	15	2	43
May 2, 1560.	——, Robert, Swillington, Mar. 12, 1559.	16		52
No date.	——, Robert, Tankersleye, Jun. 18, 1553.	14		85
May 6, 1557.	——, Robert, Upsall, par. Kilwington, Mar. 18, 1556.	15	1	241
July 15, 1560.	——, Robert, Whelehowse, par. Stillingflete, Apl. 28, 1559.	16		92
Apl. 28, 1563.	——, Robert, Yearslay (bur. Cookeswold), Jan. 14, 1562.	17		239
Aug. 27, 1567.	——, Roger, Semer in Pickeringelythe, Aug. 24, 1567.	17		686
Jan. 12, 1557.	——, Symon, Everyngham, Oct. 14, 1557.	15	2	79
Aug. 27, 1557.	——, Symond, Ledshame, May 12, 1557.	15	2	115
Aug. 12, 1561.	——, Thomas, Arnold (bur. Riston), May 8, 1561.	17		60
Aug. 18, 1562.	——, Thomas, Bempton, husbandman, Apl. 3, 1561.	17		107
Mar. 20, 1565.	——, Thomas, Catwicke, husbandman, Aug. 7, 1565.	17		505
May 13, 1557.	——, Thomas, Edwalton (Notts.), husbandman, Apl. 10, 1557.	15	1	237
May 9, 1565.	——, Thomas, Kirkmayne gate, par. Long Preston, Nov. 16, 1564.	17		435
May 5, 1558.	——, Thomas, Knessall (Notts.), Sep. 15, 1557.	15	2	256
May 4, 1557.	——, Thomas, Morehouse, par. Fyshelake, Jan. 15, 1556.	15	1	280
Apl. 26, 1558.	——, Thomas, Rotheram, Feb. 16, 1557.	15	2	224
Jan. 11, 1557.	——, William, Brandesburton, husbandman, Nov. 18, 1557.	15	2	73
Mar. 30, 1559.	——, William, Catweke in Holderness, husbandman, Jan. 27, 1558.	15	3	297
Jun. 8, 1557.	——, William, Halsham, Apl. 8, 1557.	15	1	269
Oct. 13, 1558.	——, William, Knesall (Notts.), husbandman, May 6, 1558.	15	2	364
May 2, 1566.	——, William, Lokington, Dec. 19, 1564.	17		538
Jun. 21, 1561.	——, William, Schayll (bur. Longe Preston), Apl. 3, 1561.	17		73
May 18, 1559.	——, William, Seaton, Nov. 15, 1558.	15	3	394
May 9, 1566.	——, William, Nottingham. Jan. 23. 1565.	17		545
Aug. 12, 1567.	Clarkeson, John, Muston, Apl. 1, 1567.	17		695
Jan. 17, 1557.	——, Steven, Carnabye, Oct. 1, 1557.	15	2	62
Mar. 22, 1558.	Clarkson, Brian, Outwoodsyde, par. Wakefeld, Dec. 22, 1558.	15	3	294
May 5, 1557.	————, John, curate of Gisburne, Nov. 18, 1556.	15	1	242
Oct. 5, 1564.	————, Katheran (Doncaster Deanery), widow, May 9, 1564.	17		376
May 17, 1557.	————, William, Thurnne, par. Burton Agnes, Apl. 4, 1557.	15	1	244
Feb. 17, 1561.	Claton, George, Fynnyngley (Notts.), husbandman, Sep. 7, 1561.	17		13
Apl. 1, 1557.	Clatone, Richard, Rusholme. par. Drax, Oct. 6, 1556.	15	1	203
Jun. 16, 1554.	Claxton, Edmond, Balderton (Notts.), June 15, 1555.	14		303
Oct. 7, 1557.	————, Richard, Balderton (Notts.), gentleman, Jan. 4, 1556.	15	2	18
Oct. 2, 1566.	Clay, John, Lynley, par. Hnddersfeld, Oct. 23, 1565.	17		579
Apl. 26, 1558.	——, Richard, Aston, July 11, 1551	15	2	223
—— 11, 1555.	——, Robert, Kirkebye, par. Huddersfeild, Jun. 16, 1555.	14		260
Oct. 5, 1554.	——, Thomas (bur. Semor), ——, 1554.	14		45

	Vol.	Pt.	Fol.
Apl. 19, 1559. Clay, William, Hiklyng (Notts.), Dec. 3, 1558.	15	3	371
Jun. 2, 1562. ——, William, Newmalton, shomaker, Apl. 3, 1562.	17		86
July 19, 1557. Claye, Edmunde, Egmonton (Notts.), yeoman, May 10. 1557.	15	1	310
Apl. 16, 1567. ——, Henry, Walton, par. Sandall Magna, husbn., May 30, 1566.	17		626
Nov. 12, 1556. ——, John, Clayhous, par. Elande, Apl. 20, 1556.	15	1	112
Sep. 26, 1558. Clayton, Agnes, Rotherham, July 26, 1558.	15	3	53
July 9, [1555.] ——, James, Kirstall, Mar. 28, 1555.	14		260
Oct. 5, 1558. ——, John, Denby Grange, par. Heaton, yeoman, Aug. 29, 1557.	15	3	41
Oct. 5, 1564. ——, John, Over Denbe, par. Penyston, Mar. 26, 1564.	17		376
July 11, 1558. ——, John, Rotherham, Apl. 6. 1558.	15	2	320
Apl. 28, 1563. ——, John, Tinslay, par. Rotherham, Feb. 18, 1562.	17		232
Feb. 1, 1563. ——, Rauf, Hotton Robert, husbandman. Jun. 4, 1563.	17		314
Apl. 20, 1564. ——, Rauffe, Bygden, par. Penyston, clothier, Jan. 4, 1563.	17		325
Oct. 14. 1561. ——, William, Abdy, par. Waithe, Jun. 7, 1560.	17		38
July 11, 1558. ——, William, Bigden, par. Penyston, Mar. 19, 1556.	15	2	321
July 26, 1557. Clegge, William, Netheitonn, par. Thornhyll, Jun. 30, 1557.	15	1	316
Aug. 15, 1560. Cleifton, James, Menethorpe (bur. Westowe), husbn., July 21, 1560.	16		101
Jun. 22, 1568. Cleithinge, Phillippe, Galmeton, Jan. 2, 1566.	17		823
Oct. 4, 1565. Clemet, Elizabeth, Newton Rachfurth (bur. Hunmanbie), Apl. 7, 1565.	17		487
July 5, 1557. Clerke, Alice, Acghton, par. Aston, May 23, 1557.	15	1	303
Aug. 9, 1555. ——, Allanne, Sutton in Bonnington, Notts., husbn., Aug. 11, (sic), 1555.	14		17
May 18, 1559. ——, Barnard, Felkirke, Aug. 30, 1558.	15	3	396
Oct. 5, 1558. ——, Christopher, Long Preston, Feb. 27, 1557.	15	3	38
Dec. 22, 1556. ——, Elisabeth (bur. Rawmarshe), Sep. 16, 1556.	15	1	79
Oct. 22, 1560. ——, Esabell, Hunmanbie, Mar. 23, 1560.	16		127
Oct. 5, 1554. ——, George, Willerby (Dickering), Mar. 18, 1553.	14		45
Apl. 3, 1559. ——, Hugh, Harpham, Aug. 4, 1558.	15	3	315
Jan. 24, 1558. ——, Jennet, widow of Robert C., Gysbrought, May 22, 1558.	15	3	23
Feb. 9, 1557. ——, Jennett, Wethernsey, widow, Jan. 5, 1557.	15	2	122
Oct. 1, 1557. ——, John, Danbye, Aug. 3, 1557.	15	2	34
Oct. 13, 1557. ——, John, Haistrope, par. Burton Agnes, Aug. 24, 1557.	15	2	35
Jan. 13, 1558. ——, John, Laxton (Notts.), Sep. 12, 1558.	15	3	17
Apl. 7, 1554. ——, John, Prestonne, Feb. 5, 1553.	14		219
Sep. 9, 1558. ——, John, Thorne, Mar. 19, 1557.	15	3	101
May 4, 1558. ——, Raufe, Teversall (Notts.), Jan. 20, 1557.	15	2	275
Nov. 28, 1558. ——, Richard, Attenwike in Holderness, husbn., Oct. 6, 1558.	15	3	79
Feb. 10, 1557. ——, Richard, Cranswycke, par. Hoton, husbn., Aug. 9, 1557.	15	2	149
Apl. 27, 1558. ——, Richard (bur. Gyglesweke), Sep. 19, 1556.	15	2	203
Oct. 1, 1556. ——, Richard, Sharlston (bur. Warmfeld), Jun. 5, 1556.	15	1	120
Jan. 24, 1558. ——, Robert, Gisburne in Cleveland, May 6, 1558.	15	3	216
Mar. 3, 1555. ——, Robert, Kyrkeham in Preston, Nov. 24, 1555.	15	1	10
Feb. 25, 1558. ——, Robert, Tybthorp, par. Kirkeburne, Feb. 3, 1558.	15	3	278
Apl. 30, 1556. ——, Roger, Teversall (Notts.), Jan. 13, 1555.	15	1	30
Mar. 30, 1558. ——, Thomas, Gyllemore (bur. Kyrkebymoreshed), May 2, 1557.	15	2	178
Jan. 24, 1558. ——, Thomas, York, fuller, Jan. 1, 1558.	15	3	214
Oct. 6, 1557. ——, William (bur. Bunyngton, Notts.), Jun. 15, 1557.	15	2	29
Jan. 16, 1558. ——, William, senr., Goldall, (bur. Snathe), yeoman, Oct. 28, 1558.	15	3	209
Mar. 6, 1556. ——, William, Heyton (Notts.), July 31, 1556.	15	1	181
Jan. 8, 1556. ——, William, Slyngesby, Nov. 4, 1556.	15	1	86
Feb. 9, 1557. ——, William, Swyne, husbandman, Jan. 20, 1557.	15	2	124
Apl. 16, 1562. ——, William (bur. Waddington), Jan. 2, 1561.	17		169
Mar. 17, 1561. Clarkesone, Peter, Swillington, husbandman, May 12, 1561.	17		6
Mar. 4, 1560. Clerkson, Robert, Standley (bur. Wakefeld), webster. No date.	16		152
July 5, 1557. ——, Roger, Pigburne, par. Brodesworth, Jun. 6, 1557.	15	1	303
July 5, 1557. Clesbe, Arthure, Ripon, gentleman, Dec. 14, 1556.	15	1	303
Oct. 31, 1564. Cletheroo. Richard, York, Sep. 11, 1564.	17		394
Aug. 18, 1562. Clethinge, Robert, Fleiston (bur. Fol[k]ton), May 20, ——.	17		106
Oct. 10, 1560. Cleton, George, Parkeyeate, par. Rotherham, Feb. 13, 1559.	16		126
Feb. 19, 1556. Cleveland, John, Eskryge, Jan. 26, 1556.	15	1	163
Feb. 21, 1558. ——, Robert, Sutton on Darwent, May 27, 1558.	15	3	277
Mar. 2, 1561. Cleymeyt, John, Galmeton, Dec. 6, 1561.	17		2

A.D. 1554 TO 1568.

		Vol.	Pt.	Fol.
Dec. 22, 1556.	Clif, William, Thorpe, par. Badsworth, Oct. 8, 1556.	15	1	85
July 4, 1558.	Clife, John, Egbroughe (bur. Kellington), Jun. 30, 1558.	15	2	343
Apl. 3, 1559.	Cliffe, Henry, Pocklay (bur. Helmeslay), Jan. 21, 1558.	15	3	318
Oct. 10, 1566.	Clifton, Robert, Bawderston (Notts.), Sep. 20, 1566.	17		589
Oct. 5, 1558.	——, William, Hylleleys, par. Kirkelevinton, Apl. 21, 1558.	15	3	67
Apl. 3, 1559.	Clippingdayle, Richard, Brigham (bur. Foston), Jan. 3, 1558.	15	3	316
Oct. 2, 1566.	Clooght, William, West Marton, husbandman, May 8, 1566.	17		573
Mar. 24, 1567.	Cloughe, Christopher, Kellington, Oct. 27. 1567.	17		767
Apl. 11, 1559.	——, John, Yghton, par. Bardsay, yeoman, Sep. 1, 1558.	15	3	333
Oct. 4, 1564.	——, Robert, Kigheley, Apl. 12, 1564.	17		372
Apl. 11, 1559.	——, William, Estkeswyke (bur. Bardson [Bardsey]), yeoman, Dec. 15, 1557.	15	3	332
Nov. 28, 1558.	Clought, John, Kellington, Aug. 26, 1558.	15	3	135
Oct. 2, 1566.	Clowgh, Stephane, Broughton (Cleveland), Jun. 11, 1566.	17		575
Apl. 17, 1567.	——, Thomas, Broughton (Craven), July 5, 1566.	17		619
Oct. 1, 1561.	Clowighe, Sir James, Slaydburne, priest, Oct. 8, 1560.	17		48
Jan. 20, 1557.	Cloworthe, John, Clyfton, par. Cunsburghe, Dec. 28, 1557.	15	2	68
July 20, 1557.	Clublaye, Thomas, Octone (bur. Thewynge), husbn., Apl. 7, 1557.	15	1	315
May 6, 1555.	Clughe, John, Cowthorpe, yeoman, Jan. 12, 1554.	14		199
Jan. 8, 1566.	——, Robert, Broughton in Craven (bur. Ripon), Sep. 4, 1564.	17		606
July 14, 1555.	Clyf, Richard, Lighclif, par. Hallifaxe, May 16, 1555.	14		262
Apl. 27, 1559.	Clyff, William, junr., Halyfax, July 8, 1559 (sic).	15	3	362
Apl. 26, 1558.	Clyffe, Jennet, Thorpe, par. Baddesworthe, Dec. 18, 1556.	15	2	196
Oct. 7, 1557.	Clyfton, Thomas, Bekingham (Notts.), Jun. 2, 1557.	15	2	21
Jan. 28, 1562.	——, William, Newall, par. Ottley, yeoman, Nov. 26, 1562.	17		145
Mar. 23, 1557.	Clypyndall, Robert, Seton (bur. Siglistorn), Jan. 30, 1557.	15	2	153
Jun. 13, 1554.	Cobcrofte, John, Gateforde, husbandman, Aug. 8, 1553.	14		4
Mar. 8, 1557.	Cockar, Robert, Barley, par Brayton, Nov. 7, 1557.	15	2	169
Apl. 10, 1559.	Cocke, John, Thorne, Sep. 23, 1558.	15	3	329
May 13, 1557.	——, Richard, Eastredford (Notts.), mercer, Jan. 10, 1556.	15	1	231
May 5, 1558.	——, Robert, Rampton (Notts.), Aug. 6, 1557.	15	2	208
Nov. 27, 1565.	——, Thomas, Speton (bur. Bridlington), yeoman, Mar. 8, 1564.	17		491
Apl. 27, 1558.	Cockell, Isabell, Wakefelde, widow of Thomas C., Aug. 30, 1557.	15	2	189
Mar. 8, 1557.	Cocker, Agnes, Barley, par. Brayton, Dec. 16, 1557.	15	2	169
Oct. 7, 1561.	Cockerham, John, Lenton (Notts.), gentleman, Dec. 15, 1560.	17		43
Jan. 12, 1558.	Cockes, Richard, Skiray (bur. Skerne), labourer, Nov. 21, 1558.	15	3	195
Oct. 1, 1561.	Cockeshote, Robert, Bradley, par. Kildweke, Feb. 9, 1560.	17		49
May 15, 1557.	Cockesone, Robert, Tankerslay, Nov. 25, 1552.	15	1	281
July 11, 1558.	Cockesonne, William, Stamforth (bur. Haytfeyld), husbn., Sep. 15, 1557.	15	2	319
Mar. 4, 1562.	Cocking, Thomas (bur. Skecling), Dec. 26, 1562.	17		150
Feb. 1, 1563.	Cockson, Robert, Wakefeild, clothier, Sep. 24, 1561.	17		313
Mar. 23, 1557.	¹ Cockryll, George (bur. S. Peter's, Holderness), Nov. 15, 1557.	15	2	174
Sep. 30, 1563.	Cocrofte, Richard, Heptonstall, July 20, 1563.	17		282
Oct. 6, 1557.	Coggan, Thomas, Clyfton (Notts.), Apl. 18, 1557.	15	2	28
Oct. 11, 1567.	Coggreave, William, Haitfeld Woodhous, husbn., Aug. 23, 1567.	17		729
Feb. 23, 1558.	Coites, Richard, Welburne, Nov. 3, 1558.	15	3	277
Jun. 22, 1568.	Coittes, Thomas, Hunmanbie, Sep. 7, 1567.	17		826
May 2, 1560.	Coke, Robert (bur. Snaythe), Mar. 18, 1560.	16		54
Nov. 17, 1558.	——, William, Heke, par. Snathe, Aug. 15, 1558.	15	3	73
Apl. 9, 1554.	——, William (bur. Lockington), Jan. 10, 1552.	14		54
July 22, 1562.	——, William, Skeppstern (bur. Leedes), barbour, Nov. 19, 1559.	17		97
Apl. 30, 1567.	Cokell, Richard, Kirkebirton, clothier, July 21, 1566.	17		639
Oct. 20, 1558.	¹ Cokerell, Thomas, Slyghtes, par. Whitbye, Nov. 29, 1557.	15	3	96
Oct. 20, 1558.	——, William, Sprotley, Apl. 25, 1558.	15	2	351
Aug. 2, 1557.	Cokeryll, John, Sutton in Holderness, Apl. 28, 1557.	15	1	322
May 18, 1559.	Cokesonn, William, Sykehouse, par. Fishelake, Nov. 4, 1558.	15	3	401
July 15, 1556.	Cokke, William, Speton, July 28, 1552.	15	1	55
Oct. 2, 1566.	Cokroft, Edmunde, Wadsworthe, par. Heptonstall, clothier, Mar. 31, 1566.	17		580
Oct. 2, 1566.	Cokrofte, William, Wadisworthe, par. Heptonstall, clother, Apl. 5, 1566.	17		579
Dec. 3, 1557.	Cokson, Johan, S. Leonard's, Denyngton, widow, Sep. 10, 1557.	15	2	49

1 See also under letter K.

		Vol.	Pt.	Fol.
Aug. 7, 1565.	Colance, Mychell, Clarebroughe (Notts.), husbandman, Apl. 24, 1564.	17		457
Mar. 10, 1555.	Colbie, Thomas, Sutton on Lund (Notts.), Sep. 27, 1552.	14		229
July 29, 1558.	Colbrond, Roger, Swynton (bur. Waythe), Aug. 2, 1558.	15	2	293
Apl. 21, 1554.	Coldcole, John, Carleton, par. Snaith, Jan. 14, 1553.	14		62
May 14, 1560.	Coldoyke, Thomas, Etton, yeoman, Aug. 4, 1558.	16		63
May 9, 1560.	Cole, William, Normanton besyde Plumtre (Notts.), Jun. 24, 155-.	16		61
Apl. 28, 1558.	Coles, Agnes, Hull, widow, Jan. 3, 1557.	15	2	218
Apl. 14, 1558.	Coling, Thomas, Harwoodayll, par. Hackenas, Nov. 28, 1557.	15	2	282
Mar. 7, 1566.	Colison. Thomas, Beforthe, husbandman, Nov. 25, 1566.	17		515
May 4, 1558.	Colle, Alis, Flyntam (Notts.), widow, Feb. 15, 1557.	15	2	268
May 6, 1555.	——, Robert, Southwell (Notts.), Jun. 4, 1555.	14		305
May 4, 1558.	——, Roger, Flyntam (Notts.), husbandman, Jan. 18, 1557.	15	2	267
Apl. 22, 1562.	——, Thomas, Codlynstoke (Notts.), husbandman, Aug. 15, 1561.	17		180
Oct. 10, 1565.	Collen, John, Roulston (Notts.), husbandman, May 16, 1565.	17		472
May 2, 1560.	Collenson, Henry, Paullflight in Holderness, fysherman, Feb. 3, 1559.	16		50
Jun. 18, 1557.	Colleson, John, Thorgunbold, par. Paulle, Jun. 1, 1557.	15	1	294
Sep. 29, 1557.	Collier, William (bur. Paytheleybrigges), Oct. 3, 1556.	15	1	329
May 13, 1557.	Collin, John, Nottingham, inholder, Oct. 2, 1556.	15	1	223
Oct. 1, 1562.	——, Thomas, Uslet (bur. Whitgyft), Sep. —, 1562.	17		116
Jun. 22, 1568.	—— als. Horne, William, Harwoddaill, par. Hacknes, Apl. 12, 1567.	17		822
Sep. 14, 1558.	Colling, Agnes, widow of William C., Wressell, Apl. 6, 1558.	15	3	107
Jan. 16, 1558.	Collinge, John, Rocliffe (bur. Snathe), Aug. 23, 1558.	15	3	20
Mar. 29, 1568.	Collingson, Robert, York (bur. St. Margaret), preiste, Aug. 9, 1558.	17		767
Mar. 3, 1555.	Collingsone, Robert, Aytone, par. Seamer, Apl. 26, 1555.	15	1	11
Aug. 10, 1561.	Collingworth, Richard, Dunkeswoke, par. Harwod, webster, Aug. 13, 1558.	17		64
Sep. 11, 1561.	Collinson, George, Brompton, Apl. 17, 1560.	17		49
Oct. 6, 1558.	——, William, Yeddingham, par. West Haslerton, husbn., Jun. 20, 1558.	15	3	26
Apl. 22, 1556.	Collinsone, Elizabeth, Bridlington, widow, Feb. 3, 1555.	15	1	27
Apl. 20, 1556.	Collisone, Elizabeth, Snathe, Jan. 3, 1555.	15	1	18
Jun. 9, 1563.	Collman, John, Preston in Holderness, yeoman, May 9, 1563.	17		254
Nov. 21, 1560.	Collome, Hewe, Sextendaill, par. Wharrham Percie, Feb. 20, 1560.	16		130
July 22, 1555.	Collson, Christopher, Holme in Spaldingmore, Jun. 15, 1555.	14		243
No date.	Collye, John, Ecclisfelde, Nov. 16, 1553.	14		86
Apl. 28, 1558.	Collyer, Christopher, Patheleybrigges, Dec. 12, 1557.	15	2	207
Mar. 19, 1560.	——, John, Marderbye, par. St. Felix, Apl. 14, 1559.	16		154
Jun. 18, 1557.	Collyn, Antony, Kyellnesey, May 9, 1557.	15	1	295
Mar. 10, 1558.	Collyne, William, Wressill, Feb. 21, 1556.	15	1	201
Jun. 7, 1560.	Collynson, Jennat, Aitonge in Pekeringelithe, par. Seamer, Apl. 4, 1558.	16		77
Oct. 22, 1560.	——, John, Bridlington, marchant, July 15, 1560.	16		127
Feb. 26, 1555.	Collynwood, Jennet, York, Sep. 28, 1555.	15	1	8
May 9, 1566.	Colman, Frauncis, Nottingham, gentleman, Aug. 14, 1563.	17		545
Dec. 10, 1561.	——, George, Preston in Holderness, July 2, 1561.	17		28
Dec. 11, 1566.	——, Thomas, Newbie, par. Scawbie, Jan. 6, 1565.	17		604
May 2, 1566.	Colsbe, Augustin, Preston in Holderness, husbn., Feb. 20, 1565.	17		526
Jan. 14, 1564.	Colson, Elizabeth, Armethorpe, May 27, 1564.	17		401
Sep. 29, 1563.	——, Henry, Bridlington, cordwayner, May 5, 1563.	17		274
Jun. 18, 1555.	——, Henry, Harwodddaill, par. Hacknes, May 28, 1555.	14		254
Oct. 1, 1557.	——, Sir Henry, prest, Lythe, Jun. 8, 1557.	15	2	36
Sep. 30, 1563.	——, John, Beynton, Mar. 15, 1562.	17		286
May 5, 1557.	——, Richard (Cleveland), Jan. 2, 1556.	15	1	250
July 4, 1556.	——, William, Armethorpe, husbandman, Mar. 10, 1556.	15	1	53
Oct. 19, 1556.	Colsone, Henry, Stansegare, par. Whitbie, Dec. 12, 1548.	15	1	97
Mar. 13, 1558.	Colte, Issabell, Rotherham, Dec. 25, 1558.	15	3	161
Jan. 24, 1558.	——, Thomas (bur. Rotheram), Oct. 25, 1558.	15	3	119
Oct. 5, 1558.	Colthirst Henry, Edyforth (bur. Mytton), May 6, 1554.	15	3	60
May 18, 1559.	——, Thomas, Felkirke, gentleman, Dec. 16, 1558.	15	3	417
Feb. 20, 1560.	Coltman, William, Sowthorome, par. Hallyfax, Jan. 13, 1560.	16		148
Oct. 2, 1555.	Colton, John (bur. Kettlewell), May 28, 1555.	16		170
Oct. 1, 1562.	——, John (bur. Kettlewell), May 24, 1563.	17		111
Mar. 14, 1561.	——, Margaret, widow of William, C., waxchanler (bur. York), 1554.	17		1

A.D. 1554 TO 1568.

		Vol.	Pt.	Fol.
Oct. 6, 1557.	Colton, Rauffe, Glapton, par. Clyfton (Notts.), May 10, 1557.	15	2	26
July 19, 1557.	Columbell, Edward, Nettylworthe (bur. Warsoppe, Notts.), gent., Nov. 23, 1556.	15	1	308
July 17, 1556.	Colyar, John (bur. Topclif), Jun. 16, 1555.	15	1	56
Nov. 29, 1558.	———, Thomas, Rotheram, Sep. 20, 1558.	15	3	109
Oct. 11, 1565.	Come, John (bur. East Retford, Notts.), Aug. 2, 1565.	17		473
Sep. 30, 1558.	Condal, William (bur. Ripon), Aug. 11, 1558.	15	3	56
July 9, 1563.	Conne, John, Kaingham, May 12, 1563.	17		265
Dec. 20, 1558.	Connsbye, John, Kimberworth, par. Rotheram, Oct. 28, 1558.	15	3	152
Apl. 13, 1559.	Conseyt, Robert (bur. Egton), Feb. 14, 1557.	15	3	343
Jun. 12, 1561.	Constable, Edward, Rymswell in Holderness, Jan. 14, 1560.	17		71
Jan. 20, 1564.	———, Elinour, New Malton, widow, Dec. 8, 1564.	17		400
May 10, 1565.	———, Francis, Bilton, Mar. 6, 1564.	17		424
Oct. 8, 1556.	———, John, Kynaltone (Notts.), knight, Jun. 19, 1554.	15	1	148
Mar. 23, 1564.	———, Robert, Hothome, par. Northe Cave. May 25, 1564.	17		408
Mar. 27, 1560.	———, Sir Robert, Everingham, knight, Sep. 1, 1558.	16		20
Feb. 18, 1556.	———, William, Shereburne (Buckros), Jan. 20, 1555.	15	1	162
May 4, 1557.	Conwaye, Jennett, Menstrope (bur. Sowth Kyrkebie), Mar. 4, 1556.	15	1	278
Oct. 20, 1557.	Conyers, Anne, Whitbye, widow, Jun. 30, 1557.	15	2	35
Jun. 20, 1566.	———, Christopher, Skarburghe, Apl. 18, 1565.	17		555
Oct. 20, 1557.	———, Christopher, York, merchant, Aug. 20, 1557.	15	1	364
Apl. 12, 1567.	———, Grace, Scarbrughe, widow (bur. near husband Anth. C.), Nov. 24, 1566.	17		617
Aug. 16, 1566.	Conynworthe, Robert, Draxe, Aug. 4, 1565.	17		571
May 18, 1559.	[1] Coo, Hugh, Warsoppe (Notts.), Oct. 15, 1558.	15	3	423
May 18, 1559.	———, Jennet, Warsope (Notts.), Mar. 26, 1559.	15	3	420
Jan. 17, 1557.	Coogell, John, Hunmanbye, May 10, 1549.	15	2	61
Jan. 29, 1556.	Cooke, Alison, Semar, Jun. 17, 1556.	15	1	93
May 2, 1560.	———, Andro (bur. S. Mary's, Hull), Dec. 20, 1559.	16		44
May 31, 1557.	———, Edward, Barnebie on Dunne, husbandman, Apl. 22, 1557.	15	1	259
May 6, 1563.	———, Edward, Fledbrough (Notts.), yeoman, Apl. 11, 1560	17		241
Apl. 6, 1558.	———, Elizabeth, Barmby on Donne, Jan. 27, 1557.	15	2	186
Mar. 9, 1557.	———, Elizabeth, wid. of Wm. C., Speton (bur. Brydlyngton) Mar. 8, 1556.	15	2	129
Oct. 22, 1567.	———, Sir Ezache, priest, secondarie of Bonaye and Bradmere (Notts.), Aug. 14, 1567.	17		732
Dec. 5, 1566.	———, Jeffray, Ecclesfeld, Nov. 4, 1566.	17		601
Apl. 28, 1558.	———, John, Cottingham, Jan. 14, 1557.	15	2	219
July 15, 1562.	———, John, Esington in Holderness, May 3, 1562.	17		95
Jan. 12, 1558.	———, John, Jarrow (co. Durham), yeoman, Jan. 26, 1557.	15	3	174
Jun. 10, 1560.	———, John, Kylnsey, Apl. 22, 1560.	16		82
Jan. 12, 1558.	———, Nicholas, Bushopburton, Oct. 16, 1558.	15	3	199
May 5, 1557.	———, Peter, Tonger (bur. Birstall), Oct. 20, 1556.	15	1	212
Apl. 25, 1554.	———, Raufe, Ripon, Sep. 16, 1549.	14		55
Mar. 17, 1556.	———, Raufe, Thorngumbold, par. Paule, Nov. 18, 1556.	15	1	187
Feb. 6, 1558.	———, Robert, Bramwith, Oct. 3, 1558.	15	3	253
Mar. 21, 1559.	———, Robert, Burton Pydsay, Oct. 16, 1559.	16		18
Nov. 12, 1555.	———, Roger, Kirkdighton, husbandman, Nov. 24 (sic), 1555.	14		76
Nov. 29, 1557.	———, Thomas, Bradforde, Aug. 26, 1557.	15	2	101
Apl. 19, 1555.	———, Thomas, Whitleye (bur. Kellington), Jun. 20, 1551.	14		161
Jan. 23, 1567.	———, William, Clifton, Dec. 24, 1565.	17		751
Jan. 23, 1561.	———, William, Siglestorne, Dec. 20, 1561.	17		19
Apl. 7, 1557.	——— als. Atkynson, Elizabeth, Addle, Mar. 2, 1556.	15	1	204
May 2, 1555.	Cookeson, Stephen, West Halton, par. Longe Preston, Dec. 31, 1554.	14		127
Nov. 6, 1554.	Coole, Jenet, Kingston on Hull, widow, July 20, 1554.	14		292
Oct. 5, 1558.	Coore, Richard, Bolton, yeoman, May 14, 1558.	15	3	37
Jan. 24, 1558.	Cooste, John, Ardislay, par. Derfeld, husbandman, Nov. 7, 155[8].	15	3	118
Oct. 22, 1560.	Cootes, John, Harpham, husbandman, Mar. 5, 1560.	16		127
Apl. 10, 1559.	———, John, Hooton Levett, par. Maltbie, Dec. 21, 1558.	15	3	327
Oct. 5, 1558.	———, William, Marton in Cleveland, husbandman, Sep. 25, 1558.	15	3	68

1 See also under letter K.

A.D. 1554 TO 1568.

		Vol.	Pt.	Fol.
Mar. 9, 1557.	Coottes, Richard, Carnabyé, yeoman, Dec. 14, 1557.	15	2	127
Feb. 6, 1555.	Copcroft, Malde, York, widow, July 5, 1555.	15	1	6
Jun. 20, 1566.	Copeland, Robert, Bridlington, yeoman, Nov. 3, 1565.	17		557
Mar. 8, 1558.	Copelande, Thomas, Hull, draper, Nov. 4, 1558.	15	3	284
May 5, 1558.	Copestak, Dorathe (bur. Scrobie, Notts.), Aug. 22, 1557.	15	2	248
Nov. 5, 1554.	Coplande, Ellen (bur. Rypon), Jun. 24, 1554.	14		291
Oct. 4, 1558.	Coplay, Dame Margaret, Steveton, par. Sherburne, Sep. 26, 1557.	15	3	57
Sep. 26, 1558.	———, Steven, Thryber, husbandman, Aug. 16, 1558.	15	3	52
Jun. 27, 1558.	Copledyke, Leonarde, Halsham, May 23, 1558.	15	2	339
Feb. 6, 1558.	Copleie, Thomas, Emley. Dec. 28, 1558.	15	3	255
Nov. 26, 1557.	Copley, George, Doncaster, gentleman, Apl. 20, 1557.	15	2	92
Sep. 26, 1558.	———, Thomas, Derfeld, July 22, 1558.	15	3	49
Mar. 26, 1565.	———, Thomas, Emley, Aug. 1, 1564.	17		416
July 13, 1556.	———, Sir William, Sprotburghe, knight, Apl. 14, 1556.	15	1	54
Apl. 11, 1554.	Coppendale, Edmunde, Howsome, esquier, Mar. 16, 6 Edw. VI.	14		54
Jun. 10, 1562.	Copplay, John, Byrelay, par. Burstall, Feb. 8. 1561.	17		200
Mar. 23, 1556.	Copple, Olyver, Skelmanthorpe (bur. High Hulland), Dec. 2, 1556.	15	1	191
Apl. 19, 1559.	Coppocke, James, Burton Jorce (Notts.), husbandman, Feb. 16, 1558.	15	3	358
July 18, 1556.	Coppyndaill, John, Barmebie haull (bur. Bossaull), esq. July 27, 1555.	15	1	44
Mar. 30, 1560.	Corbet, Cicilie, widow of John C. Trowell (Notts.), May 5, 1559.	16		23
Jun. 11, 1558.	Corbreke, William, Over Helmesey, husbandman, Aug. 15, 1557.	15	2	310
Dec. 15, 1557.	Corbrige, James, Cowkney (Notts.), Oct. 10, 1557.	15	2	56
Apl. 12, 1559.	Cordyngley, Jennet, Toftshay, par. Brystale, widow, Feb. 13, 1558.	15	3	337
Oct. 5, 1558.	Cornefurthe, Leonerd, Gret Busby (bur. Stokeslay), Aug. 2, 1558.	15	3	68
Jun. 11, [1554].	Corney, Richard, Danby, Oct. 28, 1554,	14		72
Feb. 14, 1567.	———, Robert, Danby, husbandman, Sep. 17, 1567.	17		759
Feb. 28, 1566.	Cornforthe, Thomas, Crathorne, Oct. 28, 1566.	17		616
May 13, 1557.	Cornyng, Clement, Sanbye (Notts.), yeoman, Oct. 21, 1556.	15	2	135
July 10, 1566.	Cort, Jefferey, Cowlston (bur. Cookeswold), May 10, 1566.	17		560
Jun. 20, 1566.	Corte, William, Burnyshton, par. Scaubie, Aug. 8, 1564.	17		556
Oct. 12, 1564.	Cost, John, Mylforthe (Notts.), July 27, 1564.	17		390
Aug. 12, 1566.	Costen, John, Newton, par. Essington, Jun. 7, 1565.	17		569
Sep. 26, 1558.	Cosyn, Robert, Raumershe, yeoman, July 24, 1558.	15	3	53
Oct. 5, 1564.	———, William, Braywell, husbandman, Sep. 3, 1564.	17		377
July 18, 1560.	Cotchon, Thomas, Cayngham, May 8, 1559.	16		93
Jan. 20, 1558.	Cotes, James, Newsom (Ridall), Jun. 20, 1558.	15	3	212
Mar. 20, 1558.	———, John, Hooton Levet, par. Maltbie, Dec. 21, 1558.	15	3	247
Mar. 27, 156[3].	———, John, Naburne, Dec. 23, 1562.	17		217
Jan. 20, 1558.	———, William, Amunderbye, Dec. 26, 1557.	15	3	213
Oct. 13, 1558.	Cottame, Alice (bur. Morton, Notts.), Dec. 9, 1558.	15	2	361
Oct. 17, 1567.	Cottes, Leonard, Appelton on Wiske, Mar. 7, 1567.	17		731
Dec. 16, 1556.	Cottham, Robert, Northleverton (Notts.), husbn., Sep. 23, 1555.	15	1	196
Oct. 29, 1554.	¹Cotton, John, South Leverton (Notts.), Aug. 16, 1553.	14		285
Oct. 7, 1556.	———, Phillippe, Grove (Notts.), Mar. 13, 1555.	15	1	147
May 5, 1558.	Cottum, Elisabethe, North Leverton (Notts.), widow, May 24, 1557.	15	2	208
Oct. 10, 1566.	Coughen, Robert, Nottingham, Apl. 22, 1566.	17		590
Feb. 17, 1557.	Couk, Robert, Sandall (Doncaster), Nov. 6, 1557.	15	2	138
Oct. 2, 1555.	Coukes, Richard, Stirsthorpe, par. Kirk Sandall, Sep. 10, 1554.	14		164
Dec. 22, 1556.	———, Richard, Stirstrope, par. Kirk Sandall, Sep. 11, 1554.	15	1	76
Oct. 20, 1558.	Coundaill, William, Crambum, husbandman, Sep. 14, 1558.	15	2	345
July 20, 1564.	Couper, Bryan, Wentbrige (bur. Darryngton), husbandman and smythe, Sep. 12, 5 Eliz.	17		358
Mar. 9, 1559.	———, Richard, Tbormonbye, Oct. 2, 1559.	16		6
Dec. 11, 1566.	Coupland, Jennet, Bridlington, widow, Aug. 12, 1566.	17		602
Apl. 3, 1559.	Couse, Alice, Galmeton, widow, Oct. 20, 1558.	15	3	317
Jun. 30, 1563.	Coussen, Robert, Clyfton (bur. Hartesshead), Sep. 2, 1562.	17		261
Mar. 17, 1556.	Counstable, Christopher, Roosse, Jan. 10, 1556.	15	1	187
Aug. 18, 1562.	Covell, William, Gemlinge, par. Foston, Apl. 20, 1562.	17		106
Jan. 31, 1564.	Coverdaill, Richard (bur. Northe Lofthus), Nov. 28, 1564.	17		406

¹ John Coton of Bereling, Kent, Rochester Court, 1479. "I bequeeth to Preston Church were I was boron, in Holdernesse, a chales of sylver."

A.D. 1554 TO 1568.

		Vol.	Pt.	Fol.
Jun. 10, 1562.	Covyntre, John, Batley, clothier, May 11, 1562.	17		199
Jan. 24, 1558.	Coward, Richard, Cudworth, par. Roiston, husbandman, Nov.12,1558.	15	3	117
Dec. 13, 1554.	Cowarde, William, Pontefracte, Feb. 24, 1 Mary.	14		96
Feb. 6, 1558.	Cowdcoille, Elizabeth, Carltone, par. Snathe, Jan. 16, 1558.	15	3	263
Oct. 3, 1565.	Cowden, Robert, Bretton, par. Sandall Magna, Aug. 9, 1565.	17		476
Oct. 9, 1556.	Coweke, Conande, Warter, Aug. 14, 1556.	15	1	70
Apl. 27, 1563.	Cowhard, John, Haukesgarthe, par. Whitbie, Feb. 5, 1558.	17		225
Feb. 6, 1558.	Cowke, Agnes, Whitley (bur. Kellington), Oct. 20, 1558.	15	3	256
Aug. 17, 1557.	———, Esabell, Warter, Apl. 2, 1557.	15	2	117
May 10, 1559.	———, James, Seamer, Jan. 31, 1558.	15	3	390
Apl. 20, 1559.	———, John, Hurst Grange, par. Cowkney (Notts.), Sep. 21, 1558.	15	3	307
Oct. 4, 1558.	———, William, Towton (bur. Saxton), Apl. 8, 1550.	15	3	59
Oct. 29, 1554.	Cowle, Thomas, Cropwell Butcher, par. Tythby (Notts.), May 25, 1554.	14		286
Mar. 8, 1558.	Cowling, Thomas, Hull, porter, Jan. 19, 1558.	15	3	285
Apl. 5, 1554.	Cowlinge, Richard, Flameburghe, fisherman, Mar. 16, 1553.	14		215
Apl. 13, 1559.	Cowllinge, John, Sutton in Holderness, husbandman, Jan. 8, 1558.	15	3	345
Jun. 22, 1568.	Cowlson, William, Harwooddaill (bur. Hacknes), Apl. 23, 1568.	17		825
Dec. 1, 1558.	Cowper, Alison, Essingwold, Aug. 1, 1558.	15	3	80
Apl. 13, 1559.	———, Annas, Thorganbye, widow, Mar. 13, 1558.	15	3	342
Dec. 18, 1560.	———, Arthure, Selbie, tanner, Oct. 11, 1560.	16		136
Apl. 28, 1563.	———, Elizabeth, Thorganbye, widow, May 5, 1562.	17		248
Oct. 2, 1567.	———, George, Leedes, bocher, Mar. 31, 1567.	17		720
Mar. 23, 1567.	———, Henry, Hovengham, Nov. 10, 1567.	17		765
Oct. 2, 1567.	———, Henry, Newfeldhedge, par. Gisburne, Aug. 7, 9 Eliz.	17		712
Jun. 7, 1560.	———, Henry, Steiton, par. Willerbie, Apl. 26, 1559.	16		79
Jan. 28, 1561.	———, Jennet, Leedes, widow, Oct. 8, 1560.	17		8
Aug. 29, 1561.	———, Johan, Appelton (bur. Bolton Percye), wid., Aug. 12, 1561.	17		53
Oct. 6, 1557.	———, John, Bonney (Notts.), Apl. 14, 1557.	15	2	32
May 28, 1562.	———, John, East Haslerton, husbandman, Jan. 17, 1561.	17		200
Sep. 26, 1556.	———, John, Esingwolde, May 23, 1556.	15	1	67
Aug. 2, 1557.	———, John, Rosse, husbandman, July 16, 1557.	15	1	322
Jun. 7, 1555.	———, John, Warter, Dec. 31, 1554.	14		307
Jun. 2, 1562.	———, Margaret, Conystropp (bur. Barton), widow, Dec. 10, 1561.	17		86
Oct. 7, 1563.	———, Mychell, Torlaston (Notts.), Aug. 26, 1562.	17		294
Jan. 11, 1557.	———, Richard, Befurthe, husbandman, Nov. 4, 1557.	15	2	73
Mar. 3, 1561.	———, Robert, Appleton (bur. Bolton Percye), Feb. 15, 1561	17		5
Nov. 26, 1556.	———, Robert, Eskirke, labourer, Nov. 14, 1556.	15	1	118
Jan. 30, 1557.	———, Robert, Thorganbye, Dec. 28, 1557.	15	2	161
Apl. 20, 1559.	———, Sebell, Thrumton, par. Ordsall (Notts.), widow, July 6, 1558.	15	3	366
Sep. 13, 1565.	———, Thomas, Castley (bur. Letheley), labourer, Apl. 24, 1565.	17		464
Feb. 9, 1557.	———, Thomas, Doddington, Oct. 20, 1557.	15	2	121
July 2, 1557.	———, Thomas, Leides, yeoman, Nov. 29, 1556.	15	1	299
May 4, 1559.	———, Thomas, York, notarye, Dec. 13, 1558.	15	3	379
Aug. 29, 1561.	———, William, Appeltone (bur. Bolton Percy), Apl. 12, 1559.	17		53
May 5, 1559.	———, William, Conystrope (bur. Barton in Rydayll), husbn., Oct. 9, 1558.	15	3	380
Aug. 6, 1567.	———, William, Northcave, yeoman, Mar. 8, 1566.	17		699
Oct. 5, 1558.	———, William, Skerne, husbandman, Mar. 19, 1557.	15	3	44
May 13, 1557.	———, William, Willoughbe (Notts.), Oct. 1, 1556.	15	1	230
Dec. 1, 1558.	———, Yssabell (bur. Essingwold), July 22, 1557.	15	3	80
Apl. 26, 1558.	als. Smyth, John, Staineburne, yeoman, Dec. 18, 1557.	15	2	234
May 9, 1558.	Cowpland, John, Ledesham, Aug. 18, 1557.	15	2	274
Nov. 10, 1557.	———, Robert, Ledstone (bur. Ledsam), Sep. 18, 1557.	15	2	97
Nov. 28, 1558.	———, Thomas, Methelay, July 18, 1558.	15	3	137
Nov. 22, 1554.	Cowplande, Johane, Essingwold, Jun. 28, 1554.	14		89
May 10, 1565.	Cowtam, Robert, Cauthorne, par. Myddleton, Feb. 14, 1563.	17		420
Mar. 17, 1556.	Cowtard, John, Rymswell, husbandman, Nov. 6, 1556.	15	1	187
Oct. 2, 1567.	Cowtasse, Cuthebarte, Skeclinge als. Brustwike, Jan. 3, 1566.	17		714
Jun. 22, 1568.	Cowton, Gregorye, Bridlington, apprentice, Oct. 12, 1566.	17		819
May 28, 1568.	———, Jennet, Carnabie, spinster. Apl. 8, 1568.	17		775
Oct. 29, 1558.	———, John, Scarbrough, goldsmyth, Jan. 14, 1558.	15	3	240
[May?]30, 1562.	———, Robert, Carnetby, husbandman, Mar. 26, 1562.	17		198

		Vol.	Pt.	Fol.
Mar.31, 1562.	Cowton, Thomas, Byrlynton, butcher, Dec. 14, 1561.	17		161
Mar.20, 1558.	Coyke, Roger, Almeholme, par. Arksey, Nov. 18, 1558.	15	3	247
May 18, 1559.	Coykyn, John, Prestone in Holderness, husbandman, Nov. 26, 1558.	15	3	412
Mar.21, 1559.	Coyll, William, clerk, curate at Rosse, Sep. 14, 1559.	16		16
Feb. 15, 1558.	Coye, John, Wethernsey, husbandman, Jan. 9, 1558.	15	3	269
Dec. 9, 1556.	——, Richard, Weton, par. Welwyke, Sep. 14, 1556.	15	1	73
Aug.28, 1563.	Crabere (Crabtree, Act Book), John, Heptonstall, Feb. 20, 1562.	17		210
Oct. 2, 1560.	Crabtre, John, Heptonstall, July 29, 1560.	16		113
July 31, 1566.	———, John, Turwyn in Sourbie, par, Halifax, clothiar, Feb.11,1565.	17		563
Dec. 2, 1561.	———, Randall, Barnebe, Oct. 30, 1561.	17		31
Oct. 2, 1556.	———, Robert, Carleton neare Snaythe, Apl. 13, 1556.	15	1	132
May 2, 1566.	———, Thomas, Heptonstall, Apl. 4, 1566.	17		532
Apl. 28, 1563.	———, William, Barnebe on Dune, Feb. 2, 1563.	17		234
Apl. 21, 1554.	———, William, Carleton, par. Snaith, Apl. 5, 1554.	14		63
Mar. 4, 1560.	———, William, Heptonstall, Oct. 3, 1560.	16		152
Aug.28, 1563.	Crabtree (Registered, Crabere), John, Heptonstall, Feb. 20, 1562.	17		210
May 17, 1565.	Cracke, Robert, Kellam (Notts.), Feb. 20, 1564.	17		436
Jan. 20, 1561.	Cragges, Edmond, Kellington, May 21, 1561.	17		22
Mar.15, 1558.	———, Thomas, Newsham, par. Wresle, Dec. 18, 1557.	15	3	166
July 16, 1561.	Crake, Hewe, Hugget, Mar. 8, 1559.	17		83
Jun. 13, 1556.	——, William, Wheldryke, Dec. 4, 1555.	15	1	58
July 2, 1562.	Cramleton, Thomas, Hull, carpinter, May 24, 1562.	17		93
Oct. 6, 1557.	Cran als. Hallam, Richard, Rodeington (Notts.), Jun. 22, 1557.	15	2	33
Mar. 8, 1558.	Cransmoure, James, Wodmancye (bur. Beverlay), Oct. 29, 1558.	15	3	157
July 8, 1560.	Craushawe, Alys, widow of William C., Thornehill, May 30, 1560.	16		90
Apl. 8, 1560.	Craven, Alyson, Kylnewike, widow, Feb. 8, 1559.	16		29
Jun. 5, 1554.	———, John. Kylnewike by Watton, husbandman. Dec. 14, 1553.	14		10
Nov. 1, 1566.	———, John, Pontefract, Sep. 4, 1566.	17		597
May 2, 1560.	———, Richard, Beverlaye, tanner, Dec. 8, 1559.	16		45
Oct. 5, 1558.	———, Thomas, Whetlay, par. Ylkelay, 1558.	15	3	38
Mar. 4, 1560.	———, William, Beverlay, Feb. 6, 1560.	16		167
Apl. 14, 1562.	———, William, Kylnewike by Watton, Jan, 4, 1561.	17		166
Dec. 1, 1558.	Cravinge, Nicholas, Hull, Aug. 31, 1558.	15	3	83
Oct. 20, 1558.	Craw, Richard, Thirske, Aug. 22, 1558.	15	2	346
Aug.12, 1566.	Crawe, Bryan, Wethernsey, Feb. 24, 1564.	17		568
Sep. 30, 1562.	——, Thomas, Sherburne, Sep. 1, 1562.	17		116
July 26, 1558.	Crawfurthe, Henry, Ubram, par. Barnyston, Sep. 16, 1557.	15	3	10
Mar.11, 1562.	Crawsha, Agnes, Silkestone, Jan. 12, 1561.	17		156
Mar.20, 1558.	Crawshaught, Thomas, Thorgoland, par. Silkystone, Oct. 24, 1558.	15	3	248
July 5, 1557.	Crawshay, Thomas, Bromellye, par. Tankerslay, May 26, 1557.	15	1	300
May 5, 1558.	Crayne, John, Estmarkham (Notts.), Feb. 20, 1557.	15	2	248
May 2, 1566.	Creswicke, Edward, Stanyngton in Bradfeld, Dec. 4, 1565.	17		525
May 10, 1567.	Crochelay, Richard, Fenton (bur. Sturton, Notts.), Oct. 20, ——.	17		650
Jun. 10, 1562.	Croft, James, Churwell, par. Batley, Mar. 6, 1557.	17		199
Oct. 3, 1566.	——, William, Collingham (Ainstie), Apl. 7, 1566.	17		582
July 15, 1567.	Crofte, Edmunde, Throppe (bur. Burnesall), husbn., Sep. 12, 1563.	17		678
May 10, 1554.	——, Henry, Gildysom (bur. Batley), Dec. 29, 1553.	14		135
Apl. 26, 1558.	——, John, Barnesley, Jun. 26, 1557.	15	2	224
Sep. 28, 1557.	——, Olyver (bur. Kyrkebye in Malhamdaill), Sep. 21, 1556.	15	1	338
Nov.29, 1558.	Croke, Richard, Buttonhill, par. Sheafeld, Jun. 29, 1558.	15	3	110
Dec.29, 1558.	Crokehay, William, Hull, Aug. 28, 1558.	15	3	154
Apl. 27, 1558.	Crombocke, Dolsabelle, Egebroughe (bur. Kellington), Jan. 17, 1557.	15	2	194
Sep. 29, 1563.	Cromocke, George, Denton, par. Otley, clothier, July 31, 1563.	17		289
May 31, 1557.	Crookes, John, Brigside, par. Sheafeld, Mar. 27, 1557.	15	1	260
Aug. 6, 1562.	Cropton, Robert, Knopton, par. Wintringham, Feb. 7, 1561.	17		104
Jun. 6, 1564.	Crosbe, Mychell, Holme in Spaldingmore, Dec. 1, 1563.	17		349
July 29, 1557.	Crosbie, Robert, Waykfeld, Sep. 17, 1557.	15	2	380
Mar. 8, 1562.	Crosbye, John, Aslabye, par. Myddilton, weaver, Feb. 25, 1561.	17		151
Jun. 22, 1565.	———, Thomas, Farnedale (bur. Kirkbye Moreshed), yeom., Mar.28, 1565.	17		445
Oct. 10, 1555.	———, Thomas, Holme in Spaldingmore, Aug. 4, 1555.	14		201
Jun. 28, 1561.	Crosdaile, Elizabeth, Waddington, par. Mytton, widow, Jun. 31,1557.	17		75

A.D. 1554 TO 1568.

		Vol.	Pt.	Fol.
May 5, 1568.	Crosdaill, Thomas (bur. Waddington), July 12, 1567.	17		784
Apl. 19, 1564.	Crosdale, Henry, Bradforthe, par. Mytton, Jan. 4, 1563.	17		330
Oct. 3, 1560.	Crosdalle, Robert, Mytton, Apl. 17, 1560.	16		118
Oct. 5, 1558.	Crosfeild, Robert, Metheley, Sep. 8, 1558.	15	3	61
Sep. 9, 1561.	Crosfeld, Jenet, Methley, Aug. 23, 1561.	17		51
Apl. 3, 1559.	Crosse, John, Boynton, husbandman, Sep. 10, 1558.	15	3	317
Jun. 2, 1558.	———, John, Cransewicke, par. Hoton, labourer, Mar. 21, 1557.	15	2	312
Dec. 16, 1557.	———, Margaret, South Frothingham, par. Outthorne, singlewoman, Nov. 29, 1557.	15	2	47
Apl. 9, 1554.	———, Richard, Beverley, brasier, Jan. 14, 1553.	14		217
May 17, 1554.	———, Robert, Hogett, Jan. 16, 1553.	14		130
May 14, 1558.	———, Thomas, Boynton, Aug. 16, 1557.	15	2	282
Sep. 30, 1556.	———, Thomas, Burton Flemynge (bur. Hunmanbye), Jun. 27, 1557.	15	1	132
Oct. 2, 1560.	——— (or Casse), William, Hoton Bushell, husbn., Dec. 10, 1558.	16		110
Mar. 17, 1557.	Crossebye, Michaell, Hollme in Spaldingmore, Jan. 10, 1557.	15	2	151
Apl. 19, 1564.	Crossedaill, Gyles (bur. Gisburne), Jan. 14, 1563.	17		329
July 13, 1557.	Crosseir, Richard, Rednys (bur. Whitgifte), May 22, 1557.	15	1	308
Apl. 27, 1558.	Crosselande, Richard, Kylnehousebanke, par. Kyrkebyrton, Feb. 24, 1557.	15	2	190
Oct. 12, 1558.	Crosselay, Edward, Selston (Notts.), husbandman, Aug. 9, 1558.	15	3	13
Oct. 3, 1565.	Crosseley, Gylbert, Barkesland, par. Eland, Jan. 2, 1564.	17		476
Nov. 20, 1563.	———, John, Huddersfeild, clothear, Nov. 12, 1562	17		303
July 8, 1560.	Crosthwhate, Thomas, Dalton, par. Kyrkeheaton, Aug. 22, 1558.	16		89
May 5, 1568.	Crother, Jennet, Hallifax, widow, Mar. 11, 1566.	17		791
Nov. 28, 1558.	Crow, Stephan, Over Newton (bur. Essyngton), Sep. 15, 1558.	15	3	76
Sep. 26, 1558.	Crowder, Edmund, Warlay, par. Hallifax, priest, Jun. 4, 1557.	15	3	50
Jun. 10, 1562.	———, John, Southe Oerome, par. Halifax, Aug. 4, 1561.	17		199
Oct. 7, 1558.	———, Richard, Warter. par. Halifax, Sep. 15, 1558.	15	3	226
Oct. 13, 1558.	Crowmwell, Thomas, Morhows (Notts.), Aug. 28, 1558.	15	2	364
Feb. 26, 1556.	Crowner, Richard, St. Mariegait, York, May 3, 1550.	15	1	165
Oct. 30, 1567.	———, Robert. Northe Cave, husbandman, May 14, 1567.	17		730
Oct. 10, 1565.	Croxe, William, Gerton (Notts.), husbandman, Jun. 1, 1565.	17		472
Mar. 4, 1562.	Croyser (Crosyer), Robert, Fleston (bur. Foltton), July 10, 1562.	17		153
Jan. 18, 1556.	Croysse, Richard, Ferybrigges (bur. Fryston by water), joyner, Aug. 23, 1556.	15	1	88
Mar. 19, 1559.	Crude, James, Wytlaye (bur. Kellyngton), Jun. 10, 1559.	16		12
Oct. 31, [1555].	———, John, Kellingleye (bur. Killington), Aug. 20, 1555.	14		249
Feb. 1, 1563.	Crue, Edward, Emley, Jan. 10, 1563,	17		312
May 28, 1557.	Crumhoc, Costen, Ferneley (bur. Otlaie), Apl. 29, 1557.	15	1	211
Oct. 29, 1554.	Crumwell, Richard, Churche Marnham (Notts.), Jan. 12, 1553.	12		286
Apl. 16, 1562.	Cryer, John (bur. Adingame). *No date.*	17		169
Aug. 27, 1567.	Cudbert, Thomas, Gyllymore (bur. Kirkbemoreside), Oct. 28, 1566.	17		696
Apl. 26, 1558.	Cudworth, Robert, Catlyff. par. Rotherham, Oct. 10, 1555.	15	2	224
Feb. ult., 1563.	Cudworthe, John, Eastfeld, par. Silkeston, Nov. 13, 1562.	17		321
Apl. 28, 1558.	Culpan, John, Heddingley (bur. Leedes), Jan. 6, 1557.	15	2	233
May 4, 1555.	Cundall, Henry, Tikehill, clerke, Oct. 18, 1554.	14		78
Sep. 22, 1565.	———, Jennet. Easingwold, widow, Apl. 20, 1565.	17		468
Jan. 18, 1560.	———, Richard, Easingwolde, Sep. 22, 1560.	16		139
Oct. 3, 1566.	Cundell, Leonard, Essingwold, Jan. 7, 1563.	17		579
Mar. 20, 1560.	Currowe, Agnes, wife of William C., Skibden in Craven, Nov. 12, 1553.	16		172
Jan. 24, 1558.	Cust, Percevell, Huton Rudbie, husbandman, Aug. 16, 1557.	15	3	23
Jan. 11, 1562.	Custance, John, Skirthenbecke, labourer, May, 11, 1559.	17		139
Oct. 12, 1558.	———, Oliver, Oxton (Notts.), husbandman, Oct. 25, 1557.	15	3	228
Mar. 13, 1558.	Cusworth, John, senr., Roystone, Nov. 20, 1557.	15	3	162
Oct. 1, 1556.	Cusworthe, Elizabeth (bur. Felkirke), widow, Dec. 7, 1555.	15	1	127
Oct. 6, 1557.	———, Thomas, Scrowbye (Notts.), Mar. 23, 1556.	15	2	9
Oct. 22, 1565.	Cutbert, William, Mowerbye, par. Stillingfleite, Aug. 23, 1565.	17		483
Jan. 22, 1557.	Cuthbert, Robert, Lethome, yeoman, Aug. 1. 1557.	15	2	157
Feb. 12, 1560.	Cuthberte, William, Kirkelethome, Jan. 4, 1559.	16		147
Jun. 17, 1556.	Cutlar, John, Thornar, labourer, Dec. 31, 1555.	15	1	48
Sep. 30, 1557.	Cutler, Agnes, widow (bur. Selbye), Dec. 8, 1555.	15	1	345
May 13, 1557.	———, Jane, Wellum Morhuse, par. Clarebrough (Notts.), wldow, Feb. 12, 1556.	15	2	134

A.D. 1554 TO 1568.

		Vol.	Pt.	Fol.
Oct. 31, 1557.	Cutler, William, Dodworthe grene, par. Sylkeston, Jun. 28, 1557.	15	1	366
Jan. 14, 1557.	—— als. Dogeson, Anne, York (bur. S. Cuthbert's), Oct. 9, 1557.	15	2	81
Sep. 1, 1563.	Cutlove, Robert, Sheffeld, Jan. 23, 1563.	17		207
Jun. 3, 1558.	Cutluff, Edmund, Masbore, par. Rotherham, Aug. 23, 1557.	15	2	338
Nov. 20, 1560.	Cutluffe, John, Malton, Jun. 30, 1560.	16		130
Jun. 5, 1556.	Culpon, Richard, Sowerbye. par. Hallifaxe, Aug. 20, 1555.	15	1	41
Oct. 6, 1558.	Cutt, John, Hollbroke, par. Tankerslay, Aug. 19, 1558.	15	3	223
Oct. 20, 1558.	Cuttberte, Thomas, North Frodingham, husbandman, Aug. 8, 1558.	15	2	351
Jan. 21, 1556.	Cutte, William, Shefeld, Jun. 9, 1556.	15	1	89
Sep. 30, 1556.	Cutter, George, Flamburghe, husbandman, Dec. 15, 1555.	15	1	134
Jun. 7, 1560.	——, William, Flambrughe, husbandman, Feb. 13, 1559.	16		76
Oct. 13, 1558.	Cuttforth, Richard, Carilton in Linricke (Notts.), smyth, Oct. 10, 1557.	15	2	358
Jun. 22, 1568.	Cuyte, William, Great Kelke (bur. Foston), Apl. 23, 1568.	17		821
Feb. 15, 1558.	Cuytte, William, Ryston in Holderness, husbandman, Dec. 3, 1558.	15	3	270
Jun. 12, 1556.	Dacre, Sir Thomas, Lanercost, co Cumberland, knight, May 9, 1552.	17		559
Jun. 20, 1566.	Daels, Stephan, Gemlinge, par. Foston, Dec. 17, 1565.	17		555
Oct. 7, 1561.	Dafft, Robert, Hicling (Notts.), singleman, Jun. 30, 1560.	17		41
May 5, 1568.	Daie, James, Bisshopside, par. Paiteleybriges, yeom., Oct. 27, 1567.	17		783
Aug. 2, 1561.	Daile, James, Danby, Sep. 22, 1560.	17		65
May 22, 1557.	——, Richard, senior, Crakall (bur. Topliffe), Feb. 25, 1556.	15	1	256
Jan. 17, 1567.	——, Roger, Thornebarghe, par. Southe Kelvygton, Sep. 6, 1567.	17		754
Oct. 20, 1558.	——, William, Thornbargh, par. Kilvington, July 20, 1558.	15	2	346
Jan. 12, 1558.	Dailes, John, South Dalton, husbandman, Aug. 31, 1558.	15	3	194
Aug. 12, 1567.	Daill, Alison, Scarbrughe, widow, Oct. 17, 1565.	17		695
May 22, 1557.	——, John, son of Richard D., Crakall, May 8, 1557.	15	1	257
Aug. 31, 1560.	——, John, Eshedalesyde, par. Whitbye, Apl. 13, 1560.	16		104
May 5, 1568.	——, John, Filinge, Feb. 23, 1567.	17		774
July 27, 1564.	——, John, Fyling, Apl. 18, 1564.	17		360
Aug. 20, 1567.	Daille, Nicholas, Yrtone, par. Semer, husbandman, Jun. 2, 1567.	17		696
Oct. 13, 1558.	Dakers, Olyver, Missin (Notts.), Mar. 24, 1557.	15	2	357
Nov. 29, 1558.	Dakins, Richard, Cottingham (dated at Barwicke), July 21, 1558.	15	3	122
Sep. 30, 1557.	Dalahay, Beatrix, widow of Rauffe D., Felkyrke, May 9, 1557.	15	1	370
Apl. 20, 1559.	Dale, Agnes, Normanton on Trent (Notts.), Oct. 5, 1558.	15	3	306
July 7, 1567.	——, William, Nether Popleton, Apl. 2, 1567.	17		666
No date.	Dallaryver, Thomas, Brandsbie, esquire, Sep. 20, 1558.	16		26
Feb. 9, 1557.	Dalton, John, Northe Frodingham, Nov. 21, 1557.	15	2	123
Mar. 9, 1559.	——, Richard, Thormonbye, Nov. 17, 1558.	16		7
Oct. 1, 1556.	Daltone, Thomas, Hull, marchaunt, Aug. 18, 1556.	15	1	136
Dec. 8, 1556.	Dalyas, John, Owte Newton (bur. Esington), husbandman, 1556.	15	1	72
Mar. 14, 1560.	Damus, John, Darlton (Notts.), husbandman, Jun. 18, 1559.	16		157
Apl. 13, 1559.	Danbie, Rauff, West Heslarton, Nov. 27, 1558.	15	3	350
July 19, 1557.	——, William, Suttone on Lound (Notts.), May 4, 1557.	15	1	287
May 23, 1565.	Danby, William, Frastrope (bur. Carnabye), yeoman, Feb. 15, 1564.	17		442
Oct. 6, 1558.	Danbye, Isabell, East Heslerton, widow, Aug. 30, 1558.	15	3	225
May 2, 1560.	——, Thomas, burgess of Scarbrught, Jun. 5, 1559.	16		36
Apl. 1, 1558.	——, William, Kyrkeby Knoll, gentleman, Jan. 31, 1557.	15	2	177
Apl. 27, 1558.	Dancaster, Thomas, Wombersley, Jan. 15, 1557	15	2	191
Apl. 24, 1567.	Dande, Henry, Nottingham, Dec. 4, 1566.	17		642
Feb. 15, 1558.	——, Robert, Siglisthron, Nov. 30, 1558.	15	3	272
Feb. 15, 1558.	Dandie, Robert, Beffurth, husbandman, Nov. 28, 1558.	15	3	272
May 18, 1559.	Dandye, Margaret, Brandisburtone, widow, Oct. 13, 1558.	15	3	410
Jun. 6, 1560.	Dannyell, John, Beswicke, par. Kylnewike, gentleman, Oct. 18, 1559.	16		74
Sep. 28, 1557.	Danser, Robert, Gysburne, Apl. 9, 1557.	15	1	339
Jun. 28, 1561.	——, William, Gysburne in Craven, May 10, 1560.	17		75
Dec. 18, 1560.	Danyell, Alyson, widow of Thomas D., Towton (bur. Saxton), Nov. 17, 1560.	16		136
Oct. 3, 1564.	——, Christopher, Saxton, Apl. 16, 1564.	17		366
Sep. 30, 1557.	——, Jane, Hull, widow, July 3, 1557.	15	1	327
Oct. 10, 1565.	——, John, Easdike, par. Wighill, husbandman, Apl. 12, 1564.	17		483
Sep. 21, 1557.	——, Sir Richard, chantre priest of St. Kath., in Haitfelde church, July 26, 1557.	15	1	355
Jun. 28, 1558.	——, Thomas, Beswyke, par. Kylnewyk, gentleman, May 26, 1558.	15	2	340

		Vol.	Pt.	Fol.
Dec. 18, 1560.	Danyell, Thomas, Towton (bur. Saxton), husbandman, Sep. 22, 1560.	16		137
Apl. 28, 1558.	———, William, Beswicke, esquire, May 22, 1557.	15	2	222
Apl. 24, 1567.	Darbeshire, Luke, Selley Mylne, par. Ansley (Notts.), Nov. 30, 1566.	17		643
Aug. 24, 1558.	Darcye, Sir George, Gatefurthe (bur. Brayton), knight, Aug. 15, 1558.	15	2	291
Oct. 29, 1554.	Darkar, Henry (bur. Lytle Leeke, Notts.), July 16, 1552.	14		279
Nov. 2, 1562.	Darke, John (bur. Helay, York), Jun. 2, 1562.	17		126
Nov. 29, 1558.	Darlay, William, Sandall, Feb. 28, 1557.	15	3	139
Oct. 6, 1558.	Darley, John, Bramton, par. Wathe, ———, 1558.	15	3	46
May 4, 1555.	———, Thomas, Darfeld, *Adm.*	14		78
July 11, 1558.	Darnyll *als.* Haryngton, William, Rotherham, May 20, 1558.	15	2	304
Mar. 9, 1561.	Darrell, Richard (bur. Kirkeby Mysperton), Dec. 28, 1561.	17		6
Jun. 18, 1560.	———, William, Cowike (bur. Snathe), Mar. 2, 1559.	16		86
Oct. 7, 1557.	Darwen, Robert, Hawton by Newark (Notts.), husbn., May 7, 1557.	15	2	18
Oct. 5, 1558.	Darwend, William (bur. Gargrave), Mar. 8, 1557.	15	3	40
May 6, 1557.	Darwent, William, Heytone in Rilleston, Jan. 6, 1556.	15	1	284
Jun. 4, 1561.	Dauson, Roger, Dewisburie, Nov. 18, 1560.	17		68
Apl. 26, 1558.	———, William, Bramley, par. Leedes, Feb. 17, 1557.	15	2	237
May 4, 1558.	Davell, William, Shelford (Notts.), husbandman, Sep. 8, 1557.	15	2	269
Apl. 26, 1559.	Davenson, Lancelotte, Burton Agnes, labourer, Oct. 10, 1558.	15	3	312
Apl. 3, 1559.	Daveson, Roger, Bempton, husbandman, Dec. 27, 1558.	15	3	360
May 2, 1560.	———, William, Bempton in Brydlyngton, Oct. 22, 1559.	16		36
Jun. 7, 1560.	Davison, Alyson, Ayton, par. Seamer, Oct. 4, 1559.	16		79
Jun. 20, 1562.	———, Edmund, Shipton (bur. Overton), Jun. 26, 1561.	17		88
Jan. 12, 1558.	———, Henry, Lund, May 30, 1557.	15	3	200
Jan. 29, 1556.	———, John, Ayton, par. Semar, July 18, 1556.	15	1	94
Oct. 3, 1550.(?5).—	———, John, East Lupton, par. Weverthorpe, Mar. 25, 1555.	14		173
Jun. 20, 1566.	———, Robert, Carnabye, husbandman, Apl. 22, 1566.	17		558
[Oct.] 29, 1555.	Davye, Thomas, Gisbroughe, tanner, Aug. 9, 1555.	14		179
Jun. 7, 1560.	Davyson, Jennat, Bessingebye, Oct. 27, ———.	16		77
Sep. 30, 1556.	———, John, Southskyrley (bur. Swyne), Jun. 30, 1556.	15	1	141
Oct. 7, 1557.	Dawbegyne, Thomas, Thorney (Notts.), Mar. 28, 1557.	15	2	17
Jan. 28, 1561.	Dawbye, Christopher, Bilbroughe, husbandman, Nov. 18, 1559.	17		8
Mar. 14, 1557.	Dawcke, Roger, Warter, Oct. 6, 1557.	15	2	153
Feb. 6, 1558.	Dawes, Nicholas, Herthyll, husbandman, Jan. 21, 1558.	15	3	253
May 13, 1568.	———, Thomas, Bawderstone (Notts.), Feb. 1, 1567.	17		799
Nov. 28, 1567.	Dawkinge, Thomas, Great Edstone, husbandman, Dec. 26, 1566.	17		741
Oct. 25, 1556.	Dawnaye, Thomas, Cowicke, knight, Aug. 17, 1556.	15	1	102
Apl. 16, 1567.	Dawson, Adam, Huddersfield, May 20, 1566.	17		622
Nov. 17, 1558.	———, Agnes, wid. of Thomas D., Burlay (bur. Ledes), Sep. 4, 1558.	15	3	111
Apl. 19, 1559.	———, Agnes, Nottingham, Aug. 27, 1558.	15	3	354
Oct. 10, 1560.	———, Alis, Dalton, par. Rotherham, widow, Jun. 16, 1560.	16		126
Oct. 11, 1565.	———, Bartill, Carleton (Notts.), husbandman, Apl. 11, 1565.	17		470
May 6, 1559.	———, Christopher, Appleton, husbandman, Dec. 31, 1558.	15	3	382
Jun. 17, 1561.	———, Elizabeth, Thormonbye, May 18, 1561.	17		71
July 4, 1556.	———, Gyles, Brampton, par. Treton, Mar. 30, 1556.	15	1	52
July 29, 1560.	———, John, Collingham, July 10, 1559.	16		98
Oct. 11, 1565.	———, John, East Leake (Notts.), whelle wright, Aug. 20, 1565.	17		470
Mar. 20, 1558.	———, John, Garforth, Oct. 25, 1558.	15	3	252
July 19, 1566.	———, John, Hooton Bushell, May 9, 1566.	17		562
Nov. 12, 1556.	———, John, Lofthouse, par. Rothewell, Aug. 6, 1556.	15	1	111
Jan. 13, 1558.	———, John, Saxandall (Notts.), husbandman, Sep. 14, 1558.	15	3	179
Sep. 28, 1557.	———, John, Southe Mylforthe (bur. Sherburne), husbn., Aug. 12, 1557.	15	1	336
Apl. 27, 1564.	———, Richard, Holme Perpoynte (Notts.), Aug. 28, 1563.	17		341
July 19, 1557.	———, Richard, Mathersaye Thorpe (Notts.), Feb. 11, 1556.	15	1	312
July 8, 1560.	———, Richard, Metheleye, Jun. 3, 1560.	16		90
Mar. 10, 1566.	———, Richard, Rotherham, Aug. 31, 1558.	17		516
Sep. 21, 1557.	———, Robert, Dalton, par. Rotherham, May 10, 1557.	15	1	356
Oct. 1, 1562.	———, Robert (bur. Hubberham), May 27, 1561.	17		110
Apl. 22, 1562.	———, Robert, Scrobe (Notts.), May 17, 1561.	17		194
Sep. 15, 1557.	———, Robert, York, cordyner, Mar. 27, 1557.	15	1	332
Jan. 11, 1564.	———, Sir Robert, Ledsham, priest, Jun. 30, 1564.	17		400

		Vol.	Pt.	Fol.
Oct. 6, 1557.	Dawson, Roger, Scrobye (Notts.), Jun. 28, 1557.	15	2	7
Sep. 29, 1563.	———, Thomas, Gargrave, Apl. 13, 1563.	17		278
Oct. 3, 1565.	———, Thomas, Helmsley, inholder, Apl. 21, 1565.	17		486
Mar. 6, 1556.	———, Thomas, Mathersay (Notts.), Oct. 8, 1556.	15	1	177
May 21, 1560.	———, Thomas, Rosedaill, par. Mydleton, Oct. 18, 1559.	16		67
Apl. 27, 1558.	———, Thomas, Skeklinge, Mar. 25, 1558.	15	2	206
Mar. 17, 1558.	———, Thomas, York, Feb. 3, 1558.	15	3	243
Oct. 8, 1567.	———, Walter, Nottingham, July 17, 1566.	17		724
Dec. 20, 1558.	———, William, Gresbrowke, par. Rotheram, Oct. 28, 1558.	15	3	152
Oct. 14, 1557.	———, William, Helmesley, Aug. 20, 1557.	15	1	363
Jan. 28, 1561.	———, William, West Garforthe, Dec. 22, 1561.	17		7
Apl. 27, 1556.	Dawsone, Elyne, Ecope, par. Addle, widow, Jan. 16, 1555.	15	1	28
Jun. 4, 1561.	———, John, Morehouse, par. Garfurthe, Jan. 27, 1558.	17		67
Sep. 3, 1566.	———, Richard, Rustone, par. Wykam, ——, 1566.	17		571
Apl. 20, 1559.	———, William, Eastretford (Notts.), marcer, Jan. 11, 1558.	15	3	431
Mar. 10, 1555.	Dawsonn, John, Mattersaythorpe (Notts.), Sep. 4, 1554.	14		223
Sep. 21, 1562.	Dawsonne, Thomas, Frysinghall par. Bradefurthe, Apl. 19, 1560.	17		201
Jan. 11, 1557.	Dawton, John, Lelley, par. Preston (Holderness), Nov. 26, 1557.	15	2	73
Sep. 14, 1558.	Dawtre, Marmaduke, Bulmar, July 23, 1558.	15	3	107
May 26, 1558.	Day, Jenet, Hovingham, Mar. 15, 1557.	15	2	285
May 26, 1558.	——, Margaret, Howvingham, Apl. 16, 1558.	15	2	283
May 14, 1558.	——, Richard (bur. Bilton), Dec. 13, 1557.	15	2	279
July 27, 1567.	——, Richard, Normonbe, par. Eston, May, 8, 1567.	17		671
Nov. 17, 1558.	——, Robert, Snath, Nov. 20, 1557.	15	3	73 & 74
Mar. 29, 1555.	——, Robert, Thurnum, par. Burton Agnes, labourer, Dec. 31, 1554.	14		189
May 17, 1565.	——, Thomas, Gresley (Notts.), Mar. 6, 1564.	17		441
May 26, 1558.	——, Thomas, Hovingham, Nov. 16, 1557.	15	2	285
Dec. 1, 1561.	——, Thomas, Overpopleton, Nov. 2, 1561.	17		32
Jun. 12, 1556.	——, Thomas (bur. Rypon), May 20, 1556.	15	1	57
Feb. 14, 1555.	——, William, Busshopesydd (bur. Paythlaybriges), cowper, Dec. 30, 1555.	15	1	7
Mar. 4, 1562.	Daye, Jennet (bur. Brandesburton), Dec. 27, 1562.	17		151
Sep. 27, 1566.	——, John, Huton Wanseley, par. Marston, Jun. 24, 1566.	17		571
Jan. 12, 1558.	Dayle, Richard, Crakall (bur. Topliffe), Aug. 3, 1557.	15	3	174
Nov. 28, 1558.	Dayles, Robert, Hornesay, tanner, Apl. 26, 1558.	15	3	78
Apl. 14, 1562.	Dayll, John, Brandysburtone, Mar. 2, 1561.	17		185
Nov. 10, 1558.	Daylle, Adam, Lyllyng (bur. Sheriffhowton), Sep. 25, 1558.	15	3	233
Dec. 22, 1557.	Dayne, Persevall, Northcorome, par. Halyfax, Nov. 7, 1557.	15	2	48
Feb. 20, 1560.	———, Richard, Lightclyffe, par. Hallyfax, Jan. 2, 1560.	16		149
1554.	Dayson (Dawson), Alice, Allhallowes, York, widow, Sep. 28, 1554.	14		98
Feb. 20, 1560.	Dealtre, George, Fullsutton, gentleman, Oct. 14, 1560.	16		149
Oct. 1, 1561.	Dean, Alexander, Kettilwell, Jan. 4, 1559.	17		48
July 6, 1555.	——, Thomas, Southclif, par. North Cave, husbn.. Apl. 18, 1555.	14		259
Oct. 3, 1554.	Deane, Agnes, Wessyt Howsys (bur. Kirkbye in Mallumdale), July 8, 2 Mary.	14		39
Apl. 13, 1559.	——, Edward, Bylton, Mar. 25, 1558.	15	3	344
May 18, 1559.	——, Elizabeth, Byltone, widow, Apl. 17, 1559.	15	3	410
Oct. 2, 1560.	——, Gilbert, Warlay, par. Hallyfax, Aug. 6, 1560.	16		113
Dec. 5, 1567.	——, Katherine, Thorngumbold (bur. Paull), Nov. 6. 1567.	17		742
July 26, 1563.	——, Richard, Deyne House, par. Halifaxe, clothier, Apl. 3, 1563.	17		266
Jan. 12, 1558.	——, Thomas, Bagbie, par. Kirkbie Knowle, Aug. 19, 1558.	15	3	176
Oct. 2, 1567.	——, William, Thorgumbold (bur. Paull), July 13, 1567.	17		715
May 18, 1559.	Deay, Richard, Estretford (Notts.), Nov. 2, 1558.	15	3	406
Mar. 20, 1558.	Deconson, Robert, Birkyn, husbandman, Feb. 12, 1557.	15	3	252
Dec. 22, 1556.	Deirman, William, Braythwayte, par. Kirke Bramwith, July 24, 1556.	15	1	80
Jun. 11, 1562.	Dekeson, Richard, Scorbroughe, Feb. 3, 1559.	17		91
Sep. 23, 1554.	Denaunde, Richard, Scarbrughe, Jun. 26, 1554.	14		273
May 6, 1557.	Denbie, Robert, Utlaie, par. Kighlaie, July 12, 1556.	15	1	252
Feb. 6, 1558.	———, William, Knottingley, par. Pontefracte, Aug. 20, 1558.	15	3	256
Jun. 20, 1568.	Denbye, Thomas, Kesbrughe, par. Darton. Jan. 28, 1567.	17		816
May 5, 1558.	Denman, Richard, Ordsall (Notts.), gentleman, Sep. 6, 1557.	15	2	249
Apl. 24, 1567.	———, Thomas (bur. Staynton, Notts.), Nov. 16, 1566.	17		641

A.D. 1554 TO 1568.

		Vol.	Pt.	Fol.
Sep. 8, 1561.	Denmore, Robert, Wilberfosse, Aug. 28, 1561.	17		49
Oct. 28, 1566.	Dent, Cudbart, Southclyff, par. North Cave, husbn., May 14, 1566.	17		586
May 1, 1567.	——, Robert, Mylnehouses, par. Sheffeld, Dec. 17, 1566.	17		647
May 5, 1558.	——, William, Kellam (Notts.), husbandman, Nov. 15, 1557.	15	2	256
July 4, 1564.	Dente, Roland, Caterton (bur. Tadcaster), May 29, 1564.	17		354
Feb. 15, 1559.	Denton, Amer, Tadcaster, Sep. 28, 1559.	16		1
Mar. 19, 1559.	———, Edward, Hollywell in Staynelande (bur. Elande), Dec. 1, 1559.	16		11
Aug. 5, 1557.	———, Gylbert, Sowth Owrome, par. Halifax, Jun. 10, 1557.	15	2	131
Nov. 28, 1558.	———, James, New Milner Dame, par. Sandall Magna, Oct. 10, 1558.	15	3	134
Jun. 19, 1566.	———, James, Wakefelde, May 27, 1556.	15	1	50
Sep. 30, 1563.	———, John, Ovenden (bur. Hallifaxe), Apl. 2, 1563.	17		282
Sep. 30, 1563.	———, Robert, Waikfeld, karpenter, Aug. 26, 1563.	17		283
July 1, 1561.	———, Thomas, Leven in Holderness, Mar. 5, 1558.	17		77
Oct. 2, 1567.	———, Thomas, Ovynden, par. Halifax, clothiar, Oct. 26, 1565.	17		719
Oct. 7, 1557.	Dentt, Thomas, Kellome (Notts.), Apl. 26, 1557.	15	2	17
Oct. 22, 1556.	Denysone, Richard, Hekmundwyke, par. Byrstall, Aug. 18, 1556.	15	1	98
Jun. 23, 1563.	Deren, Mathew, Willerbie, Feb. 26, 1562.	17		259
May 18, 1559.	Deriman, Alice, Braythwith, par. Bromwith, Apl. 4, 1559.	15	3	404
Oct. 5, 1554.	Devysborn, John, Brempton (Bempton), Aug. 30, 1554.	14		45
July 5, 1557.	Dewie, Richard, Thurne, fissher, May 7, 1557.	15	1	303
Jun. 14, 1560.	——, Thurston, Boughton (Notts.), husbandman, Feb. 27, 1559.	16		85
Jun. 14, 1564.	Dewisberie, John, Bridlington, yeoman, Aug. 3, 1563.	17		352
Apl. 6, 1558.	Dey, Edmonde, Barnesley, Apl. 6, 1557.	15	2	183
May 9, 1565.	Deye, Nicholas, Sheffeld, Feb. 5, 1564.	17		428
Jun. 20, 1562.	Deyne, Elizabeth, Bagbie, Feb. 20, 1561.	17		89
Nov. 1, 1566.	———, Robert, Ovenden, par. Halifax, yeoman, Mar. 21, 1565.	17		597
Sep. 4, 1561.	Dicanson, Robert, Braton, Aug. 14, 1561.	17		52
Mar. 6, 1556.	Diccanson, William, Myssyn (Notts.), husbandman, Nov. 30, 1556.	15	1	177
Aug. 7, 1565.	Diccons, Agnes (bur. North Leverton, Notts.), widow, Dec. 4, 1558.	17		458
Oct. 13, 1558.	———, Averay, Sturton (Notts.), husbandman, Oct. 22, 1557.	15	2	376
May 5, 1558.	Dicconson, Agnes, Myssyn (Notts.), widow, Nov. 15, 1557.	15	2	247
Nov. 17, 1558.	———, Lawrance, Carleton, par. Snathe, Apl. 22, 1557.	15	3	74
Dec. 11, 1566.	———, Ranold, Burne (bur. Brayton), Nov. 13, 1565.	17		604
Mar. 20, 1565.	———, Roger, Headon in Holderness, cordiner, Oct. 10, 8 Eliz.	17		505
Feb. 8, 1557.	———, Thomas, Aerton (bur. Kyrkebye Malhamdaill), Nov. 20, 1557.	15	2	162
Nov. 12, 1556.	———, William, Chaple Hadlesaye (bur. Birkyn), Sep. 1, 1556.	15	1	113
July 20, 1557.	Dicconsone, Anne, Broxsaie, par. Hacknes, widow, May 3, 1557.	15	1	314
Apl. 22, 1556.	———, John, Harwoodedaill, par. Hackenes, Jan. 31, 1555.	15	1	26
Apl. 6, 1554.	Dicconsonne, Thomas, Areton (bur. Kirkbie Malhamdale), Feb. 1, 1 Mary.	14		155
Jan. 28, 1561.	Dice, Edward, Monke Friston, smythe, Sep. 26, 1561.	17		8
Oct. 4, 1555.	Dickandson, Robert, Burnysheton, par. Scawbie, Apl. 20, 1555.	14		19
May 9, 1565.	Dickenson, Thomas, Burton Agnes, Dec. 20, 1562.	17		425
Oct. 10, 1566.	Dickes, Adam, Sibthorpe (Notts.), husbandman, Jun. 15, 1562.	17		589
May 19, 1559.	Dickeson, Henry, Haddlesay (par. Byrkyn), Apl. 23, 1559,	15	3	426
Oct. 2, 1550(?5).	Dickesonne, George, Sourebie (bur. Hallifax), May 19, 1555.	14		171
Jun. 22, 1568.	Dickinson, John, Burnyston, par. Scawbe, Apl. 27, 1567.	17		822
Apl. 19, 1564.	Dickonson, Thomas, Horton (bur. Braswell), Dec. 24, 1563.	17		329
Jun. 4, 1558.	Dickonsonne, Henry, Hovingham, husbandman, July 18, 1557.	15	2	310
May 14, 1558.	———, William, Suffeild, par. Hackenes, Sep. 16, 1557.	15	2	282
Mar. 20, 1560.	Dickson, Dorothe (bur. Arnecliffe), Jan. 13, 1560.	16		171
Oct. 29, 1558.	———, Steven, burges of Scarbrughe, Aug. 28, 1558.	15	2	370
Dec. 21, 1562.	Dickynson, Thomas, Sandall, par. Doncaster, husbn., Dec. 2, 1563.	17		137
Dec. 18, 1560.	Diconson, Thomas, Byrkyn. husbandman, Oct. 28, 1560.	16		136
Jun. 12, 1562.	Dicson, Cuthbert, Beverley, wright, Apl. 4, 1562.	17		88
Apl. 28, 1563.	———, Edward, Sutton (bur. Kildweke), Jan. 3, 1562.	17		230
Mar. 13, 1565.	———, John, Stanburne, husdandman, Dec. 18, 1565.	17		504
Jun. 2, 1557.	———, Roger, Medilston, par. Thornell, Apl. 16, 1557.	15	1	266
Aug. 12, 1561.	———, William, Coldon (bur. Albroughe), May 12, 1560.	17		59
Dec. 16, 1566.	———, William, Helaugh, May 18, 1565.	17		601
July 12, 1558.	Dicsonne, Sir William, Carleton (Notts.), 1558.	15	2	315

		Vol.	Pt.	Fol.
Dec. 31, 1557.	Dighton, Elizabeth, Huton, par. Marston, widow, Dec. 21, 1557.	15	2	77
Dec. 4, 1566.	——, Thomas. Beforthe, husbandman, Oct. 6, 1566.	17		600
Jan. 29, 1556.	Dikson, Richard, Muston (bur. Hunmanby), Sep. 10, 1556.	15	1	93
May 4, 1558.	Dirrye, Thomas, Bingham (Notts.), Mar. 26, 1557.	15	2	268
Mar. 26, 1565.	Dison, John, Waikfeld, chapman, Nov. 4, 1564.	17		414
Nov. 17, 1558.	Dixson, Anne, widow of Christopher D., Staineburne, ——, 1558.	15	3	114
Apl. 28, 1558.	——, John, Skelton (bur. Danbye), Jan. 3, 1557.	15	2	231
Apl. 10, 1557.	——, William, Ripon, butcher, May 4, 1555.	15	1	205
Jan. 24, 1558.	——, William, Thorpe, par. Badisworth, Sep. 30, 1558.	15	3	120
May 4, 1558.	Dob, William, Huckenall Torket (Notts.), husbandman, Dec. 19, 1557.	15	2	276
Dec. 22, 1566.	Dobbe, John, Hatfeld Wodhouse, husbandman, Feb. 20, 1554.	15	1	78
Jan. 19, 1558.	Dobbinson, Robert, Eskrigge, Dec. 4, 1558.	15	3	20
Sep. 30, 1557.	Dobbye, Robert, Wodhouse (bur. Hatefelde), husbn, Aug. 6, 1557.	15	1	368
Jan. 20, 1558.	Dobbyn, Nicholas, Kirkbymoreshed, shomaker, Feb. 10, 1557.	15	3	213
Dec. 19, 1562.	Dobbynson, Ellin, Estryke, widow, Aug. 8, 1562.	17		135
Mar. 12, 1557.	Dobe, Thomas, Over Selbye, husbandman, Feb. 2, 1557.	15	2	127
May 5, 1558.	Dobleday, Henry, Blythe (Notts.), corvesor, Sep. 6, 1557.	15	2	244
Mar. 18, 1560.	Dobson, Isabell, Fulsutton, widow, Mar. 8, 1560.	16		154
Oct. 14, 1557.	——, James, Levesham, May 13, 1557.	15	1	363
Jun. 21, 1566.	——, John, Billisdaill, Dec, 6, 1565.	17		558
Sep. 29, 1557.	——, John, Shipley, par. Bradforde, Oct. 28, 1556.	15	1	329
Jun. 16, 1564.	——, John, Sikehouse (bur. Rothewell), Nov. 4, 1563.	17		350
Sep. 16, 1557.	——, Nicholas, Lofthouse, par. Rothewell, Jan. 26, 1556.	15	1	333
Mar. 4, 1562.	——, Richard, Catwicke, husbandman, Dec. 13, 1562.	17		150
Jan. 13, 1558.	——, Richard, Southwell (Notts.), carpenter, Nov. 14, 1557.	15	3	15
Oct. 13, 1565.	——, Thomas, Lithe, Feb. 18, 1565.	17		474
Jun. 22, 1568.	——, Thomas, Muston (bur. Hunmanby), husbn., Dec. 26, 1567.	17		823
Jan. 16, 1558.	——, William, Fulsotton, Dec. 26, 1558.	15	3	210
May 6, 1557.	——, William, Kaingham in Holderness, Mar. 24, 1555.	15	1	238
Apl. 26, 1558.	Dobsonne, Edmunde, Spofforth, Aug. 18, 1557.	15	2	240
Mar. 21, 1559.	——, William, Hackenes, Feb. 10, 1559.	16		14
Oct. 20, 1558.	Dockery, Elizabeth, Tunstall, widow, Apl. 10, 1558.	15	3	228
May 9, 1560.	Dodge, Roger, Gonalston (Notts.), husbandman, Aug. 6, 1559.	16		60
Oct. 9, 1567.	Dodgeson, Christopher, Mathersey Thorpe (Notts.), July 24, 1567.	17		722
May 6, 1563.	Dodshon, George, North Whetley (Notts.), Dec. 31, 1559.	17		243
Sep. 26, 1558.	Dodworthe, James, Derfeld, July 20, 1558.	15	3	51
Apl. 27, 1558.	Dogeson, William, Pathorne, par. Gysburne, Nov. 12, 1557.	15	2	199
Jan. 14, 1557.	—— als. Cutler, Anne, York (bur. S. Cuthbert's), Oct. 9, 1557.	15	2	81
Nov. 6, 1557.	Dogg, Edward, Wyston (Notts.), husbandman, Sep. 23, 1557.	15	2	109
Jan. 21, 1557.	Dogley, Peter (bur. Monckfryston), Oct. 9, 1557.	15	2	155
May 18, 1559.	Doliffe, John, Croston, Sep. 30, 1558.	15	3	413
Oct. 13, 1558.	Dollond, Alexander, Lyttlebrough (Notts.), Jan. 10, 1558.	15	2	358
Jan. 14, 1564.	Dolphin, William, Treton, Sep. 16, 1564.	17		402
May 9, 1565.	Dolphyn, Elizabeth, Treaton, Feb. 27, 1564.	17		429
Apl. 27, 1554.	——, John, Treton, Apl. 11, 1554.	14		64
Feb. 1, 1565.	Doman, Anne, Ripon, Nov. 24, 1564.	17		496
Aug. 12, 1566.	Donas, Thomas, Garton in Holderness, husbandman, May 5, 1566.	17		569
Aug. 12, 1566.	Donay, Vincent, clerk, curate of Sutton (Holderness), May 13, 1566.	17		567
May 18, 1559.	Doncaster, John, Kirksmeton, Oct. 1, 1558.	15	3	403
Mar. 8, 1558.	Done, Henry, Hyske (bur. Beverley), husbandman, Sep. 12, 1558.	15	3	285
Mar. 30, 1558.	——, Persevall, Hotonbushell, Mar. 21, 1557.	15	2	178
July 24, 1564.	——, William, Cheriburton als. Northe Burton, husbn., Nov. 21, 1563.	17		359
Dec. 5, 1567.	Donkyne, George, Hull, housewright, July 14, 1567.	17		749
Dec. 16, 1557.	Donne, Robert, South Frodingham, par. Outthorne, husbn., July 2, 1557.	15	2	44
Apl. 16, 1567.	——, William, Ottringham, July 24, 1565.	17		633
Sep. 20, 1558.	Donnington, Agnes, Dighton (bur. Eskrig), widow, Sep. 4, 1558. (completed at fol. 85).	15	3	108
May 27, 1564.	Donyngton, Antony, Eskirke, gentleman, Sep. 15, 1563.	17		345
Apl. 5, 1565.	——, Hugh, Kirkeham (bur. Westhoe), gent., Feb. 24, 1563.	17		419
Mar. 22, 1556.	Doon, Thomas, Lokington (bur. Wawkyngton), May 14, 1555.	15	1	191
May 31, 1557.	Doore, Edward, Thewhorlaie (Wherlow), par. Sheafeld, Dec. 7, 1556.	15	1	261
Apl. 19, 1559.	——, Henry, Glapton, par. Clyftone (Notts.), Sep. 1, 1558.	15	3	375

		Vol.	Pt.	Fol.
Apl. 26, 1559.	Dorman, Isabell, York, widow, Dec. 10, 1558.	15	3	313
Nov. 3, 1558.	Doughtie, Thomas, Appleton (bur. Bolton Percie), Oct. 21, 1558.	15	3	230
Apl. 22, 1559.	Doughty. John, Appilton (bur. Bolton Percie), Oct. 19, 1558.	15	3	309
Jun. 12, 1557.	———, Margret, Bondgate (bur. Selby), widow, Dec. 8, 1556.	15	1	291
Apl. 26, 1558.	Doughtye, Elsabethe (bur. Campsall), Nov. 5, 1557.	15	2	197
Jun. 14, 1560.	———, John, Bolton Percye, Dec. 1, 1559.	16		83
Dec. 14, 1557.	———, Thomas, Hessell, Sep. 29, 1557.	15	1	358
Dec. 5, 1567.	Doumler, Thomas, Preston in Holderness, husbn., Sep. 30, 1567.	17		741
July 11, 1558.	Dounwell, William, Stayneburne, husbandman, Mar. 10, 1557.	15	2	308
Oct. 12, 1558.	Doussing, Thomas, Shelforth (Notts.), labourer, Mar. 16, 1557.	15	3	33
May 6, 1557.	Dove, John, junr., Whitgift, Nov. 15, 1556.	15	1	241
Mar. 15, 1558.	———, Margaret, Ellerton, Sep. 15, 1558.	15	3	241
Aug. 25, 1558.	———, Roger, curet of Ellerton, July 31, 1558.	15	2	295
Sep. 30, 1557.	Dowe, Richard, Birdforthe, yeoman, Mar. 24, 1553.	15	1	347
Feb. 17, 1561.	———, Robert, West Stockewith (Notts.), fyshmonger, Feb. 18, 15—.	17		16
Jan. 22, 1561.	Dowgelbe, William, North Dauton, yeoman, May 13, 1561.	17		24
July 16, 1558.	Dowghtie, Thomas, Bolton Percey, May 31, 1558.	15	2	322
Jun. 23, 1568.	Dowker (or Duker) (Registered Dulker), Thomas (bur. Staingrave), Mar. 1, 1567.	17		807
Aug. 16, 1560.	Down, John, Pottow, par. Whorleton, husbandman, Apl. 15, 1560.	16		102
Oct. 1, 1557.	Downynge, Anne, Staynforde (bur. Haitfelde), Aug. 16, 1557.	15	1	369
Oct. 6, 1557.	Dowset, Edward, Orston (Notts.), husbandman, Apl. 6, 1557.	15	2	27
May 15, 1557.	Dowson, John, Eskrigge, Apl. 25, 1557.	15	1	256
Oct. 2, 1551(?5).	Dowsonne, John, Bolton nighe Bowland, Jun. 9, 1555.	14		168
No date.	Drabbyll, Christopher, Barlye Hoyle, par. Wentworthe, yeom., Feb. 5, 1554.	14		85
Feb. 4, 1556.	Drabill, Nicholas, Conesburgh, husbandman, Oct. 27, 1556.	15	1	168
Sep. 30, 1557.	Draike, John, Tykhill, Jan. 11, 1556.	15	1	368
Oct. 29, 1558.	Draipe, Edward, Gransmore (bur. Burton Agnes), labr., Jun. 29, 1558.	15	2	368
Apl. 3, 1559.	———, Thomas, Harpham, Oct. 30, 1558.	15	3	317
Feb. 4, 1556.	Drake, Robert, Tyckhill, Aug. 27, 1554.	15	1	170
Dec. 13, 1557.	Dransfelde, John, Walton, par. Sandall Magna, Sep. 19, 1557.	15	2	54
Oct. 29, 1558.	Drape, George, Gransmore (bur. Burton Agnes), husbn., Apl. 27, 1558.	15	2	372
Aug. 18, 1562.	———, Helen, Harpham, widow, Mar. 26, 1562.	17		106
May 2, 1560.	———, John, Harpham, Feb. 12, 1559.	16		36
May 9, 1566.	Draper, Alice, Cortlyngstocke (Notts.), widow, July 1, 1565.	17		550
Sep. 30, 1557.	———, Isabell, widow of Richard D., Heptonstall, Aug. 29, 1557.	15	1	324
May 5, 1568.	———, James, Wadsworthe, par. Heptonstall, husbn., Nov. 17, 1567.	17		792
Apl. 19, 1559.	———, John, Gresley (Notts.), Sep. 15, 1558.	15	3	355
Feb. 3, 1561.	———, John, Heptonstall, Dec. 21, 1561.	17		10
Mar. 15, 1560.	———, Richard, Sutton on Lounde (Notts.), Nov. 12, 1560.	16		169
Oct. 8, 1567.	———, Robert, Thorgarton (Notts.), Apl. 24, 1567.	17		725
Apl. 19, 1559.	———, William, Cortelyngstocke (Notts.), husbn., Jan. 9, 1558.	15	3	372
Nov. 26, 1557.	Drax, John, Stayneforde (bur. Haytefeld), husbn., July 22, 1557.	15	2	91
Feb. 25, 1556.	Draxe, Thomas, Nether Wodall, par. Darfeld, esq., Nov. 24, 1553.	15	1	179
Mar. 15, 1560.	Drewe, Agnes (bur. Carleton, Retford, Notts.), wid., Jan. 26, 1556.	16		167
May 13, 1557.	Drewre, Christopher, Awkelay, par. Fynnyngley (Notts.), Dec. 11, 1556.	15	2	134
May 13, 1557.	Drewrie, William, Fynnyngley (Notts.), Jan. 3, 1556.	15	2	132
Nov. 29, 1558.	Drewrye, Roger, York, sadler, Nov. 9, 1558.	15	3	127
Oct. 6, 1558.	Dring, Margaret, Wintringham, Jun. 7, 1558.	15	3	226
Mar. 22, 1560.	Dringe, John, Wyntringham Feb. 3, 1558.	16		176
May 18, 1559.	Drowlye (or Drowrye), William, Adlingflete, Apl. 9, 1558.	15	3	413
Jun. 8, 1560.	Drowrye, William, Wadworthe, May 9, 1560.	16		81
May 5, 1558.	Drurie, Thomas, Blakestone (bur. Fynyngley, Notts.), husbn., Sep. 30, 1557.	15	2	332
Aug. 13, 1558.	Drury, Henry, York, taylyer, July 26, 1558.	15	3	1
Aug. 18, 1562.	Drusdall, William, Clowghton (bur. Scawbe), Apl. 15, 1562.	17		105
Aug. 28, 1561.	Drwe, Herrie, Shadfforthe, par. Everton (Notts.), husbn., May 5, 1561.	17		58
Oct. 9, 1560.	Drye, Thomas, Beverlay, surgyon, Aug. 5, 1560.	16		121
Feb. 19, 1557.	Drynckall, John, Rednes (bur. Whytgyfte), Jan. 5, ———.	15	2	144
Feb. 24, 1559.	Drynkerowe, Thomas, Baddersbie (Ingleby Greenhow) (bur. Ungyll), Dec. 18, 1559.	16		2

A.D. 1554 TO 1568.

		Vol.	Pt.	Fol.
July 4, 1554.	Drynkkall, Hugh, Hawdenbie, Apl. 2, 1554.	14		142
Jun. 22, 1560.	Drysser, William, Acastre Selbye (bur. Styllynflete), Jun. 9, 1560.	16		86
Sep. 13, 1565.	Dryver, Thomas, Lyndley (bur. Ottley), May 4, 1565.	17		465
Sep. 16, 1564.	Ducke, Christopher, Burnysheton, par. Scawbie, Apl. 5, 1564.	17		362
Jan. 14, 1566.	——, John, Lithe, Feb. 21, 1564.	17		607
Feb. 8, 1557.	——, Margaret (bur. Egton), Jan. 13, 1557.	15	2	162
Aug. 1, 1562.	——, Peter (bur. Lithe), Apl. 23, 1562.	17		103
Oct. 5, 1558.	——, Richard, Girrike, par. Skelton, St. Andrew's Day, 1558.	15	3	68
May 21, 1560.	——, Thomas, Fernedaile, par. Lestingham, Jun. 4, 1559.	16		66
Oct. 27, 1564.	——, Thomas, Northe Lofthous, Jun. 30, 1564.	17		393
Mar. 10, 1555.	Ducker, Cartheryn, wid. of Thomas D., Myssyn (Notts.), Sep. 28, 1553.	14		229
Oct. 7, 1556.	——, Jenet, Myssyn (Notts.), widow, Aug. 4, 1556.	15	1	172
Apl. 20, 1559.	——, Rauff, Missyn (Notts.), Dec. 10, 1558.	15	3	369
Sep. 4, 1555.	——, Thomas, Missin, husbandman, May 13, 1555.	14		24
Sep. 4, 1555.	——, Thomas, Myssyn (Notts.), May 13, 1555.	14		185
May 5, 1558.	Ducket, Robert, Newarke (Notts.), tanner, Apl. 7, 1557.	15	2	257
Apl. 14, 1562.	Duffan, John, Castelfurthe, Feb. 13, 1561.	17		182
May 18, 1559.	——. Thomas, Caste!ford, husbandman, Apl. 31, 1558.	15	3	415
Dec. 13, 1557.	——, Wiliiam, Houghton (bur. Castelfurthe), Oct. 31, 4 and 5 Philip and Mary.	15	2	53
Feb. 16, 1565.	Duffeld, Robert, Northdighton (bur. Kirkdighton), husbn., Nov. 2, 1565.	17		499
Sep. 30, 1562.	Duk, George, Girrik (bur. Skelton), husbandman, Jun. 7, 1562.	17		109
May 10, 1565.	Duke (Ducke), Frances, North Lofthus [widow], Nov. 11, 1564.	17		426
No date.	——, John, Kirkeborne, husbandman, Oct. 10, 1554.	14		90
May 27, 1567.	——, Lawrance, Scawbe, Jan. 4, 1566.	17		654
Jan. 30, 1555.	——, Richard, Kymberworthe, par. Rotherham, Oct. 21, 1555.	15	1	4
Sep. 29, 1563.	——, Robert, Flambrughe, fyssherman, Jun. 14, 1543.	17		276
Mar. 18, 1556.	Dukkett, Richard, Bagby, par. Kirkbyknoll, Nov. 23, 1556.	15	1	189
Jun. 23, 1568.	Dulker (Dowker or Duker, Act Bk.), Thomas, bur. Staingrave, Mar. 1, 1567.	17		807
Jun. 10, 1560.	Dunche, Alice, Tunstall, widow, Feb. 22, 1558.	16		82
May 17, 1565.	Dunckynge, Edward, Eperston (Notts.), Feb. 28, 1564.	17		440
Feb. 19, 1557.	Dune, John, Whytgyfte in Marsland, Nov. 25, 1557.	15	2	146
Feb. 6, 1565.	——, Robert, Wistow, Jan. 24, ——.	17		497
May 9, 1560.	——, Roger, Nottingham, shearman, Mar. 4, 1560.	16		60
Jan. 12, 1558.	Dunninge, Robert, Throston, par. Feliskirke, Nov. 5, 1558.	15	3	174
Jan. 13, 1567.	Dunnyngton, Richard, Dringhouses, York, husbandman, Sep. 18, 1567.	17		751
Jan. 15, 1557.	Dunwell, Richard, Eskrige, Nov. 15, 1557.	15	2	82
Sep. 29, 1563.	——, Thomas, Ottley, yeoman, July 20, 1563.	17		289
Jan. 19, 1576.	——, William, Ottley (Codicil), May 8, 1563 (Also Invent. & Bond).	17		212-2
Aug. 3, 1563.	——, William, Ottley, May 8, 1563.	17		212
Jan. 12, 1558.	Dursay (written also Durfay), Thomas, Warter, ——, 1558.	15	3	200
Jun. 12, 1562.	Durssa (or Dursay), Robert, Warter, Apl. 17, 1562.	17		88
Jun. 18, 1557.	Dutsheborn, George, Withornsey, May 14, 1553.	15	1	294
May 2, 1560.	Duyffanbye, Agnes, Camylforthe grraynge, par. Draxe, wid., Apl. 7, 1560.	16		55
May 6, 1557.	Dybney, Bryan, Barynston (Holderness), Jan. 5, 1556.	15	1	240
Nov. 26, 1557.	Dyccons, John, Wales, par. Treton, Aug. 12, 1557.	15	2	93
Sep. 26, 1558.	Dycconson, John, Bradfeld, Dec. 10, 1555.	15	3	54
Sep. 30, 1557.	——, John, Northcave, Aug. 12, 1557.	15	1	327
Oct. 8, 1556.	Dyckens, John, Bonney (Notts.), Jun. 15, 1556.	15	1	152
Sep. 30, 1557.	Dyckenson, Richard, Shelfe, par. Halyfax, Feb. 8, 1556.	15	1	324
May 24, 1563.	Dyconson, Robert, Carleton (bur. Snayth), Apl. 3, 1 Eliz.	17		249
Nov. 5, 1554.	Dycson, Robert, Ryppon, butcher, Aug. 29, 1554.	14		291
Dec. 31, 1561.	Dyghton, John, Ackton, par. Spofforthe, Nov. 26, 1561.	17		26
July 3, 1567.	——, Steven, Slingisbie, Dec. 16, 1566.	17		668
Apl. 13, 1559.	Dyghttone, John, Befford, husbandman, Sep. 17, 1558.	15	3	344
Oct. 3, 1565.	Dykonson, John, Wakefeild, May 13, 1563.	17		481
Mar. 9, 1558.	Dyksonn, Richard, Wheldrake, July 20, 1558.	15	3	158
Apl. 28, 1558.	Dylcocke, Nicholas, Hensall (bur. Snayth), Dec. 15, 1557.	15	2	226
Apl. 16, 1562.	Dylcoke, Ales, Armethorpe, widow, gentyllwoman, Aug. 10, 1561.	17		171
Sep. 30, 1557.	——, John, Armethorpe, gentleman, Jun. 26, 1557.	15	1	368
Jun. 7, 1560.	Dymelton, William, Gemlinge, par. Foiston, Jun. 5, 1559.	16		78

A.D. 1554 TO 1568.

		Vol.	Pt.	Fol.
Dec. 13, 1557.	Dymonde, George, Wakefelde, clothyer, Sep. 12, 1557.	15	2	53
Dec. 3, 1560.	———, Olyver, Wakefeld, July 18, 1560.	16		132
Jan. 23, 1561.	Dyneley, Arthure, Swillyngton, gentleman, May 3, 1558.	17		20
Sep. 30, 1556.	Dynes, Edward, Lowthrope, husbandman, July 10, 1556.	15	1	133
Aug. 6, 1567.	Dynewell, Thomas, Cottingham, labourer. Mar. 18, 1566.	17		698
May 6, 1557.	———, Thomas, Twenge, Nov. 22, 1556.	15	1	249
Nov. 26, 1557.	Dyngley, Richard, Doncaster, Jun. 6, 1556.	15	2	91
May 2, 1555.	Dynmand, George, Skamston, par. Rillington, 1555.	14		29
Feb. 7, 1555.	Dynmor, Thomas, Over Catton, Jan. 31, 1555.	15	1	6
May 17, 1567.	Dynmore, John, Sutton on Darwent, husbandman, Dec. 26, 1566.	17		647
Oct. 2, 1561.	———, William, Newton (bur. Wilberfosse), July 30, 1561.	17		44
Jun. 15, 1557.	Dynnys, Alison, Hoddelston (bur. Sherburne), widow, May 26, 1557.	15	1	292
Jun. 28, 1558.	———, Thomas, Newton (bur. Wilberfosse), husbn., May 27, 1558.	15	2	341
July 8, 1560.	Dynyson, John, Earllesheaton, par. Dewsberie, May 23, 1560.	16		90
May 4, 1558.	Dyrrye, Robert, senr., Bingham (Notts.), husbandman, Dec. 8, 1557.	15	2	265
Apl. 16, 1567.	Dyson, Jane, Waikfeld, widow, Mar. 17, 1566.	17		623
Oct. 2, 1566.	———, John, Stubbinge, par. Rawmarshe, husbn., Jun. 21, 1566.	17		578
Apl. 20, 1564.	———, Thomas, Rawmershe, Feb. 3, 1560.	17		324
Oct. 2, 1567.	Dysone, John, Dalton, par. Heton, July 17, 1567.	17		717
Nov. 29, 1557.	Dyxson, John, Skelton (bur. Danby), May 12. 1557.	15	2	94
Jan. 22, 1562.	Ealand, Robert, Gylbathorpe, par. Rotherham, Oct. 6, 1562.	17		143
Jan. 20, 1561.	Easbye, Stephen, Pomfret, alderman, Dec. 12, 1561.	17		23
Dec. 8, 1566.	Easinwold, John, Elvington, labourer, May 24, 1566.	17		601
Oct. 20, 1558.	Easterbie, Robert, Topliffe, May 22, 1558.	15	2	346
Apl. 16, 1567.	Eastun (Registered Hestun), Francis, Hollum in Holderness, July 10, 1566.	17		634
May 18, 1559.	Eastwood, Nicholas, Fyshelake, Aug. 16, 1558.	15	3	399
Sep. 12, 1561.	1 Ebytsonne, William, Newhall, par. Bilbrough, labr. Apl. 8, 1561.	17		49
Jun. 27, 1567.	Eddrington, Richard, Holme in Spaldingmore, Nov. 12, 1566.	17		660
Aug. 2, 1560.	Eden, Henry, Loundecotte, par. Kyrkedaill, Mar. 23, 1559.	16		98
Oct. 12, 1558.	Edmonson, John (bur. Nottingham), slater, Aug. 2, 1558.	15	3	228
Apl. 20, 1559.	Edmunson, Agnes, Knesall (Notts.), Oct. 8, 1558.	15	3	305
Apl. 26, 1560.	Edrington als. Causon, Henry, Heworthe, Sep. 4, 1557.	16		33
Oct. 27, 1557.	——— als. Causon, Henry, Heworthe, York, Sep. 4, 1557.	15	1	365
July 8, 1557.	Edward, Antony (bur. Synnyngton), Jun. 12, 1556.	15	1	306
Jun. 25, 1560.	———, Jennat, Cawton (bur. Gyllinge), Oct. 8, 1558.	16		87
Oct. 25, 1558.	———, Robert, Cawton in Ridall, husbandman, Sep. 2, 1558.	15	3	237
Oct. 25, 1558.	———, Robert, Nunyngton, par. Stangrave, Sep. 17, 1558.	15	3	237
Jun. 17, 1561.	Edwardes, Edmond, New Malton, burgense, Jun. 2, 3 Eliz.	17		71
Jan. 23, 1562.	Edwyn, Oswyn, York, marchaunt, Dec. 7, 1562.	17		144
May 13, 1557.	Efam, Thomas, Eperston (Notts.), husbandman, Feb. 24, 1557.	15	1	223
Apl. 23, 1566.	Eggilsfeild, John, Sutton on Darwent, esq. ———, 1564.	17		511
Feb. 9, 1557.	Eggylfelde, Steven, Catweke, Dec. 18, 1557.	15	2	123
May 10, 1559.	Eglesfeild, Anne, Barton, par. Crambum, widow, Feb. 27, 1558.	15	3	387
May 10, 1559.	Eglesfeld, Thomas, Barton, par. Crambum, Jun. 22, 1558.	15	3	386
May 27, 1562.	Egleston, Margaret, par. Skipse, Jun. 12, 1560.	17		101
Jan. 28, 1562.	———, Robert, Gemlinge, par. Foston, Oct. 19, 1562.	17		146
July 2, 1561.	Egliston, Rowland, Burton Agnes, labourer, Dec. 9, 1560.	17		78
May 5, 1568.	Egremonde, Edward, Howke, Aug. 8, 1567.	17		793
Oct. 6, 1557.	Eire, Robert, Litell Hodsocke, par. Blythe (Notts.), July 26, 1557.	15	2	11
Jun. 3, 1558.	Eland, John, Thrynscoo, husbandman, Sep. 30, 1556.	15	2	339
Feb. 6, 1558.	———, Thomas, Carleton (bur. Snathe), Dec. 21, 1558.	15	3	264
May 9, 1565.	Elande, Elizabeth, Gilberthorphill, par. Rotherham, Feb. 13, 1564.	17		427
Oct. 16, 1557.	———, John, Carleton nere Snathe, gentleman, Sep. 9, 1557.	15	1	365
July 18, 1555.	———, Rose, Kingston on Hull, widow, Adm.	14		263
Nov. 11, 1557.	Elcote, Alison, Preston (Holderness), July 2, 1557.	15	2	98
July 12, 1554.	Elden, Thomas, Sherifhoton, gentleman, Jun. 1, 1 Mary.	14		249
Jun. 9, 1563.	Eldrethe, Thomas, Ottringham, Mar. 15, 1562.	17		254
Apl. 24, 1554.	Elethorpe, Thomas, Thek in Holme in Spawdingmore, Apl. 1, 1554.	14		61
Apl. 17, 1567.	Eliete, Robert, Molstcrofte, husbandman, Mar. 4, 1566.	17		639

1 See Ibotson.

		Vol.	Pt.	Fol.
Apl. 6, 1560.	Ellaker, Thomas, Lysset, gentleman, Mar. 12, 1557.	16		27
Oct. 21, 1554.	Ellatson, Alice, Whitwell, par. Crambum, widow, Oct. 19, 1553.	14		50
Oct. 3, 1560.	Ellell, Henry, Skyrden, par. Bolton, July 22, 1559.	16		119
Apl. 19, 1564.	——, Richard, Holden, par. Bolton nighe Bowland, Dec. 3, 1563.	17		331
Jun. 11, 1556.	Ellerby, John, Moresome (bur. Skelton), May 23, 1556.	15	1	57
Feb. 7, 1567.	Ellerker, James, Warter, Aug. 6, 1567.	17		757
Jun. 11, 1562.	——, Sir Rauff, Risbye (bur. Rowley), knight, Sep. 22, 1559.	17		91
Feb. 6, 1558.	Elles, Alice (bur. Thurnskoo), widow, Sep. 20, 1558.	15	3	254
Sep. 1, 1563.	——, John, Hymyngfelde, par. Darfelde, Jun. 22, 1563.	17		203
Apl. 26, 1558.	——, John, Ledes, Dec. 20, 1557.	15	2	233
Jun. 3, 1564.	Ellesse, John, Arthington, par. Addell, husbandman, Mar. 12, 1563.	17		347
Nov. 13, 1556.	Ellethorpe, Elizabeth, Theckes, par. Holme in Spaldingmore, Sep. 4, 1556.	15	1	110
Mar. 8, 1566.	——, Thomas, Holme in Spaldingmore, Nov. 20, 1566.	17		513
Dec. 1, 1558.	Ellethrope, Richard, Holme in Spaldingmore, Aug. 14, 1558.	15	3	146
May 2, 1566.	Ellingthorppe, Thomas, Holgill, par. Gisbourne, 1566.	17		529
July 15, 1567.	Ellinthropp, William, Gaysgill (bur. Gysburne), July 2, 1567.	17		676
Dec. 22, 1556.	Elliott, George, Tykhill, labourer, Sep. 21, 1556.	15	1	83
Sep. 18, 1565.	Ellis, Charles, Medope in Bradfeild, May 2, 1565.	17		467
Oct. 3, 1555.	——, Christopher, Foston on Wold, Jan. 16, 1555.	14		17
Dec. 17, 1557.	Ellene, Pigburne, par. Brodsworthe, widow, Nov. 6, 1557.	15	2	39
May 7, 1567.	——, George, Welborne, par. Bulmer, Apl. 17, 1567.	17		646
Jun. 22, 1568.	——, Henry, Barwicke in Elmet, Jun. 1, 9 Eliz.	17		818
May 4, 1558.	——, James, Brynsley, par. Greysley (Notts.), Feb. 24, 1557.	15	2	270
May 31, 1557.	——, John, Bentlaie, par. Arksey, Apl. 21, 1557.	15	1	262
Oct. 30, 1556.	——, John, Conystret, York, July 26, 1556.	15	1	106
Apl. 24, 1567.	——, Richard, Brymysley, par. Greasley (Notts.), Mar. 30, 1566.	17		643
Sep. 3, 1566.	——, Richard (bur. Kirkbemysperton), Jun. 2, 1566.	17		571
July 11, 1558.	——, Richard, Sylkestone (bur. Fyshelacke), Feb. 10, 1557.	15	2	320
Aug. 12, 1566.	——, Richard, Thurnscoye, husbandman, May 5, 1566.	17		566
Oct. 5, 1564.	——, Robert, Goldthorp, par. Bolton on Derne, May 9, 1564.	17		377
Nov. 8, 1557.	——, Thomas, Bolton on Darne, Aug. 29, 1557.	15	2	110
Apl. 22, 1555.	——, Thomas, Bradford, July 3, 1553.	14		123
Dec. 2, 1562.	——, Thomas, Doncaster, gentleman, Apl. 4, 1562.	17		133
May 4, 1557.	——, William, Burghwallis, smythe, Jan. 20, 1556.	15	1	276
Dec. 1, 1563.	——, William, Doncaster, July 1, 1563.	17		306
Jun. 20, 1568.	——, William, North Collingham (Notts.), Jun. 3, 1568.	17		831
Jun. 23, 1558.	——, William, Spaldington (bur. Bubwith), May 14, 1558.	15	2	340
Apl. 19, 1564.	Ellison, Henry, Haltongyll, par. Ernclyf, Oct. 1, 1563.	17		328
Aug. 1, 1565.	——, Henry, Marston als. Huton Wansley, Jun. 6, 1564.	17		455
May 2, 1566.	——, Umfrey, Litton, par. Erneclif, Oct. 30, 1565.	17		530
May 2, 1566.	Ellistonns, William, senr., Halifax, Sep. 17, 1565.	17		534
Jan. 12, 1558.	Ellow, William, Bishopburton, Nov. 16, 1558.	15	3	193
Nov. 19, 1563.	Ellsted, Henry, Eskrige, cooke, Dec. 15, 1562.	17		303
Mar. 13, 1558.	Ellvis, John, Wylsycke (bur. Tykhill), Oct. 21, 1558.	15	3	163
No date.	Ellwes, Richard, Kirk Sandall, yeoman, July 11, 1554.	14		85
Dec. 15, 1557.	Ellwes, William, Askam (Notts.), farmer, Oct. 5, 1557.	15	2	58
Feb. 17, 1557.	Ellwys, Ellen, Kyrke Sandall, Oct. 4, 1557.	15	2	141
May 12, 1559.	Ellycarr, Dame Jane, Hawtemprice, par. Kirke Elly, Sep. 18, 1558.	15	3	392
May 18, 1559.	Ellys, John, Calthorne, Mar. 2, 1558.	15	3	397
Apl. 16, 1562.	——, John, Calthorne, Mar. 2, 1558.	17		174
July 4, 1556.	——, Richard, Pigborne, par. Brodesworthe, May 24, 1556.	15	1	53
Jan. 11, 1557.	——, William, Wetherneweke, husbandman, Sep. 30, 1557.	15	2	74
Sep. 29, 1563.	Ellysson, William, Berden (bur. Bolton), Mar. 11, 1562.	17		277
Jan. 15, 1557.	Elmesley, Guye, Cawood, yeoman, Nov. 12, 1557.	15	2	82
Aug. 2, 1561.	Elome, Richard, Hensall, par. Snathe, husbandman, Jan. 1, 1559.	17		64
May 5, 1558.	Elstonne, Richard, Eperstone (Notts.), Apl. 30, 1557.	15	2	282
Feb. penult., 1556.	Elsworth, Thomas (bur. Ripon), Feb. 11, 1556.	15	1	181
Apl. 20, 1559.	Elton, Margaret, North Wheatley (Notts.), widow, Dec. 28, 1558.	15	3	367
Nov. 6, 1557.	——, William, Claworth (Notts.), Aug. 15, 1557.	15	2	108
Feb. 13, 1565.	Elwicke, Anne, Seaton, May 16, 1560.	17		500
Feb. 4, 1557.	——, John, Seaton, Nov. 29, 1557.	15	2	163

A.D. 1554 TO 1568.

		Vol.	Pt.	Fol.
Feb. 10, 1557.	Elwood, Robert, Watton, yeoman, Jan. 14, 1557.	15	2	150
May 6, 1560.	Elwoode, Robert, Bolande house, par. Watton, Aug. 5, 1557.	16		73
Sep. 29, 1563.	Elyat, Esabell, Howton Pannall, widow, July 23, 1563.	17		284
Apl. 28, 1563.	Elyed, Robert, Scorbrough, Mar. 1, 1562.	17		236
Aug. 16, 1555.	Elyot, William, Lethome, husbandman, Jan. 19, 1554.	14		205
Apl. 24, 1556.	Elyote, William, Southburtone, Mar. 8, 1555.	15	1	24
Mar. 1, 1554.	Elyotson, Henry, Est Halsume, Dec. 21, 1554.	14		300
Apl. 23, 1556.	Elyotsone, Robert, Owtthorne, Feb. 9, 1555.	15	1	25
Sep. 30, 1557.	Elyott, George, Brerley (bur. Fellchurche), Jun. 1, 1557.	15	1	368
Jun. 22, 1556.	——, John, Brackan, par. Kylnewyke, May 28, 1556.	15	1	50
Dec. 13, 1557.	——, John, Snytall (bur. Normanton), Nov. 10, 1557.	15	2	52
Feb. 17, 1557.	——, Richard, Derfeld, husbandman, Dec. 16, 1557.	15	2	138
Jun. 10, 1557.	——, Thomas, Southburton, husbandman, Mar. 4, 1557.	15	1	270
Oct. 7, 1558.	Elyson, Thomas, Marston, husbandman, Feb. 20, 1557.	15	3	92
Nov. 8, 1557.	Embrye, Robert, Tykhyll, Jun. 27, 1557.	15	2	110
Apl. 17, 1567.	Emerson, Robert, Southeburton, Mar. 31, 1566.	17		640
Nov. 26, 1558.	Emisson, Robert, Holme in Spaldingmore, Sep. 28, 1558.	15	3	122
July 9, 1560.	Emondson, John, York, yeoman, Jun. 24, 4 and 5 Philip and Mary.	16		91
May 19, 1559.	Emonson, Robert, Roclyf (bur. Snathe), Mar. 14, 1558.	15	3	428
Feb. 5, 1557.	Empson, John, Swynflete, par. Whytgyfte, Nov. 5, 1557.	15	2	164
Jan. 21, 1557.	Emson, Anne, Newton Kyme, widow, Sep. 10, 1557.	15	2	155
Jun. 28, 1554.	——, John, Newton Kyme, Jan. 22, 1553.	14		141
No date.	——, Richard, Barkston, par. Sherborne, Jan. 10, 1553.	14		96
May 19, 1559.	—— als. Watsone, Herrie, Howke, Jan. 27, 1558.	15	3	427
Dec. 30, 1556.	Emyson, William, Holme in Spaldingmore, Sep. 1, 1556.	15	1	86
May 9, 1558.	Emysonne, Thomas, Holme in Spaldingmore, Oct. 25, 1557.	15	2	279
Aug. 6, 1563.	Emysson, William, Holme Spalingmore, Feb. 28, 1562.	17		213
Apl. 16, 1567.	Endicke, Agnes, Rysse, Jan. 30, 1566.	17		633
Aug. 21, 1561.	——, Thomas, Well (bur. Beverley), Oct. 10, 1559.	17		56
May 9, 1563.	Endike, Peter, Risse, Jan. 28, 1562.	17		255
Apl. 7, 1557.	Endycke, Thomas, Thurne (bur. Beverley), Feb. 11, 1556.	15	1	205
May 4, 1558.	Enfray, Thomas (bur. Skarrington, Notts.), July 30, 1557.	15	2	210
Mar. 20, 1558.	¹England, John, Goldthorpe, par. Bolton on Derne, Oct. 30, 1558.	15	3	248
May 2, 1566.	——, Richard, Morehouse, par. Hoton Panell, Nov. 2, 1565.	17		522
Jun. 20, 1566.	——, Robert, Cauthorne, Apl. 14, 1566.	17		558
May 2, 1555.	——, Robert, Gildersum, par. Batleye, Mar. 20, 1555.	14		30
Oct. 12, 1564.	Eperston, Edmund, Lenton (Notts.), Dec. 6, 1563.	17		392
Mar. 15, 1560.	Erbe, Christopher (bur. Ascame, Notts.), ——, 1560.	16		168
Aug. 12, 1567.	Erdley, Martyn, Flambrughe, Mar. 20, 1567.	17		694
May 18, 1564.	Ermytage, Giles, Honley, par. Almonburie, Feb. 7, 1563.	17		343
Feb. 17, 1557.	Ernyng, John, Notton, par. Ruston, Dec. 31, 1556.	15	2	138
Jan. 9, 1562.	Errington, Anthony, Skelton in Cleveland, Jun. 15, 1562.	17		141
Mar. 9, 1558.	Esenwood, John, Wheldrake, Oct. 8, 1558.	15	3	158
Apl. 30, 1565.	Eshe, John, York, marchant, Jan. 19, 1564.	17		419
Aug. 20, 1554.	——, Peter, York, fisher, Jun. 30, 1554.	14		148
Aug. 12, 1567.	——, William, Harpham, husbandman, May 12, 1567.	17		692
Jun. 2, 1558.	Eskrige, Robert, Ryse, Apl. 6, 1558.	15	2	311
Jan. 13, 1567.	Esome, Agnes, Felkirke, widow, July 2, 1567.	17		750
Apl. 17, 1567.	Esshe, John, Granshay (bur. Lynton), Jan. 3, 1566.	17		619
Oct. 1, 1562.	Essheburne, William, Esington (Holderness), Jun. 18, 1562.	17		113
Jan. 21, 1554.	Essington, Christopher, Harton (bur. Bossall), husbn., Dec. 2, 1554.	14		297
Aug. 6, 1567.	Estaby, Robert, Southe Dalton, labourer, Mar. 13, 1565.	17		702
Apl. 12, 1559.	Estburne, John, Bradforth, Feb. 13, 1558.	15	3	339
Mar. 4, 1560.	Estoft, Thomas, Skorbroughe. *No date.*	16		164
Feb. 19, 1557.	Estofte, Edmund, Redenes (bur. Whytgyfte), gent., Aug. 12, 1557.	15	2	146
Feb. 15, 1565.	Eston, John, Kirkbe in Grendallith, Jan. 27, 1565.	17		498
(?1554).	——, Thomas, Eston (bur. Lethome), husbandman, July 8, ——.	14		47
Apl. 13, 1559.	Estrope, Roger, Withornwyke, husbandman, Oct. 20, 1558.	15	3	346
Apl. 20, 1559.	Estwod, Immyn, widow of John E., Bollum (Notts.), Aug. 27, 1558.	15	3	307
Apl. 20, 1559.	——, John, Bollum, par. Clarebrough (Notts.), yeom., Aug. 23, 1558.	15	3	306

¹ See also under letters I and Y.

A.D. 1554 TO 1568.

		Vol.	Pt.	Fol.
July 23, 1560.	Estwod, John, Heptonstall, May 29, 1560.	16		95
Nov.21, 1554.	———, John, the Shore in Stansfeilde, yeoman, Sep. 14, 1554.	14		294
Oct. 12, 1564.	Estwode, John, Blithe (Notts.), labourer, May 6, 1564.	17		389
May 5, 1558.	Estwood, Anne, Kirketon (Notts.), widow, Jan. 1, 1557.	15	2	241
Apl. 26, 1558.	———, Jeffray, Campsall, Nov. 16, 1557.	15	2	223
July 16, 1562.	———, Richard, Myxenden, par. Halifax, Jun. 4, 1562.	17		96
May 30, 1560.	Etrington, Thomas, Holme in Spaldingmore, May 2, 1560.	16		70
Feb. 4, 1558.	Eure, Agnes, wid. of Sir Raulfe E., knight, Jun. 28, 1558.	15	3	262
Mar.24, 1561.	Eustaige, James, Overton, yeoman, Feb. 16, 1561.	17		5
July 18, 1554.	Evans, Elizabeth, Kingstone on Hull, widow, Jan. 23, 1551.	14		146
July 18, 1550.	———, John, Kyngston on Hull. maryner, Feb. 13, 1550.	14		145
Nov.21, 1557(6).	Everat, James, Rocliff (bur. Snaithe), clerke, Aug. 21, 1556.	15	1	116
Mar.30, 1554.	Everingham, Christopher, Egglesfeld, May 5, 1553.	14		105
Nov.17, 1556.	———, Sir William, preist at Ecclesfeld, July 16, 1556.	15	1	115
Nov.18, 1555.	Evers, Lyonell, Snaythe, gentleman, Aug. 16, 1555.	14		181
Oct. 2, 1560.	———, William, Garfurthe, May 2, 1559.	16		114
Jun. 17, 1558.	Everyngham, John, Egbroughe (bur. Kellington), Mar. 6, 1557.	15	2	334
Oct. 6, 1558.	Exilbe, Thomas, senr., Spofforth, Aug. 12, 1558.	15	3	90
July 31, 1557.	Exyllbye, Jenat, Spofforthe, July 3, 1557.	15	1	321
No date.	Eycope, Robert (bur. St. Margaret's Westminster, mentions Tadcaster, &c.), Jan. 31, 1552.	14		103
Apl. 26, 1558.	Eyre, Robert, Dongworth in Bradfeld, Jan. 21, 1557.	15	2	224
Oct. 7, 1563.	———, William.(bur. Est Retford, Notts.), ———, 1562.	17		294
Mar.22, 1558.	Eyrnsha, William, Holme par. Almonbury, July 1, 1558.	15	3	295
Apl. 12, 1554.	Facebie, William, senr., Hubie (bur.Sutton in Galtresse), Jun.29,1553.	14		57
Nov.22, 1561.	———, William, Wystowe, Dec. 25, 1560.	17		33
Jan. 11, 1557.	Facebye, Thomas, Cawoodd, Dec. 1, 1557.	15	2	77
Apl. 17, 1567.	Facetts, John, Otterburne, par. Kirkbie Malham, Feb. 27, 9 Eliz.	17		619
Dec.16, 1557.	Falconer, Margerye, "Southsshyr" [Skyrley] in Holderness, widow, Nov. 24, 1557.	15	2	43
Dec.16, 1557.	———, Peter, Northe Skirley (bur. Swyne), husbn., Nov. 10, 1557.	15	2	44
Jun.25, 1568.	Falkener, Robert, Kirley (bur. Swyne), husbandman, Apl. 26, 1568.	17		811
Dec.15, 1557.	Fall. Alis, Aukeley (bur. Fynnynglay, Notts.), Aug. 28, 1557.	15	2	59
May 6, 1563.	Fallowell, Richard, Cathrope, par. Loudam (Notts.), veverr, Mar.21, 156[2-]3.	17		242
Apl. 10, 1559.	Fang, Thomas, Doncaster, Nov. 26, 1558.	15	3	328
Jan. 20, 1557.	Fange, William, Sykehouse, par. Fyshelaike, Oct. 11, 1557.	15	2	66
Apl. 3, 1559.	Farding, William, Rudston, husbandman, Apl. 8, 1558.	15	3	315
Oct. 2, 1560.	Fardinge, John, Dringe (bur. Skipsey), Jun. 12, 1560.	16		117
Apl. 8, 1566.	———, Roger, par. St. Mary, Castlegate, York, Apl. 5, 1566.	17		508
Aug.12, 1567.	Farefax, Thomas, Burton Agnes, gentleman, Nov. 22, 1559.	17		694
Aug. 6, 1567.	Farer, Alice, Neswicke (bur. Bainton), spinster, Feb. 10, 1566.	17		700
Jan. 11, 1557.	Farlay, William, Northe Frodyngham, Nov. 11, 1557.	15	2	75
May 26, 1563.	Farneworthe, Reanalde, Tickhill, Mar. 31, 1563.	17		250
Jun. 6, 1566.	Farrer, Henry, Hallifax, marchaunt, Jan. 24, 1565.	17		553
Oct. 25, 1558.	Fartham, John, York, lockesmyth, Aug. 10, 1558.	15	3	94
Jun. 14, 1564.	Farthinge, John, Brygam (bur. Foston), Mar. 14, 1563.	17		353
Oct. 6, 1558.	Farum, John, Whetlay, par. Doncaster, husbandman, Dec. 21, 1557.	15	3	47
Aug.29, 1556.	Faukes, John, Ferneley (bur. Otley), gentleman, Aug. 4, 1556.	15	1	63
May 2, 1560.	Faull, Richard, Roclyffe (bur. Snaythe), Mar. 6, 1559.	16		53
Sep. 12, 1567.	Fauset, George, Tockwithe, par. Bilton, Jan. 8, 1566.	17		706
Aug.27, 1567.	Fausyt, John, Leistingam, May 19, 1567.	17		696
May 2, 1555.	Favell, John, Burnesall, Mar. 12, 1554.	14		127
May 2, 1555.	Fawced, John, Lytton (bur. Arneclif), July 4, 1554.	14		25
Aug.27, 1554.	Fawcet, Robert, York, wever, Aug. 6, 1554.	14		270
Apl. 8, 1559.	Fawcett, Thomas, Dalton (bur. Topliffe), Dec. 21, 1558.	15	3	321
Apl. 11, 1559.	Fawchomeberd, Leonard, Streythouses, par. Bylbrough, Jan.18,1558.	15	3	334
Dec.16, 1557.	Fawconer, George, South Skirley (bur. Swyne), husbn., Nov. 14, 1557.	15	2	44
Oct. 10, 1566.	Fawkener, Robert (bur. Stapleforde, Notts.), May 28, 1566.	17		594
Nov.12, 1556.	———, Thomas, Huntslett (bur. Ledes), Sep. 22, 1554.	15	1	114
1551.	Fawkes, Anthony, Yorke, gentleman, July 19, 1551.	14		16
May 5, 1558.	———, Janett, Carleton in Lynryke (Notts.), widow, Dec. 2, 1557.	15	2	334

A.D. 1554 TO 1568.

Date	Entry	Vol.	Pt.	Fol.
Oct. 6, 1557.	Fawkes, John, Carleton in Lyndreke (Notts.), Aug. 18, 1557.	15	2	14
May 26, 1563.	Fawley, Agnes, Tankerslay, widow, Dec. 28, 1562.	17		249
July 6, 1560.	Fawll, John, Thor[n]ton (bur. Foston), yeoman, July 12, 1559.	16		88
Apl. 28, 1558.	Fawlle, William, Roclyffe (bur. Snayth), Nov. 1, 1557.	15	2	227
May 18, 1559.	Fawsehed, Issabell, Byltone, widow, Apl. 14, 1559.	15	3	409
Apl. 16, 1562.	Fawteroppe, Robert, Rome (bur. Gyglesweke), Mar. 19, 1561.	17		190
Feb. 9, 1557.	Fayrbarne, John, Attynwicke, husbandman, Sep. 23, 1557.	15	2	119
Aug. 12, 1566.	———, John, Roose (bur. Nafferton), walker, Feb. 13, 1565.	17		569
July 11, 1558.	Fayrebarne, Robert, Sykehowse, par. Fyshelacke, Apl. 8, 1558.	15	2	320
Dec. 31, 1560.	Fayrechilde, William, Wheldrike, Mar. 8, 1558.	16		137
Dec. 3, 1558.	Fayrefax, Sir William, Steton, par. Bolton Percye, knt., Mar. 3, 1557.	15	3	149
Mar. 11, 1562.	Fayrer, Thomas, Nesweke, par. Baynton, husbandman, Jan. 10, 1562.	17		156
May 6, 1559.	Fayrewether, Christopher (bur. Kirk Myspertone), Nov. 9, 1558.	15	3	381
Feb. 9, 1561.	Fayrwether, Alice, York, widow, Nov. 10, 1561.	17		9
Oct. 5, 1560.	———, William, York, Sep. 16, 1560.	16		120
Mar. 20, 1558.	Fean (Frean in Register), John, Burwne (bur. Brayton), husbn. Jan. 23, 1558.	15	3	291
Feb. ult., 1561.	Feasor, Roger, Waddyngton, Jun. 19, 1558.	17		18
May 2, 1560.	———, William, Riston in Holderness, Sep. 23, 1559.	16		50
Mar. 13, 1556.	Federston, Thomas, Selby, labourer, Jan. 15, 1556.	15	1	184
Oct. 10, 1566.	Feding, Richard, Flintam (Notts.), husbandman, July 16, 1565.	17		595
Oct. 8, 1562.	Fedynge, William, Flyntam (Notts.), husbandman, Nov. 7, 1560.	17		119
Jan. 20, 1562.	Feild, Edward, Awthwike on the streite, Dec. 15, 1562.	17		143
Feb. 18, 1556.	———, Rauff, Beistone (bur. Ledes), Nov. 25, 1556.	15	1	161
Oct. 5, 1558.	———, Robert, Crofton, Aug. 20, 1558.	15	3	63
Oct. 1, 1556.	Feilde, Margaret, Beistone, par. Ledes, Aug. 8, 1556.	15	1	135
Oct. 8, 1567.	———, Nicholas, Nottingham, inholder, Jun. 13, 1567.	17		725
July 31, 1556.	———, Raufe, Beiston, par. Leides, corvessore, Feb. 1, 1556.	15	1	60
Dec. 22, 1557.	———, Richard, Halyfax, Oct. 8, 1557.	15	2	71
Sep. 9, 1561.	Feirthe, Thomas, Risheworthe, par. Eland, Apl. 27, 1561.	17		51
July 6, 1554.	Feisher, William, Seaseye, husbandman, Jan. 8, 1552.	14		116
May 2, 1555.	Felden, James (bur. Gisburn), Nov. 14, 1553.	14		28
Oct. 19, 1558.	Fell, Thomas, Morton Bankes, par. Bynglay, Aug. 18, 1558.	15	3	96
Feb. 6, 1558.	Felle, Thomas, Brayton, husbandman, Nov. 20, 1558.	15	3	263
Oct. 12, 1558.	Felowe (Registered Selow), Thomas, Selston, Notts., Aug. 21, 1558.	15	3	14
Oct. 3, 1554.	Felton, Elyn (bur. Swyne), Mar. 12, 1553.	14		43
Aug. 6, 1567.	Fenbie, John, Holme on Wold, Apl. 22, 1567.	17		700
Jun. 10, 1557.	———, Robert, Holme on Wolde, Apl. 22, 1557.	15	1	274
Jan. 17, 1557.	Fenbye, John, Brigham, par. Foston, Aug. 15, 1557.	15	2	62
Apl. 26, 1558.	———, Thomas, Skerne, husbandman, Jan. 2, 1557.	15	2	221
Sep. 30, 1558.	Fenne, Thomas, Burne, par. Braton, husbandman, Sep. 10, 1558.	15	3	89
Oct. 12, 1558.	Fennes, Robert, Colston Bassett (Notts.), Feb. 7, 1558.	15	3	31
Mar. 16, 1556.	Fenteman, Adame, Ossindyke (bur. Rither), Jan. 18, 1556.	15	1	186
Oct. 21, 1561.	———, Peter (bur. Rither), Aug. 18, 1558.	17		44
Jun. 20, 1566.	Fenton, Agnes, Galmeton, widow, Apl. 21, 1565.	17		555
Jan. 21, 1556.	———, Anne, widow of Richard F. of Sheffeld, May 18, 1552.	15	1	90
Apl. 20, 1564.	———, Elizabeth, Hubie, Feb. 26, 1563.	17		334
May 5, 1558.	———, George, Lounde, par. Sutton (Notts.), Jan. 21, 1557.	15	2	332
Oct. 12, 1558.	———, Nicolas, Huknall Torkerd (Notts.), gent., Aug. 3, 1557.	15	3	28
Sep. 16, 1564.	———, Robert, Willerbie, Jun. 1, 1564.	17		363
Aug. 16, 1560.	Fentres, Richard, Carleton (bur. Quorleton). *No date.*	16		102
Jan. 22, 1557.	———, Richard, Danbye, Jun. 23, 1557.	15	2	156
Dec. 1, 1557.	Fentyman, John, Swyllingtonn, husbandman, Aug. 18, 1557.	15	2	85
Dec. 11, 1554.	Fenwicke, John, New Malton, Oct. 14, 1554.	14		95
Oct. 5, 1564.	———, Lawrance, Rednes (bur. Whytegyft), May 20, 1563.	17		367
Nov. 10, 1556.	Ferborne, ———, Ledsham, Mar. 28, 1556.	15	2	103
Apl. 28, 1558.	Ferding, John, Owlston, par. Cokeswold, Dec. 25, 1557.	15	2	230
Aug. 16, 1560.	Ferebie, William, Rinsweke, par. Hynderwell, May 22, 1560.	16		102
Apl. 30, 1556.	Fereman, William, Gonertone, par. Blesbye (Notts.), Mar. 17, 1555.	15	1	33
Jan. 24, 1558.	Feribie (Registered Afferby), James, par. Thourne, Nov. 26, 1558.	15	3	218
May 13, 1557.	Fermworth, Rawffe, Shelforde (Notts.), Mar. 15, 1556.	15	1	229
Oct. 3, 1564.	Fern, Elizabeth, Leedes, widow, Sep. 14, 1563.	17		366

A.D. 1554 TO 1568.

		Vol.	Pt.	Fol.
Feb. 1, 1558.	Ferne, Sir William, York, priest, Oct. 20, 1558.	15	3	23
July 8, 1560.	Ferneley, Robert, Dewesburye, Feb. 5, 1558.	16		90
Apl. 27, 1564.	Ferneworthe, Richard, Kirkbie in Ashefeld (Notts.), husbn., Dec. 25, 1562.	17		339
Apl. 27, 1558.	Fernlay, Thomas. Heaton, par. Brystall, Oct. 3, 1557.	15	2	193
Oct. 6, 1557.	Ferns, William, Tryswell (Notts.), May 16, 1557.	15	2	9
Apl. 16, 1567.	Ferrer, Henry, Heptonstall, clothier, Mar. 22, 1565.	17		629
Apl. 16, 1567.	——, James, Sourbie, par. Halifax, Sep. 5, 1566.	17		627
Jun. 4, 1561.	Ferror, Robert, Heptunstall, May 15, 1560.	17		68
Oct. 2, 1560.	Ferrowe, Walter, Horseforthe, par. Giselay, 1560.	16		113
Dec.22, 1556.	Feryby, Robert, Thorne, Aug. 16, 1556.	15	1	80
Apl. 27, 1564.	Feryman, William, Flyntam (Notts.), husbandman, May 20, 1563.	17		341
Dec. 5, 1567.	Fesar, Margaret, Catwicke, Jun. 10, 1567.	17		741
Oct. 5, 1558.	Feshweke, Agnes, Carleton (bur. Whorleton), July 13, 1558.	15	3	70
Nov.28, 1567.	Fetchett,Frauncis,Gearbe(bur.St.JohnBapt.,Caton),Apl.31(sic),1567.	17		738
Jan. 21, 1558.	Fether, Agnes, Bradforde, widow, Nov. 8, 1558.	15	3	21
Mat.17, 1556.	Fetherston, Thomas, Myddlethorpe (by York), husbn., Mar. 4, 1556.	15	1	186
Dec. 16, 1557.	Fetherstone, John (bur. Swyne), Sep. 13, 4 and 5 Philip and Mary.	15	2	46
Mar. 4, 1562.	————, Peter, Marton (bur. Swyne), Aug. 25, 1562.	17		149
Mar.17, 1556.	——, Robert, Beverlaye, Dec. 16, 1556.	15	1	189
Jan. 30, 1566.	———, Robert, West Newton (bur. Aldbrughe), Feb. 26, 1565.	17		609
Apl. 26, 1559.	Fewler, William, Semer, Jan. 10, 1558.	15	3	311
July 26, 1558.	Fewsande, William, Gansted (bur. Swyne), husbn., Jan. 30 [1557?].	15	3	11
Aug.14, 1556.	Fewster, Isabell, Gilling, widow, May 21, 1556.	15	1	61
Aug.31, 1556.	——, Jenet, Gillyng, July 26, 1556.	15	1	63
Dec.18, 1557.	Feylde, Christopher, Waikefelde, marcer, July 8, 1557.	15	2	37
Jan. 26, 1556.	Fichwilliam, Humfrey, Clayworth (Notts.), esq., Aug. 12, 1556.	15	1	91
Jan. 28, 1558.	Fidling, Thomas (bur. Wistow), Oct. 20, 1558.	15	3	220
May 20, 1556.	Fidlinge,William,Hirst Cowertney (bur.Birkyn),husbn.,Apl.18,1556.	15	1	35
Feb. 8, 1564.	Filiskirke, John, junr. (York, dying at Hovingham), May 3, 1564.	17		405
Sep. 28, 1560.	Fillingham, Bartilmewe, Cropwell Byshoppe (Notts.), Mar. 10, 1559.	16		106
Mar.14, 1560.	——, Robert, Bushopp Cropwell (Notts.), Nov. 21, 1560.	16		164
May 13, 1558.	Firmarie, Thomas, Egmanton (Notts.), Feb. 6, 1553.	15	3	18
No date.	Firthe, John, Sheffelde, Feb. 4, 1553.	14		81
Apl. 28, 1558.	Fische, John, Hull, smyth, Nov. 25, 1557.	15	2	219
May 6, 1557.	Fishe, John, Cowicke, par. Snaith, Jan. 6, 1556.	15	1	242
Jan. 12, 1558.	Fisher, Edmund, Aram (bur. Leckinfeld), husbn., Aug. 22, 1558.	15	3	199
Sep. 28, 1560.	——, Henry, Arnall (Notts.), husbandman, Dec. 12, 1559.	16		109
Oct. 12, 1558.	——, Henry, Bingham in Vale (Notts.), husbandman, July 29, 1558.	15	3	33
Dec. 9, 1556.	——, John, Eisington in Holdernes, Oct. 8, 1556.	15	1	197
Jun. 25, 1557.	——, John, Whorlowe Lane, par. Shefeld, Apl. 3, 1557.	15	1	296
May 21, 1560.	Fishere, Robert. Everingham, Apl. 1, 1560.	16		67
Jan. 21, 1556.	Fissher, John, Shefeld, Sep. 20, 1556.	15	1	89
May 31, 1557.	Fixbie, William, Rostonne, Dec. 16, 1556.	15	1	210
Sep. 13, 1558.	Fladder, Anne, Chapelltowne, par. Leedes, widow, Aug. 4, 1558.	15	3	104
Oct. 4, 1558.	——, John, Chapeltowne, par. Leides, Mar. 7, 155[7]8.	15	3	57
Oct. 2, 1560.	Fladders, John, Weston, Sep. 8, 1560.	16		113
Jun. 20, 1568.	Flader, John, Myrfeld, yeoman, Oct. 23, 1567.	17		827
Jun. 18, 1560.	Flansall, Jennat (bur. Sherburne), Apl. 15, 1556.	16		86
May 2, 1555.	Flecher, James, Heptonstall, Mar. 18, 1554.	14		31
Oct. 4, 1564.	——, William, Mytton (bur. Waddington), July 4, 1564.	17		370
Mar.18, 1556.	Flee, Robert, parson of Leven in Holderness, Dec. 10, 1556.	15	1	189
May 5, 1558.	Fleer, Thomas, Sowth Collingham (Notts.), husbn., Nov. 9, 1557.	15	2	260
May 5, 1557.	Fleming, Agnes, Croston (St. Ursula), widow, Mar. 5, 1556.	15	1	212
Jan. 22, 1557.	Flemyng, Richard, Danbye, Aug. 24, 1557.	15	2	156
Aug. 8, 1562.	Flemynge, John, Sharellston (bur. Warmfeld), husbn., May 14, 4 Eliz.	17		103
July 8, 1567.	Flenton, Thomas, Hull, marchaunt draper, Apl. 23, 1567.	17		669
May 9, 1565.	Flesher, Alice, Wymmerslay, widow, Feb. 1, 1563.	17		423
Jan. 13, 1558.	——, Thomas, Tuxford (Notts.), labourer, Nov. 20, 1558.	15	3	185
Mar.22, 1558.	Fleshere, William, Wommersley, husbandman, Nov. 20, 1558.	15	3	294
Mar.29, 1568.	Flessher, William, Ottley, May 12, 1567.	17		769
Feb. 17, 1557.	Fletcher, Christopher. Athewycke by the Streat, Dec. 27, 1557.	15	2	140

		Vol.	Pt.	Fol.
Apl. 6, 1558.	Fletcher, Elizabeth, Eddershorpe (bur. Derfelde), wid., Dec. 17, 1557.	15	2	181
Oct. 1, 1563.	———, George, Mykelefeld (bur. Shereburne), labr., Jan, 17, 1563.	17		289
Mar. 21, 1564.	———, John, Felkirke, Nov. 3, 1564.	17		410
Feb. 6, 1558.	———, John, Sowthkirkbie, Nov. 12, 1558.	15	3	253
July 19, 1566.	———, Leonard (bur. Billisdaill), May 12, 1566.	17		562
Jan. 30, 1555.	———, Richard, Aithweke by the Streat, Dec. 18, 1555.	15	1	4
May 2, 1566.	———, Richard, Commondaill, par. Gysburne, Oct. 4, 1565.	17		539
Mar. 20, 1565.	———, . Richard, Wheatley, par. Doncaster, Jan. 31, 1565.	17		506
Oct. 5, 1558.	———, Robert, Darrinton, Aug. 16, 1558.	15	3	66
Apl. 6, 1558.	———, Robert, Derfelde, Oct. 19, 1557.	15	2	184
Nov. 8, 1557.	———, Robert, Edderthroppe (bur. Derfeld), Aug. 11, 1557.	15	2	113
Dec. 2, 1561.	———, Roger, Southe Kyrkbye, July 4, 1560.	17		31
Apl. 16, 1562.	———, Thomas, Heshillwod, par. Skipton, Jan. 21, 156[1-]2.	17		188
Oct. 5, 1558.	———, Thomas, Robyn Hoodes Bay, par. Filing, panyerman, Aug. 16, 1558.	15	3	43
Sep. 26, 1558.	———, Ursula, Adwike by strete, widow, Apl. 18, 1558.	15	3	49
Sep. 18, 1564.	———, William, Hull, keilman, Mar. 25, 1564.	17		362
May 7, 1554,	———, William, Prestlinge (Halifax), clothier, Sep. 23, 1553.	14		3
Apl. 3, 1559.	Flinton, Robert, Brompton, Jan. 15, 1558.	15	3	318
Mar. 9, 1565.	Flower, Jennet, widow of John F., Wheldricke, Sep. 26, 1561.	17		501
Oct. 12, 1558.	———, Johan, Barnestonne, par. Langar (Notts.), wid., Aug. 2, 1558.	15	2	372
Oct. 12, 1564.	———, John, Langar (Notts.), yeoman, Oct. 23, 1562.	17		391
Jun. 29, 1561.	———, John, Wheldricke, yeoman, Sep. 1, 1556.	17		85
Oct. 11, 1565.	———, Margaret, Barnston (bur. Langer, Notts.), wid., Mar. 27, 1565.	17		471
Oct. 6, 1557.	———, Richard, Everton, Sep. 15, 1557.	15	2	10
May 13, 1568.	———, Thomas, Langor (Notts.), gentleman, Apl. 19, 1567.	17		801
Oct. 12, 1564.	———, William, Barniston, par. Langer (Notts.), Aug. 14, 1561.	17		390
Jun. 12, 1557.	Flownrie, Thomas, Selbie, tanner, Jan, 15, 1556.	15	1	275
Apl. 7, 1554.	Flowre, Christopher, Wheldrake, Feb. 22, 1554.	14		157
Mar. 23, 1557.	Flunders (or Flaunders), John, Sutton in Holderness, Dec. 28, 1557.	15	2	171
Oct. 20, 1561.	Flynt, John, Topclyf, Aug. 27, 1561.	17		46
Aug. 4, 1562.	———, Richard, Wistow, Jan. 7, 1558.	17		104
Oct. 19, 1557.	Flyntofte, Margaret, Langton, Sep. 16, 1557.	15	1	364
May 2, 1566.	Fodderley, James, Newham, par. Whitbie, Feb. 18, 1565.	17		540
Mar. 20, 1558.	Folly, Henry, Tankesley, May 18, 1558.	15	3	246
May 22, 1557.	Fontance, Richard, Marston, Feb. 7, 1557.	15	1	258
Apl. 27, 1557.	Fontaynes, Agnes, Marston, Mar. 31, 1557.	15	1	208
Oct. 16, 1558.	Ford, John, North Cave, Apl. 1, 1558.	15	2	354
Nov. 6, 1566.	Foreste, Thomas, Tockwith, May 4, 1562.	17		597
Jun. 13, 1588.	Forman, John, Maister of the Maysons, York Cathedral, Mar. 20, 1557.	15	2	286
Mar. 15, 1558.	———, Robert, Estcottynwith, par. Aughton, Aug. 27, 1558.	15	3	241
Jan. 20, 1557.	Fornis, Percevall, Awston, Nov. 6, 1557.	15	2	65
Dec. 1, 1557.	Forrest, Thomas, senr., Leythley, husbandman, Nov. 18, 1557.	15	2	86
Jan. 6, 1564.	Forster, Antony, Newark, esq., Codicil, Mar. 7, 1 Eliz.	15	3	305
Apl. 20, 1559.	———, Antony, Newarke (Notts.), esq., Feb. 23, 1 Eliz.	15	3	302
Nov. 22, 1557.	———, William, Catterton (bur. Tadcaster), husbn., Sep. 20, 1557.	15	2	103
Oct. 4, 1564.	Fort, John, Newby (bur. Gisborne), husbn., 1564.	17		370
No date.	Foster, Agnes, Hye Melton, widow, Mar. 30, 1554.	14		87
Sep. 30, 1556.	———, Alexander, South Frothingham, par. Outthorne, labr. May 2, 1556.	15	1	139
Oct. 16, 1558.	———, Anthony, North Cave, Apl. 13, 1558.	15	2	366
Feb. 24, 1566.	———, Sir Arthur, Sinnyngton, Sep. 18, 1564.	17		614
Oct. 13, 1558.	———, Edward, Torworth (bur. Blyth, Notts.), husbn., Sep. 20, 1558.	15	2	378
Mar. 15, 1562.	———, George, Kyldill, Jan. 16, 1561.	17		163
Feb. 4, 1557.	———, Isabell, Holme in Spaldingmore, Dec. 26, 1557.	15	2	164
Nov. 28, 1567.	———, James, Brigham (bur. Foston), July 31, 1567.	17		738
Jun. 7, 1560.	———, James, Scawbie, Oct. 9, 1559.	16		78
May 5, 1568.	———, James, Stanforthe Underhill (bur. Gyglesweke), Aug. 3, 1567.	17		785
Jun. 29, 1561.	———, Jennet, Crambum, widow, May 27, 1561.	17		85
Feb. 6, 1558.	———, Jennet, Gemlinge (bur. Fostone), Oct. 20, 1558.	15	3	262
Oct. 6, 1557.	———, Johan, Blythe (Notts.), widow, May 3, 1557.	15	2	13
Sep. 21, 1557.	———, John, Cadeby, par. Sprodbroughe, Feb. ult., 1556.	15	1	353

A.D. 1554 TO 1568.

		Vol.	Pt.	Fol.
Oct. 3, 1561.	Foster, John, Conystrope (bur. Barton), Aug. 20, 1561.	17		35
Feb. 1, 1563.	———, John, Ederthorpe, par. Derfeld, yeoman, Dec. 17, 1563.	17		314
Feb. 4, 1557.	———, John, Holme in Spaldingmore, Nov. 12, 1557.	15	2	163
Dec.10, 1562.	———, John, Howton on Darwyn (bur. Howton on hill), May18,1562.	17		132
Mar. 4, 1560.	———, John, Northe Cave, husbandman, Jun. 15, 1560.	16		166
May 2, 1555.	———, John, Wenschall (bur. Gigleswicke), Nov. 24, 1554.	14		25
May 13, 1557.	———, John, Woodborow (Notts.), Apl. 3, 1557.	15	1	236
Jun. 2, 1562.	———, Lawrance, Synnyngton, Nov. 3, 1557.	17		86
May 18, 1559.	———, Margaret, Barnesley, Dec. 5, 1558.	15	3	405
Nov. 8, 1557.	———, Margere, Cadbye par. Sprotbrugh, widow, Apl. 5, 1557.	15	2	112
Nov.20, 1555.	———, Margery (bur. St. Bantong, Bantong, ? St. Andr., Bainton), 1555.	14		182
May 15, 1555.	———, Richard, Beforthe, husbandman, Apl. 26, 1555.	14		237
July 5, 1557.	———, Richard, Bentlay (bur. Arkesay), Jun. 1, 1557.	15	1	302
Feb. 14, 1565.	———, Richard, Howkke, Aug. 20, 1565.	17		613
Oct. 10, 1560.	———, Robert, Notton, par Roiston, husbandman, Nov. 3, 1558.	16		126
Mar. 7, 1566.	———. Robert, Roos. husbandman, Dec. 15, 1566.	17		515
Nov.13, 1567.	———, Robert, Tadcaster, gentleman, Jun. 25, 1567.	17		734
Mar.31, 1558.	———, Robert, Teryngton, Jan. 25, 1557.	15	2	177
Apl. 16, 1554.	———, Robert, Whenby, Dec. 2, 1553.	14		58
May 9, 1560.	———, Robert, Wydmerpole (Notts.), Mar. 4, 1559.	16		61
Dec.22, 1566.	———, Roger, Cadby (bur. Sprotburghe), July 3, 1556.	15	1	84
Jan. 11, 1557.	———, Thomas, Aram, par. Attingweke, husbn., Nov. 17, 1557.	15	2	75
Oct. 4, 1564.	———, Thomas, Bolton nye Bollnad, ———, 1563.	17		370
May 17, 1557.	———, Thomas, Gemblinge, par. Foston, Mar. 25, 1557.	15	1	245
Mar.18, 1566.	———, Thomas, Wilberfosse, labourer, Mar. 20, 1564.	17		512
Apl. 20, 1564.	———, William, Arram (bur. Attenweke), yeoman.	17		333
July 19, 1557.	———, William, Blith (Notts.), draper, Apl. 11, 1557.	15	1	313
Sep. 21, 1557.	———, William, Caydbye, par. Sprodbroght, Feb. 18, 1556.	15	1	355
Mar. 4, 1562.	———, William, Grisestrupe (bur. Fylaie), Jan. 20, 1562.	17		154
Sep. 21, 1557.	———, William, senr., Highe Melton, Apl. 21, 1557.	15	1	352
Apl. 14, 1559.	———, William, Knapton, par Wyntryngham, Dec. 1, 1558.	15	3	351
Aug. 6, 1567.	———, William, Neswicke (bur. Bainton), singleman, Feb. 23, 1566.	17		701
July 8, 1556.	———, William, Northe Cave, May 22, 1556.	15	1	54
Mar.10, 1555.	———, William, Nottingham, Sep. 19, 1559.	14		230
May 2, 1566.	———, William, Rymiswell (bur. Owthorne), Jan. 6, 1566.	17		527
Dec.18, 1565.	———, William, St. Savior's, York, clerk, Dec. 10, 1565.	17		493
Jan. 31, 1557.	———, William, York, inolder, Dec. 15, 1557.	15	2	160
Feb. 11, 1565.	——— als. Lelley, William, Risse, Oct. 14, 1565.	17		499
Mar. 6, 1556.	Fosterde, Henry, Blithe (Notts.), Nov. 13, 1555.	15	1	183
July 15, 1556.	Fosther, William, Catton, Mar. 10, 1555.	15	1	56
Jan. 27, 1567.	Fothergaill, Jeffraye, York (bur. in the Mynster), locksmythe, Dec. 3, 1567.	17		755
May 9, 1560.	Fotted, Richard, Gertton (Notts.), husbandman, Oct. 18, 1559.	16		59
Apl. 10, 1559.	Fournes, Edmonde, Barmbie on Donne, Sep. 16, 1558.	15	3	328
Sep. 10, 1556.	———, Richard, Ayrynden (bur. Heptonstall), Aug. 30, 1556.	15	1	65
Nov. 3, 1558.	———, Thomas, Sknowgaytehede, par. Kirkeburton, Mar.17,1557.	15	3	156
May 10, 1559.	Fouster, Thomas. Bransebye, tanner, Aug 16, 1558.	15	3	388
Feb. 16, 1558.	Fowe, Richard, Gillinge, serving man. Aug. 22, 1557.	15	3	273
Oct. 3, 1564.	Fowler, John, junr., Rigton (bur. Kirkebeoverblaus), labr., Feb.1,1561.	17		366
No date.	———, John, Sherborne in Harfurth ligh, Sep. 16, 1554.	14		90
May 18, 1559.	———, Mawde, Wellingley, par. Tikhill, widow, Nov. 12. 1558.	15	3	418
Dec.15, 1557.	———, Thomas, Claworthe (Notts.), husbandman, Nov. 21, 1557.	15	2	60
Aug. 7, 1566.	———, William, Rygton, par. Kirkbie Overblause, July 2, 1566	17		565
Feb. 25, 1558.	Fox, Edward, Hutton Wanysley *als.* Marstone, Oct. 3, 1558.	15	3	280
May 5, 1559.	—, Hugh, Gromeston, par. Gilling, Oct. 20, 1557.	15	3	380
Dec. 3, 1557.	—. Jennett, Worsburghe daill, Oct. 16, 1557.	15	2	49
May 18, 1559.	—, John (bur. Austefeild), Mar. 2, 1558.	15	3	422
Aug.18, 1562.	—, John, Hacknes, Nov. 1, 1561.	17		106
Jan. 20, 1558.	—, John, Hovingham, July 28, 1558.	15	3	213
Dec.22, 1556.	—, John, Worsburghe daill, Sep. 7, 1556.	15	1	85
Feb. 21, 1558.	—, Lowrens, Roclyf (bur. Snathe), Oct. 1, 1558.	15	3	277

A.D. 1554 TO 1568.

		Vol.	Pt.	Fol.
Feb. 15, 1558.	Fox, Michell, Uppton (bur. Skypsey). Dec. 5, 1558.	15	3	271
Feb. penult., 1556.	—, Richard (bur. S. Mary's, ? Hull), Jan. 4, 1556.	15	1	180
May 6, 1559.	—, Richard, Meakill Daltone (bur. Aitone), Oct. 30, 1558.	15	3	383
Mar. 1, 1557.	—, Robert, Hovyngham, husbandman, Oct. 1, 1557.	15	2	171
Aug. 16, 1560.	—, Thomas, Mydleton (bur. Rudbye), May 18, 1560.	16		102
July 2, 1558.	—, Thomas, Threske, Jun. 28, 1558.	15	2	342
Jan. 22, 1562.	—, William, Helaugh, York, Jan. 3, 1562.	17		143
May 10, 1559.	Foxcroft, John, Cononley (bur. Kyldwycke), Apl. 1, 1559.	15	3	386
Oct. 26, 1562.	Foxe, James, Thorpe (bur. Amplefoith) gentleman, Jan 23, 1561.	17		126
July 19, 1567.	——, John, Barkesland in Eland, husbandman, Apl. 27, 1567.	17		680
Aug. 6, 1566.	——, John, Everley, par. Hacknes, ——, 1566.	17		565
Jun. 27, 1562.	——, Miles, Hovingham, husbandman, Mar. 3, 1557.	17		88
Jun. 22, 1568.	——, Robert, Lowthorpe, May 27, 1567.	17		824
Mar. 20, 1558.	——, Roger, Roclyf (bur. Snayth), Sep. 18, 1558.	15	3	250
May 17, 1565.	——, William, Burton Joce (Notts.), husbandman, Feb. 19, 1564.	17		440
Aug. 22, 1554.	Foxgaile, Robert, York, butcher, May 22, 1554.	14		269
Apl. 6, 1560.	Foxgaill, John, Styllingflete Jun. 6, 1559.	16		30
Sep. 26, 1560.	——, Symon, senr., York, butcher, Aug. 30, 1560.	16		105
July 9, 1560.	——, William, York, bocher, Jan. 19, 1559.	16		92
Apl. [?8], 1559.	France, Alice, Lyttle Howghton (bur. Darfeld), Dec. 27, 1558.	15	3	323
Oct. 20, 1558.	——, Margaret, Catton (bur. Topliffe), widow, Aug. 27, 1558.	15	2	346
Apl. 20, 1564.	——, William, Slagheweythe, par. Huddersfeild, clothier, Oct. 3, 1563.	17		327
Jan. 12, 1557.	Francis, Godfray, South Dalton, Nov. 10, 1557.	15	2	80
Apl. 19, 1566.	——, Robert, Burnebie, Oct. 19, 1565.	17		510
Dec. 3, 1567.	Franckelande, Jane (bur. Brompton), Nov. 17, 1567.	17		743
Dec. 4, 1567.	Franckland, Peter (bur. Brompton), Nov. 13, 1567.	17		743
July 4, 1565.	——, William, Beverley, shearman, Mar. 2, 1564.	17		448
Apl. 19, 1559.	Franke, John, Ratlyf on Trent (Notts.), Nov. 12, 1558.	15	3	374
May 18, 1559.	——, John, Swyne, Apl. 10, 1558.	15	3	408
Apl. 26, 1554.	——, Parcivall, Pontefracte, gentleman, Aug. 26, 1 Mary.	14		64
Jun. 20, 1566.	——, Thomas, Grauncemore (bur. Burton Agnes), yeom., Mar. 20, 1565.	17		555
Nov. 29, 1558.	——, William, Hooton on Darwent, Sep. 26, 1558.	15	3	123
Apl. 13, 1559.	——, William, Over Hooton, Aug. 9, 1558.	15	3	342
Sep. 29, 1563.	Frankelande, Roger, Heaton (bur. Reilston), May 13, 1563.	17		278
Oct. 13, 1558.	Frankis, Roger, Harworth (Notts.), gentleman, Jan. 2, 1557.	15	2	379
No date.	Frankishe, Katherine, Barlay Hoyle, par. Wyntworth, wid., Oct. 4, 1554.	14		84
May 9, 1563.	Frankland, Elizabeth, Danby, Mar. 15, 1562.	17		256
Oct. 4, 1564.	——, Elizabeth, Haltongill, par. Ernecliff, Apl. 30, 1564.	17		370
May 5, 1568.	——, George, Glaisdayll, par. Danbye, yeoman, Jan. 25, 10 Eliz.	17		773
Aug. 1, 1562.	——, Henry, Danby, Feb, 6, 1561.	17		103
Apl. 6, 1554.	——, Lionell, Haltongill (bur. Arneclif), Jan. 8, 1553.	14		153
May 23, 1562.	——, John, Esington (All Hallows), Apl. 28, 1562.	17		108
Apl. 17, 1567.	——, John, Heaton (bur. Relston), Feb. 24, 1566.	17		622
Oct. 27, 1564.	——, Peter, Danbye, May 28, 1561.	17		393
May 9, 1563.	——, Robert, Danbie, Jan. 7, 1562.	17		256
No date.	——, Thomas, Nether Popilton, Oct. 15, 1553.	14		101
Mar. 2, 1554.	Franklande, Thomas, Nether Popilton, Oct. 15, 1553.	14		299
Mar. 27, 1560.	Franklinge, Peter, Maske in Cleveland, Feb. 7, 1559.	16		22
Dec. 2, 1562.	Frankyshe, Bryan, Barlyehole (Doncaster), July 20, 1562.	17		131
Apl. 6, 1559.	Frape, Roger, Brodholme (Notts.), yeoman, July 24, 1558.	15	3	319
Aug. 6, 1567.	Frauncis, Richard, Southe Dalton, husbandman, Mar. 27, 1567.	17		701
Mar. 20, 1558.	Frean (Fean, Act Book), John, Burwne (bur. Brayton), husbandman, Jan. 23, 1558.	15	3	291
Feb. 10, 1561.	Frear, John, Westowe, husbandman, Sep. 16, 1561.	17		10
Sep. 29, 1563.	——, Robert, Rudston, husbandman, Mar. 30, 1563.	17		275
Jan. 3, 1558.	Freare, John, Wakefeld, clothmaker, Jun. 25, 1554.	15	3	35
Apl. 8, 1559.	——, Philippe, Sutton, par. St. Felix, Aug. 27, 1558.	15	3	323
May 15, 1563.	——, Robert, Sandhuton, par. Bossall, yong man, Jun. 18, 1558.	17		248
Dec. 1, 1558.	——, Thomas, Sandhowton, Aug. 16, 1558.	15	3	80
Apl. 27, 1564.	Freber, Thomas, Mathersaythorpe (Notts.), July 29, 1563.	17		336
Aug. 1, 1562.	Frecell, Rauf, Marske, husbandman, July 2, 1562.	17		103

A.D. 1554 TO 1568.

	Vol.	Pt.	Fol.
Apl. 27, 1563. Frecell, Thomas, Marske, husbandman, Feb, 14, 1562.	17		225
Jun. 22, 1568. Freckley. John, Nafferton, Feb. 5, 1567.	17		821
Apl. 28, 1563. Freer, John (bur. Kirkebie on Wiske), Dec. 16, 1562.	17		240
May 18, 1564. 1 Freman,Christopher (Dickering Act Bk.), bur. St.Alban's, Wodstreite, London, Oct. 12, 1563.	17		344
Dec. 2, 1557. ——, Johan (bur. Awghton), widow, Aug. 15. 1557.	15	2	87
Jun. 18, 1557. — — -, Peter, Spaldington (bur. Aughton), husbn., Feb. 25, 1557.	15	1	293
Mar.15, 1558. ——, Peter, Spaldington, labourer, Feb. 9, 155[8]9.	15	3	167
Jan. 26, 1564. ——, Robert, Spaldington (bur. Bubwithe), carpenter, Jan. 6, 1564.	17		406
Dec.18, 1560. ——, Thomas, Allerton Bywater, yeoman, Apl. 18, 1560.	16		137
Aug.12, 1562. ——, Thomas, Bubwithe, July 20, 1562.	17		104
Oct. 7, 1558. ——, Thomas, Spaldington (bur. Aughton), Aug. 20, 1558.	15	3	91
Nov. 7, 1558. ——, William, York, glover, Aug. 11, 1558.	15	3	95
May 25, 1554. Frere, John, Drax, Apl. 7, 1554.	14		7
Mar. 4, 1562. Friston, James, Flixton, par. Foolton, Nov. 11, 1562.	17		153
Jun. 13. 1554. ——, Thomas, Feriebrige, gent. (bur. Friston), Mar. 29, 1554.	14		3
Mar. 9, 1557. Frithe, John, Rybondeyn in Barkislande, par. Halyfax, Nov. 23, 1557.	15	2	130
Mar. 2, 1555. ——, Robert, Ardeyn, par. Bingley, Feb. 20, 1555.	15	1	12
Sep. 1, 1563. Frobyser, Francis, Doncaster, esq., Jun. 2, 1563.	17		206
May 4, 1557. Frobysher, Thomas, priest, Brodsworthe, Feb. ult., 1556.	15	1	279
Jan. 19, 1556. Frome, Robert (bur. our lady, Hull), Dec. 3, 1556.	15	1	89
Feb.22, 1555. Frost, George, Esingwold, Jan. 10, 1555.	15	1	7
Sep. 26, 1558. ——, Robert (bur. Baddesworth), gentleman, July 10, 1558.	15	3	51
Mar.30, 1560. ——. Thomas, Owlston, par. Cokeswolde, July 9, 1559.	16		25
Oct. 1, 1557. Frykley, Robert, preyst, Kyrkesmeaton, Sep. 10, 1557.	15	1	367
Oct. 1, 1567. Frythe, Edmund, Barkesland (bur. Eland), talior, Aug. 27, 1567.	17		716
Jan. 29, 1556. Fryston, Agnes. Folketon, Nov. 30, 1556.	15	1	93
Feb. 6, 1558. ——, Jaymes, Cowicke, par. Snaithe, Nov. 5, 1558.	15	3	264
May 5, 1564. ——, Robert, Snathe, Jun. 28, 1563.	17		342
Jan. 29, 1556. ——, Thomas, Folketon, Nov. 11. 1556.	15	1	93
Mar. 2, 1555. Frystone, Isabell, wid. of Wm. F., Feribrige (bur. Watter Fryston), Aug. 13, 1554.	15	1	9
Oct. 2, 1560. Fuget (or Suget),Richard,Wrelton,par.Mydleton,husbn.,July 13,1560.	16		110
Oct. 10, 1566. Fulbecke, Margaret, North Clifton (Notts.), widow, May 13, 1566.	17		589
Apl. 27, 1558. Fuller, John, Morton Bankes, par. Bingley, Feb. 20, 1557	15	2	203
May 5, 1558. Fullwood, John, Newarke (Notts.), tanner, Nov. 3, 1557.	15	2	261
May 19, 1559. ——, Nicholas, Eastwaite (Notts.), husbandman, Jan. 12, 1558.	15	3	432
Oct. 17, 1556. Fulthorpe, Margaret, Kirkebye Knoll, widow, Jun. 26, 1556.	15	1	71
Oct. 9, 1561. Fulwod, Thomas, Myssen (Notts.), Sep. 8, 1561.	17		42
Apl. 20, 1559. Fulwode, Alys, Everton (Notts.), widow, Nov. 21, 1558.	15	3	366
Oct. 8, 1556. Fulwood, Robert, Brynslaye, par. Greslaye (Notts.), Jun. 2, 1556.	15	1	152
May 13, 1568. ——, William, Bawtrye, Feb. 25, 1567.	17		804
Oct. 29, 1554. Fulwoodd, Richard, Newarke (Notts.), butcher, Oct. 14, 1553.	14		283
May 29, 1556. Funtance, Henry, Garfourthe, Aug. 29, 1555.	15	1	38
Apl. 27, 1558. ——, Robert, Gargrave, Nov. 17, 1557.	15	2	201
Feb. 14, 1558. ——, William, Ruffurthe. Oct. 19, 1558.	15	3	266
Sep. 30, 1564. Furnes, Robert, Northorpe, par. Myrfeld. *No date.*	17		362
Oct. 6, 1558. Furth, Sir John, Bolton on Derne, clerke, Sep. 9, 1558.	15	3	25
Apl. 20, 1564. Furthe, Robert, Elland, Jan. 28, 1563.	17		328
Jun. 11, 1567. Fuster, William, Sutton (bur. Brotherton), Apl. 28, 1567.	17		659
Feb. 24, 1563. Fusum (Fewson, Act Book), Thomas, Sprotley, Aug. 8, 1563.	17		320
May 17, 1557. Futie, Edward, Buckton (bur. Bempton), husbandman, Mar. 2, 1556.	15	1	245
Sep. 12, 1562. Fuvstehope (Snewsthopp, Act Book), Vincent, Buttercram, wevar, Jun. 30, 1561.	17		108
Mar. 1, 1559. Fuyster, Christopher, Kilburne, Aug. 16, 1557.	16		4
May 5, 1558. Fydeane, William, Sutton on Lounde (Notts.), Aug. 1, 1556.	15	2	241
Mar.20, 1558. Fydlyng, William, Selbie, tannere, Jan. 22, 1558.	15	3	251
Oct. 8, 1567. Fyllingham, Richard, Wysehall (Notts.), husbn., Dec. 4, 1566.	17		727
May 5, 1558. Fynnyngle, Thomas, Myssyn (Notts.), Nov. 2, 1557.	15	2	243

1 Previous Prob. Prerog. Court, Cantr., ult. April, 1564.

		Vol.	Pt.	Fol.
May 13, 1557.	Fynyngham, Nicolas, Auklaie (bur. Finningley, Notts.), husbn., Nov. 27, 1556.	15	1	234
Apl. 21, 1562.	Fyper (Fixer in Act Book), William, prest, vicar of Overhall in Northwell (Notts.), Dec. 11, 1560.	17		175
May 26, 1563.	Fyrthe, John, Carter Knowlle, par. Sheaffeld, Oct. 28, 1562.	17		251
Feb. 1, 1563.	———, John, Fyrthehouse, par. Eland, Oct. 13, 1563.	17		313
Feb. 6, 1558.	———, Ranald, Chaple Haddilsey (bur. Birkyn), Oct. 18, 1558.	15	3	265
May 29, 1563.	Fyscher, Elizabeth, Sheryfhoton, widow, Nov. 3, 1560.	17		252
Mar. 7, 1566.	Fyshe, Jennet, Holmpton, Sep. 13, 1566.	17		515
Oct. 11, 1565.	———, Richard, Nottingham, butcher, Feb. 3, 1564.	17		479
Apl. 24, 1567.	———, Richard, Nottingham, Feb. 3, 1566.	17		643
Apl. 20, 1559.	———, Robert, Claworth (Notts.), husbandman, Dec. 28, 1558.	15	3	365
July 16, 1562.	Fyshebourne, Nicholas, Waikefeild, clothier, Jun. 9, 1562.	17		96
Jun. 12, 1567.	Fysher, Bridgett, Essyngton in Holderness, widow, Mar. 12, 1566.	17		663
May 10, 1554.	———, Christopher, Sherefhoton, Feb. 22, 1554.	14		137
May 2, 1566.	———, Edmund, Besswicke (bur. Kilnwicke), labr., Feb. 1, 1565.	17		537
Mar. 22, 1557.	———, Elizabeth (bur. Seysey), widow, May 16, 1557.	15	2	175
Aug. 7, 1561.	———, Felis, Roclif, par. Snayth, widow, July 24, 2 Eliz.	17		65
Oct. 6, 1557.	———, John, Gotham (Notts.), yeoman, July 19, 1557.	15	2	29
May 25, 1560.	———, John, Kylnweke, labourer, Oct. 5, 1559.	16		67
Feb. 18, 1556.	———, John, Skamstone, par. Ryllington, 1556.	15	1	162
Feb. 25, 1556.	———, Nicholas, Barnesley, glover, Oct. 7, 1556.	15	1	167
Ang. 4, 1558.	———, Nicholas (bur. Beverley), Jun. 21, 1558.	15	3	3
Feb. 6, 1558.	———, Nicoles, Coittes, par. Snathe, Sep. 30, 1557.	15	3	264
Oct. 10, 1566.	———, Richard, Bingham (Notts.), Feb. 25, 1565.	17		592
Jan. 22, 1563.	———, Richard, Skamston, par. Rillington, July 28, 1563.	17		310
May 25, 1554.	———, Thomas, Heyton (bur. Seysay), May 3, 1554.	14		252
May 28, 1560.	———. Thomas, Thorganbie, May 21, 1559.	16		69
Aug. 13, 1555.	———, Thomas, Thorganby, July 22, 1555.	14		24
July 17, 1565.	———, William, Holmpton, Apl. 12, 1565.	17		454
Apl. 8, 1559.	———, William, Sowth Ottrington, Sep. 20, 1558.	15	3	324
Aug. 16, 1560.	Fyshweike, Robert, Huton Rudbye, husbandman, Apl. 24, 1560.	16		103
Nov. 29, 1558.	Fysshe, William, senr., Staneford (bur. Haytefeild), July 8, 1557.	15	3	143
Dec. 14, 1557.	Fyssher, James, Weell (bur. Beverley), Nov. 26, 1557.	15	1	359
Sep. 4, 1557.	———, John, Thormonbye, July 27, 1557.	15	2	118
Aug. 21, 1561.	———, Richard, Scarbroughe, tayler, July 15, 1560.	17		56
Apl. 28, 1558.	———, Thomas, Cowicke, par. Snayth, Jan. 18, 1557.	15	2	229
No date.	Fytzwilliam, Nicholas, Bentley, par. Arksey, gentleman, Nov. 4, 1553.	14		132 & 265
Feb. 18, 1556.	Fyxser, John, Newthorpe (bur. Sheirburne), mylner, Jun. 4, 1555.	15	1	161
Apl. 30, 1556.	Gabitas, John, Tuxforde (Notts.), husbandman, Apl. —, 1556.	15	1	29
May 13, 1557.	Gaile, Richard, Clifton (Notts.), Jan. 23, 1556.	15	1	229
Jun. 14, 1557.	Gaill, Thomas, York, gentleman, Dec. 3, 1556.	15	1	292
Apl. 22, 1556.	Gaire, John, Ferybrigges, par. Pontefracte, Feb. 24, 1555.	15	1	20
Apl. 27, 1563.	Gaitfold, John, Marske, husbandman, Dec. 6, 1562.	17		223
Dec. 2, 1556.	Gaithorne, Robert, Armyne (bur. Howke), May 20, 1555.	15	1	118
Jun. 12, 1557.	———, Thomas, Howcke, May 3, 1557.	15	1	275
Dec. 9, 1561.	Gale, Francis, Acome Grange (bur. Rufforth), esq. Nov. 28, 1561.	17		30
Aug. 27, 1556.	———, George, alderman of York, Jun. 11, 1556.	15	1	62
Mar. 18, 1557.	———, Dame Marye, wid. of Geo. G., alderman of York, Sep. 24, 1557.	15	2	124
Jan. 28, 1558.	———, Thomas, Thornar, Feb. 7, 1557.	15	3	220
Aug. 12, 1566.	Galland, Anthony, Benyngholme, par. Swyne, Mar. 28, 1566.	17		568
Mar. 23, 1557.	———, Barthillmew, Swyne, Jan. 19, 1557.	15	2	154
Jan. 26, 1558.	Gambell or Gamell, Robert, York, Sep. 8, 1558.	15	3	220
Oct. 2, 1555.	Gamble, John, Wheeteleye, par. Doncaster, July 26, 1555.	14		164
Oct. 13, 1558.	———, Thomas, Helstonne neather gaite (Notts.), husbn., Oct. 17, 1557.	15	2	363
Dec. 10, 1562.	Gamell, Richard (bur. Souerbie), 1561.	17		132
May 10, 1559.	———, Robert, Bagby, par. Kerkbie Knowle, July 20, 1558.	15	3	386
Jan. 26, 1558.	——— or Gambell, Robert, York, Sep. 8, 1558	15	3	220
Oct. 12, 1558.	Gamle, Agnes, Sutton (bur. Grannbie, Notts.), widow, Aug. 10, 1558.	15	2	374
Oct. 12, 1558?	Ganaga (Savage, Act Bk.), Agnes (bur. Screaton, Notts.), Aug. 14, 1558.	15	2	373

		Vol.	Pt.	Fol.
Oct. 2, 1567.	Gante, Thomas (bur. Dewisberye), Aug. 5, 1567.	17		717
Apl. 28, 1563.	Ganton, Jennet, Wetheronwicke, Dec. —, 1562.	17		238
July 12, 1564.	Gantonne, John, Seglistorne, husbandman, Mar. 7, 1562.	17		357
Oct. 9, 1560.	Garbarey, Robert, Beverley, Apl. 20, 1560.	16		121
Oct. 22, 1560.	Garbot, Bryan, Urton, par. Seymer, labourer, May 28, 1560.	16		126
Aug. 14, 1554.	Garbotte, William, Anlabie, par. Elley, Jun. 14, 1554.	14		146
Mar. 17, 1557.	Garbrey, Jennett, wid. of John G., Beverlay, watterman, Sep. 4, 1557.	15	2	167
July 4, 1565.	———, Mathewe, Beverley, tanner, Apl. 2, 1565.	17		449
May 2, 1560.	Garbut, Alyson, Helme House (bur. Hawnbye), Dec. 23, 1559.	16		34
Apl. 8, 1559.	Garbutt, John, Risdayll in Killisdayle (Billesdaill, Act Bk.), Aug. 28, 1558.	15	3	324
Apl. 11, 1559.	Garbye, Thomas, Saxton, Feb. 1, 1558.	15	3	333
Jan. 12, 1558.	Gardin, George, Scarbroughe, Nov. 10, 1558.	15	3	194
May 16, 1555.	Gardon, Robert, Weswicke (bur. Baynton), husbn., Mar. 8, 1554.	14		238
Sep. 29, 1563.	Garforthe, John, Weston, July 26, 1563.	17		276
Jan. 30, 1556.	Garfurthe, James, Skelton in Galtres, husbandman, Dec. 13, 1554.	15	1	94
May 5, 1558.	Garland, Robert, Walkringham (Notts.), Feb. 2, 1557.	15	2	334
Mar. 4, 1560.	Garleke, Elizabeth, Woodhouse, wid. of Thos. G. (bur. Normanton), Jan. 8, 1560.	16		152
Jan. 3, 1558.	Garlicke, Margaret, West Hardwicke, par. Wragbie, widow, Nov. 2, 1558.	15	3	35
Jun. 22, 1556.	———, Thomas, Wodhowse, par. Normanton, husb., Mar. 23, 2 and 3 Phil. and Mary.	15	1	21
Oct. 13, 1562.	Garlike, Nicholas, Normanton, Sep. 7, 1562.	17		125
July 26, 1557.	Garmane, Isabell, Locton, par. Myddylton, 1553.	15	1	319
Oct. 5, 1564.	Garnet, Elizabeth, Athwicke on strete, widow, Jan. 4, 1563.	17		377
Jan. 13, 1567.	———, Richard, Athwicke on Streite, Sep. 19, 1567.	17		750
Jan. 30, 1555.	Garnett, Thomas, Aithwike by the Strett, Dec. 18, 1555.	15	1	2
Oct. 29, 1554.	Garnon, John, South Carleton, par. S. Muscam (Notts.), gent., Nov. 10, 1552.	14		287
Jun. 9, 1563.	Gartham, Richard, Dunnyngton in Holdernes (St. Nicholas), yeom., Feb. 10, 5 Eliz.	17		254
July 9, 1563.	———, Robert, Humbleton, Oct. 3, 1562.	17		263
Mar. 4, 1560.	———, William, Southeclyffe, par. North Cave, July 2, 1560.	16		165
Jun. 21, 1561.	Garthe, Cuthbert, St. Saviour's, York, Mar. 21, 1561.	17		84
Jan. 12, 1558.	Garthom, Richard, Londesbrough, July 13, 1558.	15	3	200
July 26, 1558.	———, Richard, Preston in Holderness, Jun. 11, 1558.	15	2	380
Feb. 10, 1557.	———, Simon, Sowthcleffe, par. North Cave, Oct. 22, 1557.	15	2	147
Sep. 30, 1556.	———, William, Humbleton in Holderness, ——, 1556.	15	1	142
Jun. 28, 1558.	Garthome, Thomas, Esthorpe, par. Londsburghe, Apl. 26, 1558.	15	2	340
May 18, 1559.	Garton, Elizabeth, Dringhow (bur. Skypsey), Apl. 4, 1559.	15	3	408
Mar. 23, 1557.	———, George, Arnoll, par. Ryston, Sep. 18, 1557.	15	2	122
Oct. 3, 1554.	———, Gregorie, Hollome, Jun. 25, 1554.	14		42
Feb. 5, 1557.	———, Isabell (bur. Skeflynge), Nov. 2, 1557.	15	2	120
Sep. 30, 1556.	———, Jenkyn, Drynghow (bur. Skepsee), husbn., Jun. 19, 1556.	15	1	140
Mar. 23, 1557.	———, John, Attynghweke, husbandman, Jan. 11, 1557.	15	2	173
May 17, 1565.	———, John, Willoby (Notts.), Jan. 17, 1564.	17		438
Jan. 13, 1558.	———, John, Willowbie (Notts.), Mar. 12, 1558.	15	3	180
July 26, 1558.	———, Leonarde, Hollome, Aug. 17, 1558.	15	3	9
Nov. 28, 1558.	———, Margaret, Attinwike, widow, Oct. 3, 1558.	15	3	76
Aug. 13, 1567.	———, Mathewe, Sprotley, husbandman, May 9, 1567.	17		691
Mar. 30, 1559.	———, Richard, Rowth, husbandman, Feb. 24, 1558.	15	3	165
Feb. 9, 1557.	———, Robert, Attingwike, husbandman, Aug. 10, 1557.	15	2	120
Oct. 3, 1554.	———, Robert, Dringhowe (bur. Skipsey), Aug. 7, 1554.	14		44
Sep. 30, 1556.	———, Robert, Skeflinge, Jun. 19, 1556.	15	1	141
May 2, 1566.	———, Thomas, Headon, yeoman, Oct. 13, 7 Eliz.	17		527
Aug. 13, 1567.	———, Thomas, Seaton, par. Seglestorne, Feb. 17, 1566.	17		691
Feb. 6, 1558.	———, William, Nafferton, hubandman, Aug. 12, 1558.	15	3	262
May 18, 1559.	Gartone, Margaret, Dringe (bur. Skipsey), Mar. 31, 1559.	15	3	410
Apl. 24, 1559.	Gartonne, John, Towthrope (bur. Huntyngton), husbn. Aug., 8, 1558.	15	3	364
Oct. 6, 1557.	Gartside, James, Ruddington (bur. Flawforthe, Notts.), July 28, 1557.	15	2	32
Nov. 12, 1556.	Gascoigne, Rauffe, Burnbie, esq., Sep. 23, 1556.	15	1	110

A.D. 1554 TO 1568.

Vol. Pt. Fol.

Apl. 8, 1559.	Gascoigne, Rauffe, Farlington (bur. Sheriffe Hewton), gressman, Feb. 21, 1558.	15	3	323
May 6, 1566.	———, Thomas, Lasingcroft (bur. Barwicke), esq., Jun. 7, 1565.	17		536
Jun. 21, 1567.	———, William, Gawkethorpe (bur. Harwod), esq., May 23, 1567.	17		659
Apl. 17, 1556.	Gascoinge, Bridgett, Bickerton, widow, Mar. 2, 2 & 3 Phil. and Mary.	15	1	16
No date.	Gascon, William, Semer in Pickeringe Lythe, July 18, 1555.	14		16
Dec. 24, 1560.	Gascoynge, John [Old Malton], Nov. 24, 1560.	16		138
Jan. 20, 1558.	Gasken, Christopher, Swynton (bur. Amunderie), Aug. 12, 1558.	15	3	21
Mar. 4, 1560.	Gathorne, Alison, Howke, widow, Aug. 25, 1560.	16		153
May 8, 1563.	———, Robert, Howkke, Apl. 13, 1563.	17		240
Oct. 5, 1558.	Gathrope, Edward (bur. Gargrave), Jun. 28, 1558.	15	3	37
Nov.18, 1555.	Gatynbe, John, Roclyf (bur. Snaythe), July 2, 1555.	14		181
Jun. 15, 1566.	Gaull, Peter, Cottingham, Feb. 24, 1565.	17		552
Oct. 1, 1556.	Gauntt, John, senr., Tikyll, husbandman, Feb. 3, 1555.	15	1	128
Feb.penult.,1556.	Gawde, John, Northe Cave, roper, Oct. 4, 1556.	15	1	180
Oct. 1, 1562.	Gawkeman, Alice, Burneholme, widow, Aug. 25, 1562.	17		118
May 5, 1557.	Gawkroger, Robert, Birstall, Oct. 2, 1556.	15	1	213
Dec.16, 1557.	Gawll, Thomas, Brustweke (bur. Skeklynge), Nov. 11, 1557.	15	2	46
Dec.15, 1557.	Gawskwen, Umfray, Egmanton (Notts.), Oct. 10, 1557.	15	2	57
Apl. 12, 1559.	Gawthrop, Richard, Carlton (Craven), ———, 1558.	15	3	341
Nov.26, 1565.	Gawtre, William, Crambe als. Crambum, Oct. 15, 1565.	17		490 & 549
Sep. 29, 1557.	Gayer, William, Ferybrige (bur. Water fryston), carpenter, Aug. 18, 1557.	15	1	329
Mar. 2, 1554.	Gayle, Robert, Beiston (bur. Ledes), yeoman, Dec. 31, 1554.	14		301
Dec. 1, 1557.	Gavll, William, Hunslett, par. Ledes, Sep. 12, 1556.	15	2	86
July 23, 1558.	Gaythorne, Agnes, Armyn (bur. Snaythe), widow, Dec. 20, 1557.	15	2	384
Mar. 2, 1558.	Gayton, Thomas (bur. Bylton), Dec. 23, 1558.	15	3	281
Mar.30, 1560.	Gebson,John, Cauton,par.Addingbrouth (Notts.),husbn., Jun.11,1559.	16		23
May 4, 1558.	Gee, Raffe, Huckenall Torcard (Notts.), Nov. 12, 1557.	15	2	272
Sep. 30, 1557.	Geeste, Thomas, Thorpe, par. Rotherham, Sep. 5, 1557.	15	1	369
May 12, 1559.	1 Geffrason, Sir William, Cottingham, curet, Mar. 25, 1558.	15	3	392
Mar.14, 1560.	Geige, Margery, Doncaster, widow, Oct. 13, 1560.	16		160
July 2, 1565.	Gelbanke, Elline, Old Malton, Jun. 18, 1565.	17		450
Oct. 7, 1556.	Geliot, John, Serleke, par. Harworthe (Notts.), husbn., Aug. 5, 1556.	15	1	192
Jun. 22, 1568.	Gell, John, Cowthrope, husbandman, Mar. 16, 1567.	17		816
July 23, 1558.	———, John, Estofte, par. Adlyngflott, Mar. 14, 1558.	15	2	385
Mar.15, 1558.	1 Gelletson, Thomas, Ellerton, Sep. 5, 1558.	15	3	168
Mar.20, 1558.	Gelond, Edmund, Staynbrouge, par. Silkestone, Aug. 8, 1558.	15	3	246
Oct. 2, 1554.	Gelsthrope, Thomas, Whatton (Notts.), yeoman, Jun. 10, 1553.	14		196
May 4, 1558.	Gelstropp, Walter, Whatton (Notts.), husbandman, Aug. 9, 1557.	15	2	265
Jan. 10, 1558.	Gelstroppe, Ellen, Eskrigg, Jan. 4, 1558.	15	3	36
July 12, 1566.	———, John (bur. Gaite Fulforthe), Jun. 29, 1566.	17		561
Oct. 7, 1560.	———, John, York, tanner, Aug. 13, 1560.	16		120
Jan. 10, 1558.	———, Richard, Eskrigg, ———, 1558.	15	3	36
July 18, 1566.	Gene, John, Hullocke, par. Kirkeburton, Nov. 16, 1565.	17		562
Mar.15, 1560.	1 Genever, William (bur. Elksley, Notts.), 1560.	16		168
[? Jun. 1558.]	Gennys (Jennys,Act Bk.),Robert,Brighton.par.Bubwythe(incomplete), May 13, 1558.	15	2	215
Oct. 6, 1557.	Gente, Hughe, Gotham (Notts.), July 20, 1557.	15	2	30
Apl. 17, 1554.	Genys, John, Brighton, husbandman, Dec. 28, 1553.	14		59
Sep. 24, 1567.	Gerves, John, Whiston, Jun. 18, 1567.	17		708
May 4, 1557.	———, Thomas, Todweke, Aug. 20, 1556.	15	1	276
Oct. 12, 1558.	Gervis, Robert, Gouthorpe, par Lowdham (Notts.), Apl. 18, 1558.	15	3	27
Oct. 13, 1558.	Gibbon, John, Sibthorpe (Notts.), Aug. 21, 1558.	15	2	362
Oct. 13, 1558.	Gibson, Adam, Ranskhill, par. Blyth (Notts.), husbn., Sep. 16, 1558.	15	2	379
Apl. 16, 1562.	———, Anthony, Home, par. Hovengam, Nov. 25, 1561.	17		158
Apl. 28, 1559.	———, George, Wheldryke, Mar. 14, 1557.	15	3	315
Jan. 24, 1558.	———, James, Fassiby (bur. Whorleton), Oct. 19, 1558.	15	3	117
May 2, 1560.	———, Laurance, Humbleton, Mar. 13, 1560.	16		49
Jan. 21, 1556.	———, Philippe, Lunde, Jun. 4, 1556.	15	1	89

1 See also under letter J.

A.D. 1554 TO 1568.

		Vol.	Pt.	Fol.
Apl. 28, 1559.	Gibson, Robert, Wheldryke, May 10, 1558.	15	3	314
Oct. 3, 1554.	Gibsonne, John, Ryes in Holdernes, July 2, 1554.	14		43
Apl. 26, 1554.	———, Thomas, Tadcaster, husbandman, Aug. 35 *(sic)*, 1552.	14		213
Mar. 2, 1561.	———, William, Thweing, husbandman, Dec. 18, 1561.	17		1
July 17, 1556.	Gieges, Richard, Knottyngley, par. Pontefrett, husbn., Mar. 16, 1555.	15	1	56
Aug. 3, 1563.	Gilbanke, Robert, Welburne, par. Bulmer, Feb. about 9 to 14, 1562.	17		212
May 21, 1556.	Gilbarne, Robert, Clifton by York, Mar. 18, 1556.	15	1	35
No date.	Gilbathorpe, Robert, Orgrayve, par. Rotheram, Jan. 25, 1554.	14		83
Apl. 30, 1556.	Gilberde, Lawrance, Barnibie (Notts.), husbandman, Dec. 13, 1555.	15	1	32
Oct. 13, 1558.	Gilbert, Alice, Sutton on Trent (Notts.), Nov. 6, 1557.	15	2	363
May 13, 1557.	———, Beatrix, Bilstrope (Notts.), Apl. 2, 1556.	15	2	135
Jun. 11, 1555.	———, Symon, Lytle Claxston (bur. Bossall), Mar. 22, 1555.	14		210
May 18, 1559.	Gilbey, Richard, Wellie, par. Clareburgh (Notts.), husbn., Aug. 29, 1558.	15	3	406
Oct. 7, 1557.	Gilbye, William, Clyfton by Newark (Notts.), husbn., Jun. 23, 1557.	15	2	18
Apl. 7, 1554.	Gildus, William, Pattrington, husbandman, Jan. 3, 1553.	14		219
Dec. 5, 1565.	Gill, John. Felchurch, Apl. 17, 1565.	17		493
Oct. 3, 1564.	———, John, Hadlesay (bur. Birkin), Mar. 25, 1562.	17		363
July 15, 1567.	———, Myles, Kildweke, Apl. 3, 1567.	17		679
Apl. 3, 1559.	———, Roger, Sikelinghall, par. Kirkbe Overblowes, husbn., Mar. 16, 1556.	15	3	319
Dec. 4, 1554.	———, Thomas, Bracanewhait in Rygton, sherman, Dec. 18, 1553.	14		92
Dec. 16, 1556.	———, Thomas, Righton (bur. Kirkbie Overblowes), Sep. 27, 1556.	15	1	195
Apl. 28, 1559.	Gilleam, Thomas, Hyllum (bur. Fryston), Mar. 15, 1558.	15	3	315
Mar. 19, 1559.	Gilliam, Robert, Ledesham, husbandman, May 22, 1559.	16		14
Mar. 2, 1558.	Gilloo, Phillip, York, fremason, Aug. 12, 1558.	15	3	282
Jan. 14, 1564.	Gillott, James, Baurghe, par. Darton, May 1, 1564.	17		403
Oct. 10, 1566.	Gillow, Jennet, Knesall (Notts.), widow, Jun. 19, 1566.	17		589
Apl. 26, 1558.	———, William, Bentley, par. Arkesay, Nov. 6, 1557.	15	2	223
July 16, 1562.	Gillson, Richard, Ripon, Apl. 10, 1562.	17		94
Oct. 20, 1558.	Girsbie, Thomas, Howthom, Aug. 30, 1558.	15	3	121
Oct. 13, 1558.	———, William, Codington (Notts.), husbandman, Sep. 14, 1558.	15	2	364
Aug. 3, 1565.	Girsupp, Henry, Standforthebriges (bur. Catton), July 22, 1565.	17		457
May 13, 1568.	Girton, Christopher, Faryndon (Notts.), Mar. 26, 1568.	17		797
Jun. 20, 1568.	Girtwysill, Isabell, Calton, par. Kirkbe Malham, wid., Feb. 17, 1567.	17		809
Dec. 14, 1560.	Gleadowe, Richard, Cowike, par. Snaythe, Apl. 13, 1559.	16		134
May 18, 1559.	Gleadyll, Robert, Bretton Smethes, par. Silkeston, Oct. 28, 1558.	15	3	403
Feb. 6, 1558.	Gledill, Ottewell, Eland, Jan. 4, 1558.	15	3	258
Mar. 24, 1567.	Gledo, William, prentice with Myles Prince, York, cordyner, Dec. 20, 1567.	17		766
Sep. 21, 1557.	Gleidhill, Margaret, Wathe, Aug. 21, 1557.	15	1	355
Apl. 11, 1559.	Glensouer, George, Hatslett, par. Leedes, Aug. 18, 1558.	15	3	333
Jan. 23, 1558.	Glewe, Jane, York, widow, Oct. 24, 1558.	15	3	214
May 3, 1564.	———, Leonard, Knapton, par. Wyntringham, Mar. 19, 1563.	17		342
Mar. 6, 1556.	———, Richard, Myssyn (Notts.), husbandman, Sep. 12, 1556.	15	1	179
Oct. 20, 1561.	Gleydill, William, Linthwayte, par. Almonburie, Mar. 10, 1561.	17		44
Oct. 12, 1564.	Glover, Agnes, wid. of John G., Northe Wheatley (Notts.), Apl. 4, 1564.	17		389
May 5, 1557.	———, Agnes, Wakefeld, widow, Mar. 9, 1556.	15	1	213
Oct. 5, 1558.	———, Jenet, Bynglay, widow, Apl. 18, 1558.	15	3	38
Apl. 27, 1564.	———, John, Northe Wheatley (Notts.). Mar. 9, 1563.	17		335
Apl. 25, 1554.	———, John, senr., Uglebie, par. Whitbie, Jun. 3, 1553.	14		55
Apl. 20, 1564.	———, Mathew, Hunslet, par. Ledes, 1563.	17		332
May 13, 1557.	———, William, Owmton (bur. Knesall, Notts.), Mar. 8, 1556.	15	1	217
Feb. 22, 1558.	——— *als.* Hustone, John, Sandhoton, yeoman, Aug. 12, 1558.	15	3	277
Dec. 15, 1557.	——— *als.* Sharpe, Robert, Eylkesley (Notts.), July 20, 1557.	15	2	60
Jun. 13, 1554.	Glyse, Thomas, Barley, par, Braton, Jun. 25, 1550.	14		140
Mar. 11, 1562.	Godderson, Thomas, Beverley, Feb. 9, 1561.	17		156
Apl. 18, 1567.	Goder, Jane, Langside, par. Penistone, Mar. 17, ———.	17		636
Feb. 19, 1557.	Godfray, Henry, Estofte, par. Adlyngflett, Dec. 3, 1557.	15	2	146
Jun. 4, 1558.	———, Henry, Foston (bur. S. Andrew, Normanbye), Feb. 18, 1557.	15	2	287
Sep. 28, 1557.	———, John, Armeley (bur. Leedes), husbandman, Mar. 21, 1556.	15	1	336
Mar. 10, 1567.	———, Robert, Thornar, husbandman, Feb. 14, 1567.	17		762
Aug. 27, 1557.	———, Thomas, Armeley (bur. Ledes), clothyer, Feb. 23, 1556.	15	2	116
Apl. 22, 1562.	———, Thomas, Yest Leacke (Notts.), Mar. 11, 1561.	17		178

A.D. 1554 TO 1568.

		Vol.	Pt.	Fol.
July 19, 1557.	Godlay, Seth, late chantre priest of Sanby (Notts.), Mar. 17, 1556.	15	1	310
May 14, 1557.	Godley, Humphrey, Grove (Notts.), Mar. 23, 1554.	15	2	132
Apl. 4, 1560.	———, John, Trumpton (bur. Ordsall, Notts.), husbn., Dec. 29, 1559.	16		26
Apl. 20, 1559.	Godsaffe, Thomas, North Collingham (Notts.), husbn., Aug. 1, 1558.	15	3	305
Apl. 16, 1562.	Godsalff, John, Standforthebriges (bur. Catton), Jan. 20, 1561.	17		166
May 17, 1565.	Godsaue, William, Whatton (Notts.), husbandman, Sep. 30, 1560.	17		437
May 9, 1560.	Godshawe, Hewghe, Whatton (Notts.), husbandman, Apl. 16, 1560.	16		62
Nov. 4, 1565.	Godson, Elline, Beverley, widow, July 23, 1564.	17		487
July 4, 1560.	———, George, York, tapyter, Jan. 25, 1558.	16		88
Jun. 9, 1558.	———, John, Leedes, clothier, May 2, 1568 (sic).	15	2	216
Nov. 29, 1558.	Godysonne, John, Tinslow, par. Rotherham, Jun. 1, 1557.	15	3	109
July 23, 1560.	Goittes, John, Wresle, husbandman, Feb. 26, 1558.	16		95
Oct. 6, 1557.	Goland, Elizabeth, Everton (Notts.), Aug. 10, 1557.	15	2	8
Feb. 4, 1556.	Golder, Richard, Barnesbrughe, Oct. 14, 1556.	15	1	168
May 17, 1560.	Goldethorpe, Richard, York, alderman, Mar. 12, 1559.	16		64
Mar. 4, 1562.	Goldewell, Jaine, Bristwickegarthe (bur. Skeclinge), wid., Oct. 10. 1562.	17		148
Jan. 12, 1558.	Golding, John, Cranswicke, par. Huton, labourer, Dec. 13, 1558.	15	2	355
May 27, 1555.	———, William, Craunswicke, par. Hoton, husbn., May 14, 1555.	14		252
Oct. 2, 1555.	Goldrynge, Thomas, Nottingham, Sep. 6, 1554.	14		197
Jan. 4, 1558.	Goldwell, John, Brustwicke North Parke, Nov. 2, 1558.	15	3	36
Apl. 20, 1559.	Gollan, Robert, Everton (Notts.), Jan. 17, 1558.	15	3	309
Feb. 17, 1557.	Golland, Christopher, Tykhill, Dec. 15, 1557.	15	2	137
Oct. 11, 1563.	———, George, priest, curate of Ingleby under Grenehow, Jan. 8, 1562.	17		297
May 6, 1559.	———, John, Huton Rudbie, smyth, Dec. 10, 1558.	15	3	383
Apl. 11, 1559.	Golton, John, York, yeoman, Oct. 4, 1558.	15	3	334
Mar. 23, 1557.	Gondre, Thomas, Northfrothyngham, Sep. 7, 1557.	15	2	154
Dec. 4, 1557.	Good, Jennett, Brayton, Oct. 20, 1557.	15	2	49
Oct. 29, 1558.	Goodaill, Robert, Nafferton, carpenter, Aug. 12, 1558.	15	3	238
Apl. 20, 1558.	Goodayll, Margaret, Landryke, par. Drax, wid. of Thos. G., Feb. 28, 1557.	15	2	217
Jun. 17, 1554.	Goodbarne, James, Harpham, yeoman, Apl. 16, 1554.	14		11
Dec. 2, 1556.	———, William, Wyntryngham, Nov. 16, 1556.	15	1	118
Jun. 27, 1558.	Goodd, Johan, Apleton, par. Bolton Percy, Apl. 30, 1558.	15	2	216
Feb. 6, 1558.	Gooddaie, Myles, Hensall, par. Snathe, husbandman, Dec. 21, 1558.	15	3	265
Dec. 8, 1556.	Goodder, Richard, Penyston, July 3, 1556.	15	1	74
Mar. 10, 1555.	Goodgladd, Thomas, Sutton on Lounde (Notts.), Dec. 26, 1554.	14		229
Feb. 6, 1558.	Goodeles, Michell, Burton Agnes, husbandman, July 4, 1558.	15	3	261
July 10, 1567.	Goodeson, Thomas, Nether Holand (bur. Wentworthe), husbn., Mar. 30, 1567.	17		685
May 21, 1560.	Goodhall, Robert, Thorneton in Pyckeringe lythe, Feb. 11, 1559.	16		67
Oct. 6, 1558.	Goodhill, John, Thorkilby (bur. Kirkebye in Grindallyth), July 22, 1558.	15	3	225
Apl. 3, 1559.	Goodlesse, William, Harpham (bur. Burton Agnes), labr., Feb. 12, 1557.	15	3	316
May 13, 1557.	Goodwine, Richard, Kirkebie in Ashefeild (Notts.), husbn., Apl. 7, 1557.	15	1	225
Apl. 27, 1564.	Goodwyn, William, Nottingham, Mar. 12, 1563.	17		338
Apl. 19, 1559.	Goodwyne, Briand, Burton Jorce (Notts.), husbandman, Jan. 20, 1558.	15	3	378
Nov. 6, 1557.	Goodyear, John, Northe Wheytley (Notts.), Jun. 29, 1557.	15	2	107
May 5, 1557.	Goodyeare, Agnes, Aslabie, par. Middleton in Pykeringlithe, wid., Mar. 9, 1556.	15	1	251
Jun. 30, 1554.	Goodyere, John, Nether Beckhouse, par. Mydleton, yeom., Jan. 2, 1553.	14		141
Mar. 6, 1558.	———, Thomas, York, putherer, Nov. 25, 1558.	15	3	283
Mar. 26, 1557.	Gookker, John, Spawdington (bur. Bubwith), Dec. 18, 1556.	15	1	203
July 1, 1558.	Gorrell, James, Waikfeild, Feb. 21, 1557.	15	2	329
Dec. 3, 1557.	———, Jenet, Usflet (bur. Wytgyft), Sep. 6, 1557.	15	2	98
Dec. 2, 1556.	———, Nicholas, Usfleytt (bur. Whytgift), Feb. 17, 1556.	15	1	118
Jun. 12, 1557.	———, Robert, Adlinflete, May 11, 1557.	15	1	275
Jun. 12, 1557.	Gorryll, Alice, Usflyt, par. Whitgifte, Mar. 17, 1556.	15	1	291
May 18, 1555.	———, John, Usflytt, par. Whitgyfte, Dec. 26, 1554.	14		251
May 13, 1557.	Gorson, John, Arnolle (Notts.), Feb. 27, 1556.	15	1	224
Oct. 3, 1565.	Gosmay (Gosney), Thomas, Stapleton, par. Daryngton, Jan. 11, 1564.	17		479
Sep. 3, 1554.	Gosnay, Nicolas, Womerslay, July 5, 1554.	14		271
Jun. 6, 1560.	Gossope, Robert, Leaven, May 1, 1559.	16		75
Mar. 17, 1556.	Gossoppe, John, Siglisthorne (bur. Hornsay), Jan. 29, 1556.	15	1	186

		Vol.	Pt.	Fol.
Nov.28, 1567.	Goston, John, Yrton, par. Seamer, May 23, 1567.	17		739
Jun. 5, 1555.	——, Robert, Ayton, par. Seamer, Apl. 14, 1555.	14		210
Jun. 20, 1566.	Gostone, Agnes, Semer, Feb. 4, 1565.	17		556
Sep. 30, 1557.	Gotte, John, Lowthorpe, husbandman, July 14, 1557.	15	1	342
Oct. 5, 1558.	Goulden, Christopher, Newby (bur. Semer), Apl. 24, 1558.	15	3	42
May 26, 1567.	Goule. William, Scardburghe, Jun. 17, 1566.	17		654
May 3, 1565.	Gounbe, Symon, Goule (bur. Howke), yeoman, Feb. 3, 1563.	17		420
Oct. 6, 1558.	Gourwood, John, Thornethrope (bur. Berithorpe), Aug. 7, 1558.	15	3	225
Nov.25, 1556.	Gower, Constance, Stainton in Cleveland, gentlewoman, Oct. 11, 1555.	14		183
Mar.21, 1559.	——, Cuthbarte, Thormondbie, gentleman, Dec. 14, 1559.	16		15
Jan. 27, 1556.	——, George, citizen of York, Aug. 1, 1556.	15	1	92
July 2, 1561.	——, John, Bempton, par. Brydlington, husbn., Apl. 2, 1559.	17		77
May 17, 1557.	Gowland, John, Bridlyngton, draper, Oct. 16, 1556.	15	1	244
Jun. 2, 1558.	Gowseman, Robert, Kayngham, Feb. 22, 1557.	15	2	335
Jun. 18, 1566.	Gowthayte, Thomas, Rusholme, par. Drax, Feb. 1, 1554.	17		551
Aug.13, 1567.	Gowthorpe, Robert, Albrowghe, husbandman, Mar. 12, 1566.	17		692
May 2, 1560.	Goxxell, William, Aram, par. Atwycke, yeoman, Feb. 8, 1559.	16		50
Oct. 20, 1558.	Goyte, William, Catfos (bur. Siglisthron), Sep. 4, 1558.	15	2	350
May 6, 1557.	Graie, John, Scardburgh, Feb. 10, 1556.	15	1	249
May 17, 1557.	——, John, Thurnne, par. Burton Agnes, husbandman, Apl.26,1557.	15	1	244
Sep. 30, 1556.	Grandishe, John (bur. S. Oswald, Tho[r]neton), Aug. 1, 1556.	15	1	174
May 22, 1554.	Grange, Thomas, Gisborne, Feb. 12, 1553.	14		6
Oct. 10, 1560.	Granger, Heughe, Whelley (Notts.), yeoman, Sep. 19, 1559.	16		124
Apl. 27, 1564.	——, James, Westwod, par. Selstan (Notts.), May 17, 1563.	17		338
Jan. 23, 1561.	Grascroft, William, Lellaydike (bur. Preston), husbn., Oct. 20, 1561.	17		18
Apl. 26, 1559.	Grason, Thomas (bur. Rypon), Jan. 10, 1558.	15	3	364
Sep. 16, 1558.	——, Thomas, Sand Hoowton (bur. Thriske), Aug. 20, 1558.	15	3	105
Feb. 4, 1561.	——, William, Semer, carpenter, Aug. 19, 1561.	17		12
Nov. 3, 1558.	Graue, James, Byrkinshay (bur. Byrstall), Dec. 10, 1557.	15	3	154
Nov. 9, 1557.	——, Robert, Pontefract, yeoman, July 26, 1554.	15	2	90
Mar. 7, 1554.	Graunge, Agnes, widow of John G. (bur. Smeton), July 20, 1 Mary.	14		100
Sep. 29, 1557.	——, Richard, Sharowe, husbandman, Aug. 23, 1557.	15	1	330
May 16, 1554.	Graunger, William (bur. Holme in Spaldingmore), Nov. 11, 1553.	14		138
July 31, 1566.	Graunt, Frauncis, Wakefeild, mercer, Feb. 20, 1565.	17		564
July 11, 1558.	——, John, Barneby on Donne, May 19, 1558.	15	2	320
Feb. 4, 1557.	Graunte, Anne, Tadcaster, servaunte, Sep. 18, 1557.	15	2	162
Oct. 1, 1556.	Grauntt, John, Barmbe on Done, Dec. 31, 1555.	15	1	123
Jan. 4, 1557.	Grave, Anthony, Thorpe (bur. Brayton), husbn., Nov. 19, 1557.	15	2	77
May 9, 1565.	——, George, Doncaster, Jan. 31, 1564.	17		439
May 9, 1565.	——, George, Doncaster, Jan. 31, 1564.	17		429
Nov.29, 1560.	——, Henry, Thorner, labourer, Aug. 20, 1560.	16		130
Nov. 4, 1557.	——, Richard, Hyllyng (Lyllyng), par. Sheryfhoton, labr., Oct.21, 1557.	15	2	105
Feb. 1, 1563.	——, Richard, Whitley (bur. Kellington), Nov. 5, 1558.	17		312
Mar.12, 1557.	Graven, Francis, York, surgyen, Jan. 26, 1557.	15	2	126
Apl. 30, 1567.	Gravener, Syr Thomas (bur. Gaulston, ? Gonaldston, Notts.), knight, Apl. 20, 3 Eliz.	17		637
Jan. 22, 1561.	Graves, William, Beverleie, brasier, Feb. 4, 1560	17		24
Apl. 27, 1558.	Graveson, Christopher, Cray, par. Arneclyffe, Nov. 5, 1557.	15	2	202
Sep. 30, 1556.	——, John, Owghtershawe, par. Arneclif, Aug. 9, 1556.	15	1	131
Jun. 12, 1562.	Gray, Ellin, Beverley, widow, Mar. 13, 1561.	17		87
Mar.27, 1565.	——, Jane, Welwicke, Jan. 8, 1564.	17		419
July 1, 1561.	——, Joanne, Brayton, mayden, May 6, 1560.	17		76
Aug. 5, 1566.	——, John, Bainton, husbandman, July 26, 1566.	17		564
Oct. 5, 1558.	——, John, Newbrough, par. Cuckwold, Aug. 12, 1558.	15	3	71
Mar. 2, 1561.	——, John, Rudstonne, labourer, Oct. 12, 1561.	17		2
Jan. 23, 1558.	——, Lionell, Relston, July 16, 1558.	15	3	214
Nov.10, 1557.	——, Robert, Beverley, marchand, Sep. 20, 1557.	15	2	99
May 17, 1557.	——, Robert, Thurnn, par. Burton Agnes, labourer, May 2, 1557.	15	1	244
Jan. 12, 1557.	——, Thomas, Westewoodd in Beverlaye, hyrdman, Oct. 28, 1557.	15	2	80
Oct. 1, 1556.	Graye, Janett, Sonderlandwicke (bur. Hewton Cransweke), Jan.20, 1555.	15	1	137
Jun. 11, 1568.	——, John, Hamylton (bur. Braton), labourer, Jan. 20, 1567.	17		805

A.D. 1554 TO 1568.

		Vol.	Pt.	Fol.
July 9, 1561.	Graye, Thomas, Barton in the Willowes, husbandman. *No date.*	17		80
Aug. 9, 1567.	——, Thomas, Raskell, July 3, 1567.	17		688
Nov. 4, 1556.	——, Thomas, Spantone, par. Lastingham, husbn., Mar. 31, 1555.	15	1	107
May 23, 1554.	Graynge, John, Smeton, Oct. 31, 1553.	14		7
Apl. 27, 1558.	Grayson, Agnes, Erles Hetton, par. Dewesburye, Mar. 14, 1558 (*sic*).	15	2	192
Jan. 28, 1556.	——, John, New Malton, yeoman, Dec. 25, 1556.	15	1	92
July 3, 1567.	——. Margaret, New Malton, widow, Mar. 10, 1567.	17		668
Jan. 24, 1558.	——, Robert, Gysburne in Cleveland, carpenter, Jun. 13, 1558.	15	3	215
Mar. 10, 1566.	——, Thomas, Grymethorpe, par. Sheaffeld, Mar. 29, 1564.	17		516
May 6, 1559.	Graysswith, George, Braworthe (bur. Rudbie), yeom., Aug. 1, 1558.	15	3	382
Sep. 30, 1562.	Graystocke, Elizabeth, Egton, widow, Dec. 30, 1556.	17		109
Oct. 8, 1556.	————, Richard, Maplebecke (Notts.), Mar. 25, 1556.	15	1	154
No date.	Graystoke, John, Fishlake, Oct. 28, 1553.	14		152
July 11, 1558.	Greave, James, Sheffeild, husbandman, Jun. 22, 1557.	15	2	303
Oct. 2, 1566.	——, Nicholas, Hawlecarre, par. Sheaffeld, July 1, 1556.	17		577
Oct. 5, 1558.	——, Rauf, Kirkburton, Jun. 28, 1558.	15	3	41
Nov. 29, 1558.	Greaves, John, Fullwod, par. Sheafeld, Nov. 13, 1557.	15	3	144
July 15, 1561.	——, Rauf, Hinchelff, par. Peniston, yeoman, Mar. 29, 1561.	17		82
Oct. 6, 1557.	Gree, Robert, Lound, par. Sutton (Notts.), May 1, 1557.	15	2	7
Oct. 1, 1556.	Green, James, Crofton, July 10, 1556.	15	1	121
Oct. 29, 1554.	——, Robert, Newarke (Notts.), baiker, Jan. 2, 1553.	14		277
May 2, 1555.	Greene, Edmund, Meltam, par. Almunburie, Mar. 4, 1554.	14		30
May 19, 1559.	——, William, Heke, par. Snath, Feb. 6, 1558.	15	3	427
Oct. 1, 1556.	Greenfeld, Christopher, Kyllington, July 28, 1556.	15	1	121
Feb. 20, 1554.	Grege, John, Doncaster, alderman, Dec. 29, 1554.	14		151
Apl. 27, 1558.	Gregeson, Robert (bur. Gyglesweke), Aug. 2, 1557.	15	2	201
Jan. 14, 1558.	Gregson, Edmund (bur. Ripon), Aug. 22, 1558.	15	3	190
Oct. 3, 1554.	——, John, Hetton, (bur. Villstone, ? Rilston), Jan. 3, 1553.	14		37
Nov. 7, 1564.	Greinbery, John, Barnston in Holderness, Apl. 15, 1564.	17		398
July 1, 1562.	Greive, Dianes, wid. of Jo. G., of Wyndhill, par. Bradfeld. Mar. 6, 1561.	17		92
May 4, 1558.	Greme, William (bur. S. Mich., Bonnyngton, Notts.), Jan. 30, 1557.	15	2	270
Oct. 25, 1558.	Grendsyde, Esabell, Helmeslay, Sep. 10, 1558.	15	3	236
July 16, 1562.	Grene, Arthur, Whitley (bur. Kellington), Apl. 4, 1562.	17		97
Dec. 5, 1558.	——, Christopher, Old Malton, July 24, 1558.	15	3	150
Aug. 18, 1562.	——, Edward, Catlame, par. Lowthorpe, Dec. 20, 1561.	17		105
Apl. 12, 1567.	——, Edward, Eskrige, Mar. 28, 1567.	17		617
Mar. 20, 1560.	——, Francys, Sledcroft, par. Appleton (bur. Amotherbye), Mar. 1, 1559.	16		172
Apl. 23, 1556.	——, Henry, Silkiston, Feb. 24, 1555.	15	1	36
Jan. 24, 1558.	——, Hewghe, Haitefeld, husbandman, Nov. 19, 1558.	15	3	118
July 16, 1561.	——, James, Southe Dalton, mylner, Mar. 21, 1560.	17		83
Apl. 20, 1564.	——, Jennet, Wakefeild, widow, Dec. 27, 1562.	17		326
May 4, 1558.	——, Joane, Beaston (Notts.), widow, Sep. 13, 1557.	15	2	277
Apl. 27, 1558.	——, John (bur. Addingham), Jan. 10, 1555.	15	2	201
Dec. 21, 1562.	——, John, Barneby on Done, gentleman, Sep. 26, 1559.	17		138
Jun. 18, 1557.	——, John, Dymylton (bur. Esington), May 28, 1557.	15	1	294
Oct. 2, 1567.	——, John, Farnley, par. Leedes, Jan. 8, 1566.	17		720
July 16, 1562.	——, John, Hepworth, par. Byrton, Feb. 3, 1561.	17		97
Sep. 20, 1558.	——, John, Horsfurthe hall, par. Gyeslay, gentleman, July 28, 1558.	15	3	108
July 15, 1567.	——, John, Horton, Jun. 2, 1566.	17		678
Jan. 13, 1558.	——, John, Nottingham, butcher, Sep. 30, 1558.	15	3	183
Oct. 13, 1562.	——, John, Wakefeild, draper, Aug. 10, 1562.	17		124
Sep. 30, 1556.	——, John, Westmarton in Craven, Aug. 11, 1556.	15	1	173
Oct. 5, 1564.	——, John, Whitley (bur. Kellington), Jan. 16, 1563.	17		373
July 2, 1558.	——, Lawrence, Bramham, Aug. 25, 1557.	15	2	343
May 10, 1565.	——, Leonard, Wawplay, par. Lofthus, Jan. 16, 1564.	17		426
May 6, 1557.	——, Margaret, Hensall, par. Snath, Dec. 31, 1556.	15	1	241
Jan. 29, 1557.	——, Margaret, Newsom (bur. Kyrkebyewyske), wid., Nov. 21, 1557.	15	2	161
July 22, 1562.	——, Michaell, Burton Agnes, husbandman, Nov. 3, 1558.	17		97
July 11, 1558.	——, Nicholas, Wombwell, par. Darfeyld, Apl. 29, 1558.	15	2	317
Oct. 30, 1557.	——, Rauffe, Newsam (bur. Kyrkebywyske), Sep. 5, 1557.	15	1	365
July 10, 1567.	——, Richard, Barnisley, Jan. 29, 1565.	17		684

		Vol.	Pt.	Fol.
Jun. 6, 1560.	Grene, Richard, Baverlaye, Oct. 10, 1559.	16		75
Apl. 28, 1563.	——, Richard, Coolde Conyshton (bur. Gargrave), husbn., Jun. 26, 1562	17		227
Apl. 27, 1558.	——, Richard, Hooll mylle, par. Dewesburye, Jun. 16, 1557.	15	2	192
Oct. 6, 1557.	——, Richard, Ratclyffe on Trente, (Notts.) husbn., June 16, 1557.	15	2	30
Nov.10, 1557.	——, Richard, Todcaster, labourer, Aug. 10, 1557.	15	2	100
Oct. 14, 1561.	——, Richard, Warmesworthe, gentleman, Jan. 2, 1560.	17		38
Oct. 7, 1557.	——, Robert, Basseforde (Notts.), Jun. 2, 1557.	15	2	24
Oct. 28, 1566.	——, Robert, Cottingham, yong man, May 6, 1566.	17		586
Apl. 28, 1558.	——, Robert, Everthorpe, par. North Cave, Jan. 4, 1557.	15	2	218
Nov.19, 1558.	——, Robert, Hasthroppe (bur. Burton Agnes), labr., Sep. 26, 1558.	15	3	128
Jan. 14, 1558.	——, Roger, Topliffe, Nov. 20, 1558.	15	3	192
Apl. 12, 1559.	——, Thomas, Adingham, Sep. 6, 1558.	15	3	341
Apl. 27, 1558.	——, Thomas, Brystall, Mar. 15, 1557.	15	2	193
Mar.22, 1564.	——, Thomas, Fadmore (bur. Kirkbie Moreshed), husbn., Oct. 30, 1564.	17		412
May 4, 1558.	——, Thomas, Stanford (Notts.), Dec. 24, 1557.	15	2	267
Feb. 17, 1556.	——, William, Barnebie on Done, esq., Sep. 28, 1556.	15	1	159
Oct. 3, 1554.	——, William, Conunley, par. Kildwicke, Mar. 17, 1553.	14		38
Mar.20, 1565.	——, William, Demylton, par. Essington, Feb. 19, 1565.	17		506
Feb. 24, 1561.	——, William, Lyndley (bur. Ottley), priest, Aug. 8, 1561.	17		18
Apl. 23, 1556.	——, William (bur. Skypbie), Feb. 4, 1555.	15	1	24
Apl. 25, 1559.	——, als. Webster, Alice, Haistrope, par. Burton Agnes, wid., Jun. 24, 1557.	15	3	311
Jun. 23, 1564.	Grenebury, Edmund, York, draper, Jan. 12, 1563.	17		353
Oct. 1, 1556.	Grenefeld, Jenett, Kyllingley (bur. Killington), Aug. 1, 1556.	15	1	120
Oct. 4, 1554.	Grenefelde, James, Kellyngley, ——, 1554.	14		46
Sep. 30, 1562.	Grenehood, Thomas, Ripon, clarke, Apl. 7, 1562.	17		109
Nov. 4, 1565.	Grenehopp, Richard, Beverley, smithe, Dec. 12, 1564.	17		488
Apl. 10, 1557.	Grenewod, Edward, Heptonstall, Jan. 21, 1556.	15	1	206
Aug.28, 1562.	———, Richard, Overbaytingis in Eland, husbn., June 9, 1562.	17		104
Oct. 3, 1565.	———, Thomas, Acton (bur. Fetherstone), smythe, July 3, 1564.	17		476
Sep. 3, 1554.	Grenewodde, Thomas, Grenewodde, par. Heptonstall, Feb. 3, 1553.	14		272
Apl. 16, 1562.	Grenewood, Elizabeth, Loversall, wid., June 18, 1561.	17		173
Sep. 9, 1561.	————, James, Heptonstall, Dec. 17, 1560.	17		51
Nov.12, 1557.	————, John, Heptonstall, Sep. 23, 1556.	15	1	112
May 20, 1557.	————, John, Myxenden, par. Halifax, Jun. 30, 1556.	15	1	258
July 11, 1558.	————, Richard, Morlev, par. Rotherham, May 16, 1558.	15	2	316
Jun. 19, 1556.	————, William, Shakilton, par. Heptonstall, Jan. 29, 1555.	15	1	50
Sep. 29, 1557.	Grenewoodd, John (bur. Fetherstone), Aug. 19, 1557.	15	1	329
Mar. 9, 1557.	————, John, Heptonstall, Feb. 10, 1557.	15	2	130
Mar.12, 1556.	Grenfeld, John, Hallifax, Dec. 20, 1556.	15	1	199
Oct. 7, 1563.	Grenhaghe, Roger, Tevershall (Notts.), esquier, Dec. 2, 1562.	17		292
Oct. 2, 1566.	Grenhodd, Robert, Kighley, Apl. 24, 1563.	17		576
Sep. 24, 1558.	Grennall, John, Bradford, Apl. 24, 1558.	15	3	87
Nov.10, 1557.	Grenne, William, Towlston (bur. Newton Kyme), husbn., Aug.25,1557.	15	2	97
Nov.10, 1558.	Grensid, John, Sheriffhowton, husbandman, Oct. 10, 1558.	15	3	233
July 19, 1557.	Grensmyth, Roger, Mathersey (Notts.), Jan. 18, 1556.	15	1	313
Apl. 26, 1559.	Grenwood, Margere, par. Heptonstall, widow, Feb. 26, 1557.	15	3	363
Apl. 26, 1558.	Grenwoode, Johan, Morley, par. Rotherham, Apl. 14, 1558.	15	2	224
Nov.28, 1558.	Grescrofte, Watter, Ottringham Marshe, yeoman, Nov. 1, 1558.	15	3	79
Sep. 26, 1558.	Gresse, William, Todworth (bur. Hatfeld), husbn., Nov. 8, 1557.	15	3	52
Oct. 12, 1558.	Gresseley, Thomas, Stapelfurth (Notts.), Oct. 25, 1551.	15	3	228
Nov.21, 1556.	Gressome, Neniane, Pollington, par. Snaith, Sep. 24, 1556.	15	1	116
May 5, 1557.	Gretham, Christopher, Filinge, Nov. 24, 1556.	15	1	247
July 27, 1567.	————, Robert, Fyling, Apl. 4, 1567.	17		670
Apl. 20, 1559.	Greues, William, Treswell (Notts.), Mar. 20, 1558.	15	3	434
July 11, 1558.	Greves, Alice, Shepehouse, par. Penistone, widow, Feb. 13, 1556.	15	2	301
Oct. 13, 1558.	————, Christopher, Ecking (Notts.), husbandman, Sep. 2, 1558.	15	2	365
May 4, 1558.	————, Robert, Carleton in Gedling, (Notts.) July 26, 1557.	15	2	274
July 2, 1561.	Grexon, Alice, Harpham, widow, Sep. 16, 1560.	17		78
July 18, 1560.	————, William, Harpham, May 1, 1560.	16		94
Aug.14, 1566.	Greyne, Jarey (Gerard, Act Book), Berythorpe, tayler, Dec. 26, 1558.	17		565

		Vol.	Pt.	Fol.
Oct. 2, 1566.	Greyve, John, Ughillwodside in Bradfeld, Sep. 9, 1565.	17		578
Dec. 2, 1561.	———, John, Ughilwodside, par. Bradfeld, Sep. 11, 1558.	17		31
Dec. 9, 1556.	———, Nicholas, Shephouse, par. Penyston, yeoman, Jun. 9, 1556.	15	1	74
Oct. 6, 1558.	———, Sir Thomas, Bolsterston (bur. Bradfeld), priest, Dec.31, 1557.	15	3	26
Feb. 25, 1556.	———, William, Carlecoittes, par. Penystone, Jan. 6, 1556.	15	1	167
May 4, 1557.	———, William, Fayrhirst, par. Bradfeld, Sep. 2, 1556.	15	1	277
Sep. 18, 1565.	Greyves, Rauf, Hallfeild in Bradfeild, June 8, 1565.	17		467
Sep. 30, 1562.	Gricethwait, Bryan, Semer, June 11, 1562.	17		109
May 28, 1568.	Grindall, Thomas, Great Kelke (bur. Foston), July 3, 1567.	17		775
Apl. 30, 1556.	Grobe, Thomas, Balderton (Notts.), husbandman, Feb. 3, 1555.	15	1	32
Oct. 30, 1567.	Grott, Richard, Faxflett, par. Southe Cave, 1567.	17		730
Oct. 5, 1558.	Ground, Thomas, Pikton, July 25, 1558.	15	3	70
Apl. 30, 1556.	Grubbe, William, Thurgarton (Notts.), husbandman, Feb. 22, 1555.	15	1	31
May 3, 1565.	Grvce, John, Barley, par. Braton, May 15, 1564.	17		420
Oct. 29, 1554.	Grymdyche, Margret, Eaton (Notts.), widow, Aug. 9, 1554.	14		281
Oct. 24, 1554.	Gryme, David, Doncaster, Apl. 16, 1553.	14		308
Feb. 25, 1558.	———, George, Newton Kyme, Oct. 31, 1558.	15	3	279
Sep. 10, 1556.	———, William, curate of B. Trinitye, Mykelgate, York, July 22, 1556.	15	1	64
May 2, 1566.	Grymeschaye, Henry, Northowrum, par. Halifax, clothier, Apl. 18, 1565.	17		532
May 10, 1565.	Grymlon, James, Danbie, Oct. 28, 1564.	17		426
Aug. 21, 1563.	Grymston, William, Cottingham, gentleman, Mar. 27, 1563.	17		213
Jun. 2, 1558.	Grymytt, Margaret, Stoneferie, par. Sutton in Holderness, spinster, Oct. 17, 1557.	15	2	336
Jan. 29, 1556.	Gryndall, John, Kelke Magna, Oct. 20, 1556.	15	1	93
Oct. 14, 1557.	———, Roger, Harum, par. Helmesley, Sep. 1, 1557.	15	1	363
Jun. 10, 1563.	Grysewayt, Robert, Whitley (bur. Kellington), Mar. 28, 1563.	17		258
Jan. 20, 1557.	Gryssome, Robert, Brampton, par. Cantlay, husbn., Sep. 27, 1557.	15	2	68
Aug. 28, 1563.	Grystwat, John, Egbrought (bur. Kellington), Mar. 13, 1563.	17		212
May 2, 1566.	Guddaill, John, Hull, Oct. 10, 1565.	17		537
Nov. 9, 1557.	Guddall, William, Harbyre (bur. Wakefelld), Oct, 19, 1557.	15	2	102
Sep. 26, 1558.	Gudday, Edmond, Tikhill, July 24, 1558.	15	3	51
Oct. 3, 1560.	———, Henry (bur. Mytton), Apl. 10, 1560.	16		118
Oct. 7, 1557.	———, Henry, Rampton (Notts.), Mar. 10, 1556.	15	2	22
Jun. 23, 1568.	Gudgion, Thomas, Helmslay. *No date.*	17		807
Sep. 29, 1563.	Gud Jone (Gudyone, Act Book), Thomas, Snaygill, par. Skipton, April 11, 1563.	17		280
July 18, 1560.	Gudknape, Marye (bur. S. Mary's, ? Beverley), April 29, 1560.	16		93
May 24, 1565.	Gudyer, Bryan, Naburne, (bur. Acaster), husbn., June 17, 1564.	17		443
May 5, 1559.	Gulleysse, William (bur. Bolton Percye), Mar. 20, 1558.	15	3	380
Nov. 9, 1558.	Gunbie, William, senr., Harlthroppe (bur. Bubwith), Aug. 13, 1558.	15	3	123
Feb. 19, 1557.	Gunbye, Margaret, Swynflet (bur. Wydgyfte), Nov. 1, 1557.	15	2	145
May 18, 1559.	Gundre, William, Brissyd, par. Brandisburton, husbn., Mar. 25, 1558	15	3	411
Oct. 12, 1558.	Gunthorpe, William, Oxton (Notts.), husbandman, Feb. 7, 1557.	15	3	27
Oct. 8, 1561.	Gurnell, Francis, Gyrsthorpe (bur. Normanton), Aug. 9, 1561.	17		40
Mar. 10, 1555.	Gurnet, John, Tuxforth (Notts.), Apl. 19, 1554.	14		227
July 5, 1557.	Gurp (Gurrie, Act Book), John, Thurne, fissher, July 27, 1556.	15	1	301
Jun. 26, 1561.	Gurre, Elizabeth, Thorne, May 9, 1560.	17		74
May 18, 1556.	———, Roger, Thurne, Apl. 20, 1556.	15	1	34
July 5, 1557.	Gurrie (Gurp in Register), John, Thurne, fissher, July 27, 1556.	15	1	301
Dec. 22, 1556.	Gurrye, Edmunde, Rotherham, May 12, 1556.	15	1	84
Jun. 2, 1558.	Gurwold, John, Langton, husbandman, May 1, 1558.	15	2	288
Jan. 9, 1560.	Gurwolde, Robert, Norton, husbandman, Mar. 1, 1559.	16		139
Apl. 26, 1559.	Guy, Edward, Hallifax, yeoman, Oct. 25, 1558.	15	3	312
Sep. 30, 1562.	Guye, Alexander, Beverley, glover, Jun. 18, 1561.	17		117
Oct. 2, 1566.	Guvlde, Richard, Beverley, baker, Jan. 9, 1565.	17		572
Dec. 16, 1557.	Gybson, Alyson, Garton, widow, Oct. 2, 1557.	15	2	46
Jun. 12, 1560.	———, Henry, Holme in Spaldingmore, Jan. 19, 1558.	16		83
Aug. 16, 1560.	———, Henry, Yarum, May 1, 1560.	16		103
Feb. 8, 1556.	———, Jennet, widow of Richard G. of Northorom, par. Halyfax, Jun. 13, 1556.	15	1	171
Jun. 26, 1567.	———, John, Acaster Selbie, par. Stillingflete, Jan. 2, 9 Eliz.	17		657
Nov. 26, 1554.	———, John, Essingwold, Apl. 15, 1554.	14		89

		Vol.	Pt.	Fol.
July 16, 1561.	Gybson, John, Hackenes, Feb. 13, 1559.	17		83
Apl. 27, 1564.	——, John, Normanton on Trent (Notts.), husbn., Mar. 7, 1563.	17		337
July 17, 1565.	——, John, Wellwicke, Oct. 12, 1564.	17		453
Apl. 12, 1559.	——, John, Wheldrike, Feb. 24, 1558.	15	3	335
Jan. 19, 1557.	——, Richard (Hexham), *No date*.	15	2	64
Nov.29, 1558.	——, Richard, Marre, Sep. 17, 1558.	15	3	140
Jun. 25, 1568.	——, Robert, Thornegumbolde, Mar. 21, 1567.	17		810
May 27, 1562.	——, Steven, Pattrington, Jan. 20, 1561.	17		101
Sep. 30, 1557.	——, Thomas, Garton in Holderness, Oct. 20, 1556.	15	1	341
Dec. 10, 1566.	——, Thomas, Holme in Spauldingmore, Oct. 6, 1566.	17		605
Jun. 8, 1560.	—— *als.* Gylson, Robert, Stanlaye, par. Waikefelde, Apl. 30, 1550.	16		89
May 9, 1558.	Gybsonne, Steven, Hollme in Spaldingmore, Jan. 25, 1557.	15	2	279
Sep. 30, 1557.	Gye, Robert, Rednes (bur. Whytgyft), Jun. 12, ——.	15	1	346
July 8, 1557.	——, Steven, Thirske, Jun. 12, 1557.	15	1	306
Apl. 8, 1560.	Gyels, Jenat, Beswycke, par. Kylnewicke, widow, Nov. 2, 1559.	16		28
Sep. 13, 1565.	Gyer, Christopher, Barwicke, par. Skipton, Apl. 26, 1565.	17		463
July 12, 1555.	Gyfferson, Henry, Easton (bur. Bridlington), husbn., Jun. 15, 1555.	14		22
Nov.28, 1558.	Gygges, Elizabeth, Knottinglay (bur. Pontefract), Sep. 22, 1558.	15	3	136
Nov.28, 1558.	——, William, Knottinglay (bur. Pontefract), husbn., Aug.25, 1558.	15	3	134
Feb.26, 1563.	Gyige, Robert, Metheley, Jun. 30, 1563.	17		321
Apl. 20, 1559.	Gylbert, Richard (bur. Byllisthorp, Notts.), Mar. 18, 155[8-]9.	15	3	365
July 23, 1558.	Gylderdale, Robert, Howkke, Jan. 1, 1557.	15	2	385
Jun. 2, 1558.	Gyldus, Christopher (bur. Patrington), Apl. 6, 1557.	15	2	311
Dec. 1, 1558.	Gyles, Edmond, Beswike, par. Kylnewike, Apl. 26, 1558.	15	3	83
Mar.21, 1555.	——, Robert, Stillingflete, Oct. 1, 1555.	15	1	14
Oct. 3, 1566.	Gyll, Christopher, Brahamwhate in Rigton, par. Kirkbieoverblaws, webster, Aug. 10, 1566.	17		582
July 24, 1560.	——, Christopher, Ferlington, par. Sheryf huton, July 10, 1559.	16		96
Sep. 29, 1563.	——, John, Thruscrosse, par. Fuyston, May 14, 1562.	17		289
Oct. 7, 1557.	——, Richard, Elstone (bur. Stoke, Notts.), July 27, 1557.	15	2	18
Feb.24, 1559.	——, Richard, Notton, par. Roiston, Jan. 28, 1559.	16		1
Apl. 20, 1564.	——, Robert, Royston, tanner, Nov. 1, 1563.	17		324
Dec. 4, 1557.	——, Thomas, Stillingflett, Oct. 2, 1557.	15	2	51
Apl. 27, 1558.	Gylle, Myles, Glowsburne, par. Kyldweke, Nov. 20, 1557.	15	2	201
May 5, 1559.	Gyllyote, John, Thorpparche, Apl. 11, 1559.	15	3	381
Jun. 8, 1560.	Gylson *als.* Gybson, Robert, Stanlaye, par. Waikefelde, Apl. 30, 1550.	16		89
May 4, 1558.	Gymer, Thomas, Nottingham, Sep. 12, 1557.	15	2	275
Nov.13, 1566.	Gypton, Henry, Bilton, Ainsty, Oct. 21, 1566.	17		598
Sep. 10, 1560.	Gyrdler, John, York, Feb. 20, 1559.	16		104
Feb. 4, 1561.	Gysborne, Thomas, Skelton in Cleveland, Nov. 20, 1561.	17		12
Apl. 27, 1558.	Haber, Roger, Mylnthorpe, par. Sandall Magna, Jan. 21, 1557.	15	2	191
May 4, 1557.	Haberham, Thomas, Tretone, husbandman, Mar. 19, 1556.	15	1	279
Oct. 5, 1558.	Habergame, Gylberte, Steton, par. Kyldwyke, Oct. 8, 1557.	15	3	60
Feb. 28, 1566.	Hacfourthe, John, Litill Busby (bur. Stoxlay), Nov. 24, 1565.	17		616
Jan. 24, 1558.	Hackewith, Lawrence, Pikton, par. Kirkelevington, Aug. 10, 1558.	15	3	23
Oct. 13, 1558.	Hadwicke, Richard, Egmanton (Notts.), Apl. 27, 1558.	15	2	360
Apl. 16, 1567.	Hafourth, Margaret, Watterfryston, widow, Oct. 27, 1566.	17		627
Mar.15, 1558.	Hagas, Robert, Loftsome, par. Wressle, husbn., Mar. 18, 1558.	15	3	241
Jun. 11, 1562.	Haget, John, Semer, husbandman, Mar. 12, 1560.	17		87
July 2, 1561.	——, William, Muston (bur. Hunmanbye), May 2, 1561.	17		79
Mar. 1, 1557.	Hagg, William, Cawton, par. Gillinge, Dec. 2, 1557.	15	2	170
Oct. 29, 1558.	Haggat, Robert, Hummanbe, Apl. 8, 1558.	15	2	372
Aug.17, 1560.	Hagget, Nicholas, Muston, par. Hummanbie, Apl. 20, 1560.	16		104
Dec. 7, 1557.	Haghe, Edmund, Hyrste, par. Huddersfeld, Oct. 4, 1557.	15	2	83
July 1, 1558.	——, George, Dyrker, par. Sandall Magna, Apl. 2, 1558.	15	2	327
Oct. 1, 1556.	——, Robert, Dyrker, par. Sandall Magna, husbn., July 9, 1556.	15	1	142
May 13, 1557.	Haie, Mathew, of Nottingham, Apl. 9, 1557.	15	1	226
May 18, 1559.	Haigh, Elizabeth, Darton, widow, Aug. 20, 1558.	15	3	401
Dec. 9, 1556.	Haighe, John Penyston, Oct. 23, 1556.	15	1	74
No date.	——, Richard, Coldingleye, Aug. 2, 1551.	14		88
Oct. 29, 1558.	Hainworth, Robert, Cullingworth, par. Bingley, Oct. 1, 1558.	15	3	129
May 2, 1566.	Haistinges, Sir Frauncis, Haitefeild, knight, Oct. 20, 1558.	17		523

	Vol.	Pt.	Fol.
Oct.5,1559[?8]. Haite, Henry, Hooton (bur. Gisburne), Aug. 5, 1558.	15	3	68
Feb.24, 1560. Haiton, Richard, Holme in Spaldingmore, labourer, Oct. 7, 1559.	16		150
Sep.30, 1557. ———, William, Kerke Elley, Aug. 8, 1557.	15	1	327
Oct. 17, 1561. 1 Hakam (Akam in Act Book), Thomas, Marston, Jun. 10, 1560.	17		45
Mar.23, 1557. Haknay, Christopher, Halethrom, par. Leven, labr., Aug. 20, 1557.	15	2	154
Aug. 6, 1567. ———, William, Hempholme, par. Leven, May 12, 1564.	17		701
Oct. 1, 1561. Hakyll, Richard, Skypton (bur. Bolton), May 20, 1561.	17		48
Oct. 8, 1567. Halam, William, West Bridgeforthe (Notts.), husbn., Oct. 23, 1559.	17		726
Jun. 30, 1563. Haldisworthe, Alice, Sourebye, widow, Mar. 30, 1563.	17		262
Mar.21, 1564. Haldworthe, Gylbert, Sheffeld, May 20, 1564.	17		411
May 2, 1560. ———, William, Boillinge, par. Bradforde, Sep. 11, 1556.	16		42
July 16, 1562. Halewell, Thomas, Heptonstall, Apl. 22, 1562.	17		96
Oct. 3, 1565. Haliday, Richard, Ovenden, par. Hallifax, clothiar, Oct. 1, 1562.	17		480
Dec.16, 1556. Halile, Robert (bur. Saxton), Oct. 8, 1556.	15	1	195
Feb.18, 1556. ———, Thomas, Mylforth, par. Shereburn, Dec. 15, 1556.	15	1	161
May 9, 1566. Hall, Adam, Hawkesworthe (Notts.), Jan. 25, 1565.	17		549
Oct. 10, 1566. ———, Agnes, Orston (Notts.), Jan. 24, 1565.	17		592
Oct. 12, 1558. ———, Anthony (bur. Sutton Bonnington, Notts.), July 15, 1558.	15	3	32
Sep. 16, 1555. ———, Dunstone (bur. Barnebroughe), May, 18, 1555.	14		67
Apl. 18, 1567. ———, George, Rotherham, Mar. 14, 1566.	17		635
Feb. 24, 1566. ———, George, Rustone, par. Wykam, ———, 1566.	17		615
Mar.21, 1560. ———, Hew, [Hull], marchant, Aug. 17, 1559.	16		173
Oct. 31, 1565. ———, Jane, ladye, wid. of Robert H., York, marchant and alderman, deceased Oct. 8, 1565.	17		478
May 2, 1560. ———, Jennat, Appelton (bur. Bolton Percye), Nov. 25, 1558.	16		56
July 5, 1557. ———, Joan, Tikhill, widow, Oct. 12, 1556.	15	1	299
Aug. 8, 1561. ———, John, Bardsay, smythe, July 17, 1561.	17		64
Apl. 27, 1558. ———, John, Calton (bur. Kyrkbye Malhamdaill), Feb. 21, 1557.	15	2	204
Jun. 4, 1561. ———, John, West Mynlnes, par. Myrfeld, Jan. 8, 1560.	17		67
Apl. 11, 1559. ———, John, North Grymston, Oct. 13, 1558.	15	3	331
Jan. 13, 1558. ———, John, Rosington, Apl. 13, 1558.	15	3	186
Feb.15, 1558. ———, John, Rowton (bur. Swyne), carpenter, Oct. 11, 1558.	15	3	269
Oct. 2, 1560. ———, John, Ryston in Holderness, yeoman, Apl. 5, 1560.	16		116
Jun. 2, 1558. ———, John, Watton, labourer, Jan. 31, 1557.	15	2	312
Apl. 27, 1558. ———, John, Wodhouse, par. Byngley, Jan. 1, 1557.	15	2	199
Sep. 15, 1558. ———, Lawrence, Langton, husbandman, Jun. 30, 1558.	15	3	104
Nov.29, 1557. ———, Margaret, Scrayngham, widow, Aug. 11, 1557.	15	2	95
July 19, 1567. ———, Margaret, Shibden, par. Halifax, widow, Feb. 8, 1566.	17		680
Aug.28, 1561. ———, Marie, Matherseythorpe (Notts.), widow, May 27, 1561.	17		57
Nov.17, 1558. ———, Michaell, Swillington, gentleman, Aug. 8, 1558.	15	3	113
Apl. 28, 1563. ———, Rauf, Wicharslay, Mar. 12, 1563.	17		234
Oct. 5, 1564. ———, Richard, Doncaster, alderman, Apl. 17, 1564.	17		375
May 18, 1566. ———, Richard, Lathom (bur. Awghton), clerk, Mar. 1, 1565.	17		538
Dec.15, 1557. ———, Richard, Ordsall (Notts.), Mar 22, 1555.	15	2	59
Apl. 20, 1564. ———, Richard, Sheffeld, July 3, 1560.	17		325
Apl. 26, 1558. ———, Richard, Westbretton, par. Silkestone, Feb. 21, 1557.	15	2	338
Oct. 6, 1557. ———, Robert, Cottgrave (Notts.), smythe, Apl. 4, 1557.	15	2	29
Mar.15, 1560. ———, Robert, Fynningley (Notts.), yeoman, July 8, 1560.	16		169
May 5, 1558. ———, Robert, Mathersaythorpe (Notts.), Nov. 26, 1557.	15	2	241
May 9, 1566. ———, Robert, Orstone (Notts.), husbandman, Jan. 2, 1565.	17		548
Sep. 18, 1565. ———, Robert, Peniston, May 21, 1565.	17		467
Mar.22, 1558. ———, Robert, Wragbie, Jan. 25, 1558.	15	3	293
Oct. 8, 1565. ———, Robert, York, marchaunt and allderman, Oct. 25, 6 Eliz.	17		477
Jan. 23, 1558. ———, Thomas, Calton (bur. Kirkby in Mallhamdale), Nov. 10, 1558.	15	3	214
Jan. 24, 1558. ———, Thomas, Est Hirlesay, Oct. 14, 1558.	15	3	117
Oct. 16, 1558. ———, Thomas, Hothome, weaver, Feb. 3, 1557.	15	2	367
May 8, 1567. ———, Thomas, Northe Cave, husbandman, Sep. 20, 1566.	17		650
Aug.13, 1567. ———, Thomas, Ryse, husbandman, Apl. 12, 1567.	17		690
Oct. 2, 1566. ———, Thomas, Tankersley, Jun. 16, 1566.	17		578

1 This should have been entered also under letter A, but the error in the Register was not observed until after that portion of the index was printed off.

		Vol.	Pt.	Fol.
Oct. 10, 1566.	Hall, William, Hawkesworth (Notts.), husbandman, Mar. 13, 1566.	17		595
May 4, 1558.	——, William, Hawxworth (Notts.), May 8, 1557.	15	2	264
Apl. 7, 1554.	——, William, Esington, Mar. 2, 1553.	14		217
Oct. 6, 1557.	——, William, Hawxworthe (Notts.), May 7, 1557.	15	2	27
May 19, 1557.	——, William, Hedricke, par. Harwoodde, Mar. 20, 1557.	15	1	257
May 18, 1559.	——, William, Highe Hulland, Jun. 12, 1558.	15	3	399
Feb. 6, 1565.	——, William, Leppington, par. Scryngham, husbn., Aug. 13, 1565.	17		498
Mar. 19, 1559.	——, William (bur. Myrefelde), Feb. 14, 1559.	16		12
Oct. 10, 1566.	——, William, Scraton (Notts.), hnsbandman, Jun. 14, 1566.	17		594
Oct. 10, 1566.	Hallam, Mathew, Nottingham, Apl. 2 1566.	17		591
Nov. 4, 1561.	————, Robert, Brydlington Key, May 28, 1561.	17		34
Oct. 6, 1557.	———— als. Cran, Richard, Rodeington (Notts.), Jun. 22, 1557.	15	2	33
May 13, 1557.	Halle, Edward, Estbrygforth (Notts.), Nov. 12, 1556.	15	2	132
Apl. 17, 1567.	——, Edward, Scothrope, par. Kirkbie Malham, Sep. 6, 8 Eliz.	17		619
Oct. 7, 1563.	——, George, Moregate, par. Clarebrugh (Notts.), Feb. 9, 1561.	17		296
Oct. 3, 1566.	Hallele, Richard, Sherburne, July 26, 1566.	17		581
Oct. 25, 1558.	Halley, John, Rouston, par. Wikham in Pickeringlyth, husbandman, Sep. 23, 1558.	15	3	237
Jun. 8, 1565.	Halliday, John, Dugglebe, par. Kirkebye Grendall, Oct. 16, 1564.	17		444
Jan. 13, 1556.	Hallyday, Robert, Kirkby in Gryndall lith, Jan. 1, 1556.	15	1	87
Nov. 27, 1560.	Hallydone, William, Hovingham, Apl. 18, 1560.	16		130
Apl. 26, 1558.	Hallyley, Jennett, Millfurth, par. Sherburne, wid., Aug. 28, 1557.	15	2	237
May 2, 1560.	Hallywell, John, Seymer, husbandman, Jan. 30, 1559.	16		35
Dec. 1, 1563.	Halme (Holme), John, Slephill (bur. Skelbroke), Dec. 22, 1562.	17		305
Oct. 6, 1558.	Halott (or Hoclott), Richard, Wombwell, par. Darfeld, Aug. 5, 1558.	15	3	223
Oct. 28, 1563.	Halyday, Nicholas, Rivalx (bur. Helmesley), Mar. 3, 1561.	17		299
Feb. 7, 1554.	Halydaye, Peter, Atterclife, par. Sheffelde, cutler, Sep. 19, 1554.	14		74
Oct. 4, 1558.	Halylye, Edward, Sherborne, Aug. 3, 1558.	15	3	58
May 18, 1555.	Halywell, Robert, Carleton, par. Snaithe, Mar. 2, 1554.	14		251
Nov. 29, 1558.	Hamerton, Isabell, Tickhill, widow, Aug. 3, 1558.	15	3	139
Apl. 6, 1558.	Hamesha, Christopher, Thorne, Oct. 25, 1557.	15	2	188
Jun. 22, 1568.	Hamlinge, Leonarde, Farneley, par. Ottley, July 22, 1567.	17		816
Oct. 1, 1567.	————, Thomas, Lisset, July 24, 1567.	17		713
Nov. 2, 1555.	Hamonde, Anthony, Skarthingwell, par. Saxton, esq., Aug. 26, 1553.	14		246
Jun. 9, 1563.	Hampton, John, Seglistorne, husbandman, Feb. 22, 1562.	17		254
Aug. 26, 1561.	Hanbie, John, Overthwonge, par. Almonburie, Jun. 11, 1558.	17		55
Mar. 21, 1559.	Hanbye, Nicholas, Holington, Nov. 24, 1559.	16		16
Feb. 24, 1563.	Hancocke, Edward, Halsam, Dec. 20, 1563.	17		317
Oct. 1, 1560.	Handlay, Henry, West Draton (Notts.), husbn., Jun. 8, 1560.	16		115
Mar. 15, 1558.	Handley, Richard, Ellerton, Jan. 16, 1558.	15	3	167
Apl. 22, 1564.	————, Roger, Hie Melton, Feb. 6, 1556.	17		325
Dec. 16, 1557.	Handslay, Rauffe (bur. Halsham), Sep. 17, 1557.	15	2	47
Apl. 28, 1558.	Hanforthe, Margaret, Thirske, Dec. 29, 1557.	15	2	206
May 6, 1563.	Hankoke, John, Bothamsell (Notts.), Jan. 9, 1562.	17		244
Sep. 21, 1557.	Hanley, George, Wadworthe, Sep. 12, 1556.	15	1	351
Oct. 6, 1557.	————, Thomas, Scrobye (Notts.), yeoman, Aug. 8, 1557.	15	2	8
Mar. 15, 1558.	Hannan, Niccayus, Wressle, Sep. 24, 1558.	15	3	168
May 9, 1565.	Hanooke, George, Mytton, Dec. 13, 1564.	17		434
May 5, 1568.	Hansell, Peter, Gysburne, smythe, Mar. 26, 1568.	17		773
Mar. 26, 1565.	Hanson, Alice, widow of Richard H., Wolrawe in Hertyshed, par. Dewisberye, Oct. 27, 1563.	17		415
Sep. 1, 1563.	————, Christopher, Haitfeld, husbandman, Mar. 14, 1563.	17		207
May 31, 1557.	————, Edmond, Derfeld, yeoman, May 1, 1554.	15	1	211
Dec. 12, 1567.	————, John, Barnesley, yeoman, Nov. 16, 1567.	17		744
July 10, 1567.	————, John, Felkirk, May 8, 9 Eliz.	17		684
May 13, 1557.	————, John, Gresthorpe, par. Sutton on Trente (Notts.), Mar. 14, 1556.	15	1	217
Apl. 19, 1564.	————, John, Gryndleton, par. Mytton, Dec. 16, 1563.	17		328
Apl. 3, 1554.	————, John, Woodhouse, in Rastrick par. Eland, Feb. 15, 1553.	14		221
Dec. 22, 1556.	————, Laurence, Thurguland, par. Sylkeston, Aug. 12, 1556.	15	1	77
Jun. 8, 1560.	————, Lucie, Darffelde, Aug. 6, 1558.	16		81
Oct. 13, 1558.	————, Richard, Marnham (Notts.), Apl. 28, 1558.	15	2	365
Nov. 3, 1554.	————, Richard, Wolrawe, par. Hertishead, May 21, 1554.	14		290

		Vol.	Pt.	Fol.
Apl. 3, 1554.	Hanson, Robert, Wodhouse, par. Eland, July 31, 1553.	14		60
Apl. 16, 1567.	——, Robert, Wollerawe, par. Hartishead, Mar. 26, 1567.	17		628
Oct. 6, 1557.	——, William, Scrobye (Notts.), Feb. 8, 1556.	15	2	11
Oct. 24, 1561.	Harbattill, John, York, Jun. 17, 1561.	17		33
Nov. 19, 1556.	Harberde, Nicholas, Wygnam, par. Wheldrik, Aug. 11, 1554.	14		70
Oct. 4, 1558.	Harberye, Thomas, Perlington, par. Aberford, husbandman, Aug. 8, 1558.	15	3	59
Nov. 6, 1554.	Hardcastell, Marye, Womerslaye, widow, Dec. 4. 1552.	14		293
July 2, 1558.	——, Richard, Rybston (bur. Spoffurthe), Jun. 6, 1558.	15	2	342
Sep. 29, 1557.	Hardcastle, Christopher, Dacrebankes, par. Pathleybrigges, Sep. 19, 1557.	15	1	330
No date.	——, Christopher, Newbroughe, par. Cockwold, Jan. 8, 1552.	14		261
Apl. 26, 1559.	Harde, Brian, Garton on Wold, May 16, 1558.	15	3	311
Jun. 23, 1558.	——, John (bur. Bubwithe), May 27, 1558.	15	2	340
Oct. 28, 1566.	——, Roger, Stonnlunde (bur. N. Ferybie), labourer, May 16, 1566.	17		587
Mar. 31, 1563.	Hardene (?Hardinge), John, Newbie, par. Stokeslav, Dec. 11, 1562.	17		219
Feb. 24, 1560.	Hardie, Margaret, widow of Robert H., Baynton, Dec. 10, 1560.	16		150
Jan. 23, 1561.	——, Thomas, Owstwicke, par. Rosse, Nov. 18, 1561.	17		20
May 2, 1566.	——, William, Connyston, par. Gargrave, May 19, 1566.	17		529
Apl. 13, 1559.	Harding, William, Kirkeburne, Mar. 2, 1558.	15	3	347
Oct. 9, 1560.	Hardistie, William, Nether Popleton, husbandman, Nov. 5, 1558.	16		120
Oct. 6, 1557.	Hardshall, Henry, Glapton, par. Clifton (Notts.), May 2, 1557.	15	2	27
May 13, 1568.	Hardstaffe, James (bur. Oxton, Notts.), Apl. 6, 1566.	17		797
May 10, 1559.	Hardweke, Henry (bur. Hardingham), Apl. 13, 1559.	15	3	386
Oct. 21, 1557.	——, Thomas, Potternewton (bur. Leedes), gentleman, Jun. 3, 3 and 4 Phil. and Mary.	15	1	360
Mar. 12, 1555.	Hardwicke, John, Adingham, Nov. 20, 1554.	14		264
May 29, 1568.	——, Robert, Cottingham, labourer, Jan. 3, 1567.	17		794
July 2, 1556.	——, William, Ottley, joiner, May 5, 1556.	15	1	46
Dec. 18, 1556.	Hardwike, Thomas, Newleythe in Horsefurthe (bur. Giesley), Sep. 4, 1556.	15	1	175
Dec. 18, 1556.	Hardwyke, Henry, Brakantwayte, par. Kyrkbyoverblows, yeoman, July 16, 1556.	15	1	176
Mar. 20, 1560.	Hardy, James, Hardyn, par. Byngley, Nov. 13, 1560.	16		170
Mar. 4, 1560.	——, John, Rypplingham (bur. Rowley), husbn., Jan. 13, 1560.	16		165
May 18, 1559.	——, Robert, senr., Brandisburtone, husbandman, Apl. 25, 1559.	15	3	408
Feb. 9, 1557.	——, Robert, Owstwicke (bnr. Roosse), husbn., Sep. 22, 1557.	15	2	123
Oct. 11, 1565.	——, Robert, Oxton (Notts.), July 8, 1565.	17		470
Jan. 28, 1557.	Hardye, John, Baynton, Dec. 29, 1557.	15	2	155
Mar. 23, 1557.	——, John, Halsham, husbandman, Feb. 4, 1557.	15	2	172
July 2, 1561.	——, Nicholas, Gemlinge (bur. Foston), May 8, 1561.	17		78
Apl. 26, 1558.	——, Robert, Baynton, husbandman, Feb. 23, 1557.	15	2	221
Apl. 26, 1558.	——, Rosemunde, Baynton, widow, Mar. 12, 1557.	15	2	222
Sep. 30, 1563.	——, William, Sorbye, Halyfaxe, clothier, Sep. 7, 1562.	17		283
May 8, 1567.	Hare, John, Northe Cave, tayler, Oct. 18, 1566.	17		650
Mar. 20, 1558.	Harebrede, Richard, Selbie, glewer, Mar. 31, 1558.	15	3	251
Jun. 22, 1568.	Harelington, Robert, Blythe (Notts.), maltster, Jun. 5, 1568.	17		829
May 5, 1568.	Hareson, Robert, Rilston, Oct. 24, 1567.	17		783
Nov. 6, 1557.	Haresonne, William, Walkyngham (Notts.), husbn., July 23, 1557.	15	2	107
Apl. 6, 1568.	Hargell, Thomas, Sherburne, ——, 1567.	17		770
Aug. 4, 1558.	Hargill, Richard, Hull, berebruer (born at Saigefelde), Apl 15, 1558.	15	3	4
Apl. 16, 1562.	Hargraives, Christopher, Scott Hill (bur. Kildweke), Feb. 22, 1561.	17		188
Jun. 9, 1563.	Hargrave, Nicholas, Readnes (bur. Whitgyfte), Jan. 1, 1562.	17		257
Dec. 18, 1560.	——, William, Hunslet Woodhouse (bur. Leedes), Jun. 8, 1560.	16		136
Sep. 30, 1562.	Harison, John, Haitfeild, marchant, July 28, 1562.	17		114
Oct. 8, 1556.	Harisone, Robert, Upton (Notts.), Apl. 19, 1556.	15	1	155
Mar. 22, 1560.	Harkay, John, Symnyngton, husbandman, Aug. 16, 1560.	16		178
Dec. 9, 1556.	Harland, Cicile, Weton (bur. Wellweke), widow. *No date.*	15	1	72
July 7, 1567.	——, Robert, Yngilbie under Grenoo, Jan, 15, 1567.	17		671
Oct. 20, 1554.	——, Roger, Kirkby under Knoll, Sep. 20, 1552.	14		48
May 10, 1567.	Harling, Edward, vicar of Eastdrayton (Notts.), Dec. 14, 1565.	17		651
July 2, 1561.	Harlley, Jenet, Burton Agnes, widow, Jan. 11, 1559.	17		77
No date.	Harpam, William, parish clarke, Arksaye, Nov. 6, 1 & 2 Phil. & Mary.	14		88

		Vol.	Pt.	Fol.
Feb. 6, 1558.	Harpam, William, Brigham (bur. Fostone), Oct. 12, 1558.	15	3	261
Aug. 7, 1555.	Harper, Agnes, Heton Wanslaye, Jun. 6, 1554.	14		242
Jun. 2, 1558.	———, Elizabeth, Esthorpe (bur. Goodmanham), wid., Dec. 3, 1557.	15	2	335
Sep. 30, 1557.	———, Henry, Preston (Holderness), July 15, 1557.	15	1	341
Sep. 30, 1557.	———, James, Esthorppe (bur. Gudmanham), husbn., Sep. 5, 1557.	15	1	326
Sep. 30, 1562,	———, John, Lekinfeld, yeoman, Jun. 18, 1562.	17		117
May 14, 1560.	———, Richard, Escrige (bur. Stockton), Jan. 1, 1559.	16		63
Dec. 17, 1567.	———, Thomas, York, alderman and draper, Nov. 18, 1567.	17		746
Oct. 2, 1567.	———, William, Selbie, Jun. 27, 1567.	17		710
Feb.ult.,1557.	———, William, York, draper, Dec. 3, 1557.	15	2	163
Jan. 15, 1557.	Harreson, John, Nonapleton (bur. Bolton Percye), Dec. 16, 1557.	15	2	61
Mar.14, 1560.	———, Steven, Newarke (Notts.), Sep. 13, 1559.	16		157
Feb. 6, 1558.	———, Thomas, Cowicke (bur. Snathe), Oct. 15, 1558.	15	3	263
Apl. 12, 1559.	———, William (bur. Huton Bushill), Mar. 17, 1557.	15	3	342
Jan. 26, 1562.	Harrington, James, York, marchaunt and alderman, Jan. 15, 1562.	17		143
Mar.23, 1560.	———, William (bur. Sowerbie), Jan. 11, 1560.	16		175
No date.	Harrison, John, Besyngby, marchaunt, Oct. 1, 1555.	14		19
Nov.20, 1563.	———, Percivall, Halifax, inholder, May 21, 1563.	17		303
Jun. 20, 1566.	———, Robert, Rudstone, Apl. 9, 1566.	17		556
Jan. 20, 1561.	———, Thomas, Halifax, Jun. 30, 1561.	17		23
Apl. 26, 1558.	———, William, Campsall, Sep. 9, 1557.	15	2	228
Apl. 20, 1559.	———, William, Everton (Notts.), husbandman, Jan. 11, 1558.	15	3	306
Jun. 27, 1562.	———, William, Newarke (Notts.), vintener, Jan. 25, 1561.	17		90
Oct. 1, 1556.	Harrisone, Christopher, Lethelaye, Aug. 18, 1556.	15	1	135
Oct. 2, 1566.	Harrisonne, John, Thorne, Feb. 6, 1566.	17		577
Aug.27, 1557.	Harrissonne, Thomas, Barston (bur. Saxton) May 30, 1557.	15	2	115
Mar.21, 1559.	Harryngeton, Stephan, Heydon in Holderness, gent., Jan. 20, 1558.	16		17
Oct. 9, 1567.	Harryson, Alexander, Barmebie (Notts.), husbandman, May 18, 1567.	17		723
Apl. 6, 1558.	———, Christopher, Bassheall Eavys (bur. Mytton), Jan. 3, 1557.	15	2	179
Oct. 26, 1557.	———, Ellenour, Basenbye, widow, Sep. 23, 1557.	15	1	365
Jun. 17, 1556.	———, Henry, Rookeboirwight, par. Normanbye, Mar. 2, 1556.	15	1	49
Dec. 21, 1562.	———, Isabell, Trunflett, par. Sandall, Dec. 11, 1562.	17		137
Jan. 18, 1560.	———, John (bur. Sheryfton), husbandman, Sep. 1, 1560.	16		140
July 10, 1561.	———, John, Snathe, clerk, Mar. 26, 1551.	17		64
May 5, 1568.	———, Nicholas, Sandesend, par. Lithe, Jan. 24, 1566.	17		774
Apl. 19, 1559.	———, Richard, Ansley (Notts.), husbandman, Oct. 13, 1558.	15	3	358
May 31, 1566.	———, Richard, Everton (Notts.), yeoman, Feb. 14, 1565.	17		543
Mar. 2, 1558.	———, Richard, Flaxton (bur. Bossall), Jan. 8, 1558.	15	3	281
Sep. 29, 1557.	———, Richard, Standley, par. Wakefelde, Jun. 8, 1557.	15	1	328
Feb. 9, 1557.	———, Robert, Rowthe, husbandman, Jun. 11, 1557.	15	2	120
Jun. 12, 1567.	———, Robert, Stoneferrye (bur. Sutton), Mar. 18, 1566.	17		662
Apl. 27, 1558.	———, Rowland, Normunbye, Feb. 25, 1557.	15	2	226
Oct. 2, 1567.	———, Thomas, Flinton, par. Humbleton, Jun. 10, 1567.	17		713
Jan. 9, 1560.	———, Thomas, Settrington, yeoman, Oct. 4, 1560.	16		145
May 5, 1568.	———, Walter, Middle Walton (bur. Sandall), husbn., Jan. 7,1567.	17		789
Oct. 2, 1567.	———, William, Braikenwaite (bur. Kirkebe overblause), Dec. 11, 1566.	17		721
May 3, 1566.	———, William, Denton, par. Otley, Feb. 18, 1565.	17		525
Oct. 16, 1557.	———, William, Lounde, par. Brayton, Aug. 29, 1557.	15	1	366
Nov.28, 1567.	———, William, Rudston, husbandman, Jun. 28, 1567.	17		737
May 19, 1559.	———, William, Shereburne, May 4, 1558.	15	3	426
Mar.28, 1560.	———, William, West Heslerton, par. Yeddingame, Feb. 13, 1559.	16		22
Oct. 12, 1558.	Harstoffe, William, Selston (Notts.), July 28, 1558.	15	3	227
May 13, 1557.	Harston, Hewgh, East Brigforth (Notts.), husbn., Feb. 7, 1556.	15	1	230
Oct. 8, 1556.	———, Richard, Est Brygforthe (Notts.), Sep. 8, 1555.	15	1	151
May 18, 1559.	Hart, Issabell, Swyne, widow, ———, 1558.	15	3	395
May 6, 1559.	———, John, Skynnyngraff, par. Brotton, fyshareman, Dec. 7, 1558.	15	3	383
Oct. 20, 1561.	———, Thomas, Lyngardes, par. Almonburie, Dec. 29, 1560.	17		44
Apl. 28, 1558.	———, William, Malteby, par. Stayntone, Mar. 5, 1557.	15	2	231
May 5, 1558.	Hartclyf, John, Newarke (Notts.), yeoman, Mar. 26, 15[5]7.	15	2	257
Mar.27, 1560.	Harte, Elizabeth, Brotton, Feb. 2, 1559.	16		21
Sep. 29, 1560.	———, Henry, Brotton, Sep. 13, 1560.	16		106

A.D. 1554 TO 1568.

		Vol.	Pt.	Fol.
Oct. 20, 1558.	Harte, John, Swine, husbandman, Sep. 15, 1558.	15	2	351
Apl. 8, 1559.	——, Robert, Hesgayte, par. Felixkirke, Dec. 17, 1558.	15	3	322
Mar.24, 1560.	——, Thomas, Loftus (Cleveland), Mar. 13, 1557.	16		178
Dec.22, 1556.	Hartelay, William, Thorpe par. Wynteworthe, husbn., Apl. 28, 1556.	15	1	85
Jan. 28, 1556.	Harteley, Richard, Hatefeld, yeoman, Nov. 30, 1556.	15	1	92
Apl. 13, 1554.	————, Margaret, Mallome (bur. Kirkebie), Jan. 5, 1 Mary.	14		57
Sep. 30, 1557.	Hartforthe, Agnes, Selbye, widow, July 17, 1557.	15	1	345
July 18, 1556.	————, Christopher, Staynner, par. Selbye, Jun. 6, 1556.	15	1	56
Sep. 30, 1557.	Hartfurthe, Agnes, spinster, daughter of Christopher H. (bur. Selbye), July 15, 1557.	15	1	343
Mar. 3, 1555.	Harthows, Peter, Barnyston, Oct. 1, 1555.	15	1	11
Oct. 29, 1554.	Hartishorne, Thomas, Great Leyke, husbandman, July 18, 1554.	14		285
Nov.17, 1558.	Hartlay, Henry, Cawood, Mar. 26, 1558.	15	3	113
Feb. 20, 1560.	Hartley, John, Snytall, par. Normanton, Nov. 29, 1560.	16		147
Oct. 3, 1560.	——, Myles (bur. Kighley), clerk, Jun. 2, 1560.	16		119
Apl. 28, 1563.	——, Omfraye, Healey, par. Batley, Apl. 15, 1563.	17		210
May 17, 1565.	——, Richard, Cottham (Notts.), husbandman, Apl. 29, 1565.	17		436
Feb. 17, 1557.	——, Richard, Longley, par. Eglesfeld, Aug. 23, 1557.	15	2	139
Feb. 4, 1558.	——, Symond, Eskrige, yeoman, Sep. 4, 1558.	15	3	24
Feb. 20, 1560.	——, Thomas, Pryston Jacklinge (bur. Fetherstone), Jan.27,1560.	16		147
Oct. 3, 1566.	——, Walter, Hawkisworthe (bur. Ottley), Nov. 16, 1565.	17		582
Oct. 10, 1566.	Hartshorne, Robert, Ratcliff on Sore (Notts.), husbn., May 1, 1566.	17		594
Jun. 25, 1568.	Hartte, Robert, Swyne, Apl. 15, 1568.	17		810
Apl. 20, 1559.	Harttewell, John, Bestrope (bur. S. Scarle, Notts.), Mar. 4, 1558.	15	3	306
Oct. 1, 1556.	Harvey, George, Hardwicke, par. Astone, May 13, 1554.	15	1	130
Jan. 14, 1560.	Harvye, Robert, Camylfurthe, par. Drax, May 20, 1560.	16		143
July 15, 1561.	——, William, Aston Netherthorpe, Mar. 31, 1561.	17		82
Dec. 5, 1567.	Harwarde, George, Preston in Holderness, husbn., July 24, 1567.	17		741
Oct. 2, 1560.	Harwood, Alys (bur. Hotonbushell, widow, Jun. 15, 1560.	16		110
Jun. 22, 1565.	——, Jennet, Ferndale, par. Kirkbye Moreshed, Apl. 18, ——.	17		445
July 27, 1567.	——, John, Aslebie, par. Whitbie, Apl. 27, 1567.	17		672
Apl. 16, 1562.	——, Margaret, Burythorpe, Aug. 18, 1561.	17		157
July 12, 1563.	——, Martyn, Ayton par. Hoottonbushell, husbn., July 31, 1558.	17		263
Jan. 13, 1558.	——, Robert, Flosweke, par. Worsoppe (Notts.), Oct. 9, 1558.	15	3	186
Jan. 9, 1560.	——, Thomas, Edlethorpe (bur. Westowe), husbn., Nov.23,1560.	16		145
Jun. 2, 1558.	Harwoode, Robert, Hornesey, shipwright, Apl. 12, 1558.	15	2	337
May 6, 1557.	——, Steven, Cotingham, Feb. 3, 1556.	15	1	250
Sep. 30, 1557.	Haryham, William, South Oterington, Sep. 8, 1557.	15	1	347
July 11, 1558.	Haryngton als. Darnyll, William, Rotherham, May 20, 1558.	15	2	304
May 18, 1559.	Haryson, Elizabeth, Sutton in Holderness, Mar. 30, 1558.	15	3	395
Oct. 2, 1566.	——, Garrat, Headon, marchaunt, Jun. 12, 1566.	17		581
Jan. 26, 1557.	——, John, Rawden (bur.Gyesley), myllston maker, Sep.24,1557.	15	2	160
Mar.27, 1566.	——, John, Sansend, par. Lithe, Dec. 22, 1565.	17		507
May 12, 1559.	——, Michaell, Beverley, towne clarke, Aug. 16, 1558.	15	3	392
Mar.21, 1560.	——, Richard (bur. Ripon), July 31, 1560.	16		174
Oct. 1, 1566.	——, Robert, Dayltowne, par. Hawnebie, May 7, 1566.	17		583
May 18, 1559.	Harysone, Robert, Suttone in Holderness, Mar. 26, 1559.	15	3	409
Nov. 8, 1557.	Harysonne, Edmunde, Cunsbrugh, husbandman, Sep. 20, 1557.	15	2	110
Oct. 7, 1557.	Hashurst, William, Nuttall (Notts.), May 8, 1557.	15	2	23
May 5, 1558.	[1] Haslabie, Alis, Mylneton, par. West Markham (Notts.),wid., Nov. 15, 1557.	15	2	249
Oct. 7, 1556.	——, John, Mylneton (bur.West Markham,Notts.), Feb. 24, 1555.	15	1	146
May 13, 1557.	Hassard, William, Laxton (Notts.), Apl. 25, 1557.	15	1	218
Jan. 8, 1560.	Hassarde, Robert, Colwyke, par. Snaythe, July 24, 1559.	16		138
May 9, 1565.	Hasselland, Richard, Wales, par. Treaton, Apl. 1, 1565.	17		428
Dec. 1, 1558.	Hassill, William, South Clyf (bur. North Cave), milner, May 10, 1558.	15	3	148
Jun. 22, 1568.	Hassillwood, Robert, Hunmanbie, Nov. 20, 1567.	17		821
May 13, 1557.	Hasspyn, Robert, Morehowse, par. Laxton (Notts.), Apl. 10, 1557.	15	1	218
Feb. 8, 1558.	Hastinges, Robert, Hacknes, gentleman, Dec. 31, 1558.	15	3	273
Mar.10, 1554.	Hatfeilde, William, Wilfurthe (Notts.), gentleman, July 1, 1553.	14		233

1 See also under letter A.

	Vol.	Pt.	Fol
Sep. 26, 1558. Hatfeld, Nicolas, Ecclesfeld, Aug. 2, 1558.	15	3	54
May 5, 1558. Hathornewhite, William, Myssyn (Notts.), Oct. 22, 1557.	15	2	333
Jan. 5, 1567. Hatter, John, Gremstone, par. St. Nicholas, York, husbn., Dec. 4, 1567.	17		755
Jun. 21, 1567. ——, John, Wheldricke, Mar. 12, 1557.	17		665
May 31, 1557. Hatterslaie, Thomas, Penyston, Dec. 18, 1556.	15	1	261
Jan. 30, 1555. Hattursley, Nicholas, Medhope in Bradfeld, Oct. 30, 1555.	15	1	3
July 19, 1566. Hauelocke, Margaret, Wykam, ——, 1566.	17		562
Mar. 29, 1560. ——, Robert, Harlbeke mylne in Skelton, yeoman, Apl. 21, 1559.	16		2
Nov. 29, 1558. Haukeshirst, Richard (bur. Cawthorne), Mar. 25, 1557.	15	3	140
Mar. 20, 1558. Hauksworth, Edward (bur. Calthorne), Aug. 30, 1558.	15	3	246
Mar. 20, 1558. ——, John, Ottley, Nov. 8, 1558.	15	3	250
Jun. 22, 1568. Haule, John, Kirkbbe overblause, husbandman, Apl. 26, 1568.	17		816
Mar. 23, 1559. Haull, Christopher, Gargrave, Mar. 11, ——.	16		18
Jun. 4, 1568. ——, George, Skernebecke, Aug. 23, 1567.	17		811
Aug. 16, 1560. ——, James, Wersegill (bur. Kyrkelevinton), gent., Nov. 9, 1559.	16		103
Feb. 11, 1556. ——, John, Drax, yeoman, Nov. 4, 1556.	15	1	156
Jan. 30, 1555. ——, John, Dreton, Sep. 18, 1555.	15	1	3
Jan. 8, 1563. ——, John, Thorpe, par. Rotherham, Jun. 4, 1563.	17		308
Apl. 30, 1556. ——, Nicholas. Thurgartone (Notts.), husbandman, Jan. 6, 1555.	15	1	30
Feb. 9, 1555. ——, Thomas, Menythorpe, par. Westowe, May 14, 1555.	15	1	6
Oct. 3, 1566. ——, William, Kirkbe overblause, husbandman, Apl. 8, 1566.	17		583
July 15, 1556. ——, William, Wodd Apilton, par. Lastingham, husbn., Dec. 20, 1555.	15		55
Aug. 28, 1563. Hault (Hall, Act Bk.), Thomas, Gomersall, par. Burstall, Dec. 18, 1562.	17		210
Jun. 20, 1566. Haumon, Alice (bur. Baddsworthe), May 19, 1565.	17		560
Nov. 29, 1558. Hauslin, Jennet, Harlay, par. Wentworth, widow, May 14, 1558.	15	3	110
May 5, 1557. Havelocke, Thomas, Wikham, Nov. 25, 1553.	15	1	252
Nov. 20, 1557. Havercroft, Robert, Fowcarbey (bur. Adlyngflett), Dec. 8, 1557.	15	2	94
May 18, 1559. Havercrofte, William, Fokkarbe, par. Adlingflete, Jan. 13, 1558.	15	3	413
Oct. 7, 1563. Havton, George, Scrowbie (Notts.), Mar. 9, 1563.	17		295
July 11, 1558. Hawcelyn, James (bur. Thorne), Mar. 22, 1558.	15	2	316
Mar. 20, 1560. Hawghton, George, Mytton, Nov. 3, 1560.	16		172
Apl. 11, 1559. Hawke, William, Hecope, par. Athill [Adel], Jan. 6, 1558.	15	3	331
July 11, 1558. Hawkehirst, Henry, Haughe, par. Rotherham, Sep. 30, 1553.	15	2	319
Oct. 1, 1556. Hawkeryge, John, Westone, July 20, 1556.	15	1	135
Aug. 26, 1561. Hawkesworth, Charles, Nethershittiltowne, par. Thornell, July 23, 1561.	17		55
Oct. 5, 1564. ——, Henry, Thornset in Bradfeild, Dec. 31, 1563.	17		376
Oct. 24, 1554. ——, William, Dongworth in Bradfeld, May 27, 1554.	14		308
May 18, 1559. ——, William, Penystone, yeoman, Feb. 7, 1558.	15	3	419
Apl. 28, 1563. Hawkesworthe, Henry, Edlyngton, Apl. 2, 1563.	17		234
Oct. 5, 1564. ——, Robert, Sugworthe in Bradfeild, July 27, 1564.	17		376
Jan. 14, 1564. ——, Thomas, Waldershelf in Bradfeld, May 8, 1561.	17		402
Jun. 6, 1560. Hawkins, John, Beverlaye, capper, Nov. 27, 1559.	16		75
Feb. 16, 1561. Hawksworthe, William, Cauthorne, yeoman, Jun. 15, 1561.	17		11
Mar. 21, 1564. Hawle, Alice, Doncaster, widow, Feb. 22, 1564.	17		410
Nov. 28, 1567. ——, William, Nafferton, Jun. 8, 1567.	17		737
Mar. 14, 1560. Hawlenne, Edmond, Holme (Notts.), Feb. 20, 1560.	16		158
Apl. 17, 1554. Hawley, John, Bubwith, husbandman, Feb. 27, 1553.	14		58
May 28, 1567. Hawlle, Richard, Holme in Spaldingmore, Mar. 5, 1566.	17		648
Dec. 2, 1562. Hawly, Edward, Stodfold (bur. Howton), gentleman, July 21, 1562.	17		129
Apl. 10, 1559. Hawme, Agnes, Skelbrooke, widow, Oct. 22, 1558.	15	3	326
Sep. 26, 1558. ——, Godfray, Slepe hill, par. Skelbroke, husbn., Jan. 12, 1558.	15	3	52
Mar. 15, 1560. Hawmond, Richard, Carleton in Lyndreke (Notts.), husbn., Dec. 28, 1560.	16		170
Jan. 21, 1557. ——, William, Hyllome (bur. Monckefryston), Aug. 1, 1557.	15	2	155
Jun. 4, 1561. Hawmshyer, Robert, Emley, Feb. 10, 1560.	17		68
Feb. 17, 1557. Hawselin, Thomas, senr., Wentworth, yeoman, Sep. 6, 1557.	15	2	142
Apl. 26, 1557. Hawson, George. Tykhill, tanner, Aug. 17, 1557.	15	2	226
Apl. 20, 1559. ——, Thomas, Ranskyll, par. Blyth (Notts.), sheapard, Mar. 16, 1558.	15	3	365
Nov. 29, 1558. —— (or Hanson?), William, Long Sandall, par. Doncaster, Sep. 22, 1558.	15	3	138
Feb. 17, 1557. Hawsonne, Edmund, Rawmarshe, Sep. 14, 1557.	15	2	138
Apl. 8, 1560. Hawxe, Thomas, Bryghton, par. Bubwith, Oct. 20, 1559.	16		29
Mar. 16, 1558. Haxbie, Thomas, Over Hemylsay, husbandman, Nov. 13, 1558.	15	3	242

		Vol.	Pt.	Fol.
Sep. 1, 1565.	Haxwell, Robert, Danbye, Jan. 12, 1564.	17		462
Jan. 17, 1557.	Hay, John, Skarbroughe, cordwyner, Jun. 24, 1557.	15	2	62
Jan. 21, 1555.	——, William, York, gyrdler, Dec. 26, 1555.	15	1	1
Apl. 13, 1557.	Haye, Rauf, Asleby, par. Myddleton, May 10, 1556.	15	1	208
Feb. 20, 1560.	——, William, Newe Myllner Dame. par. Sandall Magna, Jan. 21, 1560.	16		149
Aug. 13, 1567.	Hayekney, George, Baswicke, par. Brandisburton, Jun. 10, 1567.	17		690
Apl. 19, 1559.	Hayley, Thomas, Annesley (Notts.), husbandman, Nov. 4, 1558.	15	3	356
Oct. 1, 1557.	Hayre, Thomas, Pykton (bur. Kyrkelevington), July 24, 1557.	15	1	362
Aug. 6, 1563.	Hayton, Clemet, Holme in Spawdermore, Feb. 16, 1562.	17		212
May 29, 1568.	———, Elline, Hessill, widow, Feb. 23, 1568.	17		794
Sep. 30, 1557.	———, Katheren, Swynflete (bur. Whytgyft), Jun. 23, 1557.	15	1	346
Sep. 30, 1557.	Haytton, Richard, Hessell, husbandman, Aug. 28, 1557.	15	1	327
Nov. 3, 1558.	Hayworthe, Roger, Burstall, Sep. 29, 1558.	15	3	155
Oct. 3, 1561.	Headon, John, Beverley, esq., Aug. 7, 1561.	17		35
Nov. 17, 1558.	Healde, Alice, wid. of Umfray H. (bur. Whitkirke), Nov. 8, 1558.	15	3	111
Oct. 3, 1565.	Heaton, Henry, Kellington, ——, 1562.	17		476
Jun. 8, 1560.	———, Roger, the Mosse, par. Campsall, Mar. 14, 1559.	16		80
Feb. 17, 1557.	———, William, Fenwycke, par. Campsall, Nov. 5, 1557.	15	2	141
Sep. 15, 1562.	Hebdayne, Henry, York, cordewayner, 1562.	17		107
Oct. 14, 1564.	Hebdeine, John, Bishopside, par. Paiteley brigges, yeom., May 20, 1564.	17		378
Dec. 22, 1554.	Hebden, Christopher, Rypon, yeoman, Oct. 22, 1554.	14		97
Mar. 20, 1558.	———, Christopher, Thornethwayt (bur. Hamstwayt), tayler, Oct. 12, 1558.	15	3	289
May 5, 1568.	———, Gilbert, Eagilcoote, par. Skipton in Craven, Nov. 28, 1567.	17		784
Oct. 5, 1558.	———, John, Owghtershawe, par. Arneclife (bur. Hobram), Apl. 20, 1558.	15	3	61
Oct. 3, 1564.	———, Richard, Leedes, Aug. 6, 1564.	17		364
July 15, 1561.	Hebdeyn, Thomas, Clyfton, par. Conesburghe, Apl. 1, 1561.	17		82
Sep. 21, 1557.	Hedeley, Richard, Dodworthe, par. Silkeston, Aug. 17, 1557.	15	1	350
Jun. 27, 1558.	Hedlame, John, Huby (bur. Sutton in Galtres), gent., Mar. 11, 1552.	15	2	327
Oct. 8, 1556.	Hefelde, Thomas, Carcolstone (Notts.), Jun. 1, 1556.	15	1	149
May 18, 1559.	Heffeld, William, Borrocotes (Notts.), Feb. 1, 1556.	15	3	405
Sep. 26, 1558.	Heirste, Margery, Hatfeld, widow, Apl. 26, 1558.	15	3	52
Apl. 13, 1559.	Heiton, Christopher, Hornsebecke (bur. Hornsey). *No date.*	15	3	344
Oct. 16, 1558.	Helbart, Robert, Everthorpe, par. North Cave, Apl. 18, 1558.	15	2	366
Sep. 30, 1557.	Helcocke, Robert, Brayton, husbandman, July 22, 1557.	15	1	346
Dec. 3, 1560.	Heldrith, John, Hayingham, Feb. 15, 1560.	16		133
Apl. 28, 1563.	Helesse, John, senr., Skibken, par. Skipton, Sep. 2, 1562.	17		226
Aug. 2, 1554.	Helies, Thomas, Skipton in Craven, Oct. 2, 1553.	14		267
Dec. 22, 1556.	Hellele, Robert, Hoton Robert, ——, 1556.	15	1	77
Dec. 5, 1565.	Hellme, Richard, Stockbrige, par. Arksay, Nov. 2, 1565.	17		492
July 27, 1564.	Helme, Richard, Heisselhead, par. Lyeth, Apl. 10, 1564.	17		360
Apl. 20, 1564.	Helmherste, William, Wourssburghe, yeoman, Nov. 9, 1563.	17		325
Oct. 30, 1554.	Helmsley, Richard, Newlande, par. Drax, Sep. 16, 1554.	14		281
July 19, 1557.	Helves, Thomas, Egmantone (Notts.), Dec. 27, 1556.	15	1	287
Apl. 20, 1559.	Helvis, Margaret, Tuxford (Notts.), widow, Mar. 22, 1558.	15	3	370
Jan. 26, 1556.	Helywell, John, Boughton, husbandman, Oct. 26, 1556.	15	1	91
Apl. 20, 1559.	———, Margery, Boughton (Notts.), widow, Aug. 28, 1558.	15	3	369
Mar. 15, 1560.	Hembroughe, John, Blithe (Notts.), husbandman, Jan. 3, 1560.	16		167
Mar. 16, 1553.	Hemburghe, Alice, Draxe, widow, Dec. 10, 1553.	14		212
Sep. 9, 1558.	Hemeslay, Thomas, Stayneborne, par. Kirkebye Overblowes, Oct. 5, 1557.	15	3	100
July 12, 1558.	Hemmyngway, Jenet, Hillom (bur. Monkefryston), Jan. 26, 1557.	15	2	314
Jun. 14, 1567.	Hemmyngwraye, Thomas, Kirkbie Overblause, husbn., May 30, 1567.	17		659
Dec. 10, 1562.	Hemslay, Henry, Wooddall (bur. Thirske), Sep. 1, 1562.	17		131
Oct. 13, 1557.	———, John, York, baker, Sep. 10, 1557.	15	2	34
Jun. 24, 1561.	———, William, Newland, par. Drax, ——. 16, 1560.	17		84
Nov. 24, 1558.	Henlayke, William, York, corne marchant, Aug. 26, 1558.	15	3	75
Apl. 13, 1554.	Henrison, John, Gipton, par. Ledes, yeoman, Oct. 10, 1553.	14		58
Oct. 6, 1557.	Henson, Gregory, Cotgrave (Notts.), husbandman, July 8, 1557.	15	2	34
Mar. 14, 1560.	———, John, Edwalton (Notts.), Dec. 23, 1560.	16		163
May 13, 1557.	——— Thomas, Wissall (Notts.), Sep. 19, 1556.	15	1	227

		Vol.	Pt.	Fol.
Oct. 8, 1556.	Hensone, John, Plumtre (Notts.), husbandman, May 31, 1556.	15	1	150
Oct. 29, 1558.	Heppell, Giles, Scarbrughe, baxster, July 1, 1558.	15	2	371
Mar. 22, 1558.	Heptinstall, Thomas, Stapletonne (bur. Darrington), husbn., Aug. 21, 1558.	15	3	295
Apl. 18, 1560.	Heptonstall, Charles, Badisworthe, husbandman, Feb. 20, 1559.	16		31
Oct. 29, 1554.	————, John, Lanamt (Notts.), Dec. 12, 6 Edw. VI.	14		286
Jan. 21, 1557.	————, Thomas, Stapleton (bur. Darryngton), Nov. 28, 1557.	15	2	155
Oct. 4, 1558.	———— als. Pomfret, Sir Edward (bur. Leedes), priest, Aug. 3, 1558.	15	3	59
No date.	Heptunstall, Robert (bur. Daryngton), Jun. 2, 1555.	14		242
Apl. 6, 1558.	Hepworth, John, Hewton Pannell, husbandman, Dec. 11, 1557.	15	2	187
Jan. 24, 1558.	————, Margaret, Sutton, par. Campsall, Aug. 10, 1558.	15	3	218
Oct. 1, 1556.	Hepworthe, John, Almonburie, May 6, 1556.	15	1	142
Dec. 16, 1556.	————, Richard, Hopton, par. Myrfeld, husbn., Nov. 12, 1556.	15	1	193
Apl. 6, 1558.	————, Robert. Sutton, par. Campsall, Oct. 26, 1557.	15	2	183
Oct. 1, 1561.	————, Thomas, Myrfeld, Aug. 15, 1561.	17		46
Nov. 26, 1555.	————, William, Kirke Heton, Jun. 25, 1555.	14		184
Jan. 3, 1558.	Herber, Agnes, Elvington. widow, Nov. 15, 1558.	15	3	35
Aug. 16, 1558.	Herbert. Gawwyn, Alvyngton, July 31, 1558.	15	3	1
May 9, 1565.	Hercher (Archer), John, Heymore House, par. Kirkeburton, Jan. 29, 1564.	17		423
May 13, 1557.	Herdeson. James, Croppill Bottler, par. Tethbie (Notts.), Apl. 10, 1556.	15	1	229
Jun. 5, 1556.	Herdey, Robert, Medley, Sep. 16, 1555.	15	1	42
Sep. 29, 1563.	Herefeld, William, Newhall (bur. Ottley), May 20, 1563.	17		289
May 19, 1559.	————, William, Snawdonne, par. Westonne, husbn., Apl. 17, 1558.	15	3	426
Jun. 10, 1560.	Herfelde, John, Appleton (bur. Bolton Percye), Jun. 4, 1560.	16		83
Oct. 4, 1565.	Hergrave, Robert, Readnes, Feb. 20, 1564.	17		485
May 1, 1555.	Hergraves, John, Depedale, par. Longe Preston, Jan. 7, 1554.	14		126
Apl. 20, 1564.	Hergreves, George, Warley. par. Halifax, webster, Jun. 10, 1563.	17		327
May 18, 1559.	Heringe, Richard, Catlyf, par. Rotherham, Jan. 26, 1558.	15	3	418
Mar. 26, 1565.	Herison, Emmot, Wragbie, Aug. 7, 1564.	17		413
Jun. 25, 1557.	————, Richard, Athwike by the strete, Apl. 18, 1557.	15	1	296
Sep. 15, 1561.	————, Robert, Beverley, "brother with the glovers," July 2, 1561.	17		54
Nov. 17, 1562.	Herkay, Rauf, junr., par. Haunbie, Sep. 24, 1562.	17		127
Oct. 2, 1567.	Herman als. Jeffrason, Francis, Befourthe, husbn., Jan. 16, 1566.	17		715
Nov. 3, 1558.	Hermelay (Chermley, Act Bk.), William, York, inholder, Oct. 27, 1558.	15	3	232
Aug. 26, 1561.	Hermytage, John, Oldfelde, par. Almonburie, Feb. 11, 1560.	17		54
Jan. 20, 1561.	Hernshay, Edward, Heptonstall, Oct. 8, 1561.	17		23
May 4, 1558.	Herot, Jeffray, Selston (Notts.), Nov. 13, 1557.	15	2	272
Jun. 12, 1557.	————, William, Whitgifte, Apl. 1, 1557.	15	1	290
Feb. 20, 1558.	Herper, Robert, Everingham, Oct. 16, 1558.	15	3	275
Feb. 15, 1558.	Herreson, Alexander, Leven, husbandman, Nov. 24, 1558.	15	3	269
Feb. 6, 1558.	————, William, Skelley, par. Ouston, Jan. 16, 1558.	15	3	253
Jun. 20, 1554.	Herrington, Emmot, Overton, widow, Jun. 9, 1554.	14		113
May 9, 1565.	————, John, Scarbroughe, ————, 1564.	17		425
May 16, 1554.	Herrison, Bartilmew, Holme in Spawdyngemore, Feb. 24, 1553.	14		137
Jan. 14, 1558.	————, Christopher, Markington (bur. Ripon), grisman, Oct. 23, 1558.	15	3	191
Jun. 25, 1557.	————, Edward. Aithwike by the strete, Apl. 23, 1557.	15	1	296
May 6, 1563.	————, Roger, Ruddington (bur. Flafurth, Notts.), Nov. 29, 1562.	17		245
Apl. 27, 1557.	————, Thomas, Mykilgate, York, Apl. 2, 1557.	15	1	209
May 20, 1557.	————, William, Sourbie, par. Halyfax, Jan. 11, 1556.	15	1	258
Nov. 16, 1558.	————, William, Thornthorpe, par. Berythorpe, husbn., July 24, 1558.	15	3	125
Apl. 13, 1559.	Herryes, Nicholas, Wawhan. husbandman, Aug. 14, 1558.	15	3	343
Aug. 18, 1562.	Herryngton, Robert, Semer, Dec. 16, 1561.	17		106
Apl. 13, 1559.	Herrys, Edmund, Cotingham, Dec. 18, 1558.	15	3	350
Sep. 6, 1561.	Herryson, Edward (bur. York), putherer, July 13, 1561.	17		52
Oct. 4, 1565.	————, John, Awdby (bur. Bossall), husbandman, May 3, 1565.	17		481
Sep. 30, 1562.	————, John, Orgrave, par. Rotherham, July 14, 1562.	17		114
Apl. 3, 1559.	————, John, Slingesbie, Nov. 30, 1558.	15	3	319
May 29, 1563.	————, John, Willytoft (bur. Bubwith), Dec. 27, 1560.	17		252
Jun. 23, 1563.	————, Leonard, Cloughton (bur. Scawbie), Jun. 25, 1562.	17		259
Jun. 23, 1563.	————, Richard, Foston, Mar. 3, 1562.	17		260
Feb. 15, 1566.	————, Robert, Buttercrame, par. Bossall, Mar. 30, 1566.	17		615

		Vol.	Pt.	Fol.
Jan. 24, 1558.	Herryson, Thomas, Aklam, yeoman, Aug. 23, 1558.	15	3	215
Oct, 7, 1556.	Herrysone, Thomas, Walcryngham (Notts.), husbn., July 1, 1556.	15	1	192
Oct. 5, 1564.	Herst, John, Cawlboell, par. Almonburie, Feb. 3, 1563.	17		374
Oct. 2, 1566.	——, Marion, Cawell, par. Almonburie, widow, Jun. 13, 1566.	17		580
Apl. 19, 1559.	Hert, John, Colson Bassett (Notts.), Apl. 9, 1557.	15	3	375
May 10, 1559.	——, Thomas, Barton, par. Crambum, Feb. 10, 1558.	15	3	386
Apl. 19, 1559.	Hertie, William, Selston (Notts.), Dec. 1, 1558.	15	3	378
May 28, 1557.	Hertlaie, Robert, Sherburne, Apl. 14, 1557.	15	1	211
Oct. 2, 1567.	Hertlay, Roger, Skyrcott, par. Halifax, Apl. 29, 1567.	17		717
May 6, 1557.	Herwoodd, Hewe, Birdsall, Feb. 2, 1556.	15	1	215
Sep. 29, 1563.	Heryne, William, Brintesfurthe, par. Rotherham, July 1, 1563.	17		287
July 21, 1558.	Heryson, Edward, Wresle, Mar. 28, 1558.	15	2	300
Oct. 7, 1563.	————, George, Mathersey (Notts.), Jun. 19, 1563.	17		295
May 5, 1557.	————, James, Ormsbie, Nov. 5, 1556.	15	1	248
Mar. 26, 1565.	————, John, Acton (bur. Fetherstone), yeoman, Sep. 15, 1564.	17		414
Oct. 4, 1565.	————, John, Cowicke, par. Snayth, Jan. 8, 1564.	17		485
Feb. 15, 1558.	————, Rauff, Leven, husbandman, Sep. 20, 1558.	15	3	272
July 26, 1558.	————, Thomas (bur. Humbleton), Apl. 25, 1558.	15	3	10
May 16, 1564.	————, Thomas, Sutton (St. James), singill man, Mar. 4, 1563.	17		343
Nov. 26, 1557.	————, William, Doncaster, Oct. 19, 1557.	15	2	93
May 4, 1557.	Herysone, John, Sprodbroughe, husbandman, Mar. 25, 1557.	15	1	278
May 19, [1554].	Heseld, John, senr. (bur. Rowlston, Notts.), Oct. —, 1553.	14		108
Oct. 20, 1558.	Heselwood, George, curate of Merton in Holderness, Sep. 22, 1558.	15	2	348
Oct. 29, 1558.	Hesilwoodde. Thomas, Muston (bur. Hunmanbe), Jun. 24, 1558.	15	2	368
Nov. 21, 1558.	Heskay, John, Nottingham, Sep. 29, 1558.	15	3	133
Oct. 5, 1558.	Hesleden, John, Easby (bur. Stokesley), husbandman, July 25, 1558.	15	3	42
Nov. 3, 1557.	Heslegray, Androwe (bur. Harswell), Sep. 30, 1557.	15	2	105
Apl. 6, 1554.	Heslet, John (bur. Sladburn), May 29, 1553.	14		153
Nov. 8, 1558.	Heslington, Marie, widow of Thomas H., Acaster Selbie, par. Stillingfleete, May 25, 1558.	15	3	125
Dec. 4, 1557.	————, Thomas, Acaster Selbye, par. Stillingflete, Oct. 8, 1557.	15	2	50
Oct. 2, 1556.	Heslope, Alexander (bur. Thryske), May 8, 1556.	15	1	132
Oct. 29, 1558.	Hesloppe, William, Lowthorpe, Aug. 4, 1558.	15	3	240
Nov. 10, 1557.	Heslup, Robert, Leveshawe (Rydale), July 21, 1557.	15	2	105
Apl. 19, 1559.	Hesome, Jenett, Eperstone (Notts.), widow, May 16, 1558.	15	3	353
Jun. 2, 1557.	Hessilwoode, John, Seaton, husbandman, May 10, 1556.	15	1	273
Apl. 16, 1567.	Hestun (Eastun, Act Book), Francis, Hollum in Holderness, July 10, 1566.	17		634
Sep. 9, 1561.	Hesylgrave, John, Byrkbye, par. Huddersfeld, Mar. 31, 1561.	17		49
July 5, 1557.	Hetton, Thomas, Fenwyke, par. Campsall, Mar. 18, 1556.	15	1	303
Mar. 4, 1562.	————, William, Urton, par. Semer, Aug. 16, 1562.	17		153
Feb. 6, 1558.	Heugh, Thomas, son of Thomas H., Rosington, Jan. 22, 1558.	15	3	262
Apl. 13, 1559.	Hevysydes, John, Leckynfeld, husbandman, Jan. 28, 1558.	15	3	349
Feb. 10, 1557.	Heward, Edward, Willerbye (bur. Cottingham), husbn., Oct. 17, 1557.	15	2	149
Mar. 30, 1560.	Hewardayne, Thomas, Owlston, par. Cookeswalde, Oct. 3, 1559.	16		24
Mar. 30, 1560.	Hewarden, Isabell, Owlston, par. Cookewolde, Sep. 20, 1559.	16		24
Feb. 6, 1558.	Hewarthe, Katherine, Hensall (bur. Snathe), Aug. 28, 1558.	15	3	264
Feb. 20, 1558.	Hewbriges, John, Skerne, husbandman, Dec. 4, 1558.	15	3	276
Apl. 28, 1558.	Hewdome, Walter, Cottingham, Jan. 30, 1557.	15	2	219
Aug. 16, 1555.	Hewerdayne, John, Kirkbye in Cleveland, yeoman, May 6, 1555.	14		205
Mar. 29, 1568.	Hewet, Edward, Aberforthe, Sep. 16, 1567.	17		768
May 12, 1559.	Hewett, John, Hull, serchar, Oct. 16, 1558.	15	3	394
Jan. 27, 1561.	————, Thomas, Fairbourne, par. Ledesham, smythe, Nov. 21, 1561.	17		7
July 27, 1564.	Hewgalle, Gyles, Oxhill (bur. Whorleton), yeoman, Apl. 6, 1564.	17		360
Dec. 13, 1557.	Hewgett, George, Hovyngham, husbandman, Aug. 21, 1557.	15	2	41
Jan. 24, 1558.	Hewghe, Thomas, Rosington, Oct. 16, 1558.	15	3	117
Jun. 7, 1560.	Hewghson, Thomas, Haistrope, par. Burton Agnes, May 23, 1559.	16		77
Jan. 31, 1564.	Hewgill, Thomas, Grenhow Parke (bur. Ingleby), Feb. 24, 1563.	17		403
Jun. 22, 1568.	Hewithwaitte, Thomas, Great Kelke (bur. Foston), Jan. 24, 1567.	17		819
Jun. 14, 1564.	Hewitson, Peter, Argame (bur. Hunmanbe), Sep. 6, 1563.	17		352
Dec. 13, 1557.	Heworthe, Alyson, Hensall, par. Kellyngton, widow, Nov. 6, 1557.	15	2	54
Jan. 20, 1557.	Hewson, Christopher, Sykehouse, par. Fyshlaike, Nov. 27, 1557.	15	2	64

A.D. 1554 TO 1568.

		Vol.	Pt.	Fol.
Oct. 2, 1560.	Hewson, John, Halsam, Feb. 14, 1560.	16		116
Jun. 14, 1560.	———, Richard, Kylnewicke, Apl. 2, 1560.	16		84
July 28, 1554.	———, Robert, Everingham, Jun. 1, 1552.	14		144
Apl. 14, 1562.	———, Thomas, junr., Bracken, Feb. 16, 1561.	17		166
Oct. 13, 1557.	———, Thomas, Burton Agnes, July 28, 1557.	15	2	35
Dec. 1, 1561.	———, Thomas, Harbor, par. Horton (Craven), July 7, 1560.	17		33
Feb. 14, 1555.	Hewsone, Richard, Elvington, Jan. 22, 1555.	15	1	7
July 13, 1558.	Hewsonne, John, All Hallowes, Pavement,York,parishclerke,Jun.15, 1558.	15	2	323
Apl. 17, 1567.	———, Thomas, Brackan (bur. Kilnewicke), husbn.,Feb.6,1564.	17		640
Oct. 1, 1561.	Hewton, John, Kelke, par. Foston, Nov. 10, 1560.	17		47
Mar.21, 1560.	———, John, Swanland (bur. North Feribie), husbn., Oct. 30, 1560.	16		174
Dec.23, 1561.	———, John,York,prentyse with Rob.Kettland,tanner,Aug.19,1561.	17		26
Mar.30, 1558.	———, Thomas, Skypulum, par. Kyrkdaill, husbn., Dec. 19, 1557.	15	2	178
Feb. 10, 1557.	Hewtye, Richard, Cottingham, Jan. 1, 1557.	15	2	150
Sep. 30, 1558.	Hewyke, William (bur. Ripon), Sep. 12, 1558.	15	3	57
Jan. 28, 1566.	Hewyt, Jennet, Southekirkbie, widow, Oct. 24, 1565.	17		608
Oct. 1, 1556.	——— William, Ledstone (bur. Kypax), July 26, 1556.	15	1	135
Oct. 1, 1557.	Hexham, John, Mydlesbroughe, clerk, Jan. 19, 1554.	15	2	36
Dec. 3, 1560.	Hey, George, Kirkeberton, Sep. 19, 1560.	16		132
Apl. 17, 1567.	———, John, Stocke (bur. Braswell), Dec. 8, 1566.	17		620
Jan. 31, 1564.	Heydlam, William, Nunthorpe (bur. Ayton), esquire, Jan. 1, 1564.	17		405
Apl. 18, 1567.	Heylewell,Richard,Overhalghe,par.Rawmarshe, husbn.,Feb.14,1566.	17		637
Oct. 8, 1562.	Heylowe, Christopher, Ansley (Notts.), husbandman, Apl. 6, 1562.	17		123
Sep. 28, 1557.	Heyton, Richard, Setle (bur. Giglesweke),, Jun. 30, 1557.	15	1	338
May 4, 1557.	Heyword, Roger, Brawell, labourer, Mar. 6, 1556.	15	1	281
Sep. 12, 1560.	Heyworthe, Henry, Ossendyke (bur. Ryther), husbn., Apl. 14, 1559.	16		105
Aug.14, 1566.	Hic, Christopher, Thorppebasset, Aug. 4, 1566.	17		566
Apl. 16, 1562.	Hicke, Jennat, Welborne, par. Kyrkdalle, May 8, 1558.	17		158
Dec. 5, 1558.	———, Leonard, Nonyngton, par. Staynegrave, husbn., Sep. 12, 1558.	15	3	150
Jun. 7, 1558.	———, William, Skackellthropp (bur. Settrington), Oct. 7, 1557.	15	2	287
July 10, 1567.	Hickman, Thomas, Doncaster, yeoman, Apl. 16, 1567.	17		685
Aug.12, 1566.	Hicson, Robert, Kaingham, husbandman, Feb. 15, 1564.	17		568
May 2, 1555.	Hide, Isabell (bur. S. Andrew, Slateburn), Dec. 31, 1554.	14		25
Sep. 26, 1558.	———, William, Ecclesfeld, Aug. 23, 1558.	15	3	49
Oct. 12, 1558.	Hides, Richard, Arnall (Notts.), gentleman, Feb. 7, 1557.	15	3	28
July 10, 1561.	Higgyn, Thomas, Over Yeadon, par. Gysley, maisone, Apl. 18, 1560.	17		63
Oct. 2, 1555.	Hileye, Peter, Attercliff, par. Shefeld, cutler, Sep. 19, 1554.	14		165
Oct. 3, 1554.	Hiliarde,Christopher, senr., Aringhame (? Ottringham),Jun.1,1 Mary.	14		274
Apl. 12, 1559.	Hililie, Edward, Harthed, Aug. 12, 1558.	15	3	336
Sep. 16, 1557.	Hill, Edward, Olde bishop hill, York, priest, Sep. 4, 1557.	15	1	335
May 9, 1565.	———, Edward, Shipley, par. Bradforthe, Sep. 18, 1560.	17		423
Mar.13, 1565.	———, George, Gysley, smythe, Feb. 4, 1565.	17		504
May 10, 1565.	———, George, the Sleight, par. Whitbye, Feb. 20, 1563.	17		427
Aug. 2, 1560.	———, George, Tunstall, husbandman, Jun. 21, 1560.	16		100
Jan. 24, 1558.	———, Henry, Thòrpe, par. Rotheram, Nov. 14, 1549.	15	3	118
Feb. 28, 1566.	———, James, Rowsbie, Jan. 26, 1566.	17		617
Apl. 30, 1556.	———, John, Balderton (Notts.), husbandman, Mar. 10, 1555.	15	1	32
July 27, 1567.	———, John, Danbe, Apl. 18,˙1567.	17		672
May 14, 1558.	———, John, Scarbrughe, Feb. 3, 1558.	15	2	279
Aug.14, 1556.	———, Martyne. Apilton (bur. Lastingham), July 12, 1555.	15	1	61
Oct. 22, 1558.	———, Rawffe, Esington, Sep. 6, 1558.	15	3	234
Jun. 28, 1563.	———, Richard, Angrame, July 31, 1562.	17		260
Sep. 12, 1558.	———, Sir Robert, Beverlay, late chantry priest of Trinite Massindow at Crossebrigge, Aug. 1, 1558.	15	3	103
Oct. 15, 1561.	———, Thomas, Lithe, ———, 1561.	17		36
July 1, 1562.	———, Thomas, Wentworthe, Apl. 7, 1562.	17		92
Jan. 13, 1558.	———, Thomas, Woodhowse, par. Blyth (Notts.), husbn., Nov.13,1558.	15	3	184
Apl. 20, 1559.	———, Thruston, Blyth (Notts.), husbandman, Jan. 10, 1558.	15	3	367
May 9, 1558.	———, William, Harsewell, Dec, 2, 1557,	15	2	279
Aug.22, 1558.	———, William, citizen and wayte of York, May 29, 4 and 5 Phil., and Mary.	15	2	290

A.D. 1554 TO 1568.

	Vol.	Pt.	Fol.
Jun. 25, 1557. Hillingworth, Margaret, Rotherham, widow, Jan. 19, 1554.	15	I	297
Apl. 10, 1555. Hilliwell, John, Sowerbie, par. Hallifaxe, Nov. 20, 1554.	14		117
May 2, 1560. Hillywell, Edward, Southowrome, par Hallyfaxe, Aug. 9, 1559.	16		41
May 5, 1568. Hilton, George, Snayth, husbandman, Dec. 30, 1567.	17		793
May 6, 1563. Himysworth, James, Blithe (Notts.), wever, Sep. 20, 1562.	17		242
Oct. 3, 1565. Hinchecliff, Henry, Crosse, par. Burton, Dec. 27, 1564.	17		475
May 13, 1557. Hincliffe *als.* Hoghton, Richard, clerk (bur. Bramcotte, Notts.), Dec. 13, 1556.	15	I	224
Oct. 29, 1558. Hinderwell, John, Scurbie (bur. St. Lawrence, Scawbie), July 7, 1558.	15	2	370
Jun. 20, 1566. ————, William, Newbye, par. Scaubie, Mar. 8, 1565.	17		558
Oct. 29, 1558. ————, William, Scawbie, Mar. 10, 1558.	15	3	239
Oct. 13, 1558. Hindlay, John, Missin (Notts.), Nov. 15, 1558.	15	2	358
Mar. 6, 1556. Hindley, Robert, Myssyn (Notts.), Dec. 20, 1556.	15	I	178
Jan. 21, 1558. Hird, John, Thorganbye, Aug. 11, 1558.	15	3	213
Jan. 11, 1558. Hirde, Christopher, Addle (bur. Harwood), Aug. 20, 1558.	15	3	170
May 2, 1560. ————, Laurence, Burnisheton, par. Scawbye, Mar. 20, 1558.	16		40
May 2, 1566. Hirst, Edward Collersley (? in Almondbury), yeoman, Jun. 18, 1565.	17		533
Oct. 2, 1550(?5). ——, James, Colmebridge, par. Huddersfield, Aug. 19, 1555.	14		172
Nov.20, 1563. ——, James, Kyrkheaton, Nov. 1, 1563.	17		303
Dec.16, 1556. ——, Jenet, wid. of Edmonde H. (bur. Womersley), Nov. 10, 1556.	15	I	175
Oct. 5, 1564. ——, John, Gretland in Eland, par. Halifax, Nov. 14, 1563.	17		375
Oct. 13, 1558. ——, Margaret, wid. of Richard H., Willowbie, par. Wallesbie, (Notts.), Apl. 27, 1558.	15	2	376
Jun. 25, 1557. ——, Roger, Rotherham, Feb. 18, 1556.	15	I	297
Mar. 6, 1556. Hirste, Grace, Walysby (Notts), widow, Jan. 27, 1556.	15	I	182
Apl. 22, 1556. ——, Robert, Skelmonthorpe, par. Emley, Nov. 13, 1555.	15	I	23
May 19, 1554. Hitchebone, Hugh, Farnefeld (Notts.), Oct. 18, 1553.	14		110
May 5, 1557. Hobbe, William, Ridker (bur. Marske), fisherman, ——, 1556.	15	I	250
Feb.ult.,1557. Hobkynson, William, Allerton, par. Bradford, Feb. 19, 1556.	15	2	145
May 7, 1554. ————, William, Hallifax, Aug. 18, 1553.	14		3
May 2, 1566. Hobman, Agnes, Burnebuttes, par. Watton, widow, Jan. 26, 1563.	17		538
Feb. 19, 1556. ————, Thomas, Burnebuttes, par. Wattone, Dec. 28, 1556.	15	I	163
July 27, 1562. Hobson, Agnes, Poole, par. Ottley, widow, Jun. 15, 1560.	17		98
Mar.23, 1560. ——, Alyson, Skypsey in Holderness, widow, ——, 1560.	16		177
Apl. 16, 1567. ——, Anthony, Aton in Cleveland, Dec. 20, 1566.	17		629
Oct. 4, 1558. ——, Christopher, Heddingley (bur. Leedes), clotheyour, July 27, 1558.	15	3	59
Mar.12, 1556. ——, George, Staynley, par. Wakefeld, Dec. 21, 1556.	15	I	200
Oct. 2, 1566. ——, James, junr., Humbleton, Apl. 21, 1566,	17		581
July 12, 1564. ——, Jane, Homylton, widow, May 14, 1564.	17		356
Nov.29, 1558. ——, Jeffray, Screth, par. Sheafeld, cutlar, Jan. 10, 1557.	15	3	109
May31, 1557. ——, John, Doncaster, alderman, Mar. 2, 1556.	15	I	263
Jan. 30, 1566. ——, John, senr., Humbleton, July 16, 1566.	17		609
July 1, 1562. ——, John, senr., Smalfeld, par. Bradfeld, Mar. 15, 1561.	17		92
Feb. 3, 1556. ——, Marion, Kirkby, par. Emlay, Sep. 21, 1556.	15	I	94
Dec. 15, 1557. ——, Percevall, Est Retforde, Notts., Nov. 13, 1557.	15	2	59
Dec. 12, 1564. ——, Peter, Haistropp (bur. Burton Agnes), labr., July 11, 1564.	17		400
Mar.12, 1558. ——, Roger, Wistowe, Nov. 28, 1558.	17		511
Nov.28, 1558. ——, Thomas, Skypse, Oct. 21, 1558.	15	3	77
Sep. 26, 1558. ——, Thomas, Swynton (bur. Wath), Apl. 13, 1558.	15	3	50
May 9, 1563. ——, Wiliam (bur. Brandisburton), Feb. 15, 156[2-]3.	17		254
Sep. 17, 1558. ——, William, Powle (bur. Ottlay), clothier, July 26, 1558.	15	3	106
Mar.26, 1565. ——, William, Standley (par. Wakefeld), yeoman, Sep. 4, 1557.	17		415
Nov.28, 1558. ——, William, Skypse, July 22, 1558.	15	3	77
Jan. 30, 1555. Hobsone, Thomas, Sheffield, hardwareman, Aug. 30, 1555.	15	I	2
May 5, 1568. Hobsonne, John, Humbleton, Jan. 26, 1567.	17		778
July 13, 1557. Hocheson, Robert, Bubwith, husbandman, Jun. 19, 1557.	15	I	307
Oct. 1, 1567. Hochonson, Adam, Little Lepton (bur. Kirkeheaton), yeom, Mar. 14, 1566.	17		715
May 6, 1568. ————, Thomas, Wolley, husbandman, Dec. 3, 1567.	17		771
Oct. 5, 1564. Hodchon, Thomas, Arksay, Aug. 19, 1558.	17		377
July 27, 1562. Hoddye, Richard, Gyesley, 1562.	17		98

		Vol.	Pt.	Fol.
Mar.21, 1558.	Hodecheon, Christopher, Marton, Sep. 23, 1558.	15	3	291
Sep. 29, 1563.	Hodegson, William (bur. Conysheton), Mar. 20, 1563.	17		278
Apl. 22, 1556.	Hodersall, John, Hensall (bur. Snaythe), Dec. 28, 1555.	15	1	31
May 2, 1560.	Hodgeson, Christopher, Kyrkefenton, mylner, Feb. 25, 1558.	16		55
Sep. 30, 1558.	———, Christopher, Markynton (bur. Ripon),husbn.,Apl.18,1558.	15	3	57
July 29, 1560.	———. John, Cowycke (bur. Snaythe), July 20, 1560.	16		96
Sep. 17, 1556.	———, Nicholas, Garforth, Aug. 16, 1556.	15	1	65
Sep. 24, 1558.	———' Rauf, Bradford, Apl. 21, 1558.	15	3	87
July 27, 1564.	———, Rauf, Great Aiton in Cleveland, 1564.	17		360
Nov. 4, 1554.	———, Raufe, Rigton, par. Kirbe Overblows, Apl. 14, 1554.	14		92
Dec. 13, 1557.	———, Richard, Newe Malton, yeoman, Oct. 10, 1557.	15	2	42
May 5, 1558.	———, Richard, Rampton (Notts,), Oct. 19, 1557.	15	2	211
Dec. 15, 1557.	———, Robert, Sandbye (Notts.), labourer, Nov. 14, 1557.	15	2	56
May 2, 1566.	———, Thomas, Lyttle Bollinge, yeoman, Oct. 24, 1565.	17		535
Dec. 11, 1566.	———, William, Burnysheton, par. Scawbie, Jan. 10, 1565.	17		603
Feb. 16, 1557.	———, William, Huntington, Dec. 25, 1557.	15	2	124
Aug.14, 1554.	———, William, Kingston on Hull, wever, May 23, 1554.	14		146
Feb. 3, 1556.	———, William, Pomfrett, alderman, Oct. 10, 1556.	15	1	168
Jun. 18, 1560.	———, William, Rednesse (bur. Whytgyft), Dec. 26, 1559.	16		86
Dec. 9, 1556.	———, William, Sutton (Holderness), Sep. 14, 1556.	15	1	119
May 1, 1568.	———, William, York, joyner, Apl. 1, 1568.	17		795
Oct. 2, 1556.	Hodgesone, John, Balln, par. Snaythe, Mar. 21, 1556.	15	1	131
Apl. 28, 1558.	Hodgesonne, Richard, Grystwat (bnr. Topclyffe), Nov. 10, 1557.	15	2	239
Oct. 13, 1558.	Hodgson, Henry, Walkringham (Notts.), Mar. 14, 1557	15	2	379
Jun. 5, 1555.	———, Jennet, Kyngston on Hull, widow, Mar. 22, 1554.	14		253
Dec. 11, 1566.	———, John, Bynnington, par. Willerbie, husbn., Apl. 28, 1565.	17		604
May 5, 1558.	———, John, Sandbie (Notts.), husbandman, Jan. 16, 1557.	15	2	247
July 2, 1561.	———, Margaret,Thurnum (bur.Burton Agnes), wid., Jan.10, 1560.	17		78
Jan. 23, 1561.	———, William, Coniston, par. Swyne, May 10, 1561.	17		19
Sep. 30, 1562.	Hodschon,Elizabeth, wid., of Wm. H.(bur. Great Aiton), Jun.25,1562.	17		109
Jun. 11, 1562.	———, John, Clowghton (bur. Scawbro), Aug. 27, 1559.	17		87
Feb. 17, 1557.	Hodshon, Agnes, Bubwyth, widow, Dec. 28, 1557.	15	2	151
Aug. 7, 1565.	———, Edward, vicar of Este Retford (Notts.), May 2, 1565.	17		458
Mar.17, 1557.	———, John, Bubwyth, yonge man, Dec. 18, 1557.	15	2	153
Jan. 17, 1557.	———, Richard, Leberston, par. Filaye, Mar. 15, 1556.	15	2	63
Mar.17, 1557.	———, Robert, Bubwyth, yonge man, Jan. 1, 1557.	15	2	153
Jan. 22, 1561.	———, Thomas, Beverley, Nov. 26, 1561.	17		25
Apl. 3, 1559.	———, Thomas, Galmeton, Nov. 15, 1558.	15	3	316
Apl. 26, 1558.	———, William, Sherburne, labourer, Mar. 10, 1557.	15	2	236
Apl. 20, 1559.	Hodshone, Tristram, Doncaster, Apl. 14, 1558.	15	3	363
Jun. 21, 1561.	———, William, Scostrope, May 18, 1560.	17		73
Aug.17, 1557.	———, William, Sowthburne (bur. Kyrkeburne), husbn., May 12, 1557.	15	2	118
Apl. 12, 1559.	Hodson, Christopher, Bradford, Dec. 20, 1558.	15	3	340
Sep. 27, 1554.	———, Jelyan (bur. Stanby) (? Scalby, Dickering Deanery), Jun. 15, 7 Edw. VI.	14		274
Oct. 11, 1565.	———, Thomas, Bylbrowe (Notts,), Feb. 10, 1564.	17		469
May 6, 1568.	Hodyswourthe, William, Woursburghe, Jan. 6, 1567.	17		772
Nov. 5, 1562.	Hogard, William, Fernedale, par. Lestingham, Sep. 4, 1561.	17		127
Oct. 28, 1563.	Hogarte, Thomas, Billisdaill, May 28, 1563.	17		299
Mar.31, 1554.	Hogeley, Robert, Adwicke on Derne, Oct. 17, 1553.	14		105
Apl. 8, 1560.	Hogeson, Agnes, widow of Thomas H., Bubwith, Oct, 29, 1559.	16		29
Jun. 7, 1560.	———, John, Burton Agnes, labourer, Apl. 3, 1559.	16		77
Feb. 3, 1561.	———, John, Pomfrett, alderman, Oct. 6, 1561.	17		10
Apl. 16, 1567.	———, John, Sneton (bur. Whitbie), Jun. 22, 1565.	17		630
Apl. 8, 1560.	———, Robert, Baynton, husbandman, Feb. 23, 1559.	16		29
Mar.10, 1558.	———, Robert, Southburne (bur. Kirkeburne), yeom., Jan. 6, 1558.	15	3	158
May 2, 1560.	———, Robert, Thurnum, par. Burton Agnes, husbn., Jan. 3, 1558.	16		35
Feb.24, 1561.	———, Rowland, Follyfet, par. Spofforthe, Feb. 16, 1558.	17		16
Jan. 31, 1564.	Hogesonne, John, Gromone, par. Egton, July 23, 1563.	17		403
Jan. 31, 1564.	———, Lawrance, Glasedaillsyde (bur. Egton), July 15, 1557.	17		404
Dec. 16, 1557.	Hogg, Margaret, Marflete, widow, Jun. 20, 1557.	15	2	43

		Vol.	Pt.	Fol.
Sep. 30, 1557.	Hogg, Robert, Marflete, clarke of the said towne, Jun. 3, 1557.	15	1	343
Oct. 21, 1558.	——, Robert, York, July 28, 1558.	15	3	95
Mar. 4, 1562.	Hoggard, Nicholas, Osgodbie (bur. Catton), July 28, 1562.	17		154
Jan. 17, 1557.	Hoggarde, William, Lowthorpe, shearman, Sep. 7, 1557.	15	2	61
July 15, 1558.	Hoggarse, Christopher, North Dalton, husbandman, Feb. 25, 1558.	15	2	307
Jun. 1, 1556.	Hoggart, Alexander, Danbie, July 16, 1554.	15	1	40
Feb. 24, 1563.	Hogge, John, Preston in Holderness, husbandman, Apl. 23, 1563.	17		320
July 18, 1560.	——, Peter, Beverlay, Jun. 17, 1560.	16		93
Sep. 30, 1556.	——, Richard, Biltone in Holderness, gentleman, July 8, 1556.	15	1	139
Jun. 8, 1557.	——, Robert, Marflett, husbandman, Apl. 25, 1557.	15	1	274
Oct. 3, 1564.	——, Stephen, Stoneferrye (bur. Sutton), yeoman, Aug. 13, 1564.	17		364
Oct. 1, 1562.	Hoggeson, Edmund, Camyllesforthe, par. Drax, May 26, 1562.	17		115
May 13, 1557.	Hoggine, William, Orston (Notts.), Sep. 23, 1556.	15	1	220
Oct. 10, 1565.	Hoggyt, Robert, Fyskertone (bur. Roulston, Notts.), Aug. 3, 1565.	17		472
Aug. 1, 1562.	Hoghon (Holgson), William, Great Aton, Feb. 8, 1558.	17		103
May 13, 1557.	Hoghton als. Hincliffe, Richard, clerk (bur. Bramcotte, Notts.), Dec. 13, 1556.	15	1	224
Jan. 24, 1558.	Hoglay, Richard, Billinglay, par. Darfeld, Aug. 10, 1558.	15	3	217
Sep. 26, 1558.	——, Thomas, Hymynfeld, par. Derfeld, Mar. 2, 1557.	15	3	51
May 4, 1555.	Hogley, Alice, Litle Houghton, par. Darfeld, widow, Sep. 11, 1553.	14		77
Apl. 16, 1562.	——, Thomas, Bylyngly, par. Derfeld, Sep. 4, 1561.	17		173
May 26, 1563.	Hogshon, James, Thorne, Mar. 8, 1562.	17		251
Oct. 2, 1566.	——, William, Skeyrne, weaver, Apl. 6, 1566.	17		572
July 2, 1561.	Hogson, John, Kelke (bur. Foston), May 14, 1561.	17		85
Feb. 20, 1560.	Hoill, John (bur. Rowthwell), Feb. 6, 1560.	16		148
Jan. 20, 1557.	——, Thomas, Wyntworthe, Nov. 8, 1557.	15	2	68
Jun. 7, 1561.	Hoime (Holme), Thomas, Haldbye (bur. Bossell), husbn., Feb. 14, 1560.	17		70
Jan. 11, 1562.	Holand, Thomas, Beverley, cordiner, May 31, 1558.	17		142
Jan. 13, 1558.	Holande, Alice, Lanaham (Notts.), widow, Dec. 21, 1557.	15	3	187
Nov. 5, 1558.	Holdaill, Richard, Mykielfeild, par. Shearburne, husbn., Oct. 16, 1558.	15	3	231
Nov. 17, 1558.	Holdell, John, Garfurthe, Aug. 15, 1558.	15	3	112
May 5, 1568.	Holden, Katheren (bur. Slaidburne), widow, Oct. 2, 1567.	17		784
Oct. 5, 1558.	——, Rauf, Chageley, par. Mytton, gentleman, Aug. 3, 1557.	15	3	37
Oct. 2, 1567.	——, Robert, Grenefold (bur. Slaidburne), Jun. 29, 1567.	17		713
Oct. 20, 1558.	Holdernes, John, Flynton, par. Humbleton, Oct. 6, 1557.	15	2	351
May 2, 1560.	——, Katheren, Styllyngflete, 1559.	16		34
Feb. 12, 1557.	——, Thomas, Kelfelde (bur. Styllyngflete), Jan. 16, 1557.	15	2	166
Oct. 2, 1560.	Holdesworthe, John, Hallyfax, clothier, Sep. 5, 1560.	16		112
Jan. 23, 1561.	——, John, Warley, par. Halyfax, Nov. 7, 1561.	17		23
May 20, 1557.	Holdisworth, James, Warlai, par. Halifax, Feb. 16, 1556.	15	1	258
July 15, 1561.	Holdon, Nicholas, Carledeoittes, par. Peniston, May 11, 1561.	17		81
May 2, 1555.	Holdsworthe, Hewe, Raskell, Mar. 1, 1554.	14		195
No date.	Hole, Ottwell, Hothersfeild, May 16, 1555.	14		263
Oct. 14, 1561.	——, Robert, Comberworthe, par. Silkeston, May 5, 1561.	17		37
May 28, 1560.	Holgait, William, Pomfret. No date.	16		68
Sep. 30, 1557.	Holgayte, William, Roclyffe (bur. Snaythe), Aug. 1, 1557.	15	1	344
Sep. 15, 1557.	Holinges, Richard, Kirskelde, par. Adle, whelewright, Aug. 6, 1557.	15	1	332
Jun. 28, 1561.	Holl, John, Kyghley, May 15, 1561.	17		75
Oct. 7, 1561.	Holland, Gabrell, Wiloughby (Notts.), Mar. 4, 1560.	17		40
Sep. 21, 1557.	——, Hughe, Barnebye on Done, Aug. 15, 1557.	15	1	353
Oct. 7, 1561.	——, Oliver, Cossall (Notts.), Oct. 5, 1558.	17		42
Oct. 29, 1555.	——, Robert, Est Retforde (Notts.), Oct. 17, 1553.	14		283
Aug. 12, 1566.	Hollgaitte, John, Cudworthe, par. Rudstone, linnen webster, Mar. 15, 1566.	17		566
Sep. 13, 1565.	Hollinges, John, Gyselay, husbandman, Nov. 24, 1560.	17		464
Jun. 22, 1556.	——, Richard, Horseforth, par. Gyseley, July 31, 1551.	15	1	50
May 2, 1566.	Hollingrake, Anthony, Gilsteid, par. Bingley, Dec. 16, 1557.	17		531
Jan. 13, 1558.	Hollingworth, William, Everton (Notts.), husbandman, Nov. 8, 1558.	15	3	185
Apl. 27, 1558.	Hollingworthe, Richard, Cauerley, Aug. 22, 1557.	15	2	191
May 13, 1557.	—— ——, William, Screton (Notts.), Oct. 1, 1556.	15	1	229
Apl. 18, 1567.	Hollm, Thomas, Sutton, par. Campsall, May 14, 1565.	17		635
Apl. 27, 1558.	Hollme, Richard, Tykhyll, Nov. 11, 1557.	15	2	196

A.D. 1554 TO 1568.

	Vol.	Pt.	Fol.
Aug. 28, 1561. Hollond, Richard, Southe Morton, par. Babworthe (Notts.), Dec. 25, 1556.	17		57
Apl. 12, 1559. Hollynges, William, Horsforth, par. Giesley, Mar. 4, 1558.	15	3	342
Apl. 14, 1562. Hollyngworthe, Richard, Calverley, Nov. 21, 1561.	17		168
May 28, 1560. Hollyns, Thomas, Methlay, Apl. 3, 1560.	16		68
Jun. 28, 1565. Holme, John, Pauleholme (bur. Paull), esq., Feb. 17, 1564.	17		445
Apl. 19, 1567. ———, John, Ripon, Feb. 6, 1560.	17		623
Mar. 10, 1555. ———, John, Stoke by Newark (Notts.), husbn., Oct. 1, 1554.	14		227
Mar. 10, 1562. ———, John, Withray, par. Fuyston, May 20, 1562.	17		152
Mar. 16, 1553. ———, Margaret, York. widow, July 8, 1552.	14		211
Nov. 3, 1557. ———, Robert, Holme in Spaldyngmor, Sep. 12, 1557.	15	2	105
May 24, 1563. ———, Thomas, Elvington, gentleman, Dec. 22, 1562.	17		215
Oct. 20, 1557. ———, Thomas, St. Crux, York, Jun. 16, 1557.	15	1	364
Jan. 31, 1557. ———, Thomas, Spofforthe, Nov. 15, 1557.	15	2	161
Mar. 15, 1560. ———, William, Howbecke Wodhouse, par. Cuckney (Notts.), Mar. 3, 1559.	16		167
July 9, 1563. ———, William, Thorngumbold (bur. Pawlle), Jun. 23, 1562.	17		264
Dec. 5, 1558. ———, William, York, alderman, Sep. 10, 1558.	15	3	229
Sep. 21, 1557. Holred, Isabell, Sykehouse, par. Fishlaike, Aug. 12, 1557.	15	1	356
Oct. 6, 1558. Holrod, Richard, Sykehowse, par Fishlaike. Sep. 11, 1558.	15	3	72
Oct. 3, 1565. Holroide, Thomas, Coccrofte. par. Eland, Feb. 20, 1564.	17		481
Sep. 16, 1562. Holstocke, Christopher, Appleton in the strete, husbn., Oct. 26, 1561.	17		107
May 9, 1565. Holt, Jennet, Fyshelake, widow, Oct. 22, 1564.	17		428
July 8, 1567. Holtbie, John, Menythorpe (bur. Westow) yeoman, May 15, 1567.	17		665
Mar. 22, 1560. ———, John, Thirkilbie (bur. Kyrkeby Gryndalythe), Sep. 23, 1560.	16		176
Oct. 14, 1561. Holtbye, Lancelott, Fryton, par. Hovingham, gent., Aug. 24, 1561.	17		37
Mar. 21, 1559. ———, Thomas, Sprotlaye, Dec. 24, 1559.	16		16
May 5, 1558. Holte, James, Rosyngton, Nov. 22, 1557.	15	2	251
May 18, 1559. ———, Robert, Workesopp (Notts.), Aug. 3, 1557.	15	3	406
Apl. 27, 1564. ———, Thomas (bur. Sutton on Lunde, Notts.), Sep. 20, 1563.	17		335
Apl. 26, 1558. ———, William, Baddisworthe, husbandman, Feb. 1, 1557.	15	2	224
Dec. 13, 1557. Holtebye, Rauffe, Fryton, par. Hovingham, Mar. 15, 1556.	15	2	41
Feb. 17, 1557. Holyngworth, Robert, Sandall (Doncaster), Jan. 14, 1557.	15	2	137
Feb. 6, 1556. Homble, Robert, Marton (All Saints). Oct. 1, 1556.	15	1	171
Feb. 9, 1557. Hompton, Christopher, Attingwyke, husbandman, Aug. 22, 1557.	15	2	121
Oct. 2, 1567. ———, Thomas, eldest son of Chris. H., Attynwicke, Jan. 21, 1567.	17		715
Nov. 9, 1556. Homs, Richard, Carleton in Lyrycke (Notts.), husbn., Sep. 12, 1556.	15	1	109
May 2, 1560. Homyll, John (bur. Albroughe), Mar. 17, 1559.	16		52
Feb. 25, 1558. Hondislay Thomas, Seaton, husbandman, July 12, 1558.	15	3	278
May 5, 1568. Hood, William, Pomfrett, Apl. 16, 1568.	17		790
Dec. 4, 1557. Hoode, George, Cowicke (bur. Snaythe), Nov. 15, 1557.	15	2	50
Jan. 14, 1564. Hooland, Nicholas, Shiregrene, par. Ecclesfeld, Oct. 5, 1564.	17		402
Apl. 18, 1560. Hoolande, Rauffe, Waldershelfe, par. Bradfelde, Jan. 22, 1559.	16		31
Jun. 6, 1560. Hoope, William, Cottingham, Sep. 3, 1559.	16		73
May 5, 1568. Hootbie, Margaret, Raskell, May 29, 1566.	17		780
Oct. 6, 1557. Hooton, Thomas, Sokam, par. Warsopp (Notts.), Feb. 11, 1557.	15	2	6
Aug. 12, 1566. Hope, Thomas, North Frothingham, Sep. 18, 1565.	17		569
Oct. 23, 1566. Hopes, Robert, Thriske, Jun. 1, 1566.	17		585
Mar. 7, 1559. Hoperton, James, York, gentleman, Dec. 10, 1559.	16		6
Apl. 24, 1567. Hopkine, Christopher, Gonalston (Notts.), husbn., Dec. 13, 1566.	17		642
Apl. 28, 1563. Hopkinson, Arthure, Badsworthe, husbandman, Mar. 13, 1562.	17		231
May 13, 1568. ———, John, Burton on Trent (Notts.), Nov. 20, 1567.	17		802
Nov. 10, 1564. ———, John, Thornton, par. Bradford, Oct. 31, 1563.	17		398
Jan. 18, 1558. ———, Richard, Sourbye, par. Hallifax, clothyer, Apl. 24, 1558.	15	3	211
Jan. 13, 1558. ———, William, Hickling (Notts.), Oct. 12, 1558.	15	3	179
Mar. 21, 1557. Hopkinsonne, Bryan, Catton, Mar. 8, 1557.	15	2	154
Oct. 11, 1565. Hopkinsunne, Margaret, Hickelinge (Notts.), widow, May 11, 1565.	17		471
May 4, 1555. Hoppaye, James, Harlington, par. Barneburghe, Apl. 29, 1555.	14		80
Nov. 8, 1555. ———, Robert, Kirke Smeton, May 16, 1554.	14		180
Oct. 3, 1554. Hoppe, Anthony, Stynton (bur. Skypton), Nov. 11, 1553.	14		39
Jan. 11, 1557. Hopper, John, Aram, par. Attnwyke, husbandman, Oct. 14, 1557.	15	2	74
Sep. 29, 1563. Hoppere, Robert, Ayton, par. Seamer, Mar. 29, 1563.	17		276

		Vol.	Pt.	Fol.
Sep. 30, 1557.	Hoppey, Sir Edward, priest, Wakefeld (bur. Halyfax), Mar. 16, 1556.	15	1	324
May 4, 1558.	Hoppkinsonne, Elsabethe (bur. Hickeling, Notts.), wid., Nov.11,1557.	15	2	269
May 18, 1559.	Hoppwood, Edmund, Cockney (Notts.), Dec. 1, 1558.	15	3	420
Apl. 28, 1563.	Hopwod, Thomas, Collingham (Aynstie), Feb. 6, 1562.	17		235
Mar. 13, 1562.	Horberye, William, Thorlebye, par. Skipton, Mar. 20, 1560.	17		151
May 2, 1560.	Horn, William, Northdyghton, par. Kyrkedyghton, Jan. 30, 1558.	16		56
Jun. 12, 1567.	Hornbie, William, Bonwike, par. Skipsey, Apl. 15, 1567.	17		683
Jan. 12, 1558.	Hornbye, John, Beuwam (bur. Nunkeeling). *No date.*	15	3	178
Mar. 27, 1560.	Horne, Christopher, Newbyggynge, par. Lythe, Apl. 18, 1559.	16		21
July 20, 1557.	———, Thomas, Bucketon (bur. Bempton), husbn., May 3, 1557.	15	1	315
Jun. 22, 1568.	——— als. Collin, William, Harwoddaill, par. Hacknes, Apl.12,1567.	17		822
Jan. 17, 1567.	Hornebie, John, Yearsley (bur. Cookeswold), July 9, 1567.	17		755
May 13, 1568.	Hornebuckell, Edward, Hawkesworthe (Notts.), Apl. 14, 1567.	17		799
Feb. 9, 1557.	Hornebye, Elsabethe, Litle Haytfelde (bur. Siglistron), Dec. 26, 1557.	15	2	119
Apl. 6, 1558.	Hornecastell, Arthure (bur. Southkyrkebye), Oct. 1, 1557.	15	2	187
Feb. 17, 1566.	Hornecastle, Henry, Hull, beare brewer, Nov. 28, 1566.	17		612
Apl. 28, 1558.	Hornelle, Thomas, Lenthorpe, par. Acclam, husbn., Nov. 22, 1557.	15	2	231
Oct. 1, 1556.	Horner, Isabell, Ripon, widow, July 3, 1556.	15	1	69
Sep. 30, 1563.	———, John, Braton, Jun. 12, 1563.	17		272
July 24, 1555.	———, Nicholas [Ripon], July 27, 1554.	14		242
Oct. 7, 1557.	———, Philipp, Codington (Notts.), labourer, Jun. 10, 1557.	15	2	17
Jun. 22, 1568.	———, Roger, Stubhouse, par. Harwood, Apl. 14, 1568.	17		818
Dec. 4, 1554.	———, Thomas, Weston, Apl. 28, 1554.	14		93
Aug. 5, 1557.	Horsefall, John, Sourby, par. Hallyfax, July 14, 1557.	15	2	118
May 18, 1564.	Horseley, John, Skyrcote, par. Halifax, clothier, Mar. 17, 1563.	17		344
Dec. 1, 1558.	Horseman, Henry, Holme in Spaldingmore, Mar. 16, 1557.	15	3	83
Oct. 8, 1561.	Horsepull, Thomas (bur. Bleasebe, Notts.), May 2, 1559.	17		39
July 31, 1566.	Horsfall, John, Stondley in Langfeild (bur. Heptonstall), Apl. 18, 1566.	17		563
Mar. 9, 1557.	———, Richard, Heptonstall, Oct. 14, 1557.	15	2	168
Jan. 18, 1557.	Horslay, Anthony, Lytlehumber (bur. Paule), Dec. 10, 1557.	15	2	82
Jan. 13, 1558.	———, Robert, Gamston, par. Bridgforth (Notts.), husbn. Sep.16,1558.	15	3	179
July 19, 1567.	Horsley, Martyn, Collinggam (Cottingham, Pontefract Act Bk.), taller, May 25, 1567.	17		680
Apl. 26, 1559.	———, Umfray, Halifax, Jan. 4, 1558.	15	3	363
Oct. 8, 1562.	———, William, Lenton (Notts.), Jun. 20, 1562.	17		122
May 5, 1568.	Horsman, Christopher (bur. Ripon), Jun. 31, 1567.	17		788
Mar. 8, 1566.	———, Elizabeth (bur. Holme in Spaldingmore), wid., Dec. 6, 1565	17		512
Apl. 25, 1554.	———, Rauf, Monke friston, Nov. 10, 1553.	14		56
Jan. 19, 1562.	Horsseman, John, Holme in Spaldingmore, yeoman, Dec. 29, 1562.	17		144
Nov. 9, 1557.	Horton, Thomas, Crosland Hyll, par. Allmonburye, Dec. 8, 1556.	15	2	96
Jan. 22, 1561.	Hothom, Thomas, Kylnewicke, labourer, Dec. 15, 1561.	17		25
Feb. 5, 1565.	———, William, Bubwithe, Dec. 15, 1565.	17		497
Mar. 30, 1555.	Hothome, William, esq., Mar. 21, 1553.	14		13
Jan. 28, 1556.	Hoton, Mawde, Old Malton, widow, Sep. 1, 1556.	15	1	92
Apl. 24, 1567.	———, Thomas, Nottingham, Nov. 8, 1566.	17		642
Sep. 16, 1564.	Hotton, Rauf, Urton, par. Seamer, Dec. 4, 1562.	17		363
Oct. 9, 1567.	Houghe, Robert, Barmebie (Notts.), gentleman, Aug. 7, 1567.	17		722
May 2, 1555.	Hought, John, Rosinton, husbandman, Jan. 13, 1553.	14		29
July 22, 1562.	Houghton, John, Mycklefeld, par. Sherburne, husbn., July 10, 1562.	17		97
Apl. 30, 1556.	———, William, Scarthorpe (Notts.), husbandman, Nov. 3, 1555.	15	1	31
Dec. 5, 1567.	Houram, Thomas, Elloughtonn, husbandman, July 18, 1567.	17		749
Aug. 16, 1566.	Housley, Harrye, Roclif (bur. Snayth), July 12, 1565.	17		570
Apl. 28, 1563.	Houton, Rauff, Souerbie, 1562.	17		240
Apl. 8, 1560.	Howbeege, Thomas, Skeyne, yonge man, May 20, 1559.	16		28
May 14, 1558.	Howbrige, John (bur. Folketon), Mar, 11, 1558.	15	2	281
Feb. 17, 1557.	Howdell, Richard, Bubwyth, Nov. 20, 1557.	15	2	148
Oct. 1, 1556.	Howden, John, Elloughton, Jun. 24, 1556.	15	1	137
Nov. 17, 1562.	Howdgeson, William, Yórk, Nov. 3, 1562.	17		128
Apl. 9, 1554.	Howdon, Thomas (bur. Elloughton), Mar. 16, 1553.	14		53
Jun. 5, 1562.	Howdonn, Leonard, Setterinton, Jan. 19, 1562.	17		86
Dec. 5, 1565.	Howe, George, Yngilbe, Undergrenehoo, gentleman, Mar. 22, 1564.	17		493
May 5, 1558.	Howet, John, Clyfton (Notts.), Sep. 29, 1557.	15	2	257

A.D. 1554 TO 1568. '

		Vol. Pt. Fol.
May 5, 1558.	Howghe, Jennett, Rosington, Nov. 3, 1557.	15 2 248
Jun. 18, 1563.	Howghton, Agnes, Myckelfeld, par. Shereborne, wid., May 26, 1563.	17 259
Dec. 1, 1558.	Howkar, William, senr., Burghe (bur. Eloughton), husbn., Oct. 4, 1558.	15 3 147
Oct. 7, 1557.	Howker, Thomas, Clyfton (Notts.), husbandman, Jun. 13, 1557.	15 2 20
July 4, 1556.	Howland, Thomas, Sheffeld, May 31, 1553.	15 1 53
Sep. 21, 1557.	———, William, Sheffelde, cutler, May 2, 1557.	15 1 357
May 6, 1557.	Howlande, Robert, Woferton, par. Kirke Elley, Mar. 4, 1556.	15 1 251
Apl. 28, 1558.	Howlbecke, William, Hull, gentleman, Feb. 19, 1557.	15 2 218
May 6, 1566.	Howldell, Lowrance, Perlington (bur. Aberforthe), Dec. 18, 1565.	17 549
Jun. 22, 1560.	Howldsworthe, Jennat, Raskell, par. Esyngwolde, wid., Apl. 15, 1560.	16 87
Mar. 13, 1558.	Howleley, Thomas, Howseley Haull, par. Eglesfeld, Jan. 20, 1558	15 3 161
Nov. 29, 1558.	Howme, Agnes, Southkirkebye, Sep. 28, 1558.	15 3 109
Oct. 6, 1558.	Howslaie, Thomas, Howslaie Hall, par. Ecclesfeld, yeom., Dec. 7, 1552.	15 3 72
Sep. 13, 1565.	Howsone, Anthony (bur. Horton), Apl. 21, 1565.	17 463
Apl. 11, 1554.	Howsonne, William (bur. Horton in Craven), Feb. 15, 1553.	14 159
May 6, 1557.	Howst, John, Otringham, Feb. 10, 1556.	15 1 240
Nov. 1, 1562.	Howthrope, Bryan, Newton, par. Wilberfosse, Dec. 1, 1561.	17 129
May 4, 1558.	Howyt, Nicholas, Ratclyfe on Sore (Notts.), May 12, 1557.	15 2 263
Jan. 30, 1555.	Hoyll, William, Steyd in Wentworthe, Aug. 15, 1553.	15 1 5
May 29, 1556.	Hoytonne, Robert, Cranswicke, husbandman, Mar. 13, 1555.	15 1 39
Apl. 24, 1567.	Hubberd, John, Cotgrave (Notts.), husbandman, Jan. 10, 1566.	17 645
May 4, 1558.	Hubbert, William, Clipstonne (bur. Plumtree, Notts.), Oct. 6, 1554.	15 2 267
Apl. 20, 1564.	Hubblebye, Isabell, Beaford, Aug. 20, 1562.	17 333
Apl. 4, 1557.	Huchatson, Richard, Esingwold, Jun. 10, 1556.	15 1 208
May 2, 1566.	Huchinson, Stephan, Kaingham, husbandman, Mar. 18, 1563.	17 525
Sep. 9, 1557.	Hudchynsone, John, Watterfryston, Aug. 8, 1557.	15 2 95
Jun. 12, 1557.	Huddersall, Richard, Hensall (bur. Snathe), husbn., Apl. 20, 1557.	15 1 290
Aug. 30, 1563.	Huddilston, Anne, More Monkton, Jan. 1, 1562.	17 260
May 5, 1558.	Huddilstone, Thomas, Estmarkham (Notts.), Aug. 4, 1557.	15 2 251
Jun. 21, 1555.	Hude, John, Swinflete (bur. Whitgifte), May 10, 1555.	14 209
Mar. 11, 1562.	Hudson, Agnes, Campsall, Dec. 26, 1562.	17 156
Sep. 24, 1558.	———, Alexander, Stutton, par. Tadcaster, July 8, 1559 (sic).	15 3 87
Mar. 10, 1566.	———, Alice, Bradfeld, widow, Sep. 15, 1564.	17 517
Oct. 7, 1561.	———, Alys, Chylwell, par. Adenboro (Notts.), wid., Oct. 25, 1560.	17 43
Jan. 22, 1557.	———, Alys, Danbye, Sep. 12, 1557.	15 2 156
July 8, 1557.	———, Christopher, Arnall (bur. Swyne), wever, May 29, 1557.	15 1 305
May 18, 1559.	———, Edmund, Norton, par. Campsall, Aug. 1, 1558.	15 3 401
Mar. 31, 1555.	———, Edmunde, Sykhows, par. Fishelake, Nov. 5, 1553.	14 106
May 5, 1568.	———, George, Barnbye, par. Lithe, Dec. 29, 1567.	17 773
Nov. 23, 1563.	———, George, Boltbie (bur. Feelixkirke), May 4, 1558.	17 305
Dec. 1, 1563.	———, George, Wormlayhill, par. Fishelake, maryner, Apl. 22, 1563.	17 305
Nov. 5, 1558.	———, James, Accaster Selbye, par. Stillingflete, Oct. 6, 1558.	15 3 96
Feb. 4, 1556.	———, Jenet, Astynthorpe, par. Fishelake, Jan. 12, 1556.	15 1 170
May 2, 1560.	———, Jennat, Tyckyll, widow, Apl. 18, 1560.	16 47
Jun. 25, 1561.	———, John, Baildon, Oct. 6, 1560.	17 74
Dec. 22, 1556.	———, John, Claybrigges, par. Fishelaike, theiker, Aug. 11, 1556.	15 1 78
Dec. 17, 1557.	———, John (bur. Hatefelde), Nov. 10, 1557.	15 2 39
Feb. 8, 1566.	———, John, Hoton Wansley als. Marston, husbn., Feb. 2, 1565.	17 611
Feb. 4, 1561.	———, John, Huby (bur. Sutton), Jan. 3, 156[1-]2.	17 11
Apl. 17, 1567.	———, John (bur. Kigheley), Jun. 3, 1563.	17 622
Mar. 20, 1560.	———, John, Kighley, clothier, Jan. 20, 1560.	16 172
Oct. 13, 1566.	———, John, Moreley, par. Rotherham, July 30, 1566.	17 588
May 1, 1567.	———, John, Rocher in Bradfeld, Feb. 5, 1566.	17 648
Mar. 14, 1560.	———, John, Sikehouse, par. Fishelaike, Nov. 21, 1560.	16 161
Nov. 8, 1557.	———, John, Sowth Kyrkby, May 5, 1557.	15 2 110
Mar. 14, 1560.	———, John, Wollaton (Notts.), Sep. 15, 1558.	16 158
Sep. 16, 1555.	———, John, Wormleye Hill, par. Fishlake, Apl. 9, 1554.	14 68
Jan. 16, 1560.	———, Margaret, Acastre Selbye (bur. Stillinflete), Dec. 27, 1560.	16 143
Apl. 26, 1558.	———, Margaret, wid. of Jo. H., Wornley hill, par. Fishelaike, Nov. 15, 1557.	15 2 207
Feb. 11, 1557.	———, Richard, Wheldryke (bur. Barneslay), Oct. 6, 1557.	15 2 166
Dec. 22, 1561.	———, Robert, Barkeston, par. Shereburne, Nov. 23, 1560.	17 27

		Vol.	Pt.	Fol.
Feb. 14, 1567.	Hudson, Robert (bur. Maske), Dec. 31, 1567.	17		759
Apl. 5, 1554.	——, Robert (Rudston church mentioned), Feb. 6, 1553.	14		155 & 162
Feb. 14, 1567.	——, Robert, Sandesend, par. Lithe, Nov. 8, 1567.	17		760
Apl. 18, 1560.	——, Robert, Thickle (Tickhill), Nov. 7, 1559.	16		31
Mar. 11, 1562.	——, Thomas, Haitfeld Woodhouse, Jan. 8, 1562.	17		156
Apl. 28, 1563.	——, Thomas, Sikhouse, par. Fyshelake, Feb. 19, 1562.	17		234
July 27, 1564.	——, Thomas, Uggleby, par. Whitbye, Jun. 11, 1564.	17		360
May 6, 1559.	——, William, Arson (bur. Acclam), husbandman, Feb. 20, 1558.	15	3	383
Jan. 20, 1557.	——, William, Campsall, Nov. 6, 1557.	15	2	67
Mar. 12, 1556.	——, William, Knottyngley (bur. Pontefract), Oct. 21, 1556.	15	1	199
May 18, 1559.	——, William, Tidworthhay, par. Fyshlake, Sep. 25, 1558.	15	3	417
Nov. 10, 1556.	Hudsone, John, Stubbes Waldinge, par. Wymberslaye, Aug. 6, 1556.	15	1	109
Nov. 8, 1557.	Hudsonne, Robert, Campsall, Sep. 18, 1557.	15	2	111
No date.	——, Sybbill, wid. of Edmounde H , Syke Howse, par. Fishlake, Aug. 4, 1554.	14		82
Aug. 12, 1567.	Huetson, William, Haistrope (bur. Burton Annas), husbn., Mar. 30, 9 Eliz.	17		694
No date.	Hugat, John, Morton, husbandman, Nov. 21, 1554.	14		187
Aug. 23, 1563.	Huggett, Elyn, Howyngham, widow, Dec. 19, 1562.	17		211
Oct. 1, 1557.	Hughtbrege, Thomas (bur. Haytefelde), Aug. 6, 1557.	15	1	369
Mar. 22, 1564.	Hugill, Thomas, Billisdaill, Oct. 8, 1564.	17		412
Sep. 29, 1563.	Hugyns, Thomas, Flambrughe, Apl. 26, 1563.	17		274
Dec. 1, 1558.	Hull, George, Hull, marchand, Sep. 28, 1558.	15	3	146
Mar. 21, 1560.	——, Jennet, Hull, widow, Mar. 12, 1560.	16		173
Jun. 22, 1568.	Hulle, John, Flambroughe, Nov. 10, 1567.	17		825
July 11, 1561.	Humble, Gylbert, Gyllymore (bur. Kyrkbye morshed), husbn., May 20, 1561.	17		80
May 26, 1563.	Humblocke, Robert, Ecclesfeild, smethyman, Dec. 18, 1562.	17		250
May 28, 1557.	——, Thomas, Burton, par. Monkfriston, Mar. 1, 1556.	15	1	211
Jan. 24, 1558.	Humfraye, John, Thornton, par. Staynton, yeoman, Aug. 7, 1558.	15	3	22
Dec. 21, 1562.	Humpilbe, Robert, Clynt (bur. Hamstwayt), Aug. 27, 1562.	17		136
Mar. 1, 1557.	Hundesley, Alis, Wressell, Dec. 19, 1557.	15	2	171
Jun. 7, 1558.	——, John, Skrethenbecke, husbandman, Jan. 3, 1557.	15	2	216
May 5, 1558.	Hunewen or Unwene, Hugh, Askham, Nov. 10, 1557.	15	2	249
Nov. 9, 1560.	Hungaite, Hewghe, Drax, Jan. 26, 2 Eliz.	16		128
Nov. 12, 1556.	Hungaitt, George, North Dalton, gentleman, bachelor, Sep. 8, 1556.	15	1	110
May 2, 1560.	Hunselay, William, Woodhouses, par. Draxe, Mar. 6, 1559.	16		52
Dec. 3, 1566.	Hunsley, Julian, Seaton, Nov. 18, 1566.	17		600
1555.	Hunsworth, John, Fishelake, Jan. 3, 1554.	14		69
Mar. 13, 1558.	Hunt, George, Arksay, Oct. 28, 1558.	15	3	160
Mar. 14, 1560.	——, John, Bramlay Grainge, par. Brawell, yeoman, Nov. 17, 1560.	16		162
Jun. 26, 1566.	——, John, Dighton, par. Eskrige, May 29, 1566.	17		551
May 4, 1558.	——, Nicholas, Papilwicke (Notts.), masson, Nov. 13, 1557.	15	2	277
July 7, 1566.	——, William, Esgrige, Jun. 24, 1566.	17		560
Sep. 1, 1558.	Huntclyf, William, York, blakesmith, Aug. 26, 1558.	15	3	97
Apl. 27, 1558.	Hunter, Agnes, Brustweke, par. Skeklinge, Sep. 7, 1557.	15	2	205
Sep. 9, 1561.	——, Antony, Thorneton in Pikeringlith, gent., Feb. 23, 1560.	17		50
Feb. 7, 1565.	——, George, Billton, Aug. 11, 1565.	17		498
Sep. 30, 1557.	——, Henry, Marflett, husbandman, Aug. 15, 1557.	15	1	340
May 9, 1560.	——, Henry, Newthorpe, par. Greislay (Notts.), husbn., Feb. 14, 1559.	16		60
Oct. 7, 1564.	——, Henry, Wyntringham, May 13, 1563.	17		372
Oct. 30, 1567.	——, Herry, Warter, July 23, 1567.	17		730
May 18, 1559.	——, Jennett (bur. Staynton), Mar. 21, 1558.	15	3	398
Oct. 5, 1558.	——, John, Haxbye, par. Cockeswold, Sep. 13, 1558.	15	3	45
Oct. 22, 1558.	——, John, Huton Rudbye, husbandman, Sep. 30, 1558.	15	3	236
Apl. 14, 1559.	——, John, Wyntryngham, July 18, 1558.	15	3	351
Sep. 30, 1556.	——, Richard, Brystweke (bur. Skeckelinge), Jun. 20, 1556.	15	1	141
May 19, 1567.	——, Robert, senr. (No place mentioned : Sir Gregorye Percye, vicar), Oct. 16, 1566.	17		647
Oct. 2, 1560.	——, Robert, Thorneton in Pickeringelythe, Jan. 28, 1557.	16		111
Sep. 5, 1565.	——, William, Ferlington (bur. Sherifhowton), Aug. 16, 1565.	17		460
July 10, 1567.	——, William, Hubie (bur. Sutton), Nov. 8, 1566.	17		684

A.D. 1554 TO 1568.

		Vol.	Pt.	Fol.
July 23, 1560.	Hyde, Richard, Thorpe, par. Burnhowne (bur.Hayton), Apl. 16, 1560.	16		96
Apl. 20, 1560.	——, Robert, Swynflete (bur. Whytgyfte), Jan. 23, 1559.	16		33
Dec. 13, 1557.	——, William, Pontefract, butcher, Sep. 13, 1557.	15	2	53
May 18, 1559.	Hydes, Richard, Moregate, par. Clarebrugh (Notts.), Aug. 20, 1558.	15	3	423
Oct. 9, 1567.	Hyefeld, Robert, Rolston (Notts.), July 12, 1567.	17		723
Feb. 17, 1558.	Hygyn, John, Wresle, weaver, Mar. 18, 1558.	15	3	275
Mar. 18, 1559.	Hyll, John, Eglesfelde, Feb. 15, 1558.	16		10
Feb. 6, 1558.	——, Oswold, South Kirkebie, Nov. 4, 1557.	15	3	254
Apl. 26, 1558.	——, Thomas, Fyshlaike, Nov. 2, 1557.	15	2	197
Oct. 14, 1561.	——, Thomas, Wombwell, par. Darfelde, Mar. 3, 1560.	17		39
Apl. 26, 1558.	Hynchcleff, George, Tykhill, Nov. 15, 1557.	15	2	228
Mar. 13, 1558.	Hynchclyf, Thomas, Carleton, par. Roystone, Oct. 1, 1558.	15	3	163
Feb. 3, 1561.	Hynchclyff, William, Chartworthe, par. Byrton, Feb. 24, 1560.	17		11
Dec. 22, 1556.	Hyncheclif, Agnes, Southkirkby, widow, May 26, 1556.	15	1	81
July 11, 1558.	————, Thomas, Habyllehaghe, par. Roystone, Mar. 21, 1557.	15	2	304
July 11, 1558.	————, William, Doncaster, Apl. 12, 1558.	15	2	304
Nov. 8, 1557.	Hynd, Edward, Estefeld, par. Tykhyll, gentleman, Sep. 11, 1557.	15	2	114
Sep. 30, 1562.	Hynde, William, Great Houghton, par. Darfeld, husbn., Nov. 27, 1559.	17		113
July 19, 1557.	——, William, Northwheatley (Notts.), Apl. 6, 1557.	15	1	310
Jan. 17, 1557.	Hynderwell, Robert (bur. Skarbroughe), May 21, 1557.	15	2	63
May 9, 1565.	Hyne, Alyson, Calton (bur. Kirkeby Malhamdaille), Nov. 16, 1564.	17		432
Dec. 22, 1556.	——, Jenet, Litle Houghton, par. Darfelde, wid., Nov. 9, 1555.	15	1	77
Oct. 2, 1560.	——, John, Braiton, husbandman, July 21, 1560.	16		114
Oct. 7, 1556.	——, John (Gamston, Notts.), Aug. 12, 7 Edw. VI.	15	1	192
Sep. 28, 1560.	Hynkeley, John, Ruddyngton (Notts.), cotiger, Jun. 13, 1560.	16		106
Apl. 13, 1559.	Hynton, Thomas, Hulbridge (bur. Beverley), Feb. 20, 1558.	15	3	349
Feb. 22, 1563.	Hype, Phillipe (Bulmer Deanery), Dec. 2, 1562.	17		317
Jun. 4, 1563.	—— (Ipe, Act Bk.), Thomas, Gaitefulfurthe, May 7, 1563.	17		252
Jun. 4, 1561.	Hyppun, Anthony, Fetherston, gentleman, Jan. 28, 1560.	17		69
Oct. 13, 1565.	Hyrd, Elizabeth, Danby, July 26, 1564.	17		474
Sep. 6, 1565.	——, William (bur. Kirkeby Mysperton), Oct. 31, 1564.	17		460
Jun. 7, 1560.	Hyrde, Elenor, Burnyshton, par. Scawbye, Feb. 17, 1559.	16		77
Mar. 27, 1560.	——, John (bur. Egton), Jun. 3, 1559.	16		21
Oct. 22, 1556.	Hyrst, Edmunde, Stubés Waldinge (bur. Woomerslay), Oct. 1, 1556.	15	1	100
Oct. 1, 1557.	——, James, Barnysley, Aug. 1, 1557.	15	1	366
Dec. 13, 1557.	——, James, Dalton, par. Heaton, Aug. 28, 1557.	15	2	53
Jun. 14, 1560.	——, James, Estretforde (Notts.), tanner, May 1, 1560.	16		84
Dec. 15, 1557.	——, John, Broughton (Notts.), husbandman, Nov. 3, 1557.	15	2	56
May 13, 1557.	——, Richard, Allerton (Notts.), husbandman, Apl. 20, 1557.	15	2	134
Dec. 13, 1557.	——, William, Walton (bur. Sandall Magna), Sep. 1, 1557.	15	2	54
Oct. 11, 1567.	Hyrste, Alice, wid. of John H., Shaftholme, par. Arkesey, Jun. 5, 1567.	17		728
Apl. 14, 1562.	————, James, Hudderfeld, Feb. 18, 1561.	17		167
Jan. 20, 1557.	——, John, Dalton, par. Thrybarghe, Aug. 19, 1557.	15	2	67
Oct. 11, 1567.	————, John, Shaftholme, par. Arkesey, May 28, 1567.	17		728
Oct. 13, 1562.	——, John, Smithie place in Honley, par. Almonburie, Apl. 24, 1562.	17		126
Apl. 6, 1558.	Hyrsthouse, Robert, Herthill, Dec. 21, 1557.	15	2	188
Nov. 7, 1566.	Hyvinson, Nicholas, Staynegrave, Aug. 14, 1566.	17		600
Sep. 26, 1558.	Hywod, Bryan, Braywell, husbandman, Aug. 12, 1558.	15	3	50
Nov. 6, 1557.	Hyydes, Nycholes, Claworth (Notts.), Sep. 13, 1557.	15	2	107
Nov. 6, 1557.	——, Richard, Claworth (Notts.), Mar. 29, 1557.	15	2	107
May 6, 1568.	[1]Ibotson, George, Ecglesfeld, Jan. 21, 1558.	17		773
Apl. 6, 1558.	————, Robert, Bramley (bur. Braythwell). *No date.*	15	2	182
Nov. 12, 1567.	Ibson (Jybson in Register), Margaret, Wheldrake. *No date.*	17		734
Nov. 10, 1557.	[2]Illingworth, Agnes, Watterfryston, ——, 1557.	15	2	102
Oct. 2, 1566.	———— Dynnis, Ovenden, par. Halifaxe, clothiar, Mar. 6, 1562.	17		580
Jan. 23, 1561.	Illingworthe, John, Hallifax, Dec. 9, 1561.	17		22
Feb. 6, 1558.	————, Thomas, Waterfreston, husbandman, Nov. 10, 1558.	15	3	257
May 13, 1557.	[2]Ingall, Henry, Newarke (Notts.), corvisor, Dec. 21, 1556.	15	1	219
Mar. 8, 1562.	Inggildowe, John, Newmalton, Aug. 30, 1562.	17		151
Oct. 10, 1566.	[2]Inggram, Lawrance, Carleton in Lynrecke (Notts.), husbn., Apl. 27, 1566.	17		588

[1] See also Ebytsonne.   [2] See also under letter Y.

A.D. 1554 TO 1568.

		Vol.	Pt.	Fol.
Apl. 6, 1558.	[1] Ingham, Thomas, Exthorpe, par. Doncaster, Feb. 7, 1557.	15	2	184
Oct. 5, 1554.	Ingildew, Edwarde, Myddleton of Leven (bur. Rudbe), ——.	14		46
Sep. 29, 1563.	[2] Ingland, Isabell, Womebwell, par. Derfeld, July 23, 1563.	17		284
Sep. 13, 1565.	——, James, Otley, Aug. 13, 1565.	17		464
May 31, 1557.	[1] Ingle, Margrett, Weton, par. Harwood, widow, Dec. 20, 1556.	15	1	259
Sep. 3, 1558.	——, Rauffe, Est keswyke, par. Harwood, Aug. 8, 1558,	15	3	97
Apl. 30, 1555.	Ingman, Thomas, Rawmarshe, clothman, Apl. 1, 1555.	14		69
Apl. 28, 1563.	[1] Ingram, Henry, Newsam, par. Kirkebie on Wiske, Dec. 22, 1562.	17		239
Oct. 1, 1556.	——, William, Rotherham, Jun. 26, 1555.	15	1	125
Apl. 19, 1559.	Inkersell, Thomas (bur. Thurgerton, Notts.), Dec. 30, 1558.	15	3	353
Nov. 29, 1558.	Inkersfeild, Thomas, Owston, Feb. 3, 1557.	15	3	140
Apl. 10, 1559.	Inkerssell, Thomas, Upper Whiston, Jan. 26, 1559.	15	3	326
Apl. 17, 1567.	[1] Inman, John, Hebden (bur. Lynton), Aug. 22, 8 Eliz.	17		621
Nov. 17, 1558.	——, Roger, Leedes, clothier, Jan. 25, 1556.	15	3	116
Mar. 6, 1556.	Inmar, William, West Retford (Notts.), Sep. 30, 1556.	15	1	177
July 20, 1565.	Inskipe, William, More Monckton, Apl. 18, 1565.	17		452
Jun. 3, 1563.	Ipe (Registered Hype), Thomas, Gaitefulfurthe, May 7, 1563.	17		252
July 31, 1566.	Ireland, James, Halifax, corvizer, Mar. 28, 1566.	17		563
Oct. 1, 1562.	Isaack, Richard, Wethernsey, May 17, 1562.	17		112
Sep. 30, 1557.	Isaake, Thomas, Kayingham, Jun. 20, 1557.	15	1	341
May 2, 1560.	Isacke, Robert, Kaengham, Mar. 12, 1559.	16		50
No date.	[1] Isabell, Margaret, Cottingham, Nov. 9, 1554.	14		90
May 17, 1554.	——, Stephan, Cottingham, Nov. 24, 1553.	14		5
Aug. 4, 1558.	——, Thomas, Hulbanke, par. Cottyngham, Feb. 25, 155[7-]8.	15	3	6
Apl. 28, 1558.	Issbell, Rauffe, Thurne, Dec. 26, 1557.	15	2	219
Sep. 29, 1563.	Ives, George (bur. Gyselay), Apl. 30, 1562.	17		289
Oct. 2, 1566.	Iveson, Symond, Lancklyffe (Craven), husbandman, Sep. 5, 1565.	17		573
Oct. 1, 1562.	——, Thomas, Settill (bur. Gygleswicke), Aug. 20, 1562.	17		110
Oct. 1, 1562.	——, William (bur. Gyglesweke) Jun. 4, 1560.	17		112
Jun. 10, 1557.	——, William, Hull, wewar, Apl. 5, 1557.	15	1	273
May 25, 1560.	Ivitson, Christopher, Warter, husbandman, Apl. 26, 1560.	16		67
Oct. 9, 1567.	Jackeson, Avarey, Syarston, par. Stoike (Notts.), yeom., May 20, 1567.	17		723
Feb. 24, 1561.	——, Christopher, Leedes, yeoman, Nov. 2, 1561.	17		17
Mar. 15, 1558.	——, Cuthbert, Spaldington, husbandman, July 26, 1558.	15	3	241
Jun. 18, 1560.	——, Edmonde, Watterfulforthe, husbandman, Mar. 25, 1558.	16		85
July 18, 1561.	——, George, Brustwike (bur. Skeklynge), Jun. 1, 1561.	17		84
Nov. 10, 1564.	——, George, Cawton, par. Gillinge, Jan. 10, 1558.	17		397
Jun. 11, 1562.	——, George, Nafferton, carpenter, Nov. 9, 1561.	17		87
May 2, 1560.	——, Laurance, Kelbye, par. Foyston, Oct. 5, 1559.	16		40
Nov. 16, 1558.	——, John, junr., Sowerbye, husbandman, July 23, 1558.	15	3	73
Jan. 29, 1561.	——, Jone (Ridall Deanery), widow, Jan. 23, 1560.	17		8
Feb. 24, 1559.	——, Rawfe, Laysynbe, par. Wilton, Dec. 20, 1559.	16		3
May 5, 1557.	——, Richard, Darrington, Feb. 21, 1557 (*sic*).	15	1	213
Nov. 17, 1558.	——, Richard (bur. Walton), Aug. 10, 1558.	15	3	111
Apl. 16, 1567.	——, Richard, Thornill, Feb. 8, 1566.	17		623
May 13, 1568.	——, Robert, Askham (Notts.), husbandman, Nov. 28, 1567.	17		803
Jun. 4, 1567.	——, Robert, Weton, par. Rowley, husbandman, May 3, 1567.	17		658
Apl. 19, 1559.	——, Thomas, Shelford (Notts.), husbandman, Oct. 8, 1558.	15	3	374
May 25, 1563.	——, William, Cawood, smythe, May 1, 1563.	17		249
July 1, 1561.	——, William, Etton, husbandman, Dec. 16, 1560.	17		76
Feb. 19, 1566.	——, William, Hull, marchant, Nov. 25, 1566.	17		612
Apl. 22, 1556.	Jackesone, Margaret, Sylpho, par. Hackenes, widow, Nov. 28, 1555.	15	1	26
Apl. 2, 1557.	——, Thomas, Daltone, par. Topclif, Sep. 9, 1556.	15	1	286
May 6, 1557.	Jackesonne, William, senr., Owstweike (bur. Roose), Jan. 16, 1556.	15	1	239
Apl. 16, 1562.	Jackman, William, Emsaye, par Skipton, Feb. 27, 1561.	17		188
Oct. 22, 1558.	Jackson, Agnes, Newton, par. Wilberfosse, Aug. 17, 1558.	15	3	122
Jan. 11, 1557.	——, Alyson, Sutcotes, par. Drypole, widow, Nov. 26, 1557.	15	2	73
Mar. 8, 1558.	——, George, Elloughton, husbandman, Jan. 7, 1558.	15	3	283
Oct. 10, 1566.	——, Henry, Nottingham, Jan. 21, 1565.	17		590
Mar. 15, 1560.	——, John (bur. Ascham, Notts.), Nov. 20, 1557.	16		167

[1] See also under letter Y.   [2] See also under letters E and Y.

A.D. 1554 TO 1568.

		Vol.	Pt.	Fol.
Nov.23, 1558.	Jackson, John, Bishopthorpe, husbandman, Oct. 14, 1558.	15	3	230
May 18, 1559.	———, John, Dringe (bur. Skipsey), Jan. 16, 1558.	15	3	410
Jan. 24, 1558.	———, John, Hilton (bur. Rudbie), Sep. 18, 1558.	15	3	23
Dec. 3, 1555.	———, John, Katterton, par. Tadcaster, ——, 1554.	14		246
Mar. 5, 1557.	———, John, Lillinge, par. Sheryfhoton, webster, Nov. 18, 1557.	15	2	169
Apl. 27, 1558.	———, John, Monkhill in Pontefract, Jan. 24, 1557.	15	2	189
May 14, 1560.	———, John, servant unto Laurance Grene, New Malton, cord-wayner, Apl. 13, 1560.	16		63
Dec. 14, 1557.	———, Martha, Everthropp, par. North Cave, Sep. 4, 1557.	15	1	359
May 6, 1557.	———, Richard, Aram, par. Leckinfeld, husbandman, Sep. 2, 1556.	15	1	250
May 26, 1567.	———, Richard, Bridlington, bowcher, Nov. 23, 1566.	17		655
Oct. 4, 1557.	———, Richard, Gatfurthe (bur. Brayton), labourer, Nov. 20, 1557.	15	2	51
Oct. 22, 1558.	———, Richard, Ingelbie Ernecliffe, Sep. 28, 1558.	15	3	235
May 10, 1565.	———, Robert, Eskrige, Mar. 1, 1564.	17		442
Jan. 13, 1558.	———, Robert, Gawlemthroppe, par. Tirrington, Aug. 28, 1558.	15	3	178
No date.	———, Robert, Holme in Spaldingmore, Dec. 5, 1553.	14		129
Sep. 30, 1557.	———, Robert, Selbye, Dec. 28, 1555.	15	1	347
Mar.20, 1565.	———, Robert, Staynford, par. Haitefeild, Dec. 26, 1565.	17		507
Apl. 27, 1558.	———, Robert, junr., Waxham (bur. Owthorne), Feb. 16, 1557.	15	2	206
Oct. 11, 1554.	———, Robert, senr., Yorke, tanner, May 26, 1554.	14		50
Oct. 12, 1554.	———, Robert, senr., York, tanner, May 26, 1554.	14		307
Sep. 6, 1563.	———, Robert, York, Jan. 26, 1558.	17		206
Nov.28, 1567.	———, Steven, Bridlington, husbandman, Mar. 25, 1567.	17		736
Sep. 30, 1563.	———, Thomas, Carlton, par. Albroughe, Jan. 21, 1562.	17		273
Jun. 23, 1558.	———, Thomas, Spoldyngton (bur. Bubwith), May 16, 1558.	15	2	340
Jun. 2, 1557.	———, Thomas, Walton, par. Sandall Magna, Oct. 22, 1556.	15	1	267
Mar. 8, 1558.	———, Thomas, Weaton, par. Rowley, Aug. 31, 1558.	15	3	285
Aug. 2, 1560.	———, Thomas, York, Apl. 17, 1560.	16		98
Apl. 22, 1556.	———, William, Darington, Nov. 4, 1555.	15	1	19
Jan. 23, 1558.	———, William (bur. Eskrige), Nov. 15, 1558.	15	3	22
Aug.23, 1558.	———, William, Robynhoodes Baye, par. Fyllinge, May 27, 1556.	15	2	294
Nov.19, 1567.	———, William, Skagilthorpe, husbandman, Apl. 19, 1567.	17		736
Oct. 1, 1556.	———, William, Thrynscoo, husbandman, Jun. 6, 1556.	15	1	126
Oct. 3, 1566.	———, William, Topclif, May 22, 1566.	17		579
Sep. 22, 1557.	———, William, York, marchante, May 29, 1557.	15	1	348
Jan. 20, 1561.	Jacksonne, Robert, Darringtonne, Feb. 15, 1559.	17		20
Sep. 30, 1563.	Jacson, Charles, Howke, husbandman, Dec. 11, 1562.	17		272
Sep. 24, 1565.	———, Jene, York, widow, Aug. 10, 1565.	17		469
Apl. 13, 1559.	———, Jenit, Aram (bur. Leckinfeld), widow, Feb. 21, 1558.	15	3	350
Dec. 1, 1558.	———, John, Beverlay, tanner, Apl. 1, 1558.	15	3	84
Jan. 30, 1566.	———, John, Hull, tyler, Oct. 27, 1566.	17		611
Sep. 13, 1558.	———, John, senr., Sowerbie, husbandman, Aug. 27, 1558.	15	3	103
May 27, 1562.	———, Richard, Halsam, Mar. 10, 1560.	17		101
Oct. 9, 1561.	———, Richard, Hayton (Notts.), husbandman, May 3, 1561.	17		42
Nov.17, 1558.	———, Robert, Farburne, Sep. 16, 1558.	15	3	114
Nov.10, 1557.	———, Robert, Newe Malton, tanner, Sep. 28, 1557.	15	2	100
Feb. 10, 1557.	Jacsonne, Alysonne, Bainton. widow, 1557.	15	2	147
Oct. 4, 1564.	Jaike, John, Bucden (bur. Hoberam), May 17, 1564.	17		370
Jun. 23, 1558.	Jakes, Christopher (bur. Bubwith), Apl. 16, 1558.	15	2	340
Jun. 30, 1558.	Jakeson, Thomas, Slingesbye, Mar. 2, 1558.	15	2	341
Feb. 4, 1556.	Jakson, Elizabeth, Crambom, single woman, Jun. 27, 1556.	15	1	168
Jan. 24, 1558.	———, James, Lasynbye, Aug. 24, 1558	15	3	215
July 28, 1554.	———, James, York, marchant, July 20, 1551.	14		143
July 4, 1556.	———, John, Eskyrke, Jun. 18, 1556.	15	1	51
Jan. 24, 1558.	———, Rafe, Lakynbye, par. Wylton, husbandman, Aug. 16, 1558.	15	3	215
Jun. 12, 1557.	———, Richard, Whitgifte, Apl. 3, 1557.	15	1	291
Dec. 20, 1554.	———, William, Wentworth, gentleman, Feb. 21, 1553.	14		151
July 19, 1557.	———— als. Taylyour, Christopher, Estretford (Notts.), May 24,1557.	15	1	311
May 4, 1558.	Jalyn, William, Whatton (Notts.), husbandman, Jun. 28, 1557.	15	2	268
May 9, 1566.	Jalyne, Thomas, Whatton (Notts.), husbandman, Jun. 27, 1565.	17		548
Oct. 7, 1557.	Jamerson, William, Paplewicke (Notts.), Sep. 13, 1557.	15	2	25
Mar.14, 1560.	James, Agnes, Wyllforde (Notts.), Sep. 20, 1559.	16		158

		Vol.	Pt.	Fol.
Mar.14, 1560.	——, Joanne, Nottingham, widow, Feb. 5, 1560.	16		163
Mar.15, 1560.	——, Rauffe, Claworthe (Notts.), husbandman, Jun. 1, 1559.	16		167
Apl. 20, 1559.	——, Raulf, Wistone, par. Claworthe (Notts.), Jan. 3, 1558.	15	3	308
Oct. 10, 1566.	——, Robert, Mylforthe (Notts.), Jun. 2, 1565.	17		596
May 17, 1565.	——, Robert, Terlaston (Notts.), Oct. 21, 1564.	17		438
Oct. 10, 1566.	——, Robert, Thrumpton (Notts.), Dec. 20, 1561.	17		595
Nov.27, 1560.	Jameson, Alexander (bur. Nonnyngton), Sep. 17, 1560.	16		130
Oct. 12, 1558.	Jamys, John, Nottingham, tanner, Nov. 15, 1557.	15	3	28
Nov.12, 1556.	Jarett, Anthony, Hutone Cransweke, Sep. 14, 1556.	15	1	110
Nov.22, 1554.	Jarome, Thomas. Essingwolde, July 10, 1554.	14		89
Aug. 6, 1567.	Jarrome, William, Watton, labourer, Jun. 30, 1567.	17		700
May 6, 1563.	Jarvis,Thomas, Willobe of the Woldes (Notts.), husbn., Dec. 16, 1562.	17		245
Oct. 7, 1557.	Jayre, Clemett, Nottingham, Sep. 24, 1557.	15	2	24
Jan. 11, 1562. 1	Jefferayson, Alice, West Elley, par. North Feribie, Oct. 4, 1562.	17		141
Feb. 25, 1560.	Jefferson, George, Speton (bur. Righton), husbandman, Feb. 20, 1559.	16		150
Jun. 20, 1566.	Jeffrason, John (bur. Nafferton), Sep. 15, 1 Eliz.	17		556
Oct. 2, 1567.	————, Margaret, Beeford, widow, July 12, 1567.	17		713
Nov.26, 1555.	————, Richard, Marston, Sep. 30, 1555.	14		184
Aug. 4, 1558.	————, Thomas, Northe Borton, Mar. 31, 1558.	15	3	5
Oct. 2, 1567.	———— als. Herman, Francis, Befourthe, husbn., Jan. 16, 1566.	17		715
Nov.28, 1567.	Jeffrasonne, Martynne, Yerton, par. Seamer, Apl. 20, 1567.	17		740
May 4, 1557.	Jeffraye, Richard, Coytworthe in Wentworthe, Mar. 1, 1556.	15	1	278
Nov.10, 1563.	Jeffrayson, Jennat, Skitbie, widow, Sep. 4, 1563.	17		301
Sep. 15, 1561.	————, John, Well (? West) Elley, par. North Feribie, Aug. 3,1561.	17		53
Jan. 19, 1556.	————, William, Cottingham, Sep. 28, 1556.	15	1	88
Apl. 27, 1558.	————, William, Egbroughe (bur. Kellington), July 30, 1557.	15	2	194
Feb. 24, 1561.	Jefrayson, Nicholas, Chappell Allerton, par. Leedes, husbn., May 28, 1553.	17		18
Mar.21, 1561. 1	Jelatson, Christopher, Elvington, Mar. 20, 1561.	17		5
May 18, 1559. 1	Jeniver, John, Westretforth (Notts.), Aug. 9, 1556.	15	3	423
Jun. 11, 1560.	Jenkenson, Bryan, York, Mar. 8, 1559.	16		83
Feb.17, 1557.	Jenkensonne, Robert, Shafton, par. Felkyrke, Aug. 1, 1551.	15	2	141
Jan. 24, 1558.	Jenkinson, Richard, Neyther Skiers, par. Derfeld, Oct. 18, 1558.	15	3	118
Oct. 10, 1560.	————, Robert, Faringdon (Notts.), May 5, 1560.	16		123
Sep. 15, 1561.	————, Thomas, Scoulscottes near Hull, mariner, Apl. 14, 1561.	17		54
Sep. 30, 1558.	Jenkynson, Christopher, chantrie preist at Magdalens (bur. Ripon), May 10, 1557.	15	3	55
Oct. 8, 1556.	————, Elizabeth, Shelford (Notts.), widow, Aug. 20, 1556.	15	1	149
Mar.22, 1554.	————, George, Fylinge, Aug. 18, 1554.	14		188
Sep. 30, 1558.	————, Marmaduke, priest at Skelton (bur. Ripon), Aug. 29, 1558.	15	3	56
Dec.17, 1557.	————, John, Kyrkebramwith, Oct. 1, 1557.	15	2	40
Sep. 30, 1558.	————, Thomas, Swanlay (bur. Ripon), Aug. 16, 1558.	15	3	55
Jan. 20, 1557.	————, William, Allholme, par. Arkesay, Dec. 30, 1557.	15	2	65
Sep. 30, 1562.	————, William, Brynsforth, par. Rotherham, July 11, 1562.	17		113
July 29, 1558.	————, William (bur. Fetherstone), Apl. 12, 1558.	15	2	383
Oct. 22, 1556.	Jenkynsone, Anne, Byrstall, May 14, 1556.	15	1	97
May 2, 1560.	Jenynge, William, Arkesay, Nov. 29, 1559.	16		45
Sep. 29, 1563.	Jenyns, John, Arksey, May 10, 1562.	17		271
Apl. 24, 1559.	Jenyson, Henry, Faundaill, par. Lastingham, Oct. 6, 15—.	15	3	378
Oct. 30, ——.	————, Robert, Southe Holme (bur. Hovingham), Sep. 12, 1556.	14		180
Apl. 20, 1559. 1	Jenyver, John, Kirketon (Notts.), widow, Dec. 14, 1558.	15	3	368
May 9, 1566.	Jepson, Henry, Warsopp (Notts.), yeoman, Apl. 10, 1565.	17		542
May 5, 1558.	————, John, Dunham on Trente (Notts.), Jan. 10, 1557.	15	2	211
Oct. 7, 1557.	————, John, S. Peter's, Nottingham, Aug. 10, 1557.	15	2	24
Dec.15, 1557.	————, Richard, Cowknay (Notts.), Jun. 19, 1557.	15	2	57
Nov.29, 1558.	————, Thomas, Melton, par. Wath, Oct. 12, 1558.	15	3	142
May 11, 1566.	————, William, Northdighton, Feb. 16, 1565.	17		521
Nov. 6, 1557.	Jesope, William, Mattersay Thorpe (Notts.), yeoman, Jun. 30, 1557.	15	2	108
Apl. 26, 1558.	Jesoppe, William, Treaton, Dec. 12, 1557.	15	2	225
Jun. 20, 1566.	Jessoppe, Thomas, Cudworthe, par. Ruston, husbn, Apl. 11, 1566.	17		559
Oct. 8, 1562. 1	Jiniver, John, West Retford (Notts.), husbandman, Dec. 16, 1560.	17		121

1 See also under letter G.

		Vol.	Pt.	Fol.
Apl. 20, 1559.	Jiniver, Roger, West Retforde (Notts.), Sep. 8, 1558.	15	3	370
Oct. 3, 1554.	Joatson, Gerrott, Marflete by Hull, Apl. 11, 1552.	14		42
Feb. 15, 1558.	Jobson, Henry, Remeswell (bur. Owtthorne), husbn., Dec. 29, 1558.	15	3	270
July 3, 1555.	———, Thomas, Rymswell, par. Outhorne, yeoman, May 12, 1555.	14		197
May 4, 1558.	Johnson, Adame, Nutthall (Notts.), Dec. 29, 1557.	15	2	215
Apl. 20, 1556.	———, Agnes, Thirkilbie, Mar. 14, 1555.	15	1	18
Mar. 21, 1560.	———, Anne, Kylnewoldegraves, Feb. 11, 1558.	16		173
Sep. 3, 1556.	———, Anthony, Nether Ousegate, York, Aug. 16, 1556.	15	1	64
Jun. 6, 1564.	———, Anthonye, Howton, par. Saunton, Nov. 25, 1563.	17		349
[?Jan.]22, 1557.	———, Bryan, Hemlynton, par. Staynton, yeoman, Nov. 14, 1557.	15	2	158
Jun. 22, 1568.	———, Christopher, Great Kelke (bur. Foston), Dec. 23, 1567.	17		821
Oct. 5, 1558.	———, Cutbert, Carleton (bur. Whorlton), Aug. 17, 1558.	15	3	70
Oct. 8, 1556.	———, Esabell, Gonalston (Notts.), widow, Sep. 10, 1556.	15	1	152
Dec. 1, 1558.	———, George, Watton, taylier, Oct. 11, 1558.	15	3	83
Oct. 3, 1566.	———, Henry, Girgarishe, par. Weston, 1566.	17		582
July 15, 1518 (sic).	———, Henry. Hull, beerbrewer, Dec, 12, 1517 (sic).	15	2	91
Aug. 17, 1564.	———, Hew, Cookeswold, Jun, 2, 1564.	17		361
Jun. 23, 1561.	———, Hewe, Helaye, May 21, 1559.	17		73
Nov. 28, 1558.	———, Isabell, Dymilton (bur. Essyngton), Jun. 26, 1558.	15	3	77
Sep. 15, 1558.	———, Isabell, Langton, widow, July 28, 1558.	15	3	105
May 5, 1568.	———, Jennet, Leckenfeild, widow, Feb. 28, 1566.	17		775
Nov. 28, 1558.	———, John, Albrough, Aug. 27, 1558.	15	3	77
Oct. 5, 1558.	———, John, Holme in Spaldingmore, Apl. 28, 1558.	15	3	71
Jun. 22, 1568.	———, John, senr., Flamburghe, husbandman, Jan. 22, 1567.	17		825
Jan. 11, 1557.	———, John, Kayngham, Dec. 6, 1557.	15	2	76
July 26, 1558.	———, John, Lysset, par. Befforde, husbandman, Sep. 27, 1557.	15	3	12
May 5, 1557.	———, John, Middleton (bur. Rudbie), Feb. 20, 1556.	15	1	250
Sep. 30, 1562.	———, John, Pannall, mylner, Sep. 27, 1560.	17		116
Jun. 20, 1568.	———, John, Paynethorpe, par. Sandall Magna, Mar. 16, 1567.	17		827
July 15, 1562.	———, John, Riall (bur. Skeclinge), Mar. 28, 1562.	17		95
May 2, 1566.	———, John, Storethes, par. Skipton, Jan, 27, 1565.	17		531
Oct. 1, 1562.	———, Margaret, Ryall (bur. Skeclinge), Jun. 28, 1562.	17		113
Mar. 30, 1559.	———, Martyne, North Frothingham, Jan. 29, 1558.	15	3	298
Jan. 24, 1558.	———, Mathew, Hemlynton, par. Staneton, husbn., Sep. 2, 1558.	15	3	22
Aug. 12, 1561.	———, Mathew, Sigelstone, 1561.	17		59
July 27, 1557.	———, Nicholas, Newmalton, cordener, Jun. 20, 1557.	15	1	321
May 9, 1566.	———, Nicholas, Ordsall (Notts.), husbandman, Dec. 29, 1565.	17		541
Jan. 30, 1566.	———, Peter, Anlabie, par. Hessill, May 24, 1566.	17		610
Sep. 3, 1566.	———, Rauf (bur. Amonderby), July 1, 1566.	17		571
May 6, 1557.	———, Rauff, Westheslerton, Jan. 24, 1556.	15	1	215
May 6, 1563.	———, Richard, Burton Joyce (Notts.), husbandman, Mar. 20, 1562.	17		242
Jun. 6, 1560.	———, Richard, Bushipeburton, Jun. 8, 1559.	16		75
Dec. 16, 1557.	———, Richard, Danthorpe (bur. Hombleton), Nov. 6, 1557.	15	2	47
Oct. 7, 1556.	———, Richard, Egmanton, Dec. 3, 1555.	15	1	146
Jun. 7, 1560.	———, Richard, Flambrughe, Sep. 30, 1559.	16		80
Jan. 12, 1558.	———, Richard, Leckinfeild, yeoman, Nov. 10, 1558.	15	3	196
Nov. 17, 1558.	———, Richard, Ledsham, Aug. 7, 1558.	15	3	112
Oct. 6, 1557.	———, Richard, Owthorpe (Notts.), Aug. 8, 1557.	15	2	30
Mar. 23, 1557.	———, Richard (Act Book), Seton (bur. Siglisthron), Jan. 26, 1557.	15	2	175
Jan. 13, 1558.	———, Richard, South Carleton, par. Soouth Muskham (Notts.), husbandman, Sep. 10, 1556.	15	3	16
Aug. 12, 1566.	———, Richard, Wyneton als. Wyton, par. Swyne, Aug. 10, 1565.	17		568
May 12, 1559.	———, Robert, Bushopburton, Mar. 12, 1558.	15	3	392
May 5, 1557.	———, Robert, Hilton (bur. Rudbie), Mar. 2, 1556.	15	1	249
Oct. 9, 1567.	———, Robert, Northe Whetley (Notts.), husbn., Feb. 25, 1567.	17		721
Jan. 22, 1561.	———, Roger, Brackan (bur. Kylnewycke), husbn., Dec. 6, 1561.	17		24
Apl. 27, 1558.	———, Roger, Hornesay, husbandman, Aug. 21, 1557.	15	2	206
Jan. 12, 1558.	———, Thomas, Bainton, husbandman, Sep. 26, 1558.	15	3	193
May 5, 1557.	———, Thomas (bur. Gisburne), Apl. 8, 1557.	15	1	248
Apl. 24, 1554.	———, Thomas, Hessilwode, Apr. 22, 1553.	14		63
Jun. 2, 1554.	———, Thomas, Howstwick (bur. Roose), Feb. ult., 1557.	15	2	337
Jun. 17, 1554.	———, Thomas, Muston, Mar. 10, 1553.	14		12

		Vol.	Pt.	Fol.
May 10, 1567.	Johnson, Thomas, North Whetlay (Notts.), Mar. 2, 1564.	17		651
May 13, 1557.	———, Thomas, Owlcottes, par. Blyth (Notts.), Apl. 20, 1557.	15	1	232
Apl. 7, 1559.	———, Thomas (bur. Stillingflete), Mar. 15, 155[8]9.	15	3	320
Sep. 3, 1554.	———, Umfray, Waikefeld, tanner, July, 10, 1554.	14		272
Sep. 30, 1557.	———, Walter, Danthropp (bur. Humbleton), Aug. 8, 1557.	15	1	341
Jun. 28, 1563.	———, William, Ayton (bur. Hooton Bushell), Mar. 12, 1562.	17		260
May 13, 1568.	———, William, Barmebie (Notts.), husbandman, Oct. 10, 1567.	17		798
Jan. 12, 1558.	———, William, Beverlaie, priest, Nov. 16, 1558.	15	3	196
Apl. 14, 1565.	———, William, Cawoode, tanner, Feb. 2, 1564.	17		419
Mar. 21, 1557.	———, William, Galmeton, Jan. 26, 1557.	15	2	175
Mar. 23, 1557.	———, William, Halsham, Jan. 14, 1557.	15	2	172
Feb. 4, 1557.	———, William, Holme in Spaldingmore, Dec. 20, 1557.	15	2	164
May 29, 1556.	———, William, Langton, Mar. 26, 1556.	15	1	38
Mar. 14, 1559.	———, William, Skelton (bur. Overton), Sep. 1, 1558.	16		9
Oct. 31, 1565.	———, William, Skelton (bur. Overton), July 13, 1565.	17		482
Jun. 12, 1567.	——— als. Kaingham, Gerat, Brustwicke (bur. Skecklinge), Feb. 22, 1566.	17		656
Apl. 28, 1558.	Johnsone, John, Stoxley in Cleveland. _No date._	15	2	230
May 21, 1558.	Johnsonne, Richard, Amplefurth, par. Oswoldkirke, husbn., Sep. 15, 1557.	15	2	283
Jan. 16, 1558.	Jolland, John, Cowike, par. Snathe, Nov. 16, 1558.	15	3	209
Dec. 4, 1557.	Jollande, Richard, Cowicke, par. Snaythe, Sep. 15, 1557.	15	2	52
May 18, 1559.	Jonge, Robert, Ordsall (Notts.), yeoman, Dec. 17, 1558.	15	3	406
Jun. 7, 1560.	Jonson, John, Scawbye, Jun. 2, 1559.	16		78
Apl. 19, 1559.	———, William, Selstone (Notts.), Jun. 10, 1558.	15	3	355
Jun. 4, 1568.	Jordayne, John, Raystrope, Mar. 31, 1567.	17		813
Oct. 5, 1558.	Jowcey, Robert, Scougdaill, par. Gisburne, July 25, 1558.	15	3	43
Oct. 6, 1558.	Jowett, Thomas, Heiton, par. Bradford, May 22, 1557.	15	3	90
Apl. 7, 1554.	Jove, Thomas, Osington, Mar. 19, 1553.	14		216
Jun. 2, 1557.	Jubbe, Anthony, West Hardwicke, par. Wragbie, husbn., Mar. 27, 1557.	15	1	267
Apl. 18, 1567.	———, John, Brodsworthe, Mar. 7, 1566.	17		636
Nov. 29, 1558.	———, John, Howton Robert, yeoman, Sep. 26, 1558.	15	3	142
July 29, 1558.	———, William, Wyntersott, par. Wragbie, husbn., Sep. 28, 1557.	15	2	382
Dec. 17, 1557.	Justice, Roger, Staynton, Nov. 25, 1557.	15	2	40
Mar. 14, 1557.	———, Thomas, priest (bur. Skerne), Dec. 19, 1557.	15	2	152
Nov. 29, 1558.	———, Thomas, Staynton, Mar. 21, 1557.	15	3	138
July 19, 1557.	———, William, Scrube (Notts.), May 28, 1557.	15	1	312
Jun. 16, 1564.	Justis, Nicholas, Staynton (Doncaster), Apl. 8, 1564.	17		350
Jun. 5, 1561.	Jvwet, William, Ripon, Apl. 18, 1561.	17		70
Nov. 12, 1567.	Jybsonne (Ibson, Act Book), Margaret, Wheldrake. _No date._	17		734
May 5, 1558.	Jyllat, Richard, Estretforde (Notts.), Nov. 9, 1557.	15	2	249
Jun. 2, 1557.	Kaie, Homfraie, Kirkleyrton, Apl. 9, 1557.	15	1	266
Jun. 12, 1567.	Kaingham als. Johnson, Gerat, Brustwicke (bur. Skecklinge), Feb. 22, 1566.	17		656
May 18, 1559.	1 Karr, Thomas, (bur. Est Retford, Notts.), Sep. 4, 1558.	15	3	421
Jun. 15, 1566.	1 Karver, Steven, South Clif, par. North Cave, mylner, Feb. 21, 1565.	17		552
Oct. 8, 1556.	1 Karyngton, John, Hawxworthe (Notts.). Apl. 15, 1556.	15	1	150
Jun. 18, 1567.	1 Katterall, Bryan, Langthorpe (bur. Swyne), gentleman, Apl. 15, 1567.	17		660
Mar. 28, 1557.	Kay, Elyne, Estharlesay, Nov. 30, 1556.	15	1	202
Mar. 9, 1557.	———, John, Fixbye in Elande, Nov. 7, 1557.	15	2	169
Oct. 12, 1558.	———, John, Gonalston (Notts.), milner, Sep. 12, 1558.	15	3	228
Apl. 13, 1559.	———, Margaret, Beswyke, par. Kylnewycke, widow, Feb. 1, 1558.	15	3	347
May 26, 1567.	———, Richard, Lebberstone, par. Fyllay, Apl. 20, 1567.	17		653
May 6, 1557.	Kaye, John, Gysburne, Nov. 6, 1556.	15	1	284
Mar. 26, 1560.	———, Peter, Thorppe, par. Almonburie, yeoman, Mar. 12, 1559.	16		19
Feb. 15, 1558.	Kaylom, Robert, Terington, Sep. 22, 1558.	15	3	273
Oct. 6, 1557.	Kayworthe, William, Cottome, par. Southleverton (Notts.), Jun. 20, 1557.	15	2	14
July 14, 1562.	———, William, Southe Leverton (Notts.), ——, 1558.	17		98
Nov. 28, 1567.	Keathe, Elliner, Seamer, wid. of John K., Apl. 9, 1567.	17		739
Nov. 28, 1567.	———, John, Seamer, Mar. 9, 1566.	17		739

1 See also under letter C.

		Vol.	Pt.	Fol.
May 2, 1566.	Kechinge, Robert, Beverley, brekelaier, Dec. 19, 1565.	17		538
Dec. 1, 1558.	Keild, Richard, Northe Cave, July 12, 1558.	15	3	81
Apl. 5, 1554.	Keld, Henry, Skipseye, husbandman, Feb. 7, 1553.	14		214
Jun. 4, 1568.	——, Richard, Skampston, par. Wintringham, Apl. 14, 1567.	17		812
Aug.13, 1567.	——, Richard, Skipsey in Holderness, Jun. 4, 1567.	17		689
Feb. 6, 1558.	Keldaill, Francis, Scarbroughe, July 15, 1558.	15	3	258
Dec.12, 1560.	Kellay, Thomas, Watton, labourer, Oct. 12, 1560.	16		135
Oct. 29, 1566.	Kellet, Richard, York, corne marchaunt, Jun. 20, 1565.	17		585
Apl. 11, 1554.	——, Thomas, Horton in Ribilsdale, Feb. 2, 1553.	14		160
Mar.16, 1556.	Kelsay, Henry, Rither, Aug. 19, 1556.	15	1	186
Apl. 14, 1562.	Kelsey, John, Ottryngham, Dec. 20, 1561.	17		184
Oct. 12, 1564.	Kelsterne, Heugh, Newarke (Notts.), draper, Aug. 11, 1562.	17		378
Oct. 10, 1566.	Kem, Thomas, Hicklinge (Notts.), Sep. 10, 1566.	17		593
Jan. 13, 1558.	Kempe, Bernerd, Rosington, Mar. 1, 1557.	15	3	185
May 14, 1555.	——, Christopher. Northe Cave, Jun. 22, 1553.	14		36
Oct. 10, 1566.	——, Randulph, Broxstowe (bur. Bilborowe, Notts.), Mar. 20, 1566.	17		591
Nov.29, 1558.	——, Richard, Braythwell, labourer. Oct. 1, 1558.	15	3	109
Apl. 13, 1559.	——, Richard, Spaldington(bur.Bubwith),sheperd, Mar.28,155[8]9.	15	3	343
Apl. 16, 1562.	——, Thomas, Kirkbe Moreshed, yeoman, Jun. 20, 1558.	17		159
Oct. 5, 1554.	Kempley, John (bur. Marske), ——, 1554.	14		275
Oct. 6, 1565.	Kemsaie, Robert, Hull, gentleman, Jun. 26, 1565.	17		484
May 5, 1568.	Kendaill, John, Otterburne, Jan. 8, 10 Eliz.	17		786
Oct. 11, 1561.	Kendall, Christopher, Northe Leverton (Notts.), gent., July 23, 1560.	17		40
Mar. 2, 1560.	——, John, Woodhouse, par. Ryston in Holderness, gent., Jan. 9, 1559.	16		152
Dec.22, 1556.	——, Richard, Tykhill, Aug. 26, 1556.	15	1	79
Jan. 5, 1558.	——, Robert, Acaster Selbie (bur. Stillingflet), husbn.,Sep.16,1558.	15	3	36
Oct. 4, 1558.	——, Robert, Askwithe, par. Weston, husbn., Aug. 11, 1558.	15	3	59
Sep. 6, 1558.	Kendell, Christopher, Wymmerslay, Apl. 18, 1558.	15	3	99
Sep. 29, 1563.	——, Henry (bur. Longe Preston), Dec. 23, ——.	17		277
Apl. 26, 1558.	Kendill, William, Askewyth (bur. Weston), Feb. 24, 1557.	15	2	236
Jan. 22, 1557.	Kendyll, Isabell, Gysburne, Nov. 30, 1557.	15	2	157
Jan. 22, 1557.	——, Jane, Gysburne, Nov. 27, 1557.	15	2	157
Apl. 5, 1563.	Kenerose, Richard, Skarburghe, Sep. 18, 1562.	17		218
Nov.14, 1561.	Kenneto, Alexander, Scarbrughe, Mar. 18, 1561.	17		34
May 2, 1560.	Kenrosse, Emmot, Scarbrughe, Jun. 5, 1558.	16		40
Sep. 6, 1558.	Kent, George, Stanelay, par. Wakefeild, July 25, 1558.	15	3	99
July 26, 1557.	——, John, Dewisburie, Jun. 21, 1557.	15	1	317
Nov.17, 1558.	——, Nicholas, Heddinglay (bur. Ledes), yeoman, 1558.	15	3	115
Apl. 27, 1564.	Kente, Henry, Gerton (Notts.), Dec. 25, 1563.	17		337
May 5, 1558.	Kepas, William, Everton (Notts.), husbandman, Feb. 13, 1557.	15	2	251
Oct. 13, 1566.	Kepis, John, Tickhill, Jun. 20, 1566.	17		588
May 5, 1558.	Keppas, Thomas, Everton (Notts.), Sep. 27, 1557.	15	2	250
Oct. 12, 1558.	Kercham, Hughe, Orston (Notts.), Aug. 12, 1557.	15	2	374
Jan. 13, 1558.	Kerchevar, William, Orston (Notts.), husbandman, Aug. 25, 1558.	15	3	178
Apl. 19, 1559.	Kerchever, Richard, Hawkeworth (Notts.), husbn., Jan. 21, 1558.	15	3	358
July 15, 1556.	Kercoppe, John, Brompton, Apl. 11, 1556.	15	1	55
Oct. 2, 1560.	Kerebye, Edward, Rosse, Jun. 1, ——.	16		116
Oct. 13, 1562.	Kerke, Richard (bur. Wakefeild), Mar. 16, 1561.	17		125
Mar.15, 1562.	Kerton, James, Welburye, yeoman, Mar. 20, 1561.	17		163
May 26, 1557.	Kettelwell, Robert (bur. Ripon), Apl. 22, 1557.	15	1	264
Sep. 30, 1558.	Kettilstringe, Christopher, Markyngton (bur. Ripon), husbn., Mar. 1, 1556.	15	3	56
Nov. 8, 1558.	Kettlewodde, Alyson, Seklethorpe (bur. Seithrington), wid., Oct. 10, 1558.	15	3	124
Oct. 2, 1566.	Key, Christopher, Mertintoyftes (Craven), husbandman, ——, 1566.	17		573
July 18, 1565.	——, George, Griswhet, par. Topclif, Jun. 13, 1565.	17		451
Aug.20, 1567.	——, Isabell (bur. Thriske), July 17, 1567.	17		702
Jun. 20, 1562.	——, John, Carlton Myniott (bur. Thriske), Jan. 27, 1562.	17		89
Jun. 14, 1564.	——, Rauf, Flambrugh, Oct. 29, 1563.	17		352
July 9, 1561.	——, Richard, Dalton, par. Topclyff, Mar. 1, 1560.	17		80
Sep. 29, 1563.	——, Richard, Dodworthe, gentleman, Sep. 7, 1563.	17		272

		Vol.	Pt.	Fol.
Mar.27, 1555.	Key, Thomas (bur. Baynton), Jan. 22, 1555.	15	1	14
Feb. 1, 1563.	——, Thomas, Fletcherhouse, par. Almanburie, husbn., Sep. 29, 1563.	17		313
July 4, 1565.	——, William, Beswicke (bur. Kilnewicke), husbn., Nov. 20, 1564.	17		448
May 5, 1568.	——, William, Crakall (bur. Topclif), Jan 18, 1567.	17		780
May 22, 1557.	——, William, senr., Dalton (bur. Topliffe), Dec. 18, 1556.	15	1	257
Sep. 20, 1554.	——, William, Maxbroughe, par. Rotherham, Dec. 27, 1553.	14		150
Dec. 10, 1562.	——, William, Skipton (bur. Topclif), Sep. 3, 1562.	17		132
Mar.22, 1560.	——, William, West Heslerton, Jun. 22, 1560.	16		176
Jun. 6, 1554.	Keye, Edmunde, Almonburie, Aug. 18, 1547.	14		11
Jun. 25, 1554.	——, Elizabeth, Estheslerton, widow, May 21, 1554.	14		115
July 8, 1560.	Keytlye, Robert, Burghewalles, husbandman, Jan. 20, 1559.	16		80
Jan. 13, 1558.	Keyworth, William, Sowthleverton (Notts.), husbn., Apl. 30, 1555.	15	3	189
Oct. 13, 1558.	Kichin, Richard, Upton (Notts.), July 15, 1558.	15	2	360
May 13, 1557.	——, Robert, Hucknall Torcard (Notts.), Sep. 18, 1556.	15	1	222
Oct. 2, 1566.	Kid, Thomas, Burnesall, Feb. 2, 1564.	17		576
May 2, 1566.	—, Thomas, Kilnesey (bur. Conyston), May 17, 1565.	17		531
May 2, 1566.	—, Thomas, Lengerhowse (bur. Rilston), Jan. 2, 1565.	17		529
Feb. 23, 1556.	Kiddall, James, Walterfulfourthe (bur. S. Martin's, York), husbn., Dec. 22, 1556.	15	1	164
May 6, 1557.	Kighlaie, Anne, Fawwedder (bur. Ottlaie), gentlewoman, Sep. 22, 1556.	15	1	256
Mar. 6, 1556.	Kighley, Robert, Walkringham (Notts.), husbn., Oct. 22, 1556.	15	1	182
May 9, 1566.	——, William, Normanton on Trent (Notts.), labr., Sep. 9, 1565.	17		546
Sep. 3, 1558.	Kilborne, Mawde, Over Catton, Aug. 20, 1558.	15	3	98
Dec. 10, 1555.	Kildaile, Francis, Scarboroughe, Feb. 15, 1555.	14		140
May 5, 1557.	Kildall, William, Westcotum (bur. Kirklethom), husbn., Jan. 28, 1554.	15	1	249
Aug. 28, 1561.	Killingbeck, Margaret, Allerton Grange, par. Leedes, wid., Apl. 30, 1561.	17		53
Mar.26, 1565.	Killingbecke, Thomas, Wakfeld, clothier, Oct. 13, 1564.	17		415
Oct. 2, 1566.	Killom, Richard, Hie Ellers, par. Cantley, Oct. 17, 1559.	17		577
Feb. 10, 1563.	Kilweke, William, Sutton on Darvent, Oct. 10, 1563.	17		315
May 13, 1557.	Kinch, William, Bingham (Notts.), brassenar, Oct. 25, 155[6?].	15	1	221
May 5, 1568.	Kinge, John, Seglestorne, Jun. 1, 1567.	17		776
May 29, 1556.	——, Richard, Wandisfurthe, husbandman, May —, 1556.	15	1	39
May 7, 1554.	——, William, senr., Skircote, Mar. 20, 1553.	14		1
[May 18?], 1559.	Kippas, William, Eyverton (Notts.), husbandman, Apl. 12, 1559.	15	3	405
Apl. 28, 1563.	Kirkbe, Alis, Thorgoland, par. Silkestone, Jun. 10, 1557.	17		233
Jun. 12, 1567.	——, Jaine, Essyngton, Sep. 5, 1566.	17		663
May 31, 1557.	Kirkbie, Robert, Thurguland, par. Silkeston, Feb. 25, 1556.	15	1	210
Apl. 10, 1554.	——, Rolland, Hothome, Apl. 14, 1553.	14		54
Oct. 2, 1566.	——, William, Rowth in Holderness, husbandman, Jun. 12, 1566.	17		581
May 6, 1563.	Kirkbye, John, Saunbie (Notts.), husbandman, May 4, 1562.	17		244
Feb. 10, 1560.	——, Richard, Houthome, husbandman, Oct. 12, 1560.	16		147
Mar.29, 1568.	——, William, Hawseworthe, par. Otley, Sep. 10, 1567.	17		767
Oct. 12, 1558.	Kirke, Henry, East bridgforth (Notts.), husbandman, Aug. 11, 1558.	15	2	372
Oct. 12, 1558.	——, John, Bridgeford on hill (Notts.), husbn., Jun. 16, 4 & 5 Phil. and Mary.	15	3	30
May 12, 1559.	——, John, Elloughtonne, husbandman, Mar. 15, 1558.	15	3	394
Oct. 2, 1567.	——, Richard, Hilston in Holderness, husbandman, July 16, 1566.	17		714
Oct. 7, 1556.	——, Robert, Carleton in Lynrycke (Notts.), husbn., Aug. 7, 1556.	15	1	192
Nov. 7, 1564.	——, Robert, Ottringham, Oct. 24, 1564.	17		399
May 2, 1566.	——, Thomas, Baynton, labourer, Aug. 12, 1565.	17		537
May 13, 1568.	——, Thomas, Care Colson (Notts.), husbandman, Nov. 21, 1567.	17		803
July 18, 1565.	——, Thomas, Mydleton (St. Andrew), Apl. 15, 1565.	17		450
Jan. 12, 1558.	——, William, Elloughton, husbandman, Nov. 8, 1558.	15	3	195
Feb. 4, 1556.	——, William, Thorne, yeoman, Aug., 1556.	15	1	169
Jan. 20, 1558.	Kirkebie, Elizabeth, Hovingham, May 28, 1558.	15	3	21
Nov.25, 1563.	Kirkebye, John, Osindike (bur. Rither), Mar. 29, 1563.	17		305
July 8, 1556.	——, Symon, North Cave, Aug. 10, 1555.	15	1	54
Oct. 17, 1558.	——, William, York, clerk, Oct. 4, 1558.	15	3	93
Aug. 6, 1567.	Kirton, Robert, Northe Cave, husbandman, Apl. 10, 1563.	17		698
May 2, 1566.	Kitchin, Christopher (bur. Lynton), May 1, 1566.	17		531
Oct. 17, 1567.	——, William, Earesham, par. Aclam, July 12, 1567.	17		730
May 13, 1557.	——, William, Hucknall Torckard (Notts.), Mar. 3, 1556.	15	1	237

		Vol.	Pt.	Fol.
Mar.27, 1566.	Kitchin, William, Staithes, par. Hinderwell, Dec. 7, 1565.	17		507
Apl. 28, 1563.	Kitchine, Thomas, Skipton in Craven, July 17, 1562.	17		230
Mar. 9, 1567.	Kitchinge, William, Mickelbringe(bur. Brathwell), husbn., July 14, 1567.	17		763
Jun. 20, 1566.	Kitchyn, Richard, Lebberstone, par. Fylay, Oct. 13, 1565.	17		557
Nov.17, 1558.	Kitson, James, Wortelay, par. Leedes, Sep. 19, 1558.	15	3	111
May 5, 1557.	———, Robert, Sandall Magna, Aug. 16, 1556.	15	1	213
Mar.22, 1566.	———, William, Liversedge, May 24, 1566.	17		519
Oct. 8, 1562.	Knages, Janne, North Wheatley (Notts.), widow, Sep. 9, 1562.	17		120
Dec.15, 1567.	———, Richard, Lithe, Sep. 13, 1567.	17		743
Nov. 5, 1556.	———, Thomas, Gillinge, Sep. 1, 1556.	15	1	108
May 5, 1568.	Knagges, Elizabeth, Lithe, Nov. 19, 1567.	17		774
Aug.14, 1566.	———, John, Knapton, par. Wintringham, Sep. 6, 1565.	17		565
July 26, 1558.	———, John, Stoneferye, par. Sutton in Holderness, Mar. 12, 1557.	15	3	11
Nov.29, 1558.	———, John, Tickill, priest, July 26, 1558.	15	3	139
Jun. 2, 1558.	———, Robert, Stoneferie, par. Sutton in Holderness, Apl. 25, 1558.	15	2	335
Oct. 1, 1557.	———, William, Lythe, Aug. 27, 1557.	15	1	361
Oct. 2, 1567.	———, William, Stoneferrie, par. Sutton, singleman, Mar. 13, 1566.	17		713
Mar.20, 1559.	Knapton, John, Clyfforde (bur. Bramham), Aug. 14, 1559.	16		15
Mar.10, 1561.	Knevet (or Syble), Anne, Semer, wid. of Chas. K. esq., Jan. 15, 1561.	17		2
Apl. 27, 1558.	Knolles, Anthony (bur. Gyglesweke), Sep. 22, 1557.	15	2	200
Sep. 29, 1563.	———, Omefray, Foxope, par. Erneclyff, ———, 1563.	17		278
May 9, 1565.	———, Richard, Over Thraynhouse (bur. Kirkeby Malhamdaille), Oct. 28, 1564.	17		433
Mar. 9, 1561.	Knot, Richard, New Malton, wheelwright, Jan. 20, 15—.	17.		4
Dec.21, 1562.	Knotsworthe, John, Sikehouse, par. Fyshelake, Nov. 29, 1562.	17		137
Apl. 13, 1559.	Knott, Thomas (bur. Bulmer), Jan. 23, 1558.	15	3	342
Oct. 12, 1558.	Knotton, Ellen, Flintham (Notts.), widow, Nov. 1, 1557.	15	3	32
May 13, 1557.	———, Richard, Flintam (Notts.), yeoman, Jan. 22, 1556.	15	1	228
Oct. 7, 1563.	———, Thomas, Thoreton (Notts.), July 24, 1563.	17		293
Apl. 19, 1559.	Knottone, Thomas, Throwton, par. Hoistone (Notts.), Feb. 18, 155[8-]9.	15	3	359
Nov. 6, 1557.	———, William (bur. Allerton in Shyrewood, Notts.), husbn., July 22, 1557.	15	2	108
Dec. 1, 1558.	Knowles, Raufe, Beverlay, Aug. 21, 1558.	15	3	82
Oct. 5, 1558.	———, William, Thornebare, par. Long Preston, Aug. 24, 1558.	15	3	61
Aug.16, 1557.	Knowlis, William, Howton Waynyslay (bur. Marstonne), July 3, 1557.	15	2	117
Apl. 28, 1558.	Knowlles, Agnes, Thorpewilloby, par. Braton, Feb. 26, 1557.	15	2	229
Nov.28, 1558.	———, William, Bylton in Holderness, knight, Sep. 1, 1557.	15	2	353
May 10, 1565.	———, William, Ferlington (bur. Sherifhoton), Feb. 25, 1564.	17		430
Apl. 27, 1564.	Knyght, George, Broughton Sulney (Notts.), yeom., Oct. 22, 1563.	17		340
Apl. 19, 1559.	———, Myles, Gounthorpe (bur. Lowdham, Notts.), Nov. 4, 1558.	15	3	355
Nov.10, 1563.	1 Kokerell, Rauf, Beverley, Apl. 22, 1563.	17		300
Aug.12, 1567.	———, Robert, Brigham, par. Foston, Oct. 31, 1566.	17		694
Sep. 26, 1558.	Koo (Coo, Act Book), Thomas, Whistone (bur. St. Mary Magd.), ———, 1555.	15	3	53
Apl. 7, 1554.	Kydbie, Anthony, Horneseye Becke, Mar. 19, 1553.	14		157
Mar.29, 1555.	Kydd, John, Nafferton, carpenter, Nov. 30, 1554.	14		189
Dec.16, 1557.	Kyddall, John, clerk, M.A., student of S. John's, Cambr. (bur. Wylberfosse), Mar. 21, 1556.	15	2	88
Apl. 12, 1559.	Kydde, Thomas, Barden, par. Bolton, Mar. 8, 1558.	15	3	340
Sep. 30, 1557.	Kydson, Charles, Barley, par. Brayton, husbandman, Aug. 2, 1557.	15	1	345
Oct. 2, 1556.	Kydsone, William (bur. Sowerbie), Aug. 22, 1556.	15	1	133
Apl. 12, 1557.	Kye, Alison, Besweke, par. Kilnewike, widow, Dec. 8, 1556.	15	1	206
Feb.14, 1567.	Kyerton, George, Brotton, Jan. 3, 1567.	17		759
May 17, 1565.	Kygheley, Agnes, Radforthe (Notts.), Feb. 19, 1564.	17		439
Feb.27, 1558.	Kyghlay, George, Cottinglay, par. Bynglay, Oct. 18, 1558.	15	3	280
July 26, 1557.	Kyghleye, John, Alverthorpe (bur. Wakefelde), Jun. 24, 1557.	15	1	317
Mar. 2, 1554.	Kylborne, William, Over Catton, Jan. 15, 1554.	14		299
Jun. 18, 1555.	Kylbroune, Martyn, Harwoddaill, par. Hacknes, May 1, 1555.	14		254
Feb. 6, 1558.	Kyldaile, Jenet (bur. Scarbrough), Apl. 30, 1558.	15	3	262

See also under letter C.

		Vol.	Pt.	Fol.
Sep. 21, 1557.	Kyndall, Ellene, Tykhill, widow, July 17, 1557.	15	1	351
Nov. 28, 1558.	Kyng, Thomas (bur. Albroughe), Oct. 24, 1558.	15	3	78
Nov. 10, 1557.	——, Thomas, Tycton (bur. Beverley), Sep. 21, 1557.	15	2	98
Dec. 9, 1558(6).	Kynge, Christopher, Tyckton, husbandman, Sep. 13, 1556.	15	1	198
May 29, 1562.	——, Thomas, Thorpe, par. Braton, Jun. 21, 1561.	17		101
Jan. 22, 1557.	Kytchynge, James, Hawnbye, Dec. 8, 1557.	15	2	158
Apl. 27, 1558.	Kytson, William, the eldest, Calverley, Feb. 8, 1556.	15	2	192
Dec. 11, 1557.	Kyrk, Richard, Ryther, Oct. 15, 1557.	15	2	88
Jun. 28, 1561.	Kyrkbe, Rauff, Wilberfosse, Sep. 28, 1560.	17		75
Sep. 16, 1557.	Kyrkbye, James, Horton, par. Bradforde, July 7, 1557.	15	1	333
Dec. 16, 1557.	——, Mathewe, Waxham, par. Outthorne, Nov. 18, 1557.	15	2	47
July 17, 1564.	Kyrke, Elizabeth, servant to James Robinson, Hull, sadler, Jun. 20, 1564.	17		358
Nov. 8, 1557.	——, George, Sykehowse, par. Fyshelake, Sep. 20, 1557.	15	2	113
Mar. 23, 1557.	——, James, Esyngton, Jan. 14, 1557.	15	2	152
Feb. 9, 1557.	——, John, Bewicke, par. Aldbroughe, ——, 1557.	15	2	122
Sep. 13, 1565.	——, John, Leedes, clothier, Sep. 19, 1564.	17		465
Oct. 1, 1556.	Kyrkebie, John, Burghe, par. Eloughtone, July 6, 1556.	15	1	137
Oct. 6, 1557.	Kyrkebye, Adam, Tryswell (Notts.), May 20, 1557.	15	2	13
Jun. 10, 1561.	——, George, Welwicke Thorpp, Jan. 17, 1560.	17		70
Jun. 6, 1560.	Kyrkehus, Roger, Anlabye, par. Kerkellay, Mar. 28, 1560.	16		74
Jan. 12, 1557.	Kyrkeman, Henry, Northe Ferybye, Nov. 30, 1557.	15	2	78
July 18, 1560.	Kyrkhus, William, West Elleye, par. Northeferibie, Jun. 24, 1560.	16		93
Jan. 10, 1557.	Kyrkupp, George, Snaynton (bur. Brompton), husbn., Nov. 15, 1557.	15	2	77
May 22, 1563.	Kyrshay, John, the litle towne, par. Burstall, May 29, 1562.	17		248
Oct. 14, 1561.	Kyrton, Thomas, Doncaster, alderman, Mar. 13, 1561.	17		36
May 19, 1559.	Labray, Thomas, Calverton (Notts.), Mar. 26, 1559.	15	3	432
Oct. 5, 1558.	Labron, Antony, Metheley, July 24, 1558.	15	3	41
Oct. 6, 1558.	Lacan, Henry, Yeddingham, husbandman, Aug. 20, 1558.	15	3	26
Apl. 2, 1567.	Lacoke, Edmond, Bingley, Dec. 1, 1563.	17		618
Apl. 6, 1554.	——, Thomas, Kighleye, Mar. 14, 1553.	14		154
May 6, 1557.	——, William, Collingworth, par. Byngley, Apl. 1, 1557.	15	1	210
May 30, 1555.	Lacoppe, Adam, Olde Malton, labourer, Apl. 27, 1555.	14		253
Dec. 5, 1558.	——, Richard, Spanton, Lestyngham, Jun. 30. 1558.	15	3	150
May 4, 1558.	Lacy, Elizabeth, Totton (Notts.), widow, Sep. 5, 1557.	15	2	277
May 9, 1556.	Lacye, Robert, Folkton, esquire, Mar. 9, 2 & 3 Phil. and Mary.	15	1	43
Apl. 22, 1556.	Laeke, Elizabeth, Meathley, widow, Jan. 16, 1555.	15	1	36
Oct. 3, 1560.	Laicocke, William, Colling, par. Kildweke, Jan. 13, 1559.	16		117
May 10, 1565.	Lakan, William, Kyrkebe Moreshed, tanner, Jan. 29, 1564.	17		421
May 18, 1559.	Lake, John, Normanton, gentleman, Dec. 24, 1558.	15	3	414
Apl. 20, 1555.	Lakenbie, Stephen, Flameburghe, yeoman, Mar. 15, 1554.	14		122
Feb. 9, 1557.	Lam[b]e, Agnes, Brandesburton, widow, Jun. 22, 1557.	15	2	120
Sep. 27, 1557.	Lambe, Jennett, Leven, widow, Sep. 10, 1557.	15	1	357
Aug. 12, 1567.	——, John, Brigham (bur. Foston), Oct. 13, 1566.	17		693
Mar. 4, 1560.	——, John, Hull, yeoman, Apl. 22, 1560.	16		167
Sep. 30, 1562.	——, Parcivall, Leytheley, May 27, 1562.	17		116
Nov. 10, 1557.	——, Roger, Sutton (bur. Tadcaster), husbn., Aug. 22, 1557.	15	2	101
July 8, 1557.	Lam[be], William, Brandesburton, Sep. 22, 1556.	15	1	305
May 2, 1555.	Lambert, James, Moregare (bur. Burnesall), Feb. 10, 1554.	14		27
May 5, 1568.	——, John, Patteleybrigges, par. Ripon, Jan. 9, 1567.	17		788
Mar. 13, 1558.	——, John, Southkirkbye, Dec. 10, 1558.	15	3	162
May 19, 1559.	——, Nicholas, Cowicke, par. Snathe, Dec. 6, 1557.	15	3	427
Jan. 11, 1560.	——, Roger, Hooton Craunsewicke, labourer, Apl. 23, 1560.	16		145
Jun. 12, 1567.	——, William, Stoneferrye, par. Sutton, Mar. 31, 1567.	17		662
Sep. 30, 1557.	——, William, Tyckhyll, gentleman, Aug. 9, 1557.	15	1	367
Apl. 29, 1568.	Lame, Agnes, Burnham [widow], Jan. 7, 1567.	17		770
Mar. 22, 1558.	——, John, Shareston, Oct. 3, 1557.	15	3	293
Apl. 19, 1559.	——, Thomas, Bassyngfeild, par. Holme Perpoynt (Notts.), younge man, Jan. 20, 1558.	15	3	375
Dec. 9, 1556.	——, William, Levyn, July 18, 1556.	15	1	72
May 4, 1558.	Lamley, John, Calverton (Notts.), husbandman, Jan. 20, 1556.	15	2	276
Dec. 9, 1557.	——, Thomas, Carlton Mynyott (bur. Thryske), July 12, 1557.	15	2	94
Nov. 15, 1566.	Lammambie, Peter, York, sadler, Oct. 25, 1566.	17		599

		Vol.	Pt.	Fol.
Oct. 29, 1554.	Lamming, Thomas, Carcolston, Jan. 20, 1 Mary.	14		278
Mar. 10, 1555.	Lammyng, Thomas, Watton (Notts.), husbandman, Jan. 30, 1554.	14		233
July 20, 1555.	Lamperthe, John, Selbye, Jun. 25, 1555.	14		244
Sep. 5, 1565.	Lamyer, Nicholas, Beverley, Feb. 23, 1563.	17		461
May 4, 1558.	Lamynge, John, Whatton (Notts.), husbandman, Aug. 8, 1557.	15	2	209
Oct. 10, 1566.	———, Robert, Skarington (Notts.), husbandman. *No date.*	17		593
Sep. 28, 1557.	Lande, William, Adingham, May 15, 1557.	15	1	338
Apl. 19, 1559.	Lan[e], John, Nottingham, gentleman, Feb. 25, 1558.	15	3	356
Jan. 13, 1558.	Lane, Richard, Bradmore, par. Bonney (Notts.), May 8, 1558.	15	3	182
July 14, 1556.	Langdaile, Anthony, Howton (bur. Santonn, Harthill), Jan. 10, 1553.	15	1	54
Aug. 4, 1558.	Langdaill, Hugh, Heslee. gentleman, Jun. 24, 1558.	15	3	3
Apl. 20, 1556.	———, Katheryne, Thirkilbie, Mar. 13, 1555.	15	1	15
Mar. 3, 1555.	———, Rauff, Catone, Sep. 22, 1555.	15	1	11
Mar. 5, 1559.	Langdon, Edmonde, Hacknes, Feb. 27, 1557.	16		5
Nov. 9, 1557.	Langfeld, John, Horburye, par. Waykefeld, Aug. 8, 1557.	15	2	101
May 9, 1565.	Langfellowe, George, Ylkeley, Feb. 20, 1564.	17		432
Apl. 26, 1558.	Langgald, Richard, Aston Netherthorpe, Aug. 22, 1557.	15	2	223
———28, 1555.	Langhorne, John, Shupton in Galtres, craftesman, Nov. 13, 1554.	14		256
Oct. 12, 1558.	Langlay, Brigit, Flyntham (Notts.), widow, May 23, 1558.	15	2	375
Oct. 1, 1557.	Langley, Emot, Stoxley, widow, Aug. 4, 1557.	15	2	36
Jun. 21, 1561.	Langskar, Agnes, Skibden, widow, May 17, 1560.	17		72
Dec. 1, 1558.	Langthorne, Peter, Drewton, par. North Cave, July 11, 1558.	15	3	83
Oct. 5, 1564.	Langton, Alice, Darington, widow, Jan. 8, 1562.	17		374
Jun. 8, 1557.	———, John, Halsham, Apl. 8, 1557.	15	1	268
Oct. 3, 1564.	———, Richard, Lynton, par. Spofforthe, May 10, 1564.	17		365
July 4, 1556.	———, Robert, Lynton, par. Spofforthe, Jun. 12, 1556.	15	1	53
May 13, 1568.	Larrannes, John, Sutton Bunnyngton (Notts.), husbn., Mar. 3, 1567.	17		800
Dec. 14, 1557.	Lasenbye, Jennet, Hunttyngton, widow, Mar. 10, 1557.	15	2	88
July 4, 1564.	Lasinbe, William, Hersweke (bur. Huntington), Jun. 8, 1564.	17		354
Feb. 7, 1564.	Lasinbie, William, Huntington, Aug. 6, 1564.	17		407
May 21, 1568.	———, William, Newsome (Bulmer), May 2, 1568.	17		796
July 4, 1564.	Lasinby, Thomas, Hersweke (bur. Huntington), May 16, 1563.	17		354
Mar. 20, 1560.	Lasselles, Dame Margaret, Brakenberghe (bur. Kyrkebye on Wyske), widow, Mar. 25, 1559.	16		155
Jan. 12, 1558.	Lasynbie, Thomas, Huntington, Jan. 4, 1558.	15	3	177 & 205
Mar. 8, 1566.	Lasyng, Thomas, Holme in Spaldingmore, Jan. 6, 1566.	17		512
Feb. 4, 1556.	Lathes, John, Stennforth (bur. Hatfeld), smythe, Dec. 9, 1556.	15	1	169
Oct. 10, 1560.	Laughton, Richard, Thorna (Notts.), husbandman, Mar. 10, 1560.	16		123
Oct. 12, 1564.	———, Roger, Thornaye (Notts.), husbandman, Sep. 28, 1564.	17		389
Apl. 28, 1558.	Laverock, Alice, Danby, Dec. 16, 1557.	15	2	231
Oct. 3, 1554.	Laverocke, Christopher, Brandsburton, husbandman, Apl. 23, 1554.	14		42
Oct. 1, 1566.	———, William, Whitbie, Apl. 19, 1566.	17		584
Oct. 5, 1564.	Laveroke, Richard, Sykehouse (bur. Fyshelake), Sep. 5, 1564.	17		378
Oct. 13, 1558.	Law, Averay, Awkelay (bur. Finningley, Notts.), Apl. 16, 1558.	15	3	222
Apl. 28, 1563.	———, John, Bramton (bur. Cantlaye), Dec. 22, 1562.	17		231
Apl. 19, 1559.	Lawe, Cabeyne (Katherine, Act Bk.), Boney (Notts.), Feb. 8, 1557.	15	3	377
Feb. 17, 1557.	———, James, Armethorpe, husbandman, Aug. 6, 1557.	15	2	142
May 13, 1568.	———, James, Fennyngley (Notts.), husbandman, Jun. 20, 1567.	17		802
May 18, 1559.	———, John (bur. Sheffeld), Mar. 12, 1558.	15	3	398
May 2, 1566.	———, Richard, Halifax, goldsmyth, Mar. 3, 1565.	17		536
Sep. 29, 1563.	———, Richard, Rymmynton (bur. Gisburne), Apl. 28, 1563.	17		280
Oct. 7, 1557.	———, William, Northe Leverton (Notts.), husbandman, Apl. 23, 1557.	15	2	21
Jun. 25, 1568.	Lawer, Emmot, Skefflinge, Apl. 6, 1568.	17		810
Mar. 27, 1565.	———, William, Skeflinge, May 13, 1564.	17		418
Oct. 5, 1558.	Lawkland, Christopher, Herton, par. Gisburne, husbn., Mar. 18, 1557.	15	3	37
Oct. 13, 1558.	Lawnd, Thomas, Wellay (Notts.), husbandman, Apl. 25, 1558.	15	2	378
Jun. 16, 1565.	Lawnde, Jennet (bur. Ripon), May 20, 1565.	17		444
Sep. 30, 1563.	Lawrance *als.* Powson, Thomas, Bishopside, par. Paitleybrigges, Jun. 1, 1563.	17		296
Dec. 2, 1561.	Lawranson, Alis, Staynforthe (bur. Haitfeld), widow, May 5, 1561.	17		31
Dec. 1, 1556.	Lawransone, Elizabeth, Thorpe, par. Barnbie Donne, wid., May 5, 1556.	15	1	129
May 9, 1566.	Lawrens, John, Selston (Notts.), Jan. 3, 1565.	17		544

		Vol.	Pt.	Fol.
Sep. 30, 1556.	Lawson, Alison, (bur. Ruston), Sep. 1, 1556.	15	1	141
Jun. 25, 1568.	———, Edward, Rowth, husbandman, Apl. 9, 1568.	17		810
Sep. 29, 1563.	———, John, Calton (bur. Kyrkebye Mallydall), May 22, 1563.	17		279
Oct. 3, 1560.	———, John, Calton (bur. Kyrkebye Malham), yeom., Jun. 30, 1560.	16		120
Mar. 11, 1562.	———, John, Kylnewicke, carpenter, Dec. 18, 1562.	17		216
Jun. 21, 1561.	———, Richard (bur. Longe Preston), Apl. 20, 1561.	17		73
Apl. 28, 1563.	———, Thomas, Handlyth (bur. Kirkebie Malham), Nov. 26, 1562.	17		229
Nov. 25, [1555].	———, William, Ormsby, Aug. 4, 1555.	14		184
Oct. 5, 1564.	Lawton, John, Echells, par. Rawmarshe, husbn., July 3, 1564.	17		378
Jan. 30, 1555.	Lawtone, John, Gressebroke, par. Rotherham, Jan. 10, 1555.	15	1	3
May 4, 1558.	Laxton, Henry (Bingham Deanery), Nov. 10, 1557.	15	2	264
Sep. 29, 1563.	Layburne, William, Nafferton, Mar. 10, 1562.	17		274
Apl. 27, 1558.	Laycoke, Christopher, Colling, par. Kyldweke, Nov. 8, 1557.	15	2	202
Jan. 30, 1560.	Laykyn, Robert, York, tanner, Aug. 12, 1558.	16		146
Apl. 17, 1567.	Layland, Thomas (bur. Conyshetone), May 6, 1566.	17		619
Feb. 17, 1561.	Layne, Edward, North Whetley (Notts.), Dec. 25, 1560.	17		14
Apl. 20, 1559.	———, John, Codyngton (Notts.), labourer, Aug. 30, 1556.	15	3	306
July 1, 1561.	———, Peter, Saundbye (Notts.), husbandman, Jun. 1, 1560.	17		61
May 5, 1559.	Layng, William, Byllesdaill, yeoman, Jan. 5, 1559.	15	3	380
Apl. 10, 1559.	Layton, Lancelott, North Cave, gentleman, Mar. 5, 1557.	15	3	330
Jun. 20, 1556.	———, Robert, Skutterskelf (bur. Rudby), Mar. 18, 1555.	15	1	58
May 21, 1560.	———, William, Sproxton, par. Helmslay, gent., Oct. 26, 1559.	16		65
May 10, 1566.	———, William, Thikitt (bur. Thorganbie), gent., Jan. 26, 1565.	17		521
May 5, 1557.	Lazing, Isabell, Womerslaie, Apl. 3, 1557.	15	1	214
Apl. 7, 1557.	Le als. Syme, William, Harwood, Aug. 29, 1554.	15	1	205
Dec. 4, 1556.	Leache, Isabell, Felicekirke, July 10, 1556.	15	1	119
July 20, 1557.	Leadbetter, Francis, Rudstone, Feb. 24, 1556.	15	1	315
Jun. 22, 1568.	Leadbitter, John, Nafferton, May 8, 1568.	17		820
July 23, 1558.	Leadlay, John, Axylbe, par. Eyssingwolde, May 9, 1558.	15	2	384
Jan. 13, 1558.	Leake, Beatrix, Feryngfeld (Notts.), widow, July 27, 1558.	15	3	15
Nov. 17, 1558.	———, Elizabeth, Ledstone (bur. Ledsham), widow, Oct. 14, 1558.	15	3	114
Nov. 10, 1563.	———, Isabell, Holme on Wold, widow, Oct. 2, 1556.	17		301
Aug. 4, 1558.	———, James, Ayke, par. Lockyngeton, Jun. 26, 1558.	15	3	3
Jan. 13, 1558.	———, John, Halam, par. Southwell (Notts.), Nov. 14, 1557.	15	3	16
Apl. 22, 1562.	Lealande, Elizabeth, Elton (Notts.), widow, Nov. 28, 1561.	17		192
Mar. 24, 1567.	Leaper, Edward, Gaitefurth (bur. Braton), labourer, Oct. 12, 1567.	17		765
May 13, 1557.	Leason, John, Gounthorpe (bur. Lowdham, Notts.), Dec. 13, 1556.	15	1	225
Apl. 19, 1559.	———, Margaret, wid. of Robert L.(bur.Gedlyng,Notts.),Aug.6,1558.	15	3	357
Jan. 14, 1566.	Leche, Thomas, Mekilwate, par. Bingley, Nov. 8, 1566.	17		607
July 18, 1565.	Ledaile, William, Molesbye (bur. Marton), Sep. 26, 1558.	17		451
Jan. 20, 1558.	Ledaill, Christopher, York, baker, Aug. 16, 1558.	15	3	213
Aug. 19, 1565.	Ledall, Elizabeth, wid. of Christopher L., York, bayker, Dec. 31, 1564.	17		457
May 8, 1562.	———, John, Belfelde, par. Stillinflete, Jan. 29, 1561.	17		197
May 9, 1563.	———, John, Rednys, par. Whitgift, Feb. 18, 1562.	17		257
Oct. 22, 1560.	———, William, Burton Agnes, husbandman, May 19, 1559.	16		128
Oct. 8, 1558.	Ledell, Adam, Kelfeld, par. Stillingflete, husbandman, Aug. 27, 1558.	15	3	92
Jun. 14, 1560.	———, James (bur. Rypon), Apl. 3, 1560.	16		83
Sep. 16, 1557.	———, Robert, Huntyngton, husbandman, Aug. 22, 1557.	15	1	332
May 6, 1557.	Ledes, Robert, Ottringham, Mar. 19, 1557.	15	1	240
Mar. 27, 1557.	Ledheham, John, Thorpe (Snathe Deanery), Sep. 24, 1556.	15	1	202
Jun. 30, 1563.	Ledyard, John, Myrfeild, clother, Nov. 27, 1561.	17		261
Apl. 27, 1558.	Lee, Anne, Batlay, Oct. 27, 1557.	15	2	192
Oct. 22, 1556.	—, Christopher, Bradford, Sep. 24, 1555.	15	1	99
Oct. 5, 1558.	—, George, Myrfeild, husbandman, July 29, 1558.	15	3	64
Sep. 24, 1562.	—, John, Elvington, yeoman, Aug. 4, 1562.	17		108
May 2, 1555.	—, Richard, Dewesbury, clother, Apl. 1, 1555.	14		31
Mar. 22, 1558.	—, Robert, Wothersonne, par. Batlay, Jun. 30, 1558.	15	3	295
Oct. 10, 1566.	—, Roger, Cromwell (Notts.), yeoman, Jun. 28, 1566.	17		590
Apl. 27, 1558.	—, Thomas, Batley, Sep. 26, 1557.	15	2	192
May 15, 1568.	—, Thomas, Elvington, yeoman, Mar. 28, 1568.	17		796
July 26, 1557.	—, Thomas, Westerton, par. Woodkirke, Apl. 30, 1557.	15	1	316
Feb. 20, 1558.	—, William, Beswicke, par. Kilnewicke, webster, Jan. 14, 1558.	15	3	276

A.D. 1554 TO 1568.

		Vol.	Pt.	Fol.
Oct. 1, 1557.	Lee, William, Doncaster, Apl. 1, 1557.	15	1	370
Nov. 24, 1558.	Leedes, Thomas, Bishopthorpe, Aug. 10, 1558.	15	3	230
Jun. 22, 1554.	Leeke, John, Thirske, Jun. 14, 1554.	14		114
Oct. 6, 1557.	Leeson, Thomas, Kayworthe (Notts.), husbandman, Apl. 3, 1556.	15	2	31
No date.	Lefton, John, Tickhill, Dec. 17, 1553.	14		162
Oct. 7, 1557.	Legate, Agnes, Rampton (Notts.), widow, Mar. 15, 1556.	15	2	21
Oct. 20, 1557.	Legg, William, Maltbye, par. Staynton, husbandman, Sep. 26, 1557.	15	2	35
Mar. 6, 1556.	Legget, William, Myssyn (Notts.), husbandman, Aug. 10, 1556.	15	1	178
Jun. 8, 1565.	Legh, Gilbert, Mydleton (bur. Rothwell), esq., Apl. 14, 1565.	17		443
Apl. 26, 1564.	Leicke, John, Hull, Dec. 3, 1563.	17		333
Aug. 6, 1565.	Leiffe, William, Harton (bur. Bossall), labourer, Mar. 13, 1564.	17		457
July 29, 1560.	Leight, John, Holbecke (bur. Ledes), Mar. 19, 1558.	16		98
Mar. 20, 1558.	——, Richard, Holbecke (bur. Leedes), Sep. 24, 1557.	15	3	252
July 6, 1556.	Leike, Agnes, Birkyn, widow, Jun. 9, 1556.	15	1	53
May 14, 1562.	——, George, Birkyn, husbandman, Apl. 1, 1562.	17		197
Apl. 13, 1559.	——, William, Ake (bur. Lockyngton), Feb. 23, 155[8-]9.	15	3	348
Oct. 15, 1563.	Lekinbie, Thomas, Flambrughe, yeoman, Aug. 31, 1562.	17		297
Sep. 28, 1560.	Leland, Rauffe, Elton (Notts.), husbandman, Oct. 4, 1558.	16		107
Feb. 11, 1565.	Lelley *als.* Foster, William, Risse, Oct. 14, 1565.	17		499
Jun. 22, 1568.	Lelome, William (bur. Staynburne), Apl. 12, 1567.	17		818
Sep. 15, 1558.	Lelum, John, Kenythorpe, par. Langton, husbandman, Jun. 12, 1558.	15	3	104
Dec. 22, 1556.	Lemyng, Jenet (bur. Thorne), May 13, 1556.	15	1	81
May 6, 1557.	Lemynge, John, Basshallevis, par. Myttone, Sep. 12, 1556.	15	1	283
Oct. 2, 1560.	——, John, Swyndon, par. Kirkebyoverblowes, Aug. 26, 1560.	16		114
Feb. penult., 1556.	——, Mathew (bur. Ripon), Oct. 28, 1556.	15	1	180
May 19, 1559.	——, Nicholas, Arnall (Notts.), Apl. 16, 1558.	15	3	432
Jun. 17, 1556.	Lenge, John, Ayton (bur. Hooton Busshell), Apl. 28, 1556.	15	1	49
July 16, 1560.	——, Thomas, York, braysser, Mar. 16, 1558.	16		92
Apl. 22, 1559.	——, William, Nether Catton, husbandman, Apl. 6, 1559.	15	3	309
Jun. 10, 1561.	Lensa (Lynsay), John, Catwike, husbandman, Jan. 13, 1560.	17		70
Sep. 3, 1555.	Leper, Henry, Bempton, husbandman, Jun. 23, 1555.	14		21
May 6, 1557.	——, John, West Haddlesaie (bur. Birkin), Mar. 21, 1556.	15	1	255
May 18, 1559.	——, William, Estofte, par. Adlingflete, Apl. 3, 1559.	15	3	416
Dec. 5, 1554.	Lepington, William, Hunmanbye, husbandman, Oct. 1, 1554.	14		94
July 30, 1567.	Lepton, George, Loversall, Jun. 6, 1567.	17		674
Feb. 1, 1563.	——, Richard, Stannyngley, par. Calverley, July 10, 1562.	17		313
May 31, 1557.	——, Robert, Thirsbie, par. Cunsburgh, yeoman, May 2, 1557.	15	1	263
Jun. 1, 1554.	Lepyngton, Robert, Hundmanby, Apl. 13, 1554.	14		8
May 10, 1559.	Leryfax, Robert, Pokthroppe (bur. Nafferton), husbn., July 18, 1558.	15	3	389
Sep. 24, 1560.	Letbye, Hewe, Awdbye (bur. Buttercram), Aug. 6, 1560.	16		105
Apl. 26, 1558.	Lethom, Elizabeth, Byrkyn, widow, Nov. 22, 1557.	15	2	235
Apl. 26, 1558.	——, Richard, Birkyn, husbandman, July 31, 1557.	15	2	235
May 14, 1562.	——, William, Birkyn, husbandman, Jan. 31, 1561.	17		198
Nov. 29, 1558.	Lethome, Richard, Sheaffeld, milner, Feb. ult., 1557.	15	3	144
Apl. 26, 1558.	——, Thomas, Monkefrystonne, Mar. 20, 1557.	15	2	234
July 12, 1558.	Lethum, Thomas, Sowthe Mylford (bur. Sherburne), ——, 1558.	15	2	313
Sep. 16, 1563.	Leuynge (Leven), Robert, Wynflet, par. Wyggyfte, Aug. 6, 1563.	17		203
May 5, 1558.	Leuyssay, Nicholas, Laxton (Notts.), Oct. 15, 1557.	15	2	262
Feb. 25, 1555.	Leven, John, Feildhouse (bur. Howke), Feb. 15, 1555.	15	1	8
Oct. 12, 1564.	Leverton, Richard, Newarke (Notts.), mercer, Jun. 4, 1564.	17		388
May 5, 1558.	Levesay, John, Southmuskham (Notts.), husbn., Oct. 16, 1557.	15	2	210
May 5, 1558.	——, William, Laxton (Notts.), Apl. 9, 1557.	15	2	256
Feb. 21, 1567.	Levit, Richard, Appilton, par. Bolton Percie, Feb. 9, 1567.	17		759
Aug. 6, 1567.	Levitte, William, Holme on Wold, singleman, Nov. 14, 1566.	17		701
Dec. 5, 1562.	Levyn, Richard, Gowle (bur. Howke), Oct. 31, 1562.	17		131
Aug. 27, 1557.	Lewes, Anne, Charterhowse next Hull, wid. of John L., alderman of York, Mar. 22, 1556.	15	2	117
July 1, 1561.	——, Thomas, Elkisley (Notts.), Mar. 3, 1560.	17		61
Dec. 1, 1557.	——, William, Thornam, husbandman, Sep. 14, 1557.	15	2	87
July 26, 1557.	Lewis, Richard, Pontefracte, May 7, 1557.	15	1	318
Mar. 16, 1558.	Lewtie, Elizabeth, Follyfet (bur. Spofforth), Dec. 20, 1558.	15	3	242
Feb. 25, 1556.	——, John, Folifett, par. Spofforthe, Feb. 4, 1556.	15	1	164

		Vol.	Pt.	Fol.
Sep. 30, 1563.	Ley, Nycholes, Chapelthorpe, par. Sandall Magna, May 28, 1563.	17		283
Mar. 4, 1567.	Leye, Richard, Cawod, Sep. 4, 1567.	17		763
July 28, 1556.	——, Thomas, Hallifaxe, Oct. 22, 1555.	15	1	46
May 14, 1560.	——, William, Dighton (bur. Eskricke), Apl. 13, 1560.	16		63
May 10, 1559.	Leyke, Richard, Nafferton, labourer, Dec. 6, 1558.	15	3	390
Nov. 10, 1563.	——, William, Ayke, par. Lokington, July 28, 1563.	17		300
Mar. 20, 1560.	Leylande, Richard, (bur. Conneston), May 21, 1560.	16		172
Jun. 22, 1568.	Leynge, Peter, Fylay, Oct. 22, 1567.	17		823
May 26, 1563.	Leyse, John, Fyshelake, Apl. 26, 1563.	17		250
Feb. 6, 1558.	Lightfoite, Raufe, Carnabie, yeoman, Nov. 4, 1558.	15	3	259
Apl. 13, 1559.	Lightfoot, Alis, Beverlay, widow, Oct. 8, 1558.	15	3	347
Oct. 5, 1563.	Lightfoote, Robert, Carnibie, yeoman, Aug. 27, 1563.	17		291
Oct. 9, 1560.	———, Thomas, Cottingham, Mar. 1, 1559.	16		122
Oct. 4, 1564.	———, William, Lynton in Craven, husbandman, Apl. 12, 1564.	17		371
Mar. 22, 1556.	Lightfote, Jenet, widow of William L., Cottingham, Jan. 25, 1556.	15	1	190
Mar. 22, 1556.	——, William, Cottingham, Nov. 9, 1556.	15	1	190
Mar. 20, 1558.	Lilburne, John, Fayrbourne, par. Ledsham, Feb. 9, 1558.	15	3	289
May 18, 1559.	Liliman, Alice, West Retforth (Notts.), Oct. 6, 1558.	15	3	407
Jun. 22, 1568.	Lilinge, Robert, Galmeton, Apl. 11, 1568.	17		826
Nov. 7, 1564.	Liliwhite, William, Bylton in Holderness, Jan. 8, 1563.	17		399
Mar. 13, 1556.	Lille, Thomas, Rotherham, Nov. 17, 1556.	15	1	184
May 2, 1566.	Lime, Robert, Camsall, July 24, 1565.	17		522
Jun. 2, 1568.	Lindalle, John, Newton, par. Wilberfosse, husbandman, Apl. 7, 1568.	17		811
Sep. 30, 1563.	Lindsey, John, Brustwick (bur. Skeclinge), Jun. 30, 1563.	17		273
Jan. 12, 1558.	Linton, Christopher, Scissaie, labourer, Sep. 21, 1558.	15	3	174
Apl. 9, 1554.	Lister, John, Baildonne, Dec. 29, 1553.	14		158
Apl. 28, 1563.	——, Thomas, Nesfeld, Oct. 16, 1562.	17		229
May 9, 1565.	——, William, Addingham, Sep. 25, 1564.	17		431
Jun. 20, 1554.	——, William, Leedes, Jan. 22, 1554.	14		113
Apl. 28, 1563.	Listere, John, Hollym in Holderness, clerk, July 7, 1562.	17		238
July 27, 1567.	Lithe, Thomas a, Sandesend, par. Lithe, Jun. 6, 1567.	17		670
Jan. 22, 1567.	Litster, John, Ulrum (bur. Skipsey), husbandman, Feb. 14, 1567.	17		754
July 9, 1562.	——, Tristram, York, inholder, Jun. 3, 1562.	17		94
July 17, 1565.	———, William, Ottringham, May 11, 1565.	17		453
May 2, 1567.	Lobley, Alice, wid. of Robert L. (bur. Tadcaster), May 5, 1560.	17		646
Jan. 21, 1556.	Lockay, Nicholas, junr., Bolton, par. Calverley, Sep. 21, 1556.	15	1	90
July 17, 1565.	Locken, Steven, Owstwicke (bur. Garton), husbn., Apl. 28, 1565.	17		454
Nov. 28, 1558.	Lockewod, Oliver, Hallstedes, par. Burton, Aug. 7, 1558.	15	3	135
Sep. 29, 1563.	Lockewood, George, Barode, par. Wathe (bur. Wentworthe), husbn., Jan. 28, 1563.	17		285
Dec. 9, 1556.	———, Marmaduke, Marflett, yeoman, Sep. 23, 1556.	15	1	156
Jun. 2, 1558.	Locking, Robert, Howstwicke (bur. Roosse), May 6, 1558.	15	2	311
Oct. 3, 1555.	——, Thomas, Aldburghe, husbandman, May 27, 1555.	14		175
Apl. 10, 1559.	Lockley, William, Bradfeild, Dec. 14, 1558.	15	3	328
Apl. 10, 1559.	Locksmyth als. Brearley, John, Barmbroughe, Jan. 22, 1558.	15	3	327
Sep. 29, 1563.	Lockwood, Christopher, Rotherham, Sep. 28, 1557.	17		286
May 5, 1568.	———, John, Hallstedes, par. Kirkeburton, husbn., July 4, 1567.	17		790
Mar. 10, 1566.	———, John (bur. Philischurche), Dec. 23, 1566.	17		513
Mar. 4, 1562.	Lockyne, Thomas, Burton Pidsey, Nov. 20, 1562.	17		150
Mar. 10, 1555.	Lockysley, John, Newarke (Notts.), Jan. 8, 1554.	14		230
Oct. 14, 1556.	Locoke, Thomas, Galmethorpe, par. Teringtone, Jan. 30, 1555.	15	1	97
Jan. 23, 1554.	Lodge, William, Oswaldkirke, labourer, Oct. 13, 1553.	14		296
Dec. 18, 1557.	Loffte, Robert, Lyncroffte (bur. York), Dec. 1, 1557.	15	2	89
Oct. 6, 1557.	Lofly, Thomas, Rosinton, Mar. 31, 1557.	15	2	7
Jun. 11, 1562.	Lofte, Annas, Scarburgh, Feb. 10, 1561.	17		87
Jan. 21, 1557.	——, Richard, Bekey, par. Aberfurthe, Oct. 10. 1557.	15	2	155
Apl. 11, 1559.	——, Richard, Saxtone, Jan. 7, 1558.	15	3	334
Jun. 14, 1567.	Loftous, John, Over Catton, May 20, 1567.	17		658
May 2, 1555.	Loge, John, Youcantwaite (bur. Hobrame), Apl. 14, 1554.	14		127
Jan. 22, 1557.	Loggayn, Marmaduke, Skynningrayve (bur. Brotton), yeom., Jun. 15, 1557.	15	2	156
July 28, 1556.	Lokwood, William, Honlay, par. Almonburye, Jun. 6, 1556.	15	1	60

A.D. 1554 TO 1568.

		Vol.	Pt.	Fol.
May 14, 1558.	Lolley, Antony, Folyfett (bur. Spofforth), Apl. 1, 1558.	15	2	280
Oct. 2, 1567.	Lome, William, Bordon, par. Addell, husbn., Feb. 24, 9, Eliz.	17		720
May 6, 1557.	Loncaster, Robert, Ellwarbie, par. Swynne, husbn., Nov. 24, 1556.	15	1	240
Jan. 22, 1557.	Londe, Elizabeth, wid. of Thomas L., Gisburne, Oct. 27, 1557.	15	2	157
Oct. 10, 1558.	———, John, York, goldsmith, Aug. 10, 1558.	15	3	132
Dec. 4, 1557.	———, Mathewe, Hamylton (bur. Brayton), Oct. 20, 1557.	15	2	50
Nov. 26, 1565.	———, Robert, Rednes (bur. Whitgifte), Aug. 19, 1565.	17		490
Sep. 30, 1556.	———, Robert, Sykes, par. Sladburne, Sep. 1, 1556.	15	1	173
Oct. 29, 1555.	———, Thomas a, Harton (bur. Bossall), Oct. 3, 1555.	14		179
Nov. 19, 1555.	Londesdale, Thomas, Lytle Armyn, par. Drax, Sep. 27, 1555.	14		181
July 15, 1562.	Londisdaile, Robert, Gaitefulforthe, May 8, 1562.	17		94
Jan. 12, 1558.	Longbayne, Richard, Skerne, Nov. 18, 1558.	15	3	197
Jan. 18, 1558.	Longbothom, Edward, Warley, par. Hallifax, Feb. 27, 1558.	15	3	211
Jan. 18, 1558.	———, Richard, Warley, par. Hallifax, Aug. 7, 1558.	15	3	212
Dec. 16, 1556.	Longbothome, Myles, Roodes, par. Rothewell, Oct. 6, 1556.	15	1	194
Mar. 9, 1557.	———, Richard, Warlay, par. Hallyfax, Feb. 6, 1557.	15	2	169
July 3, 1567.	Longhorne, John, New Malton, chapman, Mar. 20, 1566.	17		668
May 13, 1557.	Longlaie, William, Bonnaie (Notts.), Dec. 3, 1556.	15	1	227
May 9, 1566.	Longley, William, Workesoppe (Notts.), Mar. 1, 1565.	17		540
Mar. 14, 1560.	Longman, John, Starthropp, par. Averham (Notts.), husbn., Mar. 25, 1560.	16		156
Apl. 27, 1559.	Lonndesdaile, John, Spaldington (bur. Bubwith), husbn., Feb. 5, 1558.	15	3	313
Apl. 27, 1558.	Lonsdaill, Francys, Threshefelde, par. Lynton, Dec. 10, 1557.	15	2	199
Jan. 25, 1558.	Lonsdayle, Jennet, York, widow, Dec. 6, 1558.	15	3	219
Feb. 6, 1558.	Lookes, John, Wodes (bur. Normanton), Sep. 17, 1558.	15	3	258
Oct. 6, 1558.	Lookewood, James, Boltbye, par. St. Felix, Jun. 28, 1558.	15	3	91
May 5, 1558.	Loonde, John, Welley (Notts.), Jan. 7, 1557.	15	2	252
Nov. 11, 1557.	Loppon, Christopher, Sutton (Holderness), husbn., Oct. 1, 1557.	15	2	98
Oct. 2, 1567.	Lord, Robert, Selbye, Apl. 12, 1567.	17		710
Sep. 16, 1555.	Lorde, Richard, Wathe, Sep. 16, 1551.	14		65
May 19, 1554.	———, Thomas, Broughton (Notts.), Oct. 14, 1553.	14		112
Jan. 25, 1558.	Loriman, Edward, York, showmaker, Nov. 28, 1558.	15	3	219
Oct. 8, 1556.	Loscoo, Ellen, Southwell (Notts.), widow, Oct. 23, 1553.	15	1	69
May 5, 1568.	Loudge, John, Yocanthwaite in Houbram, par. Ernclif, Dec. 9, 1564.	17		784
Jan. 13, 1558.	Lound, William, Carleton (bur. Gedling, Notts.), husbn. *No date.*	15	3	14
July 10, 1566.	Louthe, Alexander, Gresley (Notts.), Apl. 26, 1565.	17		561
Oct. 7, 1557.	Lovat, Robert, alderman of Nottingham, Apl. 6, 1557.	15	2	25
Jan. 12, 1557.	Love, Oswolde, Hull, maryner, Nov. 27, 1557.	15	2	78
Nov. 24, 1554.	———, William, Clifton, par. S. Olave, Oct. 17, 1554.	14		89
Dec. 16, 1556.	Loveday, William, Ferrybrige (bur. Pontefracte), May 17, 1556.	15	1	193
Apl. 14, 1563.	Loveles, William, Cawood, Oct. 22, 1557.	17		226
Apl. 19, 1559.	Lovell, William, Bradmyre (bur. Boney, Notts.), Oct. 9, 1558.	15	3	374
May 13, 1557.	Lovett, John, Slafurth (Notts.), Apl. 6, 1557.	15	1	227
Dec. 21, 1562.	Low, Robert, Sutton in Holderness, Apl. 7, 1562.	17		135
Oct. 3, 1562.	Lowas, Thomas, Topclif, Jun. 1, 1562.	17		115
May 13, 1557.	Lowcocke, William, Ferye Marnham (Notts.), Nov. 28, 1556.	15	1	219
Jun. 13, 1554.	Lowcoke, George, Abberforth, Nov. 30, 1553.	14		11
Jan. 21, 1562.	———, Leonard, Abirforth, Dec. 20, 1562.	17		142
Apl. 17, 1567.	Lowde, Edward, Mytton, Dec. 19, 1566.	17		622
Oct. 2, 1550(? 5).	Lowde, John, Morton, par. Mytton, husbn., July 13, 1553.	14		171
Oct. 1, 1556.	Lowden, Richard, Dodworthe, par. Silkyston, Jun. 17, 1556.	15	1	124
July 15, 1567.	Lowdge, William, Yocanthwet (bur. Hubberam), Aug. 12, 1566.	17		679
Sep. 28, 1560.	Lowe, Rauffe, Eperstone (Notts.), May 12, 1560.	16		109
May 18, 1559.	———, William, junr., Bylton, Apl. 6, 1559.	15	3	408
May 26, 1554.	Lowes, Elizabeth, Brustwyke, par. Skecklynge, July 10, 1553.	14		134
Jun. 2, 1557.	Lowkes, Nicholas, Greastocke (bur. Normanton), labr., May 14, 1557.	15	1	267
Aug. 27, 1557.	Lown, Rayf (bur. St. Oswold, Sowerbe [in Thirsk]), Jun. 23, 1557.	15	2	116
May 5, 1548.	Lownde, Miles, Shelford (Notts.), Nov. 22, 1557.	15	2	266
Apl. 22, 1556.	Lownsburghe, Robert, Sylpho, par. Hackenes, Feb. 1, 1555.	15	1	26
July 9, 1563.	Lowson, John (bur. Brandisburton), Apl. 21, 1563.	17		264
Feb. 8, 1565.	———, William, Mounketon nere Ripon, Sep. 14, 1565.	17		498
Oct. 3, 1555.	Lowsonne, John, Routhe, husbandman, Mar. 9, 1555.	14		175

		Vol.	Pt.	Fol.
Nov.19, 1562.	Lowther, Katherin, Kelfeld, par. Stillingfleite, Feb. 16, 1556.	17		127
Nov.26, 1558.	Lowthrope, Robert, Hornesay. *No date.*	15	3	76
Oct. 20, 1558.	Lowthroppe, Robert, Northburton *als.* Sheriburton, yeom., July 16, 1558.	15	3	123
Oct. 4, 1565.	Lowyll, Robert, Hothom, husbandman. *No date.*	17		484
Oct. 6, 1557.	Lowys, Thomas, Screveton (Notts.), Jun. 18, 1557.	15	2	31
Oct, 6, 1558.	Loy (Boye, Act Bk), John, Conisbrughe, husbandman, Aug. 24, 1557.	15	3	223
May 26, 1563.	Lucas, John, Wheatley, par. Doncaster, husbandman, Apl. 27, 1563.	17		250
Jan. 20, 1558.	Luckoke, John, Swynton (bur. Amunderbye), Jun. 2, 1558.	15	3	212
Mar. 1, 1559.	Lucton (or Lutton, Act Book), John, Eskrige, Nov. 13, 1559.	16		4
Oct. 7, 1563.	Ludforth, John, Bowtre (Retford), Apl. 10, 1563.	17		294
Apl. 16, 1562.	Ludge, John, Myddylton, par. Ilkley, ——, 1562.	17		191
May 13, 1568.	Ludlam, Rauf, Teversall (Notts.), Jun. 4, 1567.	17		797
Apl. 19, 1559.	Ludlame, Robert, Bingham (Notts.), husbandman, Dec. 17, 1558.	15	3	360
May 13, 1568.	——, Roger (bur. Teversall, Notts.), May 6, 1567.	17		796
Nov. 5, 1562.	Lukkoke, Isabell (bur. Amunderbe), Jun. 12, 1562.	17		127
Apl. 3, 1554.	Lulley, William, citizen and merchant of York, Nov. 23, 1553.	14		221
Mar.29, 1568.	Lumbye, William, Chappell Allerton, par. Leedes, Mar. 19, 1566.	17		767
Dec. 22, 1556.	Lund, Margret, Cantley, widow, Nov. 4, 1556.	15	1	81
Apl. 28, 1563.	——, Richard, Elslacke (bur. Broughton), Nov. 6, 1562.	17		230
Jan. 13, 1558.	——, Richard, Eskrig, July 8, 1556.	15	3	189
May 24, 1564.	——, Thomas, Hamylton, par. Braton, Jan. 20, 1563.	17		345
Feb.23, 1563.	——, William, junr. Ledston, par. Ledesham, Nov. 11, 1563.	17		317
Apl. 17, 1567.	Lunde, John, Steyton (bur. Kildweke), Jan. 2, 1566.	17		620
Oct. 2, 1567.	——, Thomas [? Arnold]bigynge (bur. Gysburne), Feb. 20, 1566.	17		711
Dec.12, 1567.	——, William, Ledesham, husbandman, Aug. 8, 1567.	17		744
Oct. 7, 1557.	Lupton, Henry, Lamley (Notts.), husbandman, Jan. 31, 1551.	15	2	22
Sep. 30, 1563.	——, John, Cawdestanefawde, par. Paiteley brigges, Apl. 28, 1563.	17		296
May 2, 1560.	——, John, Hunteslet, par. Leedes, Apl. 14, 1558.	16		55
July 15, 1567.	Luptonn, Jennet, Sutton, par. Kildwike, May 2, 1566.	17		676
Dec. 13, 1557.	Lutton, Johan, wife of Step. L., Maston (bur. Hunmanbye), Nov.9,1557.	15	2	88
Sep. 13, 1557.	——, Rauffe, Knapton (bur. Wyntryngham), gent. Aug. 10, 1557.	15	1	331
Oct. 29, 1558.	——, Robert, Honanbe, gentleman, Feb. 1, 1557.	15	3	240
Mar.30, 1560.	Luvett, John, Plumtre (Notts.), Jan. 12, 1559.	16		23
Nov.10, 1557.	Lyall, John, Leckenfeld, Jun. 10, 1557.	15	2	99
Apl. 30, 1556.	Lye, Robert, Cockney (Notts.), husbandman, Mar. 3, 1555.	15	1	29
Jun. 6, 1560.	Lyell, Christopher, Beverlay, May 15, 1560.	16		74
Jun. 7, 1555.	——, Richard, Tockettes (bur. Gysbroughe), carpenter, Apl. 26, 1555.	14		254
Mar.20, 1558.	——, Thomas, Cudworth par. Roistone, Dec. 18, 1558.	15	3	245
Apl. 13, 1559.	Lyeth, George, Brandisburton, husbandman, Jan. 21, 1558.	15	3	346
May 10, 1559.	——, William, Eastcottame (bur. Lethome), fisherman, Dec.20,1558.	15	3	384
Jun. 2, 1558.	Lyethe, Henry, Brandisburton, husbandman, Jan. 20, 1557.	15	2	336
Dec. 13, 1557.	Lyghton, Robert, Ferybrigges, par. Fryston by water, Nov. 14, 1557.	15	2	54
May 10, 1554.	Lyle, Elizabeth, Walton, par. Sandall Magna, Apl. 14, 1553.	14		135
Oct. 5, 1558.	——, William, Heton, Aug. 6, 1558.	15	3	66
July 26, 1563.	Lylee, Thomas, Kirkheton, husbandman, Nov. 23, 1562.	17		267
Jun. 22, 1568.	Lylfurthe, William, Swanland, par. Elueley, yongeman, Jan. 18,1567.	17		805
Apl. 27, 1558.	Lyllywhyte, John, Thorkilbye, par. Swyne, Jan. 22, 1557.	15	2	206
Nov.26, 1557.	Lylyman, Robert, Stansall, par. Tykehell, Nov. 11, 1557.	15	2	93
Mar.14, 1560.	Lymer, Alys, Kirkebye Woodhouse, Jan. 21, 1558.	16		162
Apl. 30, 1556.	——, Thomas, Kyrkbie Woodhouse (Notts.), Mar. 8, 1555.	15	1	30
Mar.12. 1557.	Lymynge, Richard, Doncaster, inkeper, Aug. 15, 1557.	15	2	151
May 6, 1563.	Lyn, William, Chapellsyde of Stauntton (Notts.), husbn.,Feb.13,1562.	17		241
Mar.29, 1568.	Lyndley, Dorothe, Ottley, widow, Jan. 13, 1566.	17		769
Dec. 1, 1557.	——, Edward, Leatheley, clerk, Sep. 6. 1557.	15	2	85
Sep. 23, 1557.	——, Lawrance, Leathley, gentleman, May 23, 1557.	15	1	370
Mar.21, 1561.	Lyne, Thomas, Hull, meryner, May 18, 1558.	17		3
Oct. 13, 1565.	Lynhous, Christopher, Eston, May 18, 1565.	17		474
May 11, 1562.	Lynley, Jenet (bur. Ardeslow), mayden, Feb. 6, 1561.	17		198
Aug.13, 1554.	——, John, Midleton, par. Rothwell, Aug. 28, 1553.	14		268
Jun. 6, 1554.	——, Percevall, Pontefracte, Apl. 22, 1553.	14		10
Oct. 1, 1556.	——, Thomas (bur. Ardyslawe), labourer, Sep. 1, 1556.	15	1	122
May 4, 1558.	Lynne, John, Chapellsyde, Stayntonne (Notts.), husbn., Nov.16,1557.	15	2	271

		Vol.	Pt.	Fol.
Oct. 1, 1566.	Lynskyll, John Lithe, Jan. 24, 1566.	17		584
Feb. 24, 1566.	Lynslay, Thomas, New Malton, Nov. 27, 1566.	17		615
May 10, 1565.	Lynssa, John, Flaxton (bur. Foston), Nov. 6, 1564.	17		430
July 24, 1557.	Lynton, Elizabeth, Barton, par. Crambum, Mar. 12, 1557.	15	1	320
Feb. 15, 1556.	Lynwhait, Elizabeth, Tickell, widow, Jan. 2, 1556.	15	1	166
Feb. 15, 1558.	Lynwood, John, Brissell, par. Bransburton, husbn., Nov. 20, 1558.	15	3	267
Aug. 12, 1561.	———, William (bur. Riston), ———, 1561.	17		59
Apl. 8, 1559.	Lynwoodd, Henry, Nayborne, par. S. George, York, Jan. 27, 1558.	15	3	325
Mar. 23, 1560.	———, John, Ruston. No date.	16		177
May 5, 1557.	Lyoll, John, Danbie, Mar. 12, 1556.	15	1	248
Oct. 1, 1556.	Lyon, John, Warter, Jun. 26, 1556.	15	1	67
July 31, 1562.	———, Phillipe, Brandsdaill, husbn. (bur. Kirkbiemoreside), Jan. 16, 1561.	17		98
Apl. 13, 1557.	———, William, Billesdale, Jan. 9, 1556.	15	1	208
Nov. 28, 1558.	Lyrt, Thomas, Hornesay. No date.	15	3	78
May 20, 1558.	Lyster, John, Hallyfax, Mar. 16, 1557.	15	2	280
Apl. 12, 1559.	———, Thomas, Barcroft, par. Bynglay, Aug. 25, 1558.	15	3	340
July 15, 1567.	———, William, Kighley, sherman, Feb. 28, 1567.	17		678
Feb. 24, 1566.	———, William, senr., Ovynden, par. Halifaxe, Dec. 3, 1566.	17		614
Oct. 5, 1558.	———, William, Parke house, par. Gisburne, July 9, 1558.	15	3	60
May 26, 1562.	———, William, Stubhouse (bur. Harwodd), Sep. 1, 1559.	17		198
Jun. 14, 1564.	Lythe, Richard, Flambrugh, husbandman, May 25, 1564.	17		352
Oct. 5, 1558.	Lytlewood, Richard, Austonley, par. Allmonburie, July 31, 1558.	15	3	64
Aug. 4, 1554.	Lytster, Robert, Wragbye, May 11, 1554.	14		267
Oct. 6, 1557.	———, William, Blythe (Notts.), Apl. 28, 1557.	15	2	14
Dec. 4, 1557.	———, William, Pollington, par. Snaythe, Oct. 12, 1557.	15	2	51
Jan. 14, 1564.	Lyvesey, Alexander, Shaftholme, par. Arksey, Oct. 14, 1564.	17		403
Mar. 9, 1557.	Lyvocke, Rauffe, Carnabye, Jan. 10, 1557.	15	2	129
Oct. 22, 1560.	Lyvoke, Robert, Bridlington, husbandman, July 7, 1560.	16		127
May 4, 1558.	Mabelthorpe, Christopher, Bingham (Notts.), husbn., Sep. 4, 1557.	15	2	265
Sep. 26, 1558.	Macheon, Robert, Rotherham, Sep. 13, 1555.	15	3	50
May 4, 1557.	Machon, William, Ecclesfeld, Nov. 18, 1556.	15	1	280
Mar. 15, 1558.	Maddyson, William, Newton, par. Wylberfosse, taylier, May 31, 1558.	15	3	241
Nov. 17, 1558.	Maer, William, Balne (bur. Snathe), Sep. 5, 1558.	15	3	74
May 9, 1566.	Mafelde, Henry, Eastbridgeford (Notts.), Mar. 3, 1565.	17		548
Oct. 12, 1558.	Mafild, William, Newton (bur. Shelforth, Notts.), husbn. Jun. 12, 1558.	15	3	34
Oct. 4, 1554.	Mager, Peter, Buckton (bur. Bempton), husbn., Sep. 4, 1554.	14		46
Mar. 13, 1556.	Magham, Edward, Bratton, Jan. 10, 1556.	15	1	184
Apl. 22, 1556.	Maie, Henry, Marton in Cleveland, husbandman, Jan. 24, 1555.	15	1	25
Oct. 3, 1554.	———, Rauffe, Ceton (bur. Siglesthorne), Feb. 7, 1554.	14		41
Mar. 11, 1562.	Maier, William, Sikehouse (bur. Fyshelaike), Dec. 13, 1562.	17		154
Jun. 7, 1560.	Maison, Jennat, Boynton, Jan. 22, 1559.	16		80
May 5, 1557.	———, Launcelott, Aiton, Apl. 10, 1557.	15	1	284
Mar. 14, 1563.	Maister, Elizabeth (bur. Whitbie), Oct. 14, 1563.	17		323
May 9, 1563.	———, John, Southehousses, par. Whitbie, Apl. 16, 1563.	17		255
Jan. 12, 1557.	———, William, Hull, carpenter, Nov. 15, 1557.	15	2	79
Oct. 5, 1558.	Maisterman, John, senr., Great Aiton in Cleveland, Apl. 25, 1558.	15	3	66
Oct. 4, 1565.	———, Thomas, Sutton, par. Felixkirke, Jan. 25, 1564.	17		482
Jan. 31, 1567.	Makeblithe, John, Gaitefulfurthe, Mar. 20, 1566.	17		756
July 31, 1566.	———, John, Gaite Fulforthe, husbandman, Jun. 25, 1566.	17		562
Sep. 3, 1554.	Malber, John, Carleton, par. Snaythe, Jun. 15, 1554.	14		52
Apl. 12, 1559.	Malet, Robert, Normanton, gentleman, Aug. 26, 1558.	15	3	338
May 9, 1565.	Malham, Alice, widow of John M., Overbraydley, Jan. 8, 1564.	17		435
Oct. 3, 1566.	Malhome, Mawde, servant, daughter of Jo. M., Overbradley, decd., dwelling nowe with Robt. Bayldon, of Baildon, gent., Nov. 12, 1565.	17		582
Apl. 19, 1564.	Malholme, William, senr. (bur. Broughton, Craven), gent., Jan. 8, 1563.	17		329
Oct. 29, 1558.	Malin, William, Hunmanbe, Jun. 10, 1558.	15	2	372
Jan. 24, 1558.	Mallom, William, Carleton (bur. Quorlton), Oct. 14, 1558.	15	3	215
July 27, 1562.	Mallorye, Peter, Dunkeswike, par. Harwod, Mar. 31, 1562.	17		98
Mar. 10, 1555.	Maltbye, Robert, Orston (Notts.), Feb. 26, 1553.	14		226
May 10, 1565.	———, William, Driapole in Holderness, Feb. 1, 1564.	17		424
Jun. 23, 1554.	Malton, Henry, Shereburn in Herthefurthe Liethe, Apl. 15, 1554.	14		115
May 5, 1568.	———, John, Raskell, Mar. 5, 1567.	17		780

A.D. 1554 TO 1568.

		Vol.	Pt.	Fol.
Apl. 13, 1562.	Maltus, Richard. (bur. Ripon), Jan. 12, 1562.	17		170
July 11, 1558.	Malynson, Anne, Barneslay, Jun. 11, 1557.	15	2	302
Sep. 21, 1557.	———, Thruston, Wathe, July 7, 1557.	15	1	357
July 11, 1558.	Malynsonne, Nicolas, Barnesley, July 4, 1557.	15	2	318
Mar. 17, 1556.	Mamprys, John, Skypsye, husbandman, Sep. 1, 1556.	15	1	187
Jan. 13, 1558.	Man, Christopher, Scrowbie (Notts.), Oct. 11, 1558.	15	3	186
Jun. 23, 1563.	———, John a, Holme in Spaldingmore, July 25, 1562.	17		259
Mar. 15, 1562.	———, John, Semar, Mar. 1, 1561.	17		164
Apl. 1, 1556.	———, John, Weston, Feb. 20, 1553.	15	1	16
Sep. 26, 1558.	———, Lawrence, Rotherham, Feb. 18, 1557.	15	3	49
Oct. 5, 1558.	———, Raufe, Eston, husbandman, Sep. 10, 1558.	15	3	67
May 2, 1560.	———, Thomas, Myrfelde, Feb. 15, 1559.	16		41
July 29, 1558.	———, William, Myrfeld, May 14, 1558.	15	2	383
Dec. 1, 1558.	Manbye, Robert, Hull, mayster and mariner, Oct. 10, 1558.	15	3	149
Apl. 27, 1564.	Mane, Thomas a, Hikilynge (Notts.), Sep. 9, 1563.	17		340
Oct. 11, 1563.	Manfeeld, William, Mekle Atone in Cleveland, Jun. 27, 1563.	17		298
May 6, 1559.	Manfeild, John, Great Aiton, Dec. 7, 1558.	15	3	382
May 19, 1559.	Mangall, John, Bawne (bur. Snaith), Feb. 7, 1558.	15	3	424
May 25, 1554.	———, Margaret, Balne, par. Snaithe, widow, Aug. 7, 1554.	14		252
Aug. 26, 1555.	Mankine (? Maukine), Christopher, St. Mychaell, York, July 8, 1555.	14		73
July 15, 1567.	Manne, John (bur. Rilston), Apl. 1, 1567.	17		675
Oct. 20, 1558.	Manser, Robert, Riston in Holderness, Sep. 29, 1557.	15	2	351
Jun. 25, 1568.	Mantill, William, Aton, par. Hootonbushell, Feb. 17, 1567.	17		814
May 4, 1558.	Mantyll, John, Nottingham, tanner, Aug. 15, 1556.	15	2	271
Apl. 28, 1563.	Manyngham, William, Doncaster, glover, Feb. 14, 1562.	17		233
Jun. 20, 1568.	Mapples, Nicholas, Thorne, Oct. 25, 1567.	17		816
Sep. 30, 1562.	———, Thomas, Doncaster, May 10, 4 Eliz.	17		114
Feb. 17, 1561.	Mar, William, Fynnyngley (Notts.), Mar. 27, 1561.	17		15
Oct. 5, 1558.	Marcer, Richard, Spaldington, priest, July 24, 1558.	15	3	90
July 17, 1565.	———, Thomas, Lindley (bur. Otley), yeoman, May 24, 1565.	17		450
Mar. 22, 1564.	———, William, Ferndale (bur. Lestingame), Feb. 4, 1564.	17		412
Oct. 6, 1557.	Marcham, Edmond, Walkringham (Notts.), husbn., Aug. 1, 1557.	15	2	6
May 28, 1560.	Marchante, Lancelot (bur. St. Oswald, Sourbie), Oct. 10, 1559.	16		70
May 18, 1559.	Marche, Esabell, Marflete, widow, July 17, 1558.	15	3	411
Sep. 21, 1557.	———, John, Barkhe, par. Darton, July 15, 1557.	15	1	350
Aug. 2, 1557.	———, John, Merflete, July 6, 1557.	15	1	323
Jan. 16, 1558.	———, Thomas, Rillington, Sep. 17, 1558.	15	3	210
Apl. 27, 1554.	Marcheden, Nicholas, Thorgoland, par. Silkston, Mar. 12, 1553.	14		1
Nov. 28, 1558.	Mare, Christopher, Catfos (bur. Siglisthron), Oct. 2, 1558.	15	3	78
Mar. 11, 1562.	———, Isabell (bur. Fyshelaike), Dec. 19, 1562.	17		155
May 29, 1562.	———, Jhon, Bawne (bur. Snaithe), Apl. 9, 1561.	17		101
Mar. 20, 1565.	———, William, Bransburton, Aug. 27, 1565.	17		505
Oct. 8, 1556.	Mareott, Lawrannce, Nottingham, corvesser, Aug. 20, 1556.	15	1	152
Oct. 13, 1558.	Margerie, Agnes, Crowmwell (Notts.), Jun. 16, 1558.	15	2	364
May 13, 1557.	———, Richard, Cormwell (Notts.), Nov. 2, 1556.	15	1	219
Feb. 5, 1557.	Margerson, William, Swynflete (bur. Whytgyfte), Nov. 15, 1557.	15	2	165
Oct. 5, 1554.	Margeson, Leonerd, Lowthorp, Apl. 24, 1554.	14		45
Jan. 16, 1558.	———, Robert, Armyn (bur. Snath), Sep. 17, 1558.	15	3	209
May 6, 1557.	———, Thomas, Lowthorpe, husbandman, Jan. 1, 1556.	15	1	247
May 4, 1557.	Margesone, William, Doncaster, husbandman, Jan. 26, 1556.	15	1	276
Apl. 6, 1558.	Margrave, John, Thorne, Nov. 17, 1557.	15	2	183
July 22, 1554.	———, Thomas, Thoorne, yeoman, Apl. 5, 1554.	14		143
Nov. 18, 1567.	Markecome, George, Newland, par. Drax, May 16, 1567.	17		735
Apl. 23, 1562.	———, William, Newlande, par. Drax, Jan. 8, 1561.	17		195
Feb. ult., 1563.	Markenfeild, Margaret, widow (bur. Ripon), Sep. 10, 1563	17		321
May 2, 1560.	Marlaye, Thomas, Waugham, husbandman, Jan. 25, 1559.	16		50
Apl. 26, 1559.	Marley, Robert, Staxsby, par. Whitby, Aug. 26, 1558.	15	3	364
Oct. 6, 1557.	Marnam, William, Eylkisley (Notts.), July 17, 1557.	15	2	8
July 19, 1557.	Marneham, John, Elkesley (Notts.), Apl. 27, 1557.	15	1	311
July 19, 1557.	———, Elizabeth, widow of Robert M., Elkeslay (Notts.), May 1, 1557.	15	1	311
May 13, 1557.	———, Robert, Elkislay (Notts.), Feb. 17, 1556.	15	1	233

		Vol.	Pt.	Fol.
July 19, 1557.	Marneham, Robert, Elkesley (Notts.), May 1, 1557.	15	I	312
Sep. 30, 1557.	Marre, Jayne, Stansall, par. Tyckhill, widow, Sep. 12, 1557.	15	I	369
Jun. 22, 1568.	——, John, Hessill, Feb. 16, 1567.	17		805
May 5, 1558.	——, Margaret, Westretford (Notts.), Mar. 12, 1554.	15	2	252
Oct. 5, 1564.	——, Richard, Preston in Holderness, yeoman, May 16, 1564.	17		368
Sep. 21, 1557.	——, Richard, Stanshall (bur. Tychill), Aug. 15, 1557.	15	I	352
Mar. 6, 1556.	——, William, Austerfeld, Jan. 7, 1556.	15	I	179
Apl. 16, 1562.	Marschall, Gylbert, Myddleton, par. Ylkley, Mar. 28, 1561.	17		187
July 1, 1562.	Marsden, Christopher, Penyston, Mar. 28, 1560.	17		93
Oct. 2, 1566.	——, Edmunde, Carlecottes, par. Penyston, yeom., Dec. 7, 1565.	17		577
Dec. 22, 1556.	——, Henry, Grysbroke, par. Rotherham, Sep. 22, 1556.	15	I	82
Sep. 21, 1557.	——, Richard, Barnesley, Sep. 8, 1557.	15	I	353
Mar. 23, 1557.	Marser, John, Hornesey, ——, 1557.	15	2	172
May 13, 1568.	Marshall, Agnes (bur. Sutton on Trent, Notts.), Dec. 12, 1567.	17		799
Nov. 29, 1558.	——, Bryan, Rufforthe, Aug. 16, 1558.	15	3	80
Jun. 21, 1568.	——, Christopher (Nottingham Deanery), prèiste, parson of Cogenhooe, co. Northants, Jun. 1, 1568.	17		830
Jan. 18, 1554.	——, Elizabeth, Aldburghe, Mar. 1, 1553.	14		152
Sep. 28, 1560.	——, Harrye, Sutton in Bonyngton (Notts.), husbn., Sep. 6, 1559.	16		108
Oct. 7, 1556.	——, Henry, Estretforthe.(Notts.), talyour, Jun. 21, 1556.	15	I	145
Oct. 13, 1558.	——, Henry, Neyther Lodge, par. Averham (Notts.), coteger, May 4, 1558.	15	2	362
Oct. 2, 1567.	——, James, Barneston, July 28, 1567.	17		715
May 2, 1566.	——, John, Barmbie, par. Lithe, Mar. 3, 1565.	17		540
Jan. 18, 1558.	——, John, Colton (bur. Bolton Percie), Nov. 21, 1558.	15	3	20
Oct. 21, 1564.	——, John, Flaxton (bur. Bossall), Feb. 14, 1564.	17		393
Feb. 28, 1566.	——, John, Myddilton, par. Rudbie, Aug. 25, 1566.	17		616
Oct. 6, 1557.	——, John, Normanton, par. Clyfton (Notts.), July 12, 1557.	15	2	27
May 23, 1564.	——, Margaret, East Righton (bur. Bardsay), wid., Feb. 8, 1563.	17		344
May 2, 1566.	——, Mathew, Pomfret, Jan. 10, 1565.	17		535
Mar. 23, 1557.	——, Nicholas, Awdbrough, Apl. 17, 1557.	15	2	154
Oct. 13, 1558.	——, Richard, Crowmwell (Notts.), Mar. 18, 155[7-]8.	15	2	363
Oct. 24, 1566.	——, Richard, Moremonketon, July 14, 1566.	17		587
May 13, 1557.	——, Richard, Rampton (Notts.), husbandman, Apl. 10, 1557.	15	I	236
Apl. 8, 1559.	——, Richard (bur. Rascall), ——, 1558.	15	3	329
Jun. 22, 1568.	——, Richard, Thorner, slater, May 15, ——.	17		817
Apl. 28, 1563.	——, Robert, East Carleton, par. Gyesley, husbn., Feb. 26, 1562.	17		236
Apl. 27, 1558.	——, Robert, Hanworthe, par. Byngley, Nov. 22, 1557.	15	2	199
Jun. 4, 1568.	——, Robert, Sextendaill (bur. Wharompercye), husbn., May 6, 1567.	17		812
Oct. 1, 1556.	——, Robert, Tadcastre, Aug. 16, 1556.	15	I	134
Mar. 16, 1553.	——, Robert, Thorpe (bur. Braton), husbandman, Nov. 26, 1553.	14		212
Jun. 8, 1557.	——, Thomas (bur. Kirkburne), May 2, 1557.	15	I	270
Jan. 26, 1558.	——, Thomas, Lethome, husbandman, Aug. 10, 1558.	15	3	219
Jan. 21, 1557.	——, Thomas, Monkfryston, Oct. 14, 1557.	15	2	155
Apl. 28, 1563.	——, Thomas, Nunnyngton, Feb. 24, 1562.	17		226
Oct. 23, 1555.	——, Thomas, Oxton, par. Tadcaster, Aug. 16, 1555.	14		201
Oct. 1, 1561.	——, William, Albroughe in Holderness, Sep. 8, 1561.	17		47
Oct. 1, 1562.	——, William, Brayton, labourer, Feb. 25, 1562.	17		115
July 1, 1558.	——, William, Folome, par. Wimersleye, Mar. 5, 1558.	15	2	328
Oct. 1, 1566.	——, William, Glaisdall, par. Egton, Mar. 2, 1565.	17		584
Apl. 11, 1559.	——, William, Hamylton (bur. Braton), Jan. 28, 1558.	15	3	333
July 15, 1567.	——, William, Haynworth, par. Byngley, husbn., Mar. 9, 1566.	17		677
Nov. 22, 1563.	——, William, Owerbarobie, par. Lithe, Nov. 6, 1563.	17		304
May 24, 1555.	——, William, Pennyston, Apl. 1, 1554.	14		310
Sep. 16, 1555.	——, William, Pennyston, Apl. 1, 1554.	14		68
Sep. 1, 1565.	——, William, Schaylinge in Cleveland (bur. Rosbye), husbn., Jun. 24, 1565.	17		462
Dec. 3, 1560.	Marsham, John, Kyrkebirton, Feb. 25, 1558.	16		131
Apl. 19, 1558.	Marshe, Alice, Harthill, widow, Feb. 17, 1557.	15	2	240
July 20, 1557.	——, Margaret, widow of Thomas M., Dayehouse, par. Darton, May 14, 1557.	15	I	315

		Vol.	Pt.	Fol.
Nov. 9, 1557.	Marshe, Mathewe, Thurstonland (bur. Kyrkeburton), yeom., Jun. 8, 1557.	15	2	96
Oct. 9, 1567.	Marsheland, Katherin, Mathersey Thorpe (Notts.), Oct. 11, 1566.	17		722
July 9, 1563.	Marshingalie, John, Bewham (Holderness), Mar. 2, 1562.	17		265
Jun. 21, 1565.	Marsingaill, Peter, son and heir of Peter M., Hull, baxter, deceased, Feb. 7, 1564.	17		448
May 5, 1557.	Marsingall, Robert, Filing, Jan. 6, 1556.	15	1	243
July 1, 1558.	Marsingill, John (bur. Skarbroughe), May 12, 1558.	15	2	323
Jun. 14, 1560.	Marssland, Robert, Fynynglaye (Notts.), Mar. 12, 1559.	16		84
May 6, 1563.	Marston, Henry, Elkeslay (Notts.), Oct. 25, 1562.	17		245
Jan. 25, 1567.	———, William, York, sadler, May 4, 1567.	17		756
Oct. 5, 1558.	Marsyngaille, William, Newham, par. Whitby, Aug. 17, 1558.	15	3	43
Oct. 1, 1561.	Marten, Olyver, Slaidburne, Nov. 18, 1560.	17		48
Jun. 10, 1557.	Martin, John, Aram, par. Leckingfeld, husbandman, May 6, 1557.	15	1	274
May 17, 1565.	Marton, Alice, Kyworthe, par. Bonnaye (Notts.), wid., Sep. 2, 1559.	17		437
Feb. 5, 1567.	———, Henry, Leedes, chapman, Oct. 30, 1567.	17		761
Jun. 2, 1558.	———, Isabell, Hornesey, Aug. 2, 1557.	15	2	335
Nov. 25, 1562.	———, John, Aberforthe, mylner, Aug. 28, 1559.	17		129
Aug. 16, 1560.	———, John, Marton in Cleveland, July 12, 1560.	16		103
May 3, 1555.	———, William, Bradfeilde, Sep. 6, 1554.	14		84
Nov. 24, 1562.	———, William, Standforthbrige (bur. Catton), Oct. 27, 1562.	17		128
May 13, 1557.	———, William, Willforth (Notts.), Feb. 9, 1556.	15	1	228
Jun. 20, 1566.	Martson, John, Hundmanbie, Mar. 26, 1566.	17		557
Oct. 6, 1557.	Martyn, John, Ratclyffe on Trent (Notts.), July 23, 1557.	15	2	28
Dec. 22, 1556.	———, Nicholas, Todwyke, Jun. 21, 1555.	15	1	81
Jan. 21, 1557.	———, Nicholas, Wymbersley, Sep. 28, 1557.	15	2	70
Feb. 15, 1558.	———, Thomas, Humleton, Jan. 4, 1558.	15	3	268
Sep. 30, 1562.	———, William, Hemphollme, par. Leven, Feb. 24, 1561.	17		118
Dec. 9, 1556.	———, William, Holmpton, July 13, 1556.	15	1	197
Apl. 22, 1562.	———, William, Sutton in Bonyng[ton] (Notts.), husbn., Mar. 1, 1560.	17		180
Oct. 8, 1556.	Martyne, Ellyne, Southwell (Notts.), widow, Mar. 26, 1556.	15	1	155
Apl. 17, 1567.	———, James, Aram, par., Leckinfeld, husbandman, Jan. 5, 1566.	17		640
Sep. 29, 1563.	———, John, Woddhousse, par. Slaytburne, Apl. 22, 1563.	17		215
Oct. 7, 1557.	———, Margaret, Lowdam (Notts.), Aug. 1, 1557.	15	2	23
Feb. 6, 1558.	———, Mathewe, Brigham (bur. Fostone), Aug. 31, 1558.	15	3	261
Oct. 7, 1563.	———, William, Gonalstone (Notts.), husbandman, July 11, 1563.	17		293
May 28, 1567.	Martynge, Thomas, Everingham, Nov. 4, 1566.	17		648
Oct. 5, 1564.	Martynson, John, Hawdenbie, par. Adlingflete, husbn., Nov. 20, 1563.	17		367
Sep. 30, 1556.	Marwike, William, Lowthorpe, Aug. 14, 1556.	15	1	134
Apl. 28, 1558.	Marwod, Edmund, Nunthorpe (bur. Ayton), Dec. 22, 1557.	15	2	233
Apl. 22, 1556.	Marwood, George, Ugthorpe, par. Lithe, Jun. 22, 1553.	15	1	28
Mar. 15, 1558.	———, Thomas, Newsom, par. Wresle, weaver, Dec. 16, 1557.	15	3	166
Feb. 25, 1560.	———, Thomas, Ynglebie under Arnecliffe, Apl. 15, 1553.	16		151
Oct. 1, 1557.	———, Thomasyn, Ugthropp, par. Lythe, widow, Jun. 23, 1557.	15	1	362
Sep. 10, 1555.	Maryatte, Nicholas, Winckborne, husbandman, July 14, 1555.	14		249
Oct. 7, 1563.	Marysland, Jennet, Fynnyngley (Notts.), Dec. 13, 1562.	17		295
Feb. 17, 1561.	———, Margaret, Fynnyngley (Notts.), Oct. 10, 1561.	17		14
Oct. 4, 1565.	Mascall, John, Berlay, par. Brayton, whellewright, Dec. 12, 1564.	17		485
Mar. 18, 1563.	Maskalle, William, Cawodd, cordiner, Mar. 24, 1562.	17		323
May 6, 1563.	Mason, George, Fenton, par. Sturton (Notts.), husbn., Mar. 22, 1559.	17		243
May 8, 1556.	———, George, glover, York, Oct. 11, 1555.	15	1	15
May 9, 1566.	———, Henry, Kirsall, par. Knesall (Notts.), Dec. 3, 1565.	17		546
Sep. 8, 1561.	———, Jane, Nunnyngton, par. Stonegrave, widow, Mar. 8, 1559.	17		48
July 17, 1562.	———, John, Acaster Selbie (bur. Stillingfleitt), July 3, 1562.	17		96
May 13, 1568.	———, John, Bawderston (Notts.), Oct. 20, 1567.	17		797
May 17, 1565.	———, John, Newton, par. Shelforthe (Notts.), husbn., Dec. 29, 6 Eliz.	17		438
July 15, 1567.	———, John, Suton, par. Kildwike, Apl. 7, 1567.	17		676
Sep. 14, 1565.	———, John, Withstead in Holderness, husbn., May 7, 1565.	17		466
May 2, 1560.	———, Peter (bur. Boynton), Sep. 27, 1559.	16		36
Dec. 1, 1558.	———, Robert, Hull, mariner, Aug. 28, 1558.	15	3	146
May 9, 1563.	———, Robert, Kildaill, Mar. 23, 156[2-]3.	17		256
Oct. 5, 1558.	———, William, Kirklevington, Aug. 20, 1557.	15	3	43

A.D. 1554 TO 1568.

		Vol.	Pt.	Fol.
Nov. 4, 1557.	Massam, Richard, Shereffhoton, husbandman, Sep. 23, 1557.	15	2	106
Oct. 2, 1566.	Massengam, Jennet, Buholme, par. Nunkelinge, Nov. 12, 1565.	17		581
Feb. 4, 1556.	Masseray, William, West Bretton (bur. Silkston), Dec. 2, 1556.	15	1	95
May 9, 1566.	Massie, Richard, Gotham (Notts.), Dec. 28, 1565.	17		548
July 17, 1560.	Massum, John, Brandsbie, Aug. 13, 1559.	16		93
Oct. 22, 1567.	Master, William, Eastwaite (Notts.), Apl. 25, 1565.	17		731
Jun. 10, 1560.	Matchyon, John, Westhalssum, Jan. 25, 1560.	16		82
May 6, 1559.	Matherer, Robert, Rest Parke, par. Shereburne, Apl. 10, 1559.	15	3	381
Dec. 13, 1557.	Matherson, Richard, Wyckham (bur. Old Malton), husbn., Oct.5,1557.	15	2	43
Jan. 14, 1558.	Matheson, Richard, Heweke (bur. Ripon), Sep. 7, 1558.	15	3	191
Apl. 20, 1564.	Mathew, Richard, Leides, clother, Aug. 20, 1563.	17		332
May 19, 1559.	Mathewe, Henry, Otley, Jan. 14, 1558.	15	3	424
Oct. 6, 1558.	————, John, Felkirke, July 20, 1558.	15	3	45
July 1, 1555.	————, Philippe, Everley, Jun. 13, 1555.	14		258
Nov. 3, 1558.	Mathewman, Jennett, Hollinhirste, par. Thornehill, wid., Oct. 6, 1558.	15	3	155
Jan. 14, 1558.	Mathewson, Jenet, Hewicke, par. Ripon, Nov. 14, 1558.	15	3	191
May 25, 1560.	————, John, Sutton on Darwen, Mar. 29, 1560.	16		67
Oct. 28, 1566.	Mathey, Thomas, Swanland, par. Elley, Apl. 10, 1566.	17		587
Oct. 8,[1555].	Mathyman, Thomas, Thorgoland, par. Silkeston, July 18, 1555.	14		202
July 3, 1563.	Matkin, Thomas, Fyskerton (Notts.), May 11, 1563.	17		263
May 19, 1554.	Matlocke, Robert, Kirklington (Notts.), Oct. 20, 1553.	14		110
Jan. 12, 1558.	Mattinson, Thomas, Cottingham, Nov. 8, 1558.	15	3	197
Mar. 9, 1557.	Mattynson, Rollande, Garton on Wolde, husbandman, Jan. 1, 1557.	15	2	128
Mar. 16, 1559.	Maude, George, Kyrkedyghton, husbandman, July 28, 1558.	16		9
Apl. 27, 1558.	————, Jane, wid. of Arthure M., West Ridlesden (bur. Bingley), Dec. 28, 1556.	15	2	207
Aug. 26, 1555.	Maukine (? Mankine), Christopher, St. Mychaell, York, July 8, 1555.	14		73
Oct. 31, 1566.	Maumond, William, Thornton, par. Foston, husbandman, Oct.29,1565.	17		585
Nov. 29, 1562.	Maundbie, Thomas, Essedike, par. Wighell, husbn., Jun. 12, 1562.	17		129
May 6, 1557.	Maunge, Roger. Rocliffe (bur. Snaythe), Jan. 24, 1556,	15	1	242
Jan. 21, 1557.	Maunsell, William, Ossett, par. Duesburye, Dec. 30, 1556.	15	2	70
Dec. 3, 1561.	Mawd, Christopher, Woydhouse (bur. Ylkelay), Jun. 9, 1561.	17		32
Jan. 7, 1562.	————, John, Stappelton, par. Darrington, labourer, Jun. 22, 1562.	17		140
Jan. 18, 1558.	————, Richard, Ovenden, par. Halifax, Aug. 31, 1558.	15	3	20
Sep. 30, 1557.	Mawde, Agnes, Shelfe, par. Halyfax, widow, July 20, 1557.	15	1	324
Aug. 11, 1554.	————, Anthony, Otteley, Mar. 14, 1551.	14		146
Jun. 4, 1561.	————, Edmund, Ovenden, par. Hallifax, Feb. 27, 1560.	17		67
Nov. 10, 1558.	————, Edward, Darlay, par. Halifax, Oct. 12, 1558.	15	3	156
Mar. 9, 1557.	————, Edward, Lightclyffe (bur. Hallyfax), Aug. 6, 1551.	15	2	167
Jan. 29, 1562.	————, John, Brandon (bur. Harwood), Oct. 9, 1562.	17		144
Oct. 2, 1567.	————, John, Leedes, tavlior, May 24, 1567.	17		720
May 5, 1568.	————, John, Warley, par. Halifax, Feb. 10, 1567.	17		789
Jun. 22, 1568.	————, Thomas, Burley, par. Ottley, yeoman, May 5, 1568.	17		818
Sep. 23, 1558.	Mawdeslay, John, Hirst Courtenay, July 16, 1554.	15	3	85
May 2, 1555.	Mawdesleye, Richard, Longe Preston, Nov. 14, 1554.	14		27
Apl. 5, 1563. [1]	Mawe, Henry, Hor[n]ington, par. Bolton Percie, yeom., Nov. 8 or 10, 1559.	17		217
Nov. 19, 1566.	————, Mychell, Hornyngton, Sep. 22, 1566.	17		598
Feb. 6, 1558.	————, Richard, Selbie, labourer, Dec. 18, 1558.	15	3	263
Mar. 10, 1558.	————, Robert, Hornyngton (bur. Bolton Persey), Aug. 10, 1558.	15	3	287
May 2, 1560.	———— als. Robynson, Umfray Harwoode, Dec. 28, 1559.	16		55
Oct. 13, 1558.	Mawer, Agnes, Cottam, par. South Leverton (Notts.), Feb. 10, 1558.	15	2	358
Jun. 25, 1568.	————, Cecile (bur. Sutton in Holderness), Mar. 18, 1567.	17		811
Nov. 5, 1564.	————, John, Southe Dalton, May 25, 1564.	17		395
May 18, 1559.	————, Robert, Burton Pudsey, Feb. 19, 1558.	15	3	395
Oct. 16, 1558.	————, Thomas, Hothom, Oct. 22, 1557.	15	2	344
Dec. 15, 1557.	————, William, Cottum, par. South Leverton (Notts.), July 31, 1557.	15	2	55
Apl. 20, 1559.	————, William, Weston (Notts.), Jan. 7, 1558.	15	3	306
Mar. 27, 1560.	Mawghen, Robert, Pottowe, par. Whorleton, husbn., Nov. 11, 1559.	16		21
Aug. 16, 1560.	Mawlam, Richard, Carleton (bur. Qworlton), July 11, 1560.	16		102

---

1 At Newcastle on tyne, returninge furthe of the quenes maiesties warres in the north partes.

A.D. 1554 TO 1568.

		Vol.	Pt.	Fol.
May 13, 1568.	Mawlam, Richard (bur. Claweworthe, Notts.), 1568.	17		803
Oct. 1, 1566.	Mawleverey, Leonard, Yowardayll, par. Hawnbie, gent., May 10, 1566.	17		583
July 27, 1557.	Mawmande, Richard, Flaxton, par. Bossall, Jun. 28, 1557.	15	1	321
Apl. 27, 1557.	Mawmonde, Robert, Flaxton, par. Bossall, Mar. 22, 1556.	15	1	209
Oct. 3, 1554.	Mawpas, Sir William, curate of St. Gyles Marflete, Jun. 5, 1 Mary.	14		41
May 18, 1559.	Mawson, Agnes, Hawdenbye Parke (bur. Adlingflete), Jan. 24, 1557.	15	3	413
Apl. 28, 1563.	———, John, Weston, Mar. 2, 1562.	17		235
Sep. 28, 1557.	———, Myles, Weston, Aug. 3, 1557.	15	1	371
May 19, 1559.	———, Richard, Askewith (bur. Westone), but[c]her, Feb. 12, 1558.	15	3	426
Nov.13, 1556.	———, Robert, Hawdenbie Parke, par. Adlingflett, Aug. 2, 1556.	15	1	114
Jun. 22, 1555.	Mawton, Thomas, Raskell, Apl. 3, 1 & 2 Phil. and Mary.	14		254
Oct. 8, 1555.	Max, Laurence, Halton (Notts.), gentleman. Aug. 28, 1554.	14		225
May 4, 1558.	Maxwell, Cutbert, Clyfton (Notts.), Sep. 12, 1557.	15	2	269
Nov. 7, 1564.	———, George, Thorkilbe, par. Swyne, Dec. 5, 1563.	17		399
Aug.16, 1560.	———, William, Kirke Levynton, Apl. 15, 1560.	16		103
Sep. 30, 1562.	Maxy, Thomas, Cold Ynglebe (bur. Stainton), yeom., Mar. 27, 1562.	17		108
May 9, 1556.	May, Elizabeth, Newton, Apl. 26, 1556.	15	1	38
Apl. 28, 1558.	———, William (bur. Newton, Cleveland), Dec. 9, 1557.	15	2	232
May 10, 1559.	———, William (bur. Newtone, Cleveland), Feb. 6, 1558.	15	3	385
May 3, 1555.	Maye, John (bur. Newton. Cleveland), Apl. 16, 1555.	14		34
Apl. 24, 1567.	———, Richard, Hoveringham (Notts.), Oct. 27, 1566.	17		642
Aug.27, 1561.	Maykeley, Bryan, Leckinfeld, yeoman, Mar. 17, 1560.	17		54
Feb.18, 1557.	Mayneman, Anthony, York, tyler, Dec. 20, 1557.	15	2	145
Jan. 11, 1557.	Maynpreis, Robert, Ulrum (bur. Skipse), husbandman, Nov. 28, 1557.	15	2	74
July 1, 1564.	Maynyngam, Agnes, wid. of William M., Doncaster, Nov. 7, 1563.	17		354
Oct. 6, 1557.	Mayre, Roger, Walkingham (Notts.), May 30, 1557.	15	2	13
Mar.19, 1560.	Mayson, Henry, Nonnyngton, par. Stanegrave, Feb. 19, 1560.	16		154
Dec. 3, 1560.	———, James, Kynlsey, Sep. 16, 1560.	16		134
Sep. 4, 1557.	———, John, priest (bur. Olde Malton), Aug. 9, 1557.	15	1	330
Oct. 1, 1566.	———, Mawde, Kyrkeleventon, Jun. 4, 1566.	17		584
Jan. 22, 1557.	———, Thomas, Kylldaill, May 8, 1557.	15	2	158
July 18, 1561.	———, William, Rosse, Apl. 18, 1561.	17		84
May 31, 1560.	———, William, York, marchant, May 13, 1560.	16		71
Apl. 15, 1562.	Mechell, John, Owstone (bur. Cowkeswolde), Jan. 27, 1561.	17		161
Apl. 23, 1556.	Medilton, John, Kylnsey, Dec. 4, 1555.	15	1	24
Jan. 24, 1558.	Medlay, Barnard, Shafton, par. Felkirke, husbandman, Dec. 15, 1558.	15	3	117
July 12, 1558.	———, Henry, Birkyn, husbandman, May 4, 1558.	15	2	307
Apl. 20, 1558.	Medley, Richard, Camylsfurth, par. Drax, Mar. 20, 1557.	15	2	217
Apl. 6, 1558.	———, Robert, Barnesley, July 29, 1557.	15	2	183
May 5, 1568.	———, Thomas, Sandhooton, par. Thriske, Oct. 6, 1567.	17		780
Oct. 8, 1567.	Mee, Robert, Chilwell, par. Addenborow (Notts.), Sep. 25, 1566.	17		725
Oct. 2, 1556.	Megelay, Margaret, Moregrange, par. Ledes, widow, Sep. 18, 1556.	15	1	69
May 14, 1565.	Meggson, Thomas, Ruston on the wold, husbandman, Feb. 26, 1561.	17		429
Mar.14, 1560.	Megson, Nicholas, Doncaster, Feb. 19, 1560.	16		159
Jun. 4, 1568.	———, Robert, Collom, May 17, 1567.	17		812
Aug.27, 1558.	Meike, Edward, Linghowse (bur. Haiton), July 30, 1558.	15	2	294
Feb.26, 1556.	Mekylthwayt, Margaret, Swathaull in Worsburghe, wid., May 6, 1556.	15	1	165
Mar.21, 1564.	Mellar, John, Rawmarshe, wright, Jan. 20, 1564.	17		410
Dec. 2, 1562.	Melier, Edward, Tynslowe, par. Rotherham, Jun. 18, 1562.	17		131
Apl. 14, 1562.	———, James, Hudderfelde, Dec. 7, 1560.	17		167
May 9, 1565.	Mellinge, Richard, Longe Preston, Jan. 14, 1564.	17		431
Dec.22, 1556.	Mellond, Hughe, Steinforth (bur. Hatfeld), husbn., July 10, 1556.	15	1	76
Apl. 26, 1558.	Mellor, William, Acghton, par. Aston, Feb. 6, 1557.	15	2	223
Apl. 24, 1567.	Mellors, John, Nottingham, Apl. 10, 1566.	17		643
Dec. 1, 1561.	Mellynge, Richard, Herthington (bur. Burnsall), July 23, 1561.	17		33
Apl. 23, 1556.	Mellynne, Richard (bur. Gygleswicke), Feb. 13, 1555.	15	1	36
Apl. 27, 1554.	Melton, Jennet, Claxton, par. Bossall, widow, July 16, 1553.	14		54
July 22, 1560.	———, William, Skagilthrope (bur. Setterington), May 7, 1560.	16		94
Jun. 16, 1554.	Menethorpe, William, Mydleton in Pickeringelithe, husbn., Nov. 25, 1553.	14		11
July 26, 1563.	Mennell, Robert, serjaunt at the Lawe, Mar. 28, 1563.	17		265
Oct. 7, 1563.	Menvell, Thomas, Everton (Notts.), husbandman, Apl. 15, 1563.	17		294

	Vol.	Pt.	Fol.
May 10, 1567. Mer, Richard, Blakstone, co. York (bur. Fynnyngley, Notts.), Jun. 17, 1566.	17		652
Mar. 20, 1558. Merbeke, Robert, Thorpwillobie, par. Braton, Jan. 3, 1558.	15	3	252
Jan. 16, 1558. ———, William, Thorpe (bur. Braton), webster, Nov. 23, 1558.	15	3	20
Sep. 30, 1563. Merber, Jenet, Coulton (bur. Snaith), widow, Apl. 1, 1563.	17		287
May 5, 1564. ———, William, Carlton (bur. Snaythe), Mar. 14, 1563.	17		343
Apl. 8, 1559. Merchante, Thomas (bur. Sowrbie), clerk, Dec. 25, 1558.	15	3	321
May 19, 1554. Merchell, John, Bilbroughe (Notts.), Aug. 1, 1549.	14		112
Jan. 20, 1558. Mere, Elizabeth, Locton, par. Midleton, 1558.	15	3	21
Feb. 18, 1556. Merebecke, Edward, Burtone, par. Monkefristone, Aug. 8, 1556.	15	1	161
Mar. 12, 1557. ———, Henry, Thorpe (bur. Brayton), webester, Nov. 29, 1557.	15	2	151
Apl. 29, 1559. Merfeyld, William (bur. Eskrige), Jan. 31, 1558.	15	3	361
Oct. 2, 1555. Meridewe, Alice, Rosington, Oct. 22, 1554.	14		165
Apl. 22, 1562. Meriman (Registered Moryan), George, Wylforthe (Notts.), Aug. 23, 1561.	17		180
Dec. 15, 1557. Merresden, William, Awkeley (bur. Fynnynglay, Notts.), husbn., Aug. 20, 1557.	15	2	55
Dec. 1, 1558. Merriman, James, Beverlay, Oct. 8, 1558.	15	3	81
July 19, 1566. Mersgaill, Alison (bur. Kirkbemisperton), Apl. 8, 1566.	17		562
Jan. 13, 1558. Mertill, Elizabeth (bur. Steplifford, Notts.), widow, Oct. 9, 1551.	15	3	183
Aug. 29, 1554. Mery, Robert, Lokton, May 18, 1554.	14		271
Jun. 22, 1568. Merye, Robert, Bridlington, Feb. 26, 1567.	17		821
Aug. 7, 1565. Meryng, Edmund, Fenton (bur. Screton, Notts.), Mar. 2, 1565.	17		509
Oct. 7, 1557. Merynge, James, Rolston (Notts.) gentleman, Feb. 6, 1556.	15	2	16
May 4, 1558. Meryson, Raphe, Bridgeforth (Notts.), husbn., Nov. 13, 1557.	15	2	267
May 12, 1559. Metcalf, Edmund, Beverley, glover, Jan. 11, 1558.	15	3	393
May 6, 1559. ———, Edmund, Rudbie, yeoman, Mar. 5, 1558.	15	3	382
Nov. 10, 1564. ———, Jane, Haram Hawght (bur. Helmysley), wid., Apl. 16, 1564.	17		398
July 20, 1565. ———, Margaret, Wistow, widow, Feb. 26, 1564.	17		452
Jan. 24, 1558. ———, Mathewe, Yarum, Jun. 1, 1558.	15	3	216
Jun. 5, 1566. ———, Richard, Stanley (bur. Arkesey), Jan. 2, 1559.	17		551
Jun. 16, 1558. ———, Thomas, priest, Kilburne, late monk of Byland, Apl. 14, 1558.	15	2	334
July 18, 1565. ———, Thomas, Raskell, husbandman, Feb. 15, 1564.	17		451
May 26, 1561. ———, Wilfryde (bur. Cawod), Feb. 13, 1558.	17		49
Oct. 1, 1560. Metcalfe, Abraham, Carleton in Lyndreke (Notts.), July 27, 1560.	16		115
Dec. 15, 1557. ———, Christopher, Fynnynglay (Notts.), Sep. 23, 1557.	15	2	59
Jan. 13, 1558. ———, Sir Edmunde, Newarke (Notts.), priest, Mar. 15, 1557.	15	3	16
Dec. 15, 1557. ———, Margaret, Fynynglay (Notts.), widow, Oct. 22, 1557.	15	2	55
Dec. 22, 1556. Metham, James, Cadby, par. Sprotburghe, gentleman, Aug. 24, 1556.	15	1	82
Nov. 17, 1558. Methelay, Robert (bur. Brotherton), Oct. 6, 1558.	15	3	114
Oct. 3, 1555. Mewborne, Alyson, Ormsbye, widow, Jun. 10, 1555.	14		176
Oct. 13, 1558. Mewdie, William, Wellay (Notts.), May 28, 1558.	15	2	378
July 12, 1558. Mewise, John, Monkefriston, Mar. 1, 1557.	15	2	314
May 13, 1557. Mey, George, Chillwell (bur. Adinborowe, Notts.), Feb. 10, 1556.	15	1	227
May 5, 1558. Meyre, Thomas (bur. Gamulstone, Notts.), 1557.	15	2	333
Apl. 28, 1558. Micheall, Thomas, Hessell, Feb. 3, 4 and 5 Phil. and Mary.	15	2	220
Aug. 5, 1557. Michell, Jenet, Heptonstall, widow, May 28, 1557.	15	2	131
Dec. 22, 1556. ———, John, Shefeld, yeoman, Aug. 3, 1556.	15	1	78
Jun. 19, 1556. ———, Richard, Strinds, par. Heptonstall, Jun. 9, 1556.	15	1	50
Oct. 20, 1558. ———, Thomas, Beverlaie, clerke, Sep. 13, 1558.	15	3	121
Dec. 9, 1557. Michelson, John, senr., Burton Pidsey, Sep. 16, 1556.	15	1	73
Sep. 11, 1565. Middleton, John, Stockeld, par. Spofforthe, esquier, Nov. 21, 1564.	17		461
Feb. 6, 1558. ———, Richard, Rocliffe (bur. Snathe), Jan. 23, 1558.	15	3	264
May 6, 1557. ———, Robert, Polington, par. Snaithe. Sep. 12, 1556.	15	1	242
Oct. 29, 1558. ———, Thomas, Bridlington. parishe clarke, Mar. 25, 1557.	15	2	368
Jun. 11, 1568. ———, Thomas, Hamylton (bur. Braton), yeoman, Dec. 1, 1567.	17		805
Mar. 12, 1556. Midgelay, Richard, Midgeley, par. Hallifax, Dec. 20, 1556.	15	1	200
Apl. 22, 1556. Midgeley, Richard, Midgeley, par. Hallifaxe, July 28, 1555.	15	1	19
May 20, 1558. ———, Richard, Sowerbye, par. Hallyfax, May 1, 1558.	15	2	280
Aug. 20, 1567. Midleton, Christopher, Polligton, par. Snaythe, May 16, 1566.	17		687
Sep. 16, 1558. ———, Edward, Sandhowton (bur. Thriske), Sep. 6, 1558.	15	3	106
Oct. 12, 1558. ———, Francis, Wanselay, par. Selston (Notts.), gent., Aug. 6, 1558.	15	3	14

A.D. 1554 TO 1568.

		Vol.	Pt.	Fol.
Apl. 6, 1554.	Migheleye, Alice, Heddingleye, par. Leedes, widow, Jun. 14, 1553.	14		117
Jun. 7, 1558.	Miles, Henry, Wyntringham, yeoman, Sep. 24, 1557.	15	2	286
Jan. 13, 1558.	Miller, Alice, Tollarton (Notts.), widow, Sep. 11, 1558.	15	3	178
Mar.14, 1560.	Millot, Robert, Bradmeyre, par. Bonney (Notts.), husbn., Nov.20,1560.	16		163
Nov. 8, 1557.	Milner, John, Aghtton, par. Aston, Sep. 27, 1557.	15	2	112
Nov.28, 1558.	———, John, Ketlethorpe, par. Sandall Magna, Oct. 6, 1558.	15	3	136
Jan. 12, 1558.	———, John, Pontefracte, weaver, Nov. 16, 1558.	15	3	173
Oct. 16, 1558.	———, John, Sowghcleffe, par. North Cave, Apl. 4, 1558.	15	2	366
May 13, 1557.	———, William, Edwalton (Notts.), husbandman, Apl. 9, 1557.	15	1	236
Feb. 19, 1557.	——— als. Robert, Christopher, Reidnes (bur. Whytgyfte), Dec. 20, 1557.	15	2	145
Apl. 12, 1559.	Mirchell, Sir Richard, Heptonstall, priest, Feb. 28, 1558.	15	3	337
Mâr. 4, 1562.	Missin, Robert, Hornsey, husbandman, Dec. 10, 1562.	17		150
May 13, 1557.	Mitchell, George, Gonalston (Notts.), husbandman, Mar. 2, 1556.	15	1	223
Oct. 4, 1558.	———, Richard, Newall, par. Ottlay, clothyer, Aug. 21, 1558.	15	3	58
May 13, 1557.	———, William, Gonalston (Notts.), husbandman, Nov. 2, 1556.	15	1	224
Apl. 27, 1558.	Mitchelson, Bryan, Skecklinge, Mar. 20, 1558.	15	2	205
Oct. 2, 1566.	Moberlaye, Isabell, Pontefract, widow, Nov. 11, 1558.	17		580
Oct. 7, 1557.	Modye, William, Gresthorp, par. Marnham (Notts.), Oct. 22, 1556.	15	2	18
Apl. 27, 1558.	Moeslay, Gregory, Preston in Holderness, Apl. 10, 1558.	15	2	206
Dec. 20, 1558.	Mokeson, Elizabeth, Bradfeld, Oct. 5, 1558.	15	3	152
Sep. 18, 1565.	———, John, Penyston, Dec. 26, 1564.	17		466
Dec. 4, 1561.	———, John, Thorgoland, par. Silkeston, July 21, 1560.	17		31
Jan. 14, 1564.	———, Nicholas, Peniston, Jun. 30, 1564.	17		401
Feb. 17, 1557.	Mokesonne, Nycholas, Bradfeld, par. Ecclefeld (bur. Bradfeld), Oct.15, 1557.	15	2	136
May 10, 1567.	Moldson, Francis, Blakestone, co. York (bur. Fynnyngley, Notts.), husbandman, May 22, 1566.	17		652
Mar.13, 1558.	———, George, Bramton, par. Cantlay, Jan. 27, 1558.	15	3	162
May 10, 1567.	———, George, Fynnyngley (Notts.), Nov. 5, 1566.	17		652
Mar.13, 1558.	———, Isabell, Bramton. par. Cantlay, widow, Dec. 16, 1558.	15	3	160
Apl. 5, 1563.	Monke, Henry, Skrethenbecke, husbandman, Dec. 20, 1562.	17		220
Oct. 29, 1554.	———, Robert, Cottam, par. South Leverton (Notts.), Dec. 10, 1553.	14		284
Mar.22, 1558.	Monkehead, Thomas, Mere, par. Fetherston, Aug. 12, 1558.	15	3	292
May 2, 1560.	Monkman, Allan, Hacknes, Dec. 1, 1559.	16		38
Dec. 14, 1557.	Monkson, Elizabeth, Drewton, Oct. 13, 1557.	15	1	359
July 28, 1554.	Monkton, John, Hothome, Oct. 3, 1 Mary.	14		144
Feb. 14, 1558.	Monktone, Robert, Ruffurthe, husbandman, Oct. 1, 1557.	15	3	266
Jan. 14, 1558.	Monnkton, Thomas (bur. Ripon), Oct. 28, 1558.	15	3	190
Apl. 20, 1559.	Mook, Thomas, North Wheatlie (Notts.), Oct. 3, 1558.	15	3	434
May 2, 1560.	Mookeson, Thomas, Brawell, Apl. 21, 1560.	16		48
Feb. 6, 1558.	Moone, Thomas, Muston (bur. Hummanbie), Oct. 13, 1558.	15	3	259
May 5, 1557.	———, William, Billisdaill, Mar. 4, 1557.	15	1	252
May 24, 1563.	Moore, Edmond, Snaithe, cordiner, Jan. 19, 1562.	17		249
Mar. 7, 1559.	———, George, Over Hemelsay, husbandman, Feb. 21, 1559.	16		5
Oct. 6, 1558.	———, John, Burgh Wallis, husbandman, ———, 20, 1558.	15	3	25
Oct. 6, 1557.	———, John, Stirropp, par. Blythe (Notts.), July 9, 1557.	15	2	13
May 2, 1560.	———, Richard, Great Haithfelde, priest, Mar. 6, 1558.	16		49
Apl. 26, 1558.	———, Robert, Haitfeld, webster, Feb. 15, 1557.	15	2	226
Oct. 2, 1556.	———, Steven (bur. Horton in Craven), July 3, 1555.	14		168
Oct. 22, 1557.	———, William, Barnesley, yeoman, July 7, 1557.	15	1	360
Feb. 9, 1557.	———, William, priest (bur. Goxhill), Sep. 26, 1557.	15	2	123
Oct. 5, 1558.	———, William, Metheley, July 28, 1558.	15	3	62
Jan. 27, 1558.	(? Moosse, John, Calverley), Heading with the testator's name missing.	15	3	221
Dec. 10, 1562.	Morall, Henry, Heaton (bur. Seissay), Aug. 12, 1562.	17		131
Mar.17, 1556.	More, Elizabeth, Skipby, Oct. 18, 1556.	15	1	189
Aug.12, 1566.	———, John, Sprotley, husbandman, May 8, 1566.	17		568
July 1, 1558.	———, John, Stappleton (bur. Darrynton), gentleman, Jan. 14, 1558.	15	2	327
May 14, 1558.	———, John, Sulfeild, par. Hackenes, Dec. 1, 1557.	15	2	282
Mar.10, 1563.	———, John, Harton (bur. Bossall), husbandman, Jan. 19, 1563.	17		322
May 18, 1559.	———, Richard, Haywood, par. Burghwalles, Mar. 8, 1558.	15	3	399
Nov.26, 1557.	———, Richard, Rokelay Hall, par. Burghwalles, husbn., Oct. 2, 1557.	15	2	92

		Vol.	Pt.	Fol.
Feb. 28, 1566.	More, Robert, Crathorne, Apl. 15, 1560.	17		617
Mar. 16, 1558.	——, Robert, Over Hemylsey, husbandman, Sep. 30, 1558.	15	3	242
Dec. 2, 1561.	——, Thomas, Yngmanne Logge, par. Horton, Nov. 5, 1560.	17		32
May 10, 1558.	——, William, Crambum, Mar. 18, 155[7-]8.	15	2	282
May 6, 1563.	Morehous, William, Blithe (Notts.), carpenter, Mar. 26, 1563.	17		244
Jun. 20, 1568.	Morehouse, John, Estone, par. Skipton, Apl. 1, 1558.	17		809
Oct. 20, 1561.	————, Rauff, Fulston (bur. [Kirk] Byrton), Mar. 12, 1530.	17		44
Oct. 3, 1566.	————, William, Letheley, Feb. 27, 1565.	17		581
Mar. 12, 1556.	Morehowse, John, the haull, par. Kirkbyrton, Jan. 20, 1555.	15	1	199
Dec. 10, 1562.	Morell, Thomas, Little Thirkilbie, webster, July 16, 1562.	17		132
Apl. 8, 1559.	——, William, Little Thirklebye, webster. Dec. 9, 1558.	15	3	322
Nov. 26, 1558.	Mores, Henry, Thornar, husbandman, Oct. 27, 1558.	15	3	130
Oct. 2, 1567.	——, John, Ulrum (bur. Skipsey), husbandman, July 4, 1567.	17		713
July 5, 1557.	Morewod, Nycolas, Acghton, par. Aston, Jun. 5, 1557.	15	1	303
July 2, 1561.	Moris, Peter, Gemlinge (bur. Foston), Mar. 1, 1561.	17		78
Oct. 7, 1563.	Morland, John, West Retford (Notts.), Mar. 3, 1562.	17		295
Mar. 12, 1557.	Morlande, John, Hamylton (bur. Brayton), carpenter, Jan. 14, 1557.	15	2	126
May 13, 1557.	————, John, Lambcoite in Rottlaie, par. Holme (Notts.), Mar. 25, 1557.	15	1	230
Jan. 24, 1558.	Morlay, George, Sprodbrowghe, Nov. 16, 1558.	15	3	117
May 4, 1558.	Morley, Richard, Stocke Bardolf (Notts.), husbandman, Mar. 8, 1556.	15	2	275
Feb. 15, 1558.	Morrall, Richard, Burton Pidsey, Nov. 13, 1558.	15	3	268
July 17, 1558.	Morrell, Edmonde, Great Thirkilbye, webster, Dec. 26, 1557.	15	2	334
May 28, 1568.	Morres, Agnes, widow of Laur. M., Foston, Nov. 15, 1567.	17		774
Dec. 11, 1566.	——, Elizabeth, Gemlinge (bur. Foston), widow, May 25, 1566.	17		603
Nov. 28, 1558.	——, John, Dringe[how] (bur. Skipsey), husbn., Sep. 17, 1558.	15	3	79
May 28, 1568.	——, Laurance, Foston, Nov. 11, 1567.	17		774
July 12, 1558.	Morrett, Thomas, Sherburne, Apl. 26, 1558.	15	2	314
Oct. 1, 1557.	Morson, Richard, Sandsende, par. Lythe, May 7, 1557.	15	2	36
Oct. 3, 1565.	Morton, Agnes, daur. of Lawr. M., decd., Burton (Pontefract), Apl. 29, 1565.	17		475
May 5, 1558.	Morton, Henry, Austerfeilde, Aug. 25, 1557.	15	2	242
Oct. 10, 1560.	——, Henry, Bradfelde, husbandman, Feb. 1, 1559.	16		125
July 11, 1558.	——, John, Dwaryden, par. Bradfeyld, Apl. 4, 1558.	15	2	321
Apl. 16, 1562.	——, John, Moldeclyff, par. Bradfeld, May 31, 1561.	17		172
Mar. 26, 1565.	——, Lawrance, Mathorne, par. Burton, Feb. ult., 1564.	17		417
July 11, 1558.	——, Margaret, wid. of Jo. M., Dwaryden, par. Bradfeyld, Apl. 8, 1558.	15	2	320
May 18, 1559.	——, Nicholas, Rotherend in Bradfeld, Aug. 27, 1558.	15	3	419
May 11, 1555.	——, Robert, Gillinge (Ridall), Apl. 29, 1555.	14		36
May 9, 1565.	——, Thomas, Bradfeild, Oct. 2, 1563.	17		429
May 3, 1567.	——, William, Shipton, par. Overton, Apl. 16, 1567.	17		653
Mar. 22, 1560.	——, William, Yeddingham, Jun. 11, 1560.	16		176
Mar. 9, 1567.	——, als. Wodd, Elline, Bameforthe, par. Hathersage (co. Derby), Jan. 7, 1566.	17		764
May 4, 1557.	Mortone, Edward, Bradfeld, Oct. 15, 1556.	15	1	280
Aug. 6, 1567.	——, John, Beverley, carryer, Mar. 27, 1567.	17		702
Feb. 6, 1558.	Morwene, Robert, Mustone (bur. Humanbie), Jun. 1, 1558.	15	3	261
Apl. 9, 1567.	Morwyn, Lancelot, Flotinbye (bur. Folton), Nov. 21, 1566.	17		617
Apl. 9, 1567.	Morwyng, Lancelot, Flotmunbie (bur. Folton), Nov. 21, 1566.	17		618
Apl. 22, 1562.	Moryan (Meriman, Act Book), George, Wylforthe (Notts.), Aug. 23, 1561.	17		180
Nov. 5, 1558.	Moscrofte, John, senr. (bur. Neather Popilton), Oct. 19, 1558.	15	3	231
July 24, 1555.	Mose, Thomas, Folton, Feb. 17, 1553.	14		102
Oct. 3, 1554.	Moseley, Thomas, Emsay, par. Skipton in Craven, Sep. 2, 1554.	14		39
Mar. 21, 1564.	Moslay, Thomas, Sheffeld, Aug. 31, 1564.	17		411
Jan. 20, 1557.	Moslaye, John, Norcrofte, par. Cawthorne, yeoman, Aug. 22, 1557.	15	2	68
Jun. 20, 1566.	Mosley, William, Cawthorne, May 8, 1566.	17		559
Jan. 27, 1558.	Mosse, John, Calverlay, Dec. 22, 1558.	15	3	220
Jun. 22, 1568.	——, William, Bevercottes (Notts.), husbandman, May 6, 1568.	17		830
Apl. 6, 1558.	Mosseley, John, Campsall, Feb. 23, 1557.	15	2	186
Apl. 6, 1558.	————, Margaret, Campsall, Mar. 15, 1557.	15	2	182
Mar. 9, 1557.	Moston, Thomas, Gemlinge (bur. Foston), Aug. 12, 1557.	15	2	128
May 5, 1558.	Mote, George, Awkelay (bur. Finyngley, Notts.), Oct. 6, 1557.	15	2	244

A.D. 1554 TO 1568.

		Vol.	Pt.	Fol.
July 9, 1560.	Motherbie, John, Cawicke, par. Snaythe, May 17, 1560.	16		91
Mar.15, 1565.	———, Thomas, Slingsbie, Feb. 6, 1565.	17		502
Aug.20, 1567.	Motherbye, William, senr., Cowyke[par. Snaithe], yeom., May 18, 1566.	17		687
Apl. 28, 1563.	Mountfurth, Christopher, Kylnehirst, par. Rawmershe, esq. Mar.11,1560.	17		232
Nov.20, 1563.	Mourhouse, John, Fosterplace, par. Kirkburton, May 28, 1563.	17		304
Sep. 29, 1563.	Mourton, Richard, Tholme, par. Hampstwat, Feb. 18, 1561.	17		289
Apl. 20, 1558.	Mowbary, William, York, telar, Nov. 6, 1557.	15	2	240
Jan. 12, 1558.	Mowbraie, Rowland, Beverlaie, capper, July 29, 1557.	15	3	196
Apl. 15, 1559.	Mowbray, Thomas (bur. Spoffurth), Apl. 28, 1557.	15	3	352
Oct. 5, 1558.	Mowburne, William, Lethorpe, par. Middlisbrough, husbn., Sep.2,1558.	15	3	69
May 17, 1565.	Mower, Thomas, Lowdham (Notts.), Oct. 27, 1564.	17		440
July 1, 1558.	Mowre, John, Castelforthe, Apl. 11, 1558.	15	2	330
Oct. 1, 1561.	———, Richard, North Cave, Jun. 22, 1561.	17		45
Oct. 29, 1558.	Mowthorpe, Robert (bur. Carnabie), Sep. 26, 1558.	15	3	238
July 20, 1557.	Mowthrope, John, Bucketon (bur. Bemptone), husbn., Apl. 18, 1557.	15	1	315
Oct. 7, 1567.	Moxsone, Henry, Leedes Kirkegaite, singleman, Sep. 26, 1567.	17		730
Oct. 7, 1563.	Moydye, Jennet, wid. of Wm. M., Baweltrye (bur. Austerfeld), Mar. 17, 1562.	17		296
Jun. 14, 1564.	Moyne, John, Grisetrupe (bur. Fylay), Mar. 28, 1564.	17		352
Apl. 2, 1563.	Moyser, Katerin, Ferlington (bur. Sheryhooton), wid., Aug. 16, 1562.	17		217
Mar.24, 1556.	———, James, Came, par. Kilburne, Jan. 13, 1556.	15	1	198
Mar.23, 1560.	Moyses, Gabriell, Hooton (bur. Over Hooton), Jan. 4, 1559.	16		175
Oct. 18, 1558.	———, Gawen, Clyfton by York, husbandman, Mar. 5, 1557.	15	3	95
Jan. 27, 1566.	———, Richard (bur. Huton on Hill), May 3, 1566.	17		610
May 5, 1568.	Muchellsonne, Walter, Fytlenge (bur. Humbleton), Mar. 19, 1567.	17		779
Aug. 2, 1560.	Munbye, John, Riston in Holderness, Apl. 2, 1560.	16		100
May 10, 1559.	Munckman, Thomas, Newby, par. Scawby, Dec. 7, 1558.	15	3	391
Mar.22, 1558.	Muncton, Bettrys (bur. Kellington), Nov. 26, 1558.	15	3	292
Jan. 11, 1557.	Mundie, Robert, Fitlinge (bur. Humbleton), Oct. 28, 1557.	15	2	73
May 14, 1555.	Munkton, Marmaduke, Drewton, par. North Cave, gent., Jun.13,1553.	14		36
Oct. 2, 1567.	Murray, George, Harwod, May 1, 1567.	17		720
Apl. 9, 1557.	———, Hugh, S. Crux, York, Mar. 11, 1556.	15	1	205
Mar. 4, 1558.	Musgrave, Alexander, Tadcaster, Jan. 4, 1558.	15	3	282
Feb.16, 1563.	———, Florence, New Malton, yeoman, Apl. 13, 1563.	17		316
Oct. 1, 1566.	———, Margerie, Lithe, widow, Mar. 28, 1566.	17		584
Jan. 11, 1558.	———, Robert, Wortley, par. Leedes, Nov. 18, 1558.	15	3	170
Oct. 2, 1560.	———, Thomas Wortley, par. Leides, Aug. 14, 1560.	16		113
Sep. 13, 1565.	———, William, Bramley, par. Leedes, July 28, 1565.	17		465
May 13, 1557.	Muston, Nicholas, Cropwell, par. Tithebie (Notts.), Nov. 19, 1556.	15	1	228
Feb.15, 1558.	———, William, Skipsey, Nov. 7, 1558.	15	3	271
Apl. 19, 1559.	Mustyn, Eglemure, Croppwell Buttler, par. Thithbe (Notts.), Jan. 29, 1558.	15	3	372
Nov.27, 1563.	Mvre, William, Shipton, par. Overton, Sep. 10, 1563.	17		305
Feb.14, 1566.	Mycchell, Clemett, Selbie, shomaker, Apl. 7, 1566.	17		613
Jun. 22, 1556.	Mychell, John, Heptonstall, Mar. 7, 1555.	15	1	21
July 16, 1562.	———, John, Heptonstall, Jun. 12, 1562.	17		97
Apl. 19, 1559.	———, John, Lamley (Notts.), husbandman, Nov. 30, 1558.	15	3	353
Oct. 2, 1560.	———, Margret, Heptonstall, July 31, 1560.	16		111
Dec. 3, 1561.	———, Richard, Nayburne, York, Nov. 6, 1561.	17		32
July 17, 1554.	———, Thomas, Brompton, ———, 1554.	14		143
Apl. 14, 1562.	———, Thomas, Heptonstall, Feb. 14, 1561.	17		168
Apl. 12, 1559.	———, William, Stryndes, par. Heptonstall, Jan. 24, 1558.	15	3	338
Mar.16, 1567.	Mychelle, Cudberte, Roclif, par. Snaythe, glover, Feb. 10, 1567.	17		766
Oct. 5, 1564.	Mychill, Dyones, Cawthorne, Dec. 30, 1562.	17		378
July 19, 1563.	Myddilton, Thomas, Whitclif nere Rypon, gentleman, Sep. 18, 1562.	17		266
Aug.16, 1560.	Myddleton, Gilbert, Yarum, glover, Apl. 19, 1560.	16		102
May 20, 1557.	———, Robert, Norton Priorie (bur. Campsall), Apl. 2, 1557.	15	1	264
Oct. 8, 1567.	———, Robert, Wannesley (bur. Selston, Notts.), May 9, 1567.	17		725
Jun. 10, 1567.	———, Thomas, York, chandler. Dec. 14, 1560.	17		661
Mar.20, 1558.	Myddylton, John, Hamylton, par. Brayton, yeoman, Dec. 3, 1558.	15	3	290
Oct. 1, 1561.	———, William, Cranswicke, par. Hooton, husbn., Sep. 8, 1557.	17		45
May 6, 1559.	Mydelton, Robert, Est Runtone (bur. Rudbie), husbn., Dec. 11, 1557.	15	3	382

		Vol.	Pt.	Fol.
May 5, 1568.	Mydelton, Stephen, Pollington, par. Snaithe, Jan. 11, 1567.	17		793
May 10, 1559.	Mydforth, John, Est Sawcoke (Cleveland), yeoman, Aug. 12, 1558.	15	3	384
Apl. 27, 1558.	Mydlebroke, Elsabethe, Carleton (Craven), Nov. 6, 1557.	15	2	199
Sep. 25, 1557.	Mydlebroughe, James, Spofforthe, Aug. 6, 1557.	15	1	348
Jan. 31, 1557.	—— ——, Jennett, Spofforthe, Dec. 19, 1557.	15	2	161
Mar. 1, 1557.	Mydleton, Agnes, Hamylton (bur. Brayton), Oct. 29, 1557.	15	2	170
Oct. 2, 1561.	——, Annes, Hayllton, par. Braton (bur. Selbye), wid., Apl. 6, 1559.	17		46
Mar. 28, 1555.	——, Christopher, Egbroughe (bur. Kellington), Dec. 8, 1553.	14		107
Sep. 21, 1562.	——, Edmond, Fullam (bur. Womersley), Jan. 19, 1557.	17		108
Oct. 1, 1556.	——, George, Wheatley (bur. Kyllington), July 20, 1556.	15	1	142
Nov. 28, 1558.	——, James, Whitlay (bur. Kellington), Sep. 9, 1558.	15	3	135
Apl. 26, 1559.	——, Myles, Northstrete, York, tanner, Apl. 11, 1559.	15	3	310
Oct. 6, 1557.	——, Robert, Gotham (Notts.), gent., Jun. 16, 1557.	15	2	31
Feb. 11, 1557.	——, Symon, Aismonderbye (bur. Ripon), gent., Sep. 25, 1557.	15	2	119
Mar. 1, 1557.	——, William, Hamylton (bur. Brayton), Oct. 2, 1557.	15	2	171
Apl. 26, 1558.	Mydlewod, John, Langrayke, par. Drax, Jan. 1, 1556.	15	2	234
Oct. 29, 1563.	Myears, William, Coppenthorpe, par. Bysshopphill, younger, York, Jan. 12, 1563.	17		298
July 15, 1567.	Myer, Myles, Bishopside (bur. Pathelebrigges), cowper, Feb. 16, 1567.	17		679
July 10, 1561.	Myers, John, Acaster Malbis, Jun. 3, 1561.	17		80
Mar. 7, 1558.	——, John, Acaster Malbis, Sep. 16, 1558.	15	3	283
Apl. 3, 1557.	——, William, Eskrige, Jan. 4, 1556.	15	1	285
Jun. 19, 1566.	Myghcyll, Steven, Holym in Holderness, Dec. 11, 1565.	17		551
Oct. 5, 1558.	Mylborne, Rauf, Riswarpe, par. Whitby, Jun. 1, 1558.	15	3	69
Oct. 5, 1558.	Mylles, John, Dewsburie, Aug. 5, 1558.	15	3	65
Jun. 5, 1561.	——, John, Sawdon, par. Brompton, Jan. 22, 1561.	17		69
May 17, 1565.	——, Thomas, Northe Collingham (Notts.), Oct. 30, 1564.	17		436
Apl. 19, 1559.	Myllet, William, Tythbe (Notts.), Aug. 14, 1558.	15	3	374
July 10, 1566.	Myllington, John, Nottingham, inholder, Apl. 21, 1566.	17		561
Sep. 28, 1560.	——, John, Strelley parke (Notts.), Sep. 3, 1559.	16		109
Jan. 28, 1562.	Myllner, John, Denton (bur. Ottley), Jan. 2, 1562.	17		145
Oct. 2, 1555.	Myllnes, William, Boughton (Notts.), husbandman, Mar. 11, 1554.	14		193
Sep. 11, 1563.	Myllyngton, Mathew, Holme in Spaldingmore, May 30, 1563.	17		204
Apl. 19, 1559.	Mylner, Alys, Edwolton (Notts.), Mar. 30, 1559.	15	3	359
Jan. 17, 1557.	——, Christopher, Galmeton, Oct. 12, 1557.	15	2	63
May 31, 1557.	——, Edmond, Great Houghton, par. Darfelde, husbn., Mar. 25, 1557.	15	1	259
Jun. 4, 1568.	——, Henry, Collom, Sep. 15, 1567.	17		812
Jan. 20, 1557.	——, John, Fyshelake, Oct. 22, 1557.	15	2	68
Mar. 9, 1557.	——, John, Northeland, par. Elande, Feb. 20, 1557.	15	2	130
May 2, 1566.	——, John, Yeadingham, husbandman, Oct. 16, 1565.	17		520
Oct. 5, 1558.	——, Richard, Flasby (bur. Gargrave), Feb. 29, 1557.	15	3	40
Mar. 3, 1562.	——, Richard, Howke, Dec. 20, 1562.	17		148
May 2, 1560.	——, Thomas, Honmanbe, ——, 1559.	16		34
Jun. 4, 1561.	——, William, Byrley, par. Burstall, Apl. 17, 1561.	17		68
Apl. 16, 1567.	——, William, Harteshead, Oct. 21, 1566.	17		629
Apl. 27, 1564.	——, William, Langer (Notts.), husbandman, July 20, 1563.	17		340
Jan. 31, 1564.	——, William, Marske, May 20, 1564.	17		404
May 13, 1568.	——, William, Thorne, Jan. 4, 1567.	17		804
Oct. 1, 1556.	——, William, Wragbie, Jun. 1, 1556.	15	1	121
Mar. 6, 1556.	—— *als.* Robynson, John, Rosington, husbn., Aug. 6, 1556.	15	1	178
Oct. 1, 1562.	Mylnes, Isabell, Mytton, May 9, 1562.	17		111
July 23, 1556.	——, John, Penyston, Nov. 28, 1555.	15	1	37
Dec. 3, 1560.	Mylns, Alis, Leverseige, par. Burstall, Nov. 13, 1559.	16		131
Jan. 5, 1557.	Mylson, John, Skampston, par. Ryllyngton, Nov. 14, 1557.	15	2	72
Jun. 26, 1555.	——, Thomas, Tyrrington, Apl. 24, 1555.	14		256
July 1, 1555.	Myn, Richard, Slyngisbye, May 16, 1555.	14		257
Apl. 28, 1563.	Mynethorpe, William, Mydleton (Ridall), husbandman, Jan. 31, 1562.	17		226
Apl. 19, 1559.	Myntall, William, Selstone (Notts.), Dec. 4, 1558.	15	3	357
Oct. 2, 1560.	Myres, Richard, Gyesleye, ——, 1559.	16		114
May 18, 1559.	Myrfyn, Charles, Hatefeild, husbandman, Mar. 7, 1558.	15	3	418
July 11, 1558.	——, William, Doncaster (bur. Hatefeld), husbn., May 2, 1557.	15	2	305
Oct. 7, 1557.	Mytchell, Amy, Cossoll (bur. Trowell, Notts.), May 4, 1557.	15	2	26

		Vol.	Pt.	Fol.
Apl. 26, 1558.	Mytchell, Christopher, Penyston, Oct. 28, 1556.	15	2	197
May 19, 1559.	———, Thomas, Howke, Oct. 3, 1558.	15	3	424
Oct. 1, 1556.	———, Thomas, Owlerton, par. Sheffeld, arrowhead smythe, May 15, 1556.	15	1	126
Jun. 16, 1564.	———, Thomas, Stomplowe, par. Sheaffeld, Mar. 14, 1563.	17		350
Apl. 16, 1562.	Mytchill, Henry (bur. Thorneton, Craven), Nov. 1, 1561.	17		190
Jun. 4, 1561.	Myton, Annes, Hilton (bur. Rudbye), Sep. 11, 1560.	17		66
May 10, 1565.	———, Richard, Skelton, Nov. 6, 1564.	17		426
Mar. 16, 1562.	Mytton, John, the Hill (bur. Waddington), Nov. 4, 1562.	17		152
Oct. 13, 1558.	Nable, Thomas, Skegbie, par. Marnham (Notts.), Feb. 27, 1557.	15	2	363
Feb. 6, 1558.	Nailler, Lyonell, Waikefeilde, labourer, July 28, 1558.	15	3	258
Jun. 16, 1563.	Naler, Christopher (bur. Ardeslowe), husbandman, May 20, 1563.	17		259
July 11, 1558.	———, Richard, Bentyhowghe, par. Sheffeyld, Apl. 15, 1558.	15	3	318
Jun. 23, 1557.	Nandyke, Thomas, Kirkby Moreshed, gentleman, Feb. 5, 1556.	15	1	295
May 4, 1558.	Naples, William, Shellfurth (Notts.), labourer, Nov. 23, 1557.	15	2	265
Jan. 12, 1558.	Nare, Thomas, North Cave, Nov. 8, 1558.	15	3	195
July 23, 1555.	———, William, curate of Northe Cave, July 12, 1555.	14		243
Apl. 26, 1558.	Navitt, Alison, Sowth Milforth, Aug. 31, 1557.	15	2	238
Apl. 28, 1563.	Nawt, John, East Keswicke, par. Harwood, Apl. 4, 1559.	17		235
Jan. 11, 1558.	Nawte, Henry, Secrofte, Sep. 30, 1558.	15	3	169
Jan. 28, 1561.	———, John (bur. Monckefryston), Nov. 11, 1561.	17		7
Apl. 22, 1562.	Nawton (Registered Naontyll), Richard, Sutton Bonyngton (Notts.), Aug. 8, 1558.	17		178
July 8, 1560.	Nayler, James, Bollinge, par. Bradforthe, Feb. 22, 1559.	16		89
Aug. 7, 1565.	———, Lawrance, Bawtre, Jun. 15, 1564.	17		457
July 1, 1558.	———, Margaret, Westerton, par. Woodkirke, May 25, 1558.	15	2	328
Oct. 5, 1564.	———, Richard, senr., Ossett (bur. Dewysberye), yeom., July 1, 1564.	17		373
Jun. 25, 1563.	———, Thomas, Burstall, Dec. 8, 1555.	17		262
Dec. 13, 1557.	———, William, Woodkyrke, clothier, Oct. 7, 1557.	15	2	54
July 11, 1558.	Nayller, Richard, Sykehouse, par. Fyshelayke, Apl. 23, 1558.	15	2	303
May 4, 1558.	Nede, William, Arnall (Notts.), husbandman, Oct. 16, 1557.	15	2	270
Jun. 4, 1561.	Nelson, Agnes, Monkefriston, widow, Mar. 1, 1561.	17		67
Jun. 27, 1566.	———, Edward, Bainton, husbandman, Mar. 18, 1565.	17		553
Apl. 18, 1567.	———, Henry (bur. Sourbie), Jan. 25, 1566.	17		631
Apl. 6, 1566.	———, John, Eisyngwold, Aug. 3, 1565.	17		509
May 6, 1568.	———, John, Royston, Sep. 23, 1567.	17		771
Nov. 15, 1564.	———, John, Scorbye (bur. Catton), Oct. 26, ——.	17		399
Feb. 22, 1563.	———, Margaret, Baynton, widow, Nov. 25, 1563.	17		317
May 2, 1566.	———, Rauf (bur. Thirske), Apl. 12, 1565.	17		519
Mar. 11, 1558.	———, Richard, Ayrmyn, par. Drax, Dec. 15, 1558.	15	3	159
Oct. 10, 1556.	———, Richard, Wressill, Sep. 6, 1556.	15	1	70
Nov. 17, 1558.	———, Thomas, Monkefriston, Sep. 12, 1558.	15	3	116
Jun. 20, 1562.	———, Thomas, Raskell, Feb. 4, 1561.	17		89
Nov. 5, 1559.	———, William, Skelton (bur. Overton), gent., Feb. 26, 1558.	16		97
Aug. 2, 1563.	——— als. Wayneman, William, Bainton, husbn., July 14, 1563.	17		212
Feb. 25, 1558.	Nelsonn, William, Souyrby (St. Oswold), Dec. 2, 1558.	15	3	279
Apl. 21, 1554.	Nelstrope, William, Huddilston, par. Sherborne, Sep. 8, 1553.	14		61
Jan. 11, 1558.	Nelstroppe, Elizabeth, Huddleston (bur. Shearburne), wid., Nov. 1, 1558.	15	3	172
Jan. 12, 1558.	Nendicke, John, Hullbanke (bur. Cottingham), Dec. 5, 1558.	15	3	197
Aug. 23, 1563.	Nesfelde, William, Snaynton (bur. Bromppeton), Sep. 18, 1558.	17		211
Jan. 11, 1564.	Nesse, Jennet, Skampston, par. Wintringham, widow, Dec. 19, 1564.	17		400
Dec. 22, 1563.	———, John, Scampston, par. Wintringham, Aug. 27, 1563.	17		307
Feb. 6, 1558.	———, John (bur. Snathe), Jan. 10, 1558.	15	3	263
Mar. 1, 1557.	———, William, Amoderbye, Jan. 2, 1557.	15	2	170
May 9, 1565.	Netherwod, Nicholas, Kildweke, Oct. 23, 1564.	17		433
Oct. 1, 1560.	Netleshipp, Richard, Southe Leverton (Notts.), husbn., May 12, 1560.	16		115
Jan. 12, 1565.	Nettleton, Alice, Clifforthe (bur. Bramham), Jan. 6, 1565.	17		494
Mar. 21, 1565.	———, Jane, Huton Cransewicke, widow, Aug. 11, 1559.	17		501
July 12, 1558.	———, Jennet, Leedes, widow, Aug. 1, 1557.	15	2	315
Aug. 14, 1554.	———, John, Ledes, July 19, 1554.	14		147
Dec. 5, 1562.	———, Richard, Bramham, Oct. 24, 1562.	17		131
Aug. 18, 1565.	———, Thomas, Clifforthe (bur. Bramham), husbn., Feb. 27, 1564.	17		456

		Vol.	Pt.	Fol.
Oct. 2, 1567.	Nettleton, Thomas, Thornylleyes, par., Thornyll, gent., Jun. 10, 1567.	17		718
Sep. 10, 1554.	———, William, Almonburye, Mar. 28, 1 Mary.	14		273
Jan. 12, 1558.	Nevell, George, South Skirley (bur. Swyne), Oct. 4, 1558.	15	3	203
Jan. 13, 1558.	Nevill, Robert, Radnell *als.* Ragenhill (Notts.), esq., May 2, 1558.	15	3	206
Jan. 10, 1565.	Nevyll, Alexander, Mattersaie (Notts.), esq., Dec. 19, 1565.	17		493
Nov. 6, 1557.	———, Sir Anthony, Sowth Leverton (Notts.), knight, Aug. 26, 1557.	15	2	107
Feb. 1, 1565.	———, Henry, Cheit (Pontefract), esq., Aug. 10, 1565.	17		497
July 15, 1562.	Newarke, John, Fytlyn, par. Humleton, May 9, ———.	17		95
Apl. 19, 1559.	Newbold, John, Nottingham, Dec. 16, 1558.	15	3	354
Jan. 31, 1558.	Newby, George, York, cordiner, Aug. 26, 1558.	15	3	221
Apl. 27, 1558.	Newbye (Registered Nobe), Robert, Ottringham, Mar. 24, 1558.	15	2	205
Jan. 13, 1558.	Newcom, John, junr., Torwith, par. Blyth, labourer, Nov. 12, 1558.	15	3	184
Jan. 13, 1558.	———, John, Torworth, par. Blyth, husbandman, Oct. 25, 1558.	15	3	189
May 14, 1567.	Newet, Katherine, Spauldington, par. Bubwith, Apl. 21, 1567.	17		645
Dec. 15, 1567.	Newham, Thomas, Borobie (bur. Rousbie), husbn., Nov. 13, 1567.	17		743
May 6, 1557.	Newhouse, Olyver (bur. Gyglesweke), Sep. 25, 1556.	15	1	284
Oct. 5, 1564.	Newsom, Agnes, Fyshelake, July 21, 1564.	17		376
Mar. 10, 1566.	———, John, Fishelaike, husbandman, Dec. 18, 1566.	17		517
Sep. 20, 1557.	Newsome, Christopher, Slingesbie, May 4, 1557.	15	1	334
Nov. 8, 1557.	———, Robert, Barneby on Done, May 20, 1557.	15	2	110
Sep. 16, 1558.	Newson, Richard, Sand Hooton (bur. Thriske), Aug. 14, 1558.	15	3	105
Sep. 12, 1558.	Newstead, Roger, Scarbrughe, July 26, 1558.	15	3	103
May 9, 1558.	Newton, Alis, Watton, Feb. 14, 1557.	15	2	279
Mar. 27, 1566.	———, George, senr., Whitbie, Dec. 19, 1565.	17		507
Oct. 24, 1554.	———, John, Doncastre, cutler, Apl. 19, 1554.	14		309
Dec. 10, 1561.	———, John, Flinton, gentleman, Aug. 11, 1561.	17		29
May 13, 1557.	———, John, Gonalstonne (Notts.), Aug. 26, 1554.	15	1	222
Aug. 13, 1567.	———, John, Lysset, Jun. 1, 1567.	17		688
Oct. 10, 1566.	———, John, Stanford (Notts.). *No date.*	17		592
May 7, 1565.	———, John, Swillington, husbandman, Apl. 8, 1565.	17		443
Apl. 30, 1556.	———, Margaret, Wallesbie (Notts.), widow, Jan. 18, 1555.	15	1	28
May 18, 1559.	———, Myles, Warsope (Notts.), Mar. 1, 1558.	15	3	421
Mar. 10, 1555.	———, Robert, Wallesbie (Notts.), Mar. 10, 1554.	14		224
Apl. 13, 1559.	———, Thomas, Lyssett, husbandman, Nov. 28, 1558.	15	3	346
Jun. 18, 1557.	———, Thomas, Whitby, May 10, 1557.	15	1	293
Nov. 10, 1558.	———, William, Harton (bur. Bossall), husbandman, July 18, 1558.	15	3	233
Oct. 6, 1557.	———, William, Normanton on Sore (Notts.), husbn., May 8, 1557.	15	2	34
Oct. 13, 1558.	———, William, Sowth Muskham (Notts.), husbn., Jan. 13, 1557.	15	2	361
May 15, 1557.	Newtone, John, Doncaster, cutteler, Apl. 19, 1554.	15	1	283
May 6, 1564.	Nichelson, John, Stillingfleite, Jan. 26, 1563.	17		341
Jan. 13, 1558.	Nicholes, Alice, Harwood (Notts.), widow, Sep. 4, 1558.	15	3	19
Apl. 27, 1563.	Nicholson, Robert, Filing, Mar. 24, 1561.	17		225
Dec. 16, 1556.	Nicoll, William, Greatland, par. Eland, Aug. 21, 1556.	15	1	194
Oct. 13, 1558.	Nicolles, William, Harworth (Notts.), husbandman, July 20, 1557.	15	2	375
Aug. 23, 1554.	Nicolson, Anthony, Raskell, July 30, 1554.	14		269
July 12, 1558.	———, Leonard, Hesilwood, Feb. 6, 1557.	15	2	308
July 12, 1558.	———, Robert, Ledston, par. Kepax, Dec. 10, 1557.	15	2	314
Oct. 10, 1560.	———, Roger, York, puther, Apl. 27, 1560.	16		120
Apl. 26, 1559.	———, William, Garthon, yeoman, Sep. 30, 1558.	15	3	311
Apl. 2, 1557.	Nicolsone, Hewe (bur. Topclif), Oct. 18, 1556.	15	1	286
Jun. 5, 1556.	———, John, Ovenden, par. Hallifaxe, Apl. 26, 1556.	15	1	42
Apl. 22, 1556.	———, William, Flambroughe, husbandman, Dec. 1, 1555.	15	1	26
May 2, 1555.	Nicolsonne, Robert, Sawdon, par. Brompton, Oct. 24, 1554.	14		32
Jan. 18, 1558.	Nicott, Richard, Halifax, May 12, 1557.	15	3	20
Jun. 8, 1557.	Nightingaill, William, Ottringham, Mar. 3, 1557.	15	1	269
May 13, 1557.	Nixsone, Edmonde, Eperstone (Notts.), talior, Apl. 6, 1557.	15	1	225
Apl. 27, 1558.	Nobe (Newbye, Act Book), Robert, Ottringham, Mar. 24, 1558.	15	2	205
Oct. 2, 1566.	Noble, Raynold, Wakefeild, inholder, Aug. 1, 1566.	17		579
Jun. 2, 1558.	———, Roger, Langton, husbandman, May 6, 1558.	15	2	288
Apl. 19, 1559.	———, William, Flyntam (Notts.), husbandman, Jun. 7, 1557.	15	3	377
Aug. 12, 1566.	Nodder, Johan, Brearley, par. Felchurche, widow, Mar. 6, 1565.	17		566
Mar. 20, 1558.	———, John, Hymsworth, Aug. 31, 1558.	15	3	247

		Vol.	Pt.	Fol.
May 4, 1557.	Node, Richard, Cantley, Jan. 28, 1556.	15	1	278
Aug. 2, 1560.	Noderie, Roger, Esington, Mar. 3, 1560.	16		99
Jan. 24, 1558.	Noide, Richard, Bassakell, par. Cantlay, Oct. 22, 1558.	15	3	217
Oct. 3, 1554.	Nordyn, Henry, Owtethorne, Apl. 30, 1554.	14		43
May 4, 1558.	Norege, John, Flyntame (Notts.), husbandman, Sep. 12, 1557.	15	2	264
Mar. 11, 1558.	Norffolke, John, Stillingflete, husbandman, Feb. 5, 1558.	15	3	159
May 31, 1557.	Norfolke, Thomas, Hekellton, Apl. 28, 1557. .	15	1	259
Jan. 3, 1558.	Norfooke, John, Woodthorpe, par. Sandall Magna, Aug. 11, 1558.	15	3	34
Jun. 22, 1566.	Norham, William, Lofthous, Dec. 29, 1564.	17		553
Jan. 11, 1557.	Norhame, Thomas, Leven, labourer, Sep. 9, 1557.	15	2	73
Dec. 5, 1558.	Normam, Agnes, Old Malton, widow, Jan. 3, 1557.	15	3	150
May 10, 1559.	Norman, Rauff, Thorntone, par. Cookwold, Mar. 16, 1558.	15	3	387
Dec. 10, 1566.	———, Robert, Hothom, yonge man, May 15, 1566.	17		605
May 2, 1558.	Normavell, Elizabeth, Hugait on Wolde, Feb. 24, 1558.	16		57
Oct. 6, 1558.	———, Thomas, Lepington (bur. Scraingham), gent., Aug. 11, 1558.	15	3	27
Mar. 16, 1567.	———, William, Hull, Nov. 7, 1567.	17		764
Oct. 1, 1556.	Normevell, Hewghe, Derffeld, gentleman, July 4, 1555.	15	1	124
May 25, 1554.	Norram, William, Welberye, Oct. 28, 1553.	14		248
Apl. 19, 1559.	Norreg, Margery, Flyntam (Notts.), widow, Oct. 3, 1558.	15	3	375
May 4, 1558.	North, Richard, Horringham (Notts.), Sep. 16, 1557.	15	2	277
Mar. 21, 1559.	Northe, Alysson, Humbleton, widow, Feb. 12, 1559.	16		17
Apl. 23, 1556.	———, James, Humbleton, ———, 1555.	15	1	24
Aug. 23, 1558.	———, John, York, alderman, July 28, 1558.	15	2	289
July 8, 1557.	———, Marmaduke, Withornwike, husbandman, May 25, 1557.	15	1	305
Mar. 21, 1560.	———, Rauffe, Anlabie, par. Kirke Elley, July 24, 1560.	16		173
Jan. 13, 1558.	———, Richard, Loundham (Notts.), Dec. 15, 1558.	15	3	14
Mar. 30, 1559.	———, Robert, Humbleton, Oct. 25, 1558.	15	3	298
Oct. 12, 1558.	———, Stephan, Loundham (Notts.), husbandman, Sep. 12, 1558.	15	3	13
Nov. 28, 1554.	———, Symon, Anlaby, par. Hessell, Oct. 30, 1554.	14		89
Apl. 13, 1559.	———, Thomas, Anlabye, par. Kirk Ellay, Feb. 16, 1558.	15	3	349
Apl. 24, 1567.	———, Thomas, Est Leeke (Notts.), Nov. 25, 1566.	17		645
May 2, 1566.	Northend, Christopher, Hipperom, par. Halifax, Nov. 17, 1565.	17		535
Apl. 16, 1567.	———, Richard, Dewisberie, clerk, Jun. 21, 1566.	17		624
Sep. 6, 1558.	Northerbie, Robert, York, butcher, Aug. 17, 1558.	15	3	100
May 5, 1557.	Northerby, Elizabeth, York, widow, Dec. 13, 1550.	15	1	210
Oct. 1, 1556.	Northorppe, John, Parkehowse, par. Haitefeld, yeom., Feb. 20, 1555.	15	1	122
Jun. 15, 1566.	Northus, Frauncis, Cottingham, husbandman, Mar. 6, 1565.	17		552
Oct. 1, 1556.	———, George, Cottingham, Aug. 22, 1556.	15	1	138
Mar. 8, 1558.	———, John, Cottyngham, Dec. 18, 1558.	15	3	284
Feb. ult., 1560.	———, Lettys, Ecopp, par. Adle, Dec. 5, 1560.	16		151
Nov. 6, 1554.	———, Margaret, Cotingham, widow, Sep. 7, 1554.	14		292
Mar. 3, 1562.	Norton, George, Skipton, par. Topclif, Dec. 1, 1562.	17		147
Jan. 24, 1558.	———, Jennet (bur. Southe Kirkeby), widow, Feb. 9, 1556.	15	3	120
Nov. 8, 1557.	———, Thomas, Worngbourgh, par. South Kirkeby, Aug. 12, 1557.	15	2	111
Apl. 13, 1559.	Norwod, Edward, Cotingham, Jan 18, 1558.	15	3	350
Apl. 20, 1564.	Norwood, Robert, Newsum (bur. Wrissill), Sep. 27, 1562.	17		326
Apl. 1, 1558.	Nothyngham, Thomas, York, tyler, Feb. 9, 1557.	15	2	240
May 2, 1560.	Nottingham, Jenat, Snaithe, Dec. 15, 1559.	16		54
Apl. 22, 1563.	———, John, Snaith, weaver, Dec. 16, 1562.	17		223
Oct. 1, 1562.	———, William, Burithorpp, Aug. 13, 1562.	17		112
1554.	Notyngham, Robert, Snayth, July 28, 1554.	14		98
Jan. 8, 1566.	Nowell, Alexander, Horton in Craven (bur. Gysburne), gent., Oct. 10, 1561.	17		606
July 19, 1567.	———, Sir Alexander, curate of Kirkburton, May 12, 1567.	17		681
Sep. 6, 1558.	———, Charles, Balne (bur. Snathe), Aug. 5, 1558.	15	3	102
Feb. 24, 1561.	Noydes, William, Southefenton (bur. Kyrke Fenton), Jan. 27, 1561.	17		19
May 5, 1568.	Nunweke, William, Bracewell, Oct. 30, 1567.	17		784
Aug 28, 1561.	Nut, Elizabeth, Stirrop, par. Harworth (Notts.), Apl. 26, 1561.	17		57
Mar. 21, 1560.	Nutshawe, John, Walkinton, husbandman, Jan. 8, 1560.	16		174
Dec. 22, 1556.	Nutt, Thomas, Rawmarshe, Sep. 5, 1556.	15	1	82
Oct. 4, 1565.	Nuttall, William, Nevay (bur. Hemyngbrough), gent., Apl. 20, 1564.	17		485
Mar. 1, 1564.	Nycholl, Richard, Seaton, Jan. 6, 1564.	17		407

		Vol.	Pt.	Fol.
July 10, 1561.	Nycholson, William (bur. Bulmer), May 21, 1561.	17		80
Nov. 10, 1557.	Nycholsonne, Christopher, Swilinton (bur. Brompton), Sep. 17, 1557.	15	2	102
May 18, 1559.	Nyckeson, Bartillmewe, Estretford (Notts.), Oct. 20, 1558.	15	3	420
Dec. 12, 1567.	Nycollson, Bryan, Terington, Aug. 6, 1567.	17		749
Jan. 5, 1557.	———, Richard, Byrdsall, Oct. 25, 1557.	15	2	72
Sep. 30, 1557.	Nycolson, Elizabeth, Skipton, par. Topclyffe, widow, July 25, 1557.	15	1	347
Dec. 3, 1560.	———, John, Preston in Holderness, husbandman, Apl. 21, 1560.	16		132
Apl. 3, 1559.	———, Robert, Bempton, husbandman, Sep. 11, 1558.	15	3	360
Jun. 7, 1560.	———, William, Hummanbye, husbandman, Jan. 2, 1558.	16		77
Oct. 8, 1560.	———, William, York, mylner, Apl. 1, 1558.	16		132
May 16, 1554.	Nyghtscaile, Robert, Cottingham, Mar. 15, 1553.	14		138
May 9, 1563.	Obrege, Robert, Cattwicke, husbandman, Feb. 10, 1562.	17		254
Sep. 21, 1557.	Ode, Robert, Cunsburghe, July 3, 1550.	15	1	354
Apl. 27, 1558.	—, Robert, Sandall Magna, Feb. 8, 1557.	15	2	194
Apl. 6, 1558.	—, Thomas, Cunsburghe, husbandman, Jan. 20, 1557.	15	2	187
Mar. 10, 1555.	Odingyeley, Richard, Eperston (Notts.), gentleman, Aug. 24, 1554.	14		228
Mar. 20, 1558.	Ogden, Adam, North Elmesaull, par. South Kyrkbie, Sep. 20, 1558.	15	3	245
Nov. 3, 1558.	———, John, Newhall, par. Bradford, Aug. 29, 1558.	15	3	155
Feb. 20, 1560.	———, Robert, Wakefeilde, Feb. 1, 1560.	16		148
Jan. 28, 1566.	Oggdayn, Elizabeth, Athewicke by Streite, widow, Nov. 26, 1566.	17		608
May 18, 1559.	Oglay, Isabelle, Barnebrughe, Sep. 29, 1558.	15	3	405
July 23, 1558.	Oglethorpe, Mathew, Thormar [Thorner], gent., Aug. 2, 1552.	15	2	383
Jun. 2, 1558.	Ogram, Robert, Preston, May 2, 1558.	15	2	311
Sep. 26, 1558.	Oke, Alexander, Estwod Hall, par. Rotherham, ———, 1558.	15	3	52
Jun. 30, 1563.	—, William, Rotherham, July 7, ———.	17		261
Sep. 14, 1558.	Okes, John, Burnd, par. Wressell, Apl. 9, 1558.	15	3	107
Oct. 6, 1558.	———, John, Hie Ellers, par. Cantlay, Jan. 8, 1558.	15	3	72
Jun. 25, 1557.	———, Thomas, Catclif, par. Rotherham, Feb. 3, 1556.	15	1	297
Feb. 17, 1558.	———; William, Wresle, Jun. 18, 1558.	15	3	275
May 31, 1565.	Oldefeld, John, Byngley, Feb. 27, 1564.	17		443
Jan. 17, 1560.	Oldefelde, Christopher, senr., Warley, par. Hallyfax, Nov. 19, 1560.	16		141
Oct. 1, 1562.	Oldred, Peter, Barwiecke, par. Skipton, Mar. 12, 1562.	17		110
Oct. 6, 1558.	Oleshed, George, Little Houghton, par. Darfeld, Aug. 16, 1558.	15	3	224
Apl. 23, 1556.	Olfeld, John, Wentworthe, yeoman, Jun. 23, 1555.	15	1	23
Aug. 4, 1558.	Olgnes, John, Hull, couper, Apl. 11, 1558.	15	3	2
Sep. 16, 1564.	Oliver, John, Willerbie, Jan. 23, 1562.	17		363
May 29, 1568.	———, Marjorie, Hull, widow, Feb. 13, 1567.	17		794
Aug. 13, 1562.	———, Richard, Harton (bur. Boossall), husbandman, May 6, 1562.	17		105
Apl. 20, 1559.	———, Thomas, Morton, par. Bubwith, Sep. 7, 1558.	15	3	429
Apl. 20, 1559.	———, William, Mortone, par. Bubworthe, Dec. 14, 1556.	15	3	429
July 2, 1556.	Olrede, John, Bramope, par. Otley, husbandman, Mar. 16, 1555.	15	1	59
Jun. 10, 1562.	———, John, Hingynge Heaton (bur. Dewisbury), Apl. 26, 1562.	17		199
May 9, 1566.	Olyvaunt, William, Hawton (Notts.), husbandman, Nov. 23, 1565.	17		547
Dec. 15, 1557.	Olyver, Elizabeth, Stirropp, par. Blythe (Notts.), wid., Nov. 1, 1557.	15	2	56
Jun. 18, 1557.	———, George, Housom, par. Scrayngham, Jun. 9, 1557.	15	1	293
Aug. 28, 1561.	———, Henry, Northe Morton, par. Babworthe (Notts.), Mar. 26, 1561.	17		58
Oct. 9, 1560.	———, John, Beverlay, Apl. 15, 1560.	16		121
Nov. 6, 1554.	———, John, Maister of the Grammar Schoole, Hull, July 22, 1554.	14		293
Mar. 15, 1560.	———, Robert, Little Morton, par. Babworthe (Notts.), husbn., May 10, 1560.	16		167
Oct. 12, 1558.	Omfray, Laurence, Cotgrave (Notts.), husbandman, Dec. 15, 1557.	15	3	30
Sep. 18, 1564.	———, William, Hull, marchaunt, Sep. 28, 1563.	17		362
Mar. 27, 1565.	Omler, George, Lelley, par. Preston, husbandman, Jun. 28, 1564.	17		418
Aug. 13, 1567.	———, John, Ryall, par. Skeclinge als. Brustwicke, May 29, 1567.	17		689
Dec. 10, 1561.	———, William, Lellaydyke, par. Preston, husbandman, Oct. 25, 1561.	17		28
Apl. 24, 1567.	Orme, William, Clifton (Notts.), gentleman, Feb. 10, 1566.	17		641
Feb. 25, 1558.	Orran (Orray, Act Book), Thomas, Lund, Oct. 31, 1558.	15	3	279
May 31, 1554.	Orray, Robert, Fernidale (bur. Lastingham), Feb. 5, 1550.	14		132
Oct. 11, 1565.	Orton, William, Nottingham, May 4, 1565.	17		469
July 24, 1567.	Osborne, Francis, Ayton, par. Seamer, May 9, 1566.	17		667
Dec. 5, 1554.	———, Richard, Ayton, par. Seamer, Aug. 16, 1554.	14		94
Oct. 1, 1555.	Osclyffe, John, Felkirke, Jun. 4, 1555.	14		70

		Vol.	Pt.	Fol.
Dec. 16, 1557.	Osmonde, Thomas, Wethernsay, Nov. 21, 1557.	15	2	44
Jan. 16, 1558.	Ossyt, Agnes, Snath, widow, Aug. 18, 1558.	15	3	19
Oct. 6,[?1555].	Oston, William, Huntington, Sep. 6, 1555.	14		177
Dec. 22, 1563.	Oswold, Richard, Newton, par. Wintringham, Aug. 11, 1562.	17		307
Nov. 17, 1558.	Otes, Agnes, Bargraunge, par. Ledes, widow, May 28, 1558.	15	3	112
Nov. 17, 1558.	——, Miles, Garfurthe, Sep. 25, 1558.	15	3	112
Apl. 17, 1567.	Otley, William, Sunderlandweeke (bur. Hoton Chranswicke), husbn., Oct. 11, 1566.	17		640
Apl. 19, 1554.	Otterborne, Agnes, Kirkbie Moreshed, Oct. 15, 1553.	14		59
Jun. 11, 1563.	Ottes, Bryan, Thorppe, par. Whitkirke, Oct. 24, 1562.	17		258
Mar. 30, 1559.	——, John, Barnstone, Jan, 12, 1558.	15	3	298
Dec. 5, 1565.	——, Robert, Ferneley (Ainsty), July 24, 7 Eliz.	17		492
Dec. 11, 1566.	Ousten, Robert, Foxholles, husbandman, ——, 1565.	17		604
Mar. 13, 1565.	Overend, Richard, Nether Catton, July 31, 1558.	17		501
No date.	1 Overende, George, Catwayte, yeoman (bur. Sutton on Darwente), Oct. 4, 1554.	14		192
July 12, 1564.	Overton, John, Essyngton in Holderness, yeoman, Dec. 11, 1563.	17		356
Oct. 7, 1557.	Owene, William, Basfourde (Notts.), gentleman, Sep. 5, 1557.	15	2	23
Oct. 1, 1562.	Owerend, Francis, Hamilton (bur. Braton), Aug. 8, 1561.	17		115
Feb. 4, 1561.	Owers, Paulle, Kyrkbye in Cleveland, husbandman, Feb. 23, 1560.	17		13
Mar. 2, 1555.	——, Robert, Staynton in Cleveland, yeoman, Jan. 4, 1555.	15	1	10
Jan. 24, 1558.	Owres, Peter, Stainton in Cleveland, yeoman, Oct. 11, 1558.	15	3	23
Feb. 6, 1558.	Owstane, John, Staxton, par. Willerbie, husbn., Feb. 19, 1558.	15	3	259
Nov. 5, 1564.	Owstebye, Anthony, Etton, husbandman, July 21, 1564.	17		396
Jun. 4, 1568.	Owston, Peter, Sherburne, husbandman, July 5, 1567.	17		813
Apl. 18, 1560.	Oxele, Edmonde, Barnyslay, May 30, 1559.	16		32
May 9, 1566.	Oxenforthe, John, Mathersey (Notts.), Dec. 25, 1565.	17		543
May 5, 1558.	Oxlay, Thomas, Warsope (Notts.), Aug. 24, ——.	15	2	248
Jun. 11, 1555.	Oxle, Edmond, Skelmonthorpe, par. Emley, May 16, 1555.	14		255
July 15, 1561.	——, Edmunde, Clayton, par. Highe Hulland, Mar. 10, 1561.	17		81
Apl. 10, 1555.	Oxley, Henry, Skelmethorp, par. Emleye, Dec. 11, 1554.	14		118
Oct. 5, 1558.	——, William, Osset (bur. Dewsburie), Aug. 26, 1558.	15	3	62
Oct. 5, 1558.	Oxleye, John, Treton, par. Sandall Magna, Apl. 30, 1558.	15	3	63
Oct. 7, 1557.	Oxnarde, John, Clyfton by Newark (Notts.), husbn., July 4, 1557.	15	2	19
May 25, 1554.	Pacoke, Agnes, Whitbye, widow, Jan. 2, 1549.	14		133
Apl. 14, 1559.	——, John, Newton, par. Wyntryngham, Dec. 15, 1558.	15	3	351
Dec. 17, 1557.	——, John, Whytbye, Jan. 29, 1556.	15	2	83
Dec. 3, 1557.	——, William, Sutton, par. Campsall, Oct. 3, 1557.	15	2	49
May 31, 1557.	Padlay, Robert, Fishlaike, husbandman, Jan. 13, 1556.	15	1	262
Oct. 5, 1558.	Page, Michell, Thornton, par. Staneton, yeoman, Sep. 6, 1558.	15	3	67
Jun. 23, 1568.	——, Robert, South Burton, Jun. 8, 1568.	17		828
Nov. 21, 1554.	Paget, Thomas, senr., Wentbrig (bur. Darington), Sep. 18, 1554.	14		91
Dec. 17, 1557.	Pagett, Dorothe, Kirksmeaton, Nov. 23, 1557.	15	2	38
Sep. 11, 1567.	——, John, Wentbridge (bur. Baddisworthe), yeom., Mar. 30, 1567.	17		707
Jan. 24, 1558.	Pagget, Thomas, Wentebrig, par. Badsworth, gent., July 24, 1558.	15	3	217
Jan. 24, 1558.	Paicoke, Thomas, Welburye, husbandman, Mar. 9, 1557.	15	3	215
Oct. 13, 1558.	Paidge, John, South Collingham (Notts.), gentleman, May 10, 1558.	15	2	365
Dec. 17, 1557.	Paige, Lawrance, Tankarslay, Oct. 16, 1557.	15	2	38
Feb. 24, 1559.	——, Rauffe, Crathorne, Nov. 15, 1559.	16		3
Mar. 21, 1559.	Pailer, Richard, Burton Constable (bur. Halsham), yeom., Jan. 14, 1559.	16		16
Dec. 3, 1558.	Paipe, Robert, Flaxton of the more (bur. Bossall), July 18, 15—.	15	3	126
Oct. 16, 1558.	——, Robert, Sowgcliffe, par. North Cave, Apl. 11, 1558.	15	2	344
May 9, 1565.	Pala, Hew, Stamforthe (bur. Gyglesweke), July 29, 1564.	17		435
May 6, 1557.	Palay, Isabell (bur. Gigleswicke), widow, Jan. 9, 1556.	15	1	253
May 13, 1557.	Palmeare, Richard, Hucknall Torckerd (Notts.), husbn., Feb. 20, 1554.	15	1	220
May 13, 1557.	Palmer, Ellen, Hucknal Torckerd (Notts.), widow, Nov. 21, 1556.	15	1	221
Oct. 22, 1558.	——, Henry, Huton Rudbie, husbandman, Sep. 30, 1558.	15	3	235
Sep. 29, 1560.	——, James, Carleton (bur. Whorleton), Jun. 15, 1560.	16		105
Jan. 12, 1557.	——, John, Southe Burton, Nov. 21, 1557.	15	2	78
Sep. 3, 1562.	——, John, Thourne, Jun. 20, 1562.	17		107

1 " Nil valet quia ab intestato decessit."

A.D. 1554 TO 1568.

	Vol.	Pt.	Fol.
Oct. 7, 1561. Palmer, Margaret, Barnnston, par. Langar (Notts.),wid.,Jan.10,1560.	17		41
Mar.14, 1560. ——, Margaret, Nottingham, widow, May 29, 1560.	16		163
Nov.21, 1556. ——, Richard, Goldaill (bur. Snaith), Nov. 1, 3 & 4 Phil. & Mary.	15	1	116
May 9, 1566. ——, Richard, Hocknall Torkerd (Notts.), Dec. 26, 1565.	17		546
July 11, 1558. ——, William, Fosterhowsse, par. Fyshelayke, Mar. 30, 1558.	15	2	318
Dec. 14, 1566. ——, William, Sherburne, labourer, Apl. 12, 1566.	17		604
May 8, 1555. ——, William, senr., Warter, Jun. 9, 1553.	14		193
Jan. 23, 1567. Palmes, Frauncis, Lyndley (bur. Ottley), esq., Aug. 12, 1567.	17		752
May 5, 1559. Pannell, Thomas, Burne (bur. Brayton), Apl. 4, 1559.	15	3	380
May 5, 1559. ——, William, Burne (bur. Brayton), Mar. 16, 1558.	15	3	381
July 1, 1558. Pape, Jenet, Brydlington, widow, Jan. 2, 1557.	15	2	323
May 6, 1557. ——, Robert (bur. Skefflynge), Mar. 21, 1556.	15	1	240
Oct. 10, 1566. Par, John, Toxforthe (Notts.), Feb. 1, 1565.	17		588
Dec.10, 1561. Parait, John, Preston in Holderness, labourer, July 5, 1561.	17		29
Dec.16, 1556. Parishe, Richard, Cobcrofte (bur. Wimbersley), Oct. 3, 1556.	15	1	174
May13, 1557. Parkar, Richard (bur. Carlton in Lindricke, Notts.), Dec. 28, 1556.	15	1	232
Oct. 8, 1567. ——, William, Snenton (Notts.), Dec. 30, 1566.	17		724
May 9, 1565. Parke, Rauff, Arneclif, Aug. 9, 1564.	17		431
Oct. 13, 1558. ——, Thomas, Balderton, (Notts.), Aug. 16, 1558.	15	3	92
Oct. 5, 1564. ——, William, Rednes (bur. Whitgyft), May 5, ——.	17		367
Mar.16, 1556. ——, William, Spofforth, Feb. 20, 1556.	15	1	186
Mar. 6, 1556. Parkell, Christopher (bur. Bothamsall, Notts.), Oct. 20, 1556.	15	1	182
Oct. 8, 1562. Parker, Ales, Carleton (bur. Gedlinge, Notts.), Aug. 20, 1554.	17		123
Oct. 5, 1558. ——, Christopher, Roddam Parke,Craven(bur.Chepyn),Aug.3,1557.	15	3	38
July 26, 1557. ——, Edmonde, Roithewell Haie, Apl. 24, 1557.	15	1	318
Jan. 18, 1558. ——, Geffray, Heptonstall, Aug. 17, 1558.	15	3	211
Jan. 21, 1557. ——, George, Towton, par. Saxton, Oct. 4, 1557.	15	2	156
May 2, 1566. ——, James (bur. Slaidburne), Dec. 31, 1564.	17		529
May 2, 1566. ——, John, Aghton, co. Lanc. (bur. Mytton), husbn., Dec. 23, 1563.	17		530
Oct. 10, 1566. ——, John, Colstonn Bassett (Notts.), husbn., July 18, 1564.	17		593
Apl. 26, 1555. ——, John, Egglesfeld, Feb. 26, 1552.	14		123
May 2, 1560. ——, John, Nafferton, Feb. 18, 1559.	16		37
Sep. 7, 1556. ——, John, Naffreton, husbandman, Aug. 22, 1556.	15	1	64
Apl. 18, 1567. ——, John, Newbye, yeoman, Mar. 3, 1566.	17		638
Oct. 2, 1566. ——, John, Sheffeld, May 1, 1566.	17		577
Apl. 28, 1563. ——, John, Sladburne, Oct. 20, 1562.	17		230
July 15, 1567. ——, John, Stevenparke (bur. Slaidburne), Feb. 15, 1566.	17		676
May 2, 1566. ——, John, Weton, par. Welwicke, Jan. 21, 1566.	17		526
July 15, 1558. ——, Margaret, widow of Edm. P., Rothwell Hagg, Jan. 19, 1557.	15	2	322
Mar.11, 1562. ——, Mathew, Fyshelaike, Feb. 7, 1562.	17		155
Sep. 28, 1557. ——, Nicholas, Woodhouse (bur.Slateburne), die vero Mercurii 8vo, 1556.	15	1	339
Apl. 28, 1563. ——, Robert, Basshallevis, par. Mytton, husbandman, July 10,1562.	17		228
July 15, 1567. ——, Robert, Stevenparke (bur. Slaidburne), Mar. 2, 1566.	17		675
Jun. 28, 1561. ——, Thomas, Bradforthe, (bur. Waddington), Apl. 12, 1561.	17		75
May 4, 1558. ——, William, Carleton, par. Gedling (Notts.), Aug. 6, 1557.	15	2	276
Apl. 18, 1567. ——, William, Kirkdighton, husbandman, Sep. 23, 1566.	17		632
Apl. 12, 1559. ——, William, Rothwell, Aug. 28, 1558.	15	3	338
Oct. 12, 1558. ——, William, Sneynton (bur. S. Mary, Nottingham), Aug.29,1558.	15	3	13
Oct. 12, 1564. Parkes, John, Eperston (Notts.), July 16, 1564.	17		392
Oct. 12, 1564. Parkin, Alexander, Newarke (Notts.), Feb. 19, 1563.	17		388
Apl. 3, 1559. ——, Henry, Rudstonne, husbandman, Aug. 14, 1558.	15	3	316
Jun. 8, 1557. ——, Thomas, Hornsey Burton, Mar. 14, 1557.	15	1	269
May13, 1568. Parkinson, John, Wellaye (Notts.), blacksmythe, Dec. 20, 1567.	17		802
May 5, 1557. ——, Robert, Semer, Oct. 24, 1556.	15	1	248
Oct. 25, 1558. ——, Umfra, Shirofhowton, husbandman, July 21, 1558.	15	3	95
Jun. 8, 1560. Parkyn, Christopher, Owston, Apl. 22, 1560.	16		81
Apl. 26, 1558. ——, Cuthbert, Thornynghirste, par.Fishlaike,tanner,Dec.28,1557.	15	2	195
May 5, 1558. ——, Humfray, Heyton (Notts.), Oct. 12, 1557.	15	2	243
Mar.20, 1558. ——, John, Fyshlake, maryner, Oct. 11, 1558.	15	3	243
Mar.24, 1567.(sic)——, John, Fyshlake, Codicil, Oct. 11, 1558.	15	3	244
Feb. 11, 1565. ——, John, Hornsey in Holderness, Oct. 28, 1565.	17		500

A.D. 1554 TO 1568.

		Vol.	Pt.	Fol.
Mar. 22, 1554.	Parkyn, Marmaduke, Lakenbye, par. Wilton, Sep. 29, 1552.	14		187
Feb. 17, 1557.	——, Richard, Wadeslay, par. Eglesfeld, Nov. 23, 1557.	15	2	139
May 10, 1565.	——, Rauf, Lyverton (Cleveland), Feb. 10, 1564.	17		426
Nov. 21, 1562.	——, Robert, Elvington, labourer, Nov. 13, 1562.	17		128
July 18, 1560.	——, Steven, Rudstone, gressman, May 3, 1560.	16		93
Jun. 16, 1564.	——, Thomas, Gaitshadles, par. Fyshelake, husbn., Mar. 19, 1563.	17		349
Jan. 22, 1557.	——, Thomas, Newe Malton, labourer, July 29, 1557.	15	2	159
Feb. 16, 1556.	——, William, Wadslaye, par. Ecclesfeld, July 17, 1556.	15	1	159
Jun. 6, 1560.	——, William, West Elley (bur. Ellaye), Nov. 18, 1559.	16		76
No date.	Parkyne, James, Worsbroughe Dale, par. Derfeilde, May 12, 1554.	14		83
Feb. 9, 1557.	Parkyng, Agnes, wid. of Thos. P., Hornesey Burton, Jun. 24, 1557.	15	2	120
Sep. 21, 1557.	Parkynson, John, Kyrkesmeaton, Aug. 15, 1557.	15	1	353
Dec. 22, 1556.	——, John, Sykehouse, par. Fishelaike, Oct. 3, 1556.	15	1	85
Jun. 18, 1558.	——, Thomas, Cheryburton, priest, Oct. 18, 1557.	15	2	335
Jan. 11, 1557.	——, Thomas, Stoneferye, par. Sutton, Nov. 3, 1557.	15	2	74
May 9, 1566.	Parlbye, John, Whatton (Notts.), husbandman, Mar. 31, 1564.	17		546
Oct. 6, 1557.	Parnam, Alys [wid. of Robt. P.] Granby (Notts.), Jun. 27, 1557.	15	2	29
Oct. 29, 1554.	Parnell, Robert, Est Markham (Notts.), husbandman, ——, 1554.	14		280
No date.	——, Robert, Est Markham, husbandman, Jun. 17, 1554.	14		51
May 8, 1567.	Parote, Ellinor, Hull, widow, Dec. 27, 1566.	17		649
May 2, 1566.	——, William, Hull, marchaunt, Nov. 29, 1565.	17		537
Mar. 7, 1566.	Parrat, John, Paulflet (bur. Paull), Dec. 31, 1566.	17		514
May 9, 1560.	Parre, Robert, Bradmer, par. Bonnay (Notts.) Apl. 18, 1560.	16		62
July 15, 1561.	——, Thomas, Aughton, par. Aston, Nov. 22, 1560.	17		82
Jun. 21, 1565.	Parsavell, Thomas, Hull, porter, Feb. 17, 1564.	17		447
May 19, 1553.	Parsonnes, Thomas (bur. Eddingleye, Notts.), Oct. 20, 1553.	14		110
Jan. 30, 1566.	Parsonson, George, Arnold, par. Riston, Oct. 2, 1566.	17		609
Oct. 6, 1558.	Partricke, William, Barneby (Doncaster), Mar. 5, 1557.	15	3	224
Jan. 20, 1562.	Patrike, William, Pilley, par. Tankersley, Jun. 1, 1562.	17		143
Aug. 2, 1557.	Paryshe, Thomas, Rymswell (bur. Owtthorne), July 2, 1557.	15	1	323
Apl. 26, 1559.	Pashpus, Robert, Burton Agnes, labourer, Oct. 3, 1558.	15	3	312
Jun. 2, 1558.	Paslew, William, Gaytfurth (bur. Braiton), yeoman. No date.	15	2	287
May 20, 1555.	Paslewe, George (bur. Bingley), Feb. 8, 1554.	14		73
Nov. 24, 1567.	——, Stephen, Rawden (bur. Gyselay), gentleman, Oct. 21, 1567.	17		732
Oct. 1, 1556.	Passeley, John, senr., Maltbie, May 13, 1556.	15	1	124
May 5, 1558.	Passheley, Peter, Weston (Notts.), Oct. 7, 1557.	15	2	259
May 4, 1558.	Patchett, Thomas, Grandebye (Notts.), Oct. 27, 1557.	15	2	266
Dec. 22, 1556.	Pate, William, Barneslay, herdwareman, Aug. 5, 1556.	15	1	86
Sep. 6, 1558.	Paterike, Thomas, Normanton, husbandman, Nov. 9, 1557.	15	3	99
Apl. 27, 1558.	Pathnoo, Thomas, Otterburne (bur. Kyrkeby Mallodaill), Dec. 12, 1557.	15	2	202
Aug. 16, 1561.	Patricke, Robert, Tadcaster, Jun. 13, 1561.	17		62
May 19, 1554.	——, Thomas, Great Leeke (Notts.), husbandman, Aug. 10, 1553.	14		112
Oct. 16, 1558.	Pattanson, James, Etton, husbandman, Apl. 3, 1558.	15	2	344
Jun. 6, 1560.	——, Robert, Chereburton, husbandman, Mar. 8, 1558.	16		72
Nov. 4, 1565.	——, Thomas, Beverley, Jun. 10, 1565.	17		489
Mar. 15, 1562.	Patteson, John, Skynnyngrave (bur. Lafthus), Mar. 1, 1561.	17		164
Jun. 23, 1563.	——, William, Seamer, Dec. 26, 1562.	17		259
Apl. 13, 1562.	Pattryke, Agnes, Lockington, Mar. 19, 1561.	17		165
Mar. 13, 1562.	——, John, Locton (bur. Lockyngton), Mar. 12, 1561.	17		165
May 4, 1558.	Pattyesonne, John, Adbolton (Notts.), Sep. 11, 1557.	15	2	267
Dec. 16, 1557.	Pattynson, James, Waxhame, par. Outthorne, Aug. 12, 1557.	15	2	46
Jan. 15, 1561.	Patyson, Alexander, Dodworthe grene, par. Silkstone, Apl. 13, 1561.	17		26
Nov. 28, 1567.	——, Richard, Seamer, singleman, Apl. 28, 1567.	17		738
Feb. 24, 1561.	Paver, James, Wetherbye, par. Spofforthe, Aug. 20, 1559.	17		16
Dec. 7, 1555.	——, John, Spofforde, Oct. 2, 1555.	14		199
Jun. 4, 1568.	Pawle, Frauncis, Kirkbegrendallithe, Jan. 4, 1566.	17		814
Feb. 17, 1557.	Pawlmer, Lawrance, Haygrene, par. Fyshelayke, Dec. 12, 1557.	15	2	138
Jun. 25, 1568.	Pawmer, John, Preston in Holderness, husbandman, Apl. 4, 1568.	17		809
Feb. 28, 1566.	——, Robert, Carlton (bur. Quorlton), Nov. 4, 1566.	17		616
Oct. 20, 1558.	——, Thomas, Withornsey, Jun. 6, 1558.	15	2	349
Sep. 16, 1555.	Pawson, Nicholas, Ecclisfelde, Aug. 11, 1554.	14		69
Mar. 20, 1558.	——, Nicholas, Farneley (bur. Ottlay), tayler, Aug. 20, 1558.	15	3	290

A.D. 1554 TO 1568.

		Vol.	Pt.	Fol.
May 12, 1555.*	Pawson, Robert, Farneley (bur. Otley), May 27, 1554. 14	194 & 239		
May 18, 1559.	Pawsone, John, Sowcam, par. Warsop (Notts.), Dec. 1, 1558.	15	3	407
Nov. 7, 1565.	Paycocke, Jane, Kirkbie Grendaillith, widow, Aug. 22, 1565.	17		491
May 28, 1562.	Paycoke, Christopher, Mowthrope, par. Kyrkbye Grendalithe, husbn., Oct. 3, 1561.	17		200
Apl. 13, 1559.	———, Henry, Holme in Spaldingmore, Jan. 9, 1558.	15	3	347
Oct. 5, 1564.	———, William, Gowylle (Snaythe). *No date.*	17		367
Feb. 3, 1563.	Paynter, George, Hull, priest, Jan. 1, 1562.	17		315
Sep. 16, 1564.	Payspose, Robert, Stakston, par. Willerbie, Jun. 23, 1562.	17		363
Nov. 29, 1558.	Payteson, John, Skelbroke, Nov. 25, 1557.	15	3	110
Feb. 6, 1558.	Peace, William, Metheley, Aug. 21, 1558.	15	3	256
May 18, 1559.	———, William, Warsop (Notts.), Aug. 25, 1558.	15	3	422
Feb. 15, 1565.	Peacoke, Annas, Kirkebe in Grendallith, Jan. 22, 1565.	17		499
Mar. 4, 1562.	Peacott (Perrytt, Act Bk.), James, Crume (bur. Sledmer), husbn., Sep. 10, 1562.	17		152
July 11, 1561.	Pearcye, Edmund, Welbourne (bur. Kyrkedaill), husbn., Dec. 14, 1560.	17		81
Sep. 26, 1558.	Pearecye, Robert, Haram (bur. Hemselay), husbn., Aug. 21, 1558.	15	3	88
May 5, 1557.	Peares, Beatrix, Thornton (bur. Stainton), widow, Nov. 20, 1555.	15	1	248
Nov. 22, 1563.	———, Katherin, Semer, Jun. 3, 1563.	17		305
Apl. 6, 1558.	Peake, Alys, Kylholme, par. Cantley, widow, Sep. 16, 1557.	15	2	184
Sep. 21, 1557.	———, Richard, Kylholme, par. Cantley, yeoman, Jun. 4, 1557.	15	1	350
May 3, 1565.	Pease, John, Brayton, Apl. 12, 1564.	17		420
Apl. 19, 1566.	———, Richard, York, vintiner, Dec. 14, 1565.	17		511
Feb. 6, 1558.	Pears, John, Cowicke (bur. Snaithe), Sep. 9, 1558.	15	3	263
Sep. 11, 1567.	Pearson, Heughe, the Hilles, par. Sheffeld, Apl. 8, 1567.	17		707
Mar. 15, 1565.	———, Rauf, Swynton (bur. Almonburie), Sep. 10, 1564.	17		502
Oct. 22, 1558.	———, Richard, Egton, Aug. 20, 1558.	15	3	234
Nov. 28, 1567.	———, Richard, Seamer, husbandman, May 5, 1567.	17		738
Apl. 28, 1563.	———, Thomas, (bur. Sowerbie), ———, 1562.	17		239
Apl. 26, 1558.	Pearsone, Barnerd, Felkirke, Dec. 23, 1557.	15	2	225
Nov. 11, 1557.	Pearsonne, John, Brandisburtonne, husbandman, Oct. 8, 1557.	15	2	103
May 9, 1565.	Pearte, Roland, Gryssyngton, par. Lynton, Mar. 1, 1563.	17		434
May 10, 1565.	Peche, Richard, Lyverton (Cleveland), Nov. 10, 1564.	17		426
Apl. 30, 1563.	———, Thomas, Danby, Nov. 28, 1562.	17		218
Apl. 14, 1562.	Peck, Richard, Waikfeld, esq., July 29, 1561.	17		182
Apl. 22, 1562.	Pecke, George, Dalington (bur. Orston, Notts.), Jan. 3, 1561.	17		193
Feb. 17, 1558.	———, John, Wakefelde, esquire, Nov. 2, 1558.	15	3	273
Mar. 6, 1556.	———, Richard, Heyton (Notts.), Dec. 26, 1556.	15	1	178
Oct. 13, 1558.	———, Thomas, Aiton (Hayton, Notts.), Nov. 25, 1557.	15	2	377
Oct. 11, 1565.	———, William, Kneton (Notts.), husbandman, Feb. 20, 1564.	17		471
Apl. 24, 1567.	———, William, Newton (bur. Shelford, Notts.), husbn., Jan. 18, 9 Eliz.	17		644
Jan. 18, 1560.	Pecket, Henry, Tirington, Aug. 2, 1560.	16		140
Apl. 20, 1564.	———, Richard, Teryngton, Nov. 6, 1563.	17		334
July 12, 1558.	———, Robert, Shackleton (bur. Hovyngham), husbn., Nov. 20, 1557.	15	2	324
Dec. 12, 155[?4].	———, William, Appleton in the strete, husbandman, Jun. 8, 1554.	14		96
Jun. 25, 1568.	Peckit, Sir Robert, Haram (bur. Helmsley), Apl. 24, 1567.	17		814
Apl. 14, 1559.	Peerson, Thomas, Skrethenbecke, webster, Feb. 3, 1558.	15	3	351
May 30, 1560.	Pees, Robert, Parplinton, par. Abberffourthe, Mar. 26, 1560.	16		70
Apl. 26, 1558.	Pegham, William, Wentbrigg (bur. Smeton), yeoman, Jan. 9, 1557.	15	2	195
Sep. 15, 1561.	Peicke, Kathrone, Hull, widow, Jun. 3, 1561.	17		54
Oct. 3, 1566.	Peirse, Robert, Sherifhoton, wever, May 10, 1566.	17		579
Jun. 4, 1568.	Peirson, Henry, Birdsall, webster, Aug. 1, 1567.	17		813
Feb. 18, 1556.	———, Richard, Ledes, barbor, Dec. 3, 1555.	15	1	162
Jan. 4, 1557.	———, Thomas, Selbye, shomaker, Aug. 15, 1557.	15	2	76
July 20, 1564.	———, William, Methley, Feb. 5, 1563.	17		358
May 6, 1557.	Peise, Robert, Austhorpe, par. Whitkirke, Dec. 22, 1556.	15	1	214
Jun. 20, 1562.	Pekett, John, Sherifhoton, husbandman, Jan. 12, 1559.	17		89
Jan. 13, 1558.	Pell, Olyver (bur. South Muskham, Notts.), Nov. 20, 1558.	15	3	17
May 1, 1555.	——, William (bur. Kilwicke), Nov. 30, 1554.	14		126
Apl. 28, 1563.	Pennell, John, Doncaster, May 5, 1559.	17		233
Oct. 7, 1563.	———, Thomas, Southe Scarle (Notts.), Sep. 14, 1563.	17		291
May 13, 1568.	———, William, Bawderston (Notts.), husbandman, Jan. 21, 1567.	17		797

A.D. 1554 TO 1568.

Date	Name	Vol.	Pt.	Fol.
Jan. 10, 1557.	Pennocke, Christopher, Ayton (bur. Hewton Bushell), husbandman, Aug. 19, 1557.	15	2	77
Nov.28, 1558.	———, Christopher, Lyssett, par. Befford, Oct. 23, 1558.	15	3	77
Feb. 24, 1559.	———, George, Great Ayton, Nov. 21, 1559.	16		2
Aug.30, 1561.	Pennoke, Laurence, Danby, Mar. 3, 1560.	17		53
Oct. 1, 1562.	Penylburie, John, Basshall, par. Mitton, yeoman, Jun. 20, 1562.	17		111
Mar.17, 1556.	Pepper, Richard, Claxton, par. Bossall, Feb. 22, 1556.	15	1	186
Sep. 13, 1565.	———, Nicholas, Bramley, par. Leedes, July 16, 1565.	17		465
Jun. 22, 1568.	———, William, Bramley, par. Ledes, May 24, 1568.	17		817
Mar.21, 1566.	Percehay, Elizabeth, Ryton, widow, Jan. 20, 1566.	17		518
Aug. 1, 1562.	Peres, John, Semer, carpenter, Apl. 30, 1562.	17		103
Mar. 2, 1555.	———, Lawrance, Thornton in Cleveland (bur. Staynton), husbn., Jan. 25, 1555.	15	1	9
Nov.12, 1558.	———, William, Shipton in Galtres, labr., Aug. 4, 1558 (completed at fol. 73).	15	3	96
May 2, 1555.	Pereseye, Alison, Kirkbimoreshead, widow, Jan. 14, 1554.	14		32
Feb. 4, 1566.	Pereson, Agnes, Huntyngton, widow, Dec. 30, 1566.	17		615
Apl. 20, 1556.	———, Christopher, Selbie, shomaker, Mar. 16, 1555.	15	1	18
Mar.12, 1557.	———, John, Cawoodd, Sep. 28, 1557.	15	2	126
Nov.17, 1558.	———, John (bur. Selby), Nov. 12, 1557.	15	3	112
May 10, 1565.	———, John, Southe Skirlay (bur. Swyne), Apl. 29, 1565.	17		424
Feb. 19, 1554.	———, John, Wilberfosse, husbandman, Sep. 22, 1554.	14		299
Dec. 1, 1558.	———, Richard, Beverlay, Oct. 15, 1558.	15	3	81
May 6, 1559.	———, Robert, par. clarke of Skeltone, Mar. 10, 1558.	15	3	382
Mar. 2, 1555.	———, Roger, Monkefriston, Jan. 24, 1555.	15	1	8
May 18, 1559.	———, Wilfrid, Wethernsey, husbandman, Mar. 26, 1559.	15	3	412
Feb. 10, 1557.	Peresonne, Richard, Lekenfelde, yeoman, Dec. 14, 1557.	15	2	149
July 15, 1567.	Perkenson, Alice (bur. Slaidbourne), widow, Apl. 12, 1567.	17		676
Feb.20, 1558.	Perker, William, South Dalton, labourer, Jan. 30, 1558.	15	3	276
July 12, 1564.	Perkin, Peter, Horneseyburton, husbandman, Oct. 8, 1563.	17		356
Apl. 6, 1568.	Perkingson, Christopher, Wetherbie (bur. Spofforthe), yeom., Apl. 15, 1567.	17		770
Dec. 1, 1558.	Perkinson, James, Skipton in Galtres(bur.Overton),labr.,Oct.10, 1558.	15	3	125
Oct. 6, 1558.	Perkyn, William, Carrecrofte, par. Owston, Aug. 22, 1558.	15	3	45
May 2, 1560.	Perkynson, John, Stanton of the chapell syde (Notts.), husbn., Dec. 5, 1559.	16		39
May 2, 1560.	———, Richard, Staynton (Notts.), husbandman, July 31, 1559.	16		38
Mar. 6, 1556.	Pernell, John, Est Markham (Notts.), Oct. 29, 1556.	15	1	177
May 5, 1558.	———, William, Weston (Notts.), Jun. 16, 1557.	15	2	258
Oct. 7, 1561.	Perpoynt, Robert, Kneton (Notts.), husbandman, Jan. 27, 1560.	17		41
Apl. 27, 1564.	Perpoynte,Sir George, Holme Perpoynte (Notts.), knt.,Mar.19, 6 Eliz.	17		339
Mar. 4, 1562.	Perrytt (Registered Peacott), James, Crume. par. Sledmere, husbn., Sep. 10, 1562.	17		152
Nov. 3, 1561.	Person, Agnes, Hugget, widow, ———, 1561.	17		35
Jan. 12, 1558.	———, Anthony, Molscrofte (bur. Mynster church yard, Beverley), husbandman, Sep. 12, 1558.	15	3	197
Dec. 13, 1555.	———, James, Bradforthe, July 25, 1555.	14		75
Apl. 25, 1559.	———, Jenet, Selby, widow, Mar. 4, 1558.	15	3	364
Nov.28, 1558.	———, John, Holington (bur. Windrike), Sep. 22, 1558.	15	3	76
Sep. 16, 1557.	———, John, Metheley, yeoman, July 27, 1557.	15	1	333
Mar.23, 1557.	———, John, Thorkilby, par. Swyne, Nov. 20, 1557.	15	2	173
July 26, 1557.	———, John, Waldynge Stubes (bur. Womersley), Jun. 11, 1557.	15	1	319
Aug. 2, 1557.	———, Peter, Cammerton, par. Pegerlay (Paul), yeom. (bur. Yslington, Middx.), July 8, 1557.	15	1	321
Feb. 9, 1557.	———, Richard, Outthorne, Nov. 2, 1557.	15	2	122
July 28, 1567.	———, Rouland, Kirkebemoreshed, yeoman, Feb. 9, 1566.	17		668
Nov.25, 1558.	———, Thomas, Huggett, Oct. 28, 1558.	15	3	122
July 26, 1558.	———, Thomas, Thorkylbe, par. Swyne, Feb. 18, 1557.	15	3	9
Oct. 2, 1566.	———, William, Beswicke (bur. Kilnewicke), husbn., Mar. 16, 1565.	17		572
Apl. 10, 1559.	Persons, William, Felkirke, Oct. 16, 1558.	15	3	328
Apl. 26, 1558.	Personson, Christopher, Exthrope, par. Doncaster, Sep. 14, 1553.	15	2	196
Oct. 10, 1560.	———, Thomas, Warmesworthe, par. Doncaster, Aug. 6, 1560.	16		125

A.D. 1554 TO 1568.

		Vol.	Pt.	Fol.
Apl. 16, 1562.	Pert, John, junr., Grysington (Craven), Feb. 8, 1561.	17		189
Aug.27, 1557.	Perte, John, Skaylis, par. Weston, Jun. 9, 1557.	15	2	115
Oct. 12, 1558.	Pervam, William, Grannbie (Notts.), Aug. 31, 1558.	15	2	374
July 1, 1561.	Peryson, Robert, Mathersey (Notts), Mar. 17, 1560.	17		61
Oct. 13, 1565.	Petche, Henry, Grynketh, par. Esyngton, Jun. 7, 1565.	17		475
Apl. 20, 1564.	———, John, Wombleton, par. Kirkedaille, husbn., Oct. 20, 1563.	17		326
Mar. 9, 1557.	———, Rauffe, Caton, Oct. 25, 1557.	15	2	129
Nov.29, 1558.	Petet, Jane, Doncaster, Aug. 27, 1558.	15	3	141
Oct. 3, 1554.	Petie, Robert, Hessylwod (bur. Bolton), Jan. 10, 1553.	14		39
Mar.30, 1559.	Pett, Clemett, Wytton, par. Swyne, Feb. 20, 1558.	15	3	296
Dec. 4, 1557.	Pette, Thomas, Selbye, Nov. 11, 1557.	15	2	50
July 31, 1562.	Petthe (Petche), Richard, Ferndaill, par. Lastingham (bur. Esington), Dec. 21, 1561.	17		98
May 2, 1555.	Pettie, John, Estbie (bur. Skipton), Mar. 25, 1553.	14		25
May 5, 1558.	Pettinger, Alice, Thowrsbie, par. Perlethorpe (Notts.), wid., Oct. 27, 1557.	15	2	251
Feb. 17, 1561.	———, Rauf, Gamston (Notts.), husbandman, May 20, 1559.	17		13
May 19, 1554.	———, Richard, Carlton in Lynricke (Notts.), ———, 1554.	14		108
May 5, 1558.	———, Robert, Gledthorpe (bur. Warsope, Notts). Aug. 23, 1557.	15	2	333
Nov.21, 1558.	Pettye, William, Nottingham, Sep. 7, 1558.	15	3	133
May 5, 1558.	Pettyngar, Margaret, Gledthorpe (bur.Warsope, Notts.), wid., Dec. 4, 1557.	15	2	250
May 13, 1557.	Pettynggar, Edward, Thowrsbye (bur. Parlarthorpe, Notts.), Feb. 15, 1556.	15	2	134
Nov. 6, 1557.	———, George, Warsope (Notts.), Aug. 8, 1557.	15	2	106
July 19, 1557.	Petyngar, Mabell, Carleton in Lyndreke (Notts.), wid., Feb. 15, 1555.	15	1	310
July 9, 1555.	Peyrson, James, Popplewell, par. Kyrstall, Sep. 10, 1554.	14		260
July 19, 1554.	———, Johne, Flaxton, husbandman (bur. Bossall), Jun. 13, 1554.	14		140
Mar.20, 1558.	Peys, John, Garfurth, Oct. 13, 1558.	15	3	251
Oct. 6, 1558.	Philipe, John, Doncaster, glover, Nov. 7, 1557 (completed fol. 25).	15	3	48
Sep. 30, 1557.	Philipp, William, Raskell, par. Esingwold, husbandman, Oct. 4, 1556.	15	1	344
Nov.29, 1557.	Philippe, Grace, Doncaster, widow, Sep. 24, 1558.	15	3	111
Jun. 7, 1557.	———, Roger, Blithe Spittle (Notts.), yeoman, Apl. 13, 1557.	15	1	288
Feb. 16, 1556.	Phillippe, Edward, Shirtclif haull, par. Sheffeld, Mar. 18, 1555.	15	1	158
Oct. 7, 1557.	Philpotte, William, Newarke (Notts.), marchaunte, Mar. 18, 1556.	15	2	1
May 4, 1558.	Phirkyll, Isabell (bur. Colston, Notts.), Sep. 27, 1557.	15	2	271
Apl. 28, 1563.	Phylip, William, Heshilwod (bur. Bolton), Nov. 7, 4 Eliz.	17		227
Jun. 20, 1554.	Phyrkell, Richard, Colston Bassett (Notts.), May 20, 1 & 2 Phil. and Mary.	14		198
May 13, 1565.	Pickard, Christopher, Menstone, par. Ottley, Aug. 20, 1565.	17		503
Mar. 6, 1553.	———, William, Menston, Feb. 26, 1553.	14		16
Apl. 18, 1567.	Pickburne, Jennet, Brodsworthe, Feb. 6, 1566.	17		635
Oct. 22, 1556.	Pickerd, Thomas, Ossett (bur. Dewisbury), July 2, 1556.	15	1	99
Sep. 8, 1561.	Pickerne, Laurence, Scraingham, husbandman, Mar. 10, 3 Eliz.	17		60
Nov.28, 1558.	Pickering, Christopher, Brandisburton, Sep. 19, 1558.	15	3	76
Oct. 6, 1558.	———, Nicholas, Thornethorpe (bur. Berithorpe), Aug. 26, 1558.	15	3	225
Jan. 11, 1557.	Pickeringe, John, Brandsburton, husbandman, Jun. 18, 1557.	15	2	76
Oct. 7, 1557.	———, John, Farrington (Notts.), gentleman, July 1, 1557.	15	2	20
Jun. 4, 1568.	———, John, Kenethorpe, par. Langton, May 26, 1567.	17		811
Aug. 2, 1560.	———, Margaret, Brandisburton, widow, Mar. 4, 1559.	16		99
Oct. 30, 1566.	———, Thomas, Kirkebeunderdaill, husbandman, Oct. 8, 1566.	17		586
Mar.20, 1560.	Pickerynge, Antony, Carleton in Craven, esq., Apl. 19, 1558.	16		170
May 18, 1559.	Pickhaver, William, Mosse, par. Campsall, Nov. 1, 1558.	15	3	396
Oct. 2, 1567.	Pickrin, Christopher, Bilton, Apl. 22, 1567.	17		721
May 4, 1555.	Pigborne, John, Pigborne, par. Brodesworth, Nov. 23, 1554.	14		80
Jan. 13, 1558.	Pigden, Randle, Shireokes, par. Worksope (Notts.), Jan. 4, 1554.	15	3	18
Oct. 22, 1556.	Pighilles, Richard, Haworthe, Oct. 1, 1556.	15	1	101
Oct. 12, 1558.	Pight, John, Edwalton (Notts.), husbandman, Nov. 28, ———.	15	3	31
Jan. 13, 1558.	———, Richard, Plumtre (Notts.), husbandman, Oct. 18, 1558.	15	3	178
May 13, 1557.	Pike, Brian, Colson Basset (Notts.), Nov. 2, 1556.	15	1	221
Apl. 7, 1565.	Pikeringe, Richard, Ridar Parke (Ainsty), Aug. 30, 1564.	17		419
Mar.17, 1556.	———, Robert, Southburton, yeoman, Dec. 2, 1556.	15	1	188

		Vol.	Pt.	Fol.
Jun. 25, 1557.	Pikhauer, Richard, Trumflet, par. Kirke Sandall, Oct. 5, 1556.	15	1	298
Sep. 29, 1563.	Pilkington, Charles, Haystropp (bur. Burton Agnes), husbn., Jun. 29, 1563.	17		276
Nov. 1, 1566.	———, Thomas, Bradley, par. Huddersfeild, Jun. 15, 1565.	17		597
Sep. 29, 1563.	Pilkinton, Alison, Haistrope (bur. Burton Agnes), wid., Aug. 12, 1563.	17		276
May 5, 1568.	———, John, Kirke Heaton, Sep. 28, 1567.	17		790
July 1, 1558.	Pinder, Alis, Wimersleye, Mar. 15, 1558.	15	2	328
Nov.22, 1558.	———, Jenet, wid. of Wilfrid P. (bur. York), Sep. 7, 1558.	15	3	129
Jan. 24, 1558.	———, Richard, senr., Fishelake, July 24, 1558.	15	3	218
Sep. 22, 1558.	———, William, York, priest, July 18, 1558.	15	3	85
Nov.28, 1558.	———, Ysabell, Womerslay, widow, Oct. 1, 1558.	15	3	135
Apl. 26, 1558.	Pinkenay, Margaret, Birken, Oct. 14, 1557.	15	2	236
Jun. 29, 1554.	Pitt, Robert, Rooston, May 12, 1554.	14		141
Oct. 5, 1558.	Place, Thomas, Slaitburne, Mar. 19, 1557.	15	3	60
Dec. 13, 1554.	Plafforde, William, Barkston, par. Sherborne, Oct. 28, 155—.	14		97
Apl. 23, 1563.	Plaskitt, Richard, York, merchaunt, Jun. 17, 1561.	17		222
May 10, 1567.	Plasteray, Bryan, Blakston, co. York (bur. Fynnyngley, Notts.), Jan. 1. 1566.	17		651
May 13, 1557.	Plasterer, William, Fynnyngley (Notts.), July 26, 1557.	15	2	133
Sep. 19, 1555.	Plewman, Henry, York, mylner, Jun. 6, 1555.	14		202
Aug.17, 1555.	Plomptun, John, Ruffurthe, May 13, 1 Mary.	14		204
May 5, 1558.	Plomtree, George, Howbecke, par. Cuckney (Notts.), Nov. 27, 1557.	15	2	241
Oct. 7, 1561.	Plowman, Robert, Horyngham (Notts.), husbn., Jan. 11, 1560.	17		43
Oct. 6, 1557.	Plowright, Harry, Bladmore, par. Bonney (Notts.), Aug. 2, 1557.	15	2	29
Oct. 3, 1558.	Plumbar, Richard, Raskell, Mar. 16, 1553.	15	3	89
Jun. 11, 1555.	Plumber, Robert, Raskell, Aug. ——, 1554.	14		255
Oct. 8, 1556.	Plumland, John, Whattone (Notts.), husbandman, Mar. 29, 1556.	15	1	151
Nov.22, 1558.	Plumpton, William, Roclyfe, Aug. 5, 1558.	15	3	74
Mar. 5, 1567.	Pockelington, Thomas, Adlingflete, Jan. 16, 1567.	17		762
May 23, 1554.	Pocklington, William, Adlingflete, husbandman, Dec. 13, 1553.	14		7
Jan. 25, 1557.	Pocklyngton, Robert, Adlyngflete, Nov. 9, 1557.	15	2	160
Jan. 8, 1563.	Pocoke, Hughe, Sutton, par. Campsall, Nov. 10, 1563.	17		308
Oct. 10, 1556.	Pokelington, Robert, Newsum (bur. Wressell), Sep. 28, 1556.	15	1	155
July 13, 1564.	Poklington, Robert, Willytofte (bur. Bubwithe), Apl. 27, 1564.	17		355
Mar.16, 1557.	———, William, Newsum, par. Wressyll, Oct. 24, 1557.	15	2	152
Apl. 22, 1556.	Pollard, Thomas, Okynshay, par. Byrstall, Dec. 27, 1555.	15	1	21
Oct. 2, 1560.	Pollarde, George, Overwike, par. Burstall, Apl. 16, 1560.	16		111
Jun. 5, 1561.	Polle, William, Sawden, par. Brompton, Jan. 25, 1561.	17		70
July 11, 1558.	Pollerd, Agnes, High Hulland, widow, Nov. 10, 1557.	15	2	302
Jan. 17, 1558.	———, John, York, Sep. 16, 1558.	15	3	210
Apl. 2, 1554.	———, Richard, Highe Holland, July 6, 1553.	14		220
Mar.23, 1557.	———, William, Patrington, Feb. 20, 1557.	15	2	154
Dec. 13, 1557.	Pollerde, William, Wombersley, Oct. 2, 1557.	15	2	53
Jun. 21, 1561.	Polson, Humfray, Forest of Berden (bur. Bolton), May 14, 1561.	17		72
Mar.19, 1562.	Polton, Thomas, Holme Spaldingmore, Dec. 30, 1562.	17		216
May 5, 1558.	Pomfrat, Thomas, Sutton on Trent (Notts.), Sep. 1, 1557.	15	2	255
Oct. 4, 1558.	Pomfret als. Heptonstall, Sir Edward (bur. Leedes), priest, Aug. 3, 1558.	15	3	59
Mar.10, 1556.	Ponderson, William, Beverley, tanner, Dec. 9, 1556.	15	1	184
Oct. 7, 1557.	Poo, William (bur. Horingham, Notts.), July 15, 1557.	15	2	24
Mar. 8, 1559.	Poole, Charles, Fooston, Jan. 11, 1559.	16		6
Mar. 9, 1557.	Pope, Robert, Bridlington, smythe. Nov. 5, 1557.	15	2	128
Nov.28, 1567.	———, Thomas, Bridlington, husbandman, Jun. 3, 1567.	17		738
Jan. 15, 1565.	Popeley, Robert, Wolley Morehouse, gent., Dec. 8, 1558.	17		494
Oct. 2, 1560.	Poplewell, Richard, Over Shitlington, par. Thornehill, Aug. 17, 1560.	16		112
Sep. 13, 1565.	———, Robert, Holbecke, par. Leedes, Jun. 2, 1565.	17		464
Feb. 6, 1558.	———, Thomas, Waikefeld, Sep. 2, 1558.	15	3	255
May 10, 1559.	Porrett, William, Wallesgrave (bur. Scardebroughe), yeoman, Jan.23, 1558.	15	3	389
Dec. 15, 1557.	Porter, Alice, Estmarkeham (Notts.), widow, July 26, 1557.	15	2	57
Mar.19, 1562.	———, Margaret, Newsom, par. Wresill, Dec. 30, 1562.	17		216
Apl. 10, 1559.	———, Richard, Fayramore, par. Felkirke, Nov. 15, 1558.	15	3	325
May 5, 1568.	———, Richard, Ripon, cordiner, Feb. 3, 1567.	17		787

		Vol.	Pt.	Fol.
Mar.13, 1558.	Porter, Richard, Shafton, par. Felkirke, Nov. 12, 1558.	15	3	161
Aug.23, 1557.	———, Robert (bur. S. Morice, Monkgayt, York), Aug. 15, 1557.	15	2	117
May 4, 1558.	———, Thomas, Bingham (Notts.), Oct. 1, 1557.	15	2	212
Oct. 1, 1558.	———, Thomas, Brigham, par. Foston, July 9, 1561.	17		47
Feb. 27, 1566.	———, Thomas, Hewerthe York, husbandman, Aug. 2, 1558.	17		613
May 6, 1563.	———, William, Langwith, par. Cokeney (Notts.), Jan. 10, 1562.	17		243
Aug. 6, 1567.	———, William, Spaldington (bur. Bubwith), yonge man, Apl.1,1567.	17		697
May 13, 1557.	———— als. Samson, Richard, Rampton (Notts.), yeom., Apl. 12, 1557.	15	1	236
May 23, 1565.	Portington, Alice, Clowghton, widow, Dec. 1, 1564.	17		441
May 5, 1557.	Posgaite, Thomas, Gisburne, Oct. 1, 1557.	15	1	243
Oct. 1, 1566.	Posket, Christopher, (bur. Rousbye), Sep. 10, 1566.	17		584
Oct. 1, 1566.	———, John, Rousbie, Apl. 1, 1566.	17		583
Oct. 1, 1566.	———, William, Rousbie, par. Ynderwell, Aug. 14, 1566.	17		584
Feb. 10, 1562.	Poskitt, John, Risewarpe, par. Whitbie, Jan. 4, 1562.	17		146
Apl. 14, 1559.	Possdell, Robert, Knappton (bur. Wyntryngam), Dec. 26, 1559 (sic).	15	3	351
Apl. 5, 1563.	Postell, Isabell, Sherburne, widow, Nov. 26, 1559.	17		220
Oct. 6, 1558.	———, William, Shereburne in Hartfurthlith, husbn., Aug. 15, 1558.	15	3	225
May 6, 1557.	Postgaite, Christopher, Leberston (bur. Fyveley), Jan. 12, 1556.	15	1	246
Apl. 2, 1563.	———, John, Carleyhouse, par. Whitbie, Jan. 28, 1562.	17		218
Apl. 2, 1563.	———, William, Myttanhill, par. Whitbie, Oct. 3, 1560.	17		218
Sep. 2, 1558.	Postgaitte, Henry, Riswipe, par. Whittbye. Aug. 8, 1558.	15	3	97
July 21, 1555.	Postgate, Thomas, Wragbie in Filing, May 31, 1555.	14		209
Apl. 14, 1559.	Postill, Richard, Knapton, par. Wyntringham, Aug. 8, 1558.	15	3	351
Jun. 12, 1557.	Pott, John, Rednys (bur. Whitgifte), ———, 1557.	15	1	292
Mar.27, 1565.	Potter, Rauf, Headon in Holderness, butcher, July 6, 1564.	17		417
Feb. 24, 1563.	———, Stephen, Headon in Holderness, butcher, Apl. 13, 1563.	17		319
Sep. 30, 1556.	———, William, Briestweke (bur. Skeckeling), husbn., May 4, 1556.	15	1	138
Sep. 29, 1563.	Potterton, Thomas, Addingham, ———, 1563.	17		277
Feb. 6, 1558.	Pottes, John, Skarbrought, July 15, 1558.	15	3	262
July 12, 1563.	Poule, John, servant to Wm. Lound, junr., Ledesham, husbn., May 2, 1563.	17		263
Nov. 4, 1558.	Powell, John, Bramham, husbandman, Aug. 10, 1558.	15	3	230
Apl. 22, 1562.	Power, Richard, Pluntrie (Notts.), Jan. 23, 1561.	17		192
Jan. 12, 1558.	Pownswald, Robert, Thorp Brantingham, labourer, Dec. 4, 1558.	15	2	355
Sep. 30, 1563.	Powson als. Lawrance, Thomas, Bishopside, par. Paitleybrigges, Jun. 1, 1563.	17		296
Mar.23, 1560.	Powthrop, William, Catton, par. Topcliffe, Aug. 19, 1560.	16		175
Sep. 3, 1566.	Poyd, John, Gillymore (bur. Kirkbemoreside), Apl. 28, 1566.	17		571
Mar.15, 1560.	Poynton, William, Workesopp (Notts.), Dec. 27, 1560.	16		168
May 4, 1558.	Prate, Godfray, Grete Leake (Notts.) yeoman, Apl. 8, 1557.	15	2	269
Oct. 20, 1558.	Prawde, Henry, Terington May 28, 1558.	15	3	131
Nov.26, 1555.	Preistley, Grace, Sotynland, par. Eland, spinster, Oct. 31, 1555.	14		184
Oct. 1, 1556.	———, Thomas, Wordhend, par. Ecclisfeld, Dec. 7, 1555.	15	1	128
Nov.26, 1557.	Prenc, John, Wallay, Oct. 16, 1557.	15	2	91
Oct. 5, 1558.	Prentice, Waltere, Gisburne, July 12, 1558.	15	3	44
July 19, 1567.	Prestley, Henry, Soyland in Eland, par. Halifaxe, Feb. 25, 1566.	17		682
Sep. 30, 1557.	———, John, Elande, Aug. 25, 1557.	15	1	325
Jun. 5, 1561.	Prestman, Jenet. Thornton in Pikeringlithe, Feb. 11, 1559.	17		69
Nov.14, 1561.	———, John, Harpham, Jun. 6, 1561.	17		34
Apl. 27, 1558.	Preston, Adam, Ayerton (bur. Kyrkebye Malhamdaill), Feb. 8, 1557.	15	2	203
Apl. 27, 1558.	———, Adam, Ayrton (bur. Kirkbye Malhamdayll), Feb. 20, 1558.	15	2	203
Jun. 18, 1557.	———, Alison (bur. Headon), widow, May 9, 1557.	15	1	294
Mar.14, 1559.	———, Christopher, Aerton(bur.Kyrkbye Mowlamdall),Feb, 6,1559.	16		8
Sep. 30, 1556.	———, Christopher, Calton (bur. Kirkby Malhomdaill),May 16,1556.	15	1	173
Mar.14, 1563.	———, Henry, Lakinbie, par. Wilton, Oct. 24, 1563.	17		323
Sep. 28, 1557.	———, Isabell, Kyrkebye Malhamdaill, May 22, 1557.	15	1	339
Nov.29, 1554.	———, Raufe, Gryndall, husbandman, Oct. 14, 1554.	14		91
Apl. 28, 1563.	———, Richard,senr., Aerton(bur.Kirkbe Malhomdall),Jan.30,1562.	17		229
Apl. 6, 1564.	———, Richard, senr., Mearbeke (bur. Gigleswicke), Jan: 6, 1554.	14		153
May 2, 1566.	———, Thomas, son of Rog. P., dec., Airton (bur. Kirkbie Malham), July 1, 1565.	17		530
Apl. 23, 1556.	———, Thomas, Ayrton (bur. Kirkbie Mallhamdaill), Feb. 28, 1555.	15	1	37

		Vol.	Pt.	Fol.
May 9, 1565.	Preston, Thomas, Ayrton, husbn., son of Richard P., deceased (bur. Kirkbye Malhamdaill), Mar. 6, 1564.	17		433
Nov.28, 1567.	———, Thomas, Bridlington, husbandman, May 31, 1567.	17		738
Jun. 20, 1568.	———, Thomas (bur. Gigleswicke), Mar. 3, 1567.	17		809
Mar.21, 1559.	———, Thomas, Owtthorne, Dec. 6, 1559.	16		17
Jun. 10, 1561.	———, Thomas, Patrington, May 11, 1561.	17		70
May 2, 1555.	———, William, Calton (bur. Kirkbie Malhamdale), Mar. 26, 1554.	14		29
Mar.22, 1556.	———, William, Gisburne, Jan. 21, 1556.	15	1	191
May 6, 1557.	Prestone, Arthewre, Wykyngyll, par. Boltone nye Bowland, Oct. 13, 1556.	15	1	284
Apl. 20, 1558.	————, John, Thorne, Apl. 21, 1557.	15	2	217
May 6, 1557.	————, Roger, Airton (bur. Kyrkebie Malhamdaill), Jan. 16, 1556.	15	1	285
Feb. 4, 1561.	Prissicke, Germane, Thormonbye, par. Staneton, yeom., Aug. 9, 1561.	17		12
Apl. 8, 1559.	Priste, Elizabeth (bur. Bransbie), Oct. 16, 1557.	15	3	323
Mar. 7, 1566.	Priston, Annas, Owthorne, May 17, 1566.	17		516
Aug.12, 1566.	———, John, Owthorne, Mar. 24, 1566.	17		569
July 15, 1567.	———, Richard (bur. Gigleswicke), Apl. 23, 1567.	17		679
May 9, 1565.	———, William (bur. Gyglesweke), July 2, 1564.	17		433
Apl. 19, 1564.	Procter, John, Wynterburne (bur. Gargrave), Apl. 11, 1563.	17		331
May 13, 1557.	———, Robert, Bulcoitte (Notts.), husbandman, Feb. 3, 1556.	15	1	227
Apl. 27, 1564.	———, Robert (bur. Thurgerton, Notts.), Dec. 28, 1562.	17		338
Oct. 3, 1554.	Proctor, Richerd, Therkilby in Holderness, yeoman, ———, 1553.	14		44
May 2, 1555.	Proketer, Geffraye, Knowlbanke, par. Burnsall, Jan. 9, 1554.	14		28
Oct. 22, 1560.	Propter, Edmond, Hunmanbie, Sep. 17, 1560.	16		126
Oct. 25, 1558.	Prowde, Margaret, Slingesbie, Aug. 18, 1558.	15	3	236
Jun. 14, 1560.	———, Richard, Colton, par. Hovingham, husbn. Sep. 17, 1559.	16		83
Sep. 30, 1556.	———, Richard, Slyngesby, Aug. 16, 1556.	15	1	67
Sep. 30, 1557.	———, Robert, Terington, Aug. 4, 1557.	15	1	347
Jun. 19, 1554.	———, Thomas, Whenbie, Apl. 16, 1554.	14		12
Jun. 28, 1563.	———, William (bur. Kirkbemysperton), Jun. 16, 1560.	17		260
No date.	Pryde, Robert, parson of Hauxworthe (Notts), July 17, 1554.	14		277
Jan. 22, 1557.	Pryssicke, Jennett, Thormonbye, par. Staynton, wid., Aug. 24, 1557.	15	2	157
Oct. 11, 1563.	Pryston, Jennet, Tokettes, par. Gysburne, May 24, 1563.	17		297
Nov. 9, 1558.	Pulland, William, Goldaile, par. Snaithe, Oct. 26, 1558.	15	3	233
Apl. 20, 1559.	Pullay, Robert, Besingbye, singleman, July 27, 1558.	15	3	305
Apl. 10, 1559.	Pullaye, John (bur. All Hallows, Pavement, York). No date.	15	3	330
1553.	Pullen, Margaret, Goldall, par. Snaythe, widow, Oct. 16, 1553.	14		98
Dec. 16, 1555.	Pulleye, William, York, Dec. 1, 1554.	14		245
May 5, 1568.	Pulleyn, Agnes, Snaythe, widow, May 10, 1567.	17		793
Aug.27, 1557.	———, George, Newhall (bur. S. Mich., Fuston), Jun. 5, 1557.	15	2	114
Apl. 18, 1567.	Pulleyne, Myles, Norwood (bur. Fuyston), Jun. 24, 1566.	17		632
May 9, 1560.	Pulter, William, Newarke (Notts.), Apl. 7, 1560.	16		59
May 6, 1563.	Purser, Thomas, Aslackton (bur. Whatton, Notts.), husbn., Sep.21, 1562.	17		247
Apl. 18, 1567.	Purvey, John, Cawood, Nov. 14, 1566.	17		632
Nov. 6, 1556.	Pyckarde, John, Gysburne, July 12, 1556.	15	1	108
Oct. 8, 1567.	Pycke, Thomas, Colstonbasset (Notts.), husbandman, Jan. 12, 1566.	17		727
Aug.27, 1557.	Pyckerd, George, Burley (bur. Otley), May 10, 1557.	15	2	116
Dec. 1, 1557.	Pyckergyll, Richard, Farnley, par. Ledes, July 23, 1556.	15	2	86
Mar. 2, 1561.	Pyckering, Robert, Hunmanbie, May 7, 1559.	17		1
Dec. 5, 1558.	————, Roger, Tadcaster, husbandman, Nov. 22, 1558.	15	3	150
Sep. 29, 1563.	————, Thomas, Bempton, Feb. 25, 1563.	17		275
Mar. 8, 1562.	Pyckerring, Robert, Newmalton, Jan. 26, 1562.	17		151
Mar.19, 1559.	Pyghell, Richard, Darrington, Feb. 20, 1559.	16		13
May 6, 1563.	Pyghte, Thomas, Nottingham, Apl. 8, 1562.	17		242
Apl. 18, 1567.	Pygott, John, Wathe, husbandman, Jun. 11, 1566.	17		636
Sep. 21, 1557.	———, William, senr., Bolton on Derne, July 27, 1557.	15	1	352
Oct. 6, 1557.	Pyke, Edmond, Colston Bassett, July 19, 1557.	15	2	28
Sep. 15, 1557.	Pykerd, George, Otley, yeoman, Aug. 29, 1557.	15	1	332
May 4, 1558.	Pylkinton, John, Wydmerpoole (Notts.), Nov. 5, 1557.	15	2	210
Oct. 10, 1566.	————, Rauf, Hicklin (Notts.), Jun. 16, 1566.	17		592
No date.	Pynckney, Margaret, Thurnum, par. Burton Agnes, wid., Sep.26,1554.	14		289
Oct. 12, 1564.	Pyndar, John, Tithbe (Notts.), husbandman, Apl. 30, 1564.	17		390

A.D. 1554 TO 1568.

	Vol.	Pt.	Fol.
Jun. 2, 1557. Pynder,Emmott, Lyttle Smeaton, par. Wymberslay,wid., May 3,1557.	15	1	267
Apl. 13, 1557. ———, John, Great Hapton, par. Kirkby Misperton, Dec. 16, 1556.	15	1	207
Oct. 12, 1558. ———, John, Hoveryngham (Notts.), July 13, 1558.	15	3	29
Apl. 7, 1562. ———, John, Maplebek (Notts.), husbandman, Dec. 18, 1561.	17		186
Nov.12, 1556. ———, John, Wymbersley, Aug. 15, 1556.	15	1	111
Jun. 2, 1557. ———, Richard, Nalding (Walding) Stubbes (bur. Womersley), Apl. 1, 1557.	15	1	268
Apl. 20, 1554. ———, Richard, Yorke, glover, Apl. 4, 1554.	14		61
Dec.18, 1557. ———, Wylfryde, York, tapitor, Nov. 3, 1557.	15	2	48
Jun. 15, 1566. ———, William, Everingham, Feb. 9, 1565.	17		552
Oct. 8, 1556. ———, William, Newarke (Notts.), July 7, 1556.	15	1	154
Apl. 29, 1555. ———, William, Wilmersley, husbandman, Mar. 23, 1554.	14		80
May 9, 1560. Pyne, Thomas, Cropwellbyshoppe (Notts.), Aug. 10, 1558.	16		60
Oct. 7, 1557. ———, William, S. Marie's, Nottingham, Jun. 4, 1557.	15	2	24
July 28, 1567. Pyper, John, Slingisbie, May 4, 1567.	17		667
Feb. 18, 1561. ———, William, Bushopmonketon (bur.Ripon),husbn.,Apl.13,15[5]8.	17		10
Apl. 6, 1558. Pytt, Agnes, Carleton, par. Royston, wid. of Rob. P., Jun. 4, 1557.	15	2	187
May 18, 1559. ———, John, junr., Felkirke, Aug. 2, 1556.	15	3	402
May 18, 1559. ———, John, senr., Grymsthorpe (bur. Felkirke), July 23, 1558.	15	3	396
May 9, 1566. Quarnby, Umfrey, alderman of Nottingham, May 22, 1565.	17		545
Nov.29, 1558. Quithe, Jennet, Swinton par. Wathe, Aug. 25, 1558.	15	3	143
Oct. 29, 1558. Quiting (Whitting, Act Book),Robert,Wold Newton(bur.Hunnabie), Jun. 9, 1558.	15	3	239
Nov.12, 1558. Quythause (? Whitehouse), Robert, Bylburghe, husbn., Aug. 27,1558.	15	3	229
Apl. 16, 1567. Qwykupe, Agnes, Castellevington (bur. Kirkelevington),wid.,Mar.10, 1566.	17		630
Mar.29, 1555. Qwyttinge, John, Butterwicke, Nov. 2, 1554.	14		189
Sep. 30, 1562. Rabie, John, Whorlton, July 16, 1562.	17		108
May 4, 1558. Rabye, Thomas, Chilwell (bur. Adenbroughe, Notts.), husbn., Mar. 2, 1557.	15	2	213
July 9, 1563. Race, Richard, East Halsham. Apl. 15, 1563.	17		265
July 17, 1554. Radclif, John, Newland, par. Drax, Apl. 15, 1554.	14		145 & 147
Jun. 22, 1568. Radcliff, Robert, Hunmanbie. *No date.*	17		821
July 18, 1565. Ragell, Richard (bur. Thirske), Sep. 12, 1564.	17		451
Apl. 18, 1567. Ragett, Margaret, Thriske, widow, Nov. 10, 1566.	17		631
Oct. 6, 1558. Ragge, Thomas, Sikehowse, par. Fishelake, Aug. 29, 1558.	15	3	223
July 2, 1567. Raggett, Gabriell, Thirske, Jun. 6, 1567.	17		672
Apl. 19, 1559. Ragysdaile, Henry, Kneton (Notts.), yeoman, Nov. 24, 1558.	15	3	375
Jun. 2, 1562. Rakes, Richard (bur. Cawod), Sep. 8, 1560.	17		198
Mar.20, 1558. ———, Roger, Kelfeild, par. Stillingflete, Nov. 24, 1558.	15	3	248
Apl. 24, 1560. Rakys, Thomas, Lytle Moreby (bur. Styllingflete), May 20, 1559.	16		33
May 28, 1560. Raibye, Thomas, West Cottingwithe, Dec. 2, 1558.	16		70
Nov. 5, 1564. Railton, James, Southdalton, husbandman, Apl. 27, 1564.	17		395
Mar.23, 1557. Ralay, John, Drynge (bur. Skipsey), Jan. 2, 1557.	15	2	173
May 10, 1559. Ramon, William, South Ottrington, husbandman, Feb. 21, 1558.	15	3	386
Oct. 15, 1557. Ramsden, Edwarde, Horbery (bur. Wakefelde), Sep. 10, 1557.	15	1	364
Oct. 2, 1560. ———, George, Heightres in Gretelande, par. Elande, Aug.4,1560.	16		111
May 5, 1568. ———, John, Idle, par. Calverley, Dec. 31, 1567.	17		791
Jun. 10, 1561. Ramsha, Roger, Catwike, smythe, July 26, 1560.	17		70
May 27, 1558. Ramshow, Thomas, Harlethropp(bur. Bubwith), husbn.,Nov.19,1557.	15	2	285
Mar.20, 1558. Ramskar, Nicholas, Stayneborght, par. Sylkstone, Jan. 29, 1558.	15	3	245
Apl. 18, 1560. Ramysden, Thomas, Tankerslay, Sep. 21, 1559.	16		31
Jan. 15, 1566. Ranald *als.* Wright, Robert, Harswill, Dec. 30, 1566.	17		607
May 6, 1560. Ranallde, Richard, Northe Cave, mylner, Dec. 8, 1559.	16		73
Jun. 2, 1558. Ranardson, William, Burtonne (bur. Burton Pydsay), Mar. 6, 1558.	15	2	339
Mar.17, 1556. Rand, Thomas, Wythornwyke, Dec. 25, 1556.	15	1	188
Apl. 19, 1559. Randall, George, Boney (Notts.), July 23, 1558.	15	3	359
Mar.14, 1560. ———, Henry, Bonney (Notts.), husbandman, May 23, 1560.	16		164
May 13, 1557. ———, James, Bonneie (Notts.), Dec. 25, 1556.	15	1	231
Jan. 11, 1558. ———, James, Harton in Bulmer, Dec. 12, 1558.	15	3	169
Feb. 17, 1556. Rane, Robert, Harttoft, par. Myddleton, yeoman, Nov. 20, 1556.	15	1	159
May 6, 1563. Raneall, James, Bonnay (Notts.), Aug. 9, 1562.	17		245

		Vol.	Pt.	Fol.
Mar.20, 1558.	Raner, Bartholomew, Gylderston, par. Batlay, Nov. 3, 1558.	15	3	291
Jun. 3, 1558.	——, John, Athewicke by Streate, Mar. 28, 1558.	15	2	338
Apl. 13, 1559.	Ranes, Elizabeth, dau. of Thomas R., Thorkylby (bur. Swyne), Sep. 22, 1557.	15	3	343
Apl. 20, 1564.	——, Thomas, Marton (bur. Swyne), Jun. 28, 1563.	17		333
Jun. 18, 1557.	Ranke, John, Rymswell, par. Outhorne, Jan. 16, 1556.	15	1	295
Jun. 12, 1567.	Rannson, Katherin. Humbleton, Sep. 4, 1565.	17		664
Feb. 11, 1565.	Ranold, Margaret, Wistow, Feb. 2, 1565.	17		498
Sep. 23, 1564.	———, William, Easyngwold, Jan. 11, 1563.	17		362
Jun. 10, 1557.	Raper, George, Lokington, husbandman, Mar. 16, 1556.	15	1	273
Oct. 27, 1554.	——, Thomas, Thornebarghe, par. S. Kilvyngton, Sep. 15, 1554.	14		48
Jan. 12, 1558.	——, Thomas, chauntre preest of Thriske, Sep. 5, 1558.	15	3	176
Apl. 6, 1566.	Rapper, Robert (bur. Cookeswold), Jan. 4, 1565.	17		510
May 4, 1555.	Rasbie, James, Smeton, ——, 1554.	14		79
Aug.20, 1567.	Raskall, Myles, Cowike, par. Snaithe, Feb. 23, 1566.	17		687
Aug.18, 1562.	Ratchester, Gylbert, Hackenes, Jun. 14, 1562.	17		107
Jun. 3, 1554.	Ratclife, Johne, Askwith, par. Weston, Jan. 8, 1553.	14		139
Feb. 10, 1557.	Ratclyffe, Isabell, wife of Rog. R., Threshefelde, gent., (bur. Lynton), Nov. 28, 1557.	15	2	162
May 2, 1560.	Ratlyffe, Beatryxe, Hollme, widow, Mar. 11, 1559.	16		50
Sep. 2, 1563.	———, Thomas, Aubroughe in Holderness, yeoman. *No date.*	17		205
Jun. 22, 1568.	Rattell, Thomas, Speton, Feb. 27, 1567.	17		826
July 24, 1564.	Ratyll, Robert, Leven in Holderness, Dec. 12, 1563.	17		359
Sep. 30, 1556.	Rauclif, Hughe, Bayly in Aghton, par. Mytton (Lancs.), husbn., May 7, 1552.	15	1	174
May 10, 1554.	Raulinge, William, Pontefracte, cordinar, Dec. 2, 1 Mary.	14		136
Sep. 2, 1563.	Raven, Jenet wid. of Thos. R., Owstweke (bur. Gerton), Apl. 6, 1563.	17		205
Jun. 10, 1560.	——, Jennat, Owstwicke, par. Rosse, May 3, 1560.	16		82
May 18, 1559.	——, Nicholas, Owstwyke (bur. Roose), July 21, 1558.	15	3	411
Sep. 30, 1557.	——, Thomas, Burton Pidsey, July 26, ——.	15	1	341
Jun. 21, 1565.	——, Thomas, Fyshelake, Apl. 2, 1565.	17		447
No date.	——, Thomas, North Wheatley (Notts.), Oct. 11, 1555.	14		20
Sep. 30, 1563.	——, Thomas, Owstweike (bur. Garton), husbn., Dec. 31, 1562.	17		273
Jun. 10, 1560.	Ravyn, William, Owstwicke, par. Garton, May 8, 1560.	16		82
Oct. 19, 1555.	Rawdon, Richard, Bagbie, par. Kirkbie Knolles, Nov. 8, 1554.	14		178
July 29, 1560.	Rawe, John, Beswike, par. Kylnewike, husbandman, Dec. 10, 1559.	16		98
May 5, 1568.	Rawghe, Robert, Lockington, Sep. 25, 1567.	17		778
July 17, 1565.	Rawlinge, William, Lelley, par. Preston, husbn., May 13, 1565.	17		452
Dec.22, 1556.	Rawlyn, Agnes, Newton, par. Sprotburgh, Oct. 27, 1556.	15	1	79
Dec.22, 1556.	———, William, Newton, par. Sprotburgh, Aug. 20, 1556.	15	1	79
Jan. 28, 1561.	Rawlyng, Robert, Monkefriston, carpenter, Oct. 30, 1561.	17		8
May 21, 1560.	Rawlyngson, Thomas, Thorneton (Ridall), Sep. 15, 1559.	16		66
Oct. 10, 1560.	Rawlynson, John, Rotherham, Nov. 23, 1559.	16		126
Jan. 5, 1557.	Rawse, Robert, Estheslerton, Nov. 10, 1557.	15	2	72
Aug. 9, 1565.	Rawson, Agnes, Wistowe (bur. near late husb., Wm. R.), July 2, 1565.	17		456
Apl. 27, 1558.	———, Alexander, West Morton, par. Bingley, Feb. 7, 1557.	15	2	203
Jan. 22, 1557.	———, Henry, Hawnbye, Dec. 18, 1557.	15	2	158
Nov.17, 1558.	———, John, Wistow, wid., ——, 1558.	15	3	115
Oct. 5, 1558.	———, Richard, Easte Hardwicke (bur. Pontefracte), husbandman, Aug. 20, 3 and 4, Phil. and Mary.	15	3	65
Mar.20, 1560.	———, Richard, Thwaytes, par. Kighley, Dec. 2, 1560.	16		171
July 9, 1563.	———, Robert, Halsham, Apl. 11, 1563.	17		264
Feb. 24, 1563.	———, Walter, Preston in Holderness, husbandman, Sep. 29, 1563.	17		318
Oct. 1, 1556.	Rawsone, Hughe, Rotherham, Mar. 20, 1554.	15	1	129
Apl. 24, 1559.	Ray, Hugh, New Malton, corrier, Sep. 1, 1558.	15	3	310
Nov.25, 1561.	—, John, Spaldington, Oct. 22, 1561.	17		33
Apl. 27, 1559.	--, Margere, Thorpe, par. Braton, widow, Jun. 2, 1558.	15	3	362
May 2, 1560.	—, Margaret, Hunmanbe, ——, 1559.	16		35
Mar.13, 1556.	—, Symon, Thorpe Willobye, par. Braton, Feb. 8, 1556.	15	1	184
Dec. 4, 1557.	—, William, Thorpe (bur. Brayton), husbandman, Nov. 15, 1557.	15	2	50
July 21, 1558.	Raybye, John, Bryghton, par. Bubwyth, husbandman, Jun. 19, 1558.	15	2	293
Mar.21, 1559.	Rayclyffe, John, Hollome, Feb. 13, 1559.	16		16

A.D. 1554 TO 1568.

		Vol.	Pt.	Fol.
Apl. 17, 1554.	Raye, Henrie, Bubwith, husbandman, Nov. 22, 1553.	14		59
Mar.18, 1566.	Rayenton, Richard, Newton on Darwent, labourer, Jan. 2, 1566.	17		512
Jun. 18, 1557.	Raynald, William, Pattrington, cowper, Apl. 22, 1557.	15	1	294
May 4, 1555.	Raynalde, Sir John, clerke (bur. Hemesworth), Dec. 29, 1554.	14		80
Jun. 18, 1557.	Rayne, George, Hardtofte, par. Mvdleton, husbandman, May 6, 1557.	15	1	293
Jan. 20, 1558.	——, George, Hartoft, par. Mydleton, Aug. 16, 1558.	15	3	212
Sep. 21, 1557.	Raynee, Alys, Darfelde, Aug. 9, 1557.	15	1	354
Sep. 9, 1561.	Rayneforthe, Henry, Halifax, Apl. 20, 1561.	17		51
Feb. 6, 1558.	Rayner, Charles, Harthead, Oct. 6, 1558.	15	3	256
July 19, 1555.	——, Elizabeth, Birstall, Aug. 24, 1553.	14		242
Jun. 20, 1568.	——, Elizabeth, wid. of Thomas R., Norland (bur. Eland), Feb. 12, 1567.	17		827
Sep. 9, 1561.	——, John, Harperroyde, par. Ealand, July 31, 1561.	17		51
May 15, 1557.	——, Leonard, Barnabie on Done, Feb. 5, 1556.	15	1	282
Jun. 30, 1563.	——, Nicholas, Thorne, Apl. 1, 1563.	17		260
July 9, 1560.	——, Thomas, Cowike, par. Snaythe, Mar. 5, 1559.	16		91
May 5, 1568.	——, Thomas, Norland in Eland, Jan. 9, 1567.	17		792
Dec. 23, 1566.	——, Thomas, Norland. par. Eland, mylner, Dec. 16, 1566.	17		606
Jan. 7, 1552.	——, Umfray, Batley, husbandman, Aug. 1, 1562.	17		139
Oct. 2, 1567.	——, Wilfryde, Morley, par. Batley, July 7, 1567.	17		719
May 2, 1560.	——, William, Apletreweke, par. Burnstall, Apl. 3, 1560.	16		43
Oct. 8, 1555.	——, William, Wistowe, All Hallowes, Oct. 1, 1554.	14		199
Mar.31, 1558.	Raynerde, Richard (bur. Bulmer), Dec. 5, 1557.	15	2	177
Sep. 14, 1565.	Raynes, William, West Newton, par. Aldbroughe, July 10, 1565.	17		465
Apl. 1, 1557.	Raynfurth, Robert, Langracke, par. Drax, Dec. 16, 1556.	15	1	286
May 18, 1559.	Raynold, John, senr. (bur. Felkirke), Oct. 16, 1558.	15	3	416
Sep. 13, 1565.	——, John, Wistowe, Feb. 18, 1565.	17		464
Jun. 27, 1564.	Raynolde, George, Hartonne (bur. Bossall), husbn., Jun. 16, 1564.	17		353
Feb. 15, 1558.	Rayns, Roger, Roosse in Holderness, Nov. 12, 1558.	15	3	268
Feb. 6, 1558.	Raynye, John als. Jenkyn, junr. Arksey, Jan. 8, 1558.	15	3	254
July 1, 1562.	——, Thomas, senr. Bentley, par. Arkesey, Jun. 14, 1560.	17		93
Feb. 6, 1558.	Rayse, John, Mustone (bur. Humanbie), Oct. 20, 1558.	15	3	262
Sep. 29, 1563.	Raystrick, Thomas, Yeadon (bur. Gyselay), Apl. 17, 1563.	17		289
Sep. 30, 1563.	Rayven, Thomas, Elstanwicke, Oct. 7, 1562.	17		273
Apl. 8, 1559.	Read, John, Great Thirklebie, Jan. 25, 1558.	15	3	322
Aug.27, 1567.	——, John, Pockley (bur. Helmeslay), Jun. 19, 1567.	17		696
Oct. 4, 1565.	——, Richard, Binnington, par. Willerbe, May 12, 1565.	17		486
Apl. 28, 1558.	——, Thomas, Yaram, Feb. 19, 1557.	15	2	232
Nov. 6, 1562.	Readburne, Emmote, Beswick (bur. Kilnewicke), wid., Aug. 8, 1562.	17		127
Apl. 20, 1559.	Reade, Edward, North Collingham (Notts.), Jan. 7, 1558.	15	3	371
Dec. 11, 1566.	——, Margaret, Speitilehouse, par. Willerbye, wid., Feb. 16, 1565.	17		601
Mar. 4, 1562.	——, Richard, Besingbie, smythe, Jan. 1, 1562.	17		153
July 2, 1567.	Readhead, Thomas, New Malton, yeoman, Aug. 14, 1566.	17		666
May 10, 1559.	Readhede, Margaret, Scawbye, Nov. 12, 1558.	15	3	388
Jun. 20, 1566.	Readshawe, William, Houerley (Act Book, Overley)(? Everley), (bur. Hacknes), Feb. 9, 1564.	17		556
Jun. 10, 1556.	Realme, John, Marston near York, May 1, 1556.	15	1	57
Oct. 3, 1564.	Reame, Agnes, wid. of John R., Leedes, clothier, Jan. 8, 1562.	17		365
Apl. 22, 1562.	Reckles, Richard, Chillwell (bur.Addenboroughe,Notts.),Oct.16,1557.	17		177
Apl. 22, 1562.	——, Robert, Chylwell, par. Adenbor (Notts.), Mar. 7, 1561.	17		176
Feb. 5, 1567.	Red, Thomas, Levisham, husbandman, Apl. 25, 1565.	17		758
Nov. 2, 1558.	Redar, Jenett, Swillington, widow, Apl. 13, 1558.	15	3	130
Dec. 1, 1558.	Rede, John, Cottyngham, Oct. 12, 1558.	15	3	145
No date.	——, Robert, Newarke (Notts.), Sep. 27, 1555.	14		16
July 31, 1562.	——, William, Levesham, husbandman, Nov. 13, 1560.	17		100
Dec. 22, 1556.	Reder, Thomas, junr., Thorne, July 20, 1556.	15	1	76
May 6, 1557.	——, William, Swillington, Jan. 22, 1556.	15	1	214
Oct. 22, 1556.	Rediall, Robert, Hessle, par. Wragbie, husbandman, Sep. 30, 1556.	15	1	99
July 23, 1560.	Redlaye, Christopher, Lokynton, yeoman, Jun. 19, 1560.	16		95
Mar.29, 1568.	Redley, Thomas, Addle, wheilewright, Sep. 7, 1567.	17		767
Jun. 21, 1561.	Redman, Arthure, Holcottes (bur. Arneclyff), Apl. 20, 1561.	17		72
Apl. 16, 1562.	——, Richard, Hoton Robert, Aug. 7, 1561.	17		171

A.D. 1554 TO 1568.

		Vol.	Pt.	Fol.
Feb. 19, 1557.	Redshaw, William, Wytgyfte, Nov. 6, 1557.	15	2	146
Jun. 15, 1560.	Redshey, Henry, Brakanthwayte (bur. Kyrkebeouerblouse), husbn., May 13, 1559.	16		85
May 18, 1559.	Reed, Steven, Haitfeild, husbandman, Mar. 19, 1558.	15	3	411
May 5, 1564.	——, William, Snaythe, Feb. 16, 5 Eliz.	17		342
Mar. 10, 1556.	Reede, William, Bulam (bur. Helmyslay), Jan. 14, 1556.	15	1	200
Sep. 16, 1564.	Reid, Harrye, Benyngton, par. Willerbie, May 24, 1564.	17		362
Mar. 2, 1561.	——, Robert, Hunmanbie, Jan. 9, 1561.	17		1
Dec. 11, 1566.	Reidman, Thomas, Harwooddaill, par. Hacknes, bachelar, May 11, 1566.	17		604
Dec. 18, 1556.	Remington, Agnes, Stanforthebrigges (bur. Catton), wid., Sep. 22, 1556.	15	1	172
Sep. 23, 1561.	Remyngton, George, Garrabie, gentleman, July 29, 1561.	17		26
Sep. 23, 1556.	R[e]myngton, Richard, Stanforthe Brigges, Sep. 10, 1556.	15	1	66
Apl. 20, 1559.	Reper (Roper, Act Book), Christopher, Sutton on Lund (Notts.), Oct. 10, 1558.	15	3	367
Jun. 7, 1560.	Replay, John, Grandismore, par. Burton Agnes, husbn., Apl. 30, 1559.	16		78
Oct. 7, 1563.	Rest, Florence, Herstun (bur. Orston, Notts.), widow, Apl. 25, 1561.	17		294
Apl. 22, 1562.	Reuell, John (bur. Kerkebie in Ascheffelde, Notts.), Apl. 4, 1561.	17		176
Oct. 10, 1560.	Revell, William, Brynsforthe, par. Rotherham, May 29, 1560.	16		125
Jan. 28, 1566.	Revington, John, Wathe, husbandman, Nov. 18, 1566.	17		608
July 23, 1558.	Reydnes, Thomas, Roclyffe (bur. Snathe), Apl. 16, 1558.	15	2	384
Jun. 4, 1568.	Reye, John, Settrington, labourer, Mar. 2, 1566.	17		812
Apl. 6, 1558.	Reyme, Mathewe, Thorne, Jan. 19, 1557.	15	2	187
Nov. 6, 1557.	Reyn, Richard, Myssyn (Notts.), May 11, 1557.	15	2	109
Oct. 1, 1556.	Reyvell, Thomas, Stanyngton, par. Bradfeld, Mar. 27, 1556.	15	1	128
Nov. 28, 1567.	Ribie, Richard, Yrton, par. Seamer, July 11, 1567.	17		740
Apl. 26, 1559.	Ribye, Richard, Hunmanbye, ——, 1558.	15	3	312
May 2, 1560.	Ricall, Richard, Braiton, husbandman, Mar. 16, 1558.	16		54
Jan. 4, 1562.	——, Richard, Braton, Jan. 28, 1562.	17		138
Mar. 9, 1559.	——, William, Brayton, Dec. 12, 1559.	16		6
Apl. 21, 1554.	Ricarde, William, Balne, par. Snaithe, Oct. 28, 1553.	14		62
Jan. 13, 1558.	Richard, Henry, Watnow, par. Gresley (Notts.), Oct. 7, 1558.	15	3	15
Oct. 22, 1567.	Richardes, Robert, Lincroftes, par. Greisley (Notts.), webster, Apl. 10, 1567.	17		731
Nov. 10, 1564.	Richardson, Agnes, Kirkbye Moreshed, widow, Oct. 10, 1564.	17		398
Jun. 12, 1557.	————, Agnes, Swynflete (bur. Whitgifte), Mar. 19, 1557.	15	1	290
May 4, 1554.	————, Alice, Westowe, Dec. 26, 1552.	14		148
Sep. 30, 1562.	————, Alison, Wetherbie (bur. Spofforthe), wid., Oct. 21, 1558.	17		116
No date.	————, Andrew, Lambe Closse, par. Marton, Oct. 2, 1554.	14		263
Nov. 17, 1558.	————, Arthur, Brotherton, Aug. 7, 1558.	15	3	116
Jun. 17, 1568.	————, George, Sherburne, Mar. 27, 1561.	17		805
Jun. 30, 1564.	————, Henry, Sherburne, butcher, Oct. 19, 1563.	17		354
Mar. 20, 1565.	————, Isabell, Halsam (bur. West Halsam), Feb. 10, 1565.	17		505
Mar. 26, 1565.	————, Jeffray, Wakfeld, Nov. 10, 1563.	17		414
Mar. 14, 1556.	————, Jennett, Bawllme, par. Snaythe, Aug. 24, 1556.	15	1	97
Oct. 13, 1565.	————, Jennett (bur. Egton), Nov. 30, 1564.	17		474
Sep. 3, 1565.	————, John, Buttercrame, husbandman, Dec. 9, 1564.	17		460
Mar. 11, 1567.	————, John, Esingwold, Feb. 7, 1567.	17		763
Oct. 24, 1558.	————, John, Lylling, yeoman, Sep. 5, 1555.	15	3	96
May 19, 1559.	————. John, Shereburne, Sep. --, 1558.	15	3	427
Nov. 9, 1556.	————, Margaret, Bubwith, widow, July 12, 1556.	15	1	108
July 10, 1567.	————, Margaret, Ecclesfeld, widow, Oct. 9, 1565.	17		686
Apl. 15, 1559.	————, Margaret, Stanforth Brigges (bur. Catton), Jan. 4, 1557.	15	3	352
Feb. 9, 1557.	————, Nicholas, Roosse, Dec. 22, 1557.	15	2	122
Oct. 31, 1561.	————, Peter, Westow, husbandman, Aug. 20, 1561.	17		38
Sep. 3, 1557.	————, Rauffe, Skipsey, gentleman, Feb. 24, 1556.	15	1	331
May 13, 1557.	————, Richard, Hucknall Torckard (Notts.), Nov. 3, 1556.	15	1	222
Jun. 14, 1560.	————, Robert, Burton (Notts.), husbandman, July 2, 1559.	16		85
May 5, 1557.	————. Robert, Egton, Sep. 16, 1556.	15	1	247
July 18, 1565.	————, Robert (bur. Thirske), Apl. 12, 1565.	17		452
Apl. 22, 1563.	————, Thomas, Hamylton (bur. Braton), webster, Dec. 8, 1562.	17		223
May 5, 1557.	————, Thomas, Home (bur. Birstall), husbn., Sep. 15, 1556.	15	1	214
Oct. 15, 1558.	————, Thomas, North Cave, husbandman, Mar. 2, 1558.	15	2	366

		Vol.	Pt.	Fol.
Oct. 3, 1566.	Richardson, Thomas (bur. Sowerbie), July 2, 1566.	17		579
Oct. 5, 1564.	————, Thomas, senr., Swynfleit (bur. Whitgyft), Dec. 4, 1563.	17		367
Feb. 12, 1554.	————, Thomas, yongar (bur. Whitgifte), Oct. 1, 1554.	14		74
Jan. 12, 1557.	————, Thomas, York, draper, Nov. 16, 1557.	15	2	81
Jan. 12, 1558.	————, William, Burnbie, yeoman, Feb. 25, 1558.	15	3	200
Oct. 22, 1558.	————, William, Great Aiton, Sep. 23, 1558.	15	3	235
Mar. 7, 1566.	————, William, Hornesey, labourer, Dec. 6, 1565.	17		515
Feb. 9, 1557.	————, William, Ottringham, Dec. 14, 1557.	15	2	121
Sep. 30, 1562.	————, William, Skarbroughe, Jun. 24, 1562.	17		118
May 18, 1559.	Richardsone, John, Suttone in Holderness, husbandman, Sep. 18, 1558.	15	3	412
Apl. 23, 1556.	————, Robert, Owte Newtone, Dec. 31, 1555.	15	1	25
Feb. 15, 1555.	————, Thomas, Bubwith, Nov. 28, 1554.	15	1	7
Dec. 16, 1557.	Richardsonne, John, Burton Pidsey, Nov. 21, 1557.	15	2	46
May 5, 1558.	————, William, Carletone in Lynrecke (Notts.), husbn., Dec. 22, 1557.	15	2	247
May 8, 1567.	Riche, Christopher, Everingham, Dec. 12, 1566.	17		648
Sep. 14, 1565.	——, Thomas, Burton Cunstable (bur. Swyne), July 8, 1565.	17		466
Aug. 1, 1562.	——, William, Aclom, husbandman, May 22, 1562.	17		103
Apl. 10, 1555.	Richemond, Sir George, late Canon of Bolton, Nov. 27, 1554.	14		118
Mar. 8, 1558.	————, Margaret (bur. Ripon), widow, Jan. 16, 1558.	15	3	283
Mar. 4, 1560.	Richemounde, James, North Cave, husbandman, Apl. 3, 1560.	16		166
Mar. 8, 1558.	Richemund, Richard (bur. Ripon), Nov. 20, 1558.	15	3	283
Mar. 21, 1560.	Richerdson, John, Estlillinge (bur. Sherifhoton), labr., Jan. 26, 1560.	16		176
Jun. 28, 1557.	————, Robert, Northe Cave, Jun. 12, 1557.	15	1	299
Apl. 13, 1557.	————, Thomas, Slyngesby, Jan. 19, 1556.	15	1	208
Sep. 7, 1557.	————, William, Hamyllton, par. Brayton, husbn., Aug. 20, 1557.	15	1	331
Apl. 7, 1557.	————, William, Snawdon (bur. Weston), yeoman, Jan. 22, 1556.	15	1	191
Apl. 25, 1554.	————, William, Thixindall (bur. Wharome Percie), Jan. 26, 1551.	14		161
Jun. 16, 1565.	Richmond, Christopher, senr., Gokebuske (bur. Ripon), Apl. 21, 1565.	17		444
May 7, 1568.	Rickard, Charles, Bawen, par. Snaythe, May 27, 1567.	17		781
Mar. 15, 1565.	Ricketson, John, Old Malton, Jan. 23, 1565.	17		503
Apl. 19, 1564.	Ricroft, Henry, Cunnunley (bur. Kildweke), Apl. 19, 1563.	17		328
Mar. 6, 1556.	Ricrofte, Richard, Litlebrows (Notts.), Jan. 16, 1556.	15	1	177
Nov. 10, 1563.	Ridburne, Henry, Beswicke, par. Kilnwicke, husbn., Aug. 24, 1563.	17		300
Oct. 7, 1563.	Riddshey, Margaret, Crumwell (Notts.), widow, May 20, 1563.	17		291
May 31, 1557.	Ridell, Leonarde, Darfeld, Nov. 9, 1556.	15	1	260
May 17, 1554.	Rider, Jennet, Newland, par. Cottingham, widow, Apl. 6, 1553.	14		5
May 17, 1555.	——, Jennet, Newlande, par. Cottingham, widow, Apl, 6, 1553.	14		74
Sep. 11, 1567.	Ridgill, John, Stainford (bur. Haitfeld), husbandman, Mar. 24, 1566.	17		707
Mar. 26, 1565.	Ridiall, Richard, Hessell (bur. Wragbie), May 19, 1564.	17		414
July 28, 1554.	Ridley, John, Beswike (bur. Kylnewike), clerke, Oct. 27, 1553.	14		144
July 28, 1556.	Ridyall, Thomas, Spitle Harwicke, par. Pontefracte, yeom. *No date.*	15	1	46
Oct. 13, 1558.	Rie, Richard, Worsoppe (Notts.), Aug. 24, 1553.	15	2	359
July 8, 1557.	Rigg, Thomas, Newemalton, Jun. 24, 1557.	15	1	306
Feb. 24, 1561.	Righton, Margaret, Sowthe Fenton (bur. Kyrke Fenton), Dec. 26, 1561.	17		16
Apl. 6, 1558.	Rigiall, Henry, Kynnesley, par. Hymesworthe, husbn., Oct. 6, 1556.	15	2	186
Feb. 25, 1556.	————, Richard, Barnesley, marcer, May 4, 1555.	15	1	167
Jan. 24, 1558.	Riles, Thomas, Brindsworth, par. Rotheram, Sep. 14, 1558.	15	3	217
July 31, 1556.	Riley, Thomas, Helthawayte, par. Harwood, May 26, 1553.	15	1	35
Oct. 5, 1558.	Rimer, John. Stoxlay, Aug. 27, 1558.	15	3	70
Jun. 20, 1566.	Ringerosse, William, Foxhooles, Nov. 17, 1565.	17		557
Jun. 4, 1568.	Ringros, James, Sherburne, husbandman, July 1, 1567.	17		814
Aug. 18, 1562.	Ringrose, William, Benyngton, par. Willerby, Mar. 14, 1562.	17		106
Sep. 30, 1557.	Rippley, Robert, Gransemore (bur. Burton Agnes), July 6, 1557.	15	1	342
Apl. 12, 1557.	Risheworth, John, Haworthe, Apl. 6, 1557.	15	1	207
Nov. 8, 1558.	Rishworth, Jenet, Burne, par. Brayton, widow, Sep. 20, 1558.	15	3	130
Oct. 24, 1554.	————, Rauf, Hemesworth, Dec. 6, 1553.	14		308
Oct. 5, 1558.	Rispin, Edmund, Huggett, Jun. 18, 1558.	15	3	71
Oct. 4, 1554.	Roame, Henry, Methley, Oct. 30, 1553.	14		275
Apl. 19, 1559.	Robard, John, Newthorpe, par. Grasley (Notts.), Feb. 16, 1558.	15	3	356
Jan. 13, 1558.	Robert, Alice, Kirkton (Notts.), widow, Sep. 30, 1558.	15	3	185
Oct. 3, 1566.	————, Henry, Gyrgaris, par. Weston, May 23, 1566.	17		582

		Vol.	Pt.	Fol.
Nov. 9, 1557.	Robert, Robert, Acworth, Oct. 11, 1557.	15	2	96
Sep. 30, 1557.	———, Thomas, Rednes (bur. Wightgifte), Aug. 10, 1557.	15	1	344
Nov.12, 1556.	———, Thomas, Swyllington, smythe, Sep. 28, 1556.	15	1	113
Apl. 16, 1567.	———, William, Pomfret, Sep. 3, 1566.	17		623
Feb. 19, 1557.	——— als. Milner, Christopher, Reidnes (bur. Whytgyfte), Dec. 20, 1557.	15	2	145
Nov. 9, 1557.	Roberte, Lyonell, Acworth, Sep. 15, 1557.	15	2	102
Mar. 4, 1560.	Robertes, John, Hull, meryner, Jun, 9, 1560.	16		165
May 13, 1557.	———, John, Kyrketon (Notts.). Apl. 1, 1557.	15	2	135
May 4, 1558.	———, William, Ratcliffe on Sore (Notts.), husbn., Apl. 12, 3 & 4 Phil. & Mary.	15	2	211
May 9, 1560.	Robertson, Symond, Gertton (Notts.), yeoman, Feb. 21, 1559.	16		58
May 5, 1558.	———, Thomas, Kellham (Notts.), Oct. 1, 1557.	15	2	253
No date.	———, Thomas, Wasse, clerke, Jun. 4, 7 Eliz.	17		831
May 5, 1558.	Robertsonne, William, Estmarkham (Notts.), husbn., May 7, 1553.	15	2	246
Dec. 1, 1558.	Robinson, Christopher, Beverley, Aug. 3, 1558.	15	3	146
July 27, 1567.	———, Christopher, Ormisbie, May 16, 1567.	17		671
Jan. 12, 1557.	———, Edward, Hull, housewright, Dec. 29, 1557.	15	2	79
Jan. 28, 1566.	———, Elizabeth, Fyshelake, widow, Mar. 16, 1565. ·	17		607
Oct. 29, 1558.	———, George, Clyfforth, par. Bramham, July 10, 1558.	15	3	131
Nov.28, 1558.	———, Isabell, Hornesey, Aug. 7, 1558.	15	3	227
Nov.28, 1558.	———, James, Aubroughe in Holderness, yeom., Sep. 29, 1558.	15	3	79
Mar.10, 1554.	———, James, Clowghton, Dec. 5. 1554.	14		72
Nov.16, 1558.	———, Jennet, Thirkelbye, Oct. 18, 1558.	15	3	73
Apl. 16, 1567.	———, Jennet, Wadsworthe, par. Heptonstall, May 17, 1565.	17		624
Apl. 23, 1566.	———, Jennet, Yeddingham, widow, Sep. 13, 1565.	17		510
Feb. 14, 1567.	———, John, Atone in Cleveland, Aug. 9, 1567. ·	17		760
July 1, 1561.	———, John, Beverley, waterman, Feb. 7, 3 Eliz.	17		76
Nov. 5, 1564.	———, John, Holme on the Wold. labourer, Jun. 16, 1563.	17		396
Apl. 27, 1563.	———, John, senr., Holskar, par. Whitbie, Jan. 21, 1562.	17		225
Apl. 27, 1563.	———, John, junr., Holskar, par. Whitbie, Jan. 18, 1562.	17		223
Oct. 29, 1558.	———, John, Thornam, par. Burton Agnes, Aug. 3, 1558.	15	2	368
July 10, 1567.	———, John, Thorpe Aveland, par. Badsworthe, May 31, 1567.	17	·	684
Nov.28, 1567.	———, John, Yrton, par. Seamer, Dec. 17, 1566.	17		737
May 9, 1566.	———, Mrs. Marie, Ordsall (Notts.), Nov. 20, 1565.	17		541
Mar.10, 1566.	———, Mawde, Kirkbemoreshed, widow, Jan. 20, 1566.	17		514
May 10, 1565.	———, Rauf, Kilburne Parke, par. Kilburne, Jan. 4, 1564.	17		430
Oct. 27, 1564.	———, Richard, Carleton (bur. Qworleton), Aug. 29, 1564.	17		394
Jan. 15, 1565.	———, Richard, Claton, par. Fyrcley, Oct. 16, 1565.	17		494
Jun. 22, 1568.	———, Richard, Clowghton, par. Scawbye, Sep. 28, 1567.	17		825
Nov. 7, 1565.	———, Richard, West Heslerton (bur. Yeddingham), husbn., May 4. 1564.	17		491
May 28, 1560.	———, Robert, Hetton (bur. Seasay), labourer, Sep. 24, 1559.	16		69
May 2, 1566.	———, Robert, Preston in Holderness, taler, Mar. 8, 1565.	17		526
Jun. 28, 1562.	———, Robert, Roston, par. Wickham, Jan. 15, 1561.	17		88
Apl. 28, 1563.	———, Robert, Rowton in Holderness, Jan. 2, 156[2-]3.	17		238
Oct. 5, 1563.	———, Robert, Thirnholme (bur. Burton Agnes), Jun. 29, 1563.	17		290
Nov.25, 1558.	———, Roger, Huggate on Wold, Oct. 25, 1558.	15	3	122
May 2, 1566.	———, Steven, Wigglesworthe, Sep. 18, 7 Eliz.	17		528
Sep. 29, 1563.	———, Thomas, Ascebe in Nesfeld, Jun. 8, 1563.	17		280
Dec. 1, 1558.	———, Thomas, Drewton, par. Northe Cave, July 27, 1558.	15	3	145
Jun. 25, 1568.	———, Thomas, Holmpton, Oct. 8, 1567.	17		808
Oct. 1, 1562.	———, William, Astbie in Nesfeld (bur. Ilkeley), Mar. 6, 1562.	17		112
Sep. 30, 1557.	———, William, Boltbye, par. Felyskyrke, Apl. 30, 1557.	15	1	344
May 9, 1565.	———, William, Fyshelake, Jan. 20, 1564.	17		429
Oct. 22, 1560.	———, William, Lowthorpe, Jun. 12, 1560.	16		128
Sep. 13, 1561.	———, William, Olde Malton, husbandman, Oct. 6, 1561.	17		27
Sep. 29, 1563.	———, William, Thurnholme (bur. Burton Agnes), yongman, Jan. 4, 1562,	17		275
Oct. 8, 1556.	Robothom, John, Westone (Notts.), Jun. 19, 1556.	15	1	155
May 4, 1558.	Robothome, John, Kyrkebye in Ashefelde (Notts.), Jan. 14, 1556.	15	2	214
July 3, 1567.	Robson, Andrew, Slingisbie, Dec. 24, 1566.	17		668

A.D. 1554 TO 1568.

		Vol.	Pt.	Fol.
Jun. 6, 1560.	Robson, Elizabeth (bur. Welton), Sep. 2, 1559.	16		76
Oct. 5, 1558.	———, John, Stoxley, Sep. 14, 1558.	15	3	69
May 2, 1560.	———, Richard, Grandismore, par. Burton Agnes, husbn., Nov. 10, 1558.	16		37
Jun. 20, 1562.	———, Robert, Stillington, Mar. 26, 1562.	17		89
Feb. 6, 1558.	———, Stephan, Muston (bur. Hunnambie), Aug. 20, 1558.	15	3	260
Aug. 26, 1558.	———, William, Thornton in Pykryngelythe, May 1, 1557.	15	2	293
July 11, 1566.	———, William, senr., Ripon, Jun. 20, 1566.	17		561
July 11, 1558.	Robucke, Henry, Wombwell (bur. Derfeyld), Jan. 6, 1557.	15	2	318
Oct. 11, 1567.	———, John, Felkirke, Aug. 14, 1567.	17		729
May 18, 1559.	Robuke, Thomas, Wathe, Mar. 22, 1558.	15	3	416
Feb. 21, 1558.	Robynson, Alan, Sutton on Derwent, Dec. 30, 1558.	15	3	277
Jun. 21, 1554.	———, Alison (bur. Ripon), Jan. 25, 1553.	14		131
Jun. 8, 1558.	———, Anne, Weale, par. St. John, Beverley, wid., Nov. 15, 1558.	15	3	286
May 18, 1559.	———, Elizabeth, Benehome, par. Swyne, widow, ——, 1558.	15	3	409
Jan. 17, 1557.	———, Henry (bur. Skarbroughe), Aug. 18, 1557.	15	2	62
Oct. 7, 1561.	———, James, Cropwell Bottler (Notts.), Aug. 10, 1560.	17		41
Oct. 22, 1556.	———, Jennet, widow of William R., Darrington, Sep. 17, 1556.	15	1	100
Dec. 13, 1560.	———, John, Elvington, husbandman, Mar. 20, 1559.	16		135
Apl. 27, 1558.	———, John, Pontefract, Dec. 10, 1557.	15	2	192
Oct. 12, 1562.	———, John, St. Sampson's, York, Sep. 20, 1562.	17		123
July 21, 1556.	———, Lyonell, Howden Feilde (bur. Levington), Apl. 18, 1556.	15	1	58
Mar. 20, 1558.	———, Richard, Fosterhouse, par. Fyshelyke, Sep. 16, 1558.	15	3	243
Aug. 19, 1556.	———, Robert, Danby, Oct. 13, 1555.	15	1	61
Mar. 15, 1558.	———, Robert, Ellerton, Dec. 10, 1558.	15	3	168
Oct. 7, 1557.	———, Robert, Newarke (Notts.), ieronmonger, July 18, 1557.	15	2	19
Apl. 8, 1559.	———, Robert, Thyrske, Nov. 17, 1558.	15	3	322
Oct. 10, 1560.	———, Thomas, Barnesley, Nov. 6, 1559.	16		125
Dec. 4, 1557.	———, Thomas, Gowell (bur. Howeke), Oct. 12, 1557.	15	2	51
May 11, 1556.	———, Thomas, Hooton (bur. Rudbie), husbn., Mar. 10, 1555.	15	1	38
Mar. 4, 1562.	———, Thomas, Hornesay, beare brewer, Dec. 23, 1562.	17		149
Oct. 3, 1560.	———, Thomas, Thormonbye, Apl. 6, 1560.	16		110
Apl. 8, 1559.	———, Walter (bur. Brandesbie), Sep. 6, 1558.	15	3	323
Jun. 18, 1557.	———, William, South Skirlay (bur. Swyne), husbn., Mar. 14, 1556.	15	1	295
May 2, 1560.	——— als. Mawe, Umfray, Harwoode, Dec. 28, 1559.	16		55
Mar. 6, 1556.	——— als. Mylner, John, Rosington, husbandman, Aug. 6, 1556.	15	1	178
Nov. 12, 1556.	Robynsone, Thomas, Lounde (Herthill), Aug. 15, 1556.	15	1	110
Apl. 22, 1556.	———, Thomas, Rightone, Mar. 28, 1556.	15	1	26
Apl. 22, 1556.	———, William, Lakynbie, par. Wiltone, Feb. 9, 1555.	15	1	27
May 13, 1557.	Rocklay, John, Spaldforth (bur. Clyfton, Notts.), husbn., Apl. 16, 1557.	15	1	218
Mar. 9, 1558.	Roddes, William, Bradford, Dec. 23, 1558.	15	3	158
May 14, 1558.	Roderforth, John, Irton, par. Seamer, Dec. 26, 1557.	15	2	281
Mar. 2, 1553.	Rodes, Nicholas, Hawkisworthe, par. Otley, July 20, 1553.	14		301
Apl. 7, 1557.	———, William, Hirst Courtney (bur. Byrkyn), Mar. 24, 1556.	15	1	205
Oct. 1, 1556.	———, William, the parke, par. Sheffeld, Mar. 13, 1556.	15	1	125
Oct. 9, 1567.	Rodger, Richard, Northe Collingham (Notts), Aug. 23, 1567.	17		723
Jun. 10, 1568.	———, William, Ughillwoodside in Bradfeld, Nov. 17, 1565.	17		807
Apl. 22, 1559.	Rodlay, Joseph, Neyther Catton, husbandman, Apl. 10, 1559.	15	3	364
Apl. 14, 1562.	———, Wather, Bradforde, Jan. 5, 1558.	17		168
Mar. 21, 1560.	Rodmell, William, West Elley (bur. North Firibie), husbn., May 10, 1559.	16		173
May 18, 1559.	Roger, James, Prestone, labourer, Apl. 15, 1559.	15	3	411
Jan. 26, 1558.	———, Jennet, Gisburne (bur. Danby), Jan. 6, 1557.	15	3	219
May 27, 1562.	———, John, Danby, Mar. 3, 1561.	17		100
Nov. 28, 1558.	———, John, Methelay, Nov. 12, 1558.	15	3	137
Nov. 28, 1558.	———, John, Metheleye, Nov. 12, 1558.	15	1	318
Jan. 22, 1557.	———, Robert, Danbye, Oct. 1, 1557.	15	2	157
Oct. 6, 1557.	———, Robert, Eilkisley (Notts.), July 17, 1557.	15	2	7
May 13, 1557.	———, Robert, Elkysley (Notts.), Feb. 11, 1556.	15	2	132
May 5, 1558.	———, Robert, Estretford (Notts.), Aug. 1, 1557.	15	2	241
Apl. 22, 1556.	———, Robert, Fetherston, Mar. 13, 1555.	15	1	18
Apl. 16, 1567.	———, Robert, Kirkelethome, Feb. 9, 1566.	17		631
Oct. 13, 1558.	———, Robert, North Collingham (Notts.), Nov. 18, 1557.	15	2	364

		Vol.	Pt.	Fol.
Oct. 2, 1560.	Roger, Thomas, Catwike, Aug. 1, 1560.	16		116
Jan. 22, 1557.	——, William, Danbye, Aug. 25, 1557.	15	2	157
Oct. 5, 1558.	——, William, senr., Metheley, Nov. 24, 1557.	15	3	64
Apl. 17, 1558.	——, William, Smythe Feylde, par. Bingley, Mar. 16, 1557.	15	2	204
Sep. 21, 1557.	——, William, Woddall, par. Herthill, yeoman, Aug. 11, 1557.	15	1	356
Nov. 29, 1558.	——, Sir William, curate of Owston, Oct. 12, 1558.	15	3	138
Mar. 10, 1558.	Rogeres, Robert, Roclyff, clerk, Nov. 20, 1558.	15	3	288
Dec. 3, 1560.	Rogers, Henry, Ulerum (bur. Skipse), priest, Aug. 18, 1560.	16		133
Oct. 8, 1567.	——, Thomas, York, baker, May 8, 1567.	17		729
May 12, 1566.	Rogerson, William, West Morton, par. Bingley, Apl. 28, 1566.	17		549
Oct. 2, 1560.	Roiddes, Christopher, Herton, par. Bradford, Mar. 23, 1558.	16		112
May 13, 1568.	Roides, James, Lund (bur. Brayton), Oct. 8, 1567.	17		796
Dec. 7, 1565.	——, John, Workesoppe (Notts.), Oct. 28, 1563.	17		492
No date.	——, Thomas, Horton, par. Bradforthe, Aug. 23, 1554.	14		52
Nov. 28, 1558.	—— als. Siver, William, Mirfeld, July 24, 1558.	15	3	137
Apl. 27, 1558.	Roidhouse, Richard, West Hardweke, par. Wragbye, labr., Feb. 6, 1557.	15	2	193
Oct. 27, 1564.	Rokebye, Raufe, Marske, gentleman, May 17, 1564.	17		395
Feb. 1, 1556.	——, Rauf, serjaunte at lawe. No date.	15	1	94
Oct. 11, 1565.	Rokesbye, John, son and heir of Wm. R., Workesopp(Notts.), Aug. 15, 1565.	17		473
Mar. 10, 1566.	Rolande, Thomas, Fadmore (bur. Kirkbemoreshed), Dec. 12, 1566.	17		514
May 31, 1557.	Rolay, Edmond, Adwicke of Derne, husbandman, Oct. 11, 1556.	15	1	260
Apl. 19, 1559.	Rollestone, Richard, Ratclif on Trent (Notts.), Nov. 16, 1558.	15	3	373
Mar. 20, 1565.	Rolston, Lyonell, senr., Pountefret, Mar. 2, 1563.	17		507
Feb. 16, 1556.	Romans, John, senr., Cawood, Nov. 2, 1556.	15	1	157
Jan. 31, 1558.	——, John, Cawood, husbandman, Jan. 1, 1558	15	3	221
Jan. 22, 1557.	Romctre, John, Seamer, Oct. 28, 1557.	15	2	156
Jun. 4, 1568.	Rome, Nicholas, Kirkbe in Grenedaillithe, Sep. 14, 1567.	17		813
Jan. 16, 1558.	——, Nicholas, Sledmar, Sep. 19, 1558.	15	3	210
Mar. 22, 1558.	Romesden, Robert, senr., Halyfax, clothier, Jan. 12, 1557.	15	3	292
Sep. 26, 1558.	Romesker, William, Bradfeld, July 13, 1557.	15	3	53
Dec. 2, 1558.	Romons, Alison, Eskrigge, Nov. 26, 1558.	15	3	126
July 31, 1566.	Romsden, Leonard, Gretland in Eland, par. Halifax, Feb. 22, 1565.	17		563
Jan. 17, 1560.	Romseden, Edward, Highetres in Gretelande, par. Elande, Oct. 11, 1560.	16		141
Apl. 28, 1558.	Rontre, Laurance, Newbye (bur. Semer), Dec. 20, 1557.	15	2	230
Jun. 30, 1563.	Roo, John, senr., Waikefeild, Oct. 30, 1562.	17		262
Oct. 7, 1557.	——, Robert a, Colweke, par. Gedlinge (Notts.), Apl. 18, 1557.	15	2	22
Sep. 24, 1558.	Roodes, Edward, Byrill, par. Bradford, Jun. 14, 1558.	15	3	87
Oct. 13, 1558.	Rooides, Lawrence, Esteretford (Notts.), July 13, 1557.	15	3	222
Oct. 16, 1558.	Rooke, Robert, Hothome, tyler, Jan. 11, 1557.	15	2	367
Jan. 14, 1564.	——, Thomas, Hymsworthe, husbandman, Dec. 11, 1564.	17		402
Mar. 15, 1558.	Roome, Thomas, Estcotynwith (bur. Aughton), Nov. 19, 1557.	15	3	168
Nov. 11, 1557.	Roos, Edward, Rowth in Holderness, esquire, Oct. 26, 1557.	15	2	96
Jan. 26, 1566.	——, George, Kilburn, Dec. 20, 1566.	17		611
July 19, 1557.	——, Jennett, Schawftworth (bur. Evertone, Notts.), May 18, 1557.	15	1	312
Apl. 20, 1559.	——, John, Everton (Notts.), Aug. 5, 1558.	15	3	369
Apl. 20, 1559.	——, Richard, Everton (Notts.), husbandman, Nov. 6, 1558.	15	3	308
Oct. 8, 1562.	——, Richard, Weston (Notts.), July 31, 1558.	17		119
Apl. 12, 1559.	Roose, Anthony, Hesle, par. Wragbie, gentleman, Oct. 8, 1558.	15	3	337
May 4, 1554.	——, Thomas, the eldest, Helaye, par. Sheffelde, July 9, 1554.	14		83
Apl. 20, 1559.	Roper (Registered Reper), Sutton on Lund (Notts.), Oct. 10, 1558.	15	3	367
Jun. 5, 1564.	——, Edmund, Halifax, laite of London, clotheworker, Jan. 9, 1563.	17		347
May 6, 1557.	——, Edward (bur. Kildwicke), Jan. 24, 1555.	15	1	252
Oct. 29, 1558.	——, George, Homanbe, , 1558.	15	2	370
May 2, 1555.	——, Robert (bur. Kighleye), Nov. 10, 1554.	14		128
Oct. 9, 1560.	——, William, Etton, Apl. 12, 1560.	16		122
July 20, 1557.	Rosdaill, Richard, Nafferton, Apl. 5, 1557.	15	1	315
Oct. 29, 1558.	——, William, Wallesgrave, par. Skarbrugh, Aug. 8, 1558.	15	2	370
May 29, 1556.	Rose, Frauncis, Rudstone, Oct. 6, 1555.	15	1	39
Jan. 14, 1567.	——, Jane, Heslee, par. Wragbie, Aug. 20, 1564.	17		751
Oct. 12, 1564.	——, John, Averton, par. Staunton (Notts.), husbandman, May 23, 1564.	17		379
Mar. 9, 1554.	——, John, Nayburne, Feb. 3, 1554.	14		302

		Vol.	Pt.	Fol.
Oct. 22ʃ 1560.	Rose, Richard, Rudstone, husbandman, May 28, 1560.	16		128
Jun. 12, 1557.	——, Robert, Cotes, par. Snathe, Mar. 21, 1556.	15	1	290
Apl. 26, 1559.	Rosindaill, William, Cawod, Mar. 28, 1559.	15	3	310
Apl. 19, 1559.	Rosse, Richard, Flyntam (Notts.), Nov. 3, 1558.	15	3	373
May 9, 1560.	Rossell, Edmond, Ratclyffe on Trent (Notts.), Jan. 22, 1559.	16		61
Jun. 5, 1554.	Rostan, John, Hoton Crancewike, Dec. 15, 1553.	14		9
Mar. 31, 1554.	Roston, Margaret, Shallowe, par. Asby, Sep. 14, 1554.	14		105
Oct. 10, 1566.	——, Robert, Oxston (Notts.), Nov. 2, 1564.	17		590
Oct. 5, 1558.	Rosyndayll, Richard, West Marton in Craven, May 10, 1558.	15	3	40
Oct. 13, 1558.	Rothwel, Thomas, Skegbie, par. Marnham (Notts.), Apl. 5, 1558.	15	2	365
Jan. 17, 1561.	Rothwell, John, Mosse, par. Campsall, yeoman, Oct. 18, 1561.	17		25
Jan. 27, 1557.	Rought, Thomas, Wystowe, Nov. 2, 1557.	15	2	155
Aug. 5, 1555.	Rouley, Robert, Eist Righton (bur. Bardeseye), husbn., ——, 1553.	14		207
May 29, 1563.	Roull, William, Oldsteid, par. Kilburne, Nov. 26, 1562.	17		251
Nov. 26, 1558.	Roumbolde, William, Stockeld, par. Spofforth, priest, Aug. 22, 1558.	15	3	230
Mar. 6, 1556.	Rounckhorne, Robert, Cawod, glover, Nov. 28, 1554.	15	1	202
Apl. 16, 1567.	Rountre, Alison, Newbie, par. Rudbie, widow, Feb. 12, 1566.	17		630
Feb. 26, 1557.	Rouse, Richard, Eastheslerton, Jan. 8, 1557.	15	2	145
Oct. 9, 1560.	Roward, John, Thurne, par. St. John, Beverlay, husbn., Feb. 13, 1559.	16		122
Mar. 21, 1559.	Rowarde, Thomas, Hornsey Burton. *No date.*	16		17
Aug. 4, 1558.	————, William, Thurne (bur. Beverlay), May 3, 1558.	15	3	2
Oct. 8, 1567.	Rowbothome, Thomas, Sutton Bunnyngton (Notts.), smythe, Jan. 10, 1564.	17		727
Apl. 24, 1567.	Rowe, Alice, Staynton (Notts.), widow, Jan. 9, 1566.	17		644
Sep. 28, 1560.	——, Robert, Staynton (Notts.), husbandman, July 8, 1560.	16		106
May 6, 1563.	——, Thomas, Plumtre (Notts.), Feb. 14, 1562.	17		245
Sep. 10, 1558.	Rowell, Agnes, Byrnde, par. Wresle, Aug. 29, 1558.	15	3	103
July 23, 1558.	————, Guylliam, Brind, par. Wressle, July 27, 1558.	15	2	387
Aug. 12, 1561.	Rowerd, John, Hornsey Burton, Oct. 24, ——.	17		59
Nov. 18, 1561.	Rowlay, Thomas, Lynton (bur. Spofforthe), Oct. 1, 1560.	17		34
Apl. 28, 1558.	————, William, Cottingham, taylyor, Jan. 2, 1557.	15	2	218
July 2, 1558.	Rowley, Thomas, Thorparche, tanner, Oct. 16, 1557.	15	2	342
Oct. 20, 1558.	Rowning, Thomas, Beffurth [Beeford], husbandman, Nov. 15, 1558.	15	2	350
Oct. 3, 1554.	Rowninge, William, Skipsey in Holderness, husbn., Aug. 27, 1554.	14		42
Feb. 11, 1557.	Rownthwayte, Randall, Stoidlay Roger, yeoman, Oct. 1, 1557.	15	2	166
Jun. 12, 1567.	Rownyng, Agnes, Brandisburton, widow, Jun. 14, 1566.	17		663
Sep. 30, 1556.	Rownynge, Isabell, Skepsey, Feb. 21, 1555.	15	1	140
Dec. 3, 1560.	————, John, Brandisburton, husbandman, Oct. 8, 1560.	16		133
Jan. 13, 1558.	Rowood, William, Harworth (Notts.), husbandman, Aug. 14, 1558.	15	3	188
July 2, 1561.	Rowsbe, Robert, Brydlington, husbandman, Oct. 21, 1560.	17		78
Jun. 4, 1568.	Rowsbey, John, Collom, May 19, 1567.	17		814
Apl. 17, 1567.	Rowson, Thomas, Kighley, webster, Feb. 10, 1566.	17		621
Jun. 6, 1560.	Rowton, Henry, Skydbye, Oct. 1, 1559.	16		73
Nov. 20, 1563.	Roydes, Robert, Manyngam (bur. Bradforthe), Sep. 13, 1563.	17		303
Sep. 21, 1557.	——, Robert, Rawmarshe, yeoman, ——, 1554.	15	1	349
Apl. 28, 1563.	——, William, Barnesley, Nov. 12, 1562.	17		235
Oct. 5, 1558.	Roydhouse, Thomas, Westhardwike (bur. Wragby), husbn., Aug. 14, 1558.	15	3	40
Mar. 22, 1558.	Roydhowse, John, Westhardweke (bur. Wragbe), husbn., Nov. 12, 1558.	15	3	292
Mar. 22, 1558.	————, Robert, Sharleston (bur. Kirthethorp), Sep. 2, 1557.	15	3	293
May 9, 1565.	Royston, John, Clayton, par. Fryckeley, Jan. 7, 1564.	17		427
Oct. 26, 1560.	Royte, Margaret (bur. Riplay), Oct. 1, 1560.	16		128
Jan. 24, 1558.	Roythewell, Robert, Brodesworth, Oct. 15, 1558.	15	3	219
Sep. 2, 1561.	Rud, Robert, Danby, Aug. 3, 1560.	17		53
Nov. 21, 1556.	Rudde, Jane, Rocliff, par. Snath, July 3, 1556.	15	1	117
Dec. 4, 1557.	——, John, Cowicke (bur. Snaythe), Nov. 2, 1557.	15	2	50
Feb. 5, 1556.	Rudderfurth, George, Saltaughe in Kayngham Marche, Sep. 2, 1556.	15	1	170
Aug. 1, 1561.	Rudderfurthe, Elizabeth, Kayngham, Apl. 26, 1558.	17		65
Apl. 20, 1559.	Rudley, Thomas, Myssen (Notts.), Mar. 12, 1558.	15	3	309
Apl. 3, 1559.	Rudston, Robert, Besingby, labourer, July 12, 1558.	15	3	315
Nov. 27, 1565.	————, Thomas, Besynbie, husbandman, May 8, 1565.	17		490
Apl. 22, 1556.	Ruestone, John, Besingbie, labourer, Oct. 30, 1555.	15	1	25

A.D. 1554 TO 1568.

		Vol.	Pt.	Fol.
Oct. 29, 1558.	Rukell, Roger, Filey, husbandman, May 24, 1558.	15	2	371
May 2, 1566.	Rukin, John, Berden (bur. Bolton), ——, 1566.	17		529
May 17, 1560.	Rumbard, John, Scagelden (bur. Houingham), Nov. 1, 1559.	16		64
Jun. 11, 1557.	Rumfray, Edmunde, Skamston (bur. Wyntryngham), Feb. 11, 1556.	15	1	289
Jan. 5, 1557.	——, Margaret, Skampston, par. Wyntryngham, Nov. 8, 1557.	15	2	72
Nov. 3, 1557.	Rumsthwaytte, Rawfe (bur. All Hallows, Northe streytt). *No date.*	15	2	105
Mar. 9, 1556.	Runkhorne, Thomas, Cawode, glover, Feb. 6, 1556.	15	1	201
May 18, 1559.	Runlyn, John, Calthorne, Aug. 14, 1558.	15	3	398
May 29, 1566.	Runtwhayte, Henry, Leeds, chapman, Mar. 26, 1566.	17		540
Dec. 17, 1557.	Rusbie, John, Wodhouse (bur. Haytfelde), husbandman, Sep. 27, 1557.	15	2	37
Oct. 10, 1560.	——, Robert, Thorpe in Balne (bur. Barnebie on Donne), Mar. 16, 1558.	16		125
Apl. 20, 1558.	Rusholme, Richard, Newland, par. Drax, Sep. 12, 1557.	15	2	217
Sep. 30, 1563.	Russam, Phelepe, Newlande, par. Draxe, Aug. 23, 1562.	17		287
Apl. 27, 1563.	Russell, Henry, Thornton in Pickeringe Lithe, Dec. 21, 1562.	17		226
May 2, 1560.	——, John, Seymer, husbandman, Mar. 16, 1559.	16		37
May 10, 1559.	——, Robert, Cayton, Dec. 12, 1558.	15	3	389
May 2, 1560.	——, Thomas, Caiton, Mar. 18, 1559.	16		35
Apl. 17, 1567.	——, William, Hausker, par. Whitbie, Feb. 24, 1566.	17		630
Jan. 16, 1558.	Russume, John, Roclife (bur. Snathe), Oct. 6, 1558.	15	3	19
Nov. 30, 1556.	Russill, Thomas, Thyrnum, par. Burtone Agnes, Aug. 11, 1556.	15	1	134
Apl. 3, 1559.	Ruston, Henry, Harpham, Dec. 17, 1558.	15	3	317
Dec. 11, 1566.	——, William, Rudston, Sep. 1, 1566.	17		601
Oct. 5, 1558.	Rutter, Agnes, Gt. Broughton, par. Kirkby in Cleveland, wid., Feb. 18, 1555.	15	3	43
July 27, 1564.	——, Robert, Huton (bur. Rudbie), husbandman, Mar. 6, 1563.	17		361
Sep. 1, 1565.	——, William, senr., Great Broughton, par. Kirkebie in Cleveland, husbandman, Apl. 2, 1565.	17		462
Jan. 28, 1556.	Ruyke, Richard, Hemesley, glover, Dec. 23, 1556.	15	1	92
Nov. 28, 1567.	Rybie, Ellis, Yrton, par. Seamer, July 19, 1567.	17		739
Jun. 20, 1566.	Rybye, Thomas, Newton Rocheforthe (bur. Hunmanbie), Sep. 5, 1565.	17		555
Dec. 10, 1561.	Rychardson, Elizabeth, Swynflet (bur. Whitgift), Aug. 8, 1561.	17		28
Aug. 2, 1560.	——, John, Byrstwyekegarthe, par. Skecklinge, May 21, 1560.	16		99
Jun. 7, 1560.	——, Lawrance, Gemlinge, par. Foston, Aug. 5, 1558.	16		79
May 28, 1560.	Rychardsonne, Elizabeth, Lambe Close, par. Marton, wid., Jun. 12, 1559.	16		69
Apl. 25, 1558.	——, Richard, Newthroppe (bur. Shirburne), Aug. 20, 1557.	15	2	234
May 5, 1558.	——, William, Stoke next Newerke (Notts.), Mar. 26, 1558.	15	2	256
Jan. 18, 1560.	Rychenson, William, Raskell, husbandman, Sep. 15, 1560.	16		139
July 6, 1558.	Rycherdsonne, George, Westow, husbandman, May 14, 1558.	15	2	324
Aug. 2, 1558.	——, John, Brompton, May 9, 1558.	15	3	8
Sep. 29, 1563.	Rycrofte, Robert, Lodsdall, par. Carleton (Craven), Apl. 27, 1563.	17		277
Apl. 17, 1567.	——, Roger, Kildwicke, Dec. 12, 1566.	17		621
Feb. 20, 1555.	Ryddyshe, Symond, Trowell, Aug. 22, 15—.	14		304
Jun. 3, 1563.	Ryder *als.* Sckafe, Jennat, Elvington, Apl. 15, 1563.	17		252
July 14, 1564.	Rydinges, Ranold, Cottingham, mylner, Apl. 10, 1564.	17		357
May 6, 1563.	Rydishe, John, Crumwell (Notts.), Dec. 3, 1562.	17		241
Apl. 12, 1559.	Rydlay, Robert, Wheldrake, Oct. 10, 1558.	15	3	335
May 5, 1558.	Rydley, Agnes, Upton (Notts.), Aug. 20, 1557.	15	2	209
Jun. 26, 1556.	Rydyng, Thomas, Woodhall, par. Calverley, Feb. 11, 1555.	15	1	51
May 6, 1563.	Ryecroft, Richard, Norton Cuckneye (Notts.), July 20, 1561.	17		243
Oct. 1, 1560.	Ryeley, Jennat, East Retford (Notts.), maiden, Jun. 7, 1560.	16		114
May 23, 1565.	Ryemere, Symon, curat of Hollme in Spaldingmore, Sep. 2, 1564.	17		442
Mar. 21, 1560.	Rygge, Thomas [?Ripon Deanery], Jan. 25, 1560.	16		174
Apl. 16, 1567.	Rylay, Thomas, Sourbie, par. Halifax, clothyer, Mar. 26, 1566.	17		628
Mar. 31, 1558.	Ryley, Richard, Appleton, par. Bolton Percye, Jan. 5, 1557.	15	2	177
Apl. 20, 1559.	——, Robert, East Retforde (Notts.), July 16, 1558.	15	3	434
Sep. 15, 1556.	Rymer, John, Bagby, par. Kirkebyknoll, July 22, 1556.	15	1	65
Sep. 30, 1557.	——, Richard, Bagbye, par. Kirkebyknoll, Dec. 12, 1556.	15	1	345
May 10, 1559.	——, William, Bagbye, par. Kirkebye Knowle, Jan. 29, 1558.	15	3	388
May 10, 1565.	——, William, Catton (bur. Topcliff), Dec. 16, 1564.	17		429
Jan. 17, 1557.	Ryngros, Emote, Thurnum, par. Burton Agnes, widow, Nov. 2, 1557.	15	2	61

18

A.D. 1554 TO 1568.

		Vol.	Pt.	Fol
Feb. 15, 1558.	Ryra, Annas, Skipsey Burghe, Dec. 16, 1558.	15	3	271
July 8, 1557.	——, John, Skipseyburght, par. Skipsey, May 27, 1557.	15	1	305
Jan. 21, 1557.	Rysheworthe, Robert, Crofton, gentleman, Sep. 13, 1557.	15	2	69
Mar. 12, 1557.	Rysome, William. Clyfforthe (bur. Bramham), Nov. 20, 1557.	15	2	127
Oct. 2, 1566.	Ryther, William, Easte Newton, par. Aldbrughe, yeom., Jan. 3, 1565.	17		581
Aug. 17, 1558.	Sacheverell, Henry, senr., Ratclyf on Soore (Notts.), esq., Apl. 26, 1558.	15	2	296
Sep. 18, 1567.	Sadler, Richard, Hull, porter, Jun. 24, 1567.	17		705
Feb. 4, 1556.	Saile, John, Pigborne, par. Brodesworthe, Sep. 15, 1556.	15	1	168
May 4, 1555.	Saill, William, Campsall, Sep. 24, 1554.	14		80
Jan. 30, 1555.	Saille, William. Morehowse, par. Hoyton, husbandman, Oct. 22, 1555.	15	1	4
Jan. 12, 1558.	Sainctquintin, William, South Skirley (bur. Swyne), gent., Nov. 22, 1558.	15	3	204
Sep. 17, 1567.	Saintter, Robert, Hirst Courtney (bur. Birkin) yeom., May 22, 1567.	17		702
July 26, 1557.	Saivell, Elizabeth (bur. Thornill), Apl. 14, 1557.	15	1	316
Apl. 17, 1559.	Sam, Robert, Byckerton (bur. Billton), husbandman, Aug. 1, 1558.	15	3	352
Nov. 10, 1564.	Same, Jennet, (Ainsty Deanery), Oct. 17, 1564.	17		397
Aug. 28, 1561.	Sampoll, Robert, Bowtre, husbandman, July 17, 1560.	17		58
Mar. 9, 1557.	Sampson, Agnes, Kelke Magna (bur. Foston), Oct. 4, 1557.	15	2	128
Feb. 17, 1558.	————, Edmunde, Moregate, par. Clarbrowght (Notts.), Sep. 1, 1558.	15	3	275
Jan. 28, 1566.	————, Nicholas, Ecclesfeld, Nov. 19, 1566.	17		607
Oct. 8, 1562.	————, Robert, South Leverton (Notts.), Jun. 13, 1562.	17		122
Oct. 20, 1558.	————, Robert, Tunstall, May 2, 1558.	15	2	352
Jun. 7, 1560.	————, William, Burton Agnes, mylner, Sep. 7, 1559.	16		77
Feb. 17, 1558.	Sampsonn, Alexander, East Retford (Notts.), Sep. 8, 1558.	15	3	274
May 5, 1558.	Sampsonne, John, North Collingham (Notts.), Oct. 29, 1557.	15	2	258
Mar. 11, 1562.	Samson, John, Wellhill, par. Penistone. Sep. 30, 1562.	17		156
Jan. 16, 1558.	————, William, Snath, Dec. 5, 1558.	15	3	19
May 13, 1557.	———— als. Porter, Richard, Rampton (Notts.), yeom., Apl. 12, 1557.	15	1	236
May 5, 1558.	Samsonne, John, North Collingham (Notts.), widow, Apl. 12, 1558.	15	2	259
Jan. 18, 1556.	Sale, John, Tonge, par. Birstall, Oct. 6, 1556.	15	1	88
Nov. 29, 1557.	Sall, Isabell, Lytle Smeaton, widow, Sep. 20, 1557.	15	2	104
Oct. 10, 1565.	Salmon, John, senr., Laxton (Notts.), May 1, 1565.	17		472
July 8, 1562.	————, John, York, bucher, Mar. 15, 1560.	17		93
July 26, 1558.	Salsbery, Henry, Esyngton, Oct. 21, 1557.	15	3	10
Oct. 27, 1558.	Saltmarche, William, Selbie, gent., Sep. 30, 1558.	15	3	132
Apl. 14, 1562.	Saltonstall, William, Halifax, clerke, Mar. 5, 1561.	17		182
Mar. 17, 1557.	Salvan, Allan, Egton, Apl. 2, 1545.	15	2	176
May 6, 1559.	Salven, Edward, gent., servant to Sir Frauncis Salven of Newbigginge, knight (bur. Egtone), July 18, 1557.	15	3	383
May 7, 1559.	————, William, Acaster Selbie, gentleman. *No date.*	15	3	384
Oct. 7, 1557.	Salvyn, Richard, Farington (Notts.), May 6, 1557.	15	2	17
May 2, 1560.	Sanctquyntayn, Dorothe, ladye of (Doncaster Deanery), Dec. 10, 1558.	16		45
Oct. 8, 1567.	Sandall, John, Moregren, par. Greaslay (Notts.), cottier, Jan. 26, 1566.	17		724
May 5, 1568.	Sander, Richard, Sandesend, par. Lithe, Feb. 21, 1567.	17		773
Mar. 8, 1558.	————, Robert. Walkington, yonge man, Nov. 15, 1558.	15	3	157
Jan. 31, 1564.	————, Thomas, Sansend, par. Lithe, Sep. 22, 1564.	17		404
Jan. 28, 1562.	Sanders, George, Holbeck (bur. Leedes), Jan. 3, 1562.	17		145
Oct. 10, 1566.	————, John, Basford (Notts.), May 28, 1566.	17		590
Dec. 15, 1557.	Sanderson, Alexander, Babworth (Notts.), July 5, 1557.	15	2	60
Oct. 5, 1558.	————, Charles, Crofton, Aug. 19, 1558.	15	3	62
July 19, 1557.	————, Christopher, Sterrope, par. Blithe (Notts.), Aug. 12, 1556.	15	1	308
Dec. 22, 1556.	————, Jenet, Hewys, par. Malton, widow, Oct. 13, 1556.	15	1	76
Jun. 21, 1565.	————, John, Langsett, par. Penystone, Feb. 2, 1560.	17		446
May 14, 1557.	————, John, Lowdham (Notts.), Oct. 3, 155[6?].	15	1	220
July 16, 1567.	————, Jone, Loudam (Notts.), Aug. 6, 1557.	17		672
Aug. 7, 1565.	————, Nicholas, Blithe (Notts.), husbandman, Dec. 6, 1564.	17		458
May 4, 1564.	————, Margaret, Grauntley (bur. Ripon), widow, Jan. 6, 1563.	17		342
Sep. 30, 1556.	————, Robert, Gemlynge (bur. Fostone), husbn., May 6, 1556.	15	1	133
Mar. 17, 1556.	————, Robert, Lysset, par. Beford, husbandman, Dec. 22, 1556.	15	1	187
Jun. 26, 1557.	————, Thomas, Schaffurth, par. Everton, May 21, 1557.	15	1	298
Jun. 6, 1560.	————, Thomas, Walkington, husbandman, Nov. 15, 1559.	16		76
Dec. 20, 1560.	————, William, Hornesey. *No date.*	16		137

A.D. 1554 TO 1568.

		Vol.	Pt.	Fol.
Apl. 12, 1559.	Sanderson, William, Wheldrike, Dec. 27, 1558.	15	3	335
May 18, 1559.	Sandersone, Thomas, Lellay, par. Prestone, husbandman, Mar.6,1558.	15	3	410
Feb. 3, 1556.	Sandforthe, John, Byrkyn, Jan. 30, 1556.	15	1	94
Mar.22, 1564.	Sandiman, William, Rillington, Jan. 27, 1560.	17		409
May 15, 1563.	Sandwithe, Edmund, Usflytt (bur. Whitgyfte), Dec. 13, 1562.	17		248
Feb.23, 1558.	Sandwyth, Antony, York, bower, Aug. 8, 1558.	15	3	277
Feb.15, 1565.	Sandyman, Thomas, Rillington, July 11, 1565.	17		499
Jan. 12, 1558.	Sannes, William, Beverlay, Oct. 19, 1558.	15	3	199
Apl. 28, 1558.	Santon, Alice, Elaughton, Dec. 17, 1557.	15	2	219
Mar.27, 1565.	———, Elizabeth, Pattrington, widow, Sep. 12, 1564.	17		417
Jun. 10, 1560.	———, Thomas, Patringeton, husbandman, Apl. 8, 1560.	16		82
May 13, 1557.	Sargensonne, Richard, Calverton (Notts.), husbandman, Oct. 16,1556.	15	1	226
Jan. 12, 1557.	Sargeson, Richard, Hothome, Nov. 25, 1557.	15	2	78
Sep. 30, 1556.	Sarianson, John, Malhame (bur. Kirkbye Malhamdale), Apl. 28, 1556.	15	1	174
May 13, 1568.	Sarten, Thomas, Bingham (Notts.), Nov. 12, 1567.	17		799
Oct. 1, 1557.	Saunder, John, Saundesende (bur. Lithe), Sep. 5, 1557.	15	1	362
Nov. 6, 1554.	Saunderson, John, husbandman (bur. Bulmer), Sep. 13, 1554.	14		293
Apl. 8, 1559.	———, John, Harton, par. Bossall, Sep. 22, 1558.	15	3	324
Sep. 16, 1555.	———, John, Maltbye, Jan. 29, 1554.	14		67
Apl. 3, 1555.	———, Robert, Benethorpe (bur. Langton), Feb. 26, 1554.	14		191
Oct. 6, 1558.	———, Thomas, Brampton, par. Wath, Sep. 1, 1558.	15	3	222
July 22, 1558.	———, Thomas, Huntingeton, husbandman, July 4, 1558.	15	2	386
Sep. 21, 1557.	Saundersonne, Nycholas, Ewys, par. Maltbye, husbn., May 2, 1557.	15	1	348
Oct. 12, 1558.	Savage (Registered Ganaga), Agnes (bur. Screaton, Notts.), Aug. 14, 1558.	15	2	373
Aug. 6, 1567.	———, Henry, Ellerton, Nov. 26, 1566.	17		698
Feb. 17, 1557.	———, William, junr., Bubwyth, husbandman, Nov. 20, 1557.	15	2	147
Aug. 7, 1563.	Savages, Rauffe, York, gentleman, July 11, 1563.	17		213
May 26, 1557.	Savagge, Helene, Patrington, Mar. 20, 1557 (sic).	15	1	215
Jun. 27, 1560.	Savaige, John, Dighton (bur. Eskrige), May 8, ———.	16		87
Oct. 6, 1557.	———, John, Skreton (Notts.), Sep. 6, 1556.	15	2	32
July 23, 1560.	———, William, Bubwithe, yeoman, Mar. 31, 1560.	16		95
May 28, 1560.	Savayge, Jennat, Crambe, widow, Mar. 12, 1559.	16		69
May 4, 1555.	Savedge, James, Whiston, gentleman, Dec. 6, 1550.	14		77
Apl. 10, 1555.	Savell, Henry, Copleye (bur. Halifax), esquire, Feb. 20, 1554.	14		119
Apl. 6, 1558.	———, Robert, Pilley, husbandman, Oct. 25, 1557.	15	2	184
Jun. 12, 1567.	Savidge, Katherine, Bubwithe, widow, May 13, 1567.	17		657
Sep. 30, 1557.	Savill, Nicholas, the Newhall als. the Haghe, esquire, Sep. 24, 1556.	15	1	325
Jun. 12, 1567.	Savydge, Allison, Bubwithe, spinster, May 18, 1567.	17		657
No date.	Savyle, Sir Henry, Thornehill, knight, Feb. 15, 1555.	15	2	387
Apl. 16, 1567.	Savyll, Henry, Bradley in Eland, par. Halifax, Jun. 10, 1566.	17		625
May 4, 1558.	Sawcye, George, Glapton (bur. Cliftonne, Notts.), Sep. 6, 1557.	15	2	264
May 2, 1566.	Sawden, Jennett, Thornton, par. Bradford, Mar. 8, 1565.	17		532
Dec. 1, 1557.	Sawer, Agnes, Shereborne, widow, Aug. 18, 1557.	15	2	84
Feb.18, 1567.	———, Edward, Ferndayle, par. Kirkbie Moreshed, labr., Nov.14,1567.	17		759
Feb. 1, 1557.	———, Edward, Sherburne in Elmytt, Aug. 10, 1557.	15	2	162
Mar.17, 1561.	———, John, Perlington, par. Aberforthe, May 14, 1561.	17		4
Apl. 3, 1563.	———, Thomas, Parlington, par. Abberfurthe, Mar. 1, 1562.	17		220
Jun. 23, 1568.	———, Thomas, Southburton, May 17, 1568.	17		828
Mar.23, 1560.	Sawhell, John, Bursey, par. Holme in Spaldingmore, July 25, 1560.	16		178
May 5, 1558.	Sawmon, John, junr., Laxton (Notts.), Aug. 27, 1557.	15	2	260
Oct. 6, 1557.	Sawnderson, Dyonesse, Stirropp, par. Blithe, widow, Jun. 16, 1557.	15	2	10
Oct. 29, 1558.	Sawndwith, John, York, walkar, Feb. 6, 1558.	15	3	96
Oct. 8, 1562.	Sawrbie, Gilbert, Eastretford (Notts.), yeoman, Apl. 4, 1562.	17		121
Nov.29, 1558.	Sawrebye, Robert, Brighouses, par. Sheafeld, Apl. 14, 1558.	15	3	109
Apl. 19, 1559.	Sawsy, Robert, Ruddington (Notts.), Nov. 28, 1558.	15	3	372
May 4, 1558.	Sawsye, Richard (bur. Flafurth, Notts.), May, 28, 1557.	15	2	265
Dec. 3, 1557.	Sawtre, Robert, Wathe, Nov. 18, 1557.	15	2	49
Dec. 1, 1557.	Saxton, Alice (bur. Leedes), Jun. 17, 1557.	15	2	49
Feb. 1, 1563.	Sayell, John, Mosse, par. Campsall, Jan. 7, 1563.	17		314
Feb.24, 1559.	Sayer, Leonarde, Broughton (bur. Kyrkbye), Sep. 8, 1559.	16		3
Apl. 6, 1558.	Sayll, Nicholas, Campsall, Jan. 28, 1557.	15	2	185

		Vol.	Pt.	Fol.
Apl. 6, 1558.	Saynctingley, Christopher, Arkesey, Aug. 9, 1557.	15	2	185
May 31, 1560.	Saynter, Edmonde, Chapple Hadlesaye, par. Byrkyn, yeom., Jan. 11, 1559.	16		71
Dec. 20, 1558.	Sayton, John, Northing, par. Whiston, Oct. 6, 1558.	15	3	153
Nov. 8, 1557.	———, Richard, Brompton, par. Treton, Sep. 17, 1557.	15	2	112
Apl. 27, 1558.	Sayvell, Jennett, Thorne, par. Wakefelde, Mar. 14, 1557.	15	2	194
May 9, 1566.	———, Robert, Colstonn Bassett (Notts.), husbandman, Nov.10,1564.	17		548
Sep. 2, 1567.	Sayvidge, Christopher. Bubwithe, weaver, May 20, 1567.	17		705
Aug. 26, 1563.	Scaiff, John, Fulsutton, Apl. 8, 1563.	17		213
Apl. 29, 1555.	Scailles, William, Pontefract, Mar. 25, 1 & 2 Phil. and Mary.	14		125
Oct. 2, 1555.	Scamoden, John, Hunsworthe, Jun. 6, 1555.	14		166
July 15, 1567.	Scarbroughe, John, Sutton, par. Kilwike, Apl. 22, 1567.	17		675
May 4, 1558.	Scarbrughe, Elizabeth, Flyntam (Notts.), widow, Feb. 2, 1557.	15	2	268
Sep. 28, 1557.	Scarburghe, Nicholas (bur. Kyldweke), Jan. 26, 1556.	15	1	338
Sep. 20, 1558.	Scare, Thomas, Stilingfleet, Aug. 1, 1558.	15	3	108
Aug. 8, 1555.	Scarre, James, Sedall, par. Estharlesaye, Dec. 14, 6 Edward 6.	14		311
Sep. 30, 1557.	Scawbe, Agnes (bur. Raskell), Sep. 16, 1557.	15	1	345
Jun. 28, 1560.	Scayffe, Marmaduke, Ful Sutton, Jun. 2, 1560.	16		88
Jan. 18, 1565.	Sceffeld, Richard, Thorpebasset, Dec. 18, 1565.	17		496
Oct. 8, 1567.	Scelles, William, Suttonn Bunnyngton (Notts.), May 3, 1567.	17		726
Mar. 7, 1566.	Schakles, Robert, Stoneferrye (bur. Sutton), husbn., Nov. 12, 1566.	17		514
Sep. 14, 1558.	Schaling, William (bur. Bulmar), July 28, 1558.	15	3	107
Nov. 6, 1565.	Schearde, Thomas, Ovenden, par. Hallifax, wolman, Sep. 12, 1565.	17		490
Jun. 11, 1562.	Scheminge, Annas, Scarburgh, Jan. 20, 1561.	17		87
Apl. 28, 1563.	Scherwood, Rauf, Grindelton Eves, par. Mytton (bur. Waddington), Jan. 10, 1562.	17		228
Jun. 30, 1558.	Schippard, George, Newe Malton, Nov. 10, 1557.	15	2	341
Jun. 2, 1557.	Scholaie, Margrett, Brakanhill, par. Wragbie, wid., Mar. 29, 1557.	15	1	266
Feb. 19, 1567.	Scholay, Henry, Whitlay (bur. Kellington), Apl. 5, 1567.	17		761
Feb. 17, 1557.	Scholaye, Annes, Hodhowse (bur. Haytefeld), wid., Nov. 12, 1557.	15	2	137
Mar. 13, 1558.	Scholey, Richard, Armethorp, husbandman, Sep. 22, 1558.	15	3	162
Nov. 8, 1557.	Schoyre, Henry, Campsall, July 21, 1557.	15	2	110
Jun. 3, 1563.	Sckafe als. Ryder, Jennat, Elvington, Apl. 15, 1563.	17		252
May 2, 1566.	Scoffeild, Margaret, Whitwood, par. Hertishead, wid., Dec. 24, 1565.	17		534
May 2, 1560.	Scofelde, Nycholas, Lightclyffe, par. Halyfax, Dec. 20, 1558.	16		41
Mar. 16, 1557.	Scolay, Agnes, Hornecastle, par. Hymseworthe, wid., Dec. 10, 1557.	15	2	176
Oct. 6, 1558.	———, Betrix, Claiton, par. Frickelay, widow, Apl. 28, 1558.	15	3	222
Aug. 5, 1567.	———, John, Brakenhill, par. Wragbie, Jun. 11, 1567.	17		686
Mar. 9, 1567.	———, Richard, Hornecastell (bur. Hymsworthe), ———, 1563.	17		763
Dec. 17, 1557.	———, Robert, Staynford (bur. Haytfelde), Sep. 1, 1557.	15	2	38
Oct. 1, 1556.	———, Thomas, Brakynhill, par. Wragbie, husbandman, July 30,1556.	15	1	120
Nov. 29, 1558.	———, Thomas, Great Houghton, par. Darfeld, husbn., Aug. 1, 1558.	15	3	141
Oct. 31, 1555.	Scoles, William, Thorpe, par. Rothwell, clothyar, Aug. 21, 1555.	14		75
July 15, 1561.	Scoley, Henry, Hornecastle, par. Hymsworthe, yeom., Jun. 15, 1561.	17		82
Feb. 6, 1558.	———, Henry, Hymsworth, chapman, Nov. 15, 1558.	15	3	254
Dec. 22, 1556.	———, Margaret, wid. of Jo. S., Doncastre, Nov. 19, 1556.	15	1	84
Feb. 6, 1558.	———, Richard, Aithewike by Streat, Dec. 10, 1558.	15	3	253
Sep. 21, 1557.	———, Richard, Southe Kyrkebye, July 23, 1557.	15	1	353
Oct. 1, 1557.	———, Robert, Felkyrke, Mar. 2, 1556.	15	1	367
May 15, 1563.	———, Thomas, the Laynes, par. Hymsworthe, yeom., Jan. 27, 1562.	17		247
Sep. 1, 1563.	———, Thomas, Hymsworthe, yeoman, May 14, 1563.	17		206
Feb. 1, 1563.	———, William, Kynseley (bur. Hymsworthe), cowper, Jun. 27,1563.	17		312
Apl. 18, 1560.	———, William, South Kyrkbye, Sep. 12, 1559.	16		32
Nov. 14, 1555.	Scooytt, William, Clifforthe, par. Bramham, Oct. 14, 1555.	14		239
Jan. 12, 1557.	Scorbroughe, Henry, Lockington, par. Kylnweke, husbn., May16,1557.	15	2	78
Nov. 10, 1563.	Scorburghe, Roger, Lockington, labourer, May 22, 1563.	17		301
May 2, 1560.	Scorer, William, Dunham on Trent (Notts.), corviser, Feb. 13, 1559.	16		38
Oct. 7, 1556.	Scot, John, Brawell (Notts.), Jan. 13, 1553.	15	1	172
Mar. 21, 1564.	Scote, Nicholas, Barnshalle, par. Ecclesfeild, July 30, 1564.	17		411
May 18, 1559.	———, Thomas, Herwell, par. Everton (Notts.), Apl. 8, 1559.	15	3	420
Oct. 8, 1562.	Scothorn, William, Grevis Lane, par. Edyngley (Notts.), Aug.30,1562.	17		118
Mar. 12, 1556.	Scott, Alison, widow of John S., Watterfrystone, Aug. 7, 1556.	15	1	199

		Vol.	Pt.	Fol.
Apl. 27, 1558.	Scott, Edward, Skeklinge, Dec. 3, 1557.	15	2	205
Feb. 25, 1556.	——, Peter, prest at Aithwike by the Streat, Jan. 26, 1556.	15	1	166
May 1, 1557.	——, Robert (bur. Ripon), Sep. 5, 1556.	15	1	210
Jan. 24, 1558.	——, Sir Robert, curate of Marre, Dec. 4, 1558.	15	3	217
Oct. 6, 1558.	——, Rowland, Byllysdaylle, July 7, 1558.	15	3	90
July 1, 1561.	——, Thomas, Leven in Holderness, husbandman, Oct. 2, 1560.	17		76
Feb. 15, 1558.	——, Thomas, senr., Linley Hill (Holderness), Aug. 11, 1558.	15	3	269
Feb. 25, 1556.	——, William, Silkestone, yeoman, Feb. 4, 1556.	15	1	167
Apl. 7, 1557.	—— als. Smyth, John, Saxton, Jan. 14, 1556.	15	1	204
Feb. 24, 1561.	Scotte, Christopher, Wedderby (bur. Spofford), May 1, 1557.	17		18
Mar. 20, 1559.	——, Robert, Clyfforde (bur. Bramham), Feb. 8, 1559.	16		15
Feb. 24, 1559.	——, Willliam, Ormesbe in Cleveland, Jan. 7, 1559.	16		3
May 13, 1558.	——, William, Pyegresse, par. Silkestone, Nov. 17, 1567.	17		804
Apl. 10, 1555.	Scowfeld, John, Lightclif, par. Halifax, Jan. 15, 1554.	14		117
Jan. 13, 1558.	Screton, Robert, Willoughbie (Notts.), Dec. 28, 1558.	15	3	180
Aug. 6, 1554.	Scrommyn, Richard, Doncaster, Feb. 7, 1552.	14		75
Apl. 3, 1559.	Scrowston, Robert, Muston (bur. Humanbie), Nov. 27, 1558.	15	3	270
Apl. 2, 1557.	Scrutone, William, Cattone (bur. Topclif), Dec. 7, 1556.	15	1	285
Oct. 12, 1564.	Scrymshawe, John, Balderton (Notts.), husbn., July 2, 1564.	17		389
May 9, 1566.	Scrymshey, William, Cotgrave (Notts.), Aug. 3, 1565.	17		550
Apl. 12, 1559.	Scryvener, James, Wakefeld, Jan. 19, 1558.	15	3	340
Dec. 1, 1558.	Seaman (Registered Senum), John, senr., Swinland (Swanland, bur. North Feribie), husbandman, July 15, 1558.	15	3	80
May 29, 1562.	Seasby, Thomas, Golldall (bur. Snaythe), Apl. 18, 1561.	17		100
Mar. 9, 1557.	Seavear, Steven, Righton, husbandman. Feb. 18, 1556.	15	2	129
May 31, 1557.	Secker, Richard, Wombwell (bur. Derffelde), Feb. 8, 1556.	15	1	261
Oct. 5, 1564.	Sedall, William, Draxe, Jun. 17, 1563.	17		367
Aug. 2, 1565.	Sedalle, George, Naburne, par. Acaster, July 22, 1565.	17		456
Jan. 29, 1556.	Seggeswike, John (bur. Topclif), Jan. 17, 1556.	15	1	93
Nov. 4, 1565.	Segiswithe, John, Beverley, Sep. 18, 1558.	17		487
Aug. 21, 1561.	Selbe, Robert, Beverley, fyshemonger, Mar. 20, 1560.	17		56
Jun. 2, 1561.	Selbye, Elizabeth, Bingham (Notts.), widow, Apl. 2, 1561.	17		65
May 4, 1558.	————, William, Byngham (Notts.), husbandman, Jan. 29, 1556.	15	2	212
Jan. 12, 1558.	Sele, John, Bagbie, gentleman, Jun. 10, 1558.	15	3	176
Jan. 12, 1558.	——, John, Thirkerbie, par. St. Felix, Oct. 20, 1558.	15	3	174
May 21, 1560.	Seley, Margaret, Snynton (bur. Brompton), Nov. 20, 1557.	16		66
Jan. 12, 1558.	Sellars, Jenett, Beverlaie, Nov. 18, 1558.	15	3	194
Mar. 4, 1560.	Selle, Robert, Reednes (bur. Whitgift), Dec. 22, 1559.	16		153
Sep. 15, 1558.	Seller, William, Langton, husbandman, Sep. 14, 1558.	15	3	105
Aug. 11, 1558.	Sellerer, John, York, mylner, Apl. 20, 1558.	15	2	292
Nov. 10, 1557.	Seloo, Robert, Snyenton (bur. Bromptone), gent. Aug. 4, 1557.	15	2	100
Oct. 12, 1558.	Selow (Fellowe, Act Book), Thomas, Selston (Notts.), Aug. 21, 1558.	15	3	14
Oct. 3, 1555.	Selowe, Richard, New Malton, July 18, 1555.	14		194
July 15, 1561.	Selvester, John, Hunshelf, par. Penystone, Apl. 12, 1561.	17		81
Mar. 8, 1558.	Seman, Robert, Swanland (bur. N. Feribie), yeoman, Feb. 16, 1558.	15	3	286
July 15, 1561.	Semenet, Elizabeth, Aghton, par. Aston, widow, May 1, 1560.	17		82
Jun. 26, 1557.	Semer, Christopher, Over Catton, Jun. 14, ——.	15	1	299
Aug. 26, 1558.	——, Lambert, Rival (bur. Hemslaye), Aug. 10, 1558.	15	2	292
July 2, 1558.	Sener (Saner, Act Bk.), Robert, Cliffurthe, par. Bramham, Mar. 28, 1557.	15	2	343
Jan. 28, 1566.	Senior, William, Dodworthe, par. Silkstone, husbn., Sep. 28, 1566.	17		608
Dec. 1, 1558.	Senum (Seaman, Act Bk.), John, senr., Swinland (Swanland, bur. North Feribye), husbandman, July 15, 1558.	15	3	80
Oct. 1, 1556.	Senyor, Richard, Bradfeld, Mar. 25, 1553.	15	1	126
Dec. 1, 1561.	Sergentson, Robert, Handlithe (bur. Kirkebye Mallholmdale), Sep. 29, 1561.	17		33
Oct. 13, 1558.	Setan, Vincent, East Retforth (Notts.), July 26, 1557.	15	2	359
Mar. 23, 1564.	Settell, Margaret (bur. Conysheton), Feb. 18, 1564.	17		408
Mar. 7, 1566.	Settills, John, Brustwicke, par. Skeclinge, Sep. 6, 1566.	17		514
Jun. 21, 1561.	Settyll, Thomas (bur. Longe Preston), Jan. 31, 1558.	17		73
Oct. 4, 1564.	————, Thomas, Reilston, Sep. 6, 1564.	17		369
Feb. 6, 1558.	Sevyer, Ralffe, Heaton, Nov. 25, 1558.	15	3	258
Oct. 8, 1567.	Sewell, John, senr., Kyworthe (Notts.), Feb. 12, 1566.	17		728

		Vol.	Pt.	Fol.
Oct. 14, 1563.	Sewell, John, Thirske, July 7, 1562.	17		298
Jan. 22, 1561.	Seygstone, John, Aplegarthe, par. Baynton, Jan. 7, 1560.	17		25
Jun. 19, 1567.	Seymer, John, Fyrbie (bur. Westowe), husbandman, May 21, 1567.	17		656
Apl. 3, 1563.	Seyntpall, Robert, Campsall, gentleman, Apl. 7, 1559.	17		220
Apl. 27, 1564.	Sha, Roger, Gounthorpe (bur. Lowdham, Notts.), Feb. 28, 1563.	17		338
May 6, 1557.	Shackilton, Richard, Scoles, par. Kighlaie, Apl. 2, 1557.	15	1	254
July 8, 1560.	Shackleton, John, senr., Heptonstall, May 20, 1560.	16		90
Oct. 1, 1560.	Shacklocke, William, Sturton (Notts.), husbandman, Jan. 1, 1559.	16		115
Apl. 21, 1562.	Shafto, Edward (bur. Tannfeld, Notts.), Oct. 5, 1559.	17		175
Nov. 29, 1558.	Shaie, John, Great Kelke (bur. Foston), Nov. 12, 1557.	15	2	369
May 10, 1556.	Shakelton, John, Ovenden, par. Halyfaxe, Apl. 8, 1556.	15	1	34
Apl. 17, 1567.	Shakilton, John, Morton Bankes, par. Bingley, Nov. 10, 1566.	17		621
Mar. 26, 1565.	————, William, Stansfeld, par. Heptonstall, Dec. 14, 7 Eliz.	17		414
Aug. 13, 1567.	Shakles, William, Sutton in Holderness, husbandman, Apl. 15, 1567.	17		689
Mar. 6, 1556.	Shakloke, Richard, Sturton (Notts.), husbandman, Sep. 6, 1556.	15	1	182
Oct. 5, 1558.	Shanne, Robert, Metheley, Oct. 22, 1557.	15	3	64
Apl. 15, 1562.	Share, Margaret, Sheryfhuton, Feb. 8, 1560.	17		160
Sep. 23, 1557.	————, William, Sheryfhoton, husbandman, Aug. 8, 1557.	15	1	335
Apl. 28, 1563.	Sharp, Thomas, Burton Agnes, yeoman, Dec. 17, 1562.	17		231
Oct. 2, 1566.	Sharpe, Edward, Horton, par. Braddforthe, May 27, 1566.	17		580
Dec. 15, 1557.	————, Henry, Eilkeslay (Notts.), Aug. 4, 1557.	15	2	56
Jan. 13, 1558.	————, John, Colson Bassett (Notts.), Aug. 10, 1558.	15	3	180
Jun. 6, 1560.	————, John, Fymber, par. Wytwam, husbandman, Sep. 1, 1560.	16		74
Apl. 27, 1558.	————, John, Horton, par. Bradforthe, Feb. 9, 1557.	15	2	193
Nov. 14, 1561.	————, Lowrance, Lowthorpe, Mar. 13, 1560.	17		34
Feb. 17, 1557.	————, Oliver, Notton, par. Roiston, husbandman, Jan. 24, 1557.	15	2	142
Jun. 25, 1557.	————, Peter, Athwike by the strete, May 7, 1557.	15	1	298
Nov. 21, 1554.	————, Richard, Metheleye, Aug. 6, 1554.	14		294
Nov. 3, 1558.	————, Richard, Shupton (bur. Overton), husbn., Oct. 10, 1558.	15	3	96
Apl. 8, 1559.	————, Robert, Esyngwold, Dec. 29, 1558.	15	3	323
Oct. 5, 1558.	————, Robert, Metheley, May 6, 1558.	15	3	64
May 19, 1559.	————, Robert, Ottley, Apl. 12, 1558.	15	3	427
Nov. 26, 1558.	————, Stephan (bur. Overton), Sep. 26, 1558.	15	3	76
Apl. 20, 1564.	————, Thomas, Rawmarshe, husbandman, Aug. 20, 1561.	17		324
Sep. 19, 1558.	————, Sir Thomas (bur. Huggett), Aug. 2, 1558.	15	3	107
May 13, 1557.	————, William, Colson Bassett (Notts.), Nov. 14, 1556.	15	1	229
July 19, 1557.	————, William, Elkesley (Notts.), May 9, 1557.	15	1	286
Dec. 15, 1557.	———— als. Glover, Robert, Eylkeslay (Notts.), July 20, 1557.	15	2	60
Apl. 24, 1567.	Sharples, Richard, Langar (Notts.), Aug. 9, 1559.	17		645
Dec. 13, 1557.	Sharpus, Robert, Hangyngheton, par. Dewesburye, Nov. 10, 1557.	15	2	52
July 31, 1566.	————, Thomas, Hingyn Heaton, par. Dewisberie, Dec. 8, 1565.	17		563
Apl. 4, 1554.	Shauhilton [Shackleton], Agnes, Haworthe (Notts.), Apl. 27, 1553.	14		222
May 13, 1557.	Shaw, Richard, Carleton, par. Gedlinge (Notts.), Oct. 12, 1556.	15	1	220
Sep. 26, 1558.	————, Sybell, Doncastre, widow, May 30, 1558.	15	3	49
May 5, 1558.	————, Thomas, Harby (bur. S. George, Clifton, Notts.), yeom., Apl. 10, 1557.	15	2	262
Sep. 9, 1561.	————, Thomas, Mydgley, par. Halifax, May 20, 1560.	17		51
Apl. 26, 1558.	Shawcoke, John, West Hadlesay (bur. Byrken) husbn., Jun. 4, 1557.	15	2	235
Apl. 12, 1559.	Shawe, Christopher, West Halton, par. Longe Prestone, Jan. 26, 1558.	15	3	341
May 5, 1568.	————, George, Slagheweath, par. Huddersfeld, clothier, Apl. 6, 1568.	17		791
May 20, 1557.	————, Gilbert, Ovenden, par. Hallifax, Oct. 29, 1556.	15	1	211
Aug. 28, 1563.	————, John, Archerhouse, par. Hallyfax, yeoman, Mar. 21, 1561.	17		208
Dec. 22, 1557.	————, John, Warley, par. Halyfax, Sep. 17, 1557.	15	2	48
Apl. 20, 1559.	————, Raynold, Bothumsall (Notts.), Feb. 24, 1557.	15	3	307
May 4, 1557.	————, Richard, Syckehouse in Bradfeld, May 28, 1556.	15	1	278
Apl. 8, 1559.	————, Thomas, Baddisworth, smyth, Mar. 25, 1559.	15	3	330
Apl. 16, 1562.	————, Thomas, Calder (bur. Kildweke), Aug. 8, 1561.	17		187
May 19, 1554.	————, Thomas, Carlton in Gedlinge (Notts.), Mar. 9, 1553.	14		111
July 31, 1554.	————, Thomas, Overton, parish clerk, Mar. 13, 1554.	14		145
May 4, 1565.	————, William, Seacroft, par. Whitchurche, Sep. —, 1556.	17		421
Apl. 27, 1558.	Shay, John, Sandall Magna, Jan. 2, 1557.	15	2	194
Oct. 1, 1556.	————, John, Pennyston, May 16, 1555.	15	1	123

		Vol. Pt. Fol.
Jan. 20, 1561.	Shay, Roger, Huddersfeld, Jan. 19, 1557.	17 22
July 18, 1560.	Shaye, Adelyne, spinster, dau. of John S., Great Kelke, par. Foston, Apl. 28, 1560.	16 93
May 15, 1557.	———, John, Doncaster, dyer, Feb. 13, 1556.	15 1 283
Apl. 23, 1554.	———, John, Morton, par. Bingley, Apl. 12, 1554.	14 63
May 9, 1565.	Shaykylton, Edward, Morton Bankes, par. Byngley, Jan. 18, 1564.	17 434
Mar. 22, 1558.	Sheafeild, William, Waikefeild, Jan. 30, 1558.	15 3 294
Oct. 4, 1564.	Shefeld, William, Ylkley, Jun. 26, 1563.	17 369
Feb. 9, 1557.	Sheildes, Anthony, Patrington, Nov. 27, 1557.	15 2 121
May 18, 1559.	Shelleto, Nicholas, senr., Prestone Jaklinge (bur. Fetherstone), Apl. 1, 1558.	15 3 415
May 18, 1559.	———, William, Prestone Jakling (bur. Fetherstone), May 11, 1558.	15 3 414
Dec. 5, 1558.	Shellito, John, York, notarie, Aug. 24, 1558.	15 3 127
May 14, 1558.	Shemen, William (bur. Skarbroughe), Apl. 28, 1557.	15 2 281
Feb. 4, 1556.	Shepard, James, Sportburghe, husbandman, Sep. 24, 1556.	15 1 169
Dec. 22, 1556.	———, Richard, Hikkilton, Sep. 10, 1556.	15 1 84
Dec. 1, 1558.	———, Robert, Hull, cordiner, Sep. 4, 1558.	15 3 82
Jan. 13, 1558.	———, Roger, Nottingham, shomaker, Oct. 6, 1558.	15 3 205
Jan. 30, 1566.	Sheparde, Robert, Pattrington, Aug. 18, 1566.	17 610
Oct. 28, 1563.	Shepeherd, Agnes, Helmesley, widow. *No date.*	17 299
Apl. 10, 1559.	Sheperd, Agnes, Treton, widow, Dec. 19, 1558.	15 3 329
July 8, 1557.	———, Heugh, Lestingham, Mar. 4, 1556.	15 1 306
Feb. 20, 1560.	———, Richard, Heptonstall, Dec. 8, 1560.	16 148
Nov. 3, 1558.	———, Robert, Wragby, Sep. 13, 1558.	15 3 155
Jan. 30, 1566.	———, Thomas, Kylnesey, Dec. 4, 1566.	17 609
Oct. 2, 1555.	———, Thomas, Staneburghe, par. Silkeston, Feb. 14, 1555.	14 163
Oct. 1, 1560.	———, William, Eastretford (Notts.), Oct. 1, 1559.	16 114
Apl. 18, 1567.	———, William, clerk, late vicar of Howton Pannell (bur. Hickyllton), Mar. 19, 1566.	17 635
Dec. 17, 1557.	Sheperde, Alys, Sprodbroughe, Nov. 18, 1557.	15 2 41
May 26, 1563.	———, John, Treton, Aug. 7, 1558.	17 249
Jan. 20, 1557.	———, John, Wyckerslay, husbandman, Nov. 20, 1557.	15 2 64
Dec. 22, 1556.	Shephard, Hew, Brampton, par. Treton, Mar. 2, 1555.	15 1 75
Dec. 22, 1556.	Shepherd, Nicolas, Bolton on Derne, husbandman, Sep. 18, 1556.	15 1 77
Jun. 18, 1557.	Sheplay, Alexander, Esington, Apl. 24, 1557.	15 1 294
Feb. 6, 1558.	Sheppard, John, Newmylner Dame, par. Sandall Magna, Nov. 9, 1558.	15 3 257
July 1, 1562.	Shepparde, Thomas, Maltebie, Jun. 7, 1562.	17 91
Aug. 5, 1557.	Sheppeard, Genet, Sulland (bur. Elland), widow, Jan. 20, 1556.	15 2 118
Sep. 29, 1563.	Shepperd, John, Bramebar (Barnbrough) Grange, Sep. 26, 1559.	17 284
Oct. 4, 1565.	———, John, Estcottingwithe (bur. Wighton), Feb. 10, 1564.	17 483
May 6, 1563.	———, Oliver, Loudam (Notts.), Jan. 27, 1560.	17 242
Apl. 6, 1558.	Shepperde, Elizabeth, Brodsworthe, widow, Nov. 30, 1557.	15 2 186
May 5, 1568.	Shepworth, Edwarde, Kirke Heaton, Feb. 21, 1567.	17 789
Apl. 30, 1556.	Sherbroke, Richard, Stanley (bur. Teversall, Notts.), Oct. 31, 1553.	15 1 31
Aug. 4, 1565.	Sherburne, Thomas, Kelfeild (bur. Stillingfleit), Mar. 12, 1564.	17 456
Oct. 7, 1558.	Shereborne, John, Roclyfe, Aug. 4, 1558.	15 3 91
Apl. 20, 1556.	Shereburn, Thomas, Dighton, par. Escrike, Apl. 1, 1556.	15 1 15
Feb. 16, 1556.	Sherecliff, Nicholas, Ecclesfeld, yeoman, Oct. 12, 1556.	15 1 158
July 5, 1557.	Sherpe, Henry, Athwike by the strete, Jun. 19, 1557.	15 1 301
Oct. 3, 1565.	Sherppe, Thomas. Rodyshawll, par. Bradforthe, clarke, May 21, 1565.	17 481
May 17, 1565.	Sherven, John, Beston (Notts.), Dec. 27, 1564.	17 439
Jun. 22, 1568.	Sherwodd, Thomas, Bridlington Key, occupier, Jun. 15, 1567.	17 820
Apl. 13, 1559.	Sherwoode, Richard, Hornsey. *No date.*	15 3 345
Oct. 10, 1566.	———, Thomas, Nottingham, inholder, Apl. 26, 1560.	17 590
Oct. 6, 1557.	Sheven, Sir William, curate of Clyfton (Notts.). *No date.*	15 2 29
Feb. 18, 1556.	Shiersone, Thomas, Rowall (bur. Kellyngtone), Dec. 30, 1556.	15 1 160
May 19, 1559.	Shiltone, John, Whitgift, Jan. 7, 1558.	15 3 429
Oct. 29, 1558.	Shimming, John, Suffold, par. Hacknes, Mar. 5, 1557.	15 3 238
May 17, 1565.	Shipman, Henry, Gounthorpe (bur. Lowdham, Notts.), Mar. 28, 1565.	17 439
Jan. 13, 1558.	———, Rauffe, Cropwell, par. Teithbie (Notts.), husbn., Aug. 9, 1558.	15 3 179
No date.	———, Thomas, Cathorpe, par. Lowdam, husbn., Nov. 4, 1560.	17 40
July 3, 1565.	Shippabothom, Richard, Bridlington, Apl. 19, 1565.	17 449

		Vol.	Pt.	Fol.
Dec. 1, 1567.	Skelton, Steven, York, cooke, Oct. 6, 1567.	17		748
Dec. 4, 1557.	———, William, Thorpe (bur. Brayton), yeoman, Nov. 15, 1557.	15	2	52
Jun. 2, 1564.	———, William, Thorpe Willowbe, Jun. 10, 1563.	17		347
July 11, 1558.	———, William, Warngbourghe (bur. Southe Kyrkeby), Nov. 8, 1557.	15	2	318
May 13, 1557.	Skennelbie, Henry, Wiggislay, par. Thorney (Notts.), husbn., Dec. 28, 1556.	15	1	217
Sep. 18, 1565.	Skergell, Thomas, junr., Sheffeld, May 23, 1565.	17		468
Jan. 20, 1557.	Skergill, Robert, senr., Sheffelde, yeoman, Oct. 26, 1557.	15	2	63
Jan. 24, 1565.	Skerne, Edmonde, Hothome, gentleman, July 28, 1564.	17		495
Mar. 5, 1566.	Skinner, William, Skipton (bur. Topclif), Oct. 24, 1558.	17		513
Jan. 18, 1556.	Skipton, Agnes, Pontfraite, widow, Apl. 8, 1556.	15	1	87
July 29, [1555.]	———, John. Pontefracte, alderman, Jun. 9, 1555.	14		208
Oct. 5, 1558.	Skirlay, Robert, New Malton, Jun. 25, 1557.	15	3	44
Oct. 6, 1558.	Skirrow, John, Havercrofte (bur. Felkirke), yeoman, Jan. 13, 1556.	15	3	25
Oct. 12, 1558.	Skothorne, Richard, Oxen (Notts.), husbandman, Jan. 20, 1557.	15	3	13
Aug. 3, 1557.	Skotsonne, Sybbell, York, widow, July 18, 1557.	15	2	131
Mar. 8, 1562.	Skott, Henry, Cowike, par. Snathe, Jan. 12, 1562.	17		147
Dec. 22, 1556.	———, Richard, Barneshall, par. Egglesfelde, yeoman, July 12, 1556.	15	1	75
Mar. 20, 1565.	———, Robert. Brustwicke (bur. Skeclinge), Feb. 22, 1565.	17		505
Jan. 20, 1557.	———, Robert, Sykehouse, par. Fyshelaike, Sep. 3, 1557.	15	2	67
Oct. 6, 1557.	———, Thomas, Everton (Notts.), July 22, 1557.	15	2	9
Mar. 10, 1567.	Skotte, Grace, Thornar, widow, Feb. 18, 1567.	17		763
Feb. 24, 1563.	Skotter, William, Thorngumbold (bur. Pawlle), Apl. 4, 1558.	17		318
July 6, 1557.	Skrymsher, William, Northdighton (bur. Spofford), esq., July 10, 1556.	15	1	304
Jun. 6, 1560.	Skyne, Ellyne, Northecave, widow, Mar. 12, 1559.	16		75
May 4, 1558.	Skynner, William, Bridgeforth (Notts.), husbandman, Aug. 2, 1557.	15	2	263
May 2, 1560.	Skyres, John, Wentworthe, Apl. 6, 1559.	16		49
May 6, 1557.	Skyrowe, Alexander (bur. Kyghley), Jan. 24, 1556.	15	1	285
Jan. 20, 1557.	Slacke, Edward, Cawthorne, Jun. 19, 1557.	15	2	68
Jun. 20, 1568.	———, Henry, Wragbe, May 15, 1568.	17		828
Jan. 14, 1564.	———, Jennet, Worspurdall, widow, Sep. 20, 1564.	17		401
Apl. 6, 1558.	———, John, Gunnytwhat, par. Penyston, Oct. 26, 1557.	15	2	182
Oct. 1, 1556.	Sladen, Jennett, Sourbye, par. Halifaxe, widow, Aug. 8, 1556.	15	1	143
Mar. 13, 1558.	Slader, Edward, Tikhill, Nov. 12, 1558.	15	3	164
Sep. 25, 1560.	Slaiter, William, Kyrkebye Overblawse, husbn., Sep. 15, 1560.	16		105
May 5, 1568.	Slake, Margaret, Emley, Nov. 20, 1563.	17		791
Mar. 20, 1558.	———, Richard, Worsburghdayle, husbandman, Feb. 21, 1558.	15	3	244
Jan. 23, 1564.	Slater, Oliver, York, Nov. 28, 1564.	17		400
Jun. 21, 1565.	———, Richard, Sikehouse, par. Fyshelake, Apl. 7. 1565.	17		446
July 9, 1558.	———, Robert (bur. Topclyf), Oct. 23, 1557.	15	2	325
Apl. 20, 1564.	Slatter (Slater), Richard, Dongworth, par. Bradfeld, July 1, 1563.	17		324
Aug. 18, 1554.	Slee, Richard, West Heslerton, par. Yeddingham, husbn., Mar. 9, 1553.	14		147
May 17, 1560.	———, Thomas, Westheslerton, yeoman, Feb. 1, 1559.	16		64
Dec. 9, 1556.	Sleigh, Thomas, Southburton, Sep. 8, 1556.	15	1	72
Jan. 12, 1558.	Sleighe, Alice, Bushoppburton, widow, Dec. 4, 1558.	15	3	197
Aug. 6, 1567.	———, Roger, Bainton, husbandman, Apl. 23, 1567.	17		702
Jun. 22, 1565.	Sleighthom, Thomas, Fadmore (bur. Kirkebye Morshed), Apl. 28, 1565.	17		445
May 2, 1566.	Slinger, Alice, late wife of Robert S., Rughe Cloise, par. Kirkbie Malham, Oct. 3, 1565.	17		531
Jun. 21, 1561.	Slynger, John, Buckden, par. Arneclyf, Aug. 26, 1559.	17		84
Mar. 10, 1555.	Slyueld (or Slyneld), Henry, Bothamsall (Notts.), Aug. 14, 1554.	14		223
May 5, 1558.	Smalleman, John, Gettforth, par. Warkesop (Notts.), Jan. 26, 1557.	15	2	283
Oct. 8, 1562.	Smalley, James, Berton (bur. Sallow(?), Bingham Dny.), Dec. 26, 1560.	17		119
Apl. 19, 1559.	Smally, Alexander, Watnall Chuworthe (bur. Greasley, Notts.), Dec. 21, 1558.	15	3	353
July 1, 1558.	Smalpaige, Elizabeth, Waikefeild, widow, Nov. 12, 1557.	15	2	329
Sep. 28, 1560.	Smalwood, William, Wysey (? Wysall) (Notts.), Apl. 26, 1560.	16		107
Aug. 14, 1566.	Smarthwate, John, Rustone (bur. Wykam), ——, 1566.	17		565
Jan. 31, 1564.	Smaylles, Richard, Hinderwell, Apl. 2, 1564.	17		404
Mar. 8, 1558.	Smeathlay, Edward, Beverlay, Nov. 7, 1558.	15	3	157
Mar. 30, 1558.	Smedeman, John, Harum (bur. Helmesley), yong man, Jan. 22, 1557.	15	2	178
Dec. 1, 1557.	Smekergell, Anthony, Denton, Nov. 1, 1557.	15	2	85

A.D. 1554 TO 1568.

		Vol.	Pt.	Fol.
Dec. 1, 1557.	Smekergill, Agnes, Esthawlynghew in Denton, Aug. 1, 1557.	15	2	84
July 29, 1555.	Smeyton, William, Standfurthbridge, July 1, 1555.	14		208
Jan. 13, 1558.	Smith, Brian, Standforth (Notts.), Apl. 28, 1558.	15	3	182
May 6, 1557.	——, John, Utley (bur. Kighlaie), Nov. 5, 1556.	15	1	254
Oct. 7, 1558.	——, Thomas, Sowreby, par. Halifax, Apl. 17, 1558.	· 15	3	227
Sep. 30, 1558.	Smithe, John, Burne, par. Braton, clothier, Aug. 26, 1558.	15	3	89
May 2, 1555.	——, John, Elsterwicke, Mar. —, 1554.	14		33
May 13, 1557.	——, John, Laxton (Notts.), Feb. 20, 1557.	15	1	216
Apl. 7, 1554.	——, John, Prestonne (bur. All Hallows), Mar. 21, 1553.	14		155
Apl. 7, 1554.	——, John, Vinestead. *No date.*	14		217
Mar. 28, 1555.	——, Margaret, Kellington, Mar. 4, 1553.	14		107
Nov. 29, 1558.	——, Raufe, Doncaster, ——, 1556.	15	3	144
Sep. 15, 1558.	——, Richard, Thorneton in Pykeringlythe, Sep. 4, 1558.	15	3	104
Apl. 5, 1554.	——, Thomas, Burton Fleminge, May 24, 1553.	14		215
Jan. 24, 1558.	——, Thomas, Claiton, par. Friclay, Aug. 5, 1558.	15	3	119
Jan. 24, 1558.	——, William, Billam (bur. Howton Pannall), Oct. 4, 1558.	15	3	218
May 19, 1555.	——, William, Plumtre (Notts.), husbandman, Jun. 3, 1553.	14		112
Mar. 3, 1555.	——, William, Prestone (bur. All Hallows), Nov. 1, 1555.	15	1	10
Jan. 7, 1562.	Smithes, John (bur. Kellington), Aug. 22, 1562.	17		140
Oct. 6, 1558.	Smithson, Philippe, Norton (Bucros), widow, Aug. 8, 1557.	15	3	226
Nov. 14, 1561.	Smothing, John, Gemlynge (bur. Foston) draper, Aug. 11, 1558.	17		34
Oct. 5, 1558.	Smygargill, William (bur. St. Mich., Ardesley), Aug. 17, 1558.	15	3	61
Mar. 15, 1560.	Smyrell, Henry, Barmby, par. Blithe (Notts.), husbn., Jan. 20, 1560.	16		168
Jan. 20, 1558.	Smysson, Olyver, Newe Malton, mylner, Dec. 20, 1558.	15	3	212
May 1, 1554.	——, Thomas, Teryngton, Feb. 10, 1 Mary.	14		135
Oct. 8, 1567.	Smyth, Alice, Rempstone (Notts.), Jun. 7, 1567.	17		728
July 11, 1558.	——, Alis, Doncaster, Apl. 17, 1558.	15	2	306
July 15, 1558.	——, Christopher, Nunburneholme, husbandman, Mar. 18, 1557.	15	2	307
May 18, 1557.	——, Elizabeth, Brighton (bur. Bubwith), widow, May 10, 1557.	15	1	257
May 19, 1559.	——, Isabell, Camylfurth, par. Drax, widow, Jan. 13, 1558.	15	3	425
May 4, 1557.	——, James, Bramwith (bur. Haytfeld), husbandman, Sep. 22, 1556.	15	1	277
Oct. 4, 1558.	——, James, Farneley, par. Leides, Aug. 6, 1558.	15	3	58
Feb. 25, 1558.	——, James, Sowrbye (St. Oswald), Dec. 19, 1558.	15	3	279
Oct. 12, 1558.	——, John, Barneston, par. Langar (Notts.), husbn., Aug. 12, 1558.	15	3	31
Oct. 9, 1560.	——, John, Beverlay, cowper, May 19, 1560.	16		121
Aug. 20, 1555.	——, John, Claworth (Notts.), July 31, 1555.	14		195
Apl. 18, 1567.	——, John, Grymsthorpe, par. Felchurche, Feb. 7, 1566.	17		637
Oct. 3, 1565.	——, John, the Helme in Sourbe, par. Halifax, yeom., Mar. 13, 1564.	17		476
Oct. 29, 1558.	——, John, Honnanbie, Aug. 13, 1558.	15	3	238
May 5, 1558.	——, John, Myssyn (Notts.), Dec. 13, 1556.	15	2	252
Feb. 15, 1558.	——, John, Prestone in Holderness, Nov. 21, 1558.	15	3	271
July 1, 1556.	——, John, Sherburne, husbandman, May 13, 1556.	15	1	51
July 9, 1563.	——, John, Sprotley, Apl. 13, 1563.	17		265
July 17, 1565.	——, John, West Newton, par. Alburghe, husbn., May 21, 1565.	17		452
May 13, 1557.	——, John, Wieston (bur. Claworth, Notts.), ——, 1553.	15	1	232
July 16, 1562.	——, Laurance, Heptonstall, Apl. 15, 1562.	17		97
July 12, 1564.	——, Peter, Kylnsey, Mar. 20, 1564.	17		357
May 24, 1558.	——, Richard, Aunderby, Dec. 3, 1557.	15	2	283
Oct. 11, 1565.	——, Richard, Bingham (Notts.), Jan. 2, 1565.	17		471
Apl. 8, 1559.	——, Richard, Boltbie, par. Felixkirke, Nov. 21, 1558.	15	3	321
Jan. 13, 1558.	——, Richard, Bradmer (bur. Bonney, Notts.), Mar. 19, 1558.	15	3	182
May 10, 1559.	——, Richard, Brigham (bur. Fostone), Feb. 6, 1558.	15	3	391
Apl. 1, 1557.	——, Richard, Camylsfurth, par. Drax, Dec. 15, 1555.	15	1	286
Apl. 16, 1567.	——, Richard, Colton (bur. Bolton Percie), Mar. 22, 156[6-]7.	· 17		638
Apl. 26, 1558.	——, Richard, Hornbye in Cleveland, husbandman, Apl. 15, 1558.	15	2	238
May 29, 1566.	——, Richard (bur. Ripon), Apl. 11, 1566.	17		544
Apl. 12, 1559.	——, Richard, Skypton, Nov. 7, 1557.	15	3	341
Aug. 31, 1556.	——, Richard, Tykhill, Apl. 12, 1556.	15	1	63
Oct. 13, 1558.	——, Richard (bur. Warsope, Notts.), Jan. 7, 1557.	15	2	356
Feb. 4, 1555.	——, Robert, Gannsted, par. Swyne, husbandman, Aug. 10, 1555.	14		303
Jun. 2, 1558.	——, Robert, Holme in Spaldingmore, Apl. 16, 1558.	15	2	312
May 18, 1559. ·	——, Robert, Hymsworth, Oct. 12, 1558.	15	3	401

A.D. 1554 TO 1568.

		Vol.	Pt.	Fol.
Apl. 12, 1559.	Smyth, Robert, Steton, par. Kyldwycke, Dec. 24, 1558.	15	3	342
May 18, 1559.	———, Thomas, Aithwyke by strete, Jan. 21, 1558.	15	3	400
July 20, 1557.	———, Thomas, Bucketon (bur. Bempton), husbn., Apl. 29, 1557.	15	1	314
May 6, 1557.	———, Thomas, Buckton (bur. Bempton), Feb. 17, 1556.	15	1	246
Aug. 1, 1564.	———, Thomas, Burnholme, husbandman, Jun. 4, 1564.	17		361
Apl. 29, 1559.	———, Thomas, Cawode, Apl. 19, 1559.	15	3	361
Feb. 21, 1558.	———, Thomas, Dringhouses, York, inholder, Jan. 8, 1558.	15	3	277
Apl. 23, 1556.	———, Thomas, Roose, Mar. 2, 1555.	15	1	25
Oct. 29, 1558.	———, Thomas, Scawbie, July 29, 1558.	15	2	372
Mar. 23, 1557.	———, Thomas, Weton (bur. Wellweke), Feb. 8, 1557.	15	2	153
Mar. 4, 1562.	———, William, Burton Flemynge (bur. Hunmanbie), Dec. 23, 1562.	17		153
Feb. 17, 1557.	———, William, Byrlaye Carre, par. Eglesfeld, July 6, 1557.	15	2	136
No date.	———, William, vycare of Calverton (Notts.), Mar 21, 1553.	14		230
Apl. 28, 1558.	———, William, Carliton, par. Snayth, Feb. 16, 1557.	15	2	227
Jun. 8, 1565.	———, William, Helperthrop, par. Weverthorpe, Oct. 13, 1564.	17		444
Dec. 11, 1566.	———, William, Leberston, par. Filay, husbandman, May 13, 1566.	17		603
Oct. 12, 1558.	———, William, Rempston (Notts.), Aug. 22, 1558.	15	3	31
Oct. 12, 1558.	———, William, Ruddington (bur. Flafurth, Notts.), Aug. 20, 1558.	15	2	352
Jan. 12, 1558.	———, William, Skidhe, July 23, 1558.	15	2	354
July 15, 1562.	———, William, Stoneferre, par. Sutton, Jan. 1, 1561.	17	.	95
Jan. 12, 1558.	———, William, senr. Welle, par. St. John, Beverlaie, Jan. 28, 1557.	15	3	195
Apl. 26, 1558.	——— als. Cowper, John, Staineburne, yeoman, Dec. 18, 1557.	15	2	234
Apl. 7, 1557.	——— als. Scott, John, Saxton, Jan. 14, 1556.	15	1	204
May 2, 1566.	Smythe, Anthony, Mytton, Aug. 24, 1565.	17		531
Oct. 7, 1561.	———, Anthony, Wydmerpole (Notts.), husbandman, Jun. 20, 1560.	17		41
Mar. 17, 1558.	———, Sir Anthony, Ripon, clarke, Mar. 4, 1558.	15	3	242
Aug. 7, 1565.	———, Bryan, Bothumsall (Notts.), May 11, 1564.	17		459
Apl. 16, 1567.	———, Christopher, Harteshed, Nov. 17, 1566.	17		624
Oct. 27, 1564.	———, Cicilie, Rudbye, widow, July 15, 1564.	17		394
Mar. 18, 1559.	———, Edmonde, Campsall, Feb. 9, 1559.	16		10
Nov. 28, 1567.	———, Edward, Bourton Flemynge (bur. Hunmanbie), Nov. 11, 1566.	17		740
May 15, 1555.	———, Edward, Stonefeyre, par. Sutton, Apl. 20, 1555.	14		237
Aug. 9, 1565.	———, Elline, Wistowe, widow, July 9, 1565.	17		456
Aug. 24, 1558.	———, Francis, Colton (bur. Bolton Percie), July 25, 1558.	15	2	295
July 19, 1557.	———, George, Allerton (Notts.), Jun. 1, 1557.	15	1	309
Feb. 9, 1557.	———, George, Thorkylbye, par. Swyne, husbn., Jan. 12, 1557.	15	2	122
Aug. 29, 1554.	———, Gregorye, Brighton (bur. Bubwith), husbn., Feb. 12, 1552.	14		271
Apl. 12, 1559.	———, Henry, Adingham, Mar. 24, 1559[?8].	15	3	341
Oct. 7, 1557.	———, Henry, Bekingham (Notts.), Jun. 14, 1557.	15	2	21
Jun. 20, 1558.	———, Henry, Connyston, par. Gargrave, Apl. 8, 1568.	17		808
Apl. 28, 1563.	———, Henry, Kirkbeoverblause, glover, Nov. 15, 1562.	17		235
Feb. 17, 1561.	———, Henry, Lytle Hodsacke (Notts.), Feb. 7, 1561.	17		14
Nov. 19, 1555.	———, Henry, Newsome, yeoman, Oct. 8, 1555.	14		76
July 15, 1567.	———, Hewgh, Collinge, par. Kelweke, Nov. 20, 1566.	17		674
Nov. 9, 1560.	———, Hughe, Attercliffe, par. Sheffelde, Sep. 8, 1560.	16		129
Jun. 9, 1563.	———, Isabell, Hedon, widow, Jan. 26, 1562.	17		253
Oct. 23, 1565.	———, James, Lawe Bishophill, par. Paiteleybriges, talyer, Feb. 26, 1564.	17		482
Dec. 16, 1556.	———, James, Spofforthe, Oct. 8, 1556.	15	1	195
Mar. 11, 1562.	———, Jennet, Aithwike by streite, Nov. 12, 1562.	17		155
Mar. 10, 1566.	———, Johan, Doncaster, widow, Feb. 16, 1565.	17		516
Oct. 7, 1561.	———, Johan, wid. of Wm. S., Ruddyngton (Notts.), Apl. 6, 1561.	17		41
No date.	———, John, Aston, Sep. 4, 1553.	14		88
Sep. 24, 1567.	———, John, Boynton, husbandman, Aug. 12, 1560.	17		706
Apl. 17, 1567.	———, John, Calton, par. Kirkbie Malham, Mar. 10, 9 Eliz.	17		620
May 5, 1558.	———, John, Carleton in Lyndryk (Notts.), husbn., Nov. 20, 1557.	15	2	246
Apl. 6, 1558.	———, John, Clytton, par. Fryckley, Sep. 5, 1557.	15	2	180
Oct. 8, 1567.	———, John, Cotgrave (Notts.), Dec. 18, 1566.	17		727
Oct. 1, 1561.	———, John, Cottingham, Mar. 10, 1560.	17		45
July 23, 1558.	———, John, Cowyk, par. Snayth, Nov. 10, 1557.	15	2	385
Sep. 30, 1557.	———, John, Esthorpe (bur. Loundesburghe), Aug. 17, 1557.	15	1	327
July 10, 1567.	———, John, Felkirke, May 24, 1567.	17		685

		Vol.	Pt.	Fol.
May 10, 1565.	Smythe, John, Hornesey, labourer, Dec. 6, 1562.	17		424
Aug. 23, 1563.	———, John, Howingham, May 20, 1563.	17		211
Aug. 8, 1562.	———, John, Hudderfeld, May 16, 1562.	17		104
Apl. 16, 1567.	———, John, Kaingham, husbandman, Feb. 4, 1566.	17		634
Dec. 9, 1556.	———, John, S. Nicholas, Beverlay, Nov. 11, 1556.	15	1	198
July 17, 1555.	———, John, North Frothingham, husbandman, Jan. 12, 1555.	14		244
Aug. 7, 1565.	———, John, North Whetley (Notts.), Jan. 14, 1564.	17		459
Apl. 22, 1562.	———, John, Plumtrie (Notts.), husbandman, Oct. 18, 1561.	17		178
Aug. 2, 1557.	———, John, Preston (Holderness), Jun. 19, 1557.	15	1	323
May 9, 1565.	———, John, Sourebie, par. Halifax, clothier, Dec. 18, 1564.	17		423
Feb. 4, 1556.	———, John, Steynford [par. Hatfield], Dec. 21, 1556.	15	1	170
Oct. 6, 1557.	———, John, senr., Sturton (Notts.), husbandman, Aug. 16, 1557.	15	2	10
Oct. 7, 1557.	———, John, Thurgarton (Notts.), Apl. 2, 1557.	15	2	24
May 13, 1557.	———, John, Wigthorpe, par. Karilton in Linricke (Notts.), husbn., Mar. 8, 1556.	15	1	232
Jan. 15, 1561.	———, John, Wyrspure, May 25, 1561.	17		25
Dec. 18, 1562.	———, John, York, butcher, Oct. 26, 1562.	17		135
Apl. 27, 1563.	———, Lawrance, Rudbye, husbandman, Jan. 20, 1562.	17		225
July 15, 1567.	———, Myles, Kigheley, husbandman, Feb. 10, 1566.	17		677
May 23, 1565.	———, Nicholas, Londisburghe, husbandman, Jan. 16, 1564.	17		442
Dec. 15, 1557.	———, Nicholas, Warsopp (Notts.), Nov. 23, 1557.	15	2	56
Feb. 17, 1561.	———, Olyver, North Wheatley (Notts.), labourer, Nov. 10, 1560.	17		15
Nov. 5, 1564.	———, Peter, Weill, par. St. Jo., Beverley, Sep. 15, 1564.	17		396
Feb. 17, 1561.	———, Richard, Bothumsall (Notts.), Aug. 21, 1561.	17		14
Jan. 29, 1555.	———, Richard, Brighton (bur. Bubwith), husbn., Aug. 10, 1555.	15	1	2
Oct. 7, 1557.	———, Richard, Darleton, par. Dunham (Notts.), Jun. 29, 1554.	15	2	20
Mar. 2, 1555.	———, Richard, Fernell, par. Kildewicke, Mar. 4, 1554.	15	1	12
Jun. 12, 1557.	———, Richard, Goldall (bur. Snath), Apl. 23, 1557.	15	1	291
Jun. 24, 1561.	———, Richard, Halles, par. Drax, July 8, 1560.	17		85
Dec. 13, 1561.	———, Richard, Knapton (bur. Trinity, York), Apl. 14, 1561.	17		27
May 9, 1565.	———, Richard, Nether Bradley (bur. Kildweke), Mar. 27, 1565.	17		433
Oct. 7, 1556.	———, Richard, North Clifton (Notts.), husbandman, Mar. 28, 1556.	15	1	146
Apl. 30, 1556.	———, Richard, Plumtre (Notts.), smythe, Feb. 3, 1555.	15	1	30
Feb. 19, 1556.	———, Richard, Skerne, Jan. 3, 1556.	15	1	163
Oct. 1, 1560.	———, Richard, Sturton (Notts.), husbandman, May 12, 1560.	16		115
Oct. 6, 1557.	———, Richard, senr., Sturton (Notts.), labourer, May 5, 1557.	15	2	14
Oct. 6, 1557.	———, Richard, Thoroton (Notts.), Aug. 5, 1557.	15	2	30
Feb. 6, 1558.	———, Robert, Aberforthe, Oct. 17, 1558.	15	3	265
Oct. 1, 1561.	———, Robert, Beverley, watterman, Sep. 20, 1561.	17		45
Jun. 7, 1561.	———, Robert, Braton, husbandman, May 12, 1561.	17		70
Feb. 24, 1563.	———, Robert, Burton Constable (bur. Swyne), Aug. 3, 1563.	17		318
May 18, 1555.	———, Robert, Carleton, par. Snaithe, Mar. 25, 1555.	14		238
Dec. 10, 1567.	———, Robert, Catwicke, "Intendinge to remove and flytt to Wibberton in Lincolnshire." *No date.*	17		744
July 7, 1555.	———, Robert, Catwick, Apl. 5, 1555.	14		71
Oct. 7, 1557.	———, Robert, Fiscarton, par. Rolston (Notts.), Jun. 6, 1557.	15	2	19
Jun. 7, 1560.	———, Robert, Lowthrope, husbandman, Mar. 17, 1559.	16		77
Jan. 23, 1560.	———, Robert, Nayburne, May 26, 1560.	16		139
Apl. 14, 1562.	———, Robert, Rysse, Jan. 21, 1561.	17		185
Feb. penult., 1560.	———, Robert (bur. Ryther), Sep. 20, 1559.	16		151
Apl. 20, 1564.	———, Robert, Slaghweythe, par. Huddersfeld, clothier, Jan. 31, 156[3]4.	17		327
Apl. 27, 1558.	———, Robert, Somerhouse, par. Kyldewike, Nov. 30, 1557.	15	2	202
Apl. 16, 1567.	———, Robert, Thornton in Pickeringe lithe, Jan. 6, 1566.	17		639
Oct. 10, 1566.	———, Robert, Torworthe, par. Blithe (Notts.), husbn., Dec. 1, 1564.	17		589
Aug. 17, 1564.	———, Robert, Warley, par. Halifax, clothier, Dec. 25, 1563.	17		361
Apl. 14, 1562.	———, Rowlande, Wynesteyde, Dec. 2, 1561.	17		184
Jan. 29, 1556.	———, Symon, Flambrughe, wever, Oct. 18, 1556.	15	1	94
Apl. 6, 1558.	———, Thomas, Adweke of Derne, labourer, Aug. 9, 1556.	15	2	188
Sep. 28, 1562.	———, Thomas, Ayrmen (bur. Snaythe), fisher, Aug. 6, 1562.	17		108
Dec. 3, 1567.	———, Thomas, Burley, par. Otley, Jun. 20, 1567.	17		744
Sep. 30, 1557.	———, Thomas, Conyston, par. Swyne, Sep. 10, 1557.	15	1	343

A.D. 1554 TO 1568.

		Vol.	Pt.	Fol·
Apl. 22, 1556.	Smythe, Thomas (Gillinge), Mar. 26, 1556.	15	1	19
Dec. 3, 1561.	———, Thomas, Gisburne, Sep. 23, 1561.	17		27
July 27, 1562.	———, Thomas, Horsforthe (bur. Gyesley), yeom., Jun. 8, 1562.	17		98
Apl. 14, 1562.	———, Thomas, Lyghtclyf, Feb. 12, 1558.	17		181
Jun. 5, 1561.	———, Thomas, New Malton, Sep. 20, 1560.	17		69
Sep. 28, 1557.	———, Thomas, Romesgill, par. Ylkelay, Mar. 28, 1557.	15	1	339
Oct. 5, 1558.	———, Thomas, Seamer, July, 18, 1558.	15	3	66
Dec. 4, 1554.	———, Thomas, Spofforthe, July 13, 1553.	14		92
Aug. 28, 1563.	———, Thomas, Stapleton (bur. Darington), husbn., Dec. 28, 1563.	17		211
Dec. 2, 1563.	———, Thomas, Sutton on Darwent, Nov. 9, 1563.	17		306
Dec. 15, 1557.	———, Thomas, Walkringham (Notts.), husbandman, Nov. 6, 1556.	15	2	60
May 10, 1567.	———, Thomas, Walkringham (Notts.), Jun. 10, ———.	17		651
Sep. 30, 1557.	———, William, Armyne, par. Snaythe, Aug. 21, 1557.	15	1	343
Apl. 7, 1562.	———, William, Beysthorpe (bur. South Scarle, Notts.), Dec. 15, 1561.	17		185
Jan. 22, 1561.	———, William, Bisshop Burton, Oct. 31, 1561.	17		25
Jun. 23, 1563.	———, William, Burton Flemynge (bur. Hunmanbie), Sep. 9, 1562.	17		260
July 8, 1560.	———, William, Carrehowse, par. Heptonstall, Aug. 15, 1559.	16		91
July 10, 1561.	———, William, Denton, par. Ottley, husbandman, Nov. 28, 2 Eliz.	17		64
Aug. 2, 1557.	———, William, Hedon in Holderness, mylner, Jun. 30, 1557.	15	1	323
Oct. 1, 1560.	———, William, Heydon in Holderness, gentleman, July 19, 1560.	16		110
Mar. 21, 1559.	———, William, Hollome, Dec. 20, 1559.	16		16
Apl. 12, 1559.	———, William, Letham, husbandman, Mar. 15, 1558.	15	3	335
Feb. 24, 1560.	———, William, Londisbourghe, Jan. 16, 1560.	16		150
Apl. 26, 1559.	———, William, Northowrom, par. Hallifax, Aug. 16, 1558.	15	3	313
Apl. 24, 1567.	———, William, Owthorpe (Notts.), husbandman, Feb. 5, 1566.	17		645
Mar. 2, 1555.	———, William, Skackilton (bur. Hovingham), labr., Nov. 22, 1555.	15	1	9
May 2, 1560.	———, William, senr., Stenford (bur. Hatfelde), Jan. 25, 1558.	16		46
Sep. 28, 1557.	———, William, Swyilden, par. Gysburne, husbn., Jun. 10, 1557.	15	1	340
May 4, 1557.	———, William, Upton, par. Badisworth, Jan. 28, 1556.	15	1	276
Aug. 9, 1565.	———, William, Wistowe, Jun. 13, 1565.	17		455
Oct. 6, 1557.	———, William, Yedwalton (Notts.), husbandman, Jun. 29, 1557.	15	2	27
Apl. 2, 1558.	———, William, York, tanner, Mar. 22, 1557.	15	2	179
May 17, 1567.	———, William, York, weaver, May 2, 1567.	17		646
Jun. 18, 1567.	——— *als.* Walker, John, Ferburne (bur. Ledsham), husbn., Apl. 27, 1567.	17		657
July 26, 1557.	Smytherson, Jenat, Kerkbe Misperton, Jun. 6, 1557.	15	1	320
Nov. 19, 1567.	Smytheson, Nycholes, Setteryngton, husbandman, Apl. 14, 1566.	17		736
Sep. 17, 1556.	———, Robert, Appleton in the strete, Dec. 26, 1554.	15	1	66
Jan. 21, 1557.	———, Robert, Fowlbin, par. Wragbye, Nov. 22, 1557.	15	2	70
Jan. 22, 1557.	———, Symonde, Thorneton in Pyckeryngelythe, Nov. 26, 1557.	15	2	159
Dec. 13, 1557.	Smythson, Charles, Snytall (bur. Normanton), Nov. 19, 1557.	15	2	52
Jan. 22, 1557.	———, Emote, Thorneton in Pickeringe lythe, Nov. 24, 1557.	15	2	160
Apl. 28, 1568.	———, Isabell (bur. Ripon), Mar. 30, 1568.	17		770
Nov. 10, 1564.	———, Thomas (bur. Kirkbemysperton), Jun. 3, 1564.	17		398
Feb. 18, 1556.	Smythsone, John, Nortone (Buckros), husbandman, Nov. 18, 1556.	15	1	162
Nov. 7, 1566.	Smytson, Robert (bur. Kirkbie Mysperton), Aug. 6, 1566.	17		599
Oct. 3, 1554.	Snaithe, Peter, Sutton in Holderness, Jan. 22, 1552.	14		40
Mar. 23, 1557.	———, William, Conyston, par. Swyne, husbandman, Feb. 24, 1557.	15	2	173
May 5, 1568.	Snape, George, Baeldall, par. Burton (Pontefract), Feb. ult., 1567.	17		790
Oct. 8, 1556.	Snarde, Robert, Newarke (Notts.), husbandman, Mar. 20, 1556.	15	1	154
Oct. 7, 1557.	———, Thomas, Balderton (Notts.), husbandman, May 10, 1557.	15	2	19
Mar. 2, 1555.	Snare, William, Kelfeld (bur. Stillingfleet), Sep. 24, 1555.	15	1	8
Apl. 3, 1559.	Snarrie, Sawnder (bur. Kirkbe Mysperton), Jan. 9, 1558.	15	3	318
Sep. 30, 1557.	Snart, Robert, Stillingflete, July 10, 1557.	15	1	346
July 4, 1556.	Snaw, Thomas, Eskyrke, Jun. 2, 1556.	15	1	51
Jan. 3, 1558.	Snawden, Omfray, Walton, par. Sandall Magna, Aug. 6. 1558.	15	3	34
Dec. 11, 1566.	Snawdon, Anne, York, Dec. 1, 1566.	17		604
Feb. 4, 1561.	———, George, Scallyng Hole (bur. Esyngton) Nov. 15, 1561.	17		13
Feb. 4, 1561.	———, John, junr., Est Cotum, husbandman, Jan. 8, 1561.	17		12
Oct. 14, 1563.	———, John, Seyssay, husbandman, July 17, 1563.	17		298
Dec. 10, 1557.	———, Richard, Northdyghton, smyth, Nov. 17, 1557.	15	2	83
Mar. 22, 1554.	———, William, (bur. St. Nicholas, Cleveland), Nov. 16, 1554.	14		187

		Vol.	Pt.	Fol.
Oct. 29, 1554.	Snawdon, William, Kirkdighton, Jun. 2, 7 Edw. 6.	14		283
Apl. 29, 1559.	Snawe, John, Eskrige, Mar. 13, 1558.	15	3	361
May 7, 1568.	———, John, Roclif (bur. Snaythe), Jun. 17, 1566.	17		781
Jun. 19, 1557.	Snawsell, Brian, Esingwold, gentleman, Jun. 10, 1557.	15	1	295
Oct. 5, 1564.	Snayth, John, Sutton (Holderness), Sep. 3, 1564.	17		368
Jan. 16, 1560.	Snell, Isabell (bur. Stillingflete), Mar. 16, 1559.	16		143
Apl. 27, 1558.	———, John, Wagill (bur. Gargrave), Sep. 15, 1557.	15	2	198
Oct. 2, 1566.	———, Leonard, Waygell, par. Gargrave, Mar. 10, 1566.	17		574
May 6, 1557.	———, Richard, Panbeke, par. Longe Prestone, Jan. 15, 1556.	15	1	284
Dec. 2, 1562.	———, John, Rotheram, yeoman, Sep. 6, 1562.	17		130
Apl. 28, 1563.	———, Thomas (bur. Rilston), clerk, Apl. 4, 1563	17		228
Feb. 5, 1555.	———, William, Grubthorpe, par. Bubwith, July 21, 1555.	15	1	5
Sep. 12, 1562.	Snewsthopp (Fuvstehope in Register), Vincent, Buttercram, wevar, Jun. 30, 1561.	17		108
Jan. 13, 1558.	Sneynton, John, Burton (Notts.), gentleman, Apl. 22, 37 Henry VIII.	15	3	187
Oct. 13, 1558.	Snoden, William, Norton Cuckney (Notts.), May 30, 1558.	15	2	356
May 22, 1563.	Snowe, Mathew (bur. Ripon), Apl. 30, 1563.	17		248
Sep. 1, 1563.	Snydall, Issabell, wid. of Thomas S., Almeholme (bur. Arkesey), Aug. 21, 1562.	17		206
Dec. 22, 1556.	———, Thomas, Awmehalme, par. Arkesay, Aug. 15, 1556.	15	1	77
Aug. 13, 1567.	Snype, Peter, Wynestead, May 1, 1567.	17		690
May 2, 1560.	Sodybie, William, Burton Pidsey, Apl. 6, 1559.	16		48
July 27, 1564.	Solate, John, Egton, Jun. 10, 1563.	17		361
May 5, 1557.	Sollaie, Thomas, Seamer, Mar. 4, 1556.	15	1	248
May 6, 1557.	Somerscall, Sir Richard, preest (bur. Gigleswicke), Mar. 30, 1557.	15	1	252
Apl. 2, 1554.	Somerscalles, Robert, Settell, par. Gigleswicke, foller, Oct. 29, 1553.	14		219
Dec. 3, 1560.	Sonderland, Richard, Shelfe, par. Hallyfax, Aug. 21, 1560.	16		131
July 27, 1564.	Sonley, Henry, Welborne, par. Kirkedaill, husbandman, Mar. 20, 1563.	17		359
Nov. 25, 1555.	Sonnlaye, Henry, Hinderwell, Sep. 18, 1555.	14		183
Oct. 13, 1562.	Sonyer, John, Weston, clothear, May 14, 1562.	17		125
Jan. 12, 1558.	Sorogon, Nicholas, Sprotlay, Nov. 16, 1558.	15	3	202
July 20, 1564.	Sotehill, John, Kirkeburton, Aug. 4, 1562.	17		358
Feb. 4, 1557.	Sotheron, John, Seaton, husbandman, Dec. 10, 1557.	15	2	164
Mar. 8, 1566.	Soulle, Robert, Holme in Spaldingmore, Jan. 11, 1566.	17		512
May 9, 1566.	Sourbey, Hew, Grenley, par. Clarebroughe (Notts.), Dec. 9, 1565.	17		541
July 3, 1567.	Sourbie, John, Kirkebemoreshed, smythe, Jan. 10, 1566.	17		669
Oct. 29, 1554.	Southwort, Robert, Kirton (Notts.), clerk, Nov. 26, 1553.	14		280
July 19, 1567.	Sowden, Edward, Woddall, par. Calverlay, Mar. 2, 1566.	17		681
Nov. 9, 1557.	———, Richard, Thorton, par. Bradforth, Dec. 26, 1556.	15	2	95
Apl. 18, 1567.	———, Robert, Gresgarthis, par. Weston, Dec. 19, 1566.	17		632
Jan. 7, 1562.	———, Thomas, Allerton, par. Bradford, Aug. 12, 1562.	17		141
Oct. 13, 1562.	Sowdon, John, Thornton, par. Bradford, July 23, 1562.	17		126
Oct. 6, 1558.	Sowerby, John, Little Houghton, par. Darfeild, Aug. 18, 1558.	15	3	222
July 27, 1567.	Sowlay, John, Skelton in Cleveland, May 17, 1567.	17		671
May 3, 1556(?5).	Sowley, Robert, Little Aytonne in Clevelande, Mar. 17, 1554.	14		34
Dec. 18, 1556.	Sowrby, William, Estrigton (bur. Berdsay), labourer, Oct. 9, 1556.	15	1	176
Jan. 13, 1558.	Sowre, Henry, Normanton on Soore (Notts.), husbn., May 24, 1558.	15	3	181
May 18, 1559.	Sparke, Thomas, Thorpe, par. Barnebie on Done, Jan. 22, 1558.	15	3	396
Feb. 10, 1566.	Sparrowe, Nicholas, Brinde, par. Wressill, Oct. 26, 1566.	17		612
Jun. 21, 1568.	———, Robert, Beverley, glover, Aug. 16, 1567.	17		815
May 2, 1566.	Spawnton, Thomas, Wombleton (bur. Kirkdaill), husbn., Oct. 8, 1564.	17		519
July 11, 1560.	Specke, Henry, Wheldrike, Mar. 22, 1559.	16		92
Jan. 15, 1557.	———, Raynolde, Dighton (bur. Eskrige), Oct. 20, 1557.	15	2	82
Mar. 9, 1557.	Speghte, Edward, Warleye, par. Hallifax, Dec. 12, 1557.	15	2	168
Apl. 27, 1558.	Speight, Agnes, Gomersall (bur. Brystall), widow, July 20, 1557.	15	2	195
Jan. 28, 1562.	———, Robert, Addle, labourer, Dec. 22, 1562.	17		145
Apl. 10, 1557.	———, William, Chidsill, par. Dewesburye, Jan. 26, 1556.	15	1	207
Jun. 20, 1568.	———, William, Overthownge, par. Almonburye, Oct. 5, 1567.	17		828
Sep. 3, 1554.	Speighte, Robert, Sothill, par. Dewesburye, husbn., Jun. 16, 1554.	14		272
Dec. 1, 1558.	Spence, John, Beverlay, Sep. 10, 1558.	15	3	147
May 6, 1557.	———, Robert, Glusborne, par. Kyldwike, Nov. 30, 1556.	15	1	283
Mar. 6, 1556.	Spencer, Alverey, Scrowby (Notts.), Nov. 23, 1556.	15	1	183

		Vol.	Pt.	Fol.
May 4, 1555.	Spencer, Edward, Treton, Dec. 12, 1554.	14		81
Nov. 17, 1558.	——, Henry, Wistow, Sep. 7, 1558.	15	3	113
Apl. 3, 1559.	——, John, Wistow, Sep. 8, 1556.	15	3	319
Jan. 13, 1558.	——, Mawde, Scrobie (Notts.), Sep. 23, 1558.	15	3	184
Jan. 13, 1558.	——, William, Willowbie (Notts.), Aug. 15, 1558.	15	3	181
Apl. 16, 1562.	Spencs, Nicholes, Roston, par. Wykhame, Feb. 8, 1561.	17		158
Sep. 20, 1557.	Spenley, Thomas, Tho[r]neton in Pyckeringe lythe, Apl. 22, 1557.	15	1	335
Mar. 21, 1561.	Spens, Adam, Beverley, Jun. 10, 1561.	17		6
Apl. 28, 1563.	Spenser, Jennette, Gaunsted, par. Swyne, Dec. 9, 1562.	17		238
Mar. 20, 1560.	——, John, Aerton (bur. Kirkbye Malhomedaill), Jan. 4, 1560.	16		172
Dec. 17, 1557.	——, John, Aghton, par. Aston, May 19, 1557.	15	2	39
Oct. 2, 1560.	——, John (bur. Kyrkebymysperton), May 5, 1560.	16		111
May 4, 1558.	——, Thomas, Gothame (Notts.), husbandman, July 28, 1557.	15	2	209
May 5, 1558.	——, Thomas (bur. Teversall, Notts.), Nov. 20, 1557.	15	2	283
Feb. 16, 1563.	——, Thomas, Wikeam (bur. Old Malton), July 5, 1563.	17		316
Oct. 7, 1557.	——, William, Northe Leverton (Notts.), yeoman, Jan. 17, 1556.	15	2	15
Oct. 1, 1562.	——, William, Sutton (bur. Kildweke), Jun. 6, 1562.	17		110
Oct. 25, 1558.	Spenslaie, Robert, Newton, par. Kirkdaill, husbandman, Sep. 11, 1558.	15	3	238
Aug. 26, 1558.	Spenslay, Christopher, Helmeslay, Aug. 8, 1558.	15	2	293
Oct. 20, 1558.	Sperling, Anne, Thirske, Sep. 26, 1558.	15	2	346
July 8, 1557.	Speth, Nicolas, Befurthe, husbandman, Mar. 7, 1557.	15	1	305
Aug. 6, 1567.	Spicer, Elline, Anlaby, par. Elueley. widow, May 9, 1567.	17		698
Jan. 30, 1566.	——, William, Anlabie, par. Hessill, May 3, 1566.	17		611
Jun. 11, 1558.	Spincke, Bryan, Bilton, May 22, 1558.	15	2	216
Jan. 20, 1560.	Spinke, Isabella, Sutton, par. Tadcaster, widow, Mar. 7, 1559.	16		141
Sep. 6, 1558.	——, Nicholas, Normanton, Jun. 1, 1558.	15	3	98
Jan. 17, 1558.	——, Richard, Stutton, par. Tadcaster, tanner, Nov. 20, 1558.	15	3	210
Aug. 28, 1561.	——, Richard, York, pynner, Aug. 4, 1561.	17		52
Jan. 3, 1558.	——, Thomas, Acastre Selbie, par. Styllingflet, Oct. 16, 1558.	15	3	36
Apl. 5, 1559.	——, Thomas, Howke, Aug. 20, 1557.	15	3	319
Nov. 27, 1560.	——, Thomas, Nether Popleton, ——, 1560.	16		130
Jun. 2, 1564.	Spittall, Nicholas (bur. Snaythe), clerk, Dec. 21, 1563.	17		347
Feb. 6, 1555.	Spofforth, Elizabeth, Hamylton (bur. Brayton), wid., May 14, 1555.	15	1	6
Oct. 29, 1558.	——, Thomas, Cawoode, Mar. 17, 1557.	15	3	232
Jan. 3, 1556.	[1] Spofforthe, Brian, clerke, Kyrby, ——, 1554.	15	1	171
Sep. 11, 1563.	——, John, Hamelton (bur. Brayton), yeoman, May 31, 1563.	17		204
May 30, 1560.	——, Robert, Haddlesay (bur. Byrkyn), Oct. 26, 1559.	16		70
Jan. 11, 1558.	Spoffurth, George, Haddilsay (bur. Birkin), July 6, 1558.	15	3	171
Oct. 2, 1555.	Spownare, William, Sheffeld, sheather and yeoman, Feb. 12, 1554.	14		104
Aug. 16, 1566.	Sprouston, William, Barlay (bur. Braton), Apl. 24, 1566.	17		570
Feb. 24, 1563.	Sproxton, John, Nafferton, Apl. 12, 1563.	17		320
Apl. 10, 1557.	——, Richard, Wakefeld, yeoman, Mar. 1, 1556.	15	1	206
July 28, 1556.	——, William (Hymmesworthe), preist, May 28, 1556.	15	1	47
Apl. 22, 1562.	Spurr, William, Babworthe (Notts.), yeoman, Aug. 27, 1561.	17		193
Sep. 28, 1560.	Spybye, Robert, Newton (bur. Shelforthe, Notts.), Apl. 16, 1560.	16		106
Nov. 11, 1557.	Spyer, William, Preston (Holderness), Sep. 26, 1557.	15	2	95
Jan. 29, 1556.	Spynes, John, Nafferton, husbandman, Apl. 10, 1556.	15	1	93
Jun. 11, 1558.	Spynke, Agnes (bur. St. Ellenges, York), widow, May 31, 1558.	15	2	286
Sep. 28, 1557.	——, John, Castley (bur. Leythley), Aug. 1, 1557.	15	1	336
Jun. 13, 1564.	——, Margaret, widow of Nicholas S., Altoftes (bur. Normanton), May 21, 1564.	17		348
Nov. 5, 1567.	——, Nycholas, Overpopulton, par. Bphill. junr., York, Jan. 1, 1566.	17		733
Jun. 27, 1565.	——, William, York, tapyter, Jun. 9, 1565.	17		445
May 1, 1567.	Spyvye, Thomas, Doncaster, smythe, Apl. 4, 1567.	17		647
Mar. 21, 1565.	Squier, Agnes, Skoulskottes, widow, May 4, 1564.	17		500
Oct. 31, 1566.	——, Robert, Owsom (bur. Skraingham), wright, Jun. 29, 1562.	17		586
Sep. 30, 1556.	Squire, Thomas, Welwyke, husbandman, Apl. 4, 1556.	15	1	138
May 9, 1566.	Squyer, James, Colstonn Bassett (Notts.), smythe, Jan. 2, 1565.	17		549
Nov. 28, 1558.	Squyre, William, Waxham, par. Outthorne, husbn., Oct. 20, 1558.	15	3	78
Apl. 13, 1559.	Sqwiar, Thomas, Rostone in Holderness, husbandman, Aug. 9, 1557.	15	3	344

[1] This Will is in three portions ; the second is dated South Dalton, Oct. 18, 1556, and the third Nov. 15, 1556.

		Vol.	Pt.	Fol.
July 1, 1567.	Stabill, Bartilmew, Sherifhoton, husbandman, Apl. 13, 1567.	17		684
May 2, 1566.	Stable, Christopher, Astlay, par. Swillington, Dec. 15, 1565.	17		520
Apl. 11, 1554.	———, Edmund, Wiglesworthe, par. Longe Preston, Dec. 20, 1553.	14		160
July 8, 1560.	———, Rawffe, Outwoodsyde, par. Waikefelde, Jun. 2, 1560.	16		91
Oct. 13, 1558.	———, Richard, Fernesfeld (Notts.), Mar. 28, 1558.	15	2	360
July 15, 1561.	———, Roger, Wombwell (bur. Darfeld), husbn., Aug. 10, 1560.	17		83
May 18, 1559.	Stables, John, Armethorp, Oct. 29, 1558.	15	3	397
Jan. 21, 1558.	———, William, Selbie, July 28, 1557.	15	3	192
Jun. 20, 1568.	Stachouse, Henry, Meaniley (bur. Slaiteburne), Apl. 21, 1568.	17		808
Apl. 17, 1567.	———, John (bur. Slaitburne), Nov. 15, 1566.	17		619
July 15, 1567.	Stackhous, Robert, Gigleswike, May 24, 1567.	17		674
Jan. 12, 1558.	Stafford, Thomas, Kirkheaton, yeoman, Oct. 11, 1558.	15	3	174
May 5, 1568.	Stafforth, Thomas, Baynton, husbandman, Aug. 28, 1567.	17		777
Nov. 29, 1558.	Stafurth, Owmfray, Hallfeild, par. Sheafeld, Sep. 7, 1558.	15	3	142
July 19, 1567.	Staible, Thomas, Pomfret, Jun. 10, 1567.	17		681
May 17, 1565.	Staipilton, George, Rempstone (Notts.), Dec. 3, 1564.	17		439
May 4, 1558.	Stampe, Thomas, Byngham (Notts.), husbandman, Jan. 2, 1558.	15	2	212
Feb. 11, 1563.	Stamper, John, York, tealer, Jan. 19, 1562.	17		314
Mar. 26, 1565.	Stancefeld, Thomas, Hyginchamber in Sourbie, yeom., Oct. 11, 1564.	17		413
Apl. 10, 1559.	Stancefeyld, Robert, Felkirke, Dec. 10, 1556.	15	3	326
May 5, 1568.	Standen, Elline, Woodhouse (bur. Slaidburne), Feb. 26, 1567.	17		785
Apl. 11, 1554.	———, Margaret, widow (bur. Slaytburn), Mar. 26, 1551.	14		159
Sep. 4, 1567.	Standeven, Thomas, alderman of York, Dec. 30, 1566.	17		705
Aug. 13, [1555.]	Standfeild, Rauf, Otleye, yeoman, July 8, 1555.	14		206
Sep. 21, 1557.	Standfurthe, Thomas, Treton, Aug. 10, 1557.	15	1	355
July 13, 1558.	Staneforth, Stephen, Wressell, May 24, 1558.	15	2	323
May 18, 1559.	Staneland, Robert, Shyrokes, par. Workesop (Notts.), ———, 1558.	15	3	420
Apl. 22, 1562.	Stanfeld, Sethe (bur. Colwyke, Notts.), May 21, 1561.	17		178
Oct. 5, 1558.	Stanford, Thomas, Snydall (bur. Normanton), husbn., Aug. 18, 1558.	15	3	63
May 9, 1563.	Stangoo, Thomas, Barnebie, par. Lithe, May 11, 1563.	17		256
May 6, 1563.	Stanley, Jone, Sutton Bonnyngton (Notts.), widow, Oct. 19, 1562.	17		246
Oct. 12, 1564.	———, Myghell, Sutton Bonyngton (Notts.), yeom., May 31, 1564.	17		391
May 13, 1568.	Stannewaye, Christopher (bur. Rosington), Dec. 8, 1567.	17		803
Apl. 20, 1564.	Stanrige, William, Filinge, Oct. 27, 1563.	17		335
Apl. 7, 1557.	Stansfeld, Alice, Otlay, widow, Mar. 8, 1556.	15	1	204
May 10, 1567.	———, John, Barmbie, par. Blithe (Notts.), husbn., Sep. 23, 1566.	17		652
May 19, 1568.	———, John, Fairburne, par. Ledesham, talier, May 2, 1568.	17		796
Nov. 10, 1558.	———, Thomas, Heptonstall, Aug. 21, 1558.	15	3	156
Mar. 14, 1560.	Stansfelde, Edwarde, Whiston, Jun. 28, 1560.	16		159
Dec. 4, 1557.	———, William, Polyngton (bur. Snaythe), Nov. 5, 1557.	15	2	52
May 31, 1554.	Stanus, William, Fernedall (bur. Lastingham), ———, 1553.	14		132 & 265
Apl. 27, 1558.	Stanworthe, John, Bradforthe, par. Mytton, Nov. 7, 1557.	15	2	203
Oct. 7, 1563.	Stanybanke, Umfrey, Ranskell, par. Blithe (Notts.), husbn., Aug. 7, 1563.	17		295
Feb. 15, 1558.	Stapilton, Alse, Brandisburton, late nun of Nunkelyng, Oct. 24, 1558.	15	3	271
No date.	Staples, Thomas, Fernesfeld (Notts.), Aug. 31, 1561.	17		40
Sep. 15, 1567.	Stapleton, Bryan, Burton Jorce (Notts.), esq., Aug. 20, 1567.	17		709
Oct. 4, 1565.	———, Edmond, Carlton (Snaythe), gentleman, Mar. 13, 1564.	17		485
July 21, 1557.	———, Sir Robert, Wighill, knight, Jun. 6, 1557.	15	1	307
Apl. 13, 1559.	———, Thomas, North Skirley, husbandman, Feb. 26, 1558.	15	3	346
Sep. 30, 1556.	Stapper, Robert (bur. Kettilwell), Apl. 20, 1556.	15	1	131
July 15, 1567.	———, William (bur. Kettilwell), May 19, 1567.	17		674
Jan. 28, 1562.	Stappilton, Anthony, Busterdbanke in Denton (bur. Ottley), Dec. 12, 1562.	17		145
Jan. 30, 1566.	Stark, Robert, Brustwickegarth, par. Skeclinge, Dec. 23, 1566.	17		610
Jan. 6, 1554.	Starke, Thomas, Halsham, ———, 1554.	14		306
Oct. 6, 1558.	Statham, Hugh, Barnburgh on Derne, yeoman. *No date.*	15	3	46
Dec. 14, 1557.	Stather, John, North Cave, Oct. 8, 1557.	15	1	358
July 1, 1561.	———, Marthay, Northe Cave, Jun. 17, 1560.	17		76
Dec. 22, 1556.	Stathom, Edward, Barneburghe, Aug. 3, 1556.	15	1	85
Mar. 23, 1560.	Stauker, John, Ottryngham marshe, Jan. 15, 1560.	16		177
Oct. 5, 1558.	Stavelaie, Jenet (bur. Thormonbie), Sep. 1, 1558.	15	3	71

A.D. 1554 TO 1568.

		Vol.	Pt.	Fol.
Apl. 8, 1559.	Stavelay, William, Crambie, Dec. 7, 1558.	15	3	321
Aug. 15, 1560.	Staveleye, Alyson, Rypon, widow, Feb. 20, 1559.	16		101
May 6, 1555.	Stawe, Robert, Rowlston (Notts.), Mar. 9, 1554.	14		195
July 1, 1558.	Stayfley, Robert, Bemptonne, inholder & husbandman, Dec. 25, 1557.	15	2	323
May 11, 1565.	Staynbourne, Richard, Cawod, Jun. 1, 1563.	17		421
Feb. 26, 1557.	Stayneburn, John, Tockwyth, whelewright (bur. Bylton), Jan. 24, 1557.	15	2	137
Dec. 2, 1558.	Stayneburne, Thomas, Bilton, husbandman, Aug. 3, 1558.	15	3	149
Dec. 10, 1557.	Staynforth, Jeffray, York, cordyner, Aug. 11, 1557.	15	2	84
May 9, 1565.	Staynrige, Robert, Scarbroughe, Nov. 21, 1564.	17		425
Oct. 29, 1554.	Staynton, John, Ferndon (Notts.), Jun. 10, 1554.	14		284
May 8, 1567.	———, Peter, Cottingham, husbandman, Jan. 27, 1566.	17		649
Jan. 14, 1556.	———, Richard, Gatefulforthe, husbandman, Oct. 12, 1556.	15	1	87
Apl. 13, 1559.	———, Peter, Cottingham, Feb. 10, ———.	15	3	350
Dec. 12, 1556.	———, Robert, Whedryke, ———, 1556.	15	1	197
May 7, 1558.	———, William, Gaytfullfurth, husbandman, Oct. 22, 1557.	15	2	279
Mar. 15, 1562.	Staynus, John (? Skelton in Cleveland), Feb. 21, 1561.	17		164
Apl. 8, 1560.	Stayringe, John, Pousworthe (bur. Lynton (Act Book, Hooton), Cranswycke), yeoman, Nov. 19, 1559.	16		28
May 10, 1565.	Steade, Christopher, Ferlington (bur. Sheriffhoton), Mar. 3, 1564.	17		430
Mar. 22, 1558.	———, Thomas, Dighton, par. Hudderfeild, Oct. 26, 1558.	15	3	293
Apl. 14, 1563.	Steadman, Thomas, Sherburne, yeoman, Dec. 1, 1562.	17		221
Jun. 2, 1558.	Steale, Sir John, chauntre prest of Esington, Mar. 24, 155[7-]8.	15	2	336
Jan. 20, 1561.	Sted, Richard, par. Huddersfeld, May 27, 1560.	17		20
Feb. 26, 1563.	Stede, Christopher, Huddersfeild, husbandman, Apl. 23, 1563.	17		321
May 18, 1559.	Stedman, John, South Leverton (Notts.), Oct. 4, 1558.	15	3	407
Feb. 10, 1557.	Steell, James, York, Jan. 17, 1557.	15	2	166
Jun. 25, 1561.	Steid, William, Baildon, par. Ottley, Apl. 12, 1559.	17		74
Nov. 17, 1558.	Steide, Richard, Wike (bur. Harwood), husbandman, Sep. 1, 1558.	15	3	111
Sep. 23, 1558.	Steille, Thomas, Scellton (bur. Rippon), yeoman, Aug. 19, 1558.	15	3	85
July 16, 1562.	———, William, Haddockstones (bur. Ripon) yeoman, Apl. 4, 1562.	17		94
Oct. 2, 1555.	Stele, Richard, Stoke by Newarke (Notts.), husbn., Mar. 1, 1554.	14		193
Mar. 10, 1566.	———, Robert. Ousten, gentleman, Mar. 2, 1564.	17		517
Sep. 29, 1563.	Stell, John, senr. (bur. Kighley), Apl. 10, 1563.	17		279
Oct. 2, 1566.	———, John, Kighley, Aug. 12, 1566.	17		574
Aug. 7, 1556.	Stelle, Raufe, Hotter Stoodley (bur. Ripon), clarke, Mar. 18, 1553.	15	1	60
Aug. 6, 1557.	Steniland, John, Wayth, Apl. 15, 1557.	15	2	118
Mar. 29, 1555.	Stenson (? Stevenson), Richard, Butterwyke, Oct. 31, 1554.	14		190
May 2, 1566.	——— ———, Thomas, Pattrington, husbn., Jan. 26, 8 Eliz.	17		526
Apl. 5, 1554.	Stephenson, Christopher, Butterwik, Oct. 24, 1553.	14		214
Jun. 21, 1565.	———, John, Hollme in Spaldingmore, Mar. 18, 1564.	17		448
May 2, 1566.	———, John, Neswicke (bur. Bainton), husbn., May 1, 1565.	17		538
May 31, 1566.	———, John, Swynflete, gentleman, Mar. 25, 1566.	17		544
Apl. 12, 1559.	———, John, Wragby, July 29, 1558.	15	3	340
Apl. 28, 1558.	———, Robert, Hull, carpenter, Dec. 24, 1557.	15	2	220
Mar. 4, 1560.	Stephinson, John, Hull, glover, Sep. 26, 1560.	16		166
July 11, 1558.	Stere, Elizabeth, Thorne, widow, Oct. 20, 1557.	15	2	304
May 23, 1564.	———, Robert, senr., Ormesbie, Mar. 5, 1563.	17		346
Apl. 6, 1558.	———, Roger, Thorne, Jan. 2, 1557.	15	2	188
Aug. 4, 1558.	———, Thomas, Lekenfelde, husbandman, Jun. 6, 1558.	15	3	3
May 13, 1557.	Sterland, Thomas, Selston (Notts.), husbandman, Apl. 14, 1557.	15	1	224
May 26, 1562.	Sterley, Sir Nicholas, Sterley (Notts.), knight, Aug. 21, 1561.	17		194
Apl. 28, 1559.	Steven, Richard, West Cottingwith (bur. Thorganby), Oct. 11, 1558.	15	3	315
Feb. 10, 1557.	———, Thomas, Sowthecleffe, par. Northe Cave, Nov. 7, 1557.	15	2	150
Oct. 16, 1558.	———, William, Everthorpe, par. North Cave, yonge man, Apl. 3, 1558.	15	2	344
Apl. 19, 1559.	Stevenson, Agnes, Boney (Notts.), Nov. 14, 1558.	15	3	376
May 9, 1565.	———, Agnes, Grisetrope (bur. Fylay), Jan. 20, 1564.	17		425
Jun. 22, 1568.	———, Alice, Thorner, widow, May 27, 1568.	17		817
Aug. 2, 1560.	———, Alison (bur. Skipsey). Sep. 22, 1559.	16		100
Mar. 20, 1565.	———, Amon, Weton, par. Welwicke, Oct. 23, 1564.	17		504
Oct. 2, 1567.	———, Elizabeth (bur. Howke). *No date.*	17		710
Dec. 1, 1558.	———, Elizabeth, Hull (bur. Trinity), widow, Sep. 8, 1558.	15	3	145
Oct. 9, 1560.	———, George, Etton, Apl. 10, 1560.	16		122

A.D. 1554 TO 1568.

		Vol.	Pt.	Fol.
Aug.11, 1567.	Stevenson, Henry, Neswicke (bur. Bainton), husbn., Apl. 12, 1567.	17		697
Oct. 4, 1565.	————, John, Butterwicke, May 25, 1565.	17		486
May 2, 1566.	————, John, Filinge, Mar. 21, 1565.	17		539
Oct. 6, 1557.	————, John, Kynston (Notts.), Sep. 2, 1555.	15	2	30
Dec. 5, 1567.	————, John, Skipsey in Holderness, Aug. 15, 1567.	17		742
May 2, 1560.	————, John (bur. Whitgyfte), Apl. 1, 1 Eliz.	16		53
Mar. 9, 1557.	————, Mychaell, Leberston, par. Fyley, *No date.*	15	2	128
Dec. 10, 1561.	————, Pattryk (Hompton, Holderness), Sep. 29, 1561.	17		30
Nov. 4, 1563.	————, Richard, Birkbie, par. Thorner, Aug. 19, 1558.	17		299
Mar. 3, 1562.	————, Richard, Feildhouses, par. Snaithe, Dec. 29, 1563.	17		148
Jan. 17, 1557.	————, Richard, Galmeton, Aug. 3, 1557.	15	2	61
Mar. 1, 1564.	————, Robert, Holme in Spaldingmore, Jan. 10, 1562.	17		407
Jun. 18, 1557.	————, Robert, Patrington, Apl. 12, 1557.	15	1	295
Mar.31, 1555.	————, Thomas, Doncaster, tanner, Oct. 3, 1553.	14		106
Feb. 6, 1558.	————, Thomas, Gristrope (bur. Fyveley), husbn., Jun. 3, 1558.	15	3	260
Aug. 2, 1560.	————, Thomas, Pattrington, husbandman, July 12, 1560.	16		101
Mar. 4, 1560.	————, Thomas, Whytgyft, Aug. 12, 1559.	16		153
Feb. 7, 1567.	————, William, Baynton, husbandman, Nov. 6, 1567.	17		757
Oct. 6, 1557.	————, William, Bonney (Notts.), Mar. 14, 1556.	15	2	33
Sep. 30, 1556.	————, William, Great Kelke, par. Fostone, Aug. 20, 1556.	15	1	133
May 27, 1562.	————, William, Kayngham, Dec. 1, 1561.	17		101
Mar. 4, 1555.	————, William, Kingston on Hull, butcher, May 2, 1546.	15	1	12
May 10, 1559.	Stevensone, Richard, Seamer, Jan. 23, 1558.	15	3	388
Jun. 5, 1561.	Stevinson, Christopher, Thornton in Pikeringlithe, Nov. 27, 1560.	17		69
Oct. 19, 1558.	————, John, Wilberfosse, husbandman, Oct. 3, 1558.	15	3	121
No date.	————, William, Kingston on Hull, butcher, May 2, 1556.	14		241
July 9, 1563.	————, William, Skeclinge, May 7, 1563.	17		264
Nov.11, 1557.	Stevynson, John, Skecklynge, Oct. 10, 1557.	15	2	99
Sep. 9, 1561.	Steyd, William, Eland, Jun. 17, 1561.	17		52
Apl. 16, 1562.	Steyfinesone, William, Loctonne, par. Myddyltone, ————, 1561.	17		159
May 2, 1560.	Steyll, Henry, Roclyffe (bur. Snathe), Apl. 28, 1559.	16		55
Jun. 2, 1558.	————, Sir John, chauntry preyst of Esington, Mar. 24, 1558.	15	2	311
Feb. 5, 1567.	Steynson (Stevenson), Francis, Lastingham, Oct. 5, 1567.	17		758
May 17, 1560.	Stibbinge, John, Cawtton (bur. Houingham), Nov. 25, 1559.	16		65
Apl. 13, 1559.	Stiring, John, Cawkeld, par. Watton, yeoman, Feb. 16, 1558.	15	3	348
July 15, 1567.	Stirke, Edmunde, Halton, par. Skipton, Jan. 21, 1566.	17		678
Dec. 16, 1557.	S[t]irke, John, Halsham, Nov. 9, 1557.	15	2	47
Nov. 29, 1558.	Stirman, Henry, Tickhill, Oct. 9, 1558.	15	3	140
Oct. 13, 1558.	Stirop, William, Lounde, par. Sutton (Notts.), Mar. 29, 1558.	15	2	377
Dec. 15, 1557.	Stirrop, Alis, Lounde, par. Sutton (Notts.), Nov. 2, 1557.	15	2	58
May 6, 1563.	Stirrope, John, Lund (bur. Sowtton on Lund, Notts.), butcher, Feb. 25, 1562.	17		242
Oct. 6, 1557.	Stirropp, Thomas, Lounde, par. Sutton (Notts.), July 13, 1557.	15	2	7
Dec. 5, 1558.	Stirtill, Richard, Lillin (bur. Sherifhowton), webster, Sep. 26, 1558.	15	3	151
Sep. 29, 1557.	Stockall, William, Mon[k]hill (bur. Pontefract), shomaker, July 26, 1557.	15	1	328
Dec. 29, 1563.	Stockdaill, Alexander, Hull, merchant, Sep. 20, 1563.	17		307
Sep. 17, 1557.	————, Anthony (bur. Topclyffe), July 3, 1557.	15	1	332
Dec. 16, 1563.	————, Bryan, Thirske, Aug. 11, 1563.	17		306
Oct. 5, 1554.	————, Christopher (bur. Topclif), Aug. 7, 1554.	14		275
May 6, 1557.	————, John, West Marton in Craven, Feb. 22, 1556.	15	1	253
Feb. 28, 1566.	————, Rauf, Rudbie, carpenter, May 16, 1566.	17		616
Nov. 5, 1561.	Stockdell, John, senr. (bur. Whenby), Nov. 4, 1558.	17		34
Oct. 15, 1561.	Stockedall, Philles, Gretame, co. Durham, widow, Apl. 20, 1561.	17		36
Sep. 17, 1558.	Stockedayl, Alice, Thorpe, par. Topclyf, July 23, 1558.	15	3	106
Apl. 6, 1566.	Stockedell, Alison, Whenbie. widow, Jun. 27, 1565.	17		509
Jun. 2, 1561.	Stockeles, Agnes, Kynston (Notts.), Jun. 14, 1560.	17		66
Apl. 19, 1559.	Stockeley, William, Kynstone, par. Radclyf on Soore (Notts.), husbn. *No date.*	15	3	373
Apl. 18, 1560.	Stockes, Richard, Great Houghton, par. Derfelde, Mar. 14, 1560.	16		32
Apl. 6, 1558.	————, Richard, Houghton (bur. Derfelde), Aug. 1, 1557.	15	2	183
Sep. 28, 1560.	————, Richard (bur. Hucnall Torcard, Notts.), Apl. 23, 1560.	16		109
Dec. 18, 1556.	Stodley, Thomas, Rowley (bur. Bardsey), yeoman, Aug. 27, 1556.	15	1	175

		Vol.	Pt.	Fol.
May 5, 1558.	Stofing, Richard, Weston (Notts.), Nov. 30, 1557.	15	2	261
Jun. 22, 1565.	Stoinehouse, Thomas, Ferndale, paſ. Lestingham, Nov. 15, 1564.	17		445
Feb. 15, 1565.	Stokell, Robert, Kirkbe in Grendallithe, Dec. 2, 1565.	17		499
July 16, 1558.	Stokell, William, Bolton Percye, Apl. 11, 1558.	15	2	322
Feb. 24, 1563.	Stoker, George, Headon in Holderness, Nov. 4, 1562.	17		318
May 5, 1559.	Stokes, Charles, Tykhill, yeoman, Sep. 11, 1558.	15	3	393
Oct. 6, 1557.	———, George, Thorowton, par. Orston (Notts.), husbn., Apl. 10, 1557.	15	2	28
Mar. 26, 1560.	Stoketon, Thomas, New Malton, yeoman, Feb. 9, 1559.	16		18
Nov. 26, 1557.	Stokkes, John, Tykhyll, Aug. 4, 1557.	15	2	94
Jan. 20, 1561.	Stone, Alison, Kelfeld, par. Stillingflet, Jan. 2, 1561.	17		23
Jan. 20, 1561.	———, John, Kelfeld, par. Stillingfleite, May 9, 1561.	17		24
July 11, 1558.	Stones, Nicholas, Wombewell, par. Darfeyld, May 5, 1558.	15	2	319
Nov. 12, 1556.	———, Richard, Byrkyn, husbandman, Aug. 1, 1556.	15	1	114
May 6, 1568.	———, Richard, senr., Haitfeld Woodhouse, husbn., Sep. 13, 1567.	17		772
July 11, 1558.	———, William, Thorne, mylner, May 1, 1558.	15	2	317
Sep. 21, 1557.	———, William, Treton, Aug. 22, 1557.	15	1	351
Jan. 13, 1557.	Stonnes, Beatrix, Birkynge, widow, Mar. 31, 7 Edw. VI.	15	2	81
Oct. 28, 1563.	Stonus, William, Farnedaile, par. Lastingham, Aug. 18, 1563.	17		298
Feb. 24, 1560.	Store, Thomas, Bubwythe, July 7, 1560.	16		150
May 2, 1560.	Stores, Elizabeth (bur. Braiton), widow, Aug. 30, 1559.	16		52
Feb. 6, 1558.	———, Richard, Burne, par. Braiton, Aug. 20, 1558.	15	3	263
May 2, 1560.	Storie, Alys, Burton Grainge, par. Roiston, widow, Feb. 20, 1558.	16		48
Apl. 3, 1559.	———, John, Griestroppe (bur. Filey), husbandman, Aug. 8, 1558.	15	3	316
May 13, 1557.	———, Robert, Clifton (Notts.), Jan. 7, 1556.	15	1	228
Jun. 12, 1562.	———, Vergus (bur. Beverley), Mar. 31, 1562.	17		88
Nov. 7, 1565.	Storke, Herrye, West Lutton (bur. Weverthorpe), May 25, 1565.	17		492
Jun. 22, 1568.	Storme, John, Scarburghe, Oct. 21, 1567.	17		823
Oct. 6, 1558.	Storr, Thomas, Steynford (bur. Haitfeld), Aug. 3, 1558.	15	3	72
Oct. 6, 1557.	Storres, William, Lounde, par. Sutton (Notts.), Aug. 3, 1557.	15	2	11
Oct. 29, 1558.	Storrie, John, Bridlinton, panyer man, Oct. 14, 1558.	15	3	239
May 15, 1557.	Storris, Christopher, the Foldes, par. Tykhill, Sep. 8, 1556.	15	1	282
Feb. 5, 1557.	Storrye, John, Adlingflete, ———, 1557.	15	2	165
Apl. 19, 1554.	———, John, Kellington, May 12, 1552.	14		161
Oct. 1, 1556.	Storthe, Richard, Sheffeld, yeoman, Apl. 25, 1556.	15	1	125
Aug. 12, 1566.	———, Thomas, senr., Bolsterston in Bradfeld, yeom., Feb. 15, 1560.	17		567
July 15, 1556.	Storye, George, Harpham, Feb. 15, 1555.	15	1	56
Oct. 8, 1562.	———, Heughe, Orston (Notts.), Mar. 20, 1561.	17		120
Mar. 13, 1558.	———, John, Burton Grange (bur. Roistone), yeoman, Jan. 31, 1558.	15	3	160
May 10, 1559.	———, John, Hawnbie, Mar. 19, 1557.	15	3	384
Oct, 7, 1557.	———, John, Horyngham (Notts.), July 2, 1557.	15	2	25
Jun. 13, 1561.	———, John (bur. Scarbrughe), Nov. 20, 1560.	17		71
Apl. 22, 1562.	———, Margaret, Clyfton (Bingham, Notts.), Nov. 30, 1561.	17		192
May 26, 1567.	———, Robert, senr., Bridlington, occupier, Dec. 6, 1566.	17		654
Apl. 24, 1567.	———, Walter, Orstone (Notts.), husbandman, Sep. 2, 1566.	17		644
July 28, 1567.	———, William, Locton, par. Myddleton, Mar. 15, 1566.	17		667
Jan. 16, 1561.	———, William, Scarbroughe, Nov. 19, 1561.	17		26
Mar. 14, 1563.	Stott, Thomas, Sourbie, par. Halifaxe, labourer, Nov. 20, 1562.	17		323
Jan. 13, 1558.	Stoughton, Margaret, Cromwell (Notts.), Sep. 17, 1558.	15	3	207
Oct. 7, 1557.	———, Thomas, Cromwell (Notts.), gentleman, Oct. 30, 1556.	15	2	20
July 4, 1562.	Stow, Elizabeth, Cawod, widow, Jun. 22, 1562.	17		93
Oct. 29, 1558.	Stowe, John, Cawood, husbandman, Dec. 5, 1557.	15	3	231
Oct. 7, 1557.	———, Roger, Rowlston (Notts.), Aug. 20, 1557.	15	2	17
May 5, 1558.	———, Thomas, Clyfton (Notts.), Feb. 13, 1557.	15	2	258
Nov. 22, 1563.	Stowpeis, Thomas, Rysewarpe, par. Whitbie, Sep. 1, 1563.	17		304
Oct. 16, 1558.	Stowte, John, Beverlaie, smyth, Mar. 14, 1558.	15	2	366
Mar. 22, 1566.	Straker, Marke, Skrethenbecke, husbandman, Jan. 15, 1566.	17		516
Jun. 20, 1564.	———, Robert, Oxeton, par. Tadcaster, husbn., May 16, 1564.	17		351
July 4, 1560.	———, William, York, tanner, Jan. 26, 1559.	16		88
May 24, 1563.	Stranger, Robert, Carleton (bur. Snathe), Mar. 12, 1562.	17		248
Aug. 31, 1555.	Strahggar, Thomas, Selbye, Aug. 1, 1555.	14		241
Aug. 4, 1558.	Strangwais, Sir Richard, Sneton, knight, Aug. 20, 1557.	15	2	289
Oct. 10, 1560.	Strawson, Henry (bur. Averham, Notts.), July 8, 1560.	16		124

		Vol.	Pt.	Fol.
Oct. 7, 1556.	Strea, Rauf, Harworthe (Notts.), husbandman, Sep. 4, 1556.	15	1	172
Apl. 4, 1560.	——, Richard, Harworthe (Notts.), husbandman, Oct. 12, 1559.	16		26
Oct. 13, 1558.	Stred (Stree), William, Mathersay, Sep. 15, 1558.	15	2	376
Apl. 20, 1559.	Stree, Alice, Mathersay (Notts.), Oct. 7, 1558.	15	3	307
Apl. 12, 1559.	Strengar, John, Heckmondewyke, par. Byrstall, husbn., Mar. 9, 1558.	15	3	336
Apl. 27, 1564.	Strete, Margaret, Clypston (Notts.), May 14, 1558.	17		340
Sep. 16, 1555.	——, William, Langside, par. Penistone, Dec. 10, 1554.	14		67
Oct. 12, 1558.	St[r]ey, William, Kimberley Grey (bur. Gresley, Notts.), husbn., Dec. 2, 1556.	15	3	28
July 8, 1561.	Strickeland, Peter, of Woodalle, par. Byrton, Apl. 13, 1561.	17		79
Nov. 28, 1554.	Stricklande, Thomas, Wilberfosse, esq., Oct. 3, 1554.	14		90
May 13, 1557.	Stringar, Edmonde, Parlethorpe (Notts.), husbandman, Apl. 17, 1557.	15	1	233
May 13, 1557.	——, Thomas, Parlethorpe (Notts.), husbandman, Feb. 1, 1556.	15	1	216
May 18, 1559.	Stringer, Brian, Haitfeild, husbandman, Aug. 16, 1557.	15	3	400
Jun. 4, 1561.	——, John, Cottingley, par. Leides, yeoman, Jun. 6, 1555.	17		63
Oct. 29, 1558.	——, John, Harpham, labourer, May 18, 1558.	15	2	368
Jun. 20, 1568.	——, Robert, Wakefeild, labourer, May 9, 1568.	17		827
July 19, 1557.	——, Thomas, Parlethorpe (Notts.), husbandman, May 2, 1557.	15	1	310
Sep. 26, 1558.	——, William, Fosterhouse, par. Fishelake, Jun. 16, 1558.	15	3	54
Aug. 23, 1562.	Stringfellay, Henry, Kirkebieoverblause, husbandman, July 20, 1562.	17		104
Jun. 17, 1554.	Stubbes, John, Ayton in Semer, ——, 1554.	14		12
Oct. 15, 1561.	——, Marmaduke, Greyn Ryg (bur. Leverton), Jan. 7, 1560.	17		35
Jan. 28, 1557.	——, Rowland, York, butcher, Nov. 26, 1557.	15	2	159
Aug. 6, 1567.	——, William, Beverley, butcher, Apl. 2, 1567.	17		700
Jun. 18, 1561.	——, William, Normanbye, par. Fyling, Mar. 12, 1554.	17		72
Mar. 4, 1560.	Stubbs, Mathewe, Beverlay, brasyer, Apl. 18, 1560.	16		165
Mar. 9, 1564.	Stubley, John, Birstall, marchaunt, Aug. 22, 1563.	17		407
May 8, 1556.	Studderd, John, Bigginge, par. Fenton, ——, 1556.	15	1	32
Oct. 5, 1564.	Stuerdson, Christopher, East Newton, par. Auldburghe, husbn., Aug. 6, 1564.	17		368
Feb. 17, 1561.	Stuffyn, John, Kyrckton (Notts.), May 5, 1561.	17		15
Apl. 27, 1564.	——, Mychaell, Weston (Notts.), Jun. 15, 1563.	17		337
May 2, 1566.	Sturdie, Christopher, Upsall, par. Ormesbie, Mar. 3, 1565.	17		539
Apl. 18, 1562.	Sturdye, Robert, Eskrycke, wreter, Nov. 27, 1561.	17		196
Apl. 20, 1564.	——, William, Kilburne, Aug. 8, 1563.	17		334
Apl. 24, 1567.	Sturley, Richard (Notts.), gentleman, Apl. 11, 1567.	17		642
Oct. 8, 1556.	Sturtevant, William, junr., Northwell (Notts.), Aug. 4, 1556.	15	1	70
Feb. 9, 1557.	Stutt, Robert, Wellweke, Nov. 4, 1557.	15	2	122
Mar. 17, 1556.	——, William, Tunstall, husbandman, Jun. 7, 1556.	15	1	188
1555.	Styring, Esabell, widow (bur. Barneburghe), Feb. 28, 1554.	14		87
May 10, 1559.	——, Henry, Swynckyld, par. Wattone, Aug. 13, 1556.	15	3	385
May 5, 1568.	Styringe, Agnes, Swinkelde, par. Watton, widow, Aug. 11, 1567.	17		777
Nov. 10, 1563.	——, Alexander, Kilnwicke, husbandman, Feb. 27, 1562.	17		301
Oct. 2, 1567.	Styrke, Thomas, Hawhouse, par. Skipton in Craven, yeom., Nov. 30, 1566.	17		711
Oct. 4, 1564.	——, Thomas, Steadhouse, par. Skipton (bur. Bolton), May 9, 1564.	17		372
Sep. 28, 1560.	Styrley, Henry, Wodborow (Notts.), esq., Nov. 23, 1558.	16		108
Oct. 8, 1562.	——, Joanne, wid. of Chris. S. (bur. Bestonn, Notts.), Apl. 25, 1562.	17		123
May 2, 1560.	Styrtdwen, Thomas, Dunyngton, husbandman, Mar. 5, 1559.	16		51
Feb. 17, 1557.	Styryng, John, Great Houghton (bur. Derfeld), Jun. 11, 1557.	15	2	136
Oct. 1, 1555.	Sudbere, William, Kyrton (Notts.), Sep. 18, 1555.	14		305
Jan. 13, 1558.	Sudberie, Graice, Egmonton (Notts.), widow, Nov. 9, 1558.	15	3	19
Oct. 13, 1558.	——, John, Egmanton (Notts.), May 30, 1558.	15	2	359
Aug. 7, 1565.	Sudberye, Thomas, Egmonton (Notts.), Jan. 11, 1564.	17		458
Jan. 26, 1556.	Sudbore, John, Egmanton, Oct. 10, 1556.	15	1	90
No date.	Sugate, Alison, wid. of Rob. S., Ridker, ——, 1554.	14		192
Oct. 22, 1556.	Sugden, Agnes, Bradford, widow, Jun. 4, 1556.	15	1	100
May 2, 1566.	——, Robert, Keighley, Aug. 16, 1565.	17		529
Mar. 9, 1559.	——, Thomas, S. Olyve's, York, Jan. 18, 1558.	16		7
Oct. 2, 1560.	Suget (or Fuget), Richard, Wrelton, par. Mydleton, husbn., July 13, 1560.	16		110
Oct. 3, 1565.	Sulbie, Richard, Kirkebemoreshead, shomaker, Mar. 4, 1564.	17		486
Jun. 5, 1556.	Sunderland, John, Heptonstall, May 2, 1556.	15	1	43

		Vol.	Pt.	Fol.
May 5, 1568.	Sunderland, Robert, Shelffe, par. Halifax.	17		788
Apl. 28, 1558.	Sunter, Henry (bur. Sowerbye), Apl. 1, 1558.	15	2	229
July 16, 1558.	———, John, Owtthorne, Apl. 26, 1558.	15	3	9
Dec. 10, 1562.	———, Thomas (bur. Souerbie), July 26, 1562.	17		132
May 9, 1566.	Surflit, William, Laxton (Notts.), husbandman, Mar. 27, 1566.	17		547
May 5, 1558.	Surphelet, Elizabeth, Weston (Notts.), Oct. 6, 1557.	15	2	255
Sep. 3, 1555.	Surphelett, Robert, Weston, Jun. 9, 1555.	14		306
Oct. 6, 1557.	Sussance, John, Moregaite, par. Clarebrughe (Notts.), labr., July 6, 1557.	15	2	6
May 2, 1566.	Sutclif, Henry, Wadsworthe, par. Heptonstall, clothier, Dec. 7, 1565.	17		532
May 7, 1554.	———, Thomas, Hirste, par. Heptonstall, Jan. 24, 1549.	14		2
Apl. 17, 1563.	Sutcliff, John, Hirst, par. Heptonstall, Oct. 10, 1562.	17		222
Nov. 29, 1558.	Sutclyffe, John, Haworthe, Nov. 10, 1558.	15	3	80
May 28, 1560.	———, William, Heptonstall, Apl. 22, 1560.	16		68
Sep. 30, 1563.	———, William, Heptonstall, July 24, 1563.	17		283
Apl. 27, 1563.	Sutton, Christopher, Staynsagar, par. Whitbie, Jan. 2, 1562.	17		225
Mar. 8, 1558.	———, Jennett, Bentlay, par. Rowlay, widow, Aug. 9, 1558.	15	3	288
Mar. 21, 1559.	———, Richard, Hornsay. *No date.*	16		17
May 10, 1565.	———, Robert, Rosse, Feb. 20, 1564.	17		424
Feb. 10, 1557.	———, Robert, Wetton, par. Rowlay, husbandman, Dec. 28, 1557.	15	2	150
Mar. 8, 1558.	———, Robert, Wotton (bur. Rowlay), husbandman, Jan. 19, 1558.	15	3	284
Mar. 19, 1562.	———, William, Ellerton, Feb. 4, 1562.	17		216
Jun. 30, [1555].	Swaill, John, Askham Richarde, Jun. 16, 1555.	14		207
Mar. 15, 1560.	Swaley, John, Carleton in Lyndreke (Notts.), husbn., Oct. 9, 1560.	16		168
July 10, 1564.	Swalle, John, Billisdaill, Mar. 7, 1563.	17		355
Jan. 7, 1562.	Swallowe, Roger, Kirkeheton, Oct. 8, 1562.	17		141
Dec. 22, 1556.	Swalowe, William, Wentworthe, labourer, May 20, 1556.	15	1	84
May 29, 1563.	Swane, Christopher, Seissay, Feb. 20, 1562.	17		252
Sep. 6, 1561.	———, Robert, Eskrigge, yong man, Mar. 8, 1560.	17		52
Dec. 4, 1557.	———, William, Acaster Selbye, par. Stillingflete, Sep. 24, 1557.	15	2	50
Oct. 8, 1554.	Swann, Margret, S. Mary's, Castelgate, York, widow, Feb. 28, 1553.	14		276
Jan. 24, 1558.	Swanne, Hew, Attercliffe, Sep. 29, 1557.	15	3	118
Jun. 22, 1568.	———, Thomas, Gaitefulfurthe, Mar. 3, 1567.	17		806
Feb. 15, 1566.	———, William, Gaitefulforthe, Jan. 15, 1566.	17		615
Sep. 16, 1557.	Swanson, Thomas, Wakefeilde, Sep. 1, 1557.	15	1	333
Jun. 20, 1562.	Swayn, John, Hubye (bur. Sutton), Apl. 15, 1562.	17		89
Mar. 20, 1565.	Swayth, Robert, senr., Rotherham, Jun. 10, 1564.	17		506
Dec. 15, 1557.	Swickett, Thomas, Tuxfurthe (Notts.), husbandman, Nov. 22, 1557.	15	2	60
May 2, 1555.	Swier, Richard, Thorneton (in Craven), Feb. 9, 1554.	14		128
Sep. 30, 1562.	Swift, Robert, Baynton, husbandman, ———, 1562.	17		118
Nov. 29, 1558.	Swifte, Matild, Archerfeld, par. Sheafeld, widow, Oct. 2, 1558.	15	3	143
May 31, 1557.	———, Robert, the Archerfelde, par. Sheaffeld, Jun. 24, 1554.	15	1	261
Apl. 10, 1559.	Swinden, John, Shipmanthorpe, par. Tankerslay, Sep. 30, 1558.	15	3	325
Nov. 29, 1558.	Swinnow, John, Hie Melton, singleman, May 6, 1558.	15	3	143
Apl. 27, 1558.	Swyer, Adam, Ayrton (bur. Kyrkbye Mallodaill), Mar. 9, 1558.	15	2	200
May 2, 1566.	———, Roger, Gargrave, Dec. [29?], 1565.	17		530
Oct. 1, 1562.	———, Thomas, Marton, Jun. 27, 1562.	17		110
Apl. 19, 1559.	Swyfft, Isabell, Eperstone (Notts.), widow, Oct. 17, 1558.	15	3	354
Sep. 24, 1567.	Swyffte, Robert, Sheffeld, July 18, 1567.	17		708
May 1, 1567.	Swyft, John, Sheffeld, Nov. 7, 1566.	17		647
Jan. 7, 1562.	———, Robert, Ouththorpe (bur. Wakefeild), Oct. 1, 1562.	17		139
May 18, 1559.	Swyfte, John, the Nabes, par. Silkestone, Sep. 4, 1558.	15	3	404
Oct. 1, 1560.	———, John, Ratcliffe, par. Wylberfosse, Apl. 23, 1559.	16		114
Sep. 21, 1557.	———, John, Rotherham, Jun. 27, 1557.	15	1	355
Dec. 2, 1561.	———, Robert, Rotherham, esq., Feb. 11, 1559.	17		28
Jan. 21, 1561.	Swynden, Margaret, Stirton, par. Skipton, widow, Apl. 14, 1561.	17		19
Mar. 14, 1560.	———, Thruston, Bradfelde, Feb. 13, 1559.	16		159
Oct. 2, 1566.	Swyngilhirst, Agnes, Hallefeld in Helyfeld (bur. Preston in Craven), widow, March 2, 1565.	17		575
Sep. 29, 1563.	———, John, Hallefelde, par. Longe Preston, yeom., Jan. 8, 1562.	17		281
Apl. 28, 1563.	Swynlerust, John, senr., Grindelton, par. Mytton (bur. Waddington), Jan. 12, 1562.	17		228

A.D. 1554 TO 1568.

		Vol.	Pt.	Fol.
Mar.29, 1555.	Swyre, Rebert Seamor, ——, 1554.	14		189
Mar.10, 1561.	Syble, Anne, Semer, wid. of Chas. Knevet, esq., Jan. 15, 1561.	17		2
May 2, 1560.	Sybrey, Richard, Heke (bur. Snaythe), Nov. 12, 1558.	16		53
May 6, 1568.	Sycke, Robert, High Hulland, Nov. 16, 1567.	17		772
Dec. 1, 1557.	Syckesfurth, Barnard, Brig Lane, par. Drax, Oct. 1, 1557.	15	2	86
Aug.23, 1555.	Syddall, Esspham, Tadcaster, widow, July 24, 1555.	14		204
Oct. 17, 1565.	Sydes, Thomas, St. Saviors, York, tapitor, July 10, 1565.	17		483
Jan. 13, 1558.	Sye, Agnes, Nottingham, widow, May 21, 1555.	15	3	205
May 31, 1566.	Syedes, John, Elvington, May 23, 1566.	17		544
Apl. 15, 1559.	Sygestone, John, Foston, husbandman, Jan. 13, 1558.	15	3	352
Apl. 28, 1558.	Sygesweke, Sir Michaell (bur. Ripon), Nov. 29, 1557.	15	2	207
Oct. 5, 1558.	Sygeswicke, Edward (bur. St. Mich., Ardeslow), husbn., Sep. 13, 1558.	15	3	65
Aug.27, 1557.	Syke, Isabell, Burley, par. Otley, Jun. 30, 1557.	15	2	116
Sep. 28, 1557.	Sykes, Agnes. Southe Mylforthe, Aug. 1, 1557.	15	1	371
Apl. 16, 1562.	——, John, Cudworthe, par. Royston, Feb. 10, 1561.	17		170
Apl. 9, 1554.	——, John, Greesegarthes, par. Westonne. *No date.*	14		158
May 2, 1560.	——, John, Shearborne, Oct. 12, 1559.	16		52
Feb. 6, 1558.	——, Margaret, Walton (bur. Sandall Magna), Oct. 18, 1558.	15	3	256
Apl. 16, 1567.	——, Richard, New Hey, par. Almonburie, Jun. 28, 1566.	17		629
Nov. 9, 1557.	——, Robert, Wytley (bur. Kellyngton), Sep. 20, 1557.	15	2	98
July 11, 1558.	——, William, Tickhill, May 30, 1558.	15	2	317
Oct. 3, 1560.	Sylson, Alys, Lytton (bur. Arnecliffe), Mar. 26, 1560.	16		119
Sep. 21, 1557.	Sylvester, John, preist, Bramwythe, July 29, 1557.	15	1	354
Apl. 7, 1557.	Syme *als.* Le, William, Harwood, Aug. 29, 1554.	15	1	205
Nov. 8, 1564.	Symkenson, Margaret, Doncaster, widow, Dec. 15, 5 Eliz.	17		397
May 2, 1560.	Symkinson, Thomas, Doncastre, alderman, Jan. 29, 1558.	16		46
May 2, 1560.	Symon, Henry, Wetherby (bur. Spofforthe), Sep. 16, 1559.	16		54
Jan. 24, 1558.	——, John, Kirklevington, Aug. 10, 1557.	15	3	215
Jun. 20, 1554.	Sympson, Barthilmewe, Marton, par. Senington, Oct. 12, 1552.	14		114
Sep. 6, 1556.	————, Edward, Selby, yeoman, Oct. 4, 1555.	15	1	65
Jan. 12, 1557.	————, Hugh (bur. South Burton), Nov. 29, 1557.	15	2	80
Mar. 8, 1558.	————, Jennett, Elloughton, widow, Aug. 10, 1558.	15	3	285
Jan. 12, 1557.	————, John, Hull, fuller, Dec. 15, 1557.	15	2	79
Nov.30, 1555.	————, Richard, Brafferton, May 20, 1554.	14		185
Apl. 26, 1558.	————, Richard, Norton (Bucros), Sep. 7, 1557.	15	2	204
Jun. 14, 1564.	————, Robert, Buckton (bur. Benton), husbandman, Jan. 10, 1563.	17		351
Sep. 29, 1557.	————, Robert, Ryley, par. Wragbye, Jan. 28, 1556.	15	1	327
Jan. 22, 1557.	————, Thomas, Egton, Sep. 24, 1557.	15	2	158
Oct. 3, 1554.	————, William, Appelbewike, par. Burnsall, Mar. 15, 1553.	14		37
Oct. 7, 1557.	————, William, Faryndon (Notts.), Apl. 1, 1557.	15	2	18
Jun. 20, 1566.	Symson, Bartilmew, Boynton, labourer, Mar. 3, 1565.	17		556
May 27, 1562.	——, Edward, Hawsam (Halsham), Jun. 12, 1559.	17		101
Jan. 28, 1562.	——, Edward, Saxton, Dec. 14, 1562.	17		145
Jun. 18, 1560.	——, Edward, Selbye, butcher, Sep. 20, 1559.	16		86
Nov.12, 1556.	——, George, Leddes, clother, Mar. 6, 1553.	15	1	114
Mar.27, 1566.	——, George, Whitbie, Jan. 5, 1565.	17		508
Apl. 27, 1558.	——, Henry, Harum, husbandman, Jan. 29, 1557.	15	2	228
Aug.16, 1560.	——, Henry, Tillisbie, par. Marton, Jun. 6, 1560.	16		103
Sep. 4, 1567.	——, James, alderman of York, Aug. 9, 1567.	17		703
May 9, 1565.	——, John, Broughton (Craven), Jan. 1, 1564.	17		431
Apl. 17, 1563.	——, John, Holdene, par. Batlaye, Jan. 7, 1562.	17		222
Nov.25, 1555.	——, John, Lethom, coytman, July 8, 1555.	14		183
Nov.29, 1557.	——, John, Norton (Bucros), husbandman, Mar. 24, 1557.	15	2	94
Oct. 3, 1558.	——, John, Rielle, par. Wragby, husbandman, Aug. 19, 1558.	15	3	68
Aug.16, 1560.	——, John, Ynglebye Arnecliffe, husbandman, Oct. 18, 1558.	16		102
Sep. 23, 1564.	——, Margaret, Brafferton, widow, Aug. 23, 1562.	17		362
May 10, 1566.	——, Richard, West Dratton (Notts.), Jan. 2, 1566.	17		652
Nov.12, 1556.	——, Robert, son of Jennett S., Ellowghton, Oct. 23, 1556.	15	1	110
Aug.12, 1567.	——, Robert, Hunmanbie, May 3, 1567.	17		695
Dec. 11, 1566.	——, Robert, Hunmanbie, Aug. 23, 1566.	17		603
Jan. 24, 1558.	——, Robert, Kirklevington, Aug. 13, 1558.	15	3	215
July 27, 1555.	——, Robert, Sandhuton, husbandman, July 10, 1555.	14		243

		Vol.	Pt.	Fol.
Oct. 11, 1563.	Symson, Robert, Thormondbie, par. Staneton, July 7, 1563.	17		297
Apl. 3, 1559.	———, Thomas, Aram, schutler, Nov. 2, 1558.	15	3	317
Oct. 4, 1564.	———, Thomas, Lynton (St. Michael), Feb. 26, 1564.	17		369
Oct. 2, 1560.	———, William, Brandisburton, labourer, Aug. 24, 1560.	16		116
Oct. 5, 1558.	———, William, Kirklevington, Apl. 9, 1558.	15	3	42
Aug. 16, 1555.	———, William, husbandman (bur. Lofthous), Nov. 12, 1554.	14		204
Aug. 2, 1561.	———, William, Pollington, par. Snathe, Mar. 26, 1561.	17		64
Mar. 2, 1561.	Symsonne, Christopher, Octon (bur. Thweing), husbn., Nov. 29, 1561.	17		2
May 10, 1554.	Synger, Raufe, Shepeley, par. Kyrkbyrton, Feb. 23, 1553.	14		136
Jun. 5, 1555.	Syssetson, William, senr., Cotingham, Apl. 28, 1555.	14		253
Jun. 8, 1560.	Sysson, Agnes, Derfelde, widow, Nov. 14, 1558.	16		80
Dec. 23, 1561.	———, Rauff, Shadwell, husbandman, Aug. 15, 1561.	17		26
July 8, 1567.	———, Robert, Shadwell (bur. Thorner), yeoman, Apl. 12, 1567.	17		673
Apl. 28, 1563.	Syssotson, John, Willerbie, par. Cottingham, Mar. 1, 1562.	17		236
Apl. 26, 1564.	Syssyson, William, Cottingham, tanner, Oct. 27, 1563.	17		334
Feb. 6, 1558.	Syvier, Jaymes, Righton, Oct. 24, 1558.	15	3	260
Apl. 3, 1559.	Tadman, John, Garton on Wolde, husbandman, Aug. 23, 1557.	15	3	315
Sep. 26, 1558.	Tage, Robert, Dalton, par. Rotherham, Aug. 24, 1558.	15	3	50
Oct. 13, 1558.	Tailer, Johan, Thornay (Notts.), May 28, 1558.	15	2	362
Aug. 6, 1567.	———, Robert, Lockington (bur. Kilnewicke), labr., Mar. 6, 1566.	17		701
Jun. 27, 1562.	———, Thomas, Eskrige "Our ladie even, the fyrst in harvest last past," 1561.	17		90
Oct. 17, 1567.	Tailerson, Richard, Carleton (bur. Worlton), Mar. 17, 1566.	17		730
May 4, 1560.	Tailier, John, Kelfelde, par. Stillingflet, Nov. 25, 1559.	16		57
Sep. 29, 1557.	———, Richard, Sandall Magna, Aug. 19, 1557.	15	1	327
May 13, 1557.	Tailior, Christopher, North Collingham (Notts.), Mar. 8, 1556.	15	1	216
Oct. 1, 1556.	———, James, Healay, par. Sheffeld, July 26, 1554.	15	1	130
Apl. 5, 1554.	Taillor, Edmunde, Thur[n]um, par. Burton Agnes, labr., Dec. 2, 1553.	14		216
Apl. 9, 1554.	———, Margaret, Lockinton, widow, Dec. 20, 1551.	14		218
Oct. 29, 1554.	Tailour, William, Laxton (Notts.), husbandman, Nov. 27, 1553.	14		279
Jun. 25, 1561.	Tailyer, Robert, Bayldon, ———, 1560.	17		74
Oct. 3, 1565.	Tailyour, Mychaell, Pomfret, Jun. 17, 1565.	17		480
Oct. 10, 1566.	Talbot, William, Eykeringe (Notts.), Aug. 11, 1556.	17		589
Apl. 28, 1563.	Talbott, Thomas, Westhalton (bur. Longe Preston), gent., Feb. 16, 1562.	17		227
Dec. 9, 1556.	Taler, Isabell, Tykton, widow, Aug. 12, 1556.	15	1	73
Dec. 3, 1560.	Talier, Christopher, Womersley, labourer, Apl. 20, 1560.	16		131
July 23, 1560.	———, Elenour, Lockington, par. Kylweke, May 3, 1560.	16		95
Oct. 16, 1557.	———, Isabell, Roclyffe (bur. Snaythe), Sep. 4, 1557.	15	1	366
Mar. 4, 1562.	———, James, Flambrugh, labourer, Dec. 10, 1562.	17		153
Oct. 16, 1560.	———, Jennatt, Appleton (bur. Bolton Percye), Sep. 25, 1560.	16		123
Oct. 16, 1560.	———, John, Apleton (bur. Bolton Percye), Apl. 12, 1559.	16		123
Nov. 21, 1566.	———, Leonard, Hornebie (bur. Smeton), Dec. 24, 1565.	17		598
Jan. 17, 1560.	———, Ottewell, Mylnethorpe, par. Sandall Magna, Nov. 26, 1560.	16		141
May 6, 1557.	Talior, Elizabeth, Waddyngton, widow of Richard T., Dec. 12, 1556.	15	1	255
Oct. 20, 1558.	———, John, Holmpton, Aug. 14, 1558.	15	3	228
July 16, 1554.	———, Richard, Kyngston upon Hull, maryner, Feb. 16, 1553.	14		142
Dec. 16, 1557.	———, Thomas, Nessehouse, par. Drax, Oct. 2, 1557.	15	2	37
Jan. 3, 1555.	———, William (bur. Alne), Apl. 14, 1555.	14		240
Mar. 11, 1559.	Talyeor, John, Welburie, Sep. 18, 1558.	16		8
Apl. 7, 1554.	Talyer, Edward, Hooke, Jan. 1, 1553.	14		157
Apl. 23, 1556.	———, Robert, Thurne, yeoman, Jan. 20, 1555.	15	1	24
Oct. 22, 1556.	Talyor, Brian, Heatone, par. Bristall, Sep. 1, 1556.	15	1	101
Feb. 12, 1556.	———, Sir Robert, prest, Waddingtone, Sep. 20, 1556.	15	1	157
Mar. 2, 1558.	Tarne, Margaret, Welburne (bur. Kirdall), ———, 1558.	15	3	281
Mar. 4, 1562.	Tathewell, Thomas, Burton Flemynge (bur. Hunmanbie), Nov. 16, 1562.	17		153
Jun. 22, 1568.	Tathwell, Thomas, Nafferton, Sep. 18, 1565.	17		825
Sep. 29, 1563.	Tatam, Robert, Calton (bur. Kyrkbye Mallydall), May 11, 1563.	17		278
Sep. 29, 1563.	Tattersall, George, Morehouse, par. Huton Pannall, Jun. 29, 1563.	17		286
Oct. 3, 1554.	———, Thomas, Gisbourne, Jun. 18, 1554.	14		39
Apl. 16, 1567.	Taverner, William, Ottringham, Aug. 17, 1566.	17		634
May 9, 1563.	Tawell, Robert, Linthorpe (bur. Aclom), husbandman, Mar. 20, 1562.	17		256

		Vol.	Pt.	Fol.
Jun. 2, 1558.	Tawernar, John, Skeclynge, Dec. 20, 1557.	15	2	337
Apl. 20, 1559.	Tayler, Elsabeth (bur. Marnham, Notts.), Jan. 7, 1558.	15	3	370
Mar.20, 1558.	———, George, Kelfeld, par. Stillingfleit, Dec. 20, 1558.	15	3	250
May 4, 1558.	———, George, Nottingham, tanner, Aug. 22, 1557.	15	2	278
Aug.30, 1558.	———, John (bur. Bulmer), July 23, 1558.	15	2	293
July 19, 1567.	———, John, Neltham, par. Almonburie, Dec. 20, 1566.	17		681
Jun. 12, 1567.	———, Robert, West Halsam, May 8, 1567.	17		664
May 9, 1566.	———, Umfrey, Newarke (Notts.), tanner, Oct. 20, 1565.	17		547
Dec.20, 1558.	Taylier, Elizabeth, Badsworthe, widow, Aug. 10, 1558.	15	3	152
Mar.22, 1558.	———, John, Melthame, par. Almonbury, Jan. 12, 1558.	15	3	291
Oct. 5, 1558.	Taylior, Christopher, Hornebie (bur. Smeaton), Mar. 26, 1558.	15	3	69
Aug. 1, 1562.	———, Robert, Welburye, husbandman, Apl. 17, 1562.	17		103
Dec. 5, 1567.	Tayliour, William, Brustwicke (bur. Skeclinge), May 5, 1567.	17		742
Aug. 6, 1567.	———, William, Moscrofte (bur. Beverley), husbn., May 1, 1567.	17		700
Mar. 1, 1562.	Tayllyer, Agnes, Byrdsall, servaunt, Jan. 13, 1562.	17		147
May 18, 1555.	———, Taylor, Jenet, Howke, Apl. 18, 1555.	14		238
Dec. 4, 1555.	Taylor, John, Brokholes, par. Drax, May 24, 1555.	14		246
Aug.14, 1561.	———, John, Newhouse, par. Horton in Reblisdaille, Nov. 16, 1560.	17		62
Apl. 13, 1559.	———, Margaret, Beswyke, par. Kylnewycke, widow, Aug. 28, 1558.	15	3	348
Mar.10, 1554.	———, Reynold, Bevercotes (Notts.), husbandman, Dec. 3, 1554.	14		223
Apl. 27, 1559.	———, Richard, Howsom, par. Skrayngham, Mar. 11, 1558.	15	3	314
May 18, 1559.	———, Roger, Darringtone, husbandman, Mar. 20, 1558.	15	3	413
Apl. 20, 1559.	——— *als.* Burdon, John (bur. Wallesby, Notts.), Mar. 19, 1558.	15	3	366
July 26, 1556.	Taylore, Richard, Beverley, merchant, Jun. 24, 1556.	15	1	35
Feb. 10, 1557.	Taylour, Cecill, daughter of Bryan T., Beswycke, par. Killnewycke, servaunt, Jan. 13, 1557.	15	2	149
Jun. 11, 1555.	———, Christopher, Westerton, par. Wodkirke, Oct. 8, 1554.	14		255
Jan. 12, 1558.	———, Isabell, Lockington, par. Kilnewicke, widow, Nov. 21, 1558.	15	2	355
Nov.28, 1564.	———, Margaret, Bulmer (bur. Burythorpe), widow, Jun. 22, 1564.	17		399
May 13, 1557.	———, Peter, Tuxford (Notts.), Jun. 29, 1556.	15	2	136
Jan. 13, 1558.	Taylyer, Edward, Laxton, Jun. 28, 1558.	15	3	207
Mar.20, 1566.	———, Edward, Stillingfleite, Nov. 8, 1566.	17		514
Sep. 22, 1556.	———, John, Marske, ———, 1556.	15	1	66
July 5, 1558.	———, John, senr., Spofforth, May 22, 1558.	15	2	326
Apl. 8, 1559.	———, John, Treton, Jan. 13, 1558.	15	3	330
Apl. 3, 1567.	———, Thomas, Fraystroppe, yeoman, Dec. 29, 1566.	17		618
Aug.12, 1566.	———, Thomas, Tykhill, Apl. 5, 1566.	17		567
Apl. 4, 1560.	———, Umfraye, Egmunton (Notts.), husbandman, Dec. 21, 1558.	16		25
Mar.20, 1564.	Taylyor, Henry, Thorner (bur. Barwicke in Elmet), clerk, Jan.13,1564.	17		412
Jan. 13, 1558.	———, John, Egmanton (Notts.), Sep. 10, 1558.	15	3	185
Nov.23, 1557.	———, John, Kyrke Dightone, Aug. 30, 1557.	15	2	103
Sep. 12, 1558.	———, Katherin, Spofforthe, Aug. 16, 1558.	15	3	104
Dec. 1, 1557.	———, Richard, Drax, husbandman, Apl. 26, 1557.	15	2	86
July 18, 1565.	———, Robert, Flaxton (Bulmer), Jun. 13, 1563.	17		451
May 5, 1558.	———, Rowland, Laxton (Notts.), husbandman, Oct. 20, 1556.	15	2	255
Oct. 4, 1558.	Taylyour, Robert, Kepax, May 20, 1558.	15	3	58
July 19, 1557.	——— *als.* Jakson, Christopher, Estretford (Notts.), May 24, 1557.	15	1	311
Jun. 4, 1561.	Teale, John, Fernley (bur. Otley), Apl. 6, 1560.	17		67
Apl. 24, 1559.	Teasdale, Henry, Wicham, par. Old Malton, Mar. 12, 1558.	15	3	379
Oct. 14, 1563.	Teb, Marmaduke, Dalton (bur. Topclif), Sep. 2, 1563.	17		298
Apl. 19, 1559.	Tebale, Jane, Normanton (bur. Plumtre, Notts.). Feb. 1, 1558.	15	3	371
Apl. 19, 1559.	———, Robert, Normanton (bur.Plumtre,Notts.),husbn.,Jan.12,1558.	15	3	371
Feb. 11, 1557.	Tebb, Ellene, Skelton (bur. Ripon), widow, Sep. 30, 1557.	15	2	119
Jun. 23, 1568.	Teele, John, Redcarre, par. Marske, Apl. 6, 1568.	17		829
Jan. 12, 1558.	Teile, Margaret, Bardsaie, smythe, Aug. 27, 1558.	15	3	170
Sep. 8, 1565.	Teisdaille, Thomas, Settrington, Dec. 27, 1564.	17		461
Apl. 28, 1563.	Tele, John, Letheley, Dec. 10, 1562.	17		235
May 2, 1566.	Telyer, Hewe (bur. Slaydburne), Feb. 22, 1565.	17		529
Jan. 24, 1558.	Telyerson, Thomas, Thornton, par. Stainton, husbn., Sep. 9, 1558.	15	3	23
May 5, 1558.	Telyour, William, Warkesopp (Notts.), Aug. 17, 1557.	15	2	276
Dec. 14, 1555.	Tempeste, Anne, wid. of Stev. T., Broughton in Craven, esq., Feb. 16, 1554.	14		245

A.D. 1554 TO 1568.

		Vol.	Pt.	Fol.
Apl. 27, 1558.	Tenaunde, Kyrchyan, wid. of Jo. T.,Depedaill (bur.Hobram),Sep.16, 1557.	15	2	200
Apl. 28, 1563.	Tenaunt, Oswald (Craven), Feb. 12, 1561.	17		229
Mar.30, 1559.	——, Richard, Woodhall in Holderness, Dec. 14, 1558.	15	3	296
Oct. 5, 1558.	Tenaunte, Alexander, Cray, par. Arnclif (bur. Hubream), July 21,1558.	15	3	37
Oct. 5, 1558.	——, James, Bukeden (bur. Hubberham), May 12, 1558.	15	3	37
Mar.17, 1556.	——, John, Sutton in Holderness, Mar. 4, 1556.	15	1	188
Jan. 17, 1560.	Tendale, Thomas, Leppington (bur. Scraingham), husbn., Aug. 19, 1560.	16		142
Feb. 11, 1565.	Tenderyng, John, Sprottley, husbandman, Jun. 29, 1565.	17		500
Oct. 20, 1558.	Teneson, Thomas, Thorningbold, par. Paule, Aug. 20, 1558.	15	2	350
Apl. 14, 1562.	Tenison, Richard, Ryhill (bur. Sceklynge), Jan. 7, 1561.	17		183
Oct. 6, 1557.	Tenman, Thomas, Carcolson (Notts.), husbandman, May 17, 1557.	15	2	30
Apl. 10, 1557.	Tennand, John, Methelay, Mar. 22, 1556.	15	1	205
Apl. 12, 1559.	——, Richard, Over Bordley (bur. Relston), Jan. 15, 1558.	15	3	341
May 9, 1565.	——, Rauf, Beggermondes, par. Arneclif, Dec. 4, 1564.	17		431
Apl. 17, 1567.	Tennant, Elizabeth, Haultongill (bur. Arnclif), wid., Oct. 26, 1566.	17		621
Sep. 1, 1567.	——, Thomas, York, gentleman, Apl. 16, 1567.	17		704
May 2, 1555.	Tennante, Edward (bur. Kettlewell), Jan. 2, 1554.	14		28
Jun. 12, 1567.	Tennyson, Richard, Headon, butcher, Apl. 3, 1567.	17		664
Apl. 20, 1564.	Tenyson, Agnes, Kaingham, widow, Mar. 5, 1563.	17		333
Mar.23, 1557.	——, William, Ryall, par. Skeklynge, Jan. 7, 1557.	15	2	174
Jun. 2, 1558.	Tenyssonne, John, Kayngham, yeoman, Apl. 11, 1558.	15	2	311
July 10, 1555.	Testes, Nicholas, St. Martin's, York, glover, May 13, 1555.	14		81
Feb. 12, 1557.	Tewe, Edward, Cawodd, yeoman, Nov. 13, 1557.	15	2	165
Oct. 2, 1567.	——, George, Eassingwold, Apl. 1, 1567.	17		711
Apl. 26, 1558.	——, Johane, Cawod, wid. of Edward T., Feb. 9, 1557.	15	2	181
July 8, 1557.	Tewer, Robert, Barton (Ridall), husbandman, May 13, 1557.	15	1	306
Mar. 4, 1562.	Tewney, Heline, Kaingham, widow, Apl. 15, 1562.	17		149
Nov.28, 1558.	Teyle, Robert, Hornesay, Oct. 2, 1558.	15	3	77
Dec. 5, 1558.	Teysdayle, Christopher, Old Malton, husbandman, ——, 1558.	15	3	150
Dec. 1, 1558.	Teysdayll, Edmound, Everyldeshame [Everingham], Jun. 17, 1557.	15	3	145
Aug.27, 1557.	Thacwro, Mylles, Burley nyghe Ottley, Jun. 7, 1557.	15	2	115
Mar.29, 1568.	Thackwraye, Peter, Colthrope, Nov. 24, 1567.	17		768
Mar. 9, 1559.	——, Richard, Schupton in Galtrese (bur. Overton), Mar. 10, 1557.	16		6
Jan. 11, 1558.	Thackwroo, Richard, Burley, par. Ottley, clothier, Aug. 20, 1558.	15	3	171
Feb. 15, 1566.	Thakewraye, Wylfryde, Shipton, par. Overton, Sep. 5, 1566.	17		615
Feb. 6, 1562.	Thakkwrey, John, Woodhouse, par. Swillington, Jan. 18, 1562.	17		146
Mar. 2, 1554.	Thaurton, Henry, Holbecke, par. Leedes, clothier, Oct. 6, 1554.	14		301
May 5, 1568.	Theaker, Richard, Sutton, par. Kildweke, July 20, 1567.	17		783
Aug. 6, 1567.	Theare, Vincent, Cottingham, yeoman, Jan. 26, 1566.	17		699
Apl. 28, 1558.	Theker, Robert, Roclyf (bur. Snayth), Aug. 23, 1557.	15	2	227
Feb. 4, 1561.	Themlynson, Elizabeth, Hubye (bur. Sutton), Jan. 22, 1561.	17		11
Apl. 27, 1559.	Theokepeny, Richard, Braton, husbandman, Mar. 16, 155[8-]9.	15	3	362
Dec. 4, 1557.	Thewe, John, Goldall, par. Snaythe, Oct. 10, 1557.	15	2	51
May 29, 1562.	——, Margaret, Golldall, par. Snaithe, Mar. 21, 1560.	17		100
July 26, 1563.	Thewles, George, Kirkheton, Feb. 11, 1562.	17		267
Apl. 10, 1557.	——, George, Kirkburton, Dec. 13, 1556.	15	1	205
Aug.26, 1561.	Thewlesse, Roger, Dalton, par. Heaton, Jun. 26, 1561.	17		55
Jun. 14, 1554.	Thex, Thomas, Scurthe, par. Drax, Feb. 19, 1552.	14		4
Oct. 12, 1560.	Thexton, Lawrance, Wighell, Mar. 3, 1559.	16		121
Apl. 27, 1563.	——, Peter, Esington, Nov. 1, 1562.	17		225
Aug. 2, 1560.	Thirgatson, Allyson, Skeflinge, July 2, 1560.	16		99
Nov.28, 1564.	Thirkild, Joes, Lowthorpe, par. Londsborghe, widow, May 20, 1559.	17		399
Jun. 17, 1556.	Thirkylde, Christopher, Esthorpe (bur. Goodmanham), esq., Jun. 19, 1555.	15	1	48
Mar.21, 1561.	Thirske, John, Weaton, par. Rowley, Mar. 5, 1558.	17		4
Dec. 2, 1560.	——, Thomas, Shupton, par. Overton, Mar. 10, 1559.	16		132
Oct. 12, 1558.	Thistles, Lawrence, Hull, maryner, Sep. 15, 1558.	15	3	198
Nov.28, 1558.	Tholle, Francis, Tunstall in Holderness, juvenis, Sep. 16, 1558.	15	3	77
Feb.23, 1563.	Thomas, Leonard, Bingley, Jan. 10, 1563.	17		317

21

A.D. 1554 TO 1568.

		Vol.	Pt.	Fol.
Sep. 4, 1565.	Thomas, Lewys, Semer, serving man, Jan. 26, 1563.	17		469
Apl. 14, 1558.	Thomell, John, Myton on Swaile, Jan. 13, 1557.	15	2	229
Dec. 15, 1557.	Thomkinson, Alis, Walkringham (Notts.), Jan. 12, 1553.	15	2	60
Oct. 4, 1564.	Thomlingson, John, Cold Conyston (bur. Gargrave), husbn., Apl. 16, 1564.	17		371
Sep. 30, 1556.	——————, Sir Robert, preist (bur. Mytton), Dec. 7, 1555.	15	1	144
July 18, 1562.	Thomlinson, Anne, Bureford, widow, Feb. 14, 1557.	17		99
Nov.28, 1558.	——————, John, Walton, par. Sandall Magna, Jun. 15, 1558.	15	3	137
Jan. 24, 1558.	——————, Marmaduke, Harton, par. Bossaull, Oct. 9, 1558.	15	3	219
Oct. 6, 1558.	——————, Robert, Birdsaull, Aug. 31, 1558.	15	3	225
Oct. 12, 1558.	Thomlyn, William, Bilborough (Notts.), May 18, 1558.	15	3	29
Mar.10, 1555.	Thomlynson, Thomas, Newark (Notts.), glover, Feb. 8, 1549.	14		231
Jun. 15, 1560.	—— ——, William, junr., Hubie (bur. Sutton in Galtres), Apl. 27, 1560.	16		85
Oct. 2, 1555.	Thomplingsonne, Richard, Woodhouse (bur. Hatefeld), husbn., Sep.9, 1555.	14		168
Mar.20, 1560.	Thomplynson, Richard (bur. Gargrave), Feb. 15, 1560.	16		171
Sep. 30, 1557.	——————, Thomas, servaunte to Jo. Stevenson (bur. Paull), July 19, 1557.	15	1	341
Dec. 4, 1557.	——————, Thomas, Selbye, maryner, Oct. 10, 1557.	15	2	51
Dec. 3, 1560.	——————, Thomas, Waughan, husbandman, May 31, 1560.	16		134
Apl. 27, 1558.	Thompson, Agnes, Gargrave, widow, Jan. 18, 1557.	15	2	201
Apl. 27, 1558.	——————, Agnes, Ossett, widow of Steven T., Sep. 1, 1557.	15	2	192
Oct. 18, 1560.	——————, Alyson, Angram (bur. Marston), July 20, 1560.	16		123
Oct. 1, 1557.	——————, Christopher, Esington, Aug. 22, 1557.	15	1	362
Oct. 28, 1566.	——————, Christopher, Hull, glasier, May. 22, 1566.	17		586
Mar.15, 1558.	——————, Elsabeth, Brackan, par. Kylnewicke, wid., Jan. 24, 1558.	15	3	166
Oct. 1, 1566.	——————, Frauncis, Hinderwell, Mar. 22, 1566.	17		583
Dec. 17, 1557.	——————, James, Wombewell, par. Darfelde on Derne, Sep. 24,1557.	15	2	39
Mar. 1, 1557.	——————, John, Eastnes (bur. Hovyngham), husbn., July 20, 1557.	15	2	170
Oct. 2, 1567.	——————, John, Heidon, butcher, Apl. 4, 9 Eliz.	17		714
Dec. 11, 1566.	——————, John, Leberston, par. Filay, husbandman, May 13, 1566.	17		601
Feb. 15, 1558.	——————, John, Leaven, husbandman, Feb. 10, 1557.	15	3	271
Aug.12, 1561.	——————, John, Wawhan, husbandman, July 20, 1561.	17		59
Apl. 14, 1559.	——————, Leonard, Huton Granseweycke, labr., Jan. 23, 1558.	15	3	347
Apl. 5, 1554.	——————, Margaret, Flamburghe, widow, Dec. 3, 1553.	14		214
Mar.20, 1565.	——————, Richard, Headon in Holderness, tailor, Dec. 18, 1565.	17		505
Dec. 1, 1558.	——————, Robert, Skipby (Skidby), husbandman, May 28, 1558.	15	3	146
No date.	——————, Robert, Ruddington, Notts. (bur. S. Peter's, Stanford), Jun. 17, 1554.	14		149
Jan. 28, 1566.	——————, Thomas, Bentley (bur. Arksay), Sep. 19, 1566.	17		608
Dec. 12, 1560.	——————, Thomas, Beswicke, par. Kylweke, labr., Sep. 12, 1560.	16		135
Aug.22, 1556.	——————, Thomas, Brackan, par. Kylnewike, husbn., Aug. 2, 1556.	15	1	61
May 18, 1559.	——————, Thomas, Brandisburtone, yongeman, Apl. 2, 1559.	15	3	409
Oct. 22, 1557.	——————, Thomas, Tybthorpe (bur. Kyrkburne), Aug. 4, 1557.	15	1	365
Dec. 24, 1557.	——————, William, Angram (bur. Hooton Wanseley als. Marston), Nov. 3, 1557.	15	2	72
Mar. 3, 1555.	——————, William, Preston in Holderness, Nov. 16, 1555.	15	1	11
Feb.17, 1558.	——————, William, Wresle, Apl. 17, 1558.	15	3	275
Jun. 6, 1558.	Thompsonne, Brian, Eskedayll Hawle, par. Whitbye, Mar. 23, 1557.	15	2	285
Sep. 1, 1565.	Thomson, Allison, Hynderwell, widow, May 26, 1565.	17		463
Apl. 13, 1559.	——————, Barbery, Paullflett, (bur. Pagule), widow, Jan. 17, 1558.	15	3	343
Oct. 8, 1562.	——————, Davie, Stoke (Notts.), labourer, Sep. 21, 1562.	17		119
Sep. 18, 1567.	——————, Edward, Hessill, Jun. 20, 1567.	17		706
Jun. 7, 1560.	——————, George, Bridlington, weafer, July 16, 1559.	16		78
Jun. 25, 1568.	——————, Henry, Bramsburton, husbandman, Apl. 20, 1568.	17		809
Jun. 25, 1567.	——————, Henry, Esholte, esquier, May 27, 1567.	17		658
Jan. 18, 1556.	——————, Henry, Wakefeld, Aug. 23, 1556.	15	1	88
Jun. 9, 1563.	——————, John, Bowrhousehill (bur. Pall), Feb. 13, 1562.	17		253
Jan. 16, 1556.	——————, John, Bykkerton (bur. Bylton), Nov. 30, 1556.	15	1	87
Apl. 13, 1559.	——————, John (bur. Esyngton), Nov. 20, 1558.	15	3	346
May 23, 1564.	——————, John, Gisburne, Oct. 19, 1563.	17		346

		Vol.	Pt.	Fol.
July 2, 1561.	Thomson, John, Gristrope, par. Fyley, Apl. 13, 1561.	17		77
Apl. 13, 1559.	———, John, Hessill, yeoman, Aug. 24, 1558.	15	3	349
Oct. 27, 1564.	———, John, senr., Kirkelevington, yeoman, Sep. 20, 1564.	17		394
Nov. 10, 1563.	———, John, Newland, par. Cottingham, Jun. 22, 1563.	17		300
Mar. 12, 1557.	———, John, Selbye, yeoman, Nov. 16, 1557.	15	2	126
Apl. 20, 1564.	———, John, Thornton in Pickeringlithe, butcher, Mar. 10, 1563.	17		326
July 2, 1561.	———, John, York, May 8, 1561.	17		79
Jun. 14, 1564.	———, Richard, Bridlington, occupier, Nov. 8, 1563.	17		352
Oct. 27, 1558.	———, Richard, Essingwolde, Sep. 4, 1558.	15	3	234
July 30, 1567.	———, Robert, Catton (bur. Topclif), Feb. 6, 1567.	17		686
Mar. 31, 1563.	———, Robert, Hinderwell, July 1, 1562.	17		218
July 8, 1555.	———, Robert, Seymer in Pyckering Lythe, labr., Apl. 10, 1555.	14		259
Jan. 30, 1566.	———, Thomas, Gt. Cowdon (bur. Albroughe), husbn., Jun. 5, 1566.	17		610
Feb. 15, 1558.	———, Thomas, Preston in Holderness, Nov. 23, 1558.	15	3	271
July 2, 1561.	———, Thomas, Rudstonne, labourer, Jan. 2, 1560.	17		78
May 13, 1557.	———, Thomas, Skreton (Notts.), Aug. 6, 1556.	15	1	230
Nov. 17, 1558.	———, Thomas, Snathe, May 11, 1558.	15	3	74
July 20, 1561.	———, William, senr. (bur. Cottingham), May 2, 1561.	17		63
Jan. 11, 1563.	———, William, Cottingham, husbandman, Sep. 27, 1563.	17		309
July 23, 1560.	———, William, Darrington, labourer, Jun. 25, 2 Eliz.	16		95
Sep. 1, 1565.	———, William, Gisburne, July 13, 1565.	17		462
July 1, 1555.	———, William, Pockley, par. Helmsleye, Apl. 30, 1555.	14		257
May 21, 1560.	———, William, Thorneton in Pyckeringe Lythe, Apl. 29, 1560.	16		66
Mar. 27, 1565.	Thomsone, Richard (bur. Paulle), Oct. 6, 1564.	17		418
May 4, 1558.	Thomsonne, Agnes (bur. Flafurth, Notts.), Jan. 17, 1557.	15	2	263
Nov. 10, 1557.	———, William, Brotherton, yeoman, Aug. 16, 1557.	15	2	104
Oct. 14, 1557.	Thorley, William, Holme on Wolde, Aug. 9, 1557.	15	1	364
Oct. 1, 1556.	Thormonbye, Christopher, Thormanby of the Teise (bur. Staynton), gentleman, Jun. 18, 1556.	15	1	68
Apl. 21, 1554.	Thornabie, Thomas, Beverlaye, tanner, Nov. 10, 1553.	14		62
July 29, 1558.	Thornay, Anthony, Haylywell (bur. Castellfurthe), gent., Jun. 3, 4 and 5 Phil. and Mary.	15	2	381
Dec. 14, 1557.	Thorne, Elizabeth, Hull, Sep. 17, 1557.	15	1	357
July 19, 1567.	Thornehill, John, Fyxebie (bur. Eland), esquier, Apl. 22, 1567.	17		682
Nov. 23, 1558.	Thornell, Jane, Burley, par. Otlay, widow, Sep. 22, 1558.	15	3	129
Oct. 21, 1558.	———, John, York, merchant, July 25, 1558.	15	3	94
May 26, 1565.	———, Richard, Otley, Mar. 31, 1565.	17		435
Apl. 6, 1558.	Thornes, Robert, Sykehouse, par. Fyshelaike, Nov. 20, 1557.	15	2	182
May 5, 1558.	Thorneton, John, Northe Leverton (Notts.), Oct. 21, 1557.	15	2	211
Mar. 25, 1555.	———, Thomas, Burstwike, par. Skecklinge, Nov. 10, 1555.	15	1	13
Jun. 3, 1556.	———, Thomas, Christall (bur. Ledes), May 20, 1556.	15	1	40
Jun. 23, 1554.	———, Thomas, Roodes Hall, par. Bradford, Sep. 30, 1552.	14		115
Oct. 3, 1555.	———, Robert, Pattrington, shomaker, May 2, 1555.	14		176
Jan. 30, 1557.	Thornhill, Robert, Woodhall in Holdernes, Jun. 25, 1557.	15	2	71
Sep. 14, 1565.	Thornholme, Thomas, senr., Pattrington, tanner, May 24, 1565.	17		466
Feb. 15, 1558.	———, William, Pattrington, husbandman, Dec. 24, 1558.	15	3	268
Apl. 28, 1563.	Thornlay, Avera, Sutton (Holderness), Aug. 15, 1562.	17		239
Apl. 18, 1567.	Thornton, Elizabeth, Holbeke, par. Ledes, Jan. 18, 1566.	17		633
May 11, 1566.	———, Francis, Thornton of the Hill, Apl. 12, 1566.	17		458
Apl. 6, 1560.	———, John, Acastre Malbis, Nov. 22, 1559.	16		27
Jan. 3, 1558.	———, John, Almonburie, clothier, Jun. 13, 1558.	15	3	34
Oct. 1, 1561.	———, John, Horsforthe, par. Gresley, sherman, Aug. 4, 1561.	17		46
May 15, 1563.	———, John, Hymsworthe, husbandman, May 6, 1560.	17		247
Jan. 23, 1558.	———, John, Presthrope, par. Byngley, Aug. 8, 1558.	15	3	214
May 9, 1560.	———, Nycholas, Gybsemyre (bur. Bleasebye, Notts.), Apl. 2, 1560.	16		59
Oct. 5, 1558.	———, Richard, Bingley, Aug. 15, 1558.	15	3	61
Aug. 12, 1567.	———, Richard, Nafferton, husbandman, Feb. 18, 1567.	17		692
Sep. 29, 1563.	———, Richard, Tyresall, par. Calverlay, gent., July 30, 1563.	17		276
Oct. 29, 1558.	———, Robert, Cawodd, yongeman, Sep. 27, 1558.	15	3	130
May 18, 1559.	———, Thomas, Smeaton, husbandman, Oct. 18, 1558.	15	3	416
Mar. 19, 1559.	———, William, Bollynge, par. Braydfourthe, Sep. 14, 1559.	16		13
Apl. 11, 1559.	———, William, Bryghton (bur. Bubwith), husbn., Jan. 19, 1559.	15	3	334

		Vol.	Pt.	Fol.
July 8, 1562.	Thornton, William, Hull, marchaunt, Aug. 30, 1561.	17		94
Feb. 6, 1558.	———, William, Muston (bur. Hummanbie), Oct. 28, 1558.	15	3	259
Jan. 12, 1558.	———, William, Smeaton (bur. Wimmerslay), Aug. 20, 1557.	15	3	173
Jun. 21, 1568.	———, William, South Burton, Feb. 6, 1567.	17		815
May 18, 1559.	Thorns, Robert, Horbyre (bur. Wakefeild), ———, 1558.	15	3	415
Oct. 8, 1556.	Thoroton, Robert, Carcolston (Notts.), May 8, 1556.	15	1	149
Oct. 13, 1558.	Thorp, John, Barmbie (Notts.), May 25, 1558.	15	2	365
May 5, 1558.	Thorpe, Agnes, Beastropp (bur. S. Skaryll, Notts.), Aug. 10, 1557.	15	2	261
July 30, 1567.	———, Christopher, Thorpe next Welwicke, gent., May 2, 1566.	17		666
Jan. 19, 1556.	———, Elizabeth, Hull, widow, Sep. 10, 1556.	15	1	88
Nov. 9, 1558.	———, Jenet, wid. of John T., Bubwith, husbandman, May 12, 1558.	15	3	123
Oct. 8, 1556.	———, Johan, Barmbe (Notts.), widow, July 27, 1556.	15	1	153
Dec. 3, 1560.	———, John (bur. Aubroughe), Jun. 18, 1560.	16		133
Mar. 27, 1555.	———, John, Hull, alderman, Feb. 4, 1554.	15	1	14
May 6, 1557.	———, John, Ruddeston, Dec. 6, 1556.	15	1	247
Oct. 6, 1557.	———, Sir John, Litle Hodsocke, par. Blith (Notts.), Aug. 21, 1557.	15	2	10
Dec. 11, 1566.	———, Katherin, Rudstone, widow, May 17, 1566.	17		602
Dec. 13, 1557.	———, Laurance, Mydleton in Pickeringe Lythe, husbn., Aug. 19, 1557.	15	2	42
May 2, 1560.	———, Richard, Albroughe, Mar. 21, 1560.	16		49
Apl. 24, 1567.	———, Richard, Thourgourton (Notts), husbandman, Dec. 18, 1566.	17		643
Jan. 12, 1558.	———, Robert, Albrought in Holderness, Apl. 28, 1558.	15	3	202
Nov. 12, 1567.	———, Robert, Apleton in the More (bur. Lestingham), Apl. 20, 1567.	17		734
May 13, 1568.	———, Robert, Cortelingstocke (Notts.), Feb. 15, 1567.	17		799
Oct. 12, 1558.	———, Roger, Gotham (Notts.), husbandman, Sep. 27, 1558.	15	3	30
May 13, 1557.	———, Thomas, Barton in fabis (par. Clifton, Notts.), Jan. 11, 1556.	15	1	229
May 16, 1554.	———, Thomas, Holme in Spawdingmore, Nov. 13, 1553.	14		138
Jan. 30, 1555.	———, Thomas, Hymsworthe, Aug. 31, 1555.	15	1	3
Oct. 2, 1566.	———, William, Aldbrough in Holderness, May 12, 1566.	17		581
Feb. 17, 1557.	Thorppe, John, Bubwyth, husbandman, Dec. 8, 1557.	15	2	151
Nov. 28, 1558.	Thow, John, Out Newton (bur. Essington), Aug. 18, 1558.	15	3	78
Nov. 9, [1555.]	———, Thomas, Owston (bur. St. Michael's 1), Oct. 8, 1555.	14		203
Mar. 23, 1560.	Thowthropp, John (? N. Kilvington), Nov. 14, 1559.	16		174
Oct. 1, 1556.	Thranum (Tranholme), Richard (bur. Yngleby Arneclif), Sep. 8, 1556.	15	1	68
Apl. 17, 1567.	Threpland, John, Colingworthe, par. Bingley, Feb. 26, 1566.	17		620
Dec. 1, 1558.	Threske, William, Shiplay, husbandman, July 5, 1558.	15	3	146
Oct. 5, 1558.	Threston, John, Hoton Cransweke, Sep. 6, 1558.	15	3	71
July 23, 1556.	Thriske, John Shupton in Galtres, husbandman, Jun. 10. 1556.	15	1	59
Dec. 13, 1557.	Thryston, Sir John, curate of Norton (bur. Olde Malton), Nov. 12, 1557.	15	2	41
Dec. 22, 1557.	Thurbrande, John, Hull, maryner, Nov. 21, 1557.	15	2	43
Nov. 23, 1563.	Thurisbie, Richard, West Cottinwithe, par. Thorganbie, Nov. 25, 1558.	17		305
Mar. 17, 1556.	Thurland, John (Hornesay, notary public), May 2, 1544.	15	1	186
Jun. 15, 1566.	Thurske, Thomas, Weaton, par. Rowley, Mar. 30, 1566.	17		552
Apl. 13, 1559.	Thurstone, John, Wellweke, Jan. 22, 1558.	15	3	345
Jun. 28, 1562.	Thwaites, Thomas, Marston, esquire, Aug. 5, 1557.	17		99
Oct. 1, 1557.	——— als. Webster, John, Estbecke, par. Whytbye, fysherman, May 23, 1557.	15	1	363
Oct. 4, 1558.	Thwattes, Richard, Gledowe (bur. Leedes), Aug. 12, 1558.	15	3	60
Feb. 10, 1557.	Thwaytes, William, Lunde on Wolde, esquire, Jun. 1, 1557.	15	2	148
Dec. 20, 1560.	Thwinge, George [Overhemylsey], Jan. 16, 1559.	16		137
Jan. 12, 1557.	Thyrke, John, Beverlay, Aug. 16, 1557.	15	2	80
Jun. 25, 1560.	Thyrkylbye, John, Slingesbie, Apl. 19, 1560.	16		87
May 4, 1558.	Tillinge, John, Skarryngton (Notts.), July 22, 1557.	15	2	212
Sep. 30, 1556.	Tillitson, James, Lodsdaill, par. Carleton (Craven), May 16, 1556.	15	1	173
May 5, 1568.	———, William, Lodsdaill (bur. Carlton), Jan. 28, 156[7-]8.	17		787
Feb. 14, 1567.	Todd, George, Danby, carpenter, Oct. 17, 1567.	17		760
Dec. 30, 1556.	———, John, Santon, Dec. 7, 1556.	15	1	86
Apl. 3, 1559.	———, Richard, Spreton (bur. Righton), husbandman, Dec. 26, 1558.	15	3	316
Oct. 1, 1562.	———, Robert, Depedale (bur. Houbram), ———, 1562.	17		111
July 12, 1565.	———, Thomas, Wintringham, Mar. 4, 1564.	17		450
May 18, 1559.	———, William, Norton, par. Campsall, Mar. 28, 1559.	15	3	419
Aug. 12, 1567.	———, William, Scaubie, Apl. 28, 1567.	17		695

1 The Dedication of Owston is said to be All Saints.

A.D. 1554 TO 1568.

		Vol.	Pt.	Fol.
Apl. 19, 1555.	Todde, Agnes, Flameburghe, widow, Feb. 2, 1554.	14		120
May 21, 1560.	———, Christopher, Thorneton in Pyckeringelithe, Sep. 30, 1559.	16		67
Jun. 22, 1560.	———, John, Huggat, May 1, 1558.	16		87
May 2, 1555.	———, Miles, Depedall (bur. Hobrame), Nov. 7, 1553.	14		26
Oct. 2, 1556.	———, Richard, Owlston, par. Cockewolde, July 10, 1556.	15	1	132
Mar. 27, 1565.	———, Robert, Lellay, par. Preston, husbandman, Nov. 6, 1564.	17		417
Aug. 6, 1567.	———, Thomas, Hempholme, par. Leven, July 28, 1564.	17		702
May 6, 1557.	———, Thomas, Thriske, Sep. 17, 1556.	15	1	242
May 26, 1567.	Tode, John, Clowghton, par. Scawbe, Jan. 20, 1566.	17		653
Oct. 2, 1566.	———, John, Raysgill (bur. Hubberham), May 20, 1566.	17		576
Jun. 9, 1558.	———, Katheren, Hempholme, par. Leven, widow, Oct. 23, 1557.	15	2	310
Feb. 15, 1558.	———, Robert, Sprotley, Dec. 31, 1558.	15	3	272
Jun. 12, 1567.	Togge, John, West Halsam, May 1, 1567.	17		663
Sep. 30, 1558.	Toine, Thomas (bur. Acam), Jun. 17, 1558.	15	3	89
May 13, 1557.	Toknkinson, Thomas, Walkringham (Notts.), husbn., Apl. 20, 1555.	15	1	234
Oct. 20, 1558.	Toll, Robert, Tunstall, May 24, 1558.	15	2	349
Jan. 23, 1561.	———, Thomas, Pall (Holderness), Dec. 3, 1561.	17		19
Sep. 5, 1554.	Toller, John, Gisburne, Jun. 12, 1554.	14		149
Oct. 5, 1558.	Tollerton, Robert, Cokeswold, May 24, 1558.	15	3	45
Nov. 10, 1558.	Tolson, James, Rastrike, par. Halyfax, Sep. 11, 1558.	15	3	156
July 28, 1563.	———, Jennett, widow of Jas. T., Rastricke, Jan. 31, 1562.	17		210
Jun. 9, 1563.	Tombler, John, Seglestorn, husbandman, Mar. 26, 1563.	17		253
May 9, 1566.	Tomisman, Thomas, Broughton Soulney (Notts.), husbn., ———, 1565.	17		550
Oct. 13, 1558.	Tomkinson, John, Walkringham (Notts.), Mar. 9, 1557.	15	2	379
Mar. 6, 1556.	Tomkynson, Richard, Walkringham (Notts.), husbn., Sep. 6, 1556.	15	1	183
Mar. 13, 1567.	Tomlingson, Edward, Sesaye, Sep. 16, 1567.	17		763
Jun. 11, 1556.	Tomlinson, John, Hamylton, par. Brayton, May 19, 1556.	15	1	57
Sep. 29, 1563.	———, Richard, Nappaye (bur. Gisburne), serving man, Apl. 23, 1563.	17		281
Oct. 1, 1562.	———, Thomas, Hamylton, par Braton, Apl. 3, 1561.	17		115
May 17, 1557.	Tomlynson, William, Bridlington, husbandman, Feb. 8, 1556.	15	1	244
Mar. 14, 1557.	Tomlynsonne, William, Ellerton, Dec. 26, 1557.	15	2	152
July 21, 1556.	Tompson, Rawffe, Stathes, par. Hynderwell, Dec. 12, 1555.	15	1	44
Nov. 3, 1561.	———, Thomas, Leven in Holderness, husbandman, Sep. 20, 1561.	17		35
Oct. 8, 1556.	Tompsone, Emerie, Ruddingtone (bur. St. Peter's, Slafurthe, Notts), Dec. 2, 1555.	15	1	150
Apl. 27, 1562.	Tomson, Alexander, Whitgifte, Nov. 22, 1561.	17		196
May 9, 1566.	———, Avarye, Fenton (bur. Sturton, Notts.), Oct. 16, 7 Eliz.	17		542
July 14, 1564.	———, Elizabeth, Carleton (bur. Helmsley), widow, Aug. 6, 1561.	17		358
Oct. 2, 1566.	———, Emmot, Thornesett in Bradfeild, widow, Aug. 19, 1566.	17		578
May 6, 1557.	———, Isabell, Skytbie, widow, Mar. 12, 1557.	15	1	238
May 5, 1557.	———, John, Ayton (bur. Howtonbushell), Sep. 25, 1556.	15	1	251
Apl. 12, 1559.	———, John, Crathorne, Nov. 29, 1558.	15	3	336
Jan. 14, 1558.	———, John, Eskrig, July 19, 1558.	15	3	192
Oct. 13, 1558.	———, John, Warsoppe (Notts.), Nov. 10, 1557.	15	2	357
Jun. 22, 1568.	———, Leonard, Gamston (Notts.), May 12, 1568.	17		829
Apl. 21, 1562.	———, Margaret, Raskell, widow, Apl. 11, 1562.	17		196
Jun. 12, 1568.	———, Mathewe, Eskerigge, Oct. 11, 1567.	17		806
Dec. 1, 1564.	———, Richard, Egbrough (bur. Kellington), Nov. 14, 1564.	17		400
Jan. 12, 1558.	———, Robert, Beverlaie, marchante, Nov. 26, 1558.	15	3	196
Oct. 1, 1556.	———, Stephan, Osset, (bur. Dwysburie), July 16, 1556.	15	1	120
Oct. 16, 1558.	———, Walter, Hesle, yeoman, Jun. 5, 1558.	15	2	345
Aug. 12, 1566.	———, William, Sheaffeld, Mar. 26, 1566.	17		567
Jun. 31, 1561.	Tomsone, Margaret, Selbie, Apl. 28, 1561.	17		85
Apl. 28, 1558.	Tomsonne, William, Danby, Nov. 12, 1557.	15	2	232
Oct. 7, 1557.	Tonge, Nicholas, Knesall (Notts.), husbandman, May 2, 1557.	15	2	17
Oct. 5, 1564.	———, William, East Halsame, July 10, 1563.	17		368
Sep. 30, 1557.	Toodd, Edward, Brantingham Thorpp, July 28, 1557.	15	1	325
Jan. 17, 1567.	———, William, Kirkbie under Knoll, husbandman, May 31, 1567.	17		755
Mar. 24, 1560.	Toos, Richard, Skelton in Cleveland, Oct. 30, 1560.	16		178
July 16, 1561.	Topham, John, Stooydlay Roger, Dec. 7, 1560.	17		83
Apl. 27, 1564.	Toples, Robert, West Leeke (Notts.), Nov. 22, 1563.	17		341

A.D. 1554 TO 1568.

		Vol.	Pt.	Fol.
Feb. 6, 1558.	Topliffe, Henry, Bynnyngton (bur. Willerbie), Feb. 10, 1557.	15	3	260
Apl. 16, 1562.	Toppan, John, Hebden, par. Lynton, Jan. 28, 156[1-]2.	17		191
Dec. 1, 1561.	———, John, Kettewell, Jun. 1, 1561.	17		33
Apl. 28, 1563.	———, Thomas, Heton (bur. Relston), July 28, 1562.	17		229
Apl. 16, 1562.	Toppclyffe, Richard (bur. Brompton), Aug. 13, 1561.	17		158
May 10, 1565.	Toppham, William, Topclif, clerk, Apl. 6, 1565.	17		430
Mar. 14, 1559.	Toppon, Thomas (bur. Ketlewell), Jan. 31, 1559.	16		8
Oct. 10, 1566.	Torner, Richard, Hawkesworthe (Notts.), husbandman, July 23, 1562.	17		594
Dec. 17, 1557.	Tornholme, Thomas, Kyrkehouse grene, par. Bramwith, Nov. 3, 1557.	15	2	40
Apl. 6, 1558.	Totill, John, Norton, par. Campsall, Mar. 11, 1557.	15	2	182
May 29, 1562.	Tottie, Gylbert, Selbye, shereman, Feb. 20, 1562.	17		100
Jan. 11, 1558.	———, John (bur. Bardsay), Jan. 10, 1 Mary.	15	3	170
May 21, 1554.	———, William, Birkyn, Dec. 17, 1552.	14		6
Mar. 29, 1568.	Tottye, Elizabeth, Allerton Gledowe, par. Leedes, husbn., Jan. 23, 1567.	17		768
Oct. 4, 1554.	Totyll, John, Crofton, Aug. 1, 1554.	14		46
Mar. 22, 1558.	Touned, Jefferay, Staynland, par. Eland, Mar. 23, 1557.	15	3	295
Feb. 15, 1558.	Tourner, Richard, Terington, Aug. 18, 1558.	15	3	272
May 6, 1557.	Tovie, Steven, Burton Agnes, yeoman, Apl. 9, 1557.	15	1	246
May 13, 1568.	Towbe, John, Lanham (Notts.), Jan. 1, 1566.	17		802
Apl. 28, 1563.	Tower, Mathew, Watterhouse (bur. Kirkbie Malham), Mar. 3, 1562.	17		228
Sep. 28, 1557.	———, Thomas, Wessythouses (bur. Kyrkebye Malhamdaill), Sep. 2, 1557.	15	1	339
Apl. 30, 1556.	Towle, Cicilie, Stapleforthe (Notts.), widow, Feb. 20, 1555.	15	1	30
May 13, 1568.	Towler, William, Southe Skerell [Scarle] (Notts.), Jan. 27, 1567.	17		798
Nov. 9, 1557.	Towller, Richard, Waykfeld, Aug. 14, 1557.	15	2	98
Apl. 28, 1563.	Towllerton, Bryane, Cookeswold, July 7, 1562.	17		240
July 27, 1562.	Townend, Herrye, Weston, Apl. 5, 1562.	17		98
Mar. 26, 1565.	———, John, Warley, par. Halifax, fletcher, Oct. 7, 1564.	17		417
Aug. 5, 1557.	To[w]nhend, Thomas, Heptonstall, Jun. 16, 1557.	15	2	118
Mar. 24, 1567.	Towrie, Frauncis, Selbie, Sep. 24, 1567.	17		767
Feb. 28, 1566.	Tows, Elline, Garton, Dec. 8, 1566.	17		615
July 18, 1565.	———, Thomas, senr., Garton, May 3, 1565.	17		450
Sep. 21, 1557.	Towtill, William, Kyrkesmeaton, Aug. 16, 1557.	15	1	352
Aug. 21, 1561.	Toye, Roger, Cottingham, husbandman, May 10, 1561.	17		56
Mar. 26, 1560.	Toyes, John (bur. Leverton), Nov. 14, 1559.	16		19
May 3, 1555.	Traneholme, Thomas (bur. Est Harlesey), Nov. 1, 1554.	14		34
Nov. 4, 1566.	Tranmer, John, Ereley (bur. Hacknes), Oct. 21, 1566.	17		598
Oct. 29, 1558.	Trate, John, Sawbie, Aug. 25, 1558.	15	2	369
Nov. 14, 1561.	Tratt, Henry, Thrusterby, par. Scawbe, Aug. 8, 1558.	17		34
Apl. 14, 1562.	Trawghton, John (bur. Beverley). *No date.*	17		165
Mar. 10, 1556.	Trayne, Hughe, Roisdall, par. Lastingham, Dec. 17, 1556.	15	1	201
Oct. 15, 1563.	Treasure, Peter, Garton in Holderness, yeoman, Dec. 25, 1562.	17		296
May 27, 1567.	———, William, Garton in Holderness, Apl. —, 1560.	17		647
Oct. 11, 1565.	Treis, Robert, Stapelford (Notts.), Apl. 24, 1565.	17		479
Jun. 8, 1557.	Treste, John, Ottingham, Apl. 21, 1557.	15	1	269
Oct. 12, 1558.	Trew, Edward, Nottingham, tanner, Aug. 23, 1558.	15	3	227
Aug. 2, 1560.	Trewe, Richard, Burton Pidseye, May 16, 1560.	16		100
May 28, 1560.	Trewthe, Thomas, Essingwolde, Apl. 18, 1560.	16		70
Feb. 14, 1567.	Tristram, Robert, Gisburne, gentleman, Jan. 9, 1567.	17		760
Apl. 27, 1564.	Troppe, Thomas, Throppe neare Newarke (Notts.), Mar. 27, 1564.	17		337
May 27, 1562.	Trosdell, Robert (bur. Gysbourne), Feb. 28, 1561.	17		100
Apl. 8, 1560.	Trotte, Alyson, Everyngham, widow, Feb. 13, 1559.	16		29
Sep. 16, 1564.	———, John, Scarbroughe, Dec. 28, 1563.	17		363
Jan. 8, 1562.	Trotter, Henry, Ugthorpe, par. Lithe, Jun. 8, 1560.	17		141
May 4, 1558.	Trowell, Thomas, Cottgrave (Notts.), husbandman, July 14, 1557.	15	2	268
Oct. 13, 1558.	———, Thomas, senr., Sutton (Notts.—St. Bartholmew), Ang. 9, 1558.	15	2	360
Jun. 20, 1566.	Trowsedalle, William, Burton Flemynge (bur. Hunmanbie), clerk, Feb. 4, 1565.	17		556
Jun. 28, 1557.	Truman, William, Sneton, par. Felicekirke, Apl. 24, 1557.	15	1	299
May 2, 1560.	Truscros, Henry, Hull, marchant and alderman Sep. 8, 1559.	16		43
July 15, 1558.	Truslove, John, Londsbroughe, husbandman, May 16, 1558.	15	2	307

		Vol.	Pt.	Fol.
Aug. 2, 1560.	Truslowe, Katherene, Waugham, widow, Mar. 8, 1559.	16		101
No date.	Trymyngham, John, Fishelake, Dec. 3, 1554.	14		81
Oct. 9, 1567.	Tub, William, Northe Clifton (Notts.), labourer, July 25, 1567.	17		723
Jun. 10, 1558.	Tubley, Steaven, York, doctor of phisicke, Apl. 20, 1558.	15	2	286
Oct. 13, 1558.	Tunman, Peter, Welley (Notts.), husbandman, Apl. 24, 1558.	15	2	356
Oct. 20, 1555.	Tunstall, Thomas, curate of Slaitborne, Jan. 2, 1551.	14		248
Nov. 21, 1556.	Tupman, John, Pollington, par. Snaith, Oct. 14, 1556.	15	1	116
Apl. 24, 1567.	Turnar, John, Thorpe (Notts.), husbandman, Dec. 22, 1566.	17		641
Nov. 22, 1558.	———, Robert, Flaxton (bur. Bossall), yeoman, Sep. 24, 1558.	15	3	75
Mar. 31, 1554.	Turnaye, Johane (bur. Burghwalles), Mar. 26, 1550.	14		106
Apl. 28, 1563.	Turnebull, Thomas, Stirton, par. Skipton, Jan. 3, 1562.	17		228
Oct. 19, 1558.	Turnell, William, Este Markham (Notts.), Mar. 28, 1557.	15	3	94
Oct. 3, 1554.	Turner, George, Bingley, Sep. 18, 1552.	14		37
Apl. 16, 1562.	———, George (Craven), Jun. 26, 1561.	17		169
Oct. 29, 1558.	———, John, Bointon, Mar. 8, 155[7-]8.	15	2	371
Sep. 16, 1555.	———, John (bur. Burghwallis), Mar. 26, 1550.	14		68
Feb. 10, 1557.	———, John, Cottingham, Dec. 23, 1557.	15	2	150
May 14, 1562.	———, John, Owsom (bur. Skryngham), husbandman, Apl. 17, 1562.	17		197
Jun. 4, 1568.	———, Margaret, Sledmer, widow, Jan. 10, 1567.	17		813
Mar. 15, 1558.	———, Robert, Wressle, labourer, Jan. 2, 1558.	15	3	166
Jun. 21, 1558.	———, Thomas, Carleton nere Snaythe, husbandman, Jan. 3, 1557.	15	2	384
Dec. 1, 1558.	———, William, Holme in Spaldingmore, Nov. 16, 1557.	15	3	147
May 28, 1562.	———, William, Norton (bur. Campsall), Dec. 1, 1561.	17		102
Oct. 14, 1557.	———, William, Ryton, par. Kyrkebymysperton, Sep. 11, 1557.	15	1	363
Apl. 20, 1562.	Turnill, Roger, East Markham (Notts.), husbandman, Mar. 16, 1561.	17		187
Feb. 9, 1554.	Turpin, Elizabeth, widow of Robert T., Towton (bur. Saxton), Aug. 20, 1551.	14		298
Sep. 7, 1558.	———, John, Lund, par. Braton, July 16, 1558.	15	3	101
Apl. 26, 1558.	Turpine, Robert, Monkefryston, Feb. 6, 1557.	15	2	238
May 3, 1558.	Turpyn, Elsabethe, Stutton, par. Tadcaster, widow, Nov. 12, 1556.	15	2	278
May 20, 1556.	———, Margaret, Towton (bur. Saxton), widow, Mar. 27, 1556.	15	1	35
Jan. 18, [? 1555.]	———, Robert, Towton, husbandman, Aug. 8, 1551.	14		70
May 26, 1563.	———, William, Mosse, par. Campsall, Apl. 27, 1563.	17		250
Aug. 4, 1565.	———, William, Stutton (bur. Tadcaster), July 22, 1565.	17		455
Aug. 5, 1562.	Turton, Annes, Denby, wid., of Wm. T. (bur. Penyston), Mar. 13, 1560.	17		102
Jan. 20, 1557.	———, Elizabeth, Barneslay, widow, July 14, 1556.	15	2	67
Oct. 2, 1555.	———, Robert, Doncaster, smithe, Jun. 30, 1555.	14		163
July 5, 1557.	Turvyn, Robert, Tykhill, husbandman, Aug. 28, 1556.	15	1	302
Sep. 21, 1557.	———, Robert, junr., Tikhill, Jun. 19, 1557.	15	1	350
Jan. 20, 1557.	———, Thomas, Tykhyll, Nov. 14, 1557.	15	2	69
May 18, 1559.	Turwhyte, Robert, Hilstone, Dec. 14, 1558.	15	3	395
Dec. 12, 1567.	Turwyn, Elizabeth, Tikhill, widow, Sep. 12, 1567.	17		745
Aug. 24, 1554.	Tutell, Richard, Campsall, July 16, 1553.	14		270
Apl. 18, 1560.	———, Robert, Staynforde (bur. Haitefelde), carpenter, Nov. 28, 1559.	16		31
Jun. 6, 1560.	Tuvye, Thomas, Beverlay, Nov. 29, 1559.	16		72
Dec. 13, 1554.	Twaites, John, Pontefracte, yeoman, Nov. 4, 1554.	14		96
Oct. 1, 1556.	Twaytes, Richard, Darynton, Aug. 7, 1557.	15	1	120
Nov. 10, 1563.	Tweddell, John. Nunkelinge, Aug. 10, 1563.	17		302
Feb. 17, 1561.	Twell, Jennet, Misson (Notts.), Aug. 10, 1561.	17		13
Jan. 13, 1558.	Twelues, Sir Thomas, Blithe (Notts.), priest, Nov. 16, 1558.	15	3	18
Oct. 7, 1563.	Twelves, John (bur. Estrettford, Notts.), Jan. 3, 1562.	17		294
May 2, 1555.	Twene, William, Beverleye, draper, Mar. 24, 1554.	14		33
Dec. 17, 1565.	Tweynde, Robert (bur. Kirkeburne), Jan. 6, 1564.	17		493
Sep. 20, 1554.	Twigge, Thomas, Sheffeld, Feb. 23, 1552.	14		150
Mar. 4, 1562.	Twilton, Edward, Paull, Dec. 26, 1562.	17		150
Apl. 7, 1554.	Twuy, James, Kaingham, Dec. 13, 1553.	14		216
Dec. 5, 1567.	Twynam, William, Sutton in Holderness, May 6, 1566.	17		742
Mar. 10, 1566.	Twyge, Thomas, Ecclesfeld, Apl. 20, 1566.	17		516
Oct. 29, 1554.	Tyas, John, Osset, husbandman, July 3, 1554.	14		281
Dec. 12, 1554.	———, William, Melton on Hill, Apl. 6, 1554.	14		95
Oct. 6, 1557.	Tybbott, John, Ollcotes, par. Blythe (Notts.), husbn., July 1, 1557.	15	2	12
Oct. 8, 1562.	Tyes, Robert, Myssen (Notts.), Jun. 8, 1559.	17		120

		Vol.	Pt.	Fol.
Oct. 29, 1554.	Tyll, William, Stanfford (Notts.), Dec. 25, 1548.	14		282
Apl. 27, 1564.	Tyllett, Edmund, Stoke (Notts.), Jan. 12, 1564.	17		336
Apl. 17, 1567.	Tyllitson, Margaret, Leadensdale, par. Carlton, Oct. 12, 1566.	17		622
Sep. 28, 1557.	Tyllytson, John, Lodersdaill, par. Carleton (Craven), May 15, 1556.	15	1	338
Jan. 21, 1557.	Tyndaill, James, Dyghton (bur. Eskrige), Dec. 18, 1557.	15	2	64
Oct. 9, 1567.	———, Robert, Ceasay, Aug. 25, 1566.	17		731
May 22, 1557.	———, Thomas, Newton on Derwine, par. Wilberfosse, labr., Mar. 3, 1556.	15	1	257
Jan. 31, 1563.	Tyndalle, Henry, Beverley, baker, Sep. 8, 1563.	17		312
Nov. 16, 1558.	Tyndayle, William, Langton, husbandman, Sep. 20, 1558.	15	3	124
Jan. 18, 1565.	Tyndyll, Thomas, Lepinton, par. Scryngame, Dec. 12, 1565.	17		496
Oct. 5, 1558.	Tyngill, Adame, Carlingall, par. Batley, Aug. 14, 1558.	15	3	65
Sep. 18, 1565.	Tynker, Hughe, Mylnehouse, par. Darfeld, husbn., Jun. 2, 1559.	17		468
May 4, 1557.	———, Nicholas, Astone, Dec. 4, 1557.	15	1	281
Apl. 28, 1558.	Tynslay, Richard, Skelton, husbandman, Feb. 15, 1557.	15	2	233
Oct. 5, 1558.	Typladye, Thomas, Pikton, par. Kirklevington, Aug. 17, 1558.	15	3	68
Nov. 16, 1562.	Tyson, William, York, cooke, Sep. 29, 1562.	17		128
Feb. 17, 1561.	Ulliatt, Gacyon, Walkringham (Notts.), husbn., Oct. 20, 1561.	17		15
May 6, 1557.	Umfray, John, Hildeston in Holderness, Feb. 20, 1556.	15	1	239
Jun. 25, 1568.	———, Thomas, Holme in Holderness, Mar. 28, 1568.	17		811
July 19, 1557.	Unde, Thomas, Gamilstone (Notts.), May 21, 1557.	15	1	287
Mar. 20, 1555.	Underell, John, Hooton Busshell, Dec. 23, 1555.	15	1	13
Oct. 27, 1564.	Underne, Robert, Averham (Notts.). *No date.*	17		393
May 20, 1564.	Underwod, Henry, Brinde (bur. Wressill), Apl. 27, 1564.	17		343
Aug. 28, 1561.	Undie, Robert, Cassall, par. Hayton (Notts.). *No date.*	17		58
Jun. 6, 155-.	Unter, Johan, Tanckersleye, widow, Mar. 22, 1553.	14		241
Jun. 20, 1568.	Unwen, Robert, Grayestones, par. Sheffeld, Mar. 25, 1568.	17		815
May 5, 1558.	Unwene (Hunewen, Act Book), Hugh, Askham (Notts.), Nov. 10, 1557.	15	2	249
May 26, 1567.	Uppilby, John, Bucton (bur. Bempton), Nov 26, 1566.	17		653
Dec. 22, 1556.	Upton, Alice, Brockholl, par. Cantley, widow, Aug. 16, 1556.	15	1	81
May 18, 1559.	———, Christopher, Moregate, par. Clarebrughe (Notts.), Aug. 3, 1558.	15	3	422
May 5, 1558.	———, John (bur. Westretford, Notts.), Oct. 26, 1557.	15	2	246
Mar. 6, 1556.	———, Thomas, West Retfurth (Notts.), Oct. 27, 1556.	15	1	178
Dec. 22, 1556.	———, William, Broke, par. Cantley, Aug. 12, 1556.	15	1	79
May 5, 1558.	———, William, Stocke (Notts.), Apl. 2, 1558.	15	2	259
Oct. 6, 1557.	Upsall, Margaret (bur. Lanham, Notts.), Sep. 5, 1557.	15	2	8
Apl. 22, 1562.	———, Robert, Lanham (Notts.), Dec. 1, 1561.	17		193
Dec. 5, 1554.	Ure, Nicholas, Wandisforde, husbandman, Feb. 8, 1553.	14		94
Oct. 13, 1558.	Urrie, Richard, Ferrie Marnham (Notts.), May 11, 1558.	15	2	362
Oct. 8, 1556.	Urrye, John, Ferye Marnham (Notts.), Jun. 2, 1556.	15	1	154
Mar. 23, 1557.	Uscher, Thomas, North Frodingham, July 16, 1557.	15	2	153
Aug. 13, 1567.	¹ Usher, Agnes, Northe Frothingham, Mar. 31, 1567.	17		689
Nov. 28, 1558.	———, Alis (bur. Fetherstone), Sep. 2, 1558.	15	3	135
Sep. 30, 1557.	———, John, Hastropp, par. Burton Agnes, husbn., Jun. 21, 1557.	15	1	342
Feb. 9, 1557.	———, Robert, Attyngweke, smythe. *No date.*	15	2	120
Nov. 10, 1563.	———, Steven, Northe Frothingham, May 31, 1563.	17		302
Mar. 13, 1558.	Ussherewood, James, Rither, yeoman, Oct. 10, 1558.	15	3	165
Jan. 11, 1557.	Ustwayte, John, Ringboroughgarthe, par. Awdbroughe, Oct. 29, 1557.	15	2	75
May 29, 1568.	Utie, John, Cottingham, yeoman, Jan. 19, 1567.	17		794
Sep. 23, 1558.	Uttlay, Bryan, Ilkelay, May 1, 1558.	15	3	86
Oct. 1, 1556.	Uttley, John, Langefeld, par. Heptonstall, singleman, Aug. 18, 1556.	15	1	143
Oct. 10, 1556.	Vallance, James, Newland, par. Drax, Sep. 22, 1556.	15	1	70
July 11, 1558.	Vance, Thomas, Barneby on Done, Feb. 25, 1557.	15	2	306
July 11, 1558.	Vardon, Robert, Sheffeild, Jun. 14, ——.	15	2	303
Apl. 27, 1560.	Vase, Edward, Lytle Claxton, par. Bossall, husbandman, Apl. 17, 1559.	16		33
Jun. 7, 1560.	Vasser, Philippe, Nafferton, widow, Aug. 16, 1559.	16		79
May 29, 1563.	Vauce, John, Galmthorpe, par. Teryngton, Dec. 26, 1562.	17		251
Sep. 30, 1561.	Vavasor, George, Spaldington, gentleman, Jun. 22, 1561.	17		60
Mar. 29, 1560.	———, John, Spaldington, esquire, May 2, 1558.	16		22
Dec. 6, 1560.	Vavasour, John, Appleton (bur. Bolton Percye), gent., Mar. 16, 1559.	16		134

¹ See also under letter H.

		Vol.	Pt.	Fol.
Apl. 8, 1567.	Vavasour, John, Spaldington (bur. Bubwithe), gent., Feb. 8, 1566.	17		620
Apl. 30, 1557.	———, Peter, Spaldington (bur. Bubwith), knight, Jan. 25, 1556.	15	1	209
Aug. 5, 1563.	———, Richard, Askham Richard, gentleman, May 6, 1563.	17		267
Jun. 6, 1560.	Vawse, Jaine, Walkington, spinster, Sep. 30, 1559.	16		73
May 5, 1568.	———, John, South Dalton, smythe, July 10, 1567.	17		775
May 2, 1560.	Vayll, John, Albroughe, husbandman, Feb. 25, 1559.	16		51
Jan. 30, 1560.	Vekers, William (Ripon Deanery), May 20, 1560.	16		139
Jun. 14, 1564.	Vendivall, Robert, Bempton, husbandman, Jan. 12, 1563.	17		351
May 18, 1559.	Vescie, Robert, Treton, Feb. 15, 1558.	15	3	397
Nov. 8, 1557.	Vescye, Jane, Tykhyll, widow, Jun. 20, 1557.	15	2	113
July 10, 1560.	Vesse, John, Skrethenbecke, husbandman, Jan. 15, 1559.	16		92
Feb. 18, 1563.	Vessie, Alice, Hull, spinster, Dec. 7, 1562.	17		316
Jan. 18, 1556.	Vevers, Richard, Pudsaye, par. Calverlay, Mar. 28, 1555.	15	1	87
July 12, 1558.	———, Robert, Huslyt (bur. Leedes), Apl. 14, 1557.	15	2	315
Jun. 4, 1561.	———, William, Loufthous, par. Rodwell, Feb. 20, 1560.	17		67
Jun. 5, 1565.	Vicarman, Robert, Haistropp (bur. Burton Agnes), yeom., Apl. 28, 1565.	17		443
Sep. 16, 1557.	Vicars, George, Stapleton (bur. Darrington), husbn., Aug. 3, 1557.	15	1	333
Oct. 2, 1555.	———, Jenet (bur. Athewicke), Jan. 14, 1554.	14		166
Jan. 12, 1558.	———, John, Acton, par. Fetherstonne, Jan. 5, 1558.	15	3	173
Sep. 24, 1567.	———, John, Carleton, par. Royston, husbandman, Apl. 26, 1567.	17		708
Jan. 12, 1558.	———, William (bur. Fetherstonne), Sep. 28, 1558.	15	3	173
Nov. 28, 1567.	——— als. Bickers, Thos., Griestorpe, par. Fylay, husbn., Jun. 12, 1567.	17		740
Mar. 14, 1560.	——— als. Cartwright, William (bur. Athewyke), Sep. 9, 1560.	16		161
Sep. 23, 1558.	Vickarman, John, Humonbye, Aug. 19, 1558.	15	3	86
May 18, 1559.	Vincent, Thomas, Breathwell, Apl. 17, 1559.	15	3	404
Jun. 25, 1560.	Vycars, Rawffe, Olde Malton, Apl. 2, 1560.	16		87
Apl. 4, 1560.	Waces, John, Trumpton, par. Ordsall (Notts.), Mar. 5, 1559.	16		26
May 6, 1557.	Wadbie, William, Foston (S. Andrew), Jan. 18, 1556.	15	1	246
Oct. 20, 1558.	———, William, Sprotley, Sep. 19, 1558.	15	2	350
Sep. 30, 1557.	Waddingham, Richard, Hoton Cranswike, husbandman, Sep. 13, 1557.	15	1	325
Jan. 9, 1562.	Waddington, William, Arthington (bur. Addell), clothier, Jun. 26, 1562.	17		139
Oct. 16, 1558.	Waddisworth, Jane, Hull, widow, Jun. 17, 1558.	15	2	344
May 20, 1557.	———, Richard, Waddysworth, par. Heptonstall, Mar. 10, 1556.	15	1	258
Dec. 2, 1562.	Wade, Alexander, Adweke on Dern, husbandman, Nov. 8, 1561.	17		131
Oct. 6, 1558.	———, John, Wath, Sep. 15. 1558.	15	3	222
Apl. 20, 1559.	Wadsley, John, Lond, par. Sutton (Notts.), ———, 1558.	15	3	365
Jan. 10, 1557.	Wadson, Jeffray, Helmesley, Aug. 18, 1557.	15	2	77
Feb. penult., 1556.	Wadworthe, James, Hull, draper, Jan. 9, 1556.	15	1	180
Feb. 19, 1563.	Waett, William, Huntington, July 19, 1563.	17		316
Oct. 11, 1565.	Wagden, Thomas, Clarworthe (Notts.), Jun. 22, 1565.	17		473
Oct. 13, 1558.	Waid, John, Laine[ham?] (Notts.), husbandman, Apl. 23, 1558.	15	2	357
Mar. 2, 1561.	———, Rayfe, Ganton (bur. Brandisburton), labourer, Sep. 2, 1560.	17		2
Apl. 22, 1556.	Waide, Agnes, Wakefield, wid. of Costyn W. of Whitkirk, Oct. 15, 1555.	15	1	23
Sep. 30, 1557.	———, James, Badesworthe, Aug. 15, 1557.	15	1	369
Apl. 28, 1558.	———, Raufe, Bushopmonckton, Jan. 1, 1558.	15	2	207
Jan. 27, 1558.	———, Thomas, Farselay, par. Calverley, Dec. 10, 1558.	15	3	221
Oct. 31, 1565.	Waikefeild, Thomas, St. Olave's, York, cordinar, Apl. 4, 1564.	17		482
May 26, 1558.	Waire, Elizabeth, Threske, Apl. 5, 1558.	15	2	226
May 6, 1557.	Wairinge, Nicholas, Rudstone, singleman, Feb. 12, 1556.	15	1	249
Dec. 22, 1556.	Waite, John, Barmby of Don, Dec. 28, 1555.	15	1	78
Apl. 6, 1558.	———, Thomas (bur. Barnby on Donne), Feb. 10, 1557.	15	2	183
Aug. 13, 1554.	Waith, Richard, Hardington, par. Addell, Oct. 15, 1553.	14		269
Oct. 7, 1556.	Wakefeld, Robert, Holbecke Woodhouse, July 4, 1556.	15	1	143
May 3, 1565.	———, William, Cowike (bur. Snaythe), Apl. 16, 1563.	17		420
Mar. 14, 1560.	Waker, John, Oldhall in Woursburghe, husbandman, Sep. 25, 1560.	16		161
Oct. 8, 1562.	Wakfeld, John, Walkeringham (Notts.), Jun. 14, 1562.	17		121
Jan. 13, 1558.	Walch, Nicholas, Carlton, par. Gedling (Notts.), husbandman, Dec. 22, 1558 (twice).	15	3	184
May 2, 1566.	Walcoites, Richard, Skrethenbecke, husbandman, Jan. 16, 1565.	17		510
Jan. 12, 1558.	Waldbe, Ellen, Santon, Sep. 18, 1558.	15	2	355
Oct. 28, 1566.	Waldbie, Bryan (bur. Santon), Apl. 24, 1566.	17		586
Sep. 2, 1567.	———, William, Waldebie (bur. Ellington), gent., Jun. 26, 1567.	17		704

22

A.D. 1554 TO 1568.

		Vol.	Pt.	Fol.
Nov. 17, 1558.	Walde, Thristram (bur. Wistow), Sep. 30, 1558.	15	3	115
May 18, 1559.	Walkar, Anne, wid. of Robt. W., Clarebrugh (Notts.), May 12, 1558.	15	3	424
Sep. 16, 1555.	———, Nicholas, Staynburghe, par. Sylkiston, Feb. 20, 1551.	14		65
Nov. 29, 1558.	———, Roger, Darnell, par. Sheafeld, Nov. 15, 1556.	15	3	109
Dec. 1, 1558.	———, Thomas, Beverley, tanner, July 8, 1558.	15	3	147
Feb. ult., 1563.	Walkengton, Thomas, Bulmer, husbandman, Jan. 26, 1563.	17		322
May 4, 1558.	Walke[r], Nicholas, Gedling (Notts.), Sep. 8, 1557.	15	2	273
Feb. 9, 1563.	Walker, Agnes, Doncaster, Sep. 14, 1557.	17		315
Oct. 5, 1558.	———, Alexander, Raysgill (bur. Huberham), Apl. 19, 1558.	15	3	39
Feb. 24, 1561.	———, Alexander, Werdlay, par. Harwood, Oct. 30, 1561.	17		16
Jun. 2, 1557.	———, Alice, Santynglaie, par. Wragbie, widow, Oct. 6. 1556.	15	1	266
Jun. 4, 1561.	———, Alis, wid. of Edward W., Huddersfeld, Apl. 10, 1561.	17		68
Sep. 27, 1565.	———, Christabell, wife of John W., and late wife of Thos. Sharpe, Burton Agnes, Mar. 6, 1564.	17		469
Oct. 6, 1558.	———, Christopher, Wheatelay, par. Doncaster, Jun. 11, 1558.	15	3	223
May 4, 1557.	———, Edmunde, Doncaster, alderman, Sep. 26, 1556.	15	1	280
Oct. 5, 1558.	———, Edward, Gowlecar, par. Hudderfeild, Aug. 6, 1558.	15	3	67
May 4, 1558.	———, Edwarde, Papilwicke (Notts.), Nov. 13, 1557.	15	2	214
May 5, 1568.	———, Elizabeth, Beswicke, par. Kylnewicke, wid., Feb. 27, 1567.	17		777
Nov. 22, 1563.	———, Elizabeth, wid. of Peter W., Gisburne, May 25, 1558.	17		304
Oct. 20, 1558.	———, Elizabeth, Hornesey, widow, Aug. 20, 1558.	15	2	349
Jun. 16, 1564.	———, Emmot, Balne, par. Burghwalles, Feb. 27, 1563.	17		351
Jan. 22, 1557.	———, Henry, Brotton, husbandman, Mar. 21, 1556.	15	2	158
Aug. 18, 1562.	———, Hewe, Gransmore (bur. Agnes Burton), yeom., May 31, 1562.	17		105
Mar. 22, 1558.	———, Hughe, Eland, Dec. 10, 1558.	15	3	294
Mar. 8, 1557.	———, Isabell (bur. Breton), widow, Feb. 20, 1557.	15	2	169
Sep. 29, 1557.	———, James, Duesburye, clothyer, Aug. 13, 1547.	15	1	328
May 25, 1554.	———, James (bur. Yngelby under Erneclef), Jan. 16, 1554.	14		130
Oct. 8, 1562.	———, Jane, Eperston (Notts.), Jan. 15, 1561.	17		122
Apl. 16, 1567.	———, Jennet, Osset, par. Dewisberie, widow, May 30, 1566.	17		626
Feb. 6, 1558.	———, Johane, wid. of Jo. W., Ferborne, par. Ledsham, Nov. 19, 1558.	15	3	265
Mar. 3, 1555.	———, John, Barnyston, Dec. 10, 1555.	15	1	11
Jan. 13, 1558.	———, John, Bilstroppe (Notts.), yeoman, Dec. 7, 4 and 5 Phil. and Mary.	15	3	188
Aug. 18, 1558.	———, John, Bradford, July 27, 1558.	15	2	296
May 14, 1557.	———, John, Eperston (Notts.), gentleman, —— 24, 1557.	15	1	237
Apl. 6, 1566.	———, John, Essingwold, Jan. 15, 1565.	17		510
July 1, 1562.	———, John, Exthorpe, par. Doncaster, Feb. 21, 1561.	17		92
July 29, 1560.	———, John, Ferneley (bur. Leedes), husbandman, Nov. 13, 1559.	16		96
Jun. 20, 1566.	———, John, Foston, Mar. 22, 1565.	17		557
May 9, 1563.	———, John, Gisburne, May 14, 1563.	17		255
Oct. 22, 1556.	———, John, Hecmundwyke, par. Bristall, Apl. 3, 1556.	15	1	100
Apl. 3, 1559.	———, John, Hilderthrope (bur. Bridlyngton), labr., Sep. 8, 1558.	15	3	360
Jun. 12, 1556.	———, John (bur. Kirkedaille), July 16, 1553.	15	1	57
Oct. 4, 1558.	———, John, Ledsham, Aug. 3, 1558.	15	3	58
Sep. 9, 1561.	———, John, Longwod, par. Huddersfeld, Mar. 23, 1561.	17		49
1555.	———, John, parson of St. Margeret's, York, Jun. 20, 1555.	14		244
Mar. 30, 1560.	———, John, Owlston, par. Cookeswolde, Sep. 3, 1559.	16		24
May 5, 1568.	———, John (bur. Ripon), Nov. 11, 1567.	17		783
Apl. 18, 1567.	———, John, Rosyngton, husbandman, Nov. 25, 1566.	17		633
Jan. 31, 1564.	———, John, Semer, Oct. 4, 1564.	17		404
No date.	———, Katherine, Folden, par. Bolton nighe Bowlande, Oct. 3, 1555.	14		84
Sep. 20, 1557.	———, Margaret, wid. (bur. Collthorpp), Aug. 7, 1557.	15	1	335
Oct. 16, 1558.	———, Margaret, Hull, wid. of Rob. W., merchant, Jun. 12, 1558.	15	2	367
Mar. 20, 1558.	———, Nicholas, Sykehouse, par. Fyshelake, Oct. 20, 1558.	15	3	248
May 22, 1557.	———, Peter, Crakall, par. Topliffe, Apl. 27, 1557.	15	1	264
Jun. 16, 1564.	———, Richard, Baulme, par. Burghwalles, Jan. 8, 1562.	17		351
Mar. 23, 1565.	———, Richard, Marflet, yeoman, Feb. 17, 1565.	17		504
Apl. 26, 1564.	———, Richard, Newland, par. Cottingham, husbn., Nov. 6, 1563.	17		334
May 2, 1560.	———, Richard, Rednes (bur. Whitgyft), Apl. 11, 1560.	16		53
May 3, 1560.	———, Richard, Wheldryke, Apl. 9, 1559.	16		34
Apl. 22, 1556.	———, Robert, Hawke, par. Whorleton, smythe, Dec. 2, 1555.	15	1	28

A.D. 1554 TO 1568.

		Vol.	Pt.	Fol.
Oct. 28, 1563.	Walker, Robert, Helmesley, Mar. 18, 1562.	17		299
Mar.23, 1560.	———, Robert, Hoton Bushell, husbandman, Apl. 18, 1559.	16		156
Apl. 28, 1558.	———, Robert, Hull, marchaunt, Mar. 1, 1557.	15	2	220
Jan. 24, 1558.	———, Robert, Kirklevington, Apl. 25, 1557.	15	3	216
Mar.10, 1562.	———, Robert, Kypaxe, Dec. 6, 1562.	17		152
Oct. 1, 1556.	———, Robert, Newlande, par. Cottingham, Jun. 18, 1556.	15	1	137
Jun. 25, 1557.	———, Robert, Rotherham, Jun. 11, 1557.	15	1	297
July 17, 1565.	———, Robert, Whysted (bur. Braiton), yeoman, Jan. 6, 1564.	17		453
Dec. 1, 1563.	———, Thomas, Bredgate, par. Rotherham, Nov. 7, 1563.	17		306
Oct. 6, 1557.	———, Thomas, Langar (Notts.), July 26, 1557.	15	2	26
Nov.17, 1558.	———, Thomas, Ledsham, Oct. 13, 1558.	15	3	114
Aug. 4, 1558.	———, Thomas, Northe Cave, May 6, 1558.	15	3	6
Dec. 12, 1567.	———, Thomas, Southe Kilvington, Sep. 28, 1567.	17		748
Oct. 14, 1563.	———, Thomas, junr., Southe Kilvyngton, Dec. 20, 1562.	17		298
May 9, 1565.	———, Thomas, Swillington, July 7, 1564.	17		422
Nov.15, 1557.	———, Thomas, Swyllyngton, Aug. 27, 1557.	15	2	96
May 31, 1557.	———, Thomas, Wombwell (bur. Darfeld), Mar. 6, 1556.	15	1	263
Sep. 28, 1557.	———, Umfray, Cowhousehyll, par. Bolton (Craven), Apl. 11, 1557.	15	1	340
Oct. 13, 1562.	———, Wilfride, Osset, par. Dewisburie, Feb. 26, 1561.	17		125
Jun. 17, 1556.	———, William, Athill (bur. Addill), Nov. 3, 1555.	15	1	48
Oct. 20, 1561.	———, William, Brestwell, par. Thornhill, July 14, 1561.	17		44
Mar. 8, 1557.	———, William, Burley (bur. Brayton), Aug. 11, 1557.	15	2	151
Apl. 22, 1563.	———, William, Burstall, Dec. 18, 1562.	17		209
Apl. 28, 1558.	———, William, Catton (bur. Topclyfe), Feb. 27, 1555.	15	2	239
Oct. 13, 1565.	———, William, Kirkelevington, husbandman, Mar. 18, 1563.	17		473
Mar.25, 1557.	———, William, Kylwyngton, Nov. 25, 1556.	15	1	202
July 29, 1558.	———, William, Nychous, par. Myrfeld, Feb. 24, 1554.	15	3	12
May 24, 1562.	———, William, Oswaldkirke, yeoman, Apl. 28, 1561.	17		86
Dec. 16, 1557.	———, William, Pattrington, Aug. 6, 1557.	15	2	47
May 9, 1565.	———, William, Spofforthe, Dec. 6, 1564.	17		422
Jun. 18, 1567.	——— *als.* Smythe, John, Ferburne (bur. Ledsham), husbn., Apl.27, 1567.	17		657
Jun. 13, 1560.	Walkewood, Robert, Estoft, Jan. 22, 1559.	16		83
Apl. 9, 1554.	Walkington, Nicholas, Hothome, Dec. 24, 1553.	14		53
Feb. 18, 1557.	Walkynton, Edmond, York, glaysuer, Jan. 23, 1557.	15	2	147
July 5, 1558.	Wall, Agnes, wid. of Jo. W. Cawood, Apl. 29, 1558.	15	2	326
May 10, 1559.	——, John, Ake, par. S. John, Beverlay, Dec. 8, 1558.	15	3	385
Mar.12, 1557.	——, John, Cawood, husbandman, Jan. 8, 1557.	15	2	126
May 10, 1559.	——, Robert, Besingbye, tailer, Mar. 14, 1558.	15	3	389
Jan. 24, 1558.	Waller, Cuthbert, Hemlynton, par. Staynton, yeoman, Sep. 23, 1558.	15	3	216
Jan. 24, 1558.	——, John, Hemlynton, par. Stainton, yeoman, Sep. 31 *(sic)*, 1558.	15	3	22
Aug. 4, 1558.	Walles, Elsabethe, Aike (bur. Beverley), widow, Apl. 16, 1558.	15	3	4
Jun. 5, 1554.	———, Raufe, Lockington, May 18, 1553.	14		9
Feb. 24, 1563.	———, William, Ottringham, May 30, 1563.	17		320
July 8, 1561.	Wallis, Edward, Lockinton, husbandman, Mar. 20, 1560.	17		79
May 10, 1565.	———, John, Westhoe, webster, Dec. 1, 1564.	17		422
May 16, 1554.	———, William, senr. (bur. Kylnewike), Feb. 8, 1553.	14		139
Nov.10, 1557.	Walls, John, Birkyn, Apl. 15, 1557.	15	2	104
Oct. 2, 1566.	Walmesley, William (bur. Mytton), Apl. 4, 1566.	17		573
Aug.28, 1561.	Walshay, Germane, Addle, Sep. 7, 1560.	17		53
Dec. 1, 1557.	———, Richard, Ledes, Nov. 16, 1554.	15	2	85
Oct. 8, 1562.	Walshe, John, Scrobye (Notts.), Sep. 14, 1559.	17		120
Aug.12, 1558.	Walshefurth, Myles, York, priest, Jun. 23, 1558.	15	3	2
Jan. 18, 1557.	Walshefurthe, Robert, Water Fulfurthe, Oct. 2, 1557.	15	2	65
Jun. 21, 1561.	Walterworth, Robert, Broughton, Mar. 7, 1558.	17		73
Nov.10, 1557.	Walton, John, Broughton (bur. All Hallows), Aug. 4, 1557.	15	2	100
Aug.12, 1555.	———, Robert, Pontefracte, clothedryver, ——— 17, 1555.	14		206
Sep. 1, 1563.	———, Thomas, Penyston, Feb. 27, 1562.	17		207
Apl. 23, 1567.	Walworth, G[r]ace, Raventoftes (bur. Ripon), widow, Mar. 24, 1566.	17		638
Mar. 5, 1555.	Walworthe, Ellene (bur. Ripon), Feb. 7, 1555.	15	1	12
Jun. 22, 1568.	————, Thomas, Muston (bur. Hunmanbie), husbn.,Feb.27,1568.	17		819
May 2, 1560.	Wamslay, Peter, Haitffelde, Mar. 21, 1559.	16		47

		Vol.	Pt.	Fol.
Oct. 2, 1555.	Wande, Percivall, par. St. Peter, Smeaton, May 5, 1555.	14		167
Aug. 26, 1558.	——, Richard, Amuderbye, May 1, 1558.	15	2	291
July 15, 1557.	Waneman, Thomas, Elvington, May 18, 1557.	15	1	308
Jun. 10, 1560.	Wanfflete, John, Pattrington, husbandman, Mar. 28, 1560.	16		82
Jun. 10, 1561.	Wanflyt, Thomas, Patryngton, May 12, 1561.	17		71
Apl. 28, 1558.	Wanton, Thomas, Nunthorpe, par. Aiton, Jan. 6, 1557.	15	2	230
May 4, 1558.	Waplingtonne, Henry, Beyston (Notts.), Oct. 13, 1557.	15	2	273
May 2, 1560.	Warcopp, William, Thurham (bur. Burton Agnes), husbn., Sep. 13, 1559.	16		37
Sep. 30, 1558.	Ward, Alyson, Mulwath (bur. Ripon), widow, Nov. 14, 1558.	15	3	55
Sep. 26, 1558.	——, Christopher, Wollay, par. Hymmysworth, tanner, Aug. 16, 1557.	15	3	54
Apl. 20, 1564.	——, George, Hamer in Hertoft (bur. Myddleton), Mar. 30, 1563.	17		326
May 22, 1557.	——, John, Dalton (bur. Topliffe), Apl. 28, 1557.	15	1	257
Oct. 6, 1558.	—— (or Waid), John, Haighe Grene, chapelry of Worspur, July 26, 1558.	15	3	222
May 25, 1558.	——, John, Langrake, par. Drax, Mar. 1. 1557.	15	2	283
May 9, 1563.	——, John, Ruston, smythe, Jan. 4, 5 Eliz.	17		255
Oct. 12, 1558.	——, John, Skarbrough (Skarrington, Notts., Act Book), Aug. 28, 1558.	13	2	374
Oct. 4, 1558.	——, Margaret, Barley, par. Braton, widow, Jun. 27, 1558.	15	3	59
May 10, 1565.	——, Mychaell, Skewesbe, par. Dalbye, Nov. 7, 1564.	17		430
Oct. 8, 1562.	——, Oliver, Eastwayth (Notts.), labourer, July 10, 1561.	17		123
Oct. 5, 1558.	——, Robert, Metheley, Nov. 13, 1557.	15	3	67
Mar. 15, 1558.	——, Robert, Old Malton, Nov. 21, 1558.	15	3	241
Nov. 29, 1558.	——, Roger, Stayneburghe, par. Silkestone, Sep. 9, 1556(?).	15	3	145
Dec. 6, 1557.	——, Thomas, Overyeadon, par. Gyeslay, Mar. 4, 1556.	15	2	84
Mar. 10, 1556.	——, William, Brandisdale, par. Kirkbye Morishead, Apl. 22, 1548.	15	1	200
Oct. 13, 1558.	——, William, Gamstonne (Notts.), Feb. 4, 1557.	15	2	377
Aug. 12, 1566.	——, William, Skeflinge, Mar. 30, 1566.	17		568
May 19, 1559.	——, William, Sneynton (Notts.), Jun. 27, 1558.	15	3	432
Mar. 1, 1557.	Wardaill, Thomas, Newe Malton, tanner, Nov. 17, 1557.	15	2	170
Oct. 15, 1563.	Wardall, John, Flamborughe, tanner, May 11, 1563.	17		297
Nov. 26, 1557.	Warde, Alys, Ardesley (bur. Derfyld), widow, Sep. 14, 1557.	15	2	93
May 13, 1557.	——, Dunston (bur. Hucknall Torkarde, Notts.), Dec. 31, 1556.	15	1	223
Oct. 22, 1556.	——, Elizabeth, Bradford, widow, Apl. 8, 1556.	15	1	100
Feb. 24, 1563.	——, Frauncis, Headon in Holderness, cowper, Jan. 17, 6 Eliz.	17		319
Jun. 21, 1567.	——, George, Follyfayt (bur. Spoffurth), May 25, 9 Eliz.	17		660
Nov. 12, 1556.	——, John, Barley, par. Braitone, Sep. 28. 1556.	15	1	112
Oct. 2, 1550 [? 5].	——, John, Beleye, par. Mytton, husbandman, ——, 1545.	14		171
July 27, 1564.	——, John, Farnedaill, par. Lastingham, ——, 1564.	17		359
Jan. 13, 1558.	——, Lawrence, Carcolstonne (Notts.), husbandman, Oct. 4, 1558.	15	3	181
Apl. 6, 1558.	——, Margaret, Woodhouse (Doncaster Dnry.), Nov. 10, 1557.	15	2	180
Jun. 21, 1565.	——, Mathew, Kesbrughe, par. Darton, Nov. 21, 1564.	17		447
Aug. 12, 1567.	——, Peter, Hunmanbie, May 26, 1567.	17		695
Jun. 22, 1568.	——, Peter, Hunmanbie, Nov. 13, 1567.	17		826
May 25, 1558.	——, Raufe, Langrake (bur. Drax), Nov. 22, 1557.	15	2	284
Oct. 12, 1558.	——, Rauffe, Elton (Notts.), yeoman, Aug. 19, 1558.	15	3	33
Dec. 22, 1556.	——, Richard, Edlington, husbandman, July 31, 1556.	15	1	78
Apl. 22, 1556.	——, Richard, Hunmanbye, May 5, 1555.	15	1	25
Mar. 14, 1560.	——, Richard, Treton, Apl. 9, 1560.	16		162
May 25, 1555.	——, Robert, Lamebie, par. Shereburn, Dec. 10, 1554.	14		163
Sep. 30, 1557.	——, Thomas, Balbie, par. Doncaster, Apl. 12, 1557.	15	1	369
Sep. 28, 1557.	——, Thomas, Barley, par. Mytton, husbandman, Jan. 28, 1556.	15	1	338
Aug. 27, 1556.	——, Thomas, Gaitforthe (bur. Braiton), Jun. 25, 1556.	15	1	62
Jan. 18, 1554.	——, Thomas, Preston (Holderness), Jun. 2, 1554.	14		295
May 4, 1558.	——, Thomas, Skarrington (Notts.), Aug. 15, 1557.	15	2	209
Feb. 9, 1556.	——, Thomas, York, barbour, Aug. 16, 1553.	15	1	157
Apl. 14, 1562.	——, William, Boirhouse Hyll, par. Pall, Feb. 15, 1561.	17		184
May 27, 1566.	——, William, Bulmer, husbandman, May 5, 1566.	17		536
——, 9, 1555.	——, William, Cookeswolde, Oct. 14, 1555.	14		200
May 9, 1566.	——, William, Gattforth, par. Worksoppe (Notts.), Mar. 2, 1564.	17		541
Jun. 10, 1557.	——, William, Watton, labourer, Dec. 16, 1552.	15	1	274
Jan. 12, 1557.	Wardell, John, Beverlay, tanner, Aug. 13, 1557.	15	2	80

A.D. 1554 TO 1568.

		Vol.	Pt.	Fol.
Sep. 3, 1558.	Wardell, Margaret. Nether Catton, Aug. 13, 1558.	15	3	97
Oct. 6, 1557.	Wardisworthe, Richard, Austerfeld, July 21, 1557.	15	2	7
Oct. 3, 1564.	Wardman, Richard, Ardington (bur. Addill), Mar. 26, 1559.	17		366
May 5, 1568.	Ware, Rauff, Newbye, par. Semer, Mar. 13, 1567.	17		773
Sep. 30, 1562.	Waren, Robert, Notton, par. Roiston, Feb. 2, 1561.	17		113
Apl. 22, 1556.	Waringe, William, Rudstone, husbandman, Mar. 12, 1556.	15	1	26
May 10, 1559.	Warke, Thomas, Seamer, Nov. 30, 1558.	15	3	388
Jan. 3, 1555.	Warmothe, John (bur. Alne), Feb. 14, 1554.	14		240
Aug. 12, 1567.	Warner, Christopher, Wold Newton (bur. Hunmanbie), Nov. 11, 1566.	17		693
Mar. 22, 1556.	———, Elizabeth, Cottingham, Nov. 8, 1556.	15	1	190
July 16, 1561.	———, John, Cottingham, bucher, Apl. 13, 1561.	17		83
May 4, 1558.	———, John, Flyntam (Notts.), husbandman, Oct. 13, 1557.	15	2	264
Oct. 4, 1565.	———, John, Newton Rachfurth (bur. Hunmanbie), Dec. 12, 1563.	17		486
Mar. 10, 1555.	———, Thomas, Eykring (Notts.), husbandman, Oct. 18, 1554.	14		231
Apl. 27, 1558.	———, William, Bilton, Mar. 5, 1558.	15	2	205
Jan. 12, 1558.	Warplay, Thomas, Beswicke, par. Kilnwicke, weaver, Oct. 7, 1558	15	3	202
Nov. 10, 1563.	Warplaye, John, Beswicke (bur. Kilnwicke), webster, July 28, 1563.	17		300
Dec. 16, 1557.	Warreson, Richard, North Skirley (bur. Swyne), husbn., Nov. 15, 1557.	15	2	47
July 15, 1556.	Warring, Edward, Rudstone, yong man, Jun. 7, 1556.	15	1	56
Jun. 11, 1562.	Warter, Johanne (bur. Nafferton), widow, Jun. 10, 1561.	17		86
Dec. 11, 1566.	———, Robert, Nafferton, husbandman, Apl. 2, 1565.	17		602
Sep. 30, 1557.	———, Thomas, Raskell, par. Esingwolde, Aug. 6, 1557.	15	1	344
Mar. 4, 1562.	Warton, Elizabeth, Hunmanbie, Jan. 7, 1562.	17		154
Apl. 22, 1556.	Warton, John, Hundmanbie, July 10, 1555.	15	1	27
Mar. 2, 1561.	———, William, Burton Flemyng (bur. Hunmanbie), Oct. 24, 1561.	17		2
Aug. 13, 1554.	Wasche (? Waithe), Benedic, Kirkstall, par. Addell, Aug. 10, 1553.	14		269
Apl. 19, 1555.	Wassand, Johanne, Hacknes, Oct. 26, 1553.	14		120
July 31, 1565.	Waste, John, Carleton, par. Snaythe, ———, 1565.	17		454
May 2, 1560.	Wastnes, Robert, Siglistorne, Nov. 3, 1559.	16		49
Jan. 12, 1558.	Wastray, Henry, Hull, Sep. 2, 1558.	15	3	198
May 6, 1563.	Wat, John, Barmbie (Notts.), July 6, 1562.	17		241
Apl. 13, 1557.	Waterhous, Elizabeth (bur. Bayldon), widow, Mar. 16, 1556.	15	1	207
Oct. 1, 1561.	———, John, Meltham, par. Almonburye, Jun. 9, 1561.	17		46
Jan. 18, 1558.	Waterhouse, Edmond, Sourbye, par. Hallifax, Sep. 24, 1558.	15	3	212
Apl. 16, 1567.	———, James, Shelley, par. Kirkeburton, clothier, July 17, 1566.	17		627
Apl. 16, 1562.	Waterhows, Thomas, Wentworthe, hardewaireman, Feb. 10, 1561.	17		172
May 19, 1554.	Wathead, William, Kneasall, (Notts.), yeoman, May 15, 1553.	14		109
Nov. 23, 1556.	Watherhowse, John, Hollynges in Warley, gentleman, Apl. 14, 1556.	15	1	75
Sep. 30, 1563.	Watkinson, John, Hull, tanner, Jun. 28, 1563.	17		288
Jan. 23, 1558.	———, Thomas (bur. Gigleswicke), July 10, 1558.	15	3	214
Mar. 23, 1560.	Watkyn, Christopher, Sutton (Holderness), Mar. 29, 1560.	16		177
Feb. 6, 1558.	———, John, Baddisworth, yeoman, Jan. 15, 1558.	15	3	255
Oct. 2, 1560.	Watkynson, Christopher, Brandisburton, labourer, July 26, 1560.	16		116
Sep. 23, 1557.	Watlys, John, Sheryfhoton, husbandman, Sep. 2, 1557.	15	1	348
Jan. 11, 1563.	Watman, Isabell, Cottingham, Aug. 3, 1563.	17		309
May 2, 1560.	———, John, Newland, par. Cottyngham, butcher, Nov. 12, 1559.	16		44
Sep. 18, 1567.	———, Richard, Newland, par. Cottingham, butcher, Apl. 21, 1567.	17		705
Dec. 13, 1557.	Watson, Allan, Thornton (Rydall), Oct. 30, 1557.	15	2	42
Sep. 14, 1565.	———, Annas (bur. Sutton, Holderness), widow, Aug. 13, 1565.	17		466
Sep. 30, 1558.	———, Christopher (bur. Ripon), Jun. 16, 1557.	15	3	56
Jan. 31, 1564.	———, Clement, Great Busbie, par. Stokesley, Nov. 25, 1564.	17		403
Nov. 25, 1558.	———, Edmond, York, glover, Mar. 27, 1558.	15	3	127
Apl. 7, 1557.	———, Edward, Southmylforth (bur. Sherburne), Dec. 28, 1556.	15	1	204
Feb. 11, 1557.	———, Emote, Thorpe (bur. Rippon), widow, Dec. 6, 1557.	15	2	119
Jan. 27, 1560.	———, George, Bransdaill (bur. Kirkbye Moreshead), yeom., Feb. 5, 1559.	16		139
Oct. 4, 1565.	———, George, Gaite Fulforthe, Aug. 17, 1565.	17		483
Aug. 6, 1562.	———, Gylbert, Westheslerton, Feb. 20, 1561.	17		104
July 11, 1561.	———, Jenet, Great Edston, widow, Jan. 14, 1555.	17		81
Jun. 23, 1568.	———, Jennet, Staingrave, maiden, Nov. 23, 1567.	17		807
Mar. 23, 1560.	———, John, Barton lee Willowes, par. Crambome, Apl. 12, 1560.	16		175
May 19, 1559.	———, John, Drax, Mar. 6, 1558.	15	3	425

A.D. 1554 TO 1568.

		Vol.	Pt.	Fol.
Oct. 3, 1566.	Watson, John, Ecope (bur. Adhill), May 22, 1566.	17		582
Dec. 2, 1562.	———, John, Holbroke, par. Tankersley, Jun. 14, 1562.	17		130
Oct. 4, 1564.	———, John, Kilbrough (bnr. Thornton), Sep. 2, 1564.	17		372
May 6, 1559.	———, John (bur. Lenton, Cleveland), Mar. 27, 1559.	15	3	382
Feb. 15, 1558.	———, John, Leven, wryght, Dec. 26, 1558.	15	3	272
Sep. 29, 1560.	———, John, Lytle Ayton in Clevelande, Mar. 20, 1559.	16		106
Mar. 17, 1567.	———, John, Malton, Dec. 30, 1567.	17		764
Mar. 21, 1555.	———, John, Over Selbie, husbandman, ———, 1555.	15	1	12
Aug. 13, 1567.	———, John, Pattrington, husbandman. *No date.*	17		692
Mar. 11, 1562.	———. John, Skorebroughe, Dec. 29, 1562.	17		156
Dec. 13, 1554.	———, John, Wakefeilde, carier, July 12, 1554.	14		97
Dec. 22, 1563.	———, John, Wintringham, Mar. 18, 1562.	17		307
Nov. 25, 1557.	———, John, York, Aug. 17, 1557.	15	2	90
Aug. 7, 1556.	———, Syr John, Ripon, preist, Jun. 26, 1556.	15	1	60
Dec. 13, 1557.	———, Lawrance, Rosedaill (bur. Mydleton), Sep. 24, 1557.	15	2	42
Jun. 26, 1554.	———, Margaret (bur. Cokeswoold), May 1, 1553.	14		115
Feb. 27, 1561.	———, Margaret, Marston, Jan. 22, 1561.	17		18
May 6, 1554.	———, Margaret, Nov. 1. 1553.	14		73
May 18, 1559.	———, Peter, Pattrington, Mar. 1, 1558.	15	3	408
Jan. 18, 1560.	———, Rauffe, Bransdaill, par. Kyrkbemoresheade, Dec. 18, 1559.	16		139
Mar. 4, 1560.	———, Raynolde, Bruntcliffe, par. Batley, smythe, Nov. 7, 1560.	16		152
Oct. 1, 1557.	———, Richard, Bolton on Derne, Apl. 23, 1557.	15	1	369
May 9, 1566.	———, Richard, Granby (Notts.), husbandman, ———, 1563.	17		550
Feb. 4, 1557.	———, Richard, Holme in Spaldingmore, Dec. 6, 1557.	15	2	163
Aug. 13, 1567.	———, Richard, Holmpton (bur. Trinity, Hull), Sep. 16, 1566.	17		692
Jun. 22, 1568.	———, Richard, Staynburne, July 18, 1566.	17		818
May 6, 1557.	———, Robert, Besyngbie, labourer, Feb. 11, 1556.	15	1	246
Oct. 8, 1561.	———, Robert (bur. Bleasebe, Notts.), Jan. 5, 1560.	17		39
Aug. 7, 1554.	———, Robert, Eperston (Notts.), husbandman, May 11, 1554.	14		268
Dec. 15, 1557.	———, Robert, Estretforde (Notts.), Nov. 9, 1557.	15	2	37
Mar. 18, 1557.	———, Robert, Spaldyngton (bur. Awghton), labourer, Jan. 17, 1557.	15	2	176
Nov. 28, 1558.	———, Robert, Withornwike, July 24, 1558.	15	3	78
Oct. 30, 155[?5].	———, Roger, Ferlington, par. Sherifhuton, clerk, Oct. 8, 1555.	14		179
Oct. 11, 1564.	———, Thomas, Barley, par. Brayton, July 20, 1564.	17		367
Oct. 10, 1566.	———, Thomas, Basford (Notts.), Apl. 22, 1563.	17		593
Sep. 30, 1557.	———, Thomas, Bolton on Derne, Jun. 24, 1557.	15	1	369
Mar. 8, 1558.	———, Thomas, Cottingham, Dec. 26, 1558.	15	3	157
May 13, 1557.	———, Thomas, Cropwell Butler (bur. Tithbie, Notts.), Apl. 8, 1557.	15	1	230
May 28, 1560.	———, Thomas, Ferlington (bur. Sheryfhewton), husbn., Mar. 17, 1559.	16		70
Dec. 24, 1557.	———, Thomas, Marston, Dec. 8, 1557.	15	2	83
Jan. 12, 1558.	———, Thomas, Sutton in Holderness, July 24, 1558.	15	3	204
Apl. 16, 1562.	———, Thomas, Wevirthorpe, husbandman, Oct. 5, 1561.	17		157
Jun. 2, 1556.	———, Sir Thomas, Nonnyngton, preiste, May 6, 1556.	15	1	40
May 25, 1554.	———, Umfray, Littell Actone in Cleveland, Mar. 3, 1553.	14		130
Mar. 5, 1555.	———, Walter, Thorpe (bur. Ripon), husbandman, Feb. 9, 1555.	15	1	12
Jun. 20, 1566.	———, William (bur. Hackenes). *No date.*	17		556
Jun. 7, 1560.	———, William, Harpham, Nov. 21, 1559.	16		80
Dec. 11, 1556.	———, William, Helaughe, gresman, Sep. 25, 1556.	15	1	156
May 23, 1565.	———, William, Holme in Spaldingmore, Sep. 26, 1564.	17		442
May 5, 1568.	———, William, Kelbroke (bur. Thornton), Jan. 31, 1567.	17		786
Oct. 2, 1566.	———, William, Norton, par. Campsall, May 2, 1566.	17		578
Aug. 2, 1557.	———, William, Ryall, par. Skecklynge, July 3, 1557.	15	1	322
Jun. 11, 1557.	———, William, Sherborne in Harfordlithe, Apl. 8, 1557.	15	1	289
Jun. 6, 1560.	———, William, West Elley, par. Kirk Ellay, Jun. 2, 1559.	16		76
Jun. 19, 1562.	———, William, York, marchaunt, Mar. 5, 1561.	17		89
Apl. 23, 1556.	Watsone, Arthure (bur. Gisburn), Sep. 11, 1555.	15	1	36
Mar. 3, 1555.	———, John, Wythornwyke, Nov. 20, 1555.	15	1	10
May 19, 1559.	——— *als.* Emson, Herrie, Howke, Jan. 27, 1558.	15	3	427
July 11, 1558.	Watsonne, John, Barnebie on Done, Mar. 16, 1557.	15	2	317
Oct. 2, 1554.	———, Robert, Stockbrig, par. Arkseye, July 28, 1554.	14		72
May 2, 1555.	———, Roger, Thorneton, Apl. 15, 1554.	14		25

		Vol.	Pt.	Fol.
May 26, 1567.	Watt, William, Besyngbe, weaver, Jan. 9, 1566.	17		654
Apl. 23, 1556.	Watter, John, Wodhouse, par. Burnesaull, Dec. 17, 1555.	15	1	36
Feb.ult.,1558.	———, Robert, Newsted, par. Kylburne, Sep. 2, 1558.	15	3	281
Oct. 2, 1567.	———, William, Askwithe, par. Weston, Aug. 11, 1567.	17		721
Dec. 3, 1560.	Watterhouse, Richard, senr., Skercote, par. Hallyfax, Aug. 27, 1559.	16		130
Nov.29, 1558.	Watterhowse, John, Wadeslay, par. Eglesfeld, Oct. 23, 1558.	15	3	138
Apl. 6, 1560.	Watterson, Richard (? York), May 26, 1559.	16		27 & 28
Oct. 15, 1561.	Watterton, Thomas, Pottowe (bur. Whorlton), yeom., Nov.18,1560.	17		36
Apl. 20, 1559.	Wattes, George, Bothomsall (Notts.), Mar. 2, 1558.	15	3	367
Jan. 21, 1558.	Wattson, Richard, Selbie, yeoman, Oct. 15, 1558.	15	3	192
Apl. 16, 1567.	Waune, William, Normanbie, Dec. 1, 1566.	17		639
Apl. 10, 1559.	Wauwen, William, Rawmarshe, Feb. 1, 1558.	15	3	329
July 8, 1561.	Wawde, Thomas, Newsome (bur. Wressle), husbn., Dec. 18, 1560.	17		80
Jun. 10, 1557.	Wawker, Henry, Beswicke by Watton, husbandman, Apl. 10, 1557.	15	1	270
Apl. 14, 1562.	———, John, Rowton (bur. Swyne), Jan. 28, 1561.	17		183
July 28, 1567.	Wawne, John, Auknes, par. Kirkebemoreshed, Dec. 15, 1566.	17		667
Nov.29, 1558.	Wayd, Isabell, Billinglay, par. Darfeld, widow, Oct. 10, 1558.	15	3	141
Nov. 8, 1557.	———, Robert, Kyllyngley (bur. Darfeld), husbn., Aug. 26, 1557.	15	2	111
Oct. 4, 1558.	———, William, Harwood, Aug. 11, 1558.	15	3	89
Jan. 17, 1560.	Wayde, Gilbert, Warley, par. Hallyfax, Dec. 15, 1560.	16		142
May 28, 1567.	———, Robert, Hollingthorpe (bur. Sandall), Apl. 27, 1567.	17		646
Feb. 11, 1557.	———, Robert, Monkton (bur. Ripon), Aug. 20, 1554.	15	2	166
July 12, 1564.	Wayll, William, Dowthrope, par. Swyne, Nov. 9, 1563.	17		355
Apl. 16, 1562.	Wayneman, Henry, Ryddinges (bur. Bolton), servant to Ellin W., wid. of John W., Feb. 8, 156[1-]2.	17		189
Oct. 3, 1560.	———, John, Ryddinges (bur. Bolton), Mar. 8, 1558.	16		118
Apl. 16, 1562.	———, Peter (bur. Bolton), Feb. 2, 1561.	17		191
Apl. 28, 1563.	———, Richard, Estby, par. Skipton, Nov. 9, 1562.	17		227
Aug. 2, 1563.	——— als. Nelson, William, Bainton, husbn., July 14, 1563.	17		212
Nov.12, 1556.	Waynman, Richard, Pontefracte, Mar. 14, 1556.	15	1	111
July 10, 1567.	Waynwright, Henry, Staynton, par. Bradfeld, Nov. 3, 1566.	17		685
May 26, 1556.	Wayrde, Walter, Mulwathe (bur. Ripon), gent., Mar. 1, 1555.	15	1	35
Mar.17, 1557.	Wayrdroper, John, Rippon, widow, Jun. 1, 1557.	15	2	152
Jun. 20, 1568.	Wayringe, Christopher, Mytton, May 25, 1568.	17		809
Sep. 23, 1558.	Wayryne, Rauffe (? Chester) (Ainsty Deanery), Oct. 24, 1557.	15	3	88
Mar.19, 1564.	Wayt, John, Thornton (bur. Foston), Sep. 5, 1564.	17		412
Mar.20, 1558.	———, Thomas, Bramwith, par. Haitfeild, Oct. 20, 1558.	15	3	247
Apl. 26, 1558.	———, Robert, Fyshlaike, Sep. 18, 1557.	15	2	196
Feb. 11, 1557.	Webster, Agnes, York, singlewoman, Dec. 18, 1557.	15	2	165
May 9, 1560.	———, Ales, Welleye, Jun. 18, 1559.	16		58
Jan. 20, 1562.	———, Emm, Sheaffeld, widow, Mar. 8, 1555.	17		143
May 17, 1557.	———, George, Hasthrope, par. Burton Agnes, yeom, Mar. 30,1557.	15	1	244
July 5, 1557.	———, George, Thunshelf, par. Penyston, Nov. 17, 1555.	15	1	301
May 27, 1562.	———, Isabella, Albrowghe in Holderness, Jan. 29, 1562.	17		102
Nov. 3, 1561.	———, John, Beverley, tanner, Sep. 19, 1561.	17		35
Feb. 4, 1561.	———, John, Brotton, Dec. 10, 1560.	17		12
Oct. 2, 1560.	———, John, Esington, July 21, 1560.	16		116
May 29, 1566.	———, John, Est Cottingwithe, par. Aughton, Mar. 24, 1565.	17		543
July 4, 1558.	———, John, Litle Claxton (bur. Bossall), Jan. 28, 1557.	15	2	326
Aug. 2, 1560.	———, John, Ryston in Holderness, Apl. 12, 1560.	16		100
Feb. 5, 1555.	———, John, Spawdington, gresman, Jun. 4, 1555.	15	1	5
Dec. 17, 1557.	———, Nicholas, Penyston, singleman, Oct. 15, 1557.	15	2	40
July 12, 1564.	———, Richard, Essyngton, Mar. 25, 1564.	17		356
Apl. 7, 1556.	———, Richard, Farbarne (bur. Ledsham), Dec. 31, 1555.	15	1	17
May 14, 1558.	———, Robert, Flamebroughe, yeoman, Sep. 2, 1557.	15	2	273
Apl. 13, 1559.	———, Robert, Hollome in Holderness, Jan. 18, 1558.	15	3	344
Jun. 8, 1557.	———, Robert, Rowth, Mar. 15, 1557.	15	1	268
Nov.20, 1557.	———, Robert, Yorke, Nov. 15, 1557.	15	2	101
Mar. 5, 1556.	———, Thomas, Hamylton, Brayton, Dec. 13, 1556.	15	1	176
Mar.13, 1565.	———, Thomas, Ledeston (bur. Kepax), Nov. 1, 1565.	17		504
Aug.12, 1556.	———, William, Estcottingwithe (bur. Aughton), Jun. 1, 1556.	15	1	60
Apl. 25, 1559.	——— als. Grene, Alice, Haistrope, par. Burton Agnes, wid., Jun. 24, 1557.	15	3	311

		Vol.	Pt.	Fol.
Oct. 1, 1557.	Webster *als.* Thwaites, John, Estbecke, par. Whytbye, fysherman, May 23, 1557.	15	I	363
May 10, 1559.	Webstere, Thomas, Warter Hall (bur. Warter), Mar. 20, 1558.	15	3	385
July 30, 1560.	Wedall, Isabell, Nafferton, July 10, 1560.	16		98
Nov. 10, 1556.	Wedderald, Thomas, senr., Coptheweke (bur. Ripone), yeom, Oct. 17, 1556.	15	I	109
Jan. 23, 1558.	Wedderall, Frances, Eskrige, Aug. 11, 1558.	15	3	22
Apl. 13, 1559.	———, Harry, Holme in Spaldingmore, Aug. 6, 1558.	15	3	348
Dec. 2, 1561.	Wedderarde, Myles, Yngmanne Logge, par. Horton, Aug. 22, 1561.	17		32
Oct. 2, 1567.	Wedderhead, Myles, Shaddwell (bur. Thorneover). *No date.*	17		721
Oct. 2, 1567.	Wedderhirde, Isabell, late wife of Jo. W., Browghton, July 11, 1567.	17		711
Dec. 14, 1557.	Weddrell, Jaine, Hull, singlewoman, Nov. 10, 1557.	15	I	359
Apl. 28, 1563.	Wedhoppe, John, senr., Kighley, Dec. 20, 1562.	17		226
Dec. 1, 1558.	Wedlay, Hugh, Elowghton, husbandman, Oct. 8, 1558.	15	3	146
Oct. 6, 1557.	Wedosone, Alis, Sutton (bur. Granbe, Notts.), widow, May 21, 1557.	15	2	32
Apl. 6, 1566.	Wedowes, John, Thormonbie, Aug. 20, 1565.	17		510
May 9, 1565.	Wegan, Edward, Pothouse (bur. Kirkby Malhamdale), Jan. 21, 1560.	17		434
Mar. 4, 1560.	Weidley, Robert, Bentley, par. Rowley, Nov. 12, 1559.	16		165
May 6, 1557.	Weilsbie, Isabell, Hull, widow, Feb. 3, 1556.	15	I	251
Dec. 12, 1567.	Weire, Thomas, senr., Essingwold, Jan. 29, 1566.	17		748
Jun. 16, 1561.	Welbanke, James, Knapton (bur. Wyntringham), Dec. 5, 1559.	17		71
Jun. 2, 1557.	Welbecke, William, Sutton on Lownde (Notts.), gentleman, Nov. 22, 3 and 4 Phil. and Mary.	15	I	271
Oct. 11, 1563.	Welbere, Christabell, Rudbye, widow, May 16, 1563.	17		297
Mar. 15, 1562.	———, Thomas, Rudbye, husbandman, Sep. 2, 1558.	17		164
Oct. 1, 1557.	Welberye, William, Wylton in Clevelande, Aug 27, 1557.	15	I	363
Nov. 26, 1557.	Welbore, Richard, Bentley, par. Arkseay, Aug. 8, 1557.	15	2	90
No date.	Welborne, Johne (bur. Lounde), Mar. 16, 1553.	14		129
Jun. 19, 1567.	Welburne, John Westowe, May 10, 1567.	17		656
Jun. 14, 1564.	———, Robert, Bridlington, glover, Nov. 28, 1563.	17		353
Aug. 21, 1561.	———. Thomas, Kirke Elley, Apl. 13, 1561.	17		57
Aug. 4, 1567.	Weldricke, William, Birken, husbandman, Jun. 27, 1567.	17		688
Apl. 12, 1559.	Welfett, Robert (bur. Crathorne), Jan. 31, 1558.	15	3	335
Oct. 2, 1567.	Welle, John, Routhe, husbandman, July 14, ——.	17		715
Apl. 17, 1567.	———, Robert, Welle, par. St, John, Beverley, Jan. 18, 1566.	17		640
May 16, 1554.	Welles, Edward, Arswell (bur. Horswell, ? Harswell), 1553.	14		139
Feb. 17, 1557.	———, Margett, Toumflett par. Sandall, Oct. 18, 1557.	15	2	137
Oct. 10, 1566.	———, Richard, Wysall (Notts.). May 14, 1566.	17		595
Apl. 19, 1559.	———, William, Colson Bassett (Notts.), Aug. 15, 1558.	15	3	359
Apl. 26, 1558.	Wells, Esabell, Byrkyn, widow, Sep. 28, 1557.	15	2	237
Sep. 26, 1558.	———, Umfray, Fishlake, July 17, 1558.	15	3	52
Apl. 26, 1558.	———, William, Campsall, Nov. 22, 1557.	15	2	197
May 2, 1566.	Wensper, John (bur. Trinity, Hull), Sep. 4, 1565.	17		537
Nov. 23, 1558.	Wentworth, Elizabeth (bur. Waddington), widow, Aug. 10, 1558.	15	3	128
Feb. 3, 1561.	Wentworthe, Christopher, Sheffeld, gentleman, Nov. 25, 1561.	17		9
July 5, 1557.	————, John, Hangetwayte (bur. Athwike), gent., Aug. 28, 1556.	15	I	301
Jan. 20, 1562.	————, Richard, Balbye, par. Doncaster, husbn., Dec. 11, 1562.	17		144
Sep. 21, 1557.	————, Thomas, West Bretton, par. Sylkestone, esq., Aug. 19, 1557.	15	I	349
Oct. 1, 1556.	Wenwright, John (bur. Cauthorne), Jun. 15, 1556.	15	I	128
Apl. 18, 1560.	Wesse, Thomas, Kesbrughe, par. Darton, Mar. 6, 1559.	16		32
Jan. 8, 1563.	West, Charles, Hatefeild, ——, 1563.	17		308
Jan. 31, 1561.	———, Edward, Brodholme (Notts.), yeoman, Jan. 12, 1561.	17		9
Mar. 21, 1560.	———, Jennett, Lekenfelde, widow, July 11, 1560.	16		174
Apl. 20, 1559.	———, John, Bestrope (bur. S. Scarle, Notts.), husbn., Feb. 27, 1558.	15	3	305
May 8, 1567.	———, John, Ellerton, Nov. 17, 1566.	17		650
July 15, 1567.	———, Marmaduke, Rilston, May 26, 1567.	17		678
May 20, 1568.	———, Rauf, Langton, husbandman, Apl. 10, 1568.	17		795
Oct. 12, 1558.	———, Thomas, Rempstonne (Notts.), Apl. 23, 1558.	15	3	32
May 9, 1566.	———, William, Wollaton (Notts.), July 18, 1565.	17		544
Jun. 22, 1568.	Westabie, William, Flotmanbie (bur. Folton), Dec. 6, 1567.	17		820
Jun. 25, 1557.	Westall, Robert, Gresbroke, par. Rotherham, Jun. 14, 1557.	15	I	297

A.D. 1554 TO 1568.

		Vol.	Pt.	Fol.
Oct. 3, 1554.	Westbie, Laurens, Beverley, glover, Sep. 4, 1553.	14		43
May 4, 1558.	Westbowrow, Robert, Gedling (Notts.), Sep. 1, 1551.	15	2	272
Oct. 12, 1558.	Weste, Philippe, Silston (Notts.), Nov. 10, 1557.	15	3	30
Aug. 6, 1567.	———, Robert, Kirkeburne, Mar. 12, 1567.	17		700
Dec. 15, 1557.	———, William, Saundby (Notts.), husbandman, Jun. 14, 1557.	15	2	58
Feb. 17, 1556.	Westerdaill, Mungo, Bridlington, gentleman, Dec. 10, 1556.	15	1	159
July 26, 1557.	Westerdale, John, Aslabye, par. Mydleton, Jun. 10, 1557.	15	1	319
Nov. 21, 1556.	Westerman, Alysone (bur. Snaithe), widow, ———, 1556.	15	1	115
Mar. 22, 1558.	———, Margaret, Wakefeild, Dec. 22, 1558.	15	3	295
Oct. 26, 1564.	Westmorlande, Hy. erle of, K.G. (bur. Stayndropp), Aug. 18, 1563.	17		833
Apl. 16, 1567.	Westoby, Henry, Beverley, ropemaker, Aug. 23, 1566.	17		639
Oct. 6, 1557.	Weston, William, Lounde, par. Sutton (Notts.), May 18, 1557.	15	2	14
Apl. 28, 1563.	Westwood, John, Heton (bur. Reilston), Feb. 24, 1562.	17		230
Jan. 30, 1566.	Wetherall, Bryan (Hull), Sep. 13, 1566.	17		611
Jun. 21, 1560.	———, Esabell, York, Apl. 9, 1559.	16		86
Feb. 24, 1559.	———, Henry, Heworthe, gentleman, Jan. 1, 1559.	16		2
Apl. 8, 1559.	———, Isabell, Eskrig, widow, Feb. 3, 1558.	15	3	324
July 21, 1564.	———, Umfray, Thorngumbold, par. Paulle, Oct. 24, 1563.	17		358
Aug. 13, 1567.	Wethernwicke, Agnes, Bewham, par. Nunkelinge, May 22, 1567.	17		691
Dec. 1, 1558.	Wetum, John, Beverlay, Oct. 8, 1557.	15	3	83
Jun. 12, 1557.	Wever, John, Goldall (bur. Snath), Jan 12, 1556.	15	1	291
Apl. 28, 1563.	Weygilsworthe, Roger (bur. Long Preston), Nov. 21, 1562.	17		230
No date.	Whalley, Margret, Newarke (Notts), widow, Jun. 12, 1554.	14		285
Jan. 28, 1561.	———, William, Bullingthroppe (bur. Leedes), Mar. 14, 1559.	17		7
Jan. 31, 1560.	Whalleye, Richard, Dalby, gentleman, Dec. 3, 1557.	16		146
Apl. 26, 1558.	Wharton, Anthony, Helaugh, yeoman, Nov. 26, 1557.	15	2	237
Dec. 19, 1555.	———, Edmounde (bur. Hunmanbye), July 15, 1555.	14		247
May 2, 1566.	———, Jane, Maltbie, widow, Mar. 12, 1565.	17		522
May 6, 1557.	———, John, Healthwathill (bur. Harwood), yeom., Feb. 6, 1556.	15	1	255
Oct. 29, 1558.	———, John, Staxton (bur. Willerbie), husbandman, Feb. 6, 1557.	15	2	371
Mar. 6, 1556.	———, Nicholas, Est Retford (Notts.), marser, Oct. 28, 1556.	15	1	177
Sep. 28, 1557.	———, Richard, Leathley, Feb. —, 1557.	15	1	371
July 21, 1565.	———, Richard, Maltbye, Dec. 24, 1564.	17		446
May 13, 1557.	———, Robert, Everton (Notts.), Jan. 28, 1557 (sic).	15	1	233
Dec. 17, 1567.	———, William, Brakenwhate in Rigton, par. Kirkbe Overblaus, Oct. 18, 1567.	17		745
May 29, 1562.	Whaytes, William, Snaith, Apl. 6, 1562.	17		101
Sep. 29, 1563.	Whearter, Nicholas, Yeadon, par. Gyselay, Apl. 3, 1563.	17		289
Jan. 28, 1558.	Wheatelay, William, Ripon, Sep. 9, 1558.	15	3	221
Apl. 27, 1558.	Wheatley, Jennet, widow of John W., Emlay, Feb. 3, 1549.	15	2	193
Sep. 30, 1563.	Whebter, Jennett, Rowth, widow, Apl. 9, 1563.	17		274
Jun. 9, 1558.	Wheldraike, William, Bubwith, labourer, May 10, 1558.	15	2	215
Dec. 13, 1557.	Wheldrek, John, York, kouke, Oct. 17, 1557.	15	2	88
Sep. 30, 1563.	Whelpdaill, Lourance, Burton Pidsey, Aug. 8, 1563.	17		273
May 5, 1568.	Whelpdrake, Robert, Beverley, Dec. 5, 1567.	17		775
Mar. 23, 1557.	Whelpedaill, Robert, Skeklynge, Dec. 25, 1557.	15	2	175
Jun. 2, 1558.	Whelpedayll, Antony, Brandisburton, husbandman, Sep. 26, 1557.	15	2	310
Apl. 28, 1563.	Whetherwicke, Alexander, Beweum (bur. Kelinge). No date.	17		238
Jun. 22, 1568.	Whetston, Jarret, Holme in Spauldingmore. No date.	17		806
July 19, 1557.	Wheytherbie, Robert, North Wheatley (Notts.), Mar. 2, 1556.	15	1	313
Sep. 30, 1562.	Whit, Thomas, Howton Pannell, Aug. 19, 1562.	17		113
May 2, 1566.	Whitacars, William, Shipley (bur. Bradforth), Apl. 11, 1566.	17		536
Oct. 3, 1554.	Whitaker, Roger (bur. Gargrave), July 20, 1554.	14		37
Aug. 12, 1566.	Whitakers, Thomas, Kymberworthe, par. Rotherham, Feb. 19, 1566.	17		567
Oct. 22, 1558.	Whitbie, John, Gisburne in Cleveland, Sep. 24, 1558.	15	3	235
Mar. 10, 1564.	White, Edmund, Wrissill, May 15, 1564.	17		408
Apl. 20, 1559.	———, Gregory, Ordsall (Notts.), husbandman, Jun. 23, 1558.	15	3	308
Feb. 19, 1557.	———, James, Spawldington (bur. Aughton), husbn., Feb. 10, 1557.	15	2	140
Dec. 5, 1567.	———, Jeffray, Skipsey in Holderness, Aug. 2, 1567.	17		741
Feb. 17, 1557.	———, John, Styrsthorp (bur. Sandall), husbandman, Nov. 17, 1557.	15	2	138
Mar. 13, 1558.	———, Richard, Cantlay, husbandman, Jan. 1, 1558.	15	3	164
Oct. 1, 1560.	———, Richard, Sutton on Lounde (Notts.), Dec. 21, 1558.	16		115

		Vol.	Pt.	Fol·
Jun. 21, 1565.	White, Robert, Hull, glover, Mar. 28, 1565.	17		448
May 13, 1568.	———, Robert, Marnham (Notts.), Dec. 18, 1567.	17		798
Apl. 18, 1567.	———, Robert, Nether Cantley, Feb. 18, 1567.	17		636
Apl. 28, 1563.	———, Thomas, Cantley, bacheler. Feb. 9, 1562.	17		234
Jun. 30, 1563.	———, William, Beiston (bur. Leedes), Apl. 16, 1563.	17		260
July 2, 1561.	———, William, Bridlington, maison, Apl. 4, 1561.	17		77
Dec. 9, 1556.	Whitehead, Alexander, Penyston, Aug. 18, 1556.	15	1	74
Jun. 10, 1568.	———, William, Adlingfleite, Feb. 18, 1567.	17		805
Jan. 13, 1558.	Whiteheade, James, Fornisfeild (Notts.), husbandman, Aug. 31, 1558.	15	3	16
Feb. 14, 1554.	———, John, Whitwell, par. Crambum, yeom., Nov. 20, 1554.	14		298 & 300
Sep. 16, 1555.	———, Richard. Branton, par. Treton, July 22, 1554.	14		65
Apl. 19, 1564.	Whitfeild, Leonard, Skipton in Craven, Nov. 1, 1563.	17		330
Feb. 16, 1563.	———, Thomas, Westnes, husbandman, Apl. 14, 1563.	17		316
Feb. 16, 1565. [1]	Whithawse, Christopher, Ruffurthe, Jan. 8, 1565.	17		499
Jun. 5, 1563.	———, Richard, Ruffurthe. *No date.*	17		253
Jun. 16, 1556.	Whitheade, John, Wheateley, par. Ylkeley, Mar. 21, 2 and 3 Phil. and Mary.	15	1	58
Mar. 6, 1556.	Whitdede, Ellen, Triswell (Notts.), widow, Sep. 20, 1556.	15	1	182
Jun. 21, 1561.	Whitiker, William, Banke Newton, par. Gargrave, July 11, 1561.	17		73
Oct. 4, 1565. [1]	Whitinge, Robert, Wandisforthe (bur. Nafferton), Mar. 26, 1564.	17		486
Jan. 20, 1561.	Whitlay, Arthure, Risheworth (bur. Ealand), Oct. 20, 1561.	17		23
Jan. 23, 1561.	Whitley, John, senr., Oveden, par. Hallifax, Nov. 29, 1561.	17		22
Aug. 24, 1554.	———, Robert, Tickhill, July 30, 1553.	14		270
Apl. 8, 1559.	Whitstonne, William, Whitwell, par. Crambum, Jan. 26, 1558.	15	3	323
May 2, 1560.	Whitsyde, John (bur. Ripon), clerk, Sep. 24, 1559.	16		57
Jan. 20, 1561.	Whitt, John, Hee Egbrought, yeoman, Dec. 25, 1560.	17		23
May 13, 1568.	Whitte, Robert, Spaldington, servinge man, May 4, 1567.	17		795
May 9, 1565.	Whittikers. Robert, Chickingley (bur. Dewisburie), Nov. 8, 1563.	17		423
Oct. 5, 1558.	Whittillie, William, Thirkelbie, Aug. 3, 1558.	15	3	72
July 20, 1557.	Whittinge, John, Bucketon, husbandman, Mar. 20, 1556.	15	1	314
Oct. 10, 1560.	Whittington, John, Southehovingham (Notts.), husbn., July 26, 1560.	16		123
Jan. 24, 1558.	Whitton, Elizabeth, Kirke Levington, widow, Nov. 5, 1558.	15	3	22
Oct. 1, 1556.	Whitwell, Jenet, widow of Wm. W. of Stayngrave, Aug. 18, 1556.	15	1	67
No date.	———, Thomas, Irton, par. Seamer (imperfect), Nov. 1, 1554.	14		302
Oct. 12, 1564.	Whitworthe, Richard, Kinston (Notts.), Apl. 4, 1564.	17		390
Oct. 8, 1562.	———, William, Whoidhouse, par. Cokeney (Notts.), Dec. 21, 1561.	17		121
Oct. 20, 1558.	Whorlton, Thomas, Sowth Ottrington, Aug. 25, 1558.	15	2	347
Oct. 13, 1558.	Whright, Denis, Walkringham (Notts.), husbn., Apl. 20, 1558.	15	2	377
Feb. 4, 1558.	Whrightson, William, Eskrigge, Dec. 11, 1558.	15	3	24
Feb. 6, 1558.	Whyet, John, Beriwod, par. Haitfeilde, labourer, Dec. 2, 1558.	15	3	255
Feb. 6, 1558.	———, Thomas, Cantley, Dec. 2, 1558.	15	3	255
Dec. 15, 1557.	Whyett, John, Wyllowbye, par. Wallesbye (Notts.), July 20, 1557.	15	2	54
July 26, 1557.	Whypham, John, Stapleton (bur. Dayryngton), husbn., July 18, 1557.	15	1	318
Mar. 30, 1560.	Whyppe, Robert, Skipton (bur. Topclyffe), Jan. 6, 155—.	16		24
Feb. ult., 1557.	Whypphame, Agnes, Stapleton (bur. Darryngtonne), widow. Oct. 15, 1557.	15	2	146
Apl. 10, 1567.	Whyt, John, Goonbye, par. Bubwithe, yeoman, Aug. 11, 1566.	17		617
Apl. 26, 1558.	Whyte, Costyn, Swynton, par. Wathe, Dec. 6, 1557.	15	2	224
Aug. 23, 1563.	———, George, York, Jan. 10, 1561.	17		215
Oct. 1, 1557.	———, Richard, Danbye, Aug. 28, 1557.	15	2	34
Jun. 23, 1558.	———, William, Spawldington (bur. Bubwith), May 26, 1558.	15	2	336
Oct. 8, 1556.	Whytefoitte, William, Stoike, par. Gedlinge (Notts.), Aug. 9, 1556.	15	1	152
Jan. 6, 1557.	Whyteheade, Nicholas, Tynslowe, par. Rotherham, Sep. 16, 1557.	15	2	68
Apl. 14, 1562.	Whytelay, Edmunde, Yealand, Jan. 16, 1561.	17		167
May 2, 1566.	Whyteley, Henry, Stanyngden, par. Ealand, Mar. 8, 1564.	17		534
May 19, 1559.	Whytesyde, Issabell, Roclyf (bur. Snaith), Jan. 10, 1558.	15	3	428
Oct. 23, 1557.	———, John, Roclyffe (bur. Snaythe), Oct. 1, 1557.	15	1	366
Mar. 27, 1560.	Whytfeilde, William, Egton, Apl. 18, 1559.	16		21
Mar. 18, 1559.	Whythead, Robert, Sykehouses, par. Fysshlake, Jun. 3, 1559.	16		11

1 See also under letter Q.

		Vol.	Pt.	Fol.
Oct. 13, 1558.	Whytlam, Robert, Middleton (bur. West Markham, Notts.), husbn., Sep. 23, 1558.	15	2	359
May 18, 1559.	Whytley, William, Sandall (Doncaster), Aug. 8, 1553.	15	3	398
Mar. 2, 1559.	Whytous, William, Bylbroughe, gresman, Sep. 20, 1559.	16		4
Sep. 28, 1557.	Whytquam, Henry, Over Bradley, par. Kyldweke, Aug. 25, 1549.	15	1	338
Apl. 20, 1559.	Whytton, Christopher, Blythe (Notts.), Mar. 24, 1558.	15	3	368
Apl. 12, 1559.	————, John, senr., Kirklevington, Aug. 18, 1558.	15	3	335
Nov. 29, 1558.	Wicam, Thomas, Howton Pannell, husbandman, Oct. 2, 1558.	15	3	142
July 27, 1567.	Wiclyff, Margery, Lithe, Aug. 26, 1566.	17		671
May 19, 1554.	Widdowson, Richard, Sutton, par. Grambe (Notts.), Jan. 14, 1553.	14		111
May 13, 1557.	Widnett, Robert, Lowdam (Notts.), Dec. 4, 1556.	15	1	225
Feb. 6, 1558.	Wielles, Robert, Foston, Oct. 11, 1558.	15	3	259
Oct. 4, 1564.	Wiggylsworthe, Roger, Stanton North Coote, par. Gargrave, May 18, 1564.	17		371
July 15, 1567.	Wighanne (or Wighame), John, Kirkbemawlomdaill, May 18, 9 Eliz.	17		675
Mar. 14, 1560.	Wightman, John, Rotherham, Dec. 27, 1560.	16		160
Sep. 30, 1563.	————, Robert, Southe Otterington, Jun. 11, 1563.	17		271
Mar. 20, 1565.	————, Thomas, Connesbrughe, May 17, 1565.	17		506
May 25, 1560.	————, Thomas (bur. Thyrske), Mar. 3, 1559.	16		68
Oct. 2, 1555.	Wigleswoorthe, Christopher, clerk (bur. Gargrave), Aug. 23, 1555.	14		170
Oct. 2, 1566.	Wiglesworth, William (bur. Gysburne), May 2, 1566.	17		573
Feb. 5, 1557.	Wiglesworthe, Dorothe, Roclyffe (bur. Snaythe), Dec. 3, 1557.	15	2	164
Oct. 10, 1560.	Wigsall, Richard, Brigside Byerlawe, par. Sheffelde, Feb. 5, 1559.	16		126
May 2, 1566.	Wilbarne, William, Knottinley (bur. Pontefract), Jan. 28, 8 Eliz.	17		535
May 19, 1559.	Wilbastone, John, Ruddington (bur. Flafurth, Notts.), Dec. 23, 1558.	15	3	432
Apl. 8, 1559.	Wilbere, John, Rosyngton, Mar. 4, 1558.	15	3	329
Nov. 25, 1558.	Wilberfosse, Anne, Over Catton, widow, Sep. 16, 1558.	15	3	123
Sep. 27, 1560.	————, John, Wylberfosse, Apl. 7, 1560.	16		110
Sep. 1, 1557.	————, William, Wylberfosse, gentleman, Aug. 3, 1557.	15	1	337
Apl. 18, 1567.	Wilbore, Elline, Bentley (bur. Arkesaye), widow, July 8, 1566.	17		636
Nov. 8, 1564.	————, John, Bentley, par. Arksay, July 22, 1561.	17		397
July 1, 1558.	————, Thomas, Helaye, par. Batley, Dec. 8, 1557.	15	2	330
Oct. 10, 1566.	Wilcocke, John, Workesoppe (Notts.), Apl. 22, 1566.	17		588
May 2, 1558.	————, Sir Myles, New Malton, priest, Apl. 10, 1557.	15	2	275
Apl. 7, 1559.	————, Thomas, St. Dionesse, York, Mar. 7, 1558.	15	3	320
Sep. 29, 1563.	Wilcoke, Hughe, Gysburne, Jun. 14, 1563.	17		277
Sep. 30, 1556.	————, Richard, Gisburne, July 31, 1556.	15	1	173
July 1, 1561.	Wild, John, Bole (Notts.), Mar. 5, 1560.	17		60
May 5, 1558.	Wilde, John, Blithe (Notts.), Nov. 13, 1557.	15	2	248
Sep. 28, 1560.	————, Peter, Eperston (Notts.), Apl. 1, 1560.	16		109
Apl. 10, 1559.	————, Thomas, Grisbroke, par. Rotheram, Apl. 4, 1557.	15	3	328
May 13, 1557.	————, William, Eastleake (Notts.), husbandman, Dec. 3, 1556.	15	1	231
July 5, 1557.	Wildman, Agnes, Thornour (bur. S. Nicholas, Thurne), wid., Feb. 26, 1556.	15	1	302
Feb. 15, 1558.	Wildon, Jenet, Mowthrope, par. Terrington, Dec. 7, 1558.	15	3	267
Nov. 17, 1558.	Wile, William, Wile, par. Bardsay, husbandman, Aug. 16, 1558.	15	3	111
Oct. 5, 1558.	Wilfurthe, Christopher, Mydleton, gentleman, Sep. 6, 1558.	15	3	44
Sep. 30, 1562.	Wilie, John, Weille (bur. Beverley), May 31, 1562.	17		117
Apl. 28, 1558.	Wilkes, John, Thorpbrantyngham, syngilman, Dec. 17, 1557.	15	2	220
Jun. 10, 1560.	————, Merialle, Bandisburton, widow, July 4, 1559.	16		81
Apl. 13, 1559.	————, William, Brandisburton, husbandman, Sep. 22, 1558.	15	3	345
May 13, 1557.	Wilkin, William, Sybthorpe (Notts.), Apl. 8, 1557.	15	1	218
Jan. 24, 1558.	Wilkinson, Anne, Fishelake, widow, July 31, 1558.	15	3	120
Jan. 23, 1558.	————, Anne, Nappaye, par. Gysborne, widow, May 16, 1558.	15	3	21
Sep. 28, 1560.	————, Edward, Woodborowe (Notts.), Feb. 20, 1560.	16		109
Mar. 22, 1566.	————, Elizabeth, Stockton, Dec. 27, 1566.	17		518
Dec. 1, 1558.	————, Ellin, Hullbanke, Oct. 16, 1558.	15	3	148
Nov. 5, 1562.	————, George, Leveshame, husbandman, Jun. 25, 1562.	17		127
Dec. 10, 1561.	————, George, Rowthe, husbandman, Aug. 18, 1561.	17		30
Oct. 5, 1558.	————, Henry, Nappay (bur. Gysburne), Feb. 26, 1557.	15	3	40
Apl. 27, 1564.	————, John, Blithe (Notts.), carpenter, Mar. 29, 1564.	17		335
Oct. 6, 1558.	————, John, Bolton on Derne, Jan. 10, 1558.	15	3	47

A.D. 1554 TO 1568.

		Vol.	Pt.	Fol.
Dec. 5, 1566.	Wilkinson, John, Ecclesfeild, Nov. 2, 1566.	17		600
Oct. 2, 1567.	———, John, Halifax, swyne seller, May 1, 1567.	17		716
Apl. 8, 1559.	———, John, Kilburne, Oct. 24, 1558.	15	3	321
Oct. 5, 1558.	———, John, Mydleton on Wold, yeoman, Sep. 3, 1558.	15	3	45
Feb. 6, 1558.	———, Margaret, Whitwood, par. Fetherston, Aug. 11, 1558.	15	3	257
Apl. 20, 1564.	———, Nicholas, Ottley, Nov. 10, 1563.	17		332
Feb.penult.,1556.	———, Richard, Stanforthbrigges (bur. Catton), Feb. 4, 1556.	15	1	180
Dec. 20, 1558.	———, Robert, Atterclyffe par. Sheafeld, Nov. 25, 1558.	15	3	153
July 17, 1565.	———, Steven, Preston in Holderness, husbandman, Feb.21,1564.	17		452
Apl. 13, 1559.	———, Thomas, Beverley, armerer, Oct. 9, 1558.	15	3	348
Oct. 11, 1563.	———, Thomas, Egton, Dec. 20, 1559.	17		297
Jan. 31, 1554.	———, Thomas, Witwod, par. Fetherstone, Sep. 28, 1554.	14		297
Oct. 1, 1561.	———, Thomas, Staynland in Eland, par. Hallifax, Feb. 25, 1560.	17		47
Oct. 11, 1567.	———, William, Bolton on Derne, gentleman, Jun. 22, 1567.	17		729
Mar.22, 1556.	———, William, Hulbanke, par. Cottingham, Feb. 14, 1556.	15	1	190
Jun. 20, 1568.	———, William, Panedoe (? Paynthorne), par. Gisburne, Dec. 10, 1567.	17		808
Jan. 15, 1557.	Wilkynson, George, Naburne, Nov. 13, 1557.	15	2	81
Aug.26, 1561.	———, James, Wakefeld, July 12, 1561.	17		55
July 8, 1557.	———, John, Northfroddingham, May 22, 1557.	15	1	305
Apl. 10, 1557.	———, William, Kellington, Feb. 18, 1556.	15	1	206
Sep. 30, 1556.	———, William, Nappay, par. Gisburne, May 29, 1556.	15	1	172
Oct. 1, 1556.	Wilkynsone, John, Barneslay, tanner, Jun. 15, 1556.	15	1	129
Oct. 1, 1556.	———, John, Fishlaike, May 24, 1556.	15	1	122
Oct. 10, 1566.	Willde, Richard, Est Leake (Notts.), husbn., May 20, 1566.	17		596
Oct. 19, 1556.	Wille, Peter, Whitbie, Nov. 8, 1551.	15	1	97
July 11, 1558.	Willes, Richard, Yringthorpe, par. Whistone, yeoman, Dec. 2, 1557.	15	2	301
Mar.20, 1565.	Williamson, Barnard, Sheffeild, Oct. 7, 1565.	17		506
Aug.13, 1567.	———, Elizabeth, Pattrington, widow, Mar. 18, ———.	17		689
Apl. 28, 1559.	———, Esabell, Wheldrake, widow, Oct. 4, 1558.	15	3	361
Feb.25, 1558.	———, Henry, Thormonbye, Oct. 22, 1558.	15	3	280
Apl. 26, 1559.	———, Isabell, Gransmore (bur. Burton Agnes), wid., Mar. 20, 1557.	15	3	363
May30, 1555.	———, Isabell, Great Ayton in Clevelond, Oct. 13, 1552.	14		252
Mar.19, 1564.	———, James, Boultby, par. Feliskirke, Mar. 27, 1564 (sic).	17		412
Feb.23, 1556.	———, Jeffraye, York, talyer, July 2, 1554.	15	1	164
Oct. 20, 1558.	———, Jenet, Tunstall, widow, Apl. 4, 1558.	15	2	348
Jun. 17, 1556.	———, Jenet, Wykam in Pykerinlythe, widow, Mar. 6, 1556.	15	1	49
July 29, 1556.	———, John, Bubwithe, gresseman, July 23, 1556.	15	1	47
May 2, 1560.	———, John, Harpham, Sep. 11, 1559.	16		34
May10, 1559.	———, John, Lethome, labourer, Oct. 18, 1558.	15	3	384
July 3, 1567.	———, John, Nunyngton, July 10, 1565.	17		668
Mar.27, 1565.	———, John, Ottringham, husbandman, Feb. 9, 1564.	17		417
Oct. 13, 1565.	———, John, Stanghow in Cleveland (bur.Skelton), Nov.17,1564.	17		474
Sep. 6, 1560.	———, John, York, wrighte, Dec. 20, 1559.	16		104
July 12, 1564.	———, Peter, Sutton in Holderness, Nov. 22, 1563.	17		357
July 17, 1554.	———, Richard, Ruyston, par. Wicham, May 13, 1554.	14		143
Sep. 29, 1563.	———, Robert (bur. Hunmanbie), Feb. 3, 1562.	17		275
Aug.27, 1561.	———, Robert, Skeyrne, shepherd, Jun. 29, 1561.	17		54
May29, 1563.	———, Thomas, Boultbye, par. Feliskyrke, Jan. 4, 1562.	17		251
Mar. 3, 1556.	———, Thomas, Esingwold, Jan. 24, 1556.	15	1	181
Feb. 6, 1558.	———, Thomas, Shereburne, Nov. 26, 1558.	15	3	266
Mar.20, 1560.	———, William, Estcottingwythe (bur. Aughton), Dec. 8, 1560.	16		155
Nov.23, 1558.	———, William, Gayte Fulforthe, husbandman, Oct. 7, 1558.	15	3	80
Nov.19, 1566.	———, William, Hull, marchaunt, May 28, 1566.	17		598
Feb.25, 1558.	———, William, Over Catton, husbandman, Nov. 28, 1558.	15	3	280
Apl. 3, 1554.	Williamsone, Richard, York, cordyner, Aug. 30, 1552.	14		129
Apl. 28, 1558.	Williamsonne, Thomas, Nunthorpe, par. Aiton, Jan. 14, 1558.	15	2	230
Dec.21, 1562.	Willman, Thomas, Staneborne, Oct. 5, 1559.	17		136
Oct. 8, 1567.	Willobye, George, Cottgrave (Notts.), Apl. 6, 1567.	17		726
May 2, 1560.	Willois, Nycholas, South Loufthous, Mar. 9, 1559.	16		42
Oct. 14, 1561.	Willous, Edward, West Cottingwithe (bur.Thorganbye), Aug.11,1561.	17		46

		Vol.	Pt.	Fol.
Apl. 28, 1558.	Willows, Richard, West, Cottingwyth (bur. Thorganby), Mar. 30, 1557.	15	2	239
Oct. 7, 1563.	Willowughbie, John, Nottingham, tanner, Feb. 4, 1563.	17		292
Feb. 19, 1557.	Willse, William, Hawdynbye, Dec. 20, 1557.	15	2	145
Mar. 16, 1554.	Willshe, Richard (Deanery of Harthill), Feb. 19, 1553.	14		138
Jun. 17, 1556.	Willson, Christopher, Synnyngton, husbandman, July 16, 1555.	15	1	49
Jan. 4, 1562.	——, John, Gatforthe (bur. Braton), ——, 1561.	17		138
No date.	——, John, Tollerton (bur. Alne), Apl. 11, 1555.	14		240
Sep. 21, 1557.	——, Margaret, Bromeheade in Bradfelde, widow, Apl. 9, 1553.	15	1	356
Aug. 13, 1567.	——, Robert, Pattrington, Jun. 7, 1567.	17		692
Jan. 20, 1557.	——, Thomas, Wolthwayte, par. Tyckhill, Sep. 23, 1557.	15	2	63
May 5, 1568.	Willsonne, Agnes, Pattrington, widow, Mar. 6, 1567.	17		779
Apl. 14, 1558.	——, Thomas, Thornbarshe, par. Kilvington, Apl. 30, 1557.	15	2	229
Dec. 1, 1558.	Willye, John, Beverlay, Sep. 25, 1558.	15	3	148
Oct. 3, 1560.	——, Robert, Oversilton, Apl. 22, 1560.	16		117
May 13, 1557.	Willymote, Thomas Beston (Notts.), Feb. 2, 1556.	15	1	226
May 2, 1566.	Wilman, Rainbrowne, Wilden (bur. Bradforde), Nov. 14, 1565.	17		533
Dec. 10, 1566.	Wilshe, Thomas (bur. Holme in Spaldingmore), May 8, 1566.	17		605
Jun. 20, 1566.	Wilson, Agnes, Ecclesfeld, widow, May 28, 1564.	17		559
July 27, 1567.	——, Alan, Filing, Mar. 3, 1566.	17		670
Oct. 13, 1558.	——, Alexander, Great Markham (Notts.), carpenter, Oct. 8, 1558.	15	2	375
Jun. 25, 1557.	——, Arthure (bur. Sheffeld), Jun. 5, 1557.	15	1	298
Mar. 30, 1559.	——, Denys, North Skirley (bur. Swyne), tayllyour, Dec. 8, 1558.	15	3	299
Sep. 18, 1565.	——, Elizabeth (bur. Sheaffeld), Aug. 5, 1564.	17		468
May 29, 1562.	——, Georg, Armen (bur. Howke), May 8, 1561.	17		101
Jun. 28, 1566.	——, George, Hirstcourtneye, husbandman, Jan. 8, 1562.	17		551
Feb. 4, 1562.	——, Henry, Farnedall (bur. Kyrkbymoreside), Jun. 20, 1562.	17		146
May 10, 1565.	——, Henry, Newmalton, powderer, Feb. 3, 1564.	17		421
May 13, 1557.	——, Isabell, Torlaston (Notts.), Feb. 6, 1556.	15	1	229
Apl. 22, 1563.	——, John, Barley, husbandman, Dec. 26, 1562.	17		223
May 12, 1559.	——, John, Chereburton, husbandman, Feb. 15, 1558.	15	3	391
Oct. 3, 1560.	——, John, Draghton (bur. Skipton), May 8, 1559.	16		119
Jun. 22, 1568.	——, John, Everingham, Jan. 19, 1567.	17		806
Oct. 6, 1558.	——, John, Follyfeat, par. Spofforthe, Sep. 12, 1558.	15	3	91
May 23, 1564.	——, John, Great Ayton in Cleveland, husbandman, Apl. 12, 1564.	17		346
Jun. 2, 1564.	——, John, Litle Ribston, par. Spofforthe, May 25, 1564.	17		347
July 17, 1565.	——, John, Preston in Holderness, carpenter, Feb. 23, 1564.	17		453
Jan. 12, 1558.	——, John, South Cliffe, par. North Cave, Dec. 8, 1558.	15	3	196
Jan. 24, 1558.	——, John, Skellay, par. Owston, Nov. 4, 1558.	15	3	120
No date.	——, John, Tollerton, par. Alne, Apl. 11, 1555.	14		239
Apl. 19, 1559.	——, John, Whatton (Notts.), husbandman, Aug. 21, 1557.	15	3	375
Mar. 14, 1563.	——, John, Yarhame (Cleveland), Oct. 15, 1563.	17		323
Apl. 27, 1558.	——, Katheren, Hollome, widow, Mar. 10, 1558.	15	2	205
Mar. 23, 1567.	——, Katherine (bur. Old Malton), widow, Jan. 10, 1567.	17		765
Feb. 6, 1558.	——, Margaret, Gaitfurth (bur. Braiton), Dec. 26, 1558.	15	3	263
Apl. 19, 1564.	——, Nicholas, Cunnunley (bur. Kildwecke), Apl. 14, 1563.	17		331
May 18, 1559.	——, Nicholas, East Retford (Notts.), Aug. 25, 1558.	15	3	407
Apl. 10, 1559.	——, Nicholas, Sandal, par. Doncaster, Jan. 22, 1557.	15	3	326
Jan. 12, 1558.	——, Rauffe, the provostre of Walkington, husbn., Sep. 30, 1558.	15	3	195
Jun. 10, 1568.	——, Richard, Adlingfleite, Jan. 10, 1567.	17		804
Nov. 17, 1558.	——, Richard, Mickelfe[i]d (bur. Shereburne), Sep. 13, 1558.	15	3	115
Apl. 3, 1559.	——, Robert, Aram, labourer, Oct. 25, 1558.	15	3	318
May 2, 1566.	——, Robert, Barneybie, par. Gysburne, Jan. 6, 1565.	17		539
Dec. 1, 1558.	——, Robert, Cherriburton, husbandman, Sep. 10, 1558.	15	3	82
Jan. 24, 1558.	——, Robert, Egton, Feb. 9, 1558.	15	3	117
Jan. 13, 1558.	——, Robert, Kelham (Notts.), Sep. 13, 1557.	15	3	17
Aug. 27, 1556.	——, Roger, Gaiteforth (bur. Braton), June 16, 1556.	15	1	61
Aug. 20, 1561.	——, Roger, Myton, near Hull, Mar. 1, 1559.	17		62
Jun. 22, 1566.	——, Roger, Wistowe, July 9, 1566.	17		550
Mar. 15, 1562.	——, Rowland, Skelton in Cleveland, Jan. 12, 1561.	17		164
Mar. 17, 1556.	——, Thomas, Burton Pidsey, Dec. 16, 1556.	15	1	187
Jan. 19, 1556.	——, Thomas, Newland, par. Cottingham, Nov. 2, 1556.	15	1	89
Apl. 13, 1557.	——, Thomas, Nunnyngton (Act Book), Feb. 20, 1556.	15	1	208

A.D. 1554 TO 1568.

A.D. 1554 TO 1568.

		Vol.	Pt.	Fol.
Jan. 7, 1562.	Wode, John, senr., Lepton, par. Kirkheton, yeoman, Mar. 6, 1558.	17		140
May 6, 1563.	Wodhouse, Agnes, Tuxfurthe (Notts.), Feb. ult., 1562.	17		243
Apl. 27, 1563.	———, James, Ibrounedaille, par. Whitbie, May 28, 1559.	17		224
Jan. 29, 1556.	Wodmosse, James, Foston, Dec. 18, 1556.	15	1	94
Feb. 4, 1561.	Wodows, Mathew, Leverton, par. Esyngton, Mar. 27, 1561.	17		12
Mar.15, 1560.	Wodsmythe, Agnes, Est Retford (Notts.), widow, Oct. 12, 1560.	16		170
May 18, 1559.	Wodson, John, Cudworth, par. Roistone, Nov. 8, 1558.	15	3	402
May 10, 1565.	Wodward, Katherine, Myton on Swale, Sep. 9, 1564.	17		429
[Feb.—,1561.]	Wodwerd, Robert, Raskell, Nov. 26, 1561.	17		12
May 2, 1560.	Woffyndaille, James, Otlay, Apl. 18, 1559.	16		56
Oct. 8, 1567.	Wolhouse, Nicholas, Nottingham, Aug. 4, 1567.	17		724
Apl. 4, 1560.	Wollay, Richard, Westockwith (bur. Mysterton, Notts.), yeom., Jan. 24, 1559.	16		26
Oct. 6, 1558.	Wolley, Thomas, Owston, Aug. 17, 1558.	15	3	46
May 13, 1557.	Wollffytt, Gefferay, Wysall (Notts.), Jan. 15, 1557.	15	2	133
May 5, 1558.	Wolraye, Thomas, South Collingham (Notts.), husbn., Sep. 30, 1557.	15	2	260
Sep. 18, 1565.	Wombwell, Elline, West Melton, par. Wathe, Jun. 23, 1565.	17		466
Apl. 10, 1559.	———, Robert, Armthorpe, Feb. 27, 1558.	15	3	325
Dec. 20, 1558.	———, Roger, West Melton (bur. Wathe), gent., Aug. 5, 1558.	15	3	153
July 20, 1561.	Womersley, Steven, Hullbanke, par. Cottingham, bucher, Mar.2,1560.	17		62
Jun. 21, 1565.	Wommocke, Robert, Balne, par. Burghwalles, Mar. 15, 1564.	17		447
Nov. 8, 1557.	Womok, Robert, Anston, Oct. 8, 1557.	15	2	111
May 4, 1557.	Womwell, Thomas, Haitfeld, butcher, Mar. 15, 1557.	15	1	279
Mar.20, 1558.	Wood, Addam, Pollyngton, par. Snaith, Jan. 16, 1558.	15	3	250
Jun. 19, 1562.	——, Agnes, Camylfurth, par. Drax, widow, Apl. 13, 1562.	17		91
Mar.12, 1562.	——, Alexander, Est Morton (bur. Byngley), Nov. 20, 1561.	17		152
July 12, 1558.	——, Annas, Bramley, par. Leedes, widow, Mar. 13, 1555.	15	2	315
Jan. 18, 1558.	——, Christopher, Warley, par. Halifax, Oct. 4, 1558.	15	3	211
May 10, 1559.	——, Christopher, Wollerbye, yeoman, Feb. 7, 1558.	15	3	390
Nov.17, 1558.	——, Elizabeth, Pollington (bur. Snathe). *No date.*	15	3	74
May 4, 1557.	——, Elyne, Bradfeld, widow, Jan. 8, 1556.	15	1	279
Nov.29, 1558.	——, George, Wathe, Oct. 10, 1558.	15	3	138
Oct. 26, 1558.	——, Gylbert, York, Sep. 20, 1558.	15	3	95
Jun. 21, 1563.	——, James, Kirkby Moreside, Apl. 26, 1563.	17		258
Nov. 8, 1558.	——, Jennett, York, widow, Mar. 28, 1558.	15	3	95
Oct. 5, 1558.	——, John, Dryghlyngton, par. Burstall, Feb. 15, 1557.	15	3	62
Jun. 6, 1554.	——, John, Lepton, par. Kirkheton, Oct. 24, 1552.	14		10
May 20, 1558.	——, John, Mixenden, par. Hallifax, Mar. 21, 1557.	15	2	280
Jun. 8, 1560.	——, John, the More, par. Hymsworthe, yeoman, Apl. 21, 1560.	16		80
Dec. 17, 1567.	——, John, Normanbie, Mar. 10, 1566.	17		749
Apl. 28, 1554.	——, John, Yorke, inholder, Mar. 28, 1554.	14		55
Dec. 2, 1562.	——, Luke, Baddisworthe, husbandman, Oct. 13, 1562.	17		129
Apl. 19, 1559.	——, Richard (bur. Clyftone, Notts.), May 30, 1558.	15	3	372
Mar.29, 1568.	——, Richard, Cowkrigge Graunge, par. Adle, husbn., Dec. 14,1567.	17		768
May 21, 1558.	——, Richard, son of John W., Myxenden, par. Hallyfax, Feb. 10, 1555.	15	2	284
Jun. 21, 1566.	——, Robert, senr., Bransdaile (bur. Kirkbie Moreside), husbn., Apl. 13, 1566.	17		558
July 26, 1557.	——, Roger, Leptone, par. Kyrkeheaton, May 25, 1557.	15	1	316
Nov.20, 1563.	——, Thomas, Chappelthorpe, par. Sandall Magna, husbn., Nov. 4, 1563.	17		303
Sep. 13, 1555.	——, Thomas, Kellington, Apl. 28, 1555.	14		203
Mar.20, 1558.	——, Thomas, Roclyff (bur. Snaith), Dec. 12, 1558.	15	3	290
May 18, 1559.	——, Thomas, Rosington, July 18, 1558.	15	3	396
Aug.13, 1567.	——, Thomas, Ulrum (bur. Skipsey), husbandman, July 23, 1567.	17		688
Mar.20, 1558.	——, William, Drax Maner, par. Drax, Mar. 23, 1557.	15	3	251
May 2, 1566.	——, William, Drighlington, par. Birstall, Sep. 19, 1565.	17		534
Jan. 27, 1562.	——, William, Farnley, par. Leedes, Dec. 15, 1562.	17		144
Dec. 9, 1556.	——, William, Flyntone, par. Humbleton, Oct. 12, 1556.	15	1	156
Sep. 18, 1565.	——, William, Haldworthe in Bradfeild, May 21, 1565.	17		468
Jun. 23, 1565.	Woodburne, John, Spofforthe, May 12, 1565.	17		444
Oct. 31, 1557.	Woodcoke, William, Denbye, par. Penyston, Apl. 24, 1557.	15	1	366

		Vol.	Pt.	Fol.
Sep. 30, 1557.	Wodd, Robert, Baynton, husbandman, ——, 1557.	15	1	326
Jan. 13, 1558.	——, William, Donham on Trent (Notts.), Oct. 25, 1558.	15	3	206
Jan. 24, 1558.	Wooddall, John, Hellyby (bur. Stayneton), Oct. 16, 1558.	15	3	218
[? Oct.] 2, 1560.	——, William, Hornesey. *No date.*	16		116
Feb. 9, 1557.	Woodde, John (bur. Elsterweke), Dec. 10, 1557.	15	2	121
Mar. 23, 1557.	——, Thomas, Dodyngton, husbandman, Jan. 9, 1557.	15	2	172
July 21, 1566.	Wooddus, Richard, Ibrondaile, par. Whitbye, Sep. 24, 1555.	15	1	59
May 18, 1559.	Woode, Edward, Wakefeild, priest, Apl. 11, 1559.	15	3	416
Apl. 17, 1562.	——, Richard, Bowthorod, par. Dewisbury, Feb. 28, 1545.	17		166
July 1, 1558.	——, Robert, Hessle, par. Wragbye, carpenter, July 31, 1556.	15	2	330
Apl. 18, 1560.	——, William, Attercliffe, par. Sheffelde. Feb. 25, 1560.	16		31
Mar. 9, 1557.	Woodemasse, Isabell (bur. Foston), July 18, 1557.	15	2	129
Oct. 3, 1565.	Woodhead, Nicholas, Scamonden, par. Huddersfeild, Oct. 5, 1564.	17		479
Mar. 6, 1556.	Woodhouse, Raulf, West Markham (Notts.), Sep. 18, 1556.	15	1	176
Oct. 18, 1555.	——, William, Shereborne, Mar. 14, 1554.	14		178
Mar. 21, 1561.	Woodhowse, Cuthbert (bur. Whitby), Aug. 8, 1561.	17		3
Apl. 13, 1559.	Woodmasse, Robert, Cotingham, Nov. 10, 1558.	15	3	349
Dec. 13, 1557.	Woodroffe, James, Pryston Jacklynge, par. Fetherston, gent., July 30, 1557.	15	2	53
July 11, 1558.	——, Richard, Tickehill, Jan. 27, 1557.	15	2	303
Mar. 10, 1555.	Woodsmythye, Thomas, Estredforth (Notts.), shomaker, Dec. 12, 1551.	14		225
Nov. 11, 1557.	Woodward, Thomas (bur. Holym), Sep. 26, 1557.	15	2	98
Jan. 27, 1566.	——, William (bur. Myton), Jun. 18, 1565.	17		611
Feb. 7, 1555.	Woodwarde, William, senr., Myton on Swaill, Sep. 14, 1553.	15	1	6
Oct. 12, 1564.	Woollay, Mechell, West Stokwithe (Notts.), carpenter. July 28, 1562.	17		389
Apl. 13, 1559.	Worblington, James, Hull, fyshemonger, Mar. 9, 1558.	15	3	346
Feb. 25, 1556.	Wordesworth, Thurstone, Penistone, Jan. 25, 1556.	15	1	166
July 11, 1558.	Wordesworthe, Rauf, Penyston, yeoman, Sep. 9, 1557.	15	2	302
Oct. 22, 1560.	Worleton, Jennat, Burton Flemynge (bur. Hunmanbie), Sep. 14, 1560.	16		128
Apl. 17, 1563.	Wormall, Edward, Staynland, par. Elland, Nov. 25, 1562.	17		221
Aug. 8, 1562.	——, Heugh, Warley, par. Halifax, clothier, Mar. 4, 1561.	17		103
Mar. 19, 1559.	——, Richard (bur. Dewysburie), Oct. 15, 1559.	16		13
July 11, 1558.	Wormeley, Margaret, Haytfeyld, widow, May 9, 1558.	15	2	317
Dec. 18, 1567.	Wormlay, John (bur. Haitfeld), Jun. 16, 1557.	17		746
Dec. 22, 1556.	Wormley, John, Hayfeld (bur. Haitfeld), husbn., Oct. 2, 1556.	15	1	81
Dec. 12, 1567.	Worrall, John, Rotherham, Aug. 1, 1566.	17		745
Dec. 7, 1556.	——, Thomas, Grysbroke, par. Rotherham, Sep. 13, 1556.	15	1	119
May 27, 1562.	Worstocke, Rauf, Bolbie, par. Esyngton, Mar. 29, 1562.	17		100
No date.	Wortlaye, Nicholas, Hardwick, par. Aston, Jan. 26, 1554.	14		82
Apl. 28, 1556.	Wottone, Richard, Burne (bur. Braytone), Apl. 23, 1555.	15	1	28
Mar. 4, 1560.	Wourlington, Henry, Hull, yongman and fishemonger, July 23, 1560.	16		167
Jun. 2, 1558.	Wover, Christopher, Ottringham Masse, Apl. 16, 1558.	15	2	312
Aug. 2, 1560.	Wowls, Thomas, Ryse, July 5, 1559.	16		99
Sep. 30, 1558.	Woyde, William (bur. Paithlaybrigges), Apl. 19, 1558.	15	3	56
Apl. 27, 1564.	Wragbie, Thomas, Byngham (Notts.), May 8, 1563.	17		340
May 5, 1557.	Wraith, Brian, Crofton, husbandman, Jan. 20, 1556.	15	1	214
Dec. 1, 1558.	Wrangham, John, Spellow Hill, par. Marton, July 7, 1558.	15	3	126
Apl. 12, 1559.	Wrathe, James, Bradford, Dec. 13, 1558.	15	3	336
Sep. 17, 1558.	Wray, John, senr., Clifforth (bur. Bramham), July 26, 1558.	15	3	106
Nov. 5, 1558.	——, John, junr., Clifforth (bur. Bramham), husbn., Aug. 20, 1558.	15	3	231
Sep. 12, 1556.	——, Robert, Cliffurthe (bur. Bramham), husbn., Sep. 4, 1556.	15	1	65
Oct. 25, 1558.	Wreith, Thomas, Sheriff Howton, carpenter, July 22, 1558.	15	3	234
Jan. 12, 1558.	Wren, John, Crowgarth (bur. Skipsey), Nov. 23, 1558.	15	3	203
Dec. 21, 1562.	——, Thomas (bur. Beforde), July 15, 1562.	17		135
Apl. 13, 1559.	Wrenshe, John, Bennyngham (bur. Swyne), labourer, Dec. 12, 1558.	15	3	346
Jun. 12, 1557.	Wresill, Robert, Rednys (bur. Whitgifte), Apl. 8, ——.	15	1	291
Oct. 27, 1564.	Wreye, Agnes, Hornebie, par. Great Smeton, May 3, 1560.	17		393
Sep. 30, 1561.	Wreythe, Thomas, Ripon, wooleman, Aug. 5, 1561.	17		48
Apl. 26, 1558.	Wright, Agnes, Lotherton (bur. Sherborne), Nov. 12, 1557.	15	2	234
Apl. 26, 1558.	——, Alice, Barnebrough, widow, Nov. 30, 1557.	15	2	223
Aug. 18, 1562.	——, Alis, widow of John W., Carnaby, Mar. 20, 1561.	17		105
May 2, 1562.	——, Anthony, Kyrke Dighton, husbandman, May 20, 1561.	17		196

		Vol.	Pt.	Fol.
Oct. 10, 1566.	Wright, Anne, Ratclif on Trent (Notts.), widow, Apl. 19, 1566.	17		596
Oct. 12, 1568.	——, Barthillmewe, Hawton (Notts.), husbandman, Apl. 19, 1568.	17		829
Mar. 7, 1561.	——, Christopher, Ellerton, Nov. 18, 1561.	17		3
Feb. 17, 1557.	——, Edmond, Norton, par. Campsall, Nov. 26, 1557.	15	2	139
Feb. 25, 1560.	——, Elizabeth, Burton Agnes, widow, Oct. 17, 1560.	16		150
May 4, 1557.	——, Elizabeth, Campsall, Nov. 16, 1556.	15	1	277
May 31, 1557.	——, Elizabeth, Fishelaike, widow, Jan. 17, 1556.	15	1	261
Jun. 18, 1557.	——, George, Flynton (bur. Humbleton), Jun. 8, 1557.	15	1	295
Dec. 11, 1566.	——, Henry, Flambrughe, Jun. 15, 1566.	17		602
May 24, 1555.	——, Henry, Herthill, Jan. 20, 1550.	14		310
May 9, 1560.	——, Hewghe, Hauton (Notts.), husbandman, Apl. 6, 1560.	16		58
Mar. 3, 1555.	——, Isabell, dau. of Jo. W., late of Beverley, merchant, Dec. 22, 1555.	15	1	10
Dec. 17, 1562.	——, Jane, wid. of Thos. W., Righton, Nov. 9, 1562.	17		134
May 2, 1560.	——, Jane, Waltonhead in Kyrkbyoverblawse, wid., Dec. 5, 1559.	16		56
May 31, 1559.	——, Janet, Seamer, Jan. 14, 1558.	15	3	435
Oct. 3, 1555.	——, John, Beverleye, marchaunte, Jan. 8, 1554.	14		174
May 5, 1568.	——, John, Bolton, Craven, bur. Appilbie (co. Westmd.), Aug. 13, 1567.	17		786
July 17, 1565.	——, John, Camerton, par. Pawlle, Dec. 15, 1563.	17		454
Sep. 30, 1556.	——, John, Drynghoo (bur. Skypsey), ——, 1556.	15	1	140
May 13, 1568.	——, John, Knesall (Notts.), Jan. 12, 1567.	17		798
Jan. 9, 1560.	——, John, priest, curate of Leppington, Sep 10, 1560.	16		138
Apl. 7, 1557.	——, John, Lotherton, par. Sherborne, Apl. 13, 1556.	15	1	204
Jun. 25, 1566.	——, John, Marston, Sep. 6, 1565.	17		551
Oct. 6, 1558.	——, John, Orgrave, par. Rotheram, Jan. 8, 1557.	15	3	223
Apl. 20, 1564.	——, John, Preston in Holderness, husbandman, Sep. 10, 1563.	17		332
July 15, 1562.	——, John, Pudsay, par. Calverley, Nov. 6, 1560.	17		96
Jun. 25, 1557.	——, John, Shefeld, yeoman, Jun. 3, 1557.	15	1	297
Nov. 8, 1557.	——, John, Skelbrocke, husbandman, Oct. 18, 1557.	15	2	112
July 8, 1561.	——, John, Standley (bur. Wakefeld), labourer, Jun. 4, 1561.	17		79
Dec. 16, 1557.	——, Margaret, Litle Haitfelde (bur. Selstorne), May 1, 1556.	15	2	46
Oct. 1, 1561.	——, Mawd, Burton Pudsey, Jun. 28, 1561.	17		47
May 9, 1563.	——, Nicholas (bur. Welwicke), Sep. 9, 1561.	17		254
Oct. 7, 1557.	——, Randley, Trowell (Notts.), Aug. 20, 1557.	15	2	25
May 12, 1559.	——, Rauff, Beverley, mylner, Mar. 8, 1558.	15	3	393
Jan. 13, 1558.	——, Richard, Brancrofte, par. Austerfeld, May 28, 1558.	15	3	189
Apl. 6, 1566.	——, Richard, Myton on Swaylle, Jan. 15, 1565.	17		509
May 13, 1557.	——, Richard, Rolston (Notts.), Oct. 1, 1556.	15	1	218
Oct. 6, 1558.	——, Richard, Spofforthe, Aug. 28, 1558.	15	3	91
May 6, 1563.	——, Richard, Walkeryngham (Notts.), Oct. 30, 1562.	17		244
May 13, 1557.	——, Richard, Wilforde (Notts.), Nov. 4, 1556.	15	1	227
Oct. 12, 1558.	——, Richard, Willebe (Notts.), Mar. 18, 155[7-]8.	15	3	33
Dec. 15, 1557.	——, Robert, Brancrofte, par. Austerfelde, husbn., Oct. 22, 1557.	15	2	57
Apl. 7, 1554.	——, Robert, Burton Pidseye, husbandman, Jan. 11, 1553.	14		218
Mar. 27, 1565.	——, Robert, Est Newton, par. Albroughe, Jun. 4, 1563.	17		418
Oct. 13, 1558.	——, Robert, Hockerton (Notts.), husbandman, Nov. 10, 1557.	15	2	362
Apl. 27, 1556.	——, Robert, Hull, draper, Oct. 21, 1555.	15	1	14
Jan. 12, 1558.	——, Robert, Thirlbie, par. St. Felix, Nov. 4, 1558.	15	3	176
Oct. 13, 1558.	——, Robert, Walkringham (Notts.), husbandman, Aug. 3, 1557.	15	2	361
Jun. 25, 1568.	——, Robert, Welwicke, husbandman, Nov. 2, 1568.	17		811
Mar. 12, 1556.	——, Roger, Fullum, par. Womerslay, Nov. 20, 1556.	15	1	200
Apl. 27, 1563.	——, Thomas, Appleton of Wiske, husbandman, Sep. 10, 1562.	17		224
Oct. 10, 1566.	——, Thomas, Hawkesworthe (Notts.), husbandman, Jun. 26, 1566.	17		591
Jan. 11, 1562.	——, Thomas, Holme in Spauldingmore, Dec. 4, 1562.	17		142
Jan. 24, 1558.	——, Thomas, Pikton (bur. Kirklevyngton), July 16, 1558.	15	3	22
Dec. 17, 1562.	——, Thomas, Righton, Sep. 14, 1562.	17		135
Oct. 3, 1564.	——, Thomas, Sherburne, yeoman, May 27, 1563.	17		366
Apl. 9, 1554.	——, Thomas, Yorke, haberdasher, Mar. 14, 1553.	14		53
Sep. 6, 1558.	——, William, Altoftes, par. Normanton, Aug. 24, 1558.	15	3	99
May 4, 1558.	——, William, Brbdmore, par. Bonney (Notts.), Sep. 19, 1557.	15	2	266
Oct. 22, 1556.	——, William, Campsall, Sep. 26, 1556.	15	1	101

		Vol.	Pt.	Fol.
Jan. 28, 1555.	Wright, William, Campsaull (Act Book).	15	1	1
Oct. 7, 1557.	———, William, Fiscarton, par. Rolston (Notts.), July 10, 1557.	15	2	18
Mar.10, 1555.	———, William, Hawton (Notts.), Oct. 16, 1554.	14		227
Mar. 6, 1556.	———, William, Mathersaye (Notts.), Jan. 18, 1556.	15	1	181
Jun. 8, 1557.	———, William (bur. Skefling), Mar. 2, 1556.	15	1	269
Apl. 16, 1567.	———, William, Waltonhead, par. Kirkbe Overblause, yongman, Apl. 2, 1567.	17		633
Oct. 14, 1561.	——— als. Allen, John, Fyshelake, July 12, 1561.	17		36
Jan. 15, 1566.	——— als. Ranald, Robert, Harswill, Dec. 30, 1566.	17		607
Jan. 13, 1558.	Wrighte, John, Gotham (Notts.), husbandman, Sep. 30, 1558.	15	3	180
Mar.27, 1557.	———, John, Wehell. No date.	15	1	203
Apl. 4, 1560.	———, Richard, Egmanton (Notts.), yeoman, Aug. 23, 1558.	16		25
Oct. 3, 1554.	———, Thomas, Elwarby (bur. Swyne), Jun. 6, 1553.	14		40
Aug. 1, 1560.	———, William, Aitonne, par. Seamer, Oct. 3, 1558.	16		98
May 18, 1559.	———, William, Norton, par. Campsall, Nov. 24, 1558.	15	3	403
Jan. 17, 1557.	Wrighteson, William, Galmeton, Oct. 11, 1557.	15	2	61
Oct. 24, 1554.	Wro, Thomas, Bretton, par. Silkeston, Jan. 17, 1553.	14		309
Dec. 14, 1557.	Wryght, Agnes, Elloughton, widow, Nov. 10, 1557.	15	1	358
No date.	———, John, Hawxworth (Notts.), July 28, 1555.	14		21
May 6, 1557.	———, John, West Halton, par. Longe Preston, Feb. 8, 1556.	15	1	252
Oct. 9, 1561.	———, John, Wheatley (Notts.), yeoman, May 2, 1559.	17		41
Apl. 27, 1558.	———, Richard, Mydle Shillington, par. Thornhill, Apl. 8, 1558.	15	2	192
Apl. 19, 1559.	———, Richard, Ratclyf on Trent (Notts.), husbn., Jan. 6, 1558.	15	3	377
Mar.13, 1561.	———, Richard, Weghell, Sep. 1, 1559.	17		7
Oct. 30, 1556.	———, Richard, York, baker, Oct. 18, 1556.	15	1	106
Jan. 11, 1557.	———, Robert, Brandesburton, husbandman, Nov. 16, 1557.	15	2	74
Dec. 18, 1557.	———, Thomas, Crakall (bur. Topclyff), Oct. 6, 1557.	15	2	83
Feb. 15, 1558.	———, Thomas, Leven, husbandman, Aug. 28, 1558.	15	3	272
May 5, 1558.	———, Umfraye, Wyston, par. Claworthe (Notts.), Dec. 23, 1556.	15	2	242
Apl. 6, 1558.	———, William, Barnebroughe, husandman, Sep. 11, 1557.	15	2	183
May 9, 1560.	———, William, Eastbridgeforde (Notts.), husbn., Feb. 15, 1560.	16		61
Oct. 3, 1561.	———, William, Thweyng, batcheler, Apl. 11, 1561.	17		37
Feb. 17, 1557.	Wryghte, William, Campsall, Oct. 16, 1557.	15	2	142
Aug.16, 1555.	Wrythe, John, Ellarbye, par. Lythe, Jun. 6, 1555.	14		205
Aug. 7, 1554.	Wulfet, George, Dr. of Lawe (bur. Ribchester, eff I dye there), Feb. 1, 1552.	14		268
Oct. 22, 1556.	Wybsaye, John, Byrstall, May 17, 1556.	15	1	98
May 6, 1563.	Wycam, Hew, Austerfeld, son of Jo. W. of Bawltre, husbn., Mar. 12, 1562.	17		244
Sep. 21, 1557.	———, William, Hulley (bur. Aston), Aug. 19, 1556.	15	1	356
Sep. 30, 1557.	Wyddows, John, Neway (bur. Hemyngbrought), May 21, 1557.	15	1	346
Oct. 3, 1565.	Wydoppe, Edward, Wakefeild, Jun. 2, 1565.	17		480
Aug.16, 1566.	Wyelles, John, Burton, husbandman, Jun. 30, 1565.	17		570
Apl. 17, 1563.	Wygane, Christopher, Heptonstall, Aug. 8, 1562.	17		221
Mar.27, 1560.	Wyghtman, William, Southe Otryngton, Sep. 3, 1559.	16		22
Jun. 6, 1560.	Wykam, Thomas, Cottingham, husbandman, Sep. 24, 1559.	16		74
May 25, 1560.	Wykes, Marmaduke, Everingham, May 10, 1559.	16		67
Apl. 8, 1560.	———, Thomas, Everingham, July 22, 1559.	16		28
Nov.10, 1557.	Wykfeld, Thomas, Beverlay Parke, Aug. 25, 1557.	15	2	98
Jun. 6, 1564.	Wykys, Pattricke, Everingham, Sep. 20, 1563.	17		349
Sep. 28, 1560.	Wylbaston, Henry, son and hayre to John W., Ruddington (Notts.), freholder, May 24, 1559.	16		106
Sep. 30, 1556.	Wylbert, Thomas, Aram, par. Leckenfeld, Mar. 12, 1556.	15	1	138
Aug. 4, 1558.	Wylberte, Nicolas, Aram, par. Lekenfeld, husbandman, Apl. 14, 1558.	15	3	8
Apl. 8, 1559.	Wylcocke, John, Comshode, par. Cuckwold, Dec. 20, 1559 (sic.)	15	3	322
Mar.20, 1560.	———, William, Kelbroughe (bur. Thorneton), husbn., Jan.13, 1561.	16		171
May 13, 1557.	Wyld, John, Lytle Leake (Notts.), husbandman, Apl. 8, 1557.	15	2	133
Apl. 22, 1562.	———, Julian, West Leaske (Notts.), Oct. 13, 1561.	17		178
Oct. 6, 1557.	Wylde, Martyne, Blythe (Notts.), yeoman, May 26, 1557.	15	2	12
Oct. 8, 1567.	———, Robert, Little Leake (Notts.), Dec. 26, 1566.	17		728
Apl. 27, 1558.	Wyldman, John, Celsied (bur. Horton), Jan. 27, 1556.	15	2	199
Sep. 3, 1558.	Wyle, Christopher, Kesweke, par. Harwood, Sep. 8, 1556.	15	3	98

A.D. 1554 TO 1568.

		Vol.	Pt.	Fol.
Mar.27, 1565.	Wyle, Thomas, Risse, Sep. 6, 1564.	17		418
Oct. 1, 1561.	Wyles, John, Lockyngton, Aug. 20, 1561.	17		45
Sep. 26, 1558.	Wylice, Roger, Wistone (Whiston, bur. St. Mary Magdl.), Sep. 6,1558.	15	3	54
Dec. 20, 1560.	Wylie. Thomas, Ottringham, Oct. 15, 1560.	16		137
Nov.25, 1555.	——, Umfrey, Vu'be [Yearby], par. Lethome, husbn., Aug.28, 1555.	14		183
Apl. 11, 1559.	——, William, Bylbrough, Nov. 20, 1558.	15	3	333
Sep. 28, 1557.	Wylkinson, Henry, Kelbroke (bur. Thorneton), Feb. 23, 1556.	15	1	340
Sep. 28, 1557.	————, Thomas, Allerton, par. Kepax, Aug. 20, 1557.	15	1	371
Feb. 9, 1557.	Wylkyn, Robert, Goxill, Oct. 4, 1557.	15	2	124
Mar.30, 1559.	Wylkynson, Christopher, Routh, husbandman, Feb. 6, 1558.	15	3	299
Sep. 26, 1558.	————, Edmond, Atterclif, par. Shefeld, Aug. 2, 1558.	15	3	51
Jan. 22, 1557.	————, John, Carleton in Clevelande, Nov. 7, 1557.	15	2	158
Dec. 16, 1557.	————, Lyonell, Rowthe, husbandman, Nov. 8, 1557.	15	2	43
Apl. 15, 1559.	————, Richard, Roydhall, par. Bradford, Dec. 21, 1558.	15	3	351
Feb. 17, 1561.	————, Robert, Carlton in Lyndreke (Notts.), yeoman, Nov. 20, 1561.	17		13
Nov.11, 1557.	Wylkynsonne, Thomas, Preston, Oct. 6, 1557.	15	2	101
Jan. 22, 1557.	————————, William, Gysburne, Dec, 1, 1557.	15	2	159
Apl. 9, 1562.	Wylliamson, Nycholas, Barton, par. Crawme, Jan. 7. 1561.	17		161
Nov.14, 1555.	————, Thomas, Mikelfeilde, par. Shereborne, Jan. 25, 1554.	14		200
Oct. 1, 1557.	Wyllson, Jennett, Wylton in Cleveland, widow, Jan. 14, 1557.	15	1	362
Oct. 3, 1555.	——, John, Barnabye (Cleveland), Aug. 27, 1555.	14		177
Sep. 28, 1557.	——, John, Carleton (Craven), July 7, 1557.	15	1	336
Apl. 27, 1558.	——, Leonerd, Buckdayne, Oct. 2, 1557.	15	2	203
Dec. 14, 1557.	——, Leonerd, Hull, sherman, Sep. 13, 1557.	15	1	359
Dec. 13, 1557.	——, Myles, Snytall (bur. Normanton), gentleman, Nov. 17,1557.	15	2	53
Sep. 21, 1557.	——, Richard, Atheweke by the streite, May 20, 1557.	15	1	354
Oct. 22, 1560.	——, Thomas, Hunmanbe, labourer, Mar. 12, 1559.	16		128
Jan. 10, 1557.	——, William, Appleton in the strete, Nov. 1, 1557.	15	2	77
Nov. 6, 1557.	Wyllsonne, John, Elkysley (Notts.), July 2, 1557.	15	2	109
May 28, 1560.	Wyllye, Thomas, South Oterington, Mar. 17, 1560.	16		68
Apl. 13, 1559.	Wylshe, Michill, Holme in Spaldingmore, Dec. 29, 1558.	15	3	348
Mar.30, 1560.	Wylson, Elizabeth, Thornbawrghe (bur. S. Kylventon), Oct. 14,1559.	16		24
Apl. 27, 1558.	——, Heugh, preist, Kirkburton, Mar. 20, 1557.	15	2	190
May 28, 1560.	——, John, keper of the great parke of Topclyffe, Mar. 27, 1560.	16		68
Mar.19, 1559.	——, Robert, Kyrkbie Overblows, husbandman, Jun. 5, 1559.	16		13
Mar.24, 1555.	——, Robert, Ottringham Ma[r]she, Mar. 16, 1555.	14		306
Mar.14, 1560.	——, Robert, Shelforthe (Notts.), labourer, Dec. 16, 1560.	16		163
Oct. 10, 1560.	——, Thomas, Westhorpe, par. Southwell (Notts.), husbn., 1560.	16		124
Apl. 18, 1560.	——, William, Braywell, May 28, 1559.	16		32
Mar.10, 1555.	Wylsonn. John, Newarke (Notts.), marcer, Aug. 3, 1546.	14		226
May 12, 1559.	——, Margaret, wid. of Robt. W., Chereburton, husbn., Jan. 20, 1558.	15	3	392
Jun. 22, 1568.	Wylye, Henry, Bridlington, husbandman, July 22, 1567.	17		826
Mar.27, 1560.	——, Peter, Urbye, par. Kirkelethome, Nov. 16, 1559.	16		20
Jan. 14, 1560.	Wymake, John, Eastretford (Notts.), drovier, Oct. 22, 1560.	16		144
Apl. 24, 1559.	Wynchope, Peter, Lynton (bur. Spofforthe), Nov. 2, 1558.	15	3	310
May 9, 1565.	Wyndle, Christopher, Thornton (Craven), Apl. 25, 1565.	17		432
Apl. 26, 1558.	Wyndros, Thomas (bur. Kirkeham), Apl. 1, 1558.	15	2	204
Sep. 28, 1557.	Wynklay, Roger, Aighton, par. Mytton (Lanc.), gent., Aug. 1, 1556.	15	1	339
May 2, 1566.	Wynkley, Alice. Haughton, par. Mitton, widow, Mar. 1, 1564.	17		530
Oct. 6, 1557.	Wynney, John, Plumtrey (Notts.), Aug. 14, 1557.	15	2	31
No date.	Wynsley, Isabell, Wytley (bur. Kellington), wid., Aug. 10, 1558 (incomplete).	15	3	67
May 6, 1563.	Wyntchbecke, William, Cottam (Notts.), husbandman, Jan. 7, 1562.	17		243
Jan. 30, 1555.	Wynter. Thomas, Brynnesforth, par. Rotherham, Jun. 26, 1555.	15	1	2
May 17, 1565.	——, Thomas, Kilvinton (Notts.), husbandman, Nov. 30, 1564.	17		436
Oct. 23, 1566.	Wynterskaylle, Edward, Rypon, Aug. 30, 1566.	17		586
Jun. 27, 1567.	Wynterskill, Richard, Rippon, glover. Jun. 20, 1567.	17		660
July 26, 1558.	Wynteryngham, John, Thorngombaley, par. Paule, Feb. 8, 1557.	15	3	11
Dec. 5, 1567.	Wyntringham, Henry, Camerton (bur. Paull), Sep. 14, 1567.	17		741
Oct. 30, 1554.	Wyntryngham, Elizabeth, Cottingham, widow, July 22, 1554.	14		288

A.D. 1554 TO 1568.

		Vol.	Pt.	Fol.
July 2, 1561.	Wyntryngham, John, Morehouse, par. Burton Agnes, Oct. 20, 1560.	17		77
Mar. 13, 1558.	————, Robert, Carcroft, par. Owston, Sep. 23, 1558.	15	3	162
Dec. 22, 1556.	————, Thomas, Athwyke by the strete, Aug. 23, 1556.	15	1	84
Feb. 17, 1561.	Wyntworthe, Richard, Bawtre, Jan. 20, 1561.	17		13
No date.	Wynytte, Robert, Sykehowse par. Fishelake, Jan. 30, 1554.	14		85
May 21, 1565.	Wysdall, William, curat of Welwicke, Mar. 31, 1564.	17		442
Oct. 3, 1554.	Wyske, Martyn, Barniston (Holderness), Aug. 22, 1554.	14		43
Mar. 8, 1558.	Wyst (? West), John, Leckenfeild, husbandman, Feb. 12, 1558.	15	3	157
May 5, 1558.	Wytheid, Richard, Langwith, par. Cowknay (Notts.), Mar. 6, 1557.	15	2	283
May 18, 1559.	Wyttakeres, William, Hueton Pannell, husbandman, Sep. 26, 1558.	15	3	398
Apl. 20, 1559.	Wytton, Robert, Southleverton (Notts.), husbandman, Feb. 20, 1558.	15	3	366
May 9, 1565.	————, Thomas, the Rawffeholles als. Alderhouse or Paynehill, par. Slaidburne, Apl. 17, 1561.	17		434
Mar. 21, 1559.	Wytwange, William, Wethernseye, husbandman, Dec. 14, 1559.	16		17
May 2, 1560.	Wyvell, John, Cayton, Oct. 26, 1559.	16		41
Aug. 26, 1558.	————, Marmaduke (bur. Massham), esquire, Aug. 8, 1558.	15	2	292
Apl. 4, 1555.	————, Peter, Cottingham, Jan. 10, 1554.	14		23
Oct. 6, 1557.	Yaittes, John, Missyn (Notts.), July 20, 1557.	15	2	7
Aug. 4, 1558.	Yates, Thomas, Hull, lyghterman, Mar. 31, 1558.	15	3	5
Aug. 12, 1566.	Yarwithe, Thomas, Fishelaike, talier, Dec. 28, 1563.	17		566
May 6, 1557.	Yeadon, Thomas, Over Yeadon (bur. Gieslaie), Apl. 12, 1557.	15	1	256
Feb. 4, 1561.	Yeates, William, Great Thirklebe, husbandman, Aug. 20, 1558.	17		11
Oct. 20, 1558.	————, William, Topliffe, Aug. 9, 1558.	15	2	345
July 1, 1556.	Yedall als. Chasterton, Thomas, Kyrkestall, par. Ledes, Aug. 7, 1555.	15	1	51
Dec. 22, 1556.	Yeewith, Thomas, Barnby (Doncaster), May 6, 1554.	15	1	76
May 19, 1554.	Yemondson, James, Kirklington (Notts.), husbandman, Feb. 18, 1552.	14		110
Mar. 30, 1555.	Yevot, William, Bradmore, bur. Bonney (Notts.), Aug. 20, 1546.	14		15
Oct. 6, 1557.	Yevott, James, Bradmore, par. Bonney (Notts.), Aug. 2, 1557.	15	2	28
Apl. 16, 1562.	Ygkeson, John (bur. Thornton, Craven), Jan. 18, 156[1-]2.	17		190
Mar. 6, 1556.	Ykson, Edward, West Retfurth (Notts.), Oct. 31, 1556.	15	1	183
Feb. 3, 1561.	[1] Yllingworthe, John, Waterfriston, Aug. 21, 1561.	17		10
Oct. 5, 1558.	————, Robert, Manyham, par. Bradford, Aug. 7, 1558.	15	3	65
Dec. 3, 1560.	Yllytson, William, Wylberfosse, labourer, Jan. 10, 1558.	16		134
May 5, 1558.	[1] Yngald, Thomas, Gamulstone (Notts.), Sep. 6, 1556.	15	2	245
Aug. 7, 1565.	[1] Yngall, Thomas, Scrobye (Notts.), Mar. 22, 1564.	17		459
Jan. 13, 1558.	Yngilbie, William, Blythe (Notts.), yeoman, Sep. 24, 1558.	15	3	18
Feb. 6, 1558.	Yngill, William, Rosyngton, Oct. 12, 1558.	15	3	254
Jan. 18, 1558.	[1] Yngham, Richard, Heptonstall, Sep. 23, 1558.	15	3	212
Sep. 26, 1558.	[2] Yngland, Christopher, Wombwell, par. Darfeld, July 29, 1558.	15	3	53
May 4, 1557.	————, Thomas, Bentley (bur. Arkesaye), Feb. 18, 1556.	15	1	280
May 4, 1557.	————, William, Howtone Pannell, husbandman, Jan. 21, 1556.	15	1	281
Feb. 4, 1556.	[1] Yngle, Nicholas, Rotherham, tanner, Dec. 24, 1556.	15	1	170
Oct. 20, 1558.	————, William, Stoiles, par. Rotheram, Nov. 18, 1558.	15	3	152
Jun. 30, 1567.	Yngolbie, William, Huton Wandslay, par. Marston, Mar. 15, 1566.	17		661
May 5, 1558.	[1] Yngrame, Robert, Karyltone in Lynreke (Notts.), Oct. 10, 1557.	15	2	244
Feb. ult., 1560.	[1] Ynman, John, Garnshay, par. Lynton, Sep. 25, 1557.	16		151
Apl. 11, 1559.	Yoille, Thomas, Saxton, Jan. 10, 1558.	15	3	332
Jan. 12, 1558.	Yole, Robert, Wheldrike, Sep. 8, 1558.	15	3	172
Jan. 14, 1558.	Yong, George, Ripon, tanner, Nov. 16, 1558.	15	3	191
Oct. 22, 1558.	————, John, Great Ayton, Sep. 12, 1558.	15	3	234
Jun. 18, 1557.	————, Thomas, Harelthrope (bur. Bubwith), husbandman, Jun. 2, 1557.	15	1	293
Jan. 22, 1567.	Yonge, Andro, Skipseyburghe, Dec. 10, 1567.	17		751
May 2, 1566.	————, Anthony, Appiltrewicke, par. Burnsall, gent., Apl. 5, 1566.	17		528
Oct. 1, 1556.	————, Christopher (bur. Newton in Cleveland), July 6, 1556.	15	1	68
Feb. 18, 1558.	————, Eling (bur. Rypon), widow, Nov. 25, 1558.	15	3	275
Mar. 7, 1554.	————, Henry, Topclif, Mar. 15, 1552.	14		302
Oct. 13, 1565.	————, John, Ormesbe, Apl. 12, 1565.	17		475
May 19, 1554.	————, John, Sutton on Darwent, husbandman, May 2, 1554.	14		6
Jun. 2, 1568.	————, John, Wilberfosse, husbandman, Feb. 25, 1563.	17		806
Apl. 20, 1564.	————, Percivall, Inglebie, Nov. 1, 1563.	17		335

[1] See also under letter I.   [2] See also under letters E. and I.

A.D. 1554 TO 1568.

	Vol.	Pt.	Fol.
May 10, 1567. Yonge, Richard, Hayton (Notts.), Oct. 11, 8 Eliz.	17		653
May 26, 1564. ———, Robert, Ellerton, singleman, Apl. 25, 1564.	17		345
Jun. 4, 1561. ———, Rowland (bur. Kildaill), Dec. 11, 1560.	17		66
Aug. 2, 1560. ———, Thomas, Brissell, par. Brandisburton, husbn., Apl. 28, 1560.	16		99
May 10, 1565. ———, Thomas, Rosse in Holderness, mylner, Mar. 25, 1565.	17		423
Dec. 14, 1557. ———, Vyncent, Beverlay, glover, Nov. 20, 1557.	15	2	49
Feb. 10, 1557. ———, William, Beverlay, mariner, Jan. 7, 1557.	15	2	149
May 10, 1559. ———, William, Garthone, gentleman, Jun. 21, 1558.	15	3	390
Jun. 11, 1562. ———, William, Great Kelke, par. Foston, Dec. 9, 1561.	17		87
July 18, 1567. Yonger, Thomas, York, labourer, Mar. 20, 1566.	17		673
Oct. 14, 1556. ———, Richard, York, gentleman, Sep. 20, 1554.	15	1	104
May 10, 1565. Yorke, Thomas, Kirkby Knowlle, yeoman, Dec. 15, 1564.	17		430
Mar. 8, 1558. Younge, Edward, Cottingham, July 3, 1558.	15	3	158
Mar. 21, 1560. ———, Hewghe, Brantingham, Dec. 17, 1558.	16		173
Apl. 28, 1558. ———, Peter, Santon, millner, Mar. 2, 1557.	15	2	220
Dec. 15, 1557. Yourle, John, Eylkeslay (Notts.), Jun. 28, 1557.	15	2	58
Mar. 16, 1559. Yoye (Joye, Act Bk.), William, Huntyngton, husbn., Feb. 3, 1558.	16		10
Dec. 1, 1563. Yoyle (Yowle), John, Rotherham, Jun. 6, 1563.	17		306
Dec. 5, 1567. [1] Ysbell, Henry, Hulbanke, par. Cottingham, butcher, July 4, 1567.	17		749
Sep. 26, 1558. Ysott, Richard, Thribargh, Aug. 8, 1558.	15	3	54
Aug. 9, 1563. Yssott, John, Dirtcar, yeoman, Apl. 10, 1563.	17		271

[1] See also under letter I.

APPENDIX.

Index to the Administration Acts taken from the Act Books, 1553 to 1568.

Jan. 19, 1557. Atkynson, Hughe, Haitfeld, Process, *Doncaster*.
July 20, 1560. ———, Joanne als. Jane, Womerslay, infant, *Vacancy*, Fol. 62.
Sep. 30, 1558. ———, Thomas, Ripon, cook, *Craven*.
Nov. 7, 1564. ———, William, Wethernesay, *Holderness*.
Oct. 1, 1557. Atkynsone, Agnes Semer, widow, *Cleveland*.
Jan. 27, 1560. ———, Leonard, Byrdsall, *Vacancy*, Fol. 98.
Oct. 1, 1557. ———, Ralph, Semer, *Cleveland*.
May 5, 1558. Austeler, Alexander, Rampton, *Southwell*.
Nov. 5, 1558. Awbraye, Adam, Barneslaye, *Doncaster*.
Feb.penult.,1556. Awchon, John, Hull, *Harthill*.
Apl. 4, 1565. Awmonde, Thomas, London, *Holderness*.
Sep. 24, 1563. Awnebie, Robert and Joan, Sherwod hall, infants, *Pontefract*.
Feb. 4, 1567. Babthorpe, Guy, Gowle, *Bulmer*.
Feb. 17, 1560. Backus, Thomas, Esington in Cleveland, *Vacancy*, Fol. 103.
Nov. 6, 1560. Baildon, Nicholas, Baildon, par. Ottley, *Vacancy*, Fol. 85.
Mar.29, 1568. Baiteman, Henry, Myklefeild. *Ainsty*.
Oct. 5, 1558. Baites, William, *Pontefract*.
May 5, 1559. Baitman, John, Kellington, priest, *Pontefract*.
May 29, 1562. Balay, Robert, Howke, *Bulmer*.
Sep. 28, 1557. Baley, Thomas, Bradforth, par. Mitton, *Craven*.
Sep. 30, 1557. Bambroghe, John, Pollyngton, par. Snathe, *Bulmer*.
Oct. 27, 1563. Bancke, William, Diocese of Worcester, *Pontefract*.
Dec. 1, 1558. Bankes, Henry, Beverley, *Beverley*.
May 5, 1559. ———, William, Rotherham, infant, *Doncaster*.
Nov. 9, 1557. Barbar, William, Duysburye, *Pontefract*.
Feb. 9, 1557. Barcharde, Dionisius, Skeftlynge, *Holderness*.
Jan. 16, 1566. Barker, Elizabeth, Gisburne, *Cleveland*.
Apl. 6, 1566. ———, Henry, Great Thirklebye, *Bulmer*.
July 30, 1567. ———, Isabella, Tadcaster, *Ainsty*.
Sep. 30, 1557. ———, Peter, Rednes, *Bulmer*.
May 5, 1568. ———, Thomas, Lund, *Harthill*.
Mar.18, 1562. ———, William, Snathe, infant, *Bulmer*.
Dec. 11, 1566. Barmebye, Roger, Hunmanbye, *Dickering*.
Oct. 25, 1560. Barnard, Laurence, Egton, *Vacancy*, Fol. 84.
Apl. 18, 1566. Barnarde, Christopher, Farnelay, *Ainsty*.
Jan. 16, 1556. Barnebie, Edward, Hull, schoolmaster, *Harthill*.
Oct. 7, 1557. Barrytt, Robert, Newarke, tanner, *Newark*.
Apl. 29, 1568. Bassett, Michael, Felicekirke, *Bulmer*.
Oct. 23, 1557. Bateman, Adam, Swynflet, *Bulmer*.
May 5, 1559. ———, John, Kellington, *Pontefract*.
Sep. 4, 1557. ———, Richard, Worsoppe, *Retford*.
Apl. 7, 1559. Battell, Joan, Lumbie, widow, *Ainsty*.
Apl. 26, 1563. Baxster, John, Sherpehill, par. Drax, *Ainsty*.
Dec. 22, 1556. ———, Richard, Aston, *Doncaster*.
May 14, 1557. Bayley, Edward, Roulston, *Newark*.
Mar.27, 1568. ———, Elizabeth, daughter of Robert B., Gowle, Curation, *Bulmer*.
May 19, 1559. Baylyer, Edward, Howke, *Bulmer*.
Apl. 22, 1562. Bayne, George, Ferybye, *Retford*.
Jan. 18, 1560. ———, William, Spofforth, *Vacancy*, Fol. 96.
Nov. 8, 1557. Bayns, Ralph, Calcoottes, par. Leedes, *Ainsty*.
Nov. 3, 1558. Baytes, William, Dunyngton, *Pontefract*.
Feb. 10, 1562. Beall, William, Egbroughe, *Pontefract*.
Aug.13, 1562. Beamond, John, Hipperom, par. Hallyfax, *Pontefract*.
Sep. 23, 1561. ———, Thomas, Myrfeld, *Vacancy*, Fols. 132 and 133.
Oct. 2, 1561. Beamonde, Thomas, Myrfede, *Pontefract*.
Mar.22, 1558. Beamonte, Leonard, Brighouse, *Pontefract*.
Sep. 4, 1557. Beckewithe, Peter, Ledes, *Ainsty*.
Nov.23, 1558. Becrofte, James, Appletrewicke, Caveat, *Craven*.
Jun. 15, 1557. Bedfurthe, Anne, Staynbor, par. Silkeston, singularis, *Doncaster*.
Dec. 12, 1556. & Mar. 27, 1557. Beilbie, Anna, Cayton, widow, *Dickering*.
Apl. 26, 1559. Beilbie, John, Thweing, *Dickering*.
Aug.19, 1557. Beilbye, Peter, Caton, *Rydall*.
May —, 1567. Bell, James, Hull, *Harthill*.
July 5, 1557. ———, John, Oborne, par. Bridlington, priest (Will afterwards), *Dickering*.

Feb. 27, 1566.	Bell, Robert, Hull, *Harthill*.
Sep. 30, 1557.	——, Robert, Hull, *Harthill*.
May 6, 1563.	Bellamy, John, junr., Tuxford, *Retford*.
Mar. 31, 1557.	——, Thomas, Hull, Oath of Admx., *Harthill*.
Apl. 22, 1562.	——, Thomas, Laneham, *Retford*.
Sep. 1, 1565.	Beneson, Joan, Kylton, widow, *Cleveland*.
Aug. 11, 1562.	Benson, John, Medston, co. Kent, *Bulmer*.
Feb. 24, 1567.	——, Margaret, Beverley, widow, *Harthill*.
May 5, 1568.	——, Thomas, Beverley, *Harthill*.
Feb. 18, 1567.	Benthame, Laurence, Horton in Riblesdaill, *Craven*.
Aug. 4, 1558.	Bentley, Peter, Hesill, *Harthill*.
May 13, 1557.	Bett, Alice, North Wheatlie, widow, *Retford*.
Dec. 20, 1565.	Beuerley, Agnes, Brystweke, infant, *Holderness*.
Jan. 17, 1565.	——, Thomas and Alice, *Holderness*.
Oct. 2, 1560.	Billamye, Edward, Rosse, *Vacancy*, Fol. 76.
Jun. 21, 1563.	Bilbowe, Robert, York, *City*.
May 30, 1560.	Birkhead, Agnes, Leedes, *Vacancy*, Fol. 45.
May 26, 1561.	Bladworthe, William, Bramwith, *Doncaster*.
Jan. 14, 1564.	Blaike, Anne, Scoreby, infant, *Harthill*.
Aug. 22, 1558.	——, Thomas, Scoreby, *Bulmer*.
Oct. 12, 1562.	Blaiston, Henry, Etton, *Holderness*.
Jan. 30, 1560.	——, Henry, Etton, *Vacancy*, Fol. 100.
Dec. 3, 1567.	Blakburne, Edward, Myrfeld, *Pontefract*.
Jan. 5, 1557.	Blakwell, Christopher, Skamston, *Buckrose*.
Aug. 28, 1561.	Blankenall, John, Eaton, *Retford*.
Feb. 16, 1558.	Blansherd, Christopher, Bubwith, *Harthill*.
Mar. 2, 1559.	Blith, John, Hutton Wandislay *als.* Marstone, *Vacancy*, Fol. 3.
Sep. 24, 1566.	Blythe, John, Robert, and Elizabeth, Elloughton, *Harthill*.
Mar. 19, 1564.	Bodye, Robert, Burton Agnes, *Dickering*.
May 18, 1559.	Boithe, John, Langwith, *Retford*.
May 13, 1557.	Bolton, Margaret, Est Retford, widow, *Retford*.
Oct. 2, 1560.	——, William, Bolton Percie, *Vacancy*, Fol. 75.
July 29, 1558.	—— *als.* Powton, William, Byland Abbey, *Bulmer*.
Oct. 6, 1564.	Borfoyt, Peter, Gowxhill, *Holderness*.
Oct. 10, 1562.	Bosomworthe, Bartholomew, Sutton sub. Whistonclyffe, *Bulmer*.
Apl. 27, 1558.	Bothe, Thomas, Mylshay, *Pontefract*.
Oct. 5, 1558.	——, Thomas, Netherton, *Pontefract*.
Sep. 16, 1560.	Bouthe, Matilda, Shiplaye, par. Bradforth, spinster, *Vacancy*, Fol. 69.
Sep. 10, 1563.	Bowes, Edward, York, *City*.
Jun. 26, 1557.	——, William, Rowston, *Doncaster*.
Sep. 1, 1558.	Bowne, Cuthbert, Heyldinglay, *Rydall*.
Sep. 23, 1558.	Boyce, John, Kyrkebymisperton, *Rydall*.
Apl. 15, 1562.	Boys, William, Semer, *Clevelavd*.
Nov. 25, 1558.	Boythe, Edmond, Roclif, par. Snathe, *Bulmer*.
Apl. 20, 1559.	Bradford, Agnes, Retford, *Retford*.
Feb. 17, 1561.	——, John, and Agnes, his wife, *Retford*.
Dec. 1, 1564.	Bradfurthe, Elizabeth, Tichill, widow, *Doncaster*.
Oct. 4, 1564.	Bradley, Richard, Waterfryston, *Pontefract*.
May 2, 1566.	——, Robert, Skeflynge, *Holderness*.
Apl. 3, 1566.	——, Thomas, Egton, clerk, *Cleveland*.
Jun. 12, 1564.	—— *als.* Clarke, Richard and Elizabeth, Watterfryston, *Pontefract*.
Mar. 30, 1558.	Braithwait, Robert, Womelton, *Rydall*.
Sep. 22, 1558.	Brandesbie, Richard, student at Lovanium, *Ainsty*.
Mar. 15, 1559.	Brasse, Peter, Stokesley, *Cleveland*.
Feb. 22, 1566.	Brereton, Humphrey, York, *City*.
Apl. 27, 1564.	Brian, Elizabeth, *Retford*.
Aug. 4, 1558.	Brige, John, Ovenden, *Pontefract*.
Sep. 30, 1556.	Brigge, Christopher, Staynton, *Craven*.
Apl. 14, 1562.	Brigham, Robert, North Dalton, *Harthill*.
Oct. 1, 1558.	Brighous, John, Hipperom, *Pontefract*.
Apl. 12, 1559.	Broke, John, Dalton, par. Kirkeheaton, *Pontefract*.
May 1, 1557.	Brokelsbie, Robert, Glentworthe, co. Linc., esquire, *Harthill*.
Dec. 10, 1561.	Brokes, William, Welburne, *Ridall*.
Apl. 30, 1556.	Brombe, Johan, Nottingham, widow, *Nottingham*.

Sep. 25, 1560. Brooke, Joan, Huddersfeld, widow, *Vacancy*, Fol. 69.
Aug. 20, 1556. ———, Thomas, Hull, merchant, *Harthill*.
Jan. 6, 1558. Broud, Richard, Selbie, to Costance, relict, *Bulmer*.
Oct. 1, 1567. Browne, Frances, Donnyngton, *Holderness*.
Sep. 6, 1558. ———, Gilbert, Wakefeld, *Pontefract*.
Apl. 28, 1558. ———, Johan, Ripon, *Craven*.
Sep. 29, 1557. ———, Johan, Ripon, widow, *Craven*.
Sep. 24, 1561. ———, Katherine, Moremonkton, widow, *Ainsty*.
Dec. 17, 1563. ———, Margaret, Lepyngton, *Buckrose*.
May 18, 1559. ———, Ralph, Sutton, *Holderness*.
Apl. 24, 1559. ———, Thomas, Sutton, par. Brotherton, *Ainsty*.
Jun. 18, 1562. ———, Thomas, York, tanner, *City*.
Mar. 7, 1561. Brownrigg, William, Lokington, *Harthill*.
Feb. 22, 1563. Bryscoo, Thomas, North Burton, *Harthill*.
Aug. 2, 1557. Bucke, William, Hompton, *Holderness*.
Dec. 18, 1556. Buckshawe, Richard, York, cook, *City*.
May 9, 1566. Buckton, William, New Malton, *Ridall*.
Oct. 7, 1558. Bulloke, Richard, Hovingham, Adm. with Will, *Rydall*.
Feb. 6, 1558. Bulsone, Thomas, Burton Agnes, *Dickering*.
Jun. 20, 1568. Bunbye, John, Lanam, *Retford*.
Mar. 26, 1567. Bunnye, George, Ferybrigges, *Pontefract*.
July 11, 1558. Burdheed, Robert, Doncaster, *Doncaster*.
Jan. 16, 1561. Burdsall, Joan, Cottingham, infant, *Harthill*.
Dec. 6, 1561. ———, Joan, Dunsall, infant, *Harthill*.
Dec. 17, 1561. Burgh, Alexander, Rither, *Ainsty*.
Apl. 16, 1565. Burland, Agnes and Jane, children of John B. of Stokton (Peculiar of Bugthorpe), Tuition, *City*.
Dec. 8, 1561. Burne, Margaret, Bramwith, *Doncaster*.
Nov. 10, 1563. ———, William, Chereburton, *Harthill*.
Feb. 7, 1560. Burnet, Henry, Esingwold, *Vacancy*, Fol. 101.
July 8, 1559. Burton, Giles, Wakefeld, *Pontefract*.
July 23, 1567. ———, Joan, Heslington, widow, *City*.
Mar. 6, 1556. ———, John, Mathersay, *Retford*.
Jun. 30, 1561. ———, Robert, Catton, *Bulmer*.
Sep. 23, 1557. ———, Thomas, Kirkbie Moreshead (*sic*), *Craven*.
May 13, 1558. ———, Thomas, Wistowe, *Ainsty*.
July 18, 1562. ———, William, Nonapleton, *Ainsty*.
May 26, 1567. Buryman, Joan, Wycame, *Ridall*.
Mar. 24, 1563. Butler, Christopher, Wheldrike, *Bulmer*.
Feb. 4, 1561. ——, Edward, Byngley, *Vacancy*, Fol. 146.
Mar. 4, 1561. ——, Edward, Bingley, *Ainsty*.
Mar. 19, [1556]. ——, Thomas, West Norton, par. Bingley, *Craven*.
Jun. 26, 1556. Butterfeld, William, West Morton, *Craven*.
Dec. 14, 1565. Butterfelde *als.* Persye, John, Newcastle on Tyne, *Ainsty*.
Mar. 6, 1560. Byer, Isabell, Basinbie, widow, *Vacancy*, Fol. 112.
Jan. 9, 1562. Bylott, William, Kylnsey, *Holderness*.
Jan. 22, 1567. Bylton, John, Pattrington, *Holderness*.
May 10, 1566. Bylytt, Robert, Swyne, *Holderness*.
Oct. 6, 1557. Byngham, William, Burton, *Retford*.
Feb. 4, 1567. Bynkes, John, and Elizabeth his wife, York, *City*.
July 11, 1558. Bynnyngley, John, Sandall, par. Doncaster, *Doncaster*.
Apl. 27, 1558. Byns, Isabella, widow, *Craven*.
Aug. 13, 1567. Byrkebye, William, Selbye, *Bulmer*.
Dec. 10, 1566. Bywell, William, York, *City*.
Apl. 23, 1563. Cade, William, Allerton, *Retford*.
Apl. 27, 1558. Calie, Christopher, Hollegille, *Craven*.
Oct. 3, 1565. Calverley, Christopher, Ferybrigges, *Pontefract*.
Aug. 25, 1564. ———, William, Calverley, *Pontefract*.
Feb. 9, 1558. Calvert, Brian, Tunstall, par. Aiton, *Cleveland*.
July 2, 1566. Calverte *als.* Cawood, Joan and William, Hull, infants, *Harthill*.
Feb. 10, 1558. Cannabye, Matilda, Haitfeld, *Holderness*.
Mar. 23, 1556. Capper, Agnes, Wyeston, par. Claworthe, widow, *Retford*.
Mar. 2, 1560. Care, Stephen, Welweke in Holderness, *Vacancy*, Fol. 107.
Nov. 12, 1566. Carlell, John, Rillington, *Buckrose*.

25

Oct. 6, 1564, & Jun. 13, 1565. Constable, Marmaduke, Cottingham, esq., *Adm. de bonis non, Harthill.*
Jan. 18, 1565. Constable, Marmaduke, Wassan, esquire, *Adm. de bonis non, Holderness.*
Mar.29, 1559, & Aug. 8, 1564. Constable, Marmaduke, Wassand, esquier, *Holderness.*
Mar.24, 1567. Constable, Thomas, Burdsall, *Buckrose.*
Oct. 18, 1558. ———, Thomas, Stillingflete, *Bulmer.*
Sep. 30, 1558. Cony *als.* Meltynby, John, Order to exhibit inventory, *City.*
Nov.30, 1566. Conyers, Antony, Scarbroughe, *Dickering.*
July 9, 1565. ———, Rogers, Lythe, infant, *Cleveland.*
July 15, 1559. Cooke, John, Haywod, par. Burghwalles, *Doncaster.*
Apl. 18, 1560. ———, William, Howghton, *Vacancy,* Fol. 22.
May 10, 1559. ———, Thomas, Warter, *Harthill.*
July 17, 1561. ——— *als.* Ward, John, Naburne, *Bulmer.*
Mar. 5, 1555. Cootes, Thomas, Wyntryngham, *Dickering.*
July 18, 1556. Coppindale, John, Barnebie haull, Adm. with Will, *Bulmer.*
May 5, 1564. Corner, Thomas, Upledam, *Cleveland.*
Feb. 17, 1561. Cornyng, Hugh, Sawnbye, *Retford.*
Aug. 1, 1566. Cotes, Thomas, Helmesley, *Cleveland.*
Feb.ult.,1561. Cowerd, Alice, widow of William C., Cudsworth, *Doncaster.*
Aug. 2, 1561. Cowke, John, Pollington, par. Snath, *Ainsty.*
Apl. 13, 1559. Cowling, Tristian, Wawghan, *Holderness.*
Nov. 8, 1565. Cowpeland, Robert, Brydlington, Sequestration, *Dickering.*
Oct. 7. 1557. Cowper, Richard, Rampton, *Southwell.*
Oct. 29, 1558. ———, Robert, Scardbroughe, *Dickering.*
Mar.17, 1563. Cowton, Mary, Carnetbye, *Dickering.*
July 27, 1563. Coye, John, Weton, par. Wellweke, infant, *Holderness.*
July 27, 1567. Coyne, Peter, Danby, *Cleveland.*
July 27, 1567. ———, William, Danbye, *Cleveland.*
Feb. 18, 1556. Coyttes, William, Skampston, *Buckrose.*
Oct. 7, 1558. Crabtre, Thomas, Heptonstall, *Pontefract.*
Mar.13, 1567. Craike, Walter, Ganton, *Holderness.*
Nov.19, 1567. Crane, George, *Retford.*
Feb.12, 1560. Crawe, Joan, Marske, *Vacancy,* Fol. 103.
Oct. 16, 1558. Crawshaye, John, Sutton, par. Nortone, *Buckrose.*
Dec. 14, 1562. Cressewell, Henry, Hull, alderman, *Harthill.*
Oct. 7, 1558. Grier, William, Ovenden, par. Hallifax, *Pontefract.*
May 2, 1566. Crofte, John, Emsay, par. Skipton, *Craven.*
Dec. 4, 1564. Crombocke,John,junr.,son of Antony and Dulsabella C.,Kellington, *Pontefract.*
Apl. 17, 1567. Crosdaill, John, *Craven.*
July 15, 1567. Crosedaill, John, Langbar, *Craven.*
Apl. 3, 1559. Crosse, Thomas, Bucketon, *Dickering.*
May 19, 1559. Crowston, William, Roclife, *Bulmer.*
Sep. 2, 1567. Cudbert, Agnes, Gillimore, *Ridall.*
Feb.16, 1558. Cudworth, Richard, Silkeston, *Doncaster.*
Apl. 28, 1568. Curtis, Barnard and Janet, Cawood, *Ainsty.*
Jan. 10, 1561. Curtys, John, Little Ribston, *Ainsty.*
Jun. 9, 1563. Cusson, John, Pollington, *Bulmer.*
July 14, 1558. Cute, Richard, Foston, *Dickering.*
May 18, 1559. Cutforthey, William, Gylfoite, par. Rotheram, *Doncaster.*
July 22, 1567. Cuthbert, Mathew, Gillinge, *Ridall.*
Sep. 30, 1557. Cutler, William, Dodworthe, *Doncaster.*
Sep. 4, 1565. Dacre, Thomas, Lord, Hynderskelfe, *Bulmer.*
Sep. 9, 1556. ———, Thomas, Lord, Kyrkeoswolde, Dioc. Carlisle, *Bulmer.*
Jun. 10, 1564. ———, William, kt., Ld. Dacre of Grastock and Gylsland, Kyrkeoswolde, Dioc. Carlisle, *Bulmer.*
Feb. 1, 1557. Dakyns, Edward, Bransburtone, *Holderness.*
Jan. 24, 1561. Dalton, Margaret, infant, *Harthill.*
Aug.26, 1561. ———, Margaret, dau. of John D., North Froddyngham, *Vacancy,* Fol. 130.
July 23, 1563. Dannyell, Sir John, Doncaster, Sequestration, *City.*
Feb.12, 1563. Danyell, Agnes, Barmbowe, widow, *Pontefract.*
Jun. 27, 1558. ———, Anne, Beswicke, widow, *Harthill.*
Nov. 2, 1563. ———, Sir John, Doncaster, clerk, *Doncaster.*
Sep. 29, 1563. ———, Margaret, Skerdingwell, par. Saxton, *Ainsty.*
Sep. 23, 1566. Darley, James, Brampton, *Doncaster.*

Nov. 13, 1563.	Darley, William, Awstrop, but dying in London, *Ainsty*.
Mar. 8, 1559.	Darling, Walter, Hull, infant, *Vacancy*, Fol. 4.
Oct. 20, 1558.	Darnell, Joan, Welwyke, *Holderness*.
Oct. 17, 1558.	Dawkens, Richard, Couttingham, *Harthill*.
Jun. 23, 1558.	Dawney, George, Befurthe, esq., Commission to enquire as to debts, *Holderness*.
Mar. 28, 1556.	Dawson, Elina, Ecoppe, par. Adle, widow, *Ainsty*.
Apl. 28, 1563.	———, Richard, Flamburgh, *Dickering*.
Nov. 8, 1558.	Day, Robert, Todwicke, *Ainsty*.
Oct. 16, 1557.	———, Thomas, Hessey, par. Moremonkton, *Ainsty*.
Oct. 30, 1566.	———, Thomas, Snaythe, *Bulmer*.
Sep. 29, 1563.	Deane, Richard, Denton, *Ainsty*.
Mar. 1, 1562.	———, Robert and Joane, children of Leonard D., Humbleton, *Holderness*.
Dec. 1, 1558.	Defte, John, Skerne, *Harthill*.
Apl. 3, 1559.	Delicar, Robert, Brydlington, *Dickering*.
Feb. 6, 1558.	Dennand, Thomas, Scardbroughe, *Dickering*.
Apl. 18, 1560.	Denton, George, Darton, *Vacancy*, Fol. 21.
July 5, 1557.	———, John, Silkestone, *Doncaster*.
July 19, 1557.	Depinge, Alice, Sutton on Lounde, *Retford*.
Mar. 4, 1562.	Dickson, Laurence, Bridlington Keye, *Dickering*.
Mar. 29, 1558.	Dighton, Thomas, Hooton Wanselay, *Ainsty*.
Feb. 25, 1562.	Dignell, Joan and Elizabeth, Barleweke, *Craven*.
Dec. 23, 1567.	Dobson, Edward and Joan, Tuition, *Holderness*.
Mar. 29, 1559.	———, Richard, Headon, *Holderness*.
Mar. 18, 1557.	———, Richard, Thriske, *Bulmer*.
Dec. 3, 1561.	———, Robert, vicar of Crowell, co. Linc., *Doncaster*.
Jan. 9, 1565.	Dombler, William, Aldbroughe, infant, *Holderness*.
Jan. 22, 1561.	Done, Antony, Beverley, *Harthill*.
Apl. 14, 1562.	Donne, Cicilie, Beverley, *Harthill*.
Feb. 1, 1558.	———, John, Potto, par. Whorlton, *Cleveland*.
Mar. 6, 1559.	Donnynge, John, Crofton, *Vacancy*, Fol. 4.
July 5, 1557.	——— als. Smythe, John, Doncaster, singularis, *Doncaster*.
Oct. 21, 1558.	Doonne, Thomas, *City*.
Oct. 1, 1567.	Doughty, William, Sutton, *Holderness*.
Jun. 7, 1561.	Doves, John, Whitgifte, *Ainsty*.
Oct. 17, 1567.	Draikes, William, Holey Grayne, *Pontefract*.
Jun. 15, 1565.	Drake, William, Horleygrene, par. Hallifax, Process, *Pontefract*.
Feb. 17, 1561.	Drakes, Nicolas, Fynyngley, *Retford*.
Feb. 25, 1560.	Drape, Agnes, Harpham, *Vacancy*, Fol. 106.
Mar. 23, 1560.	Drew, John, Kaingham, *Vacancy*, Fol. 124.
Oct. 3, 1558.	Drynkrawe, Ursula, Gillinge, widow, *Rydall*.
Dec. 10, 1561.	Ducheburne, Agnes, *Holderness*.
Mar. 21, 1560.	Duffeld, John, Hull, *Vacancy*, Fol. 122.
May 4, 1564.	Duffelde, Agnes, Ripon, *Craven*.
Oct. 13, 1558.	Dynge, John, Southwell, *Southwell*.
July 2, 1561.	Dynwell, John, Thweyng, *Dickering*.
Apl. 20, 1559.	Eastewoode, Thomas, Margait, par. Clarebrough, *Retford*.
Jan. 29, 1558.	Eastofte, Edward, Reidnes, *Bulmer*.
Jun. 14, 1560.	Eaton, William, Fenton, *Vacancy*, Fol. 54.
Oct. 23, 1566.	Edley, Thomas, Marton, *Bulmer*.
Apl. 4, 1565.	Edmondes, Thomas, Hull, merchant, *Harthill*
Oct. 2, 1567.	Elcocke, Thomas, Brayton, *Bulmer*.
Apl. 6, 1560.	Ellerker, Thomas, Lysset, *Vacancy*, Fol. 19.
Dec. 20, 1566.	Ellis, Anthony, Hull, *Harthill*.
Oct. 1, 1561.	Ellyson, William, Holtongill, *Craven*.
Oct. 5, 1558.	Elmden, John, Gisborne, *Cleveland*.
Jun. 12, 1566.	Elyotson, Margaret, Hollome, *Holderness*.
Nov. 19, 1561.	Emerson, Robert, Crambum, *Bulmer*.
Feb. 4, 1561.	———, Vincent, Bolby, par. Esington, *Cleveland*.
July 10, 1557.	Empson, Isabella, Gowlle. par. Snathe, widow, *Bulmer*.
Jan. 14, 1557.	———, Katherine, Holden [Howden], two Adms., *Bulmer*.
Mar. 21, 1557.	Ermette, Agnes, Holme in Spawdyngmore, widow, *Harthill*.
Jan. 22, 1567.	Escrecke, John, Skipsey, *Holderness*.
Mar. 27, 1556.	Esheton, William, Laythome, par. Awghton, *Harthill*.
Apl. 28, 1563.	Estburne, Robert, Estburne, *Craven*.

July 23, 1562.   Estoft, Elizabeth, infant, daughter of Thomas E., Scorbrughe, *Harthill*.
Aug. 5, 1562.   ——, Thomas, Estoft, esquire, *Bulmer*.
Jun. 14, 1566.   Estofte, Christopher, Southburton, esquire, *Harthill*.
Jun. 2, 1558.   Estryge, Alice, Rysse, singularis, *Holderness*.
Feb. 18, 1566.   Eyre, Dorothy, *Retford*.
May 13, 1557.   Eyton, Thomas, Tryswell, *Retford*.
Feb. 5, 1557.   Farebarne, Margaret and Isabella, Attingwike, infants, *Holderness*.
Apl. 16, 1565.   Farley, William, York, *City*.
Feb. 16, 1564.   Fawcett, Richard, Upper Hesleden, *Craven*.
Feb. 5, 1566.   Faycebye, Agnes, Hubye, *Bulmer*.
Jan. 11, 1563.   Fayrbarne, Thomas, Hull, *Harthill*.
Dec. 17, 1557.   Fayrebanke, Margery, Atwicke, *Holderness*.
July 21, 1558.   Feaser, Roger, Wadyngton, par. Mytton, *Craven*.
Jun. 25, 1567.   Feilden, James, South Mylforthe, *Ainsty*.
Apl. 22, 1556.   Feldewe, William, Gisburne, priest, *Cleveland*.
Feb. 6, 1558.   Fenbie, William, Gemlinge, *Dickering*.
Dec. 1, 1558.   Fenton, Christopher, Hubie, *Bulmer*.
Mar. 13, 1565.   Ferneley, George, Ferneley, *Ainsty*.
May 25 & Jun. 2, 1558.   Fetherstone, John, Marton, par. Swyne, infant, *Holderness*.
Oct. 6, 1557.   Firthe, Thomas, Ordsaull, *Retford*.
Jun. 3, 1558.   Fisher, John, Branton, par. Cantlay, *Doncaster*.
Aug. 30, 1558.   Fladder, Anne, Chappell towne, par. Ledes, *Ainsty*.
Nov. 13, 1556.   Flemynge *als.* Wardeman, Eufemia, York, widow, *City*.
Nov. 12, 1556.   Fletcher, Christopher, Kepax, *Ainsty*.
Nov. 13, 1556.   Fleymynge, Margaret, spinster, *City*.
Feb. 15, 1558.   Forcyttes, Thomas, Stoneferie, *Holderness*.
Jan. 25, 1560.   Fornes, John, York, *Vacancy*, Fol. 98.
Aug. 28, 1561.   Foster, Alice, Blith, *Retford*.
Mar. 20, 1558.   ——, Hugh, Gillinge, *Ridall*.
Mar. 9, 1557.   Fourenes, Robert, Skercottes, par. Hallifax, *Pontefract*.
Mar. 9, 1557.   Fournes, Robert, Skercottes, par. Hallifax, *Pontefract*.
Aug. 15, 1560.   Fowbrey, Johan, Hull, widow, *Vacancy*, Fol. 66.
Apl. 12, 1559.   Fox, John, Walton, *Pontefract*.
Feb. 15, 1558.   ——, Robert, Newton, par. Aldburghe, *Holderness*.
Oct. 27, 1562.   Foxgale, Thomas, York, *City*.
May 6, 1563.   Franckyshe, Joan *als.* Jane, Harworthe, *Retford*.
Sep. 23, 1558.   Francys, John, Beverley, *Harthill*.
Jan. 29, 1556 & May 6, 1557.   Frankishe, Thomas, Bredlington, *Dickering*.
July 24, 1561.   Freer, John, Newland, par. Drax, *Bulmer*.
Jan. 12, 1563.   Freman, William, Spaldington, infant, *Harthill*.
Jan. 20, 1561.   Froddingham, Elizabeth, Brandesbye, widow, *Bulmer*.
Sep. 17, 1561.   —————, Elizabeth, Bransbye, widow, *Vacancy*, Fols. 131, 133, 137, 139.
                 142.
May 19, 1560.   Froste, William, Fetherston, *Vacancy*, Fol. 8.
Mar. 12, 1556.   Fryston, Robert, Altoftes, *Pontefract*.
Apl. 27, 1564.   Fysher, Roland, Upton, *Retford*.
Feb. 12, 1566.   Gannton, William, Wodhouse, *Holderness*.
Jan. 14, 1566.   Garbot, John, Danby, *Cleveland*.
Jan. 22, 1566.   Garbray, Christopher, son of Mathew G., Beverley, Curation, *Harthill*.
Dec. 4, 1566.   ——, Peter, bast. son of Mathew G., Beverley, *Harthill*.
Jun. 20, 1566.   Garbrey, Christopher, son of Mathew G., Beverley, decd., Curation, *Harthill*.
Jan. 22, 1566.   Gargrave, George, Bolton, par. Calverley, *Pontefract*.
Mar. 17, 1556.   Garland, Christopher, Bossall, *Bulmer*.
Feb. 9, 1557.   Garton, Robert, Attynwike, *Holderness*.
May 2, 1560.   ——, Stephen, Great Codon, par. Albrough, *Vacancy*, Fol. 32.
Jun. 30, 1564.   ——, William, Foston, *Dickering*.
Nov. 3, 1556.   Gascoigne, Sir William, Cusworthe, knight, *Doncaster*.
Apl. 16, 1567.   Gayfayte, Ellen, Kirkelethome, *Cleveland*.
Oct. 18, 1565.   Gelder, Richard, Langton, Curation, *Buckrose*.
Oct. 6, 1557.   Gelderd, John, Lound, par. Sutton, *Retford*.
Sep. 1, 1565.   Gelderde, James, Salley, *Craven*.
July 15, 1567.   ——, John, senr., *Craven*.
Sep. 28, 1560.   German, John, Wollarton (Notts.), *Vacancy*, Fol. 72.
May 14, 1568.   Gervase, William, Whiston, *Doncaster*.

Oct. 7, 1558. **Gibson**, George, Sharow, par. Ripon, *Craven*.
Sep. 14, 1563. ———, John, Hothome, *Harthill*.
Dec. 11, 1562. ———, John, Skottershelfe, par. Rudbye, *Cleveland*.
May 27, 1558. ———, Margery, Hexham, widow, *City*.
Jun. 21, 1568. **Gilbanke**, John, Old Malton, *Ridall*.
Mar. 6, 1562. ———, Robert, Welburne (*Vacat.*), *Bulmer*.
Oct. 3, 1558. **Gilbert**, Robert, Barnbie, *Newark*.
Jan. 28, 1567. **Gill**, Elizabeth, Rigton, widow, *Ainsty*.
May 5, 1568. —, John, Heyshawe, *Craven*.
Feb. 17, 1561. —, Nicolas, Sutton on Lound, *Retford*.
Jun. 18, 1566. **Gledaie**, Mathew, Cowike, *Bulmer*.
Apl. 4, 1565. **Gledeill**, Thomas, Barsland, par. Halyfax, *Pontefract*.
Apl. 27, 1558. **Glover**, Uldred, Byngley, *Craven*.
Feb. 17, 1558. **Goityere**, Edwyne, Wressell, *Harthill*.
May 5, 1568. **Gonbye**, Thomas, Whitgifte, *Bulmer*.
Mar. 4, 1562. **Goote**, Thomas, Seglistorne, *Holderness*.
Sep. 6, 1557. **Gorrell**, Alice, Usfleytt, *Bulmer*.
Dec. 3, 1557. **Gorrell**, Johan, Usflete, widow, *Bulmer*.
Apl. 2, 1568. **Gower**, Richard, Sherifhoton, *Bulmer*.
Oct. 19, 1560. ———, Elizabeth, Burnholme, *Vacancy*, Fol. 81.
Mar. 29, 1559. **Gowsell**, George (son of John G., of Hull), *Holderness*.
Jan. 22, 1561. **Gowsell**, John, Hull, *Harthill*.
Aug. 10, 1562. **Granger**, Ralph, Newton on Darwende, *Harthill*.
Feb. 6, 1558. **Grastoke**, Gervase, Snathe, *Bulmer*.
Jan. 7, 1562. **Grave**, Amer, Bradford, *Pontefract*.
Aug. 20, 1559. ———, Richard, infant son of Geo. G., Doncaster, *Doncaster*.
Aug. 9, 1565. **Gravener**, Sir Thos., Eyton, Chester Diocese, knt., *Craven*.
July 6, 1558. **Gray**, John, Scardbrughe, marener, *Dickering*.
Dec. 1, 1558. ———, Thomas, Flaxton, *Bulmer*.
Feb. 7, 1560. **Graye**, Milla, York, spinster, *Vacancy*, Fol. 102.
July 11, 1558. **Graystocke**, Robert, Fishelake, *Doncaster*.
Apl. 7, 1562. **Greaves**, Christopher, Farindon, *Newark*.
Jan. 15, 1561. **Gree**, Barbara, Mathersay, infant, *Retford*.
Apl. 26, 1559. **Green**, John, Haistrope, *Dickering*.
July 12, 1563. **Grene**, Elizabeth, York, infant, *City*.
July 8, 1560. ———, Richard, Allerthorpe, par. Waikfeld, *Vacancy*, Fol. 58.
Jan. 31, 1564. ——— als. Webster, William, Agnes Burton, priest, *Dickering*.
Sep. 14, 1564. **Greneburye**, Millisia, York, infant, *City*.
Apl. 15, 1562. **Greneside**, Christopher, Sherifhoton, *Bulmer*.
Feb. 4, 1561. **Grenesyde**, Christopher, Sherofhoton, *Bulmer*.
May 19, 1560. **Grenewood**, Richard, Houghton, *Vacancy*, Fol. 8.
Oct. 15, 1561. **Greyne**, Reynold, West Skaling, *Cleveland*.
Sep. 16 & 29, 1557. **Greynfeld**, William, Killinglay, *Pontefract*.
Apl. 16, 1561. **Greyves**, Margaret, Bradfeld, widow, *Doncaster*.
Dec. 26, 1556. **Grycetwhait**, Alice, Killingley, widow, *Pontefract*.
May 28, 1568. **Gryndall**, Margaret, Great Kelke, widow, *Dickering*.
Jun. 22, 1568. **Gryndon**, Susanna, Danbye, *Craven*.
Apl. 26, 1564. **Guye**, William, Elley, *Harthill*.
May 10, 1564. **Gybson**, Antony, Skynnyngrave, *Cleveland*.
Dec. 3, 1566. ———, Philip, York, *City*.
Oct. 29, 1563. ———, William, Myton, *Harthill*.
Apl. 12, 1559. **Gyll**, Thomas, Darrington, *Pontefract*.
Mar. 20, 1558. **Hagge**, John, Monkebretton, par. Roiston, *Doncaster*.
Nov. 28, 1558. ———, Thomas, Emlay, *Pontefract*.
July 8, 1560. **Haigh**, Richard, Netherwike, par. Bristall, *Vacancy*, Fol. 59
July 17, 1566. **Haistinges**, Marmaduke, Flambroughe, *Dickering*.
Oct. 2, 1560. **Haldisworth**, Gilbert, Bradford, *Vacancy*, Fol. 74.
May 24, 1560. **Haldesworth**, James, Sowrebie, *Vacancy*, Fol. 41.
Sep. 23, 1561. **Hall**, Edith, infant dau. of Michael H., *Ainsty*.
July 17, 1565. ———, Henry, Beverley, *Harthill*.
Mar. 17, 1567. ———, Katherine, Northe Frodingham, *Holderness*.
July 18, 1560. ———, Thomas, Wansforth, *Vacancy*, Fol. 61.
July 12, 1564. ———, Peter, York, merchant, *City*.
Feb. ult., 1561. **Halldenby**, Robert, Halldenby (Caveat), *Vacancy*, Fol. 146.

July 15, 1562. Halmond, John, Welwike, *Holderness*.
Dec. 10, 1557. Hanselay, William, Wyestede, *Holderness*.
Jan. 25, 1565. Hanson, Richard, Hull, *Harthill*.
Oct. 7, 1557. Hardrome, Francis, Nottingham, *Nottingham*.
Dec. 22, 1557. Hargraves, Richard, Sawerbie, par. Hallifax, *Pontefract*.
Dec. 17, 1557. Harrison, John, Cliftone, par. Cunsburghe, *Doncaster*.
Feb. 25, 1562. Harryson, Alexander, Thorlebye, Caveat, *Craven*.
Apl. 28, 1563. ————, Elizabeth, Hull, *Harthill*.
Oct. 24, 1558. ————, Joan, infant, dau. of Edw. H., Wressell (imperfect), *Harthill*.
May 15, 1564. ————, Margaret, Garton, infant, *Holderness*.
July 8, 1558. ————, Margaret, infant, dau. of Johan H., Wresell, widow, *Harthill*.
Jun. 27, 1565. ————, Richard, Stanley, Tuition, *Pontefract*.
Jun. 19, 1566. Harte, Jane, Cottingwith, *Pontefract*.
May 2, 1565. Harvye, John, Hull, maryner, *Harthill*.
Jan. 13, 1558. Harwood, Thomas, Worssope, *Retford*.
Apl. 13, 1559. Hassand, John, Kirkeburne, *Harthill*.
Sep. 11, 1565. Hastinges, Sir Francis, Hatefeld, knight, Process, *Doncaster*.
July 6, 1563. ————, John, Elsinghall, co. Norfolk, infant, *Doncaster*.
May 2, 1566. Hawkesworthe, Edward, Cauthorne, *Doncaster*.
July 23, 1567. ————, Godfrey, son of Edw.H., Cawthorne, decd., Curation, *Doncaster*.
Jun. 18, 1560. Haworth, Adam, Cowike, *Vacancy*, Fol. 55.
May 6, 1563. Haworthe, George, Norton, *Retford*.
Apl. 19, 1564. ————, William, Long Preston, *Craven*.
Jan. 18, 1556. Hay, John, Sharleton, par. Warmefeld, *Pontefract*.
Jan. 19, 1567. Hayton, Henry, Kelfelde, *Bulmer*.
Mar. 14, 1559. Headlam, Alice, Hubie, widow, *Vacancy*, Fol. 6.
Aug. 17, 1556. Headon, Richard, Langton, *Buckrose*.
May 5, 1568. Hebden, John, Griston, *Craven*.
Mar. 7, 1560. ————, Robert, Hunmanbie, *Vacancy*, Fol. 112.
Sep. 28, 1557. Heles, John, Styrton, par. Skipton, *Craven*.
Mar. 10, 1564. Helme, Nicholas, Spofforthe, *Ainsty*.
Apl. 26, 1558. Hemmyngway, Alice, Byrkyn, *Ainsty*.
Jun. 30, 1563. Hepe, Edmund, Heptonstall, *Pontefract*.
May 9, 1567. Heptonstall, Edward, Rippon, *Craven*.
Apl. 14, 1559. Herdyn, John, Harum, *Rydall*.
May 6, 1559. Herte, Marmaduke, Skynnyngrave, *Cleveland*.
Jan. 26, 1558. ———, William, Shipton in Galtres, *Bulmer*.
Jan. 25, 1560. Herrison, Alexander, Thorlebie, *Vacancy*, Fol. 98.
Jan. 14, 1560. ————, Edmund, son of W. H., Campsall, *Vacancy*, Fols. 95, 102, 107, 113.
Oct. 21, 1558. ————, Edward, Cowthrope, *Ainsty*.
Feb. ult., 1561. ————, Robert, Collingham, *Ainsty*.
July 19, 1557. Herryngton, Nicholas, Whitbie Lathes, *Cleveland*.
Oct. 24, 1562. Heryson, William, York, *City*.
Feb. 23, 1565. Hesleden, Brian, Hampsthwaite, *Ainsty*.
Sep. 17, 1558. Hessey, John, Hnby, *Bulmer*.
May 5, 1558. Hetcoyttes, William, Sowth Collyngham, *Newark*.
Jan. 27, 1567. Hewson, John, York, merchant, *City*.
Sep. 29, 1563. ———, Matilda, Haistropp, widow, *Dickering*.
Apl. 17, 1567. ———, Thomas, Beswicke, *Harthill*.
Sep. 29, 1563. Hewthwaite, Thomas, Burton Agnes, *Dickering*.
July 30, 1567. Heyton, William, Elizabeth, and Ellen, children, of Wm.H., Cottingham, Bond
  for portions, *Harthill*.
July 31, 1566. Hicke, Ellene, Thorpbasset, infant, *Buckrose*.
Dec. 4, 1566. Hickson, Nicholas, Kayingham, *Holderness*.
Nov. 15, 1560. Hid, Robert, Swynflet, *Vacancy*, Fols. 86 and 87.
Apl. 20, 1560. Hide, Robert, Swynflet, *Vacancy*, Fol. 22.
Sep. 27, 1558. Hill, Walter, Oxton, par. Tadcastre, *Ainsty*.
Mar. 11, 1556. —, William, Burton, par. Monkfryston, *Ainsty*.
Mar. 12, 1566. —, William, Holme in Spaldingmore, *Harthill*.
July 1, 1561. Hirst, Thomas, Willoughby, *Retford*.
Dec. 21, 1561. Hobson, Charles, Cawthorne, *Doncaster*.
Jan. 29, 1566. ————, John, Cawodde, *Ainsty*.
May 2, 1560. ————, Thomas, Oustwicke, par. Garton, *Vacancy*, Fol. 30.
May 18, 1559. ————, William, Humbleton, clerk, *Holderness*.

Jun. 2, 1558. Hobsone, Margaret, Humbleton, *Holderness.*
Mar.29, 1563. Hodgeson, John, Thormondbye, *Cleveland.*
Apl. 6, 1566. ———, Margaret, Owlston, *Bulmer.*
Mar.17, 1557. ———, Robert, Bubwith, singularis, *Harthill.*
Sep. 30, 1558. Hodshon, Thomas, Busshopside, *Craven.*
Jun. 9, 1563. Hoge, George, Garton, *Holderness.*
Jan. 12, 1558. Hogge, John, Marflet, *Holderness.*
Sep. 26, 1558. Hogley, William, Darfeld, *Doncaster.*
Feb. 8, 1560. Holdernes, Thomas, Wheldrike, infant, *Vacancy*, Fol. 102.
Feb.25, 1560. Holgait, Nicholas, Foston, *Vacancy*, Fol. 106.
Feb. 28, 1556. Hollingraike, William, Gilsted, *Craven.*
Apl. 27, 1564. Holme, Dorothy, Southleverton, widow, *Retford.*
Mar.20, 1565. Holme, John, Doncaster, *Doncaster.*
July 1, 1563. ———, Robert, Elvington, *Bulmer.*
May 5, 1558. Holmes, Edmund, West Retford, *Retford.*
Jun. 17, 1564. Holtbye, Richard, Raskell, *Bulmer.*
Mar. 1, 1557. Hompton, Elizabeth and Isabella, Attyngwicke. infants, *Holderness.*
Feb. 19, 1557. ———, Thomas and Robert, infant sons of Chris. H., Attynwicke, *Holderness,*
Jan. 12, 1558. Hoogge, Richard, Beverley, baker, *Harthill.*
Apl. 20, 1564. Hoope, Robert, Ormesby, *Cleveland.*
Apl. 30, 1556. Hopkens, John, Eperston, *Nottingham.*
Apl. 22, 1567. Hoppay, Thomas, Kirkesmeton, *Doncaster.*
Nov. 5, 1567. ———, William, Barley, *Ainsty.*
Feb. 9, 1557. Hopper, William, Agnes, and Elizabeth, Hornesey, *Holderness.*
Apl. 14, 1562. Hornebye, Robert, Bewham, *Holderness.*
Oct. 21, 1557. Horner, William, Skelton, *Cleveland.*
Dec. 3, 1557. Horsfaull, Agnes, Haworthe, *Pontefract.*
Dec. 3, 1557. ———, Joan, Heptonstall, *Pontefract.*
Nov.28, 1567. Horsley, Robert, Wansfurthe, *Dickering.*
Sep. 27, 1557. Howland, William, Sheffeld, *Doncaster.*
Jun. 16, 1568. Howldell, Agnes, Bubwith, *Harthill.*
Mar.20, 1558. Howley, Edward, Hemsworth, *Doncaster.*
Nov.29, 1558. Howlle, John, Fyshelaike, *Doncaster.*
Oct. 1, 1561. Howson, Humphrey, *Craven.*
May 15, 1566. Hudson, Robert, Campsall, *Doncaster.*
Apl. 23, 1566. Huggett, John, Bossall, infant, *Bulmer.*
May 18, 1561. ———, Katherine, Berythorpe, *Buckrose.*
Apl. 27, 1564. Hughe, James, Rosington, *Retford.*
Aug.12, 1566. Hull, Henry, Holmpton, *Holderness.*
May 28, 1567. Hulls, William, Hull, *Harthill.*
July 30, 1561. Humbton, William, Gristhrope, par. Fylaye, *Dickering.*
Nov.17, 1558. Hummysse, Robert, Snath, *Bulmer.*
May 28, 1560. Hunte, John, Carleton, par. Rothwell, *Vacancy*, Fol. 43.
Apl. 6, 1558. Hunters, William, Hellybie, *Doncaster.*
Jan. 8, 1562. Huntroides, Thomas, Whitbie, *Cleveland.*
Feb. 7, 1555. Husey, Sir William, Belvoir, knight, *Bingham.*
Nov.29, 1558. Husone, Richard, Sykehouse, *Doncaster.*
Jan. 28, 1558. Hustler, John, Skipton, *Craven.*
Dec. 19, 1560. Hutchenson, John, Bulmer, *Vacancy*, Fol. 92.
July 2, 1563. ———, Roger, Lowthropp, *Dickering.*
Apl. 8, 1567. Hutcheson, Christopher, Hacknes, *Dickering.*
Apl. 12, 1559. Hutchingson, John, Shella, par. Kirkebyrton, *Pontefract.*
July 18, 1560. Huthwaite, Thomas, Agnes Burton, *Vacancy*, Fol. 61.
Dec. 13, 1557. Hynchclif, Thomas, Donnyngton, *Pontefract.*
Oct. 27, 1557. Hynde, John, York, *City.*
May21, 1557. Illingworth, George, Rotherham, *Doncaster.*
May 4, 1556. Ingle, William, Weton, par. Harwod, *Ainsty.*
Oct. 21, 1557. Ingledewe, James, Marske, *Cleveland.*
Oct. 26, 1564. Inglyshe, William, Hull, maryner, *Harthill.*
Jan. 20, 1558. Isabelle, Joan, Hulbanke, infant, *Harthill.*
July 18, 1565. Isott, Joan, Anne, and John, infant children of Rich. I., Thrybarghe, *Doncaster.*
Oct. 3, 1560. Iveson, James (Craven Deanery) *Vacancy*, Fol. 78.
Jun. 9, 1556. ———, John, Skipton, Renunc. and Adm., *Craven.*

Nov. 4, 1558. Jackeson, Peter, Renunciation, *City*.
Oct. 22, 1558. ———, Richard, Wressell, *Harthill*.
Apl. 28, 1559. ———, William, Hooton Cransewicke, *Harthill*.
Feb. 12, 1560. Jackesone, Thomas, Borowbie, *Vacancy*, Fol. 103.
Oct. 7, 1563. Jackson, Dionisius, East Markham, *Retford*.
Feb. 20, 1566. ———, John, York, *City*.
July 24, 1564. ———, Laurence, Bushopburton, *Harthill*.
Oct. 7, 1563. ———, Robert, Tuxforde, *Retford*.
Jun. 8, 1565. ———, Robert, York, *City*.
Aug. 13, 1567. ———, William, Barnestone, *Holderness*.
Aug. 7, 1566. ———, William, Drax, *Bulmer*.
Jan. 20, 1561. Jagger, Thomas, Lynley Cote, *Pontefract*.
Oct. 5, 1558. Jakson, William, Cauton, *Rydall*.
Mar. 14, 1560. Jamys, Robert, Newarke (Notts), *Vacancy*, Fol. 115.
May 20, 1558. Jeffrason, Elizabeth, Whitkirke, *Ainsty*.
Sep. 22, 1558. ———, Lawrence, Creskell, par. Adle, *Ainsty*.
July 3, 1566. Jeffrayson, Laurence and Anne, Paull, *Holderness*.
Mar. 21, 1561. Jelatson, Christopher, Elvington, *Bulmer*.
Sep. 18, 1567. Jenkinson, John, Cottingham, *Harthill*.
Sep. 5, 1566. Jenkynson, William, Mewse, *Holderness*.
Mar. 3, 1557. Jewet, Edward, Heaton, par. Bradfurthe, *Pontefract*.
Mar. 23, 1560. Jobson, Richard, Rimswell, *Vacancy*, Fol. 125.
Nov. 8, 1563. Johnson, John, Barley, priest, *Ainsty*.
May 18, 1559. ———, Richard, Ordsall, *Retford*.
Aug. 21, 1564. ———, Robert, York, *City*.
Sep. 30, 1563. Jubbes, John, Wragbye, *Pontefract*.
Oct. 11, 1563. Judson, Robert, Shelforthe, *Nottingham*.
Feb. 11, 1560. Judsone, Ranold, Huntington, *Vacancy*, Fol. 102.
May 12, 1563. Kay, Agnes, Holme in Spaldingmore, *Harthill*.
Oct. 4, 1558. ———, Robert, Lokington, *Harthill*.
May 5, 1564. Kellington, George, Carleton, *Bulmer*.
Jan. 14, 1558. Kenrowe, George, son of William K., Skarburgh, *Dickering*.
Feb. ult., 1558. Kighley, Joan, Cottinglay, par. Binglay, widow, *Craven*.
Oct. 29, 1558. Kilborne, John, York, draper, *City*.
Nov. 6, 1561. Kildaill, Thomas, *Dickering*.
July 11, 1561. King, Thomas, Hull Brige, *Vacancy*, Fol. 129.
May 5, 1558. Kirkbie, Thomas, Sanbye, *Retford*.
Jan. 11, 1562. Kirkebie, Nicholas, South Clyffe, *Harthill*.
Apl. 22, 1556. Kirwike, John, Hilderthorpe, *Dickering*.
Apl. 22, 1556. Kitson, Margaret and Isabella, infants (to Jo. and Eliz., Foster, of N. Frodyngham), *Holderness*.
Oct. 2, 1566. Knagges, Margery, Stonefery, *Holderness*.
May 14, 1567. ———, Thomas, Stonefery, *Holderness*.
Jan. 22, 1567. Knowles, Richard, Hull, *Harthill*.
Sep. 30, 1557. Kyender, John, Doncaster, *Doncaster*.
Jun. 13, 1559. Kynge, Thomas, Hull briges als. Sownderland, infant, *Harthill*.
Mar. 10, 1562. Kyrbie, Margaret, Saxton, *Ainsty*.
Jan. 11, 1563. Kyrkehouse, Thomas, Hull, mylner, *Harthill*.
Sep. 10, 1561. Kyldaill, Thomas, Scardbrughe, *Vacancy*, Fol. 130.
Apl. 3, 1559. Kytchingman, William, York, *City*.
Sep. 7, 1556. Laborne, Andrew, Nafferton, *Dickering*.
May 1, 1559. Laicoke, Joan, Ripon, *Craven*.
May 15, 1566. Laiken, Jane, Kirkebye Moreshed, infant, *Rydall*.
Nov. 11, 1561. Laiton, Thomas, Becka, *Ainsty*.
Apl. 28 & Sep. 30, 1558. Lambert, Robert, Ripon, *Craven*.
May 28, 1560. Langdaile, Robert, Dalbie, *Vacancy*, Fol. 44.
Feb. 24, 1561. Langton, Agnes, Linton, par. Spoffurth, *Ainsty*.
Dec. 4, 1557. Lawe als. Wentlay, John, Pollington, *Bulmer*.
Feb. 21, 1567. Lawson, Thomas, Nether Popleton, alderman of York, *City*.
Oct. 1, 1562. Lawtie, Thomas, Carleton, *Bulmer*.
Apl. 28, 1568. Leadell, Peter, Selbye, *Bulmer*.
Jun. 14, 1566. Leadley, Ralph and Margaret his wife, New Malton, *Rydall*.
Jun. 23, 1563. Leake, John, son of George L., Hadlesay, *Ainsty*.
July 20, 1566. Ledell, Bartholmew, Kelfelde, *Bulmer*.

Sep. 30, 1557.	Lee, William, Doncaster, *Doncaster*.
Mar. 6, 1556.	Legate, William, Rampton, *Retford*.
Oct. 2, 1567.	Lemynge, Thomas, Sladburne, *Craven*.
Oct. 31, 1566.	Letbye, John, Leppington, *Buckrose*.
July 8, 1561.	Leven, Thomas, Roclif, *Ainsty*.
Apl. 19, 1564.	Leyland, Katherine, *Craven*.
Jan. 13, 1558.	Lilling, Henry, Skerington, *Bingham*.
Dec. 23, 1567.	Lilliwhite, Mathew and John, Swyne, *Holderness*.
Oct. 17, 1561.	Lister, Thomas, Brakynhall, Caveat, *Ainsty*.
July 10, 1561.	——, William, Denton, *Ainsty*.
May 30, 1565.	Lokewodd, Elizabeth and Mary, Hallyfax, *Pontefract*.
Nov. 20, 1563.	Londesdaill, Laurence, Ellerton, Tuition, *Harthill*.
Jun. 11, 1567.	Londesdall, Agnes, Armyne, *Bulmer*.
Jan. 11, 1557.	Longcaster, Dorothy, Elwerbie, *Holderness*.
Feb. 15, 1558.	———, John, Hollome, *Holderness*.
Jan. 8, 1556.	———, William, Baildon, *Pontefract*.
Nov. 20, 1566.	Longley, Agnes, York, widow, *City*.
Apl. 12, 1559.	———, Richard, Heaton, *Pontefract*.
Apl. 26, 1559.	Loue, William, Thwing, *Dickering*.
Dec. 3, 1567.	Lound, William, *Ainsty*.
Apl. 28, 1563.	Lowde, Edmund, Gisburne, *Craven*.
Apl. 16, 1562.	——, Richard, *Craven*.
Feb. 6, 1560.	Lowe, Francis, Bilton, *Vacancy*, Fol. 101.
Apl. 29, 1567.	——, Percival, Heidon, *Holderness*.
Feb. 19, 1566.	——, Perceval, Heydon, Sequestration, *Holderness*.
Oct. 8, 1562.	Lume, Thomas, Owelcootes, *Retford*.
Nov. 6, 1565.	Lyghtfoote, William, Cottingham, *Harthill*.
Mar. 8, 1558.	Lylforth, Henry, Cottingham, *Harthill*.
Feb. 13, 1565.	Lyster, Thomas, junior, Brakenhall, par. Otley, *Ainsty*.
Oct. 20, 1558.	Lythe, Peter, *Holderness*.
May 13, 1558.	Madsone, Elizabeth, Holme in Spawdyngmore, *Harthill*.
Mar. 24, 1563.	Maison, Henry, Bramhopp, par. Otley, *Ainsty*.
May 5, 1558.	Malham, John, Skelton, *Newark*.
Jan. 8, 1562.	Manbye, Peter, Kirkeham, *Buckrose*.
Sep. 27, 1560.	Mangall, Richard, Snaith, bachelor, *Vacancy*, Fol. 70.
Nov. 25, 1562.	Mankyn, Ursula, York, infant, *City*.
Jan. 29, 1556.	Mannynge, William, Brydlington, *Dickering*.
May 27, 1562.	Manssell, Arthur, Eastrungton, *Cleveland*.
Aug. 6, 1561.	Marche, William, Rillyngton, *Buckrose*.
July 20, 1561.	Mare, Thomas, Epilworth, par. Cottingham, *Harthill*.
Apl. 20, 1559.	Marham, John, Mathersey, *Retford*.
Oct. 10, 1566.	Mariet, William, Bingham, *Bingham*.
July 29, 1562.	Marmaduke, William, Hull, *Harthill*.
Sep. 30, 1558.	Marsden, William, Silkstone, *Doncaster*.
Oct. 1, 1566.	Marshall, Alice, Eastbarnby, *Cleveland*.
Jan. 12, 1558.	———, Christopher, West Hardwike, *Pontefract*.
Jan. 13, 1558.	———, John, Sowthe Carleton, *Newark*.
Oct. 1, 1566.	———, Katherine, Estbarnby, *Cleveland*.
Dec. 1, 1558.	———, Ralph, Brompton, *Rydall*.
Sep. 25, 1567.	———, Richard, Thorneton in Pickeringlithe, *Rydall*.
Dec. 17, 1557.	———, Robert, Awbrughe, Caveat, *Holderness*.
May 2, 1560.	———, William, Carelton, par. Snayth, *Vacancy*, Fol. 32.
May 21, 1560.	———, William, Kyrklethome Caveat, *Vacancy*, Fol. 11.
Jan. 18, 1558.	———, William, Robinhodsbay, *Cleveland*.
May 2, 1560.	———, William, West Cottam, *Vacancy*, Fol. 27.
Apl. 6, 1558.	Marshe, Richard, Harthill, priest, *Doncaster*.
Aug. 27, 1563.	Marsingaill, William and Margaret, Hull, infants, *Harthill*.
Feb. 7, 1555.	Marton, Alexander, Maltbie, *Doncaster*.
Oct. 11, 1563.	——, Nicholas, Eston, *Cleveland*.
Nov. 10, 1558.	Mashroder, Roger, pewderer, *City*.
Feb. 12, 1555.	Mawburn, Peter, Scrayngham, *Dickering*.
Dec. 5, 1558.	Mawcus, Margaret, Hull, widow, *Harthill*.
Oct. 13, 1562.	Mawde, Brian, Warley, par. Halyfax, *Pontefract*.
July 29, 1562.	Mawton, Thomas, Raskell, Curation, *Bulmer*.

Mar. 5, 1562. Mayre, William, Bawne, par. Snaythe, *Bulmer.*
Oct. 1, 1566. Mayson, Thomas, Kirkeleventon, *Cleveland.*
Oct. 8, 1561. Mearing, John, North Scarle, *Newark.*
Aug.28, 1566. Meke, Christopher and Robert, Curation, *Holderness.*
Oct. 29, 1563. Mell, John, West Cottingwith, *Bulmer.*
Jan. 27, 1556. Melton, John, Skakkelthroppe, *Dickering.*
Sep. 30, 1558. Meltynby *als.* Cony, John, Order to exhibit inventory, *City.*
Feb.10, 1558. Menethorpe, John, Brompton, *Rydall.*
Jun. 2, 1558. Mennell, Henry, Hilton, par. Rudbye, *Cleveland.*
May 5, 1558. Merydue, Thomas, Rosyngtone, *Retford.*
Sep. 11, 1564. Metcalfe, William, London, purse maker, *Ainsty.*
Jun. 7, 1560. Middleton, Edmund, Rigton, *Vacancy*, Fol. 48.
Aug.26, 1561. Milner, Elizabeth, Lepton, *Pontefract.*
Sep. 18, 1561. Milnes, Richard, Foston, *Dickering.*
Oct. 13, 1558. Moore, Richard, and Agnes his wife, Laneham, *Retford.*
Nov.15, 1566. ——, Thomas, Mydleton, *Harthill.*
July 1, 1561. More, Agnes, *Retford.*
May 28, 1560. ——, Henry, Midle Shitlington, par. Thornell, *Vacancy*, Fol. 43.
Dec. 14, 1567. ——, John, Wyntringham, *Buckrose.*
Jun. 30, 1563. ——, Richard, Huddersfeld, *Pontefract.*
Aug.26, 1561. Morehowse, Ralph, Fulston, *Pontefract.*
Nov.10, 1557 Morlaye, Christopher, Marres, singularis, *Cleveland.*
Nov.20, 1566. Morres, Richard, Hothome, Curation, *Buckrose.*
Jun. 3, 1562. Mosse, William, Calverley, *Ainsty.*
Dec.12, 1562. Motherbie, John, Cowicke, Curation, *Bulmer.*
Jun. 27, 1558. Moundye, William, Fitlynge, *Holderness.*
Oct. 5, 1558. Mowrson, Nicholas, Whitbye, *Cleveland.*
Jun. 12, 1568. Mudde, Anthony, York, *City.*
Oct. 1, 1558. Murgatrod, James, Warley, *Pontefract.*
Apl. 27, 1558. Musgrave, Richard, Wakefelde, *Pontefract.*
Dec.22, 1556. Mychell, Christopher, Dalton, *Doncaster.*
Sep. 30, 1558. Myddilton, John, Ripon, *Craven.*
Mar. 8, 1567. Mydleton, Anthony, Beverley, *Harthill.*
Apl. 28, 1559. ——, Robert, Rungton, *Cleveland.*
Dec. 17, 1567. Myleson, John, Ferybrigges, *Pontefract.*
Sep. 6, 1558. Mylner, John, Sandall, *Pontefract.*
July 28, 1564. ——, Thomas, Eskrige, *Bulmer.*
Nov.24, 1562, Myllyngton *als.* Tomlynson, Wilfred, Holme in Spaldingmore, *Harthill.*
Feb.ult.,1558. Mynythrope, Ambrosse, Hooton Busshell, *Rydall.*
Oct. 3, 1558. Mynytt, John, Woodcottes, par. Fladburn, *Newark.*
Jan. 2, 1558. Mytchell, Henry, Elvington, *Bulmer.*
May 17, 1565. ——, Robert, Westebrydgefurthe, *Bingham.*
Jan. 23, 1556. Mytton, Robert, Bramham, *Ainsty.*
Oct. 31, 1556. ——, William, Cawood, *Ainsty.*
Jan. 31, 1558. Nawton, Agnes, New Malton, widow, *Rydall.*
Oct. 22, 1556. Nayler, Thomas, Byrstall, *Pontefract.*
May 9, 1560. Nedam, John, Marnham (Notts.), *Vacancy*, Fol. 36.
Apl. 21, 1563. Nellson, William, Rysomgarthe, par. Wethernesay, *Holderness.*
Dec. 1, 1558. Nendicke, Richard, Hullbanke, par. Cottingham, *Harthill.*
May 14, 1567. Newett, Katherine, Spaldington, *Harthill.*
May 3, 1567. Newman, Agnes, Elvington, *Bulmer.*
Jan. 5, 1558. Newnam, dame ——, widow, *Doncaster.*
Jun. 4, 1567. Newsam, Thomas, Shadwell, *Ainsty.*
July 30, 1561. Newton, Michael, Thorpe, par. Ripon, *Vacancy*, Fol. 129.
Apl. 3, 1559. Nicholson, Thomas, Cropton, par. Mydleton, *Rydall.*
Jun. 30, 1565. Nicolson, Henry, Brumpton, *Rydall.*
Nov.24, 1561. Noddall, Robert, Aighton, Account, *Harthill.*
Dec.20, 1558. Noddle, Robert, Aighton, *Beverley.*
Aug.19, 1564. Normavell, Richard, Beverley, *Harthill.*
May 3, 1557. North, Roger, Walcringham, gentleman, Caveat, *Retford.*
Sep. 30, 1557. Northe, Elizabeth, Tawthroppe, Newton, *Holderness.*
Feb.26, 1563. ——, Richard, Stanfurthe Brigges, *Harthill.*
Jan. 16, 1558. ——, Roger, Walkryngham, *Retford.*
Dec.13, 1561. ——, Roger, Walkringham, *Retford.*

Aug.27, 1556. Northus, Elizabeth, Cottingham, infant dau. of Thos. N., deceased, *Harthill*.
Mar.25, 1557. Norton, John, Norton, esq., *Craven*.
Nov.27, 1556. Nowell, Henry, Staynton, par. Gargrave, *Craven*.
Aug. 5, 1557. Oldfeld, Edward, Warlay, par. Hallifax, *Pontefract*.
Mar.21, 1560. Oliver, William (Harthill and Hull Deanery), *Vacancy*, Fol. 122.
May 13, 1557. Olyver, William, Styrroppe, par. Blithe, *Retford*.
Oct. 7, 1557. Orome, Thomas, and Margaret his wife, *Newark*.
Jan. 18, 1561. Ostclif, Francis, Breerley, par. Felkirke, *Doncaster*.
Jan. 11, 1565. Otes, Michael, Hallyfax, mercer, *Pontefract*.
Jun. 27, 1567. Otterburne, John, Hovingham, *Rydall*.
Jun. 2, 1561. Oxley, John, Beston, *Nottingham*.
Aug.13, 1567. Owmbler, Thomas, Brystwicke, *Holderness*.
Oct. 5, 1558. Pacoke, Robert, Rudby, *Cleveland*.
Sep. 30, 1558. ———, William, Studlay, *Craven*. .
Feb.ult.,1555. Padget, Walter, Hull, *Harthill*.
Jun. 28, 1563. Palmer, William, Snathe, *Bulmer*.
Jan. 22, 1567. Palmes, George, doctor of laws, *City*.
Aug. 2, 1557. Parker, John, Kylnesey, *Holderness*.
July 12, 1564. Parker, Nicholas, Welweke, *Holderness*.
Dec. 9, 1567. Parkinson, Roland, Hawnebye, *Cleveland*.
Feb. 16, 1563. Parkyn, John, Old Malton, *Rydall*.
Nov.28, 1567. ———, William, Ruston, *Dickering*.
Oct. 1, 1561. Parsons, Christopher, Sladburne, *Craven*.
Sep. 1, 1563. Pasheley, Geoffrey, Wadworthe, *Doncaster*.
Mar.20, 1565. Patrycke, John, Doncaster, *Doncaster*.
Jan. 30, 1560. Pattenson, Alice and Isabella, Chereburton, minors, *Vacancy*, Fol. 99.
Jan. 30, 1560. ———. Margaret, Lockington, minor, *Vacancy*, Fols. 99, 112, 113.
Mar. 6, 1560. Pattensone, Isabell, Chereburton, *Vacancy*, Fols. 112, 113.
Jan. 23, 1561. Pattynson. Margaret, Ellice, and Isabell, children of Robt. P., Cheryburton, *Harthill*.
May 30, 1555. Pawlinge, Peter, Hunmanbye, *Dickering*.
May 29, 1567. Paycoke, Roger, Whitby, *Cleveland*.
Sep. 2, 1563. Pearson, Ralph, Camerton, *Holderness*.
Aug. 6, 1565. Pecket, William, Craven Close, par. Marton, *Bulmer*.
Oct. 6, 1557. Pekeringe, Peter, Southleverton, *Retford*. .
Jan. 13, 1558. Penington, William, Upton, *Newark*.
Oct. 1, 1561. Penstrops, Robert, Hull, maryner, *Harthill*.
Sep. 29, 1563. Perkour (Parker), Ellen, Towton, widow, *Ainsty*.
Aug. 8, 1565. Person, Elizabeth, Howden, *Holderness*.
May 9, 1560. ———, Thomas, Fledbrough (Notts.), *Vacancy*, Fol. 37.
Dec. 14, 1565. Persye *als*. Butterfelde, John, Newcastle on Tyne, *Ainsty*.
Nov. 6, 1556. Petche, John, Leedes, *Ainsty*.
Apl. 24, 1567. Picke, Richard, Colston Bassett, *Bingham*.
May 6, 1557. Pickeringe, Geoffrey, Cawod, *Ainsty*. .
Apl. 10, 1563. Pikerynge, Thomas, Lockinton, *Harthill*.
Mar.20, 1564. Pillye, John, More Monkton, dying in London, *Ainsty*.
Apl. 24, 1559. Plewman, George, York, miller, *City*.
Sep. 10, 1558. Plummar, Richard, Raskell, *Bulmer*.
July 23, 1560. Pocklington, Richard, Wresle, *Vacancy*, Fol. 62.
Mar.11, 1559. Pollard, Thomas, Shiplaye, *Vacancy*, Fol. 5.
Apl. 10, 1559. Pollardes, John, Barnesley, *Doncaster*.
Feb. 27, 1566. Porter, Isabelle, Heworthe, widow, *City*.
Oct. 1, 1556. Portington, Ralph, Ellyngton, *Harthill*.
Oct. 4, 1565. Posket, William, Hull, *Harthill*.
Oct. 7, 1558. Postgate, Agnes, Riswarpe, widow, *Cleveland*.
Jan. 16, 1558. Pott, John, Kyrkby Overblavers, *Ainsty*.
July 29, 1558. Powton *als*. Bolton, William, Byland Abbey, *Bulmer*.
July 16, 1562. Preistley, Robert, Elland, *Pontefract*.
May 26, 1567. Preston, George, Brydlington, *Dickering*.
May 5, 1568. ———, Robert, Hullbrige, *Harthill*.
Nov.12, 1560. Procter, Richard, Bordelay, Caveat, *Vacancy*, Fol. 86.
Mar. 1, 1560. ———, Richard, Rilstone, *Vacancy*, Fol. 107.
Apl. 8, 1558. Prustwolde, Thomas, Newland, *Harthill*.
Jan. 20, 1561. Prynce, Edward, Olorthorpe, *Pontefract*.

Mar.13, 1556. Pryngle, Nicholas, and Elizabeth his wife, Cawod, *Ainsty*.
July 12, 1558. Pukeringe, William, Paynstrope, par. Kirkbie Underdalle, *Buckrose*.
Nov.24, 1565. Pynder, Robert, son of Geo. P., Wystowe, Curation, *Ainsty*.
Feb. 17, 1557. Pynnynges, John, Nutton, *Doncaster*.
Feb. 19, 1564. Rakes, Richard, Keldebrocke, *Craven*.
Oct. 24, 1565. Ralay, Edward, Weste Morton, *Craven*.
Apl. 13, 1559. Ralson *als*. Robinson, Peter, Dawncevall, *Harthill*.
Jan. 20, 1557. Ranbie, Robert, Tickehill, *Doncaster*.
Feb. 19, 1566. Randes, Judith, Bugton, Dioc. Linc., *Harthill*.
Feb. 9, 1557. Ranson, Edward, Humbleton, *Holderness*.
July 19, 1557. Ransone, John, Hombletone, *Holderness*.
Dec. 11, 1557. Ratclif, Isabella, Thrishefeild, par. Lynton, *Craven*.
Sep. 29, 1563. Ratcliffe, William, Hunmanby, *Dickering*.
May 6, 1566. Raughton, John, Wyntryngham, *Buckrose*.
Mar.13, 1561. Rawden, Robert, Brandesby, *Bulmer*.
Sep. 9, 1558. Rawson, Robert, Crofton, *Pontefract*.
Oct. 29, 1558. Raye, William, Hunmandbie. *Dickering*.
May 6, 1563. Rayner, Augustine, Stokam, *Retford*.
Mar. 4, 1562. Raynerde, John, Wethernesey, *Holderness*.
July 5, 1564. Raynford, Samuel, Halyfax, infant, *Pontefract*.
Jun. 23, 1563. Reade, William, Staxton, *Dickering*.
Nov.21, 1562. Readesdaill, Roger, Elvington, *Bulmer*.
Jan. 24, 1558. Richardson, Edward, Thurnescue, *Doncaster*.
Apl. 18, 1566. ————, John, Sherburne in Ellmytt, *Ainsty*.
May 20, 1558. ————, Thomas, Dugglebie, *Buckrose*.
July 6, 1560. ————, Thomas, junr., Swynflet, *Vacancy*, Fol. 57.
Feb. 5, 1565. ————, William, Bubwithe, *Bulmer*.
May 6, 1558. ————, William, Hunttington, *Bulmer*.
Mar.15, 1560. Rie, Alice, Barfeld, *Vacancy*, Fol. 110.
Oct. 8, 1556. Rigeley, Nicholas, Nottingham, *Nottingham*.
Oct. 23, 1557. Robert, Margaret, Rednes, *Bulmer*.
May 9, 1560. Robertson, Henry, Sowthwell (Notts.), *Vacancy*, Fol. 37.
Apl. 13, 1559. Robinson *als*. Ralson. Peter, Dawncevall, *Harthill*.
Sep. 18, 1566. Robson, Jane, Whistonclyffe, *Bulmer*.
Apl. 12, 1559. Robuke, John, Kirkeburton, *Pontefract*.
Jan. 30, 1565. Robynson, Agnes, Baynton, *Harthill*.
Aug.12, 1566. ————, John, Burton Pydsey, *Holderness*.
Mar.17, 1556. ————, John, Helsternewicke, *Holderness*.
Jan. 24, 1560. ————, Richard, Hull, *Vacancy*, Fol. 98.
Apl. 23, 1566. ————, Thomas, Agnes Burton, son of Rich. R., Yeddingham *Buckrose*.
Nov.24, 1564. ————, Thomas, Yeddyngham, *Buckrose*.
Aug. 1, 1561. Roclif, John, Howke, *Bulmer*.
May 19, 1559. Roclife, Thowas, Howke, *Bulmer*.
Jan. 12, 1558. Rodhowse, Joan, West Hardwicke, *Pontefract*.
Feb. 11, 1567. Rome, Katherine, Kirkeby in Gryndallythe, *Buckrose*.
May 11, 1568. ————, Margaret and Elizabeth, *Ainsty*.
May 9, 1565. Roobes, William, Wetherbye, *Ainsty*.
Apl. 20, 1559. Roodes, Robert, Retford, *Retford*.
Mar.28, 1558. Rookes, William, Rodishall, Acquittance by Henry Lutton and Anne his wife, *Pontefract*.
Apl. 20, 1559. Roose, Alice, Everton, widow, *Retford*.
Oct. 14, 1563. Roosse, Mary, Flambrughe, infant, *Dickering*.
Oct. 10, 1566. ————, Richard, *Nottingham*.
Jan. 24, 1565. Roper, James, Hull, *Harthill*.
Jan. 21, 1567. ————, Joan, Hull, *Harthill*.
Feb. 25, 1558. Rowlay, John, Marston *als*. Hooton Wandesley, *Ainsty*.
Sep. 24, 1558. Rud, Henry, Roclif, to Thos. Waikefeld, Pontefract, *Bulmer*.
Nov.16, 1558. Rudde, Agnes, Snathe, widow, *Bulmer*.
Apl. 28, 1558. ————, George, Danbye, *Cleveland*.
May 12, 1559. Rudston, Nicholas, Hayton. esquire. *Harthill*.
Jun. 15, 1568. Rudstone, Joan, Burnebye, widow, *Harthill*.
Nov. 3, 1557. Rumfoote, Ralph, York, glover, *City*.
Nov.20, 1566. Runkhorne, William, Cawodde, *Ainsty*.
May 20, 1560. Russell, Lawrence, York, *Vacancy*, Fol. 39.

May 30, 1564.	Rutland, Henry Manners, earl of, Comm. to collect debts, *City*.
Sep. 19, 1564.	Rydar, Isabella, Esington, infant, *Holderness*.
Oct. 30, 1564.	——, John, Hull, Tuition, *Harthill*.
Sep. 30, 1563.	Rydarr, Stephen, Cottingham, *Harthill*.
Apl. 4, 1565.	Rysheworthe, Robert, Crofton, *Pontefract*.
Mar. 5, 1561.	Salmon, William, Flaymburghe, *Dickering*.
Jan. 11, 1562.	Salmond, Isabella, Skitbie, *Harthill*.
May 15, 1562.	Salven, Sir Francis, Newbiggyn, knight, *Cleveland*.
Aug. 6, 1563.	———, William, infant son of Sir Francis S., knight, *Cleveland*.
Dec. 18, 1564.	Sam, Robert, Bicarton, par. Bylton, *Ainsty*.
Feb. 6, 1558.	Sanderson, Isabella, Gemlinge, singularis, *Dickering*.
Feb. 26, 1559.	———, Thomas, Hornsey Becke, *Vacancy*, Fol. 2.
Mar. 15, 1558.	Sandwith, William, Newsome, *Harthill*.
May 2, 1566.	Saunder, Robert, Staythes, *Cleveland*.
Oct. 1, 1560.	Sawmon, John, East Markham (Notts.), *Vacancy*, Fol. 76.
Feb. 14, 1567.	Sawnder, William, Lithe, *Cleveland*.
May 2, 1560.	Sawnders, Richard, Hull, *Vacancy*, Fol. 28.
July 8, 1562.	Scoles, James, Hull, *Harthill*.
May 18, 1559.	Scoley, Barnard, Hynseworth, *Doncaster*.
May 23, 1558.	Scotson, John, York, Adm. and Tuition, *City*.
Dec. 5, 1565.	Sekerwham, John, Robynhoodbay, *Cleveland*.
Mar. 5, 1566.	Seller, Vincent, Kennythorpe, *Buckrose*.
Mar. 1, 1558.	Selowe, Francis, Snaynton, *Rydall*.
Feb. 5, 1566.	———, Joan *als.* Jane, Heslerton, *Rydall*.
Feb. 8, 1565.	Seyner, Isabella, Clyfforthe, widow, *Ainsty*.
July 13, 1558.	Seyvell, Robert, junr., Hallifax. *Pontefract*.
Apl. 6, 1558.	———, Robert, Pille, *Doncaster*.
May 14, 1567.	Shackells, Robert, Stonfery, *Holderness*.
May 14, 1567.	Shakkells, Christopher, Stonefery, infant, *Holderness*.
Jun. 20, 1565.	Shakleton, John, Womersley, *Pontefract*.
Jan. 18, 1565.	Sharlocke, Thomas, Hull, *Harthill*.
Nov. 7, 1565.	Sharpe, James, Hull, *Harthill*.
July 15, 1556.	———, William, Hunmanbie, *Dickering*.
July 1, 1558.	Sharphouse, Anthony, Duesburye, *Pontefract*.
Dec. 12, 1567.	Shawe, Geoffrey, Topcliffe, *Bulmer*.
Apl. 12, 1559.	Shay, Roger, Kirkeburton, *Pontefract*.
Aug. 26, 1561.	Sheffelde, John, Heathe, *Pontefract*.
Aug. 22, 1566.	Sheildes, William, Esington, *Holderness*.
May 20, 1557.	Sheile, Thomas, New Sheild, *City*.
Apl. 16, 1561.	Sheperd, Thomas, Silkestone, *Doncaster*.
Dec. 3, 1560.	Shepherd, Walter, Kinsea, *Vacancy*, Fol. 89.
May 5, 1559.	Shepley, Barnard, Little Houghton, *Doncaster*.
Aug. 4, 1558.	Shepperd, Edward, Bushopburton, *Harthill*.
July 11, 1558.	———, Isabella, Bolton on Derne, widow, *Doncaster*.
Sep. 30, 1557.	———, Johan (? Skeflinge), *Holderness*.
Nov. 15, 1566.	Shepperde, John, Bolton, *Doncaster*.
Oct. 26, 1558.	Sherewod, Thomas, Walkyngton, *Harthill*.
Feb. 11, 1565.	Sherpe, Thomas, Esington, *Holderness*.
Feb. penult., 1556.	Sherwod, John, Swanland, *Harthill*.
Feb. 14, 1564.	Sherwoodd, Willam, Skarbroughe, *Dickering*.
Jun. 3, 1564.	Shippen, John, son of Thos. S., Selbye, *Bulmer*.
Jun. 19, 1556.	Shipwright, John, Waghen, *Holderness*.
July 17, 1557.	Shirlocke, William, and Ellen his wife, Usflett, *Bulmer*.
May 15, 1566.	Shotton, Margaret, Ryton, infant, *Rydall*.
Mar. 17, 1567.	Sibereye, John, Great Hecke, par. Snaythe, *Ainsty*.
July 17, 1556.	Sikes, William, Flaghwayte, *Pontefract*.
Aug. 4, 1563.	Skaife, Thomas, Averaie Parke, par. Hampeswaith, *Ainsty*.
May 6, 1560.	Skarre, Margaret, dau. of James S., *Vacancy*, Fol. 35.
Nov. 9, 1557.	Skelowe, John, Foxhoolls, *Dickering*.
Dec. 5, 1556.	Skelton, Clement, Seacroft, *Ainsty*.
Sep. 6, 1560.	———, Robert, Bolton, par. Calverley, *Vacancy*, Fol. 68.
Sep. 14, 1564.	———, Roger, Skardburghe, *Dickering*.
Aug. 19, 1557.	Skoles, William, Batley, priest, *Pontefract*.
Dec. 10, 1567.	Skott, William, Rippon, *Craven*.

Apl. 22, 1559. Skotte, John, Cawood, *Ainsty*.
Sep. 30, 1561. Slacke, Elizabeth, Brerley, *Doncaster*.
Sep. 3, 1558. Slater, Elizabeth, Bramley, par. Leedes, widow, *Ainsty*.
Sep. 22, 1565. ———, Edmund, Fewyston, *Ainsty*.
Dec. 2, 1567. ———, Edmund, Fryston, *Ainsty*.
May 5, 1568. Sleighe, William, Baynton, *Harthill*.
July 13, 1565. Smeton, Robert, Stanfurth Brigges, clerk, *Harthill*.
Oct. 29, 1558. Smyth, Agnes, widow of John S., *Dickering*.
Jan. 23, 1560. ———, Alice, York, spinster, *Vacancy*, Fol. 98.
Aug. 11, 1570(?). ———, James, son of Will. S., Londisbroughe, *Vacancy*, Fol. 105.
May 2, 1560. ———, John, Old Malton, *Vacancy*, Fol. 6.
May 2, 1560. ———, Richard, Hull, *Vacancy*, Fol. 28.
Nov. 17, 1558. ———, Robert, Monkfriston, *Ainsty*.
Jun. 7, 1560. ———, William, Buckton, *Vacancy*, Fol. 40.
Apl. 19, 1563. Smythe, Dorothy, Kirkbye Overblawes, widow, *Ainsty*.
Aug. 19, 1567. ———, Henry, City of London, *Cleveland*.
Apl. 14, 1568. ———, Isabella, Heydon, *Holderness*.
Oct. 8, 1567. ———, Joan, Styllingflete, *Bulmer*.
Feb. 24, 1563. ———, John, Foston, *Dickering*.
Aug. 27, 1557. ———, John, Heddynglay, *Ainsty*.
Apl. 31, 1567. ———, John, Hull, maryner, *Harthill*.
Dec. 16, 1556. ———, John, Monkfryeston, *Ainsty*.
May 7, 1567. ———, Margaret, Seaton, *Holderness*.
Dec. 22, 1556. ———, Nicholas, Clayton, par. Frykley, *Doncaster*.
Feb. 17, 1558. ———, Richard, Howke, *Bulmer*.
Oct. 20, 1565. ———, Richard, Selbye, *Bulmer*.
Aug. 14, 1566. ———, Robert, Burnbye, *Harthill*.
Sep. 30, 1556. ———, Robert, Skeflynge, *Holderness*.
Sep. 29, 1557. ———, Roger, Litle Smeton, par. Womerslay, *Pontefract*.
Apl. 12, 1559. ———, Thomas, Skipton, *Craven*.
Dec. 2, 1559. ———, William, infant son of Edmund S., Campsall, *Doncaster*.
Oct. 10, 1562. ———, William, Swinflete, par. Whitgyft, *Bulmer*.
Oct. 10, 1562. ———, William, Swynflete, par. Whitgift, *Rydall*.
July 5 & Sep. 30, 1557. Smythe *als.* Donnynge, John, Doncaster, singularis, *Doncaster*.
Aug. 1, 1565. Smythies, John, Beverley, *Harthill*.
Apl. 11, 1565. Smythson, Alan, Ryllyngton, *Buckrose*.
Apl. 28, 1568. ———, Robert, Bushopmonckton, *Craven*.
Jan. 28, 1562. ———, Thomas, Thirlebie, par. Feliskirke, infant, *Bulmer*.
Apl. 14, 1559. Smythsonns, Roger, Norton, *Buckrose*.
Apl. 4, 1565. Snarre, John, Olde Malton, *Rydall*.
Sep. 16, 1562. ———, Robert, Amonderbie, *Rydall*.
Mar. 21, 1566. Snarte, William, Robert, and John, Stillingflete, *Bulmer*.
May 10, 1559. ———, William, Wandisforth, *Dickering*.
Jan. 4, 1558. Snathe, John, Sutton, *Holderness*.
Apl. 3, 1557. Snawe, John, Eskryke, *Bulmer*.
Jan. 12, 1558. ———, Thomas, Eskrike, *Bulmer*.
Mar. 4, 1562. Snaythe, William, Stoneferye, *Holderness*.
Nov. 24, 1562. Sotheron, Robert, Holme in Spaldingmore, *Harthill*.
Dec. 1, 1558. ———, Robert, Seaton, *Harthill*.
Sep. 4, 1557. Sothill, Robert, North Dighton, *Ainsty*.
July 3, 1566. Sowelbye, Lucy, Anycke in Hexhamshyre, widow, *City*.
Oct. 1, 1560. Spavald, Robert, Burton (Notts.), *Vacancy*, Fol. 76.
Nov. 10, 1560. Specke, Joan, Wheldrike, widow, *Vacancy*, Fol. 85.
Oct. 10, 1566. Spedes, Richard, Moargrene, *Nottingham*.
Sep. 13, 1558. Spender, Geo[r]ge, Hunttington, *Bulmer*.
Sep. 4, 1566. Spenser, William, Wystow, *Ainsty*.
Apl. 6, 1565. Spoffurth, Richard, Application of Agnes Spoffurth *als.* Aslabye, his mother, to cancel Tuition Bond, *Rydall*.
Feb. 1, 1563. Spyve, Robert, Barnesley, *Doncaster*.
Mar. 23, 1560. Squier, Henry, Rustone, *Vacancy*, Fol. 125.
Feb. 21, 1565. Stamper, Margaret, York, *City*.
May 13, 1557. Stanley, John, Sutton Bonington, *Bingham*.
Mar. 9, 1557. Stansfeld, William, Sowerbie, par. Hallifax, *Pontefract*.
Sep. 14, 1563. Stanupp, Bartholmew, Hull, *Harthill*.

Oct. 3, 1560. Staynworth, Richard, Gisburn, *Vacancy*, Fol. 78.
July 23, 1567. Stephenson, Richard, Armyn, par. Snath, *Bulmer*.
Sep. 29, 1563. Stevenson, Henry, Flambroughe, *Dickering*.
Nov.28, 1567. ———, Margaret, Great Kelke, *Dickering*.
Jun. 23, 1563. ———, Richard, Seamer, *Dickering*.
Aug. 7, 1566. ———, William, Hull, yeoman, Compotus, *Harthill*.
Mar. 5, 1556. Stilbarnes, William, Fymber, par. Wetwange, *Buckrose*.
Jan. 22, 1561. Stiring, Ellinore, Hooton Crancewike, *Harthill*.
Nov. 7, 1556. Stockdale, John, Thyrske, *Bulmer*.
May 5, 1559. Stokes, Charles, Tykhill, Renunc. and Adm., *Doncaster*.
Feb. 5, 1557. ———, Thomas, Waikefeld, *Pontefract*.
Feb.ult.,1557. Stokhall, Agnes, Pontefract, widow, *Pontefract*.
Mar.21, 1557. Storie, Jerard, Foston, Caveat, *Dickering*.
Jun. 14, 1563. Storyes, William, Flamburgh, fisherman, *Dickering*.
May 2, 1560. Stowpes, John, Waugham, *Vacancy*, Fol. 32.
Feb. 17, 1561. Strange, Thomas, Bothamsall, *Retford*.
Mar.12, 1562. ———, Thomas, Bothomsall, *Retford*.
Oct. 27, 1558. Strynger, Thomas, and Christabella his wife, Selbye, *Bulmer*.
May 14, 1558. Stubbys, John, Irton, *Dickering*.
Apl. 11, 1559. Stubley, Peter, Warmefeild, *Pontefract*.
Sep. 26, 1565. ———, Peter, Warmefeld, *Pontefract*.
Dec. 5, 1558. ———, Thomas, Byrstall, *Pontefract*.
May 11, 1557. Sturdie, Katherine, Eskrig, widow, *Bulmer*.
May 13, 1557. Sturtyvant, William, Northwell, *Southwell*.
Apl. 4, 1559. Stybing, Thomas, Slingesbie, *Rydall*.
Jun. 23, 1558. Sugden, John, Bradfurthe, *Pontefract*.
Apl. 24, 1560. Sunderland, Agnes, Northorome, *Vacancy*, Fol. 22.
Apl. 20, 1559. Sussance, Margaret, Bollam, *Retford*.
Dec. 1, 1558. Sutton, John, Weton, *Harthill*.
Mar. 9, 1555. ———, Nicholas, Willowghton, Linc. Dioc., *Rydall*.
Dec. 22, 1556. Swyfte, Robert, Wathe, *Doncaster*.
Oct. 29, 1558. Swynborne, Leonard, Settryngton, *Rydall*.
Apl. 27, 1563. Symonde, John, Thormonbye, par. Staneton, *Cleveland*.
Oct. 5, 1558. Sympson, John, Rowley, *Harthill*.
Nov. 7, 1564. ———, John, Settrington, *Buckrose*.
Apl. 25, 1559. ———, Vincent, Hornebie, *Cleveland*.
Mar.15, 1558. Symson, John, Clowghton, *Dickering*.
Dec. 20, 1560. Tailyer, Robert, Appilton, infant, *Vacancy*, Fol. 92.
Sep. 17, 1558. Tairte, Richard, Huby, *Bulmer*.
Nov.11, 1562. Talier, James, York, merchant, *City*.
Mar.19, 1557. Talyour, Thomas, Settill, *Craven*.
Jan. 12, 1567. Tankarde, Ninian, Skewesbye, *Bulmer*.
Dec. 5, 1562. Tempest, John, Brestwessill, par. Thornehill, *Pontefract*.
Nov.18, 1565. Tempeste, Sir John, Bollynge, knight, *Pontefract*.
Oct. 1, 1562. Tenant, Humphrey, *Craven*.
Dec. 1, 1558. Tennand, John, Elleton, *Harthill*.
Jan. 23, 1561. Tennyson, John, Ryall, *Holderness*.
Mar.27, 1560. Terriman, Thomas, Ridkar, *Vacancy*, Fol. 12.
Apl. 17, 1559. Thackoray, Robert, Ramesgell, *Craven*.
Oct. 19, 1558. Thickpenney, Richard, York, *City*.
July 30, 1562. Thompson, Agnes, Hovenden, par. Ledes, *Pontefract*.
May 25, 1563. ———, Andrew, Barton in lee Willowes, par. Crambome, *Bulmer*.
July 9, 1567. ———, Ellen, Hulbanke, *Harthill*.
Oct. 7, 1557. ———, Henry, Rampton, *Southwell*.
Apl. 27, 1564. ———, James, Sturton, *Retford*.
July 17, 1562. ———, John, Beverley, infant, *Harthill*.
Aug.10, 1562. ———, John, Beverley, infant, *Harthill*.
Jun. 21, 1565. ——— John, Hulbanke, *Harthill*.
July 14, 1564. ———, Marmaduke, Everingham, *Harthill*.
Oct. 1, 1557. ——— Thomas, Rymswell, *Cleveland*.
Mar.23, 1560. ———, Thomas, Welweke, *Vacancy*, Fol. 124.
Dec. 21, 1562. ———, Walter, Flambroughe, *Dickering*.
May 5, 1559. Thomson, John, Carleton, *Rydall*.
Feb. 19, 1567. ———, John, Kellington, *Pontefract*.

May 10, 1559. Thomson, Richard, Seamer, *Dickering.*
Jan. 20, 1558. ————, Robert, Brandsdaill, *Rydall.*
Dec. 19, 1560. Thormanbie, Laurence, Thormanbie, infant, *Vacancy,* Fol. 92.
Dec. 19, 1560. Thormonbie, Edward, Thormonbie, infant, *Vacancy,* Fol. 92.
Dec. 19, 1560. ————, Thomas, Thormonbie, infant, *Vacancy,* Fol. 92.
Aug. 12, 1558. Thornehill, Hugh, Walcryngham, late City of London, Long proceedings, *Retford.*
Nov. 28, 1558. Thornes, Robert, Horburie, *Pontefract.*
Feb. 24, 1566. Thorneton, Thomas, Sherburne, *Ainsty.*
May 5, 1568. Thornybies, Agnes, widow, *Harthill.*
May 18, 1566. Thorpe, Christopher, Thorpegarthe, *Holderness.*
Jan. 24, 1558. ————, Roger, Hymsworth, mylner, *Doncaster.*
July 6, 1556. ————, William, Hull, *Harthill.*
Dec. 4, 1566. · Thwaytes, Henry, York, *City.*
Sep. 17, 1558. Thwayttes, Henry, York, gentleman, *City.*
Dec. 20, 1560. Thwenge, Francis, Estheslerton, infant, *Vacancy,* Fol. 92.
Dec. 12, 1564. Thwynge, James, Cottingham, infant, *Harthill.*
Jun. 19, 1566. Todde, John, Esington, *Holderness.*
Jan. 11, 1557. Tokke, William, Pattryngton, *Holderness.*
Apl. 4, 1560. Tomkinson, Eliseus, Retford (Notts.), *Vacancy,* Fol. 18.
Dec. 1, 1557. Tomlynson, John, Pooll, *Ainsty.*
Nov. 24, 1562. ———— *als.* Myllyngton, Wilfrid, Holme in Spaldingmore, *Harthill.*
Feb. 26, 1555. Tompson, Margaret, wid. of Jo. T., New Malton, *Rydall.*
Sep. 21, 1562. Townende, Edward, Heptonstall, *Pontefract.*
May 13, 1558. ————, Nicholas, York, *City.*
Jan. 17, 1567. Towthorpe, Joan, Thirske, *Bulmer.*
Jun. 21, 1568. Toye, Richard, Beverley, *Harthill.*
May 2, 1566. Tranam, Raginald, Magna Broughton, *Cleveland.*
Dec. 4, 1561. Tranham, Katherine, Harlesaye, *Bulmer.*
July 11, 1558. Tremyngham, Richard, Fyshelake, *Doncaster.*
Jun. 27, 1560. Trew, Thomas, Eskrige, *Vacancy,* Fol. 56.
Aug. 13, 1567. Troughet, John and George, sons of Robt. T., Hilston, decd., Curation, *Holderness.*
Dec. 3, 1560. Truslowe, Christopher, Waugham, *Vacancy,* Fol. 89.
July 27, 1566. [1] Tunstall, Elizabeth, dau. of Roger T., decd., Curation, *Cleveland.*
Nov. 10, 1557. Turner, Margaret, Owston, par. Tadcaster, widow, *Ainsty.*
Jan. 11, 1558. Turpyne, Lawrence, Newthrope, *Ainsty.*
Oct. 7, 1556. Twyvell, Johan, Barmbie, widow, *Retford.*
Nov. 12, 1556. Tyas, Christopher, Osset, par. Dewysburie, *Pontefract.*
Apl. 16, 1567. Tyndaill, Thomas, Birskerhouse, *Cleveland.*
Oct. 27, (1564?). Underne, Thomas, Stathropp, par. Averham, *Newark.*
Jun. 14, 1560. Upton, Christopher, Wolley, *Vacancy,* Fol. 54.
Aug. 13, 1558. Ussher, William, Abberforthe, *Ainsty.*
Mar. 6, 1558. Vavasor, Edward, Parokehowse, par. Kirkebieoverblaus, *Ainsty.*
Aug. 23, 1563. Veile, Nicholas, Bridlington, *Dickering.*
Dec. 8, 1566. Verealls *als.* Yonge, Stephen, Hull, *Harthill.*
Apl. 30, 1558. Vertue, Michael, Thorneton, par. Foston, *Bulmer.*
Apl. 14, 1559. Vesse, Thomas, Skerpenbeke, *Buckrose.*
Mar. 11, 1562. Vessey, Alice, Hull, *Harthill.*
Dec. 11, 1566. Vicarman, Thomas, Haistropp, *Dickering.*
Mar. 13, 1567. Vicars, William, York, *City.*
May 12, 1559. Wadingham, William, Myton, *Harthill.*
Dec. 2, 1561. Wadisworthe, William, Silkeston, *Doncaster.*
Dec. 29, 1558. Wagher, Richard, priest, late Master of Trinity Hospital, Hull, *Harthill.*
May 18, 1559. Waid, Oliver, Laneham, *Retford.*
Nov. —, 1565. Waide, Elizabeth, Staynfurth, *Craven.*
Feb. 17, 1564. Waidropper, William, Sallay, *Craven.*
May 6, 1557. Waire, John, Thriske, *Bulmer.*
May 14, 1557. Wakefeld, Elizabeth, Newarke, *Newark.*
Mar. 2, 1555. ————, Peter, Pontefract, *Pontefract.*
Aug. 16, 1563. Wald, Thomas, Wistow, *Ainsty.*
Sep. 3, 1556. Waldbe, Brian, son of William W., South Newbald, *Beverley.*
Jan. 12, 1558. Walke, Alice, Chereburton, *Harthill.*

1 After 1568.

Mar. 4, 1562. Walker, Agnes, Brustwike, *Holderness*.
May 22, 1557. ———, Alice, wid. of Peter W., Crakall, par. Toplyffe, widow, *Bulmer*.
Jun. 12, 1557. ———, Isabella, Crakell, par. Topclif, singularis, *Bulmer*.
Jan. 30, 1566. ———, John, senr., North Frodingham, *Holderness*.
Mar. 21, 1558. ———, John, and Joan his wife, Ripon, *Craven*.
Apl. 13, 1559. ———, Margaret, Cottingham, *Harthill*.
May 22, 1557. ———, Peter, Crakall, par. Topclif, *Bulmer*.
May 14, 1557. ———, Ralph, Eperstone, *Nottingham*.
Oct. 23, 1557. Wall, John, Wistowe, *Ainsty*.
Sep. 30, 1556. Walshe, William, Fernehill, *Craven*.
Apl. 23, 1567. Walworthe, Robert, Raventoftes, *Craven*.
Nov. 5, 1560. Ward, John, Esyngwold, *Vacancy*, Fol. 85.
May 21, 1560. ———, Roger, Burton Pidse, *Vacancy*, Fol. 11.
July 17, 1561. ——— *als.* Cooke, John, Naburne, *Bulmer*.
Mar. 26, 1560. Warde, Christopher, Marske, *Vacancy*, Fol. 11.
Mar. 21, 1560. ———, John, Coppulworthe, *Vacancy*, Fol. 122.
Jun. 4, 1561. ———, John, Lombye, *Ainsty*.
Mar. 3, 1566. ———, John, Monkefryston, *Ainsty*.
July 15, 1564. ———, Oliver, Pattrington, *Holderness*.
Mar. 29, 1568. ———, Robert, Addle, *Ainsty*.
Jun. 20, 1568. ———, Robert, Hampstwait, *Ainsty*.
Feb. 9, 1557. ———, William, Kylnesey, *Holderness*.
Nov. 13, 1556. Wardeman *als.* Flemynge, Eufemia, widow, *City*.
Oct. 8, 1562. Warryner, Bartholomew, Tuxforde, *Retford*.
Jun. 4, 1568. Watson, Humphrey, Sutton, *Holderness*.
Sep. 1, 1565. ———, Isabella, Magna Busbye, widow, *Cleveland*.
Apl. 13, 1562. ———, Leonard, Little Aiton, infant, *Cleveland*.
Apl. 20, 1564. ———, Thomas, Brompton, *Rydall*.
Sep. 3, 1557. ———, Walter, senr., Thorpe by Ripon, *Craven*.
May 20, 1560. Watsone, Thomas, Raskell, *Vacancy*, Fol. 9.
Dec. 9, 1562. Wawdbie, Brian, Beverley, infant, *Harthill*.
July 7, 1563. Wayrde, Joan, Swanland, par. South Feriby, infant, *Harthill*.
Dec. 7, 1557. Webster, James, Foston, *Bulmer*.
Mar. 3, 1561. ———, Joan, Foston, widow, *Rydall*.
May 14, 1558. ———, Juliana, Flambrough, widow, *Dickering*.
May 2, 1560. ———, William, Hull, *Vacancy*, Fol. 28.
Jan. 31, 1564. ——— *als.* Grene, William, Agnes Burton, priest, *Dickering*.
Dec. 11, 1566. Welborne, John, Burton Flemynge, *Dickering*.
July 23, 1560. ———, Katherine, Lunde, *Vacancy*, Fol. 62.
Dec. 4, 1557. Wentlay *als.* Lawe, John, Pollington, *Bulmer*.
Mar. 5, 1559. Wentworth, John, Empsall, *Vacancy*, Fol. 3.
Oct. 24, 1564. Westabye, Richard, Flambroughe, infant, *Dickering*.
Aug. 14, 1567. Weste, Robert, Bradford, *Pontefract*.
Feb. 19, 1556. ———, Robert, Bradforde, Sequestration, *Craven*.
Mar. 20, 1564. Wetherelde, Robert, Hull, *Harthill*.
May 2, 1566. Wetherell, Joan, Thornegumbald, *Holderness*.
Jun. 3, 1558. Wheatlay, Thomas, Aston, *Doncaster*.
Jan. 21, 1557. ———, William, Snytall, *Pontefract*.
Dec. 8, 1561. Whippe, William, Thirske, *Bulmer*.
Dec. 2, 1562. White, Thomas, Borreswod (? Brodsworth), *Doncaster*.
Feb. —, 1557. Whitehead, Anthony, Stead, par. Ottlay, *Ainsty*.
Jan. 11, 1562. Whitfeilde, William, Beverley, *Harthill*.
Jan. 27, 1555. Whithawce, Thomas, Marston, *Ainsty*.
Mar. 18, 1557. Whithead, Anthony, Wheatley, par. Ilkelay, *Craven*.
Sep. 29, 1560. Whitside, Edward, Rocliffe, *Vacancy*, Fol. 72.
Nov. 28, 1567. Whyete, Thomas, Great Kelke, *Dickering*.
Nov. 12, 1556. Whytton, Richard, Ayton, *Cleveland*.
Dec. 22, 1556. Wiggen, William, Melton on Hill, *Doncaster*.
Feb. 16, 1563. Wightman, George, Skawton, *Rydall*.
Jun. 14, 1565. Wiglesworthe, Richard, Cattonparke, *Harthill*.
Apl. 8, 1560. Wilbore. William, Kylnewyke, *Vacancy*, Fol. 20.
July 13, 1556. Wilcockes, Richard, Holland, par. Wentworthe, *Doncaster*.
Mar. 12, 1558. Wilcoke, Agnes, Womerslay, *Pontefract*.
Apl. 18, 1560. Wildsmith, John, Tankerslay, *Vacancy*, Fol. 21.

Dec. 2, 1557. Wyman, Robert, Wheldricke, *Bulmer.*
Jun. 11, 1566. Wynkley, Antony, Wynkeley, par. Mytton, *Craven.*
Oct. 7, 1557. Wynney, George, Nottingham, *Nottingham.*
Sep. 21, 1566. Wynterburne, Richard, Methley, *Pontefract.*
May 24, 1558. Wyrell, William, Askam Richard, *Ainsty.*
May 2, 1566. Yngle, Thomas, Kesweke, *Ainsty.*
Jan. 7, 1558. Yonge, Henry, Thyckehead, par. Wheldreke, *Bulmer.*
Jun. 12, 1567. ——, Richard, Esington, *Holderness.*
Jun. 17, 1565. ——, Thomas, Appletreweke, *Craven.*
Dec. 8, 1566. —— *als.* Verealls, Stephen, Hull, *Harthill.*
Aug. 22, 1565. Yorke, John, Boltby, *Bulmer.*

ROBERT WHITE, PRINTER, WORKSOP.

Date Due

Demco 293-5